ZEN BUDDHISM: A HISTORY

Volume 2
Japan

Nanzan Studies in Religion and Culture
James W. Heisig, General Editor

Heinrich Dumoulin, *Zen Buddhism: A History. Vol. 1, India and China*. Trans. by J. Heisig and Paul Knitter, 1988.

Frederick Franck, ed., *The Buddha Eye: An Anthology of the Kyoto School*. 1982.

Winston, L. King, *Death Was His Kōan: The Samurai-Zen of Suzuki Shōsan*, with a Foreword by Nakamura Hajime, 1986.

Robert E. Morrell, *Early Kamakura Buddhism: A Minority Report*, 1987.

Nagao Gadjin, *The Foundational Standpoint of Māhyamika Philosophy*. Trans. by John Keenan, 1989.

Nishitani Keiji, *Religion and Nothingness*. Trans. by Jan Van Bragt with an Introduction by Winston L. King, 1985.

Nishitani Keiji, *Nishida Kitarō: The Man and His Thought*. Trans. by Yamamoto Seisaku et al., 1989.

Nishitani Keiji, *The Self-Overcoming of Nihilism*. Trans. by G. Parkes and S. Aihara, 1989.

Nishida Kitarō, *Intuition and Reflection in Self-Consciousness*. Trans. by Valdo Viglielmo et al., with an Introduction by Joseph O'Leary, 1987.

Paul Swanson, *Foundations of T'ien-T'ai Philosophy*, 1989.

Takeuchi Yoshinori, *The Heart of Buddhism: In Search of the Timeless Spirit of Primitive Buddhism*. Trans. with Introduction by J. Heisig and a Foreword by Hans Küng, 1983.

Tanabe Hajime, *Philosophy as Metanoetics*. Trans. by Takeuchi Yoshinori et al., with an Introduction by J. Heisig, 1987.

Hans Waldenfels, *Absolute Nothingness: Foundations for a Buddhist-Christian Dialogue*. Trans. by J. Heisig, 1980.

ZEN BUDDHISM: A HISTORY

Volume 2
Japan

Heinrich Dumoulin

Translated by
James W. Heisig and Paul Knitter

Macmillan Publishing Company
New York

Collier Macmillan Publishers
London

Macmillan Publishing Company
866 Third Avenue
New York, NY 10022

Collier Macmillan Canada, Inc.

Library of Congress Catalog Card Number: 87-34834

Printed in the United States of America

printing number
1 2 3 4 5 6 7 8 9 10

Library of Congress Cataloging-in-Publication Data

(Revised for vol. 2)

Dumoulin, Heinrich.
  Zen Buddhism.

  (Nanzan studies in religion and culture)
  Translation of: Zen.
  Includes bibliographies and indexes.
  Contents: v. 1. India and China—v. 2. Japan.
  1. Zen Buddhism—History. I. Heisig, James W.,
1944–   . II. Knitter, Paul F. III. Title.
IV. Series.
BQ9262.3.D85513 1988   294.3'927'09   87-34834
ISBN 0-02-908220-X (set)
ISBN 0-02-908230-7 (set : pbk.)
ISBN 0-02-908270-6 (v. 1)
ISBN 0-02-908260-9 (pbk. : v. 1)
ISBN 0-02-908250-1 (v. 2)
ISBN 0-02-908240-4 (pbk. : v. 2)

Contents

Foreword

Zen Buddhism spread from China throughout East Asia. The process by which it came to take root and flourish in Japan just as it had done in its native Chinese soil makes a fascinating story. Its well-balanced diffusion across a relatively small area and its thorough penetration of the spiritual life of Japan are of particular historical interest. Together with the concerted effort to preserve the whole wealth of the Zen tradition, Japanese Zen stressed elements that had hitherto been little developed. In China it was the master–disciple relationship of original, robust, and strong-tempered personalities that attracted attention, while the profile cut by many a Japanese Zen master is that of a reliable educator, a true champion to those in need, enjoying the confidence of high and low social classes alike.

Of course the substance of Zen is understood fully by no more than a small nucleus of adherents, and none but a few reach true enlightenment. Yet these were enough to wield an enduring influence and spread the insights of the Zen tradition, especially the rooting of the self in the realm of the absolute and a cosmic worldview. In the West, interest in Zen has centered on these elements and their accompanying artistic achievements. A deeper study of the formative historical process can only further enrich the understanding that already exists.

No sooner does one set out to tell the story of Zen in Japan than one is faced with a veritable *embarras de richesses*. The superabundance of primary sources and an almost incalculable harvest of secondary literature prescribe selection and limitation at every turn. No more than a small ration of the total mass of material can be used. To choose is to pass judgment and hence to run the risk of oversight.

In recent years Japanese scholarship has brought to light important new source material. This has prompted me to add rather lengthy sections and make some alterations here and there for the English edition that are not in the German original. I am particularly indebted to Professor Ishii Shūdō of Komazawa University in Tokyo for making materials available to me on the Japanese Daruma school and providing additional helpful information (chapter 1). Advances in scholarship also obliged me to review and expand the chapters on Dōgen (chapter 2) and the Sōtō school (chapter 3).

After completing the German manuscript of the first volume of this work early in 1983, a series of important new disclosures regarding the early history of Zen Buddhism in China emerged one after the other in rapid succession. The sheer volume of the published materials made a reworking of the text impractical, either for the German edition or for the English translation. Still more recently, valuable contributions to the history of Zen in Korea and Tibet have appeared. The scope and focus of this second volume, however, seemed to prohibit treating these matters, even in the form of a series of appendixes or supplements. Meanwhile, an impressive collection of new information on early Zen is accumulating and will no doubt be given due treatment in the cource of time.

Given the size of this second volume, it was necessary to impose certain limits on lists, chronological tables, and bibliography. Unlike the one in the first volume, the glossary of Chinese characters is restricted to those names, titles, and expressions that have a direct bearing on the Zen movement within the intellectual and religious history of Japan. Names associated with political or local background, as well as more general Japanese expressions, have been omitted; ideograms already listed in the first volume have not been repeated. The chronological tables keep to the main traditions treated in the text and do not claim to represent the wide variety of lines of tradition mentioned in the Japanese sources. The concluding bibliography is far from complete; it merely seeks to gather together some of the principal works referred to in the text, with a few supplemental titles. (Variations in the reading of characters are indicated, consensus being virtually impossible.)

It only remains for me to reiterate my thanks to all those whose help has been invaluable in the preparation of this volume. As he had done for the first volume, Professor Dietrich Seckel read through the chapter on Buddhist art with a critical eye and suggested valuable additions. To the list of Japanese scholars who helped me with the first volume, I would add here Professor Takeuchi Yoshinori and Tamaki Kōshirō, both of whom have contributed essentially to my appreciation of Japanese Buddhism. Consciously or not, much of what I have learned through long years of personal acquaintance with Zen masters in Japan is woven between the lines of this book. Indeed one of the most appealing aspects of Zen is the fact that the fascinating figure of the Zen master is not merely a thing of the past. For their technical assistance, I am once again indebted to the many collaborators who aided me in the preparation of this volume. For their untiring attention, my sincerest gratitude.

Heinrich Dumoulin

The Zen Schools in Japan

The Planting of Zen in Japan

Japanese historians of Buddhism are fond of speaking of "Buddhism in the three lands," namely, India, China, and Japan. The phrase not only points to the extent of Buddhist presence in Asia but implies a development that peaked in Japan. It also applies to the way of Zen, the meditation school of Mahāyāna Buddhism. While the roots of Zen reach back to India and came into being in China as the flowering of a distinctively Chinese spirit, Zen underwent new developments in Japan and achieved a maturity that made it possible to open a path to the West.

As far as we can tell from its early history, East Asian culture, one of the cradles of human civilization, had its source and center in China. In great part Japan owes its own culture to this powerful neighboring land, from which numerous influences streamed to the Japanese archipelago giving impetus to all sorts of cultural developments. In the realm of religion, Buddhism exercised an enduring influence and eventually became the dominant religion in Japan. Throughout it all, Japan maintained its own spiritual and cultural identity in appropriating the religion of Buddha, a fact which is of great importance for the history of Zen.

On the one hand, Japanese Zen is cast completely in the mold of Chinese Zen Buddhism; on the other, it adopted its own native materials to transform what it had inherited from China, producing something new and different. Throughout the trials it was to face, Japanese Zen preserved a remarkable vitality that continues strong and tangible to this day.

1

The Rinzai School
in the Kamakura Period

EARLY HISTORY

The arrival of Buddhism in Japan from the Asian continent took place shortly after Japan entered the annals of history. As the ancient chronicles of Japan report, it was in the year 552, during the reign of Emperor Kinmei, that the first image of Buddha reached the imperial court of the *tennō* ("emperor") from Kudara in Korea. After a brief period of intense conflict, the new religion took root and for centuries played a leading role in the spiritual life of the Japanese people, dominating the primitive *kami* cults of Shinto. The prince-regent Shōtoku Taishi (572–621), the first major figure of Japanese history and creator of the *tennō* state, was a zealous devotee of the teachings of the Buddha. His deeply religious temperament led him to trust in the protection of *Hotoke*—as the Buddha was called in Japanese—and his political insight recognized that the law of the Buddha would provide an effective means of securing a sounder moral base and a higher quality of life for his people. Among the three sūtras that he was particularly fond of, and on which he lectured to a circle of pious friends, was the *Vimalakīrti Sūtra*, whose considerable influence on the history of Zen we examined in the first volume. We may suppose that the practice of meditation, which is so essential to Buddhism, also played a role in the spiritual life of Japanese Buddhists from the very beginning.

The first reliable reports concerning Zen in Japan come already from the earliest period of recorded Japanese history.[1] The eminent Japanese Buddhist monk Dōshō (628–670), who numbers among the founders of Buddhism in Japan, learned of Zen during his visit to China in 653 from his Chinese teacher, the famous Indian pilgrim Hsüan-tsang, with whom he had studied Yogācāra philosophy. This philosophy formed the central doctrine of the Hossō school that Dōshō introduced to Japan.[2] Dōshō studied Zen meditation with Hui-man, a disciple of the second Chinese patriarch Hui-k'o, and also came to know the Fourth Patriarch, Tao-hsin. After his return from China, he lived in the monastery of Gangō-ji in Nara, where he opened the first Zen meditation hall in Japan. During his travels across the country, Dōshō became deeply involved in practical matters like digging wells, building bridges, and setting up ferry crossings. An imposing figure held in high esteem, he is ranked today as one of the Buddhist monks of the early period to whom Japanese civilization is most indebted. Although he did not establish a line of tradition within Zen, he contributed much to the teaching of Zen meditation. In his declining years he devoted himself with renewed zeal to Zen practice and died seated cross-legged. At his request, the body was cremated, the first known instance in Japan.[3]

During the Tempyō period (722–748), the first Chinese Zen master arrived in Japan.[4] Tao-hsüan (702–760), who belonged to the Vinaya tradition and was well versed in the teachings of Tendai and Kegon, had embraced Zen under the direction of P'u-chi (651–739) of the Northern school. Arriving in Japan at the age of thirty-five, Tao-hsüan taught Vinaya and maintained contacts with the Japanese Kegon school. He taught the practice of Zen meditation to the Japanese monk Gyōhyō (722–797), who in turn transmitted it to Saichō, better known as Dengyō Daishi (767–822), the founder of Japanese Tendai.[5] During what was probably a short stay in China (804–805), Saichō became familiar with the extensive teachings as well as the esoteric rituals of Tendai—the so-called *mikkyō*. He also became familiar with Zen. He had two encounters with Zen personalities: Tao-sui (Jpn., Dōsui), who taught a mixture of Tendai and Zen meditation,[6] and Hsiao-jan (Jpn., Yūzen), who taught him the kind of meditation practiced in the Gozu school.[7] Still, it seems that Saichō kept his distance from Zen, content with the significant contemplative element preserved in the Tendai school. To be sure, Tendai meditation was reinforced in China and Japan through its contact with Zen, but it still maintained its own distinctive identity. It is going too far to speak of a "Tendai Zen," since authentic Zen requires some kind of connection with the school of Bodhidharma.[8]

A further stage in preparing the Japanese soil for the planting of Zen came in the following century when I-k'ung (Jpn., Gikū), a disciple of Yen-kuan Ch'i-an (750?–842) from the line of Ma-tsu, visited Japan at the invitation of the empress Tachibana Kachiko, wife of the emperor Saga Tennō, during the early part of the Jōwa era (834–848). While in Japan, I-k'ung taught Zen first at the imperial court and later at Danrin-ji in Kyoto, a temple built for him by the empress.[9] These first efforts in the systematic propagation of Chinese Zen did not, however, meet with lasting success. The Chinese master from the Rinzai school was not able to launch a durable movement and returned to China distraught, leaving behind an inscription at Rashō-mon in Kyoto testifying to the futility of efforts to bring Zen to the East.[10] For three centuries Zen lay dormant in Japan. During the Heian period (794–1192), the two powerful schools of Tendai and Shingon dominated and meditation was forced into the background by philosophical speculation and an extravagance of magical rites. Throughout this period signs of decay in Buddhism were everywhere in evidence. By the time the Heian period was drawing to its close, the worldliness of the court had spread to the populace and permeated the Buddhist monasteries.

BACKGROUND TO THE KAMAKURA PERIOD

The Buddhist renewal that began with the onset of the Kamakura period (1185–1333)[11] gave rise to new sects which in turn carried the renewal forward. The old schools of Hossō, Kegon, Tendai, and Shingon had built up positions of power, disseminating difficult doctrines that were incomprehensible to the common person and giving themselves over increasingly to the practice of magical rites. In the face of this situation, new tendencies arose within Buddhism in response to the pressing religious needs of the people. Aroused by the call for help that, to use the image of the *Lotus Sūtra,* came like "a cry from a burning house," religious personages undertook the task of saving human beings in the apocalyptic atmosphere of the Final Dharma (*mappō*).

Hōnen (1133–1212) and Shinran (1173–1262), founders of the Japanese Amida (Pure Land) schools, preached a message readily understood by the masses—salvation at the hands of a Buddha of light and great compassion. Nichiren (1222–1282) raised the voice of a wrathful but consoling prophet, preaching the *Lotus Sūtra* to lift the hopes of the people. The rising class of knights found the intellectually simple yet practical and aristocratic Zen religion suited to their way of life. The leaders of the Buddhist movement at this time all stemmed from the Tendai school, but had left the heights of Mount Hiei, the center of its institutional power, breaking with the old traditions in order to find their way in the world of ordinary people.

From the middle of the twelfth century, a regular exchange of Japanese and Chinese monks had come about, giving the flourishing Zen of the Sung period an entry into Japan. Kakua (born 1142), a contemporary of Eisai, traveled to China in 1171 as a young man.[12] There he practiced faithfully and attained the seal of enlightenment in 1175 under Hui-yüan (1103–1176, known by his title as Fo-hai Ch'an-shih), a master of the Yang-ch'i line of the Rinzai school. Well before the time of Eisai, Kakua returned to Japan and began to propagate Zen meditation, though meeting with little success among his fellow Japanese. As an indication of his genuinely Zen manner, the story is told of Kakua that when Emperor Takakura questioned him about the way of Zen, Kakua surprised the entire court by playing his flute in response. Resigned to his lot, Kakua withdrew to the solitude of Mount Hiei where he continued to practice Zen to the end of his life.

DAINICHI NŌNIN AND THE DARUMA SCHOOL

Historians of Japanese Zen usually begin the story of the planting of Zen in Japan with the travels to China of Myōan Eisai (1141–1215).[13] One of his elder contemporaries, Dainichi Nōnin (n. d.), had already some time earlier established a not unimportant role for himself as a Zen master.[14] He has been given little attention since the source materials related to his life and work were not accessible. Recently, writings of the Daruma school of Nōnin were uncovered among the rich collection of ancient Japanese texts in the Kanazawa Bunko library.[15] Important contributions have helped to place the school in the history of Japanese Zen.[16] Because the beginning of the school precedes Eisai, a brief account, necessarily colored by later developments, is introduced here.

THE BIOGRAPHY OF NŌNIN
Much of the course of Nōnin's life remains unclear, including the dates of his birth and death. The only certain date is 1189, the year in which he dispatched two disciples to China. This date is provided for us in a biographical notice in

the *Honchō kōsōden,* an extensive seventy-six-volume historical collection that treats more than 1,600 Buddhist monks. The work was compiled by Mangen Shiban (1626–1710) of the Rinzai school.[17] According to a brief passage in book 19, Nōnin studied Buddhist texts as a young man and "felt drawn to Zen meditation by natural disposition." After assiduous practice he achieved enlightenment and founded the monastery of Sambō-ji in the region of Settsu. Since he had not received recognition as a Zen master, he sent two of his disciples, Renchū and Shōben, to China in the year 1189 with a letter and gifts, that they might visit the Zen master Cho-an Te-kuang (1121–1203), a disciple of the famous Ta-hui Tsung-kao (1080–1163), and request recognition for their master. Te-kuang not only supplied the desired certificate of enlightenment but also arranged for the envoys to return with gifts: a Dharma robe, an inscribed portrait of himself (commissioned at the request of the two disciples), and a picture of Bodhidharma. After the disciples had returned home, the biographical note continues, the name of Nōnin spread far and wide. There follows mention of his disciple Kakuan and his works in the Buddhist center of Tōnomine in the region of Yamato. The notice closes with a report that Nōnin's nephew Kagekiyo of the Taira clan struck his uncle down with a sword during a visit, a detail that Japanese historians do not find credible. Kagekiyo died in 1196 and the probable date of Nōnin's death is 1194 or 1195.

Mention of Nōnin and his effectiveness in early writings of various origin require some enlargement on this sparse account. The learned Tendai monk Shōshin of Mount Hiei (n. d.) refers several times to the Daruma school in a comparative study of Tendai and Shingon, *Tendai shingon nishū dōi-shō,* dated 1188, where he treats the school as bound to Tendai in the same way that Shingon is and acknowledges it as an independent school.[18] In other passages he takes the Daruma school to mean a form of Zen, the sense that it often has in verbal usage. This is also the case with the Kegon monk Myōe (1173–1232), an acquaintance of Eisai who carried on a strong interest in Zen and frequently referred in general to the "Daruma school."[19]

Nichiren, the founder of the school that bears his name, places Nōnin alongside Hōnen, the founder of the Pure Land school (Jōdoshū,) in his work *Kaimokushō* (1272).[20] In his view, both diverge from true Buddhism but deserve high respect nevertheless. In any case, Nichiren gave importance to the school of Nōnin.

The term *Daruma school* is also used to designate the Zen school of Nōnin in recently discovered writings of the school. It would appear that Nōnin himself had so named his school, though this is not certain. The name *Daruma school* was used in remembrance of Bodhidharma in China and then again in Japan for Zen groups of all sorts. In order to avoid confusion, Ōkubo Dōshū, the renowned Dōgen scholar and longtime president of Komazawa University, adopted the name "Japanese Daruma school," for which tradition did not offer any support.[21] The strong Japanese stamp of the Zen style propagated by Nōnin nonetheless argues for the nomenclature.

We owe the most important report on Nōnin and his school in the early period to Eisai whose principal work, *Kōzen gokokuron* (1198) contains harsh criticisms.[22] In the third book, entitled *Seijin ketsugiron*, Eisai writes:

> Someone asked: "Some people recklessly call the Daruma-shū the Zen sect. But they [the Daruma-shū adepts] themselves say that there are no precepts to follow, no practices to engage in. From the outset there are no passions; from the beginning we are enlightened. Therefore do not practice, do not follow the precepts, eat when hungry, rest when tired. Why practice *nembutsu*, why give maigre feasts, why curtail eating? How can this be?
>
> Eisai replied that the adherents of the Daruma-shū are those who are described in the sūtras as having a false view of emptiness. One must not speak with them or associate with them, and must keep as far away as possible.[23]

This passage, which Japanese historians see as referring to the school of Nōnin, voices serious complaints against the Daruma school.[24] The doctrine of emptiness (Skt., *śūnyatā*; Jpn., *kū*) announced in the Wisdom sūtras is one of the fundamental views of Mahāyāna. Taken over from the philosophical school of the "Middle Way" (Skt., Mādhyamika), it became a basic principle in China, above all in the school of the "Three Treatises" (Chin., San-lun; Jpn., Sanron). Ancient tradition has also handed down the two sayings, that there is in the beginning no darkening of the mind and that all living beings are originally enlightened. Yanagida sees here signs of the early Chinese Zen of the T'ang period.[25] Eisai's critique is principally concerned with an insufficient attention to the precepts and a lack of zeal for the practice on the part of the Daruma school. Nōnin's spirituality had, like that of Eisai, led beyond Mount Hiei, where the religious quest had declined noticeably during the second half of the Heian period. In theory and praxis he subscribed to a free interpretation of the monastic rule. In contrast, Eisai strove earnestly for workable reforms.

The confrontation of the masters gave rise to a rivalry between their schools, witnessed in the low esteem in which Nōnin and his disciples were treated in the influential work *Genkō shakusho* (1322) of Kokan Shiren (1278–1346).[26] Shiren, who belonged to one of the main lines of the Rinzai school, set out to safeguard within Japanese Zen the preeminence of the Rinzai school of Eisai that had been brought over directly from China. For this reason he insisted emphatically that Eisai was the first in a direct line of succession to transplant the way of Zen from China. In contrast, Nōnin attained confirmation of his enlightenment experience and acceptance into the Dharma inheritance of a Chinese Rinzai line indirectly through the mediation of two disciples that he sent to China. Shiren takes this absence of generational succession as the starting point of a forceful critique aimed at Nōnin's abandonment of the precepts and rules. In addition, he reports of disputes between the two masters that ended in Nōnin's defeat.

One may well wonder why Nōnin did not himself travel to China and practice under a Chinese master as so many of his contemporaries did. Perhaps it was only in advanced age that he felt the inadequacy of having been self-taught, or perhaps his position of leadership in the Sanbō-ji monastery prohibited him from taking the long and dangerous voyage.[27] In the absence of further information the question must rest moot. In any event, personal experience of Zen practice under a recognized Chinese master was seen as indispensable in Japan at the time.

It seems that we may attribute the little attention given the Daruma school in Japanese historiography above all to the critical passage in the Genkō shakusho. The favorable notice given Nōnin later by Mangen Shiban was unable to alter the historical image that had been spread. The few scanty details known at the time about the Daruma school were unable to lend any force to the biographical report of Shiban. In our own day, the verification of writings from the Daruma school has wrought a change in our understanding of the school.

THE WRITINGS OF THE DARUMA SCHOOL

The three texts of the Daruma school appear in the first sourcebook of the Kanazawa Bunko collection. They are put together in the following order with no indication of the compiler or date: (1) Kenshō jōbutsuron (pp. 174–98), (2) Jōtōshōgakuron (pp. 201–207), (3) Hōmon taikō (pp. 211–20). These relatively brief texts provide important information on the Daruma school. After painstaking research scholars were able to determine that the first two treatises originated from within the Daruma school itself. There is good cause to argue for an early draft that gave Eisai support for the criticisms of the Kōzen gokokuron of 1198. The third text is later; because of its similarity with the two previous texts as well as certain data it contains on the history of the Daruma school, it is also to be counted as the writing of the school.

All three texts clearly support the claim that the school can be traced back to the first Chinese Zen patriarch, Bodhidharma, and his spiritual legacy. The Jōtōshōgakuron expressly refers to Nōnin's school, which carries on the generational line of Bodhidharma, as the Daruma-shū. The designation does not appear in the other two tracts, but the Kenshō jōbutsuron relies on the "Three Treatises of Bodhidharma" (Jpn., Daruma sanron) as a doctrinal foundation.[28] Like all works attributed to Bodhidharma, the treatises have since been proven apocryphal, but right up to modern times they enjoyed high esteem. Moreover, the Daruma school bases itself on the Śūraṃgama Sūtra, whence the expression ikkyō sanron, "one sūtra and three treatises."[29]

The three treatises of Bodhidharma, the underpinning of the Kenshō jō-butsuron, no doubt date back to the early years of Zen history. The Hasōron (Chin., P'o-hsiang lun) has been identified as the Kanshinron (Chin., Kuan-hsin lun) of Master Shen-hsiu of the Northern school. The Goshōron (Chin., Wu-hsing lun) rests at all events on the doctrine of the Northern school, while the Ketsumyakuron (Chin., Hsüeh-mo lun) is close to the Oxhead school.[30] In these ancient Chinese tracts discipline and practice retreat into the background. The core of the Kenshō jōbutsuron makes "seeing into one's nature and becoming a Buddha" (kenshō jōbutsu) the dominant axiom of the Zen of the T'ang period.

The school straightforwardly calls itself the "Zen school" or the "Buddha mind school" (Busshinshū). It takes as its main concern the transmission of the Buddha mind.

Ishii Shūdō, the editor of the texts of the Daruma school, considers the *Jōtōshōgakuron* as the most important. He researched the text, which he took to be a transcript of a programmatic talk delivered by a young disciple on the occasion of a celebration in honor of Bodhidharma, and devoted a long study to it. After demonstrating its authorship in the Daruma school, he clarifies the structure of its composition. A first section presents a treatment of historical succession of generations similar to that found in the Zen chronicles. Printing the texts synoptically, he draws attention to the similarities to and differences with the Chinese sources. Some strong elements of the Bodhidharma legend, such as the six years the patriarch spent seated in meditation before a wall, are omitted; no mention is made of diligent, prolonged sitting in meditation, while the altogether unbelievable detail of Bodhidharma's crossing over to Japan is mentioned.

The second section introduces the main point of the talk as captured in the phrase *jishin sokubutsu,* a formula used in the T'ang period to express the doctrine of the unity of all things. Through the identification of the self with the Buddha all of reality is acknowledged as Buddha reality. All living beings, and in increasing measure all nonliving beings, are mind and Buddha, or Buddha nature. The chronicles and kōan collections of the Sung period attribute the words particularly to Ma-tsu.[31] The train of thought of the *Jōtōshōgakuron,* as Ishii demonstrates, is similar to that of the *Sugyōroku* (Chin., *Tsung-ching lu*) of Yung-ming Yen-shou (904–975).[32] This extensive work, widely circulated in Japan, had considerable influence on the Daruma school. The saying regarding the identity of mind and Buddha allowed for wider interpretations such as those that Eisai singled out for reproach in the passage cited above.[33] The identity of mind and Buddha was taken over into the Daruma school (similar to what we see in the *Sugyōroku*), whose motif was the identity of mind and Buddha or even the Buddha nature of all living beings.

The third section of the *Jōtōshōgakuron* returns from the heights of enlightenment to the everyday world. It treats the good fortune that befalls the enlightened in this life. Its title reads "What is searched for is obtained." What is longed for is protection from natural catastrophes, sickness, and all harm; what is achieved is every imaginable good fortune. Here we see the efficacy of the school at work through the recitation of magical formulas and the carrying out of esoteric rites. Magical practices procure merit which in turn bring worldly gain and ward off bad fortune. In this section, too, the text relies heavily on the *Sugyōroku,* which gives ample room for the esoteric and teaches a rite for the praise of Bodhidharma (*Daruma-kōshiki*), the essence of the cult of the Daruma school. The esoteric element, however, reaches back to a much earlier time and in the course of the unfolding of the history of Zen came to assume an important role.[34]

The third text, *Hōmon taikō,* also a product of the Daruma school, is particularly difficult to approach since all information regarding date and com-position are lacking. Adopting the powerful manner of expression of early Zen history, it recounts the conversation that Bodhidharma had with his disciples when taking his leave of them. As in the first two texts, the proximity to the old masters of the T'ang period is striking. The writings of the Daruma school offer direct contact with the early period of Chinese Zen. This signifi-cant particularity raises the difficult question of how the Daruma school understood these texts and applied them to life at the end of the Heian pe-riod. That there is a considerable distance from the methodically cultivated style of Zen in the Sung period is clear. It remains only to lay out, in rath-er loosely ordered fashion, what remained of the Daruma school at the time that the new Buddhism broke on the scene at the start of the Kamakura period.

THE DARUMA SCHOOL WITHIN THE JAPANESE ZEN MOVEMENT

The origin and fate of the Dharma school are imbedded in the process of the transplanting of Zen from the Chinese motherland into Japan. Dainichi Nōnin, as already mentioned, dispatched two disciples to the Chinese Zen master Te-kuang and secured a certification of enlightenment together with recognition as the fifty-first Dharma heir (Te-kuang served as the fiftieth) in a line of tradition reaching back to Śākyamuni. Te-kuang carried on as a disciple of Ta-hui, who belonged to a line of Zen that devoted all its energies to the practice of the kōan and, because it was aimed at sudden enlightenment, was also known as taigo-zen or "the Zen that awaits enlightenment."[35]

Nōnin did not adopt Ta-hui's form of Zen. His own style came from the Zen meditation practiced in Tendai, which resonates with the early Zen of the Northern school first introduced from China by its founder Saichō. He drew copiously from the Sugyōroku, which was studied zealously on Mount Hiei. In this way he fused Zen and the teachings of the sūtras (zenkyō itchi). He also incorporated into his doctrine and practice elements of Tendai esotericism (taimitsu). He did not engage in the practice of kōan. The Zen of the Daruma school, as its texts show, distinguished itself in this way from the Rinzai Zen of the Sung period in the line of Ta-hui.[36]

The actual significance of Nōnin is hard to assess. Shiban praises his deeds "far and wide" in the biographical notice referred to above, but there is a lack of concrete data regarding times and places. In the light of Eisai's critique in the Kōzen gokokukuron, possibly occasioned by Nōnin's success, we may reckon the last decade of the twelfth century as a temporal point of reference and the area surrounding Kyoto as the geographical locale. Around the same time and in the same region Eisai's speedy rise began. Though not free of weaknesses, Eisai proved strong enough to overcome his rivals.[37] Not only was he unmarked by the blemish of having been self-taught—personal encounter with the master, the menju, was held to be an essential element in spiritual transmission—but after returning from his two trips to China Eisai developed an impressive range of religious and cultural activities. The Daruma school had nothing comparable to the three large monasteries Eisai founded in Hakata (Shōfuku-ji), Kyoto (Kennin-ji), and Kamakura (Jufuku-ji).

Ōkubo Dōshū, who has in the past been critical of the Daruma school, acknowledges the works of Nōnin, who, he says, "as a Zen adept was an outstanding personality."[38] He may be right. The fact that Nōnin achieved enlightenment without the aid of a master supports it. Of course, the portrait we are able to piece together of him from the sources at our disposal lacks clear contours; the same can be said of his school as a whole.[39]

The uncertainty begins with the erection of the first monastery, Sambō-ji, and carries through to the end of the school. Nōnin himself, according to the biographical note in the *Honchō kōsōden*, founded Sambō-ji in Settsu; the year is not known. The property was an annex of the Tendai center of Mount Hiei. Nōnin had a second domicile on the East Mountain in Kyoto. After his death his disciple Kakuan there instructed Ejō, later to become the main disciple of Dōgen, until he transferred to Tōnomine with him and perhaps other disciples. The place was a center of Tendai Buddhism in the Yamato region, but some time later (1228) was destroyed by enemy monks from the monastery of Kōfuku-ji in Nara. Ejō bound himself to Dōgen, who was staying in Kukakusa near Kyoto in 1234. A group of adherents of the Daruma school were living at the time with Kakuan in the area around Kyoto. After Kakuan's death, the group moved, under the leadership of Ekan, to the monastery of Hajaku-ji in the Echizen region. In 1241 Ekan and some of his associates entered the monastic community of Dōgen. The story of what took place there and Dōgen's relation to the Daruma school will be taken up in the following chapter.

The main seat of the Daruma school was clearly in Sambō-ji. Why Kakuan left the monastery and transferred to Tōnomine is a mystery. The temple property remained until the Ōnin War (1467–1477). It served to store the greater part of the rich reliquary (Skt., *śarīra*) brought over from China, which the monks esteemed highly and went to great pains to safeguard. The custodian of the Kanazawa Bunko collection almost by accident recently discovered these treasures, preserved down to the present, in an exhibit of temple art.[40] They contain "relics" of the bodhisattva Samantabhadra (Jpn., Fugen) and the first six Chinese patriarchs (whose authenticity is of course out of the question) as well as the Dharma robe of Ta-hui and the portrait of Te-kuang. The individual pieces contain certificates with dates and explanations. These expensive pieces were not lost in the flames that destroyed Sambō-ji because shortly before that they had been committed to the friendly Jōdo monastery of Shōbō-ji in Kyoto, where they remained unnoticed, but carefully guarded, until they attracted the eyes of the Buddhist historian. The wealth of the relics guarded at Sambō-ji indicate the place of preeminence of the monastery. The branch line of Hajaku-ji was in possession of only one such memorial piece.

On the papers found with the relics the names of some monks, particularly from the first decades after Nōnin, are registered. Reports of activities among the people are lacking. Esoteric writings of the temple lead one to suppose that ceremonies in the style of Tendai (*taimitsu*) or Shingon (*tōmitsu*) were carried out.[41] The monastery understood itself as a Zen temple of the Daruma school, where more weight was placed on practice (gyō) than on study (gaku).[42] In the absence of further facts the details can only be left to the imagination. Nōnin's creation clearly proved no match for the Kamakura Zen of the new era, with its numerous eminent personalities from Japan and China. One may agree with a young Japanese Buddhist scholar who concentrated his attentions for a time on the study of the Daruma school, when he tells us that he holds it in high esteem as one of the factors that challenged the new Kamakura Buddhism.[43] As an independent Zen school it could not prevail.

EISAI

The honor of having founded Zen in Japan is ascribed to the Buddhist monk Myōan Eisai,[44] though the statement cannot be used without certain reservations. One can say that Eisai took the first decisive steps leading to the formation of the Rinzai school of Zen Buddhism in Japan. But his efforts did not suffice to lay a solid foundation for the new school. The founding of the Japanese Rinzai school was a many-faceted process and extended over a long period of time, as we shall see presently. The honor of being named the founder of Zen in Japan fell to Eisai only because he stood at the beginning of an important development that proved strong enough to carry into the future. One cannot rank him among the influential founding figures in the history of Japanese Buddhism. It is more correct to say with Miura and Sasaki that "Eisai . . . later came to be considered the founder of Zen in Japan."[45]

YOUTH AND TRAVELS IN CHINA

Eisai was born into the priestly house of the Shinto shrine at Kibitsu in the province of Bitchū, present day Okayama. Early on his father entrusted the education of his son to a Buddhist friend who headed a nearby temple. From this Buddhist monk the young man learned the basics of Tendai Buddhism. At age fourteen, Eisai entered the monastic life at the main Tendai temple on Mount Hiei near Kyoto, had his head shaved, and was ordained as monk. He concentrated himself energetically to the study of the comprehensive Tendai system. He was also introduced into its secret doctrines, underwent esoteric ordination,[46] and went on to specialize in the esoteric doctrines of Tendai (tai-mitsu), mastering its theory and practice.

The well educated Tendai monk set out for China to broaden and round out his knowledge—a bold venture for those times. For more than a century no Japanese Buddhist monk had visited China. But Eisai was determined, hoping that what he would learn in China might help him revitalize the failing religion of Buddha in Japan. In April of 1168 he arrived in the land of Sung and met with the Japanese Shingon monk Chōgen (1121–1206). Together they made pilgrimages to Mount T'ien-t'ai and Mount Aśoka (Chin., A-yü-wang shan), and made brief excursions to holy places so that by September of that same year he was able to return to Japan. During this first of Eisai's visits to China he met with many Zen Buddhists and was struck by how widely Zen had spread through-out the Middle Kingdom. A further fruit of the trip were the Tendai writings he carried back with him to Japan. In the twenty rather uneventful years that followed, Eisai devoted himself tirelessly to the doctrinal study and the practice of esoteric Tendai rituals. He founded the Yōjō line within Tendai *mikkyō* and was soon declared patriarch of this line with the title of Yōjōbō. During the lengthy interlude before his second trip to China, he was also active in his home province and in Kyūshū.[47]

Eisai set out for China a second time on April 2, 1187, a trip that was to change his life. In a terse, direct style, he reported on this visit in his important work *Kōzen gokokuron* (*Treatise on the Spread of Zen for the Protection of the Nation*).[48] Composed amidst the pressures of the dramatic and painful events that followed Eisai's return to Japan, the work reflects on the foundational experiences of his trip. From the start, the purpose of this second journey to the West was to follow the stream of Buddhism back to its fountainhead in India. He states his intention in so many words, noting that he had hoped to visit the eight holy sites of Śākyamuni in India, especially the site of his enlightenment.[49] Immediately upon his arrival in China he went to the military and civilian authorities but was unable to procure the necessary permission to travel on to India.[50]

He therefore resorted to his original plan of studying Zen at its sources in China. He persevered in his conviction that the Zen that was flourishing so markedly in the land of Sung would also be able to heal the ailing state of Buddhism in Japan. He went to Mount T'ien-t'ai, where Zen was practiced in the monastery of Wan-nien-ssu (Jpn., Mannen-ji). Under the direction of Master Hsü-an Huai-ch'ang (Jpn., Koan Eshō; n. d.) he devoted himself to sitting cross-legged in meditation and to the practice of the kōan, "totally in the style of the Rinzai school," as he himself remarks.[51] When Hsü-an, who belonged to the eighth generation of the Huang-lung (Jpn., Ōryō) line of Rinzai, moved to Mount T'ien-t'ung, Eisai followed him. There, before departing for Japan, he received the insignia of succession. As the Dharma heir of Hsü-an, he was now authorized to transplant the Rinzai Zen of the Huang-lung line in his Japanese homeland.

Unfortunately Eisai does not include much about his personal experiences in his short report—nothing to reveal the relationship he had to his Chinese master. Instead, he adds the full text of his certificate of enlightenment, which is full of exuberant praise for the Japanese disciple who left his home in an effort to get a deeper understanding of the spirit of Rinzai in China.[52] Hsü-an also lauds his student's diligence in the devotional practices of Buddhism and closes the text with a statement of the authenticity of the transmission of mind from Śākyamuni up to the present time. Other reports passed down about Eisai's stay in China are embellished with legend. For example, he is extolled for using magical prayers and rituals to rid a certain region of a contagious disease and for having brought rain to an area suffering from drought.[53] As these stories would have it, the Zen disciple Eisai was gifted with wondrous powers that he owed to esoteric Tendai Buddhism. This raises the whole problem of the mixture of Zen and Tendai—a problem that was to accompany and often unsettle him during the course of his life.

Before continuing with our review of Eisai's life, we would do well to reflect on the motives and aims of his second trip to China. Eisai was part of a reform movement made up of Buddhists who were deeply disturbed by the decadence and pessimism that they saw as marking the final days of the "Last Dharma" (mappō) and set out accordingly to effect a radical renewal within Japanese Buddhism.[54] His desire to go to Indian arose not only out of a great devotion to the Buddha as founder but more particularly out of a desire to know the original "true Dharma" (Jpn. shōbō)—that is, the true teachings of the Buddha and the true fulfillment of the precepts. It was said that during the final days in Japan the Buddha-Dharma had disappeared from India and China and was flourishing only in Japan.[55] Eisai quotes the saying and explains it without expressly accepting it. While he knew only too well the abuses of Japanese Buddhism, everything he knew about India was hearsay. He had heard that most of the Indian Buddhist monks were following the dictates of the law faithfully.[56] If there was any place that the "true Dharma" was to be found, surely it was in the land of its origins. It was this conviction that distinguished Eisai as a true reformer: the most important thing in a time of religious decay was a return to origins.

Eisai's determination to bring about reform was an important factor in his turn to Zen Buddhism, convinced as he was that the renewal of Buddhism in Japan would have to rest on a strict observance of rules and precepts (Jpn., kairitsu). At the time of the "true Dharma" the Buddhist way of life had been marked by faithful observance of the rules of the order (Skt., saṅgha) as laid out in the Vinaya; Eisai saw this way of life reflected in the Zen school of China. In the beginning of his Treatise on the Spread of Zen for the Protection of the Nation he states that only a sound moral life can assure the endurance of the Dharma.[57] In the same section he speaks of the observance of rules and precepts in Zen. "For the Zen school," he remarks in another section of the Treatise, "precepts (Jpn., kai) come first and meditation (zen) at the end."[58] He finds this same great esteem for the precepts within all of Mahāyāna Buddhism: "When consciousness is still, the precepts arise, and thus enlightenment is achieved."[59] His hope was to cultivate anew in Japan the strict observance of the precepts that he admired among the Chinese, and this was what impelled him to take up life in a Chinese Zen monastery.

During Eisai's second visit to China the motivation of the reformer was especially evident in his two chief concerns—to make a pilgrimage to India and to promote Zen Buddhism. This drive lay at the very roots of his being and is perhaps more important for understanding his personality and his work than is his own Zen experience, about which we know very little in any case.

THE KŌZEN GOKOKURON

After having spent four years in China, Eisai reached the port of Hirado on the southern Japanese island of Kyūshū in 1191 and at once began preaching the way of Zen. After securing a small number of followers, he set about laying the pillars for the future of the Zen movement.[60] Already during this period in Kyū- shū, his sites were set on the capital city of Kyoto where he hoped one day to erect a Zen temple at the nation's center. But before he could even begin to realize these plans, Eisai discovered that his success in promoting the cause of Zen had aroused a mounting storm of protest from the powerful Tendai monks who had been incited against him by the complaints of Rōben, a monk from Hakosaki in Kyūshū. In 1194 the monks persuaded the court to issue an interdict against this "new sect" of "the Dharma school." Eisai replied that Zen was nothing new: "Saichō, the patriarch of the Tendai school, has already taught Zen; if the Zen school is void, then so is Saichō, and the Tendai school has no mean- ing."[61]

This same line of thought reappears in the Kōzen gokokuron. Later we will consider how Eisai developed these views and how they led him to self-contra- dictions. As the animosity of his opponents grew fiercer, he returned to Kyūshū where, with the protection and aid of the shōgun Minamoto Yoritomo, he founded the monastery of Shōfuku-ji in Hakata in 1195, which history records as the first Japanese Zen monastery. It is not clear just how long Eisai remained in the south, nor do we have much information on how he carried out his role as Zen master in Shōfuku-ji. What we do know is that in this new monastery, as in the other temples founded by Eisai, Zen was practiced side by side with esoteric rituals.[62]

The next entry in Eisai's biography is his Kōzen gokokuron, dated 1198.[63] Printed in three books, the text consists of ten sections of unequal length, each of which is written from a different perspective. Section 3 is the longest, making up the major portion of the first book and extending into the second. In this section Eisai takes up a number of questions that he most likely encountered from his opponents during earlier controversies. Many of his responses consist of citations from Buddhists scriptures, which Eisai interprets according to his own purposes. Incoherencies in composition, together with complicated argu- mentation, make the Treatise difficult reading. During the Edo period (1603– 1868), doubts were raised about Eisai's authorship of the text.[64] The controversy lasted for some time, but the case has since been closed. The work is now held to be Eisai's most important work and the clearest statement of his thought.

The Kōzen gokokuron resounds a clear apologetic tone. Eisai was defending himself against the many attacks of the Tendai monks who ever since his return from China had been accusing him of introducing a "new sect" into Japan— namely, the Chinese school of Zen—and trying to give it a higher place than traditional Buddhism, represented chiefly by Tendai and Shingon. The monks were not at all pleased with Eisai's propaganda, first in Kyūshū and then before their very eyes in the capital city of Kyoto. The fact that he was referring to this new Zen movement as the "school of the Buddha mind" was for them tantamount to the conviction that it possessed the Buddha mind in a unique way. What is more, Eisai was actively establishing Zen monasteries to serve as the centers of this new movement. All of this excited the wrath of the Tendai

monks, who in their own way were also concerned with reviving the "true Dharma." Even though there was general agreement at the time that Japanese Buddhism was ripe for reform, the monks could not accept Eisai's apparent attempts
to identify the "true Dharma" with the one school of Rinzai Zen and to slight
more traditional forms of Buddhism in Japan. Thus the question became, Was
Eisai really trying to introduce Rinzai Zen as a new school for Japan and did he
see Rinzai as the sole embodiment of the "true Dharma"?

THE TENDAI TRADITION AND CHINESE ZEN

This central question is not really given a clear answer in the *Kōzen gokokuron*.
Although Eisai defends himself with a barrage of counter-arguments, his final
position is ambiguous. On the one hand, he does not reject traditional Buddhism.
Not only did he remain a Tendai monk in the school in which he was first
ordained, but he stresses that Zen is in line with Tendai, that it corresponds to
the spirit of Tendai, and that it can contribute significantly to the renewal of
Tendai. This is one wall of his argument, behind which he retreats when attacked
by his determined opponents. On the other hand, he is aware of being the
Dharma heir of a Chinese Rinzai master from whom he learned that only Rinzai
represents the quintessence of the Buddhism and embodies the "true Dharma."
This "true dharma" is of inestimable value and provides for the self-defense of
the nation.[65] It is therefore in the national interest to promote Chinese Zen.

In the *Kōzen gokokuron* Eisai develops both sides of the argument from
several angles. He rejects the accusation that he is unfaithful to his school of
origin and points out how loyal he is to Saichō (Dengyō Daishi), the founder
of Japanese Tendai Buddhism, who recognized the great value of meditation
and practiced it zealously. Nothing could be more misleading than to sever Tendai
from meditation. Together with the "perfect teaching" (Jpn., *en*, *engyō*), the
secret rites (*mitsu*), and the precepts (*kai*), meditation (Skt., *dhyāna*; Jpn., *zen*)
is one of the four essential elements of Tendai as expressed in the formula *en-
mitsu-zen-kai*. Eisai also appeals to another fourfold pattern: precepts (*kai*), meditation (*zen*), wisdom (*hannya*), and spotless mind (*mujokushin*).[66] He gives references to support his insistence that meditation and enlightenment (*zenjō*) must
always take first place and that without them there is no attaining liberation.[67]
In the section dealing with the enlightenment of the early honored figures, he
appends ten texts from Buddhist literature (some of them from Tendai writings)
for additional proof.[68]

In the course of the decline of Japanese Buddhism during the second half
of the Heian period, both meditation and observance of the precepts had suffered
considerably. Eisai wanted to redress the situation and the best way he knew
was through promoting the practice of Zen, albeit only the authentic Zen he
had learned in China. To the protests of his opponents Eisai countered that
they were deserting what was best in their own tradition. And when he was
accused of subordinating Tendai to the new school he seemed intent on establishing, Eisai appealed to the history of Japanese Tendai, arguing that he resorted

to Rinzai Zen only in an effort to reestablish the traditional "Zen of the Patriarchs" and the masters of Mount Hiei.

Is it possible to reconcile Eisai's support of the Tendai tradition with the concern for Chinese Zen so predominant in the *Kōzen gokokuron?* We have already mentioned his account of his close contacts with the Rinzai school during his second journey to China. In addition to these personal recollections, he also supplies us with detailed explanations of the nature of the Zen school, revealing a profound knowledge of Zen. He repeats formulas that were current in Zen, especially the claim that "the school of the Buddha mind" "does not rely on words or letters but represents a special tradition outside the teaching (of the sūtras)."[69] Buddhahood was to be achieved through spiritual experience. Eisai supplies proof for this claim by citing numerous passages from a variety of sūtras (thus remaining faithful to his method of appealing to history and tradition), but also recognizes the special, direct transmission of mind *(ishin denshin)* of the Zen patriarchs, who passed on the ineffable core of their experience and evinced the Buddha nature in their daily lives—in "walking, standing, sitting, and lying" *(gyōjūzaga).*[70] He treats the generational line of Zen tradition in detail, beginning with the seven Buddhas and the twenty-eight Indian Zen patriarchs up to Bodhidharma and proceeding to the lineage in China from Bodhidharma to the Sixth Patriarch, Hui-neng. Lin-chi (Rinzai) is named as the thirty-eighth transmitter of the Buddha mind, from whom the line passes through Huang-lung to Eisai's Chinese master Hsü-an Huai-ch'ang, the fifty-second name in the traditional lineage. Eisai expressly mentions himself as the fifty-third member of this unbroken chain.[71]

His consciousness teeming with all these things, could Eisai have done other than cherish the hope of carrying on in Japan the tradition of Chinese Rinzai in which he felt so much at home? For him, Rinzai meant the "quintessence of all teachings and the summation of the Buddha-Dharma."[72] Yet despite his convictions, Eisai lacked both the ability and the will to carry out his dream of founding an independent Japanese Rinzai school. He was hindered not only by his outward and inward ties to Tendai, but also by his propensity to syncretize and harmonize, which became more of an obstacle as he advanced in years.

LAST YEARS AND DEATH

Eisai's *Kōzen gokokuron* did not lead to any kind of resolution. On the contrary, his opponents grew still more bitter. He therefore decided in 1199 to leave the capital city of Kyoto, where he had lived for some time, and move to Kamakura. There he was well received by the Minamoto clan and became the founding abbot of Jufuku-ji, which Hōjō Masako, the widow of the shōgun Minamoto Yoritomo (d. 1199) built in the year 1200 in memory of her husband and his father. The temple ranks third among the "Five Mountains" *(gozan)* of Kamakura.[73] Shortly thereafter, the capital city once again opened its doors to Eisai. At the behest of the shōgun Minamoto Yoriie, he agreed in 1202 to become the first abbot of Kennin-ji, a Zen monastery built in Kyoto by the emperor. There the early Zen movement of Japan found its center. Meantime, the nearby headquarters of Tendai and Shingon demanded concessions. By imperial decree Kennin-ji was obliged to erect, in addition to the meditation hall (Zen-in), shrines honoring Tendai (Tendai-in) and Shingon (Shingon-in).

During his final years, Eisai's activity centered around the two temples he headed in Kamakura and Kyoto. In general, he enjoyed a position of respect and the favor of the court and important offices in the Buddhist world were entrusted to him. But his interest in Zen meditation diminished. Was he admitting to himself that Zen's time had not yet come for Japan? He himself had remarked that it would take fully fifty years after his death for Zen to flower.[74] Esoteric rites become the focal point of his activities. Because of his expertise in this area he was frequently invited to important events. No longer did he seek to wield his influence for the purpose of establishing an independent Zen school. In a word, his life's work resulted in important, indeed pioneering, achievements for the implanting of Zen in Japan, but failed to accomplish the final breakthrough. In the history of Zen Eisai represents the first and foundational step in a process that, according to his own prophecy, would come to fulfillment with the establishment of the Japanese Rinzai school some fifty years after his death.

A man of many gifts, Eisai's influence extended into the cultural realm as well. Evidence of his architectural skills can be seen in Buddhist buildings constructed at that time. But it is for his contribution to the tea ceremony that he is especially remembered in the cultural history of Japan. The introduction of tea to Japan dates back to Kūkai (Kōbō Daishi, 774–835), the founder of the Shingon school about whom many legends have grown. Eisai brought tea seeds from China and began the cultivation of tea gardens on temple grounds. He wrote an essay on the advantages of tea-drinking (Kissa yōjōki, 1211) and dedicated it to the young and musically gifted shōgun of the Minamoto clan, Sanetomo (d. 1219). Not only did Eisai praise tea as a stimulant helpful for meditation, but he also claimed that it had healing effects on the entire human organism, which he understood in terms of esoteric teachings.[75]

Eisai's eventful life came to a close in an honorable death. After having predicted his end and delivered his final lecture on the precepts before a large audience, he passed away at the age of seventy-five years—as tradition has it, seated cross-legged either in Jufuku-ji in Kamakura or in Kennin-ji in Kyoto. The precise place and time of his death are uncertain. Officially, he remained a member of the Tendai school to the end. Even Kennin-ji, though intended to be a Zen monastery, was listed as a branch temple (matsuji) of the Tendai headquarters; Eisai himself named his school the "Yōjō line of Tendai Esotericism" (Yōjō taimitsu) after the Yōjō valley of Mount Hiei.[76]

Eisai (whose posthumous title is Senkō Kokushi) certainly deserves to be reckoned among the leading Buddhists of his time. His contribution to the implanting of Zen in Japan, however, was limited both by conditions of the time and by his own personality. The religious mentality of the upper classes resisted a sudden shift from the highly ceremonial type of Buddhism represented by Tendai and Shingon to a new and strange school of meditation from China. Eisai must have come to realize the impossibility of an abrupt and radical change and therefore contented himself with a mixture of Tendai and Zen—which in any case suited his syncretistic inclinations. Although some aspects of his life story require further examination, his personality and his work, minus the occasional shadow, are entirely worthy of the positive esteem that no less a figure than Dōgen accorded him, according to reliable reports. The renewal of Japanese Buddhism in the light of the "true Dharma" owes much to this man whose endeavors belonged to all of Buddhism.[77]

EISAI'S DISCIPLES

Eisai attracted numerous disciples eager to receive instruction at the hands of the renowned and gifted master so well versed in both Tendai and Zen. Particularly worthy of mention are Ryōnen Myōzen (1184–1225), Taikō Gyōyū (1162–1241), and Shakuen Eichō (d. 1247).[78] These three most important of Eisai's disciples represent very distinct personalities, whose life stories give us an insight into the complex situation that marked the outset of the Kamakura period.

Among Eisai's disciples, Myōzen, who succeeded him in Kennin-ji, was the most devoted to Zen.[79] The history of Zen remembers him chiefly as the teacher of Dōgen. Born in Ise (the district of Mie), he was orphaned at the age of eight and brought to Mount Hiei with its temples crowding in on one another. There he studied the teachings of Tendai Buddhism under the direction of the monk Myōyū. At sixteen, he received the Hīnayāna precepts on the ordination platform of Tōdai-ji in Nara (1199), and later in the Tendai monastery of Enryaku-ji he received the bodhisattva precepts of Mahāyāna. He learned Zen meditation from Eisai in the Kennin-ji temple and received the Dharma there. Had Eisai founded an independent Zen school instead of remaining with Tendai, Myōzen would have been his Dharma heir in the ninth generation of the Huang-lung line of the Rinzai school and Dōgen, who studied under Myōzen, would have also been counted in this tradition.

Dōgen remained with Myōzen in Kennin-ji for the six years from 1217 to 1223. In the chapter on practice (Bendōwa) of his major work, the Shōbōgenzō, Dōgen recounts how he began his search by visiting many teachers throughout the land until finally he came to the feet of the monk Myōzen in Kennin-ji:

> During that time I learned something of the manner of the Rinzai school. Myōzen, the chief disciple of the patriarch Eisai, was the only of Eisai's disciples who genuinely transmitted the supreme Buddha-Dharma. None of the others could compare with him.[80]

A happy master-student relationship developed between Myōzen and Dōgen. In both of them the zeal for Zen meditation soon kindled the desire to travel to China, but no sooner had they made up their minds to go than difficulties arose. Myōzen's aged teacher, ajari Myōyū, lay on his deathbed and called for Myōzen to come and be with him to the end. A report on how this news was received is given us in the *Shōbōgenzō zuimonki*, a collection of stories and sayings from the life of Master Dōgen compiled by his disciple Ejō. Myōzen called all the monks together and asked for their advice. After describing to them all the good things that his master Myōyū had done for him he said, "It is difficult to disobey a teacher's request,[81] but my going to China now at the risk of my life to seek the Way also derives from the great compassion of the bodhisattva and the desire to benefit all beings."[82] Those present all advised him to put off the voyage for six months or a year. Only the young pupil Dōgen, "the least experienced of the monks," endorsed the plan. His advice carried the day, and Myōzen announced his decision to begin the trip, explaining that his presence could not really help his sick teacher and would be of no help to those seeking to abandon the world and follow the Way.

> But if I can carry out my determination to visit China in search of the Law and can gain even a trace of enlightenment, it will serve to awaken many people, even though it means opposing the deluded wishes of one person. If the virtue gained were exceptional, it would serve to repay the kindness of my teacher. Even if I should die while crossing the sea and fail in my original plan, since my death would stem from my determination to seek the Law, my vow would not be exhausted in any future life. . . . I have, therefore, definitely decided to go to China now.[83]

In the *Shōbōgenzō zuimonki* this whole episode is offered as an example for future generations. Later, when Dōgen related this story to his disciples, he had high praise for Myōzen, in whose actions Dōgen saw the embodiment of the bodhisattva ideal.

On 22 February 1223, Myōzen, Dōgen, and their companions departed Kennin-ji. By the end of March they had embarked from Hakata in Kyūshū and within a month reached the shores of China. There they parted ways. Myōzen went to the Ching-te monastery on Mount T'ien-t'ung, where his master Eisei had practiced Zen during his second visit to China. There he celebrated a special ritual for the dead in memory of his venerated teacher. He practiced under the two masters Wu-chi Liao-p'ai and Ju-ching for three years until his health failed. On 27 May 1225 he died, sitting in meditation. As an expression of their high regard for him, the local monks erected a monument in his and Eisai's honor. When Dōgen returned home to Japan, he carried the remains of his master back with him. Dōgen's great regard for his first teacher in Zen is expressed in a short account that he wrote about Myōzen's life, entitled *Sharisō denki*.

Myōzen's untimely death was a great loss for Zen in Japan. It is hard to estimate how much this gifted, popular monk might have accomplished for Rinzai Zen in Japan had he been able to bring the wealth of his mature experience back to his native land. One may well imagine that under his guidance, the difficult process of establishing an independent Rinzai school in Japan would have taken a course quite different from the one it actually did.

Eisai's disciples Gyōyū and Eichō surpassed their master in their syncretistic tendencies. In a sense, they represent the consequences of what he taught and practiced. Although neither of them represent Zen strictly speaking, they are important for understanding the Zen movement inasmuch as some of their disciples were to become authentic and important Zen figures. Historical records mention the names of a large number of Shingon, Tendai, and Zen monks who were in contact with Gyōyū and Eichō.

Gyōyū came from around Kamakura (the district of Kanagawa). Having decided at an early age to become a Buddhist monk, he applied himself to the study of the esoteric teachings of Shingon. On orders from the shōgun Minamoto Yoritomo, the young Shingon monk took up the post of monastic assistant at the Hachiman shrine of Tsurugaoka in Kamakura, at the same time as he served as overseer of two Buddhist temples, Eifuku-ji and Daiji-ji.[84] When Eisai took up residence in Kamakura in 1200, the aging Gyōyū was his disciple and went on to succeed his master as abbot of the Jufuku-ji.

Gyōyū was active mainly in the Kamakura region, the residence of Minamoto, whose respect and trust he enjoyed. The shōgun's widow, Masako, requested Gyōyū's spiritual guidance and received ordination at his hands as a Buddhist nun. Gyōyū also had a close friend in Sanetomo, the third shōgun of the Minamoto clan. Sanetomo was a devoted follower of Buddhism and a composer of songs in the Man'yōshū style, which earned him a place in the history of Japanese literature.[85] Gyōyū was deeply disturbed when the young prince was assassinated in 1219, which may account for his retreat for a time to Kyoto and Mount Kōya. There, upon the intervention of the still influential Masako, he became head of the Kongōzammai-in temple complex, where he devoted himself both to the practice of Shingon and the study of Zen.[86] It was at this time, too, that the well-known Shinchi Kakushin (1207–1298) studied Zen meditation with him. Kakushin accompanied him on his return to Kamakura and served him faithfully until his death. During this last period of his life, a circle of influential figures gathered around Gyōyū, who, in addition to his regular duties, had also assumed direction of Jōmyō-ji. This monastery had originally been built in 1188 by Ashikaga Yoshikane as a Shingon temple but was later converted into a Zen temple by his son, Yoshiuji. In time, Jōmyō-ji would be elevated formally to the rank of one of the "Five Mountains" of Kamakura (1386).[87] Gyōyū passed away in Jufuku-ji at a ripe old age.

It is not known where or when the disciple Eichō was born. In his youth he too immersed himself in the exoteric and esoteric teachings of the Tendai system. In Kamakura he became a student of Rinzai Zen under Eisai (1199), and was so zealous and successful in his practice of Zen meditation that Eisai eventually recognized him as having the marks of his successor in the Huang-lung line. But through and through the syncretist that he was, Eichō never really sought to carry on the Zen tradition in this manner. Under him Zen was absorbed, without its own identity, into the general structure of Mahāyāna Buddhism. Personally, Eichō's chief interest lay in esoteric Tendai. At the beginning of the Jōō period (1222 or 1223), he founded and became the first abbot of the

Chōraku-ji in the district of Gumma, where he attracted a number of notable disciples, among them Jinshi Eison and Enni Ben'en who later visited China and returned to Japan to play an important role in the establishment of Rinzai Zen. Eichō's disciple Zōsō Rōyo (1193–1276) succeeded him as head of Chōraku-ji, which was considered a Tendai temple.[88] Eichō's disciples made his name known and secured for him a place in the history of Japanese Zen.

Eisai's disciples were not able to provide for the survival of Rinzai Zen in Japan. After the early death of Myōzen, a man truly animated by the spirit of Zen, only Gyōyū and Eichō remained, but neither of them succeeded any better than their master Eisai in passing the Rinzai tradition on to future generations. In the years that followed, however, the picture of Zen in Japan was to change. Contacts with China, the motherland of Zen, had not been broken off, and soon strong and life-giving winds were to blow across the seas from the Land of the Sung, helping Rinzai Zen to sink lasting roots.

ENNI BEN'EN

Enni Ben'en (1201–1280) is the pivotal figure in the history of Rinzai Zen in Japan during the thirteenth century.[89] Not as well known as other Zen masters—indeed often hardly known at all—Enni Ben'en spent most of his long life in the capital city Kyoto, where his activity was successful and influential. What qualified him above all were the seven years he spent in China studying under the famous Zen master Wu-chun Shih-fan (Jpn., Mujun Shiban, 1177–1249) of the Yang-ch'i (Jpn., Yōgi) line of Rinzai. This fact must be borne in mind for the proper evaluation of what follows. If one were to consider only Enni's study with Eichō, one would have to place him in the Huang-lung line, which Eichō and his three disciples represented and which afterward became extinct in Japan.[90] All the Japanese Rinzai masters whom we are about to consider belong to the line of Yang-ch'i.

Like most Japanese Zen Buddhists of this early period, Enni Ben'en was first trained in Tendai. Born in the Land of Suruga (in the district of Shizuoka), he ascended Mount Kunō at the tender age of five, and at age eight began study under the Tendai monk Gyōben; together with the widely-meshed Tendai system, he also studied early Buddhist writings, including such works as the foundational *Abhidharmakośa* (Jpn., *Kusharon*). At age eighteen, in the central Tendai monastery of Onjō-ji (known as Mii-dera), he entered monastic life, received the tonsure, and later was ordained a monk on the platform of Tōdai-ji in Nara. Following his ordination he spent three years in Kyoto studying Confucianism and then returned for a time to Onjō-ji, whence he retreated to the monastery of Chōraku-ji in order to learn from Eichō the mixture of Tendai and Zen that Eisai had practiced. During a second stay on Mount Kunō in 1224, he was introduced into the secret rites of Tendai by Kenzei and four years later received the seal of the esoteric teaching of Tendai from Abbot A'nin of Jufuku-ji in Kamakura.

This unusually many-faceted education provided Enni with a vast learning.

In his later years, as he went about his different activities in Kyoto, he was in fact reputed to be one of the most learned persons of his time. While his immense knowledge assured him of great respect, even more important for the promotion of Zen than all his learning was his profound experience of enlightenment, the fruit of his intense discipline in China.

The success of Enni's stay in China (1235–1241) turned out to be of extraordinary significance. He had the good fortune to be accepted as a student of the prestigious Zen master Wu-chun Shih-fan, who practiced in Manjuzen-ji (Chin., Wan-shou ch'an-ssu) on Mount Ching in the province of Chekiang, one of the "Five Mountains" of the Sung period.[91] Having practiced in his early years under well-known masters, Wu-chun became the Dharma heir of P'o-an Tsu-hsien (1136–1211). The esteemed Chinese master held his Japanese student in high regard and after an intense but short period of practice awarded him the seal of enlightenment (1237). To honor the occasion, Wu-chun presented his disciple with the precious gift of a portrait of himself, bearing a personally inscribed dedication dated 1238—a choice piece of art of the highest quality. In the words of one art historian, the painting "enables one to feel the presence of the enlightened Ch'an master. From the master's countenance, aglow with the personal qualities of his imposing personality, there emanates the power of this truly great portrait."[92] Enni was permitted to take this remembrance of his master home with him, and to this day it is preserved and revered in Tō-fuku-ji.

His seven years on Mount Ching afforded Enni the incomparable opportunity of steeping himself in the Zen that was in full flower in China at the time. The Chinese monastery of Wan-shou ch'an-ssu became one of the mainstays of the bridge across which Zen travelled to Japan. Many of the Chinese Buddhists who played crucial roles in spreading Zen in Japan had practiced on Mount Ching under Wu-chun, among them Wu-hsüeh Tsu-yüan (Jpn., Mugaku Sogen, 1226–1286), the founder of Engaku-ji (Kamakura), and Wu-an P'u-ning (Jpn., Gottan Funei, 1197–1276), the second abbot of Kenchō-ji (Kamakura). Many other Japanese monks, following the example of their countryman Enni, visited Mount Ching and studied under Wu-chun and his successors.

In addition to the portrait of his master, Wu-chun, and Buddhist and Confucian texts, Enni also returned to Japan with monastic rules and meditation texts. He remained first in Kyūshū, establishing a number of monasteries in the region around Hakata and propagating the "school of the Buddha mind" in the north part of the island. Despite the opposition mounting among local Tendai groups, Enni's reputation grew and attracted the attention of many prominent contemporaries.

In 1243 Fujiwara Michiie (1192–1252), who had withdrawn into privacy after an illustrious life of activity, summoned the good monk who had recently returned from China and whose fame was spreading in his homeland. Already for some years Michiie had nurtured the idea of erecting a grand temple to Buddha in the capital, one that would rank in splendor with the great temples of Tōdai-ji and Kōfuku-ji in Nara. In the person of Enni he had discovered his founding abbot. Although the project advanced slowly, Enni now had a powerful patron on whose effective protection he could rely. He took up residence in Fumon-in, a building put up in 1246 alongside what would one day be the completed temple complex of Tōfuku-ji.[93] It was Michiie's dream that the Buddhist tradition would find a home in the new temple, which, in addition to a Zen hall, would also include quarters for Shingon and Tendai rites.

From the start, Enni's abilities lay in this line. He presided over Shingon and Tendai rituals, lectured on the *Dainichi-kyō*, the main sūtra of Shingon Buddhism, and on the popular syncretistic treatises, the *Sugyōroku* and *Buppō-daimei-roku*. Still, Zen meditation took first place and the spiritual life of the Zen monks on Mount Ching remained his ideal. And so Zen grew in popularity, largely through the efforts of this spirited, balanced, and effective monk and the assistance of his influential patrons. Enni rejoiced as opposition weakened and Zen meditation became better known and praticed. During the decade he spent working in the capital city of Kyoto, there was a clear shift in the popular attitude toward this new school from China—not a sudden and dramatic change, but clearly an advance over the state of affairs under Eisai and his successors.

Tōfuku-ji, which later became one of the Five Mountains of Zen in Kyoto, developed into the center of the Zen movement in the capital. It was only completed after the death of Fujiwara Michiie. At the request of Ichijō Sanetsune, Michiie's third son and founder of the Ichijō clan, Enni consecrated the monastery formally in 1255. He took over its direction as abbot and extended his influence beyond the monastery walls. Among his disciples there were followers of other Buddhist schools. Enni was also the tenth of the abbots of Kennin-ji, and every day at noon, as the temple bells tolled, he would leave his headquarters at Tōfuku-ji and walk to Kennin-ji, where monastic fervor had waned after the death of Eisai and Myōzen. In 1257, at the invitation of Hōjō (1226–1263), Enni traveled to Kamakura, the other center of the nation, to reside at Jufuku-ji.

Enni's lasting accomplishments, especially his written works, are associated today with the posthumous title given him in 1312 by Emperor Hanazono: Shō-ichi Kokushi.[94] In his *Jisshūyōdōki* (*Essentials of the Way of the Ten Schools*) Enni treats ten Buddhist schools, beginning with the "school of the Buddha mind." This chapter on the Zen tradition is the heart of the work, comprising about one-third of the whole. As he explains, the school of Zen, far from being just one of the many Buddhist schools, is the only one that carries the mind of the Buddha through history. The same inspiration lay behind his collection of sayings, the *Shōichi-goroku*. Of particular importance is his collection entitled *Dharma Words of Shōichi* (*Shōichi hōgo*),[95] where Enni adopts the question-and-answer style to explain the essentials of Zen to his patron Fujiwara Michiie, and in doing shows himself to be an authentic and highly qualified Rinzai master.

As Enni sees it, Zen is the alpha and omega of the Buddhist path, the bedrock on which everything else rests. To the question, What do you mean by calling the Zen school the foundation for all things (*dharma*)? he replied:

Zen is the Buddha mind. The precepts (morality) are its external form; the teachings are its explanation in words; the invocation of the name (nembutsu) is an expedient means (Skt., upāya; Jpn., hōben). Because these three proceed from the Buddha mind, this school represents the foundation.[96]

The value of Zen is seen in its universal character. All things and all forms, it is said, take their origin from Zen and return to Zen, the "Way of Great Liberation." "When one comprehends this way, all teachings, open and secret, are fulfilled."[97] Through Zen practice, one attains the Buddha mind, which is identical with one's own mind.

When someone who has not yet attained the Way practices Zen for a time, that person is Buddha for the duration; if one practices Zen for a day, one is Buddha for a day; if one practices Zen for one's entire lifetime, one is Buddha for a lifetime. And whoever fosters this faith is a person of great capacity and is a receptacle for the Dharma.[98]

The Rinzai Zen that Enni learned in China corresponds to the teachings of the Sixth Patriarch. "The Buddha mind is without form and without attachment (musō mujaku)," and correct practice is that of "no-mind and no-thinking (mushin munen),"[99] which transcends all discriminating thought. Enni repeats the words of the Platform Sūtra: "Do not think good, do not think evil!" The person of the Tao of no-mind goes beyond all differentiation, including the difference between passion and enlightenment. Clearly, this is pure Zen, the unadulterated teaching of the Zen patriarchs. Miraculous powers are insignificant. Nothing matters but "to see into one's nature and to become the Buddha" (kenshō jōbutsu).[100] The questioning persists:

With what knowledge can one grasp what it means to see into one's nature and become Buddha?

The answer goes to the heart of the matter:

The knowledge that one attains through learning the sūtras and śāstras is called seeing, hearing, perceiving, understanding. This is the knowledge of ordinary, ignorant people (Skt., pṛthagjana; Jpn., bombu); it is not true understanding. The one who directs the light and allows the light to reflect back, such a one grasps the original Buddha nature. This is what is called the Eye of Wisdom. With this eye one sees one's nature and becomes Buddha.[101]

Toward the end of his treatise, Enni touches on the meaning of life and death. Once released from the cycle of rebirth, the enlightened person transcends the difference between life and death. "No-mind and no-thinking know neither birth nor destruction." The condition of an enlightened one is that of the great nirvāṇa.[102]

Enni's Dharma words communicate pure, undiluted Zen, the Zen that he himself strived to communicate to his disciples. How far he succeeded in particular cases is, of course, uncertain. His lectures reached very diverse audiences.

Because of the large number of Enni's disciples, the Shōichi-ha movement ramified in several directions.[103] In his *History of Buddhism*, Akamatsu lists fifteen disciples of Enni, some of whom founded their own lines of tradition. Several of them were abbots of Tōfuku-ji: Tōzan Tanshō (1231–1291), Enni's immediate successor; Mukan Gengo (also, Mukan Fumon, 1212–1291), the third abbot of Tōfuku-ji and well-known as the founding abbot of the prominent Zen temple at Nanzen-ji; Hakuun Egyō, the fourth abbot of Tōfuku-ji; Sansō E'un (1231–1301) and Zōsan Junkū (1233–1308), the fifth and sixth in the succession of abbots; and finally, the ninth and tenth abbots of Tōfuku-ji, Chigotsu Daie (1229–1312) and Jikiō Chikan (1245–1322). Mujū Dōgyō (1226–1313), distinguished for his broad knowledge of the Mahāyāna teachings, was especially interested in the syncretistic mixture of *mikkyō*. He is the author of numerous works, notably a collection known as the *Shasekishū*. Sōhō Sōgen (1262–1335), who lived in both Tōfuku-ji and Nanzen-ji, was asked by Emperor Go-Uda to elucidate the way of Zen in the imperial palace; he was the first of his time to receive the honorary title of "Zen Master" (*zenji*). To deepen their formation, most of Enni's disciples visited China where for the most part they gained a sound knowledge of Zen teaching and practice. Some of them remained attached to esoteric forms of Buddhism.[104] Jinshi Eison (1195–1272), who studied with Enni at the feet of Gyōyū, is also listed in the line of Shōichi.

By the end of Enni's life the Rinzai movement in Japan was consolidated, even though his disciples were a rather motley group. The Japanese scholar, Furuta Shōkin, well known for his extensive research in the history of Japanese Rinzai Zen, divides the complex process out of which the Japanese school of Rinzai Zen evolved into three phases. In its first phase Zen gained the upper hand and secured for itself the first place among the syncretistic mixture of different Buddhist teachings at the time. In a second phase Zen asserted itself as an independent school, and finally, in the third phase, attained a completely independent identity. Furuta maintains that "Enni can be considered the most representative architect of the bridge between a syncretistic Zen and the formation of an independent Zen school."[105] Basing this claim on a comparison between Enni and his predecessors, Eisai and Eichō, Furuta states his case meticulously but unmistakably:

Even though Enni made room for the teachings of Zen, *mikkyō*, and Tendai at Tōfuku-ji, and therefore does not seem different from Eisai, who also welcomed these three schools, things are essentially different in the case of Enni. For him, the three schools were not simply lined up alongside each other; rather, they were ranked vertically, with Zen—let it be stressed—at the top. True, Enni was strongly influenced by Tendai and *mikkyō* and drew heavily upon his great interest in the latter. Yet there remains an undeniable difference between Enni and Eichō in Enni's greater esteem for Zen than for Tendai or *mikkyō.*[106]

In this way, Furuta seeks to substantiate his argument that although Enni, who taught the Zen of his Chinese master Wu-chun, did not himself actually establish a fully independent Zen school in Japan, he did "set Zen firmly on its way to full independence."[107]

Enni Ben'en was nearly eighty when he died in his monastery of Tōfuku-ji in 1280. His departing verses express the satisfaction that he felt after a lifetime of dedicated labors in a rapidly changing society. Called "the greatest and most active propagator of the Zen of his Chinese master,"[108] he holds a lasting place in the history of Japanese Zen. At the time of his death, Rinzai Zen had already moved into the second phase of its development in Japan. That it had so quickly advanced on its way to independence was due to the dedicated efforts of Chinese Zen masters on Japanese soil.

SHINCHI KAKUSHIN

Despite his great gifts, Shinchi Kakushin (or Muhon Kakushin (1207–1298), a contemporary of Enni, did not play as important a role in Japanese Zen history, for he loved solitude and after an exciting apprenticeship took up permanent residence on a remote piece of land in his native region.[109] Born in a village of what is today the district of Nagano, he began his spiritual journey at the age of fourteen; at eighteen he received the tonsure, and at twenty-eight was ordained a monk on the platform of Tōdai-ji at Nara. From there he took up the study of Tantric teachings and rituals in the Shingon monasteries of Mount Kōya. It was there that he met his first Zen teacher—Gyōyū, a disciple of Eisai whom Shinchi was to accompany in Kamakura from 1239 to 1241. Under Dōgen he took the bodhisattva vows. After further study under several Japanese Zen masters he decided to go to China, where he remained for about six years between 1249 and 1254.

Like so many of his compatriots, Kakushin looked forward to studying with Master Wu-chun Shih-fang, who was known to be amicably disposed toward the Japanese, only to discover upon arriving in China that the famous master had died. Disappointed, Kakushin set out on a pilgrimage to the best known centers of Buddhism in China until a fellow Japanese named Genshin directed him to the most prominent Chinese Zen master of the time—Wu-men Hui-k'ai (1183–1260), the fifth-generation Dharma heir of Wu-tsu Fa-yen (1024?–1104). From the first day the relationship between the master and his Japanese disciple was uncommonly close. At their first meeting Hui-k'ai asked the newcomer, "There is no gate for getting in here. Where did you come in from?" Kakushin replied, "I came in by the non-gate (*mumon*)." "What is your name?" the master inquired. "My name is Kakushin (i.e., "enlightened mind")." At that Hui-k'ai composed the following spontaneous verse:

Mind is the Buddha.
The Buddha is mind.
Mind and Buddha, such as they are,
Are the same in past and future.

After a mere six months of practice Kakushin received the seal of succession from Hui-k'ai. At his departure the master presented him with three gifts: a robe, a portrait of himself, and a copy of the *Mumonkan* written in his own hand. Kakushin treasured these gifts as the invaluable fruit of his stay in China. The *Mumonkan* was to become the keystone of his teachings in Japan. It is said that there was a further exchange of letters across the sea in which Hui-k'ai sent his final gifts—another robe and seven portraits of the Zen masters of his line, beginning with Wu-tsu Fa-yen (whom Hui-k'ai held in special regard), passing down to Hui-k'ai himself, and ending with Kakushin.

Upon returning to Japan, Kakushin built the small monastery of Saihō-ji (later known as Kōkoku-ji) in the hilly terrain of Yura (in the district of Waka-yama), where he stayed for some forty years. He was frequently invited to Kyoto to give lectures for the retired emperors Kameyama and Go-Fukakusa and for the reigning emperor Go-Uda. Kakushin resisted the attempts to have him appointed the first abbot of the monastery destined to become the famous Nanzen-ji, and instead returned to his rural solitude. The former emperor Kameyama bestowed on him during his lifetime the honorary title of Hottō Zenji ("Zen Master of the Dharma Light"), to which Emperor Go-Daigo (who ruled from 1319 to 1338) later added the posthumous title of Emmyō ("Perfect Light") and gave him a place in history as the national master Hottō Zenji.

Shinchi Kakushin was not able to maintain Zen in its pure form. In addition to the four hours spent daily sitting in Zen meditation, his monastery of Saihō-ji also carried out Shingon ceremonies.[110] The main discipline he assigned his many Zen students was the practice of the kōan of the *Mumonkan*, among which he had a special predilection for the famous opening kōan on "nothingness." Numerous miracle stories came to be associated with the name of this versatile monk, who was also known as the founder of the Fuke sect, in which the music of the *shakuhachi* bamboo flute was used to foster enlightenment. Members of this sect, most of whom were lay persons, were called the komusō ("monks of nothingness"). In later centuries, they would include many lordless samurai, or rōnin. Eventually the sect got a bad name because of its many corrupt and unruly members until it was finally proscribed during the Meiji period (1868–1912).

For some generations the Zen disciples of Kakushin formed a school known as the *Hottō-ha*, which remained loyal to the southern court during the division of the imperial house at the end of the Kamakura period and thus incurred the displeasure of the Ashikaga lords. Because the school did not seek members in the capital city, its development was limited.[111] In its third generation it was headed by Bassui Tokushō, one of the most prominent Japanese Zen masters, of whom we shall have more to say later. Kakushin's greatest contribution to Japanese Zen was the kōan collection he brought from China—the *Mumonkan*.

Not long after, another important kōan collection of the Rinzai school, the *Hekiganroku*, would arrive.[112] Thus at the time of its initial introduction into Japan, Rinzai Zen was already assured of the two works that would prove normative for its practice.

CHINESE MASTERS

During the first half of the Kamakura period, despite numerous excursions to China by Japanese monks for study, the Zen of the Rinzai school was able to take root in Japan only in syncretistic form, that is, mixed with other Buddhist schools, especially Tendai and Shingon. This was due mainly to the cultural and religious climate of the times. The religious revival that was taking shape among the Japanese people could not simply break abruptly with widespread, indigenous customs. The esoteric rites that accounted for the dominant form of religious practice during the middle ages were deeply rooted in the feudal society of the time. New attitudes and practices could only slowly hope to replace the people's faith in the magical powers of special ceremonies and incantations. During the first half of the Kamakura period, contacts with influential figures both from the Minamoto clan as well as from the ruling family of the Hōjō were limited by the dominant social attitudes of the time.

During the Kamakura period, Zen received its warmest reception among the warrior class—the samurai. According to a popular saying of the time, "Tendai is for the imperial court, Shingon for the nobility, Zen for the warrior class, and Pure Land for the masses." We get an insight into this connection between warriors and monks from the admonition that Sasaki Sadatsuna, a vassal of Minamoto, offered his son: "The duty of a warrior, like that of a monk, is to obey orders. . . . He must consider his life not his own but a gift offered to his lord." No doubt there were also ethical reasons for why the samurai turned to Zen, with its teaching of loyalty, courage, and fearlessness even to the point of facing death. But it was not the implications for military training that account above all for Zen's popularity among the warriors. Nor do sociological factors alone suffice to explain the close relation between the samurai and Zen. Equally important were certain essential aspects of Zen that came to light during this period, especially with the Mongolian invasions.[113]

It was under the fourth regent, Hōjō Tokiyori (1227–1263), that the military regime (*bakufu*) of Kamakura became seriously interested in Zen. Tokiyori, who has been called "one of the great politicians of Japan,"[114] was strongly attracted to Zen meditation, practicing it conscientiously and finally attaining enlightenment under a Chinese master. In 1246 he assumed the office of *shikken*, a Japanese practice whereby just as the shōgun took the place of the *tennō*, so would the *shikken* act in the name and place of the shōgun (in cases where the latter was either too young or unable to exercise his office), and in effect was fully empowered to run the government. Tokiyori, as well as his two successors, Tokimune (1251–1284, ruled 1256–1284) and Sadatoki (1271–1311), were powerful, generous, and intelligent patrons who fostered the growth of the Zen of the Chinese masters in the Kamakura. The circle of Zen followers spread from the upper strata of society among the warrior class. In the city of Kamakura, which had been transformed from an impoverished fishing village into the second most important center of the nation, Japanese Rinzai Zen moved into a new phase.

The Japanese Zen monk Muzō Jōshō (1234–1306),[115] who during a fourteen-year stay in China (1252–1264) attained enlightenment under Master Shi-hsi Hsin-yüeh of the line of Sung-yüan Ch'ung-yüeh (1139–1209) and surpassed all others in his close relations with the Chinese masters of the time, reports as follows in his informative work *Kōzenki:*

> Of late, one can find there the Zen masters Daikaku, Gottan, Mugaku, and Daikyū, all of them outstanding men from the Land of Sung, pillars of the Dharma school. Outwardly, they show goodness and wisdom; inwardly, they are full of marvelous powers. Their mission is to propagate the Dharma, their heart's desire to save sentient beings. Without fear of turbulent seas, they came to this land from afar. . . . They make the Buddha's sun to shine and radiate their own deep learning widely.[116]

In this passage, Muzō mentions the four most prominent Chinese Zen masters who came to Japan during this period: Lan-hsi Tao-lung (Jpn., Rankei Dōryū, whose posthumous title is Daikaku, 1213–1278); Wu-an P'u-ning (Gottan Funei); Ta-hsiu Cheng-nien (Daikyū Shōnen, 1214–1289); and Wu-hsüeh Tsu-yüan (Mugaku Sogen). Spiritual leaders of imposing stature, these four masters taught pure, unadulterated Zen. They pursued their religious goals conscientiously and energetically, caring little for the cultural-artistic or the politico-social implications of the Zen undertaking. It was because of them that Rinzai Zen grew into an independent school and came increasingly to be recognized as such. Stemming from two related traditions of Chinese Zen, these masters remained on friendly terms with each other. "Through their cooperation the pure Zen school of the Land of Sung all of a sudden grew strong."[117] The powerful patrons of the Hōjō clan placed at their disposal all the outside help they needed. Muzō Jōshō—the Dharma brother and special friend of Ta-hsiu (Daikyū), with whom he had practiced and experienced enlightenment under Master Shih-hsi Hsin-yüeh (Sekkei Shingatsu) of the line of Sung-yüan Ch'ung-yüeh—provided the Chinese masters invaluable help as a translator. Lan-hsi Tao-lung was also of the line of Sung-yüan; he had studied directly under Wu-ming Hsu-hsing. The two other Chinese masters, P'u-ning and Wu-hsüeh, were from the frequently mentioned school of Wu-chun Shih-fan, which, like the school of Sung-yüan, traces its origins back to Mi-an Hsien-chieh (1118–1186).

Lan-hsi Tao-lung,[118] the first and most prominent of the Chinese Zen masters to work in Japan, landed at Hakata on the island of Kyūshū in 1246 and proceeded to Kamakura by way of Kyoto. The regent Hōjō Tokiyori received him warmly and promptly appointed him abbot of the Jōraku-ji, which had been converted into a Zen temple. Nearby, Lan-hsi (Rankei) erected a monks' hall (*sōdō*), the first meditation hall for Rinzai Zen in Japan. In no time the hall proved too small to accommodate the increase in students, and before long the number of practitioners at this center of pure Zen surpassed that of the syncretistic Zen center at Jufuku-ji.

Hōjō Tokiyori conceived a plan to establish a representative Zen monastery in Kamakura. When the monastery complex was completed in 1253 it was named after the Kenchō era and Lan-hsi was called upon to be its founding abbot. Modeled after Mount Ching in China, the buildings of Kenchō-ji constituted the first full-fledged Rinzai monastery in Japan. We shall have more to say about its structure and organization in connection with the system of the "Five Mountains." From the very first day, Lan-hsi established the strict observance of a Chinese Zen monastery at Kenchō-ji. Its influence across the country was enormous and the name of its Chinese founding abbot grew famous. Thus when Tokiyori invited Wu-an P'u-ning to Kamakura, Lan-hsi was able to turn over the leadership of Kenchō-ji to his countryman, while he himself moved on to Kyoto to continue his efforts for the spread of authentic Zen. Lan-hsi became the eleventh abbot of Kennin-ji (1259–1261), which Enni had rebuilt and enlarged with a monk's hall after it had been damaged by fire. Ever since the time of Eisai, Zen had been practiced at Kennin-ji together with the esoteric Tendai and Shingon rites. Lan-hsi changed all that, insisting on the practice of pure Zen, and in so doing accomplished the reform that Enni had hoped for but never succeeded in bringing about. When the emperor Go-Saga (1220–1272, ruled 1243–1246) returned from a journey on official business, Lan-hsi accepted his invitation to lecture on Zen at the imperial court; he also instructed the former emperor in Zen meditation.

Meanwhile P'u-ning[119] had matters firmly in hand in Kamakura. This highly gifted monk, one of Wu-chun's most outstanding disciples, had already made a name for himself in China before coming to Japan in 1260. At Kenchō-ji he carried on the work of his predecessor Lan-hsi energetically. Tokiyori entrusted himself to P'u-ning's spiritual guidance and attained enlightenment. Although already advanced in years, this highly original master gathered a circle of select disciples about himself. Many stories are told about him, perhaps the best known of which is how he once refused to pay respect to the bodhisattva Jizō (Skt., Kṣitigarbha) whose picture was the main object of devotion in the Buddha hall of Kenchō-ji, claiming that he himself was a Buddha in no way inferior to the bodhisattva. P'u-ning's style was pure Rinzai. Had not Lin-chi (Rinzai) impressed on his disciples that they were all—each and every one of them sitting in front of him—Buddhas? It was hard for such a capricious personality, so full of mischief, to be at home in Japan, and after Tokiyori died in 1263 P'u-ning returned to China. The tradition that developed from him was named the line of Sōkaku, after his title, Sōkaku Zenji. Among his disciples was the belligerent Tōgan E'an (1225–1277), whose reckless methods in promoting pure Zen brought him into conflict with the monks of Mount Hiei.[120] After him, the Sōkaku line died out.

When Lan-hsi returned to Kamakura, Tokiyori made him superior of the newly founded Zen monastery of Zenkō-ji, a position he held until he returned to the post of abbot of Kenchō-ji. Unfortunately, in 1265 he became the object of defamatory rumors accusing him of being a spy for the Mongol regime in China. Twice he was forced into exile. After repeated admonitions, he was permitted to live for a while in Jufuku-ji. It was only shortly before his death that he was called back to Kenchō-ji where, together with the regent Hōjō Tokimune, he selected a site for Engaku-ji, which had already been planned as the second largest Zen temple. Lan-hsi is remembered in history as the "Zen Master of the Great Enlightenment" (Daikaku Zenji). The line of his disciples (Daikaku-ha) formed a numerically strong and significant force within the Rinzai Zen of that time. The master also left his followers a collection of sayings (Daikaku zenji goroku) as well as a short introduction to Zen meditation (Zazenron).

Among the well-known Zen masters who came to Japan during this early period, Ta-hsiu (Daikyū) played a somewhat modest role while filling various positions of leadership in a number of Kamakura monasteries.[121] Ta-hsiu was first invited to Japan by Tokiyori and was received by his successor Tokimune in 1269. Lan-hsi, like Ta-hsin of the line of Sung-yüan, became his friend and helper. A Zen master of great talent and broad influence, Ta-hsiu directed numerous disciples along the path to enlightenment for some two decades. He is especially remembered in Jōchi-ji, the monastery where he had been appointed founding abbot in 1283. The first of the four Chinese masters to die, he was honored with the posthumous title "Zen Master of the Buddha Eye" (Butsugen Zenji), which also accounts for the name of his line of disciples (Butsugen-ha). He left behind a collection of sayings known as the Daikyū oshō goroku.

After the death of Lan-hsi in 1278, Hōjō Tokimune sent messengers to China to seek a suitable successor.[122] The choice fell on Wu-hsüeh Tsu-yüan, a high-ranking monk on Mount T'ien-t'ung, when the master first chosen for this important mission proved too old for the strenuous journey. Although Wu-hsüeh (Jpn., Mugaku) was highly respected, he did not figure among the leading personalities of Chinese Zen. Accompanied by his disciple Ching-t'ang Chueh-yüan and a Japanese Zen monk, he arrived in Kamakura in August of 1279. As a demonstration of his complete trust in the new arrival, Tokimune immediately appointed him abbot of Kenchō-ji.

It was the time of the Mongol peril. In 1274 the first Mongol invasion of the southern island of Kyūshū was met by Japanese warriors and, with the help of a sudden storm, repelled. As he had done before in 1268 and 1271, the regime of Kublai Khan sent messengers in 1276 and again in 1279 to urge their foes to surrender. Tokimune roundly rejected the demand but he, along with the entire Japanese nation, was deeply disturbed. In this state of emergency the Chinese Zen masters were a reassuring force and made a notable contribution to the resistance. We do not know much of the historical detail, but the following episode, recounted by D. T. Suzuki, illustrates the situation and proves how highly regarded were the Chinese Zen masters. It is said that when news reached Tokimune of the approach of a massive Mongol fleet, he went to the temple to find strength from his master Bukkō (the Master of the Buddha Light, as Wu-hsüeh was called):

"The greatest event of my life is at last here."

Bukkō asked, "How would you face it?"

Tokimune uttered, "*Katsu!*" as if he were frightening away all his enemies actually before him.

Bukkō was pleased and said, "Truly, a lion's child roars like a lion."[123]

When the Mongols launched their second invasion in 1281 the dangers were even greater. Only with great difficulty were the Japanese able to mount a defense against the enemy, who were landing in Kyūshū in even larger numbers. On 14 August, the Japanese were aided by a powerful typhoon. This "wind of the gods" (*kamikaze*)[124] inflicted serious damages on the Mongol ships; thousands drowned and those that survived were killed by the Japanese. The debacle was complete.

The following year witnessed the completion of Engaku-ji where, as we said, Wu-hsüeh became the first abbot. Two years later, in 1284, Tokimune suddenly took ill and decided to take the tonsure and assume the monastic robes. After the early death of the regent, who had taken the monastic name of Dōkō, his wife withdrew to the convent of Tōkei-ji, which she had erected in 1285 on a hill facing Engaku-ji.[125] This little convent, decked out entirely in green, was popularly known as Enkiri-dera (Temple of Divorce) or Kakekomi-dera (Temple of Runaways) since it had become a refuge for women who had been dismissed or mistreated by their husbands. Today the buildings of Tōkei-ji, like so many others, are completely new (the original wood structures having proved easy prey to the devastation of fire) and there are no longer any nuns to preserve the memory of their noble foundress. Only a beautiful bronze bust of Amida from the Muromachi period bears witness to the devotion to the Buddha of Compassion that these pious women combined with the strict practice of Zen.

With his combination of great knowledge, pedagogical know-how, and genuine friendliness, Wu-hsüeh (Mugaku) attracted many disciples. During a short but illustrious period of activity, he also directed his attentions to the court and the larger circle of Kamakura warriors. His posthumous title, "Zen Master of the Buddha-Light," also identified his successors as the Bukkō-ha. There is no doubt that this master taught the same authentic Zen he had learned so well in the monastic halls of Wu-chun. This same spirit of faithfulness was carried on by his elderly disciple Ichiō Inkō (1210–1281), who lent support to the Zen movement in northeastern Japan from the Chōraku-ji. Another of his pupils, Kian Soen (1261–1313) exercised considerable influence as the second abbot of Nanzen-ji in Kyoto; we will have more to say about him later. The most famous name in this circle of early disciples, however, is that of Kōhō Kennichi (1241–1316), the eldest son of emperor Go-Saga. After studying with Enni and P'u-ning, Kōhō entered the school of Wu-hsüeh. He is clearly responsible for an influx of syncretistic Zen.[126] He transformed the monastery of Ungan-ji in Nasu from a center for the practice of the Shugendō branch of Shingon into a Zen temple. There he set himself up as abbot, practicing and passing on to his disciples an adulterant of Zen.

The success of these four great Chinese Zen masters assured the implantation of an independent Rinzai school in Japan modeled after the Chinese Rinzai tradition. A total of sixteen Chinese Zen missionaries are said to have come over from the continent to spread Zen in the islands of Japan. While not all of them were of the same quality or achieved the same fame, the Zen they all brought with them was authentic. The number of Japanese monks who visited China was larger—fifteen for the time of the Southern Sung dynasty (1127–1279) and another fifteen for the Yüan period (1271–1368). From these Chinese and Japanese masters a total of forty-six different lines of Japanese Rinzai Zen originated.[127]

Sadatoki, the next ruler of the Hōjō clan, proved to be a zealous patron of Zen. Where his predecessors had been concerned mainly on the spiritual side of Zen, Sadatoki's interest spread to the intellectual background of the movement. Under his aegis, Zen in Kamakura took a pronounced cultural turn. One should not forget that for some time the Hōjō had eyed the capital city of Kyoto enviously as the center of Japanese culture. These "tented" rulers of the bakufu, unwilling and unable to forgo intellectual and cultural renown, at last saw their hopes fulfilled under the rule of Sadatoki.

Zen's new friendship with culture was embodied in the prominent Chinese Zen master I-shan I-ning (Jpn., Issan Ichinei, 1247–1317),[128] whom the Yüan government, without any outside prompting, had decided to send to Japan. He met with a rather unusual reception: thought to be a Yüan spy, he was confined to the monastery of Shuzen-ji on the Izu peninsula. The mistake was soon recognized, and immediately upon his arrival at Kamakura, Sadatoki appointed him abbot first of Kenchō-ji and then of Engaku-ji, where the impact of his presence soon became evident. So many were those who came from near and far to be his disciples that the rooms of the vast monastery were unable to accommodate all the applicants. To limit the number of his disciples, I-shan devised a type of entrance examination to test in particular the literary abilities of the aspirants. One of those to pass the test was Musō Soseki, the artistic star of the following epoch.

I-shan was also able to introduce his cultural-religious program in the capital city Kyoto and became the precursor of the Gozan culture so important in Japanese history. With his appointment as third abbot of Nanzen-ji by the retired emperor Go-Uda (1267–1324), his fame as a Zen master, teacher, and versatile artist reached its zenith. Through him Zen gained many friends in the imperial court and among the nobility. At the time of his death he was highly revered, as witnessed by the fact that the honorific title of "national master" (kokushi) was bestowed on him the day after his death. His sayings were gathered together in the Issan kokushi goroku, and the line of Issan formed by his disciples carried on his spirit. Thus were the foundations laid for the astonishing artistic and cultural development of Zen that was to take place during the Muromachi period.

In this context mention should be made of two Chinese Zen masters from the Sōtō (Chin., Ts'ao-tung) school who, at the invitation of the bakufu government, arrived somewhat later in Kamakura and there began important artistic and scientific activities much in the style of later Chinese Rinzai masters. The first, Tung-ming Hui-jih (Tōmyō E'nichi, 1272–1340),[129] was appointed to successive posts as abbot in the most important Zen temples of Kamakura beginning soon after his arrival in 1309. He belonged to the tradition of the Sōtō school in the fifth generation after Hung-chih Cheng-chüeh (Wanshi Shōgaku, 1091–1157). Although he taught Sōtō doctrine in the monastic halls, his artistic inclinations drew him much more in the direction of the culturally-oriented form of Zen inspired by I-shan and the regent Sadatoki. At the invitation of Emperor Go-Daigo (1287–1338) he came to the capital city of Kyoto and served as the superior of the Kennin-ji monastery. His artistic accomplishments were held in regard among the Rinzai circles of Kamakura and Kyoto, where he was in no way considered an intruder.

The same may be said of the second master from the Sōtō school, Tung-ling Yung-yu (Tōryō Eiyo, d. 1365),[130] who belonged to the same line as Tung-ming and arrived in Kamakura in 1351, the last Chinese master of the period. Also warmly received by adherents of the Rinzai school, he became close friends with the famous contemporary Zen master and artist Musō Soseki. The line that developed from these two Chinese Sōtō masters (Wanshi-ha) enjoyed the support of powerful patrons, particularly from the house of Asakura. After flourishing for a time in eastern Japan, it disappeared with the defeat of the Asakura warriors under Oda Nobunaga (1534–1582). "The style of this school is completely different from the Sōtō Zen of the Eihei-ji school,"[131] the school that originated with Dōgen and his disciples and is still active in Japan.

Takatoki (1303–1333, ruled from 1316), the last ruler of the Hōjō clan, could still be counted among the patrons of Zen inasmuch as he kept up relations with the various Zen temples and occasionally offered them assistance. But the real interests of this degenerate, brutal, and weak-willed ruler were cockfighting and dancing. His corrupt government brought great unrest across the country. The intent of the decrees he issued on Zen temples was mainly to strengthen discipline and thus keep them under his control. He gave a friendly reception to the three Chinese masters Ch'ing-cho Cheng-ch'eng (Seisetsu Shōchō, 1274–1339), Ming-chi Ch'u-chün (Minki Soshun, 1262–1336), and Chu-hsien Fan-hsien (Jikusen Bonsen, 1292–1348), to each of whom he granted a prominent post in one of the Zen temples of Kamakura.[132]

The Zen master Ch'ing-cho,[133] an illustrious figure closely related to the line of Wu-chun, arrived in Japan in 1326. His abilities were given the full recognition they deserved. He became the superior of a number of prominent monasteries in Kamakura and Kyoto—Kenchō-ji, Engaku-ji, Kennin-ji, and Nanzen-ji. A devotee of the great T'ang master Pai-chang, he worked to adapt Chinese monastic rules to Japanese customs. He composed the *Daikan shingi*, a monastic rule whose strict observance Takatoki enjoined on the Zen monasteries. The powerful Ogasawara Sadamune (1294–1350), who was entrusted with the governance of a number of provinces, invited him to the land of Shinano to become founding abbot of Kaizen-ji. The rules of the *Daikan shingi* were incorporated into the rules of etiquette of the Ogasawara school (Ogasawara-ryū), which Sadamune's uncle Nagahide among others had composed and which were still in use during the Tokugawa period. Ch'ing-cho's disciples form what is known as the Daikan-ha, after the posthumous title of their master, Daikan Zenji.

The contribution of these Chinese masters to the formation of Zen Buddhism in Japan is considerable. During the second half of the thirteenth century, the center of the Zen movement shifted for a time to Kamakura. The five monasteries known as the "Five Mountains" (gozan) of Kamakura, already mentioned severally in relation to their founding abbots, were Kenchō-ji (Lan-hsi Tao-lung, 1253), Engaku-ji (Wu-hsüeh Tsu-yüan, 1282), Jufuku-ji (Myōan Eisai, 1200), Jōmyō-ji (Taikō Gyōyū, 1212), and Jōchi-ji (Ta-hsiu Cheng-nien, 1283). Whether this list already existed during the Kamakura period is not clear. An early report dated 1299 refers to the elevation of Jōchi-ji to the rank of the gozan, leading one to surmise that the establishment of the Five Mountains extends back to the Kamakura period.[134] During the following period, under the rule of the Ashikaga, the gozan system was to reach full the height of its development.

THE RINZAI SCHOOL PRIOR TO THE END
OF THE KAMAKURA PERIOD

The three-phased development referred to earlier summarizes the essential features of the implantation of Rinzai Zen in Japan: (1) from the introduction of Zen meditation as one form of Buddhist practice among others to the primacy of the way of Zen; (2) from the superiority of Zen to the formation of a self-sufficient Rinzai school; 3) from self-sufficiency to the establishment of a fully independent Rinzai school on a par with other schools of Japanese Buddhism. This is not to say that Zen was dissected in the course of its development; it remained intact in the form in which it reached Japan from China. Each of these stages is meant only to represent the way in which Japan received Zen and should not be construed as a temporal sequence. Enni Ben'en, who, together with the "founder" Eisai, represents the first phase, appropriated the way of Zen in China, even though his activity in Japan led him to mix Zen with other forms of Buddhism. But it is important to remember that for him the practice of Zen remained primary. As we have seen, already during Enni's lifetime Chinese masters arrived and energetically went about their mission of propagating Rinzai Zen throughout Japan.[135] For the Chinese, it was self-evident that Zen practice merited an independent school of its own as they had known it in the Kingdom of the Sung.

The third phase of Zen's implantation in Japan took place during the last decades of the thirteenth century and the first decades of the fourteenth. From the beginning, the final result of this phase was clear. Japan's readiness for Zen in an authentic, unadulterated form grew from decade to decade. Among the disciples of Enni and the Chinese masters of Kamakura, there were many who pressed for an independent Japanese Rinzai school. As more and more Japanese monks trained by Chinese masters took over the direction of the great monasteries of Kamakura and Kyoto, the process of the implantation of Rinzai Zen in Japan neared its completion.

The third phase of Rinzai Zen's growth in Japan is represented in the figure of Nampo Jōmyō (1235–1308), whom Miura and Sasaki consider so important for the history of Zen in Japan that they assign him and his followers a table of their own in the list of Zen generational lines.[136] To be sure—as we shall see in detail later—the names of many significant Zen masters up to Hakuin Ekaku, the most influential leader of Rinzai Zen during the modern period, appear in this table. Nampo's personal qualities befit his unique place in the history of Japanese Rinzai Zen.

Nampo, who like Enni Ben'en came from Suruga (in the region of Shizuoka) and was said to be Enni's nephew, began his spiritual path like many other Buddhist monks in a local temple near his home. At eighteen he visited Kenchō-ji in Kamakura and studied Zen meditation under Lan-hsi. Soon afterward, in 1259, he travelled to China and practiced under the renowned master Hsü-t'ang Chih-yü (Kidō Chigu, 1185–1269) on Mount Hsüeh-tou in Chekiang. He followed his master first to the Ching-tz'u temple and then to Mount Ching, the thriving center of Chinese Zen at the time. In late summer of 1265 he experienced enlightenment and received the seal of discipleship from Hsü-t'ang in the tenth generational line of Yang-ch'i. Before his return to Japan, the master gave him a gift of some parting verses that express both the master's deep love for his Japanese pupil as well as the high hopes he held for him:

To knock on the door and search with care,
To walk broad streets and search the more:
Old Hsü-t'ang taught so clear and bright,
And many are the grandchildren on the eastern sea who received [this dharma].[137]

Having knocked bravely at the high door of a demanding master, Nampo received of the master's best. Once home, Nampo spent a number of years with his previous teacher Lan-hsi and then went to the southern island of Kyūshū to take over the direction first of Kōtoku-ji in Fukuoka and three years later of the nearby monastery of Sōfuku-ji. This temple, where Nampo spent thirty years, pales in comparison with the great complexes of Kyoto and Kamakura, yet one cannot really speak of a life spent in seclusion. Subordinate to the Dazaifu, the old regional government in Kyūshū, Sōfuku-ji served the Zen movement as a bridgehead to China. Many a Japanese and Chinese monk passed through on his travels. Nampo himself attracted many disciples and Sōfuku-ji became the site of his dedicated and successful efforts on behalf of Zen.

Details on Nampo's talks and his practice of Zen in Kōtoku-ji and Sōfuku-ji are to be found in two collections of sayings, *Kōtoku-ji goroku* and *Sōfuku-ji goroku*. Together with other reports on his activity in the monasteries of Manju-ji (Kyoto) and Kenchō-ji (Kamakura), these works form a representative work known as the *Collection of Sayings of the National Master Enzū Daiō* (*Enzū Daiō kokushi goroku*), which was later incorporated into the Sino-Japanese Buddhist canon.[138] During his days in Sōfuku-ji, Nampo developed a sense of national responsibility disclosed in such expressions as "the Great Nation of Nippon" or "the Great Country of Nippon" (Dainipponkoku).[139] Although the Zen school certainly originated in China and was brought over to Japan, he taught, Zen as such is not "Chinese" but transcends history. The Buddha manifests himself day after day; Bodhidharma comes from the West again and again. The characteristic events of Zen tradition, like the smile of Kāśyapa or the nine-year meditation of Bodhidharma, are timeless. The disciples practicing in Sōfuku-ji were told to live in the here and now; the Zen that was brought to Japan is the Zen of the present moment in Japan. The information available shows how deeply Nampo's insight penetrated during the time of his activity in Sōfuku-ji.

In 1304, at the invitation of the retired emperor Kameyama, Nampo came to Kyoto and the following year was named abbot of Manju-ji in Kyoto, where Shūhō Myōchō (1282–1338) became his disciple.[140] The collection of sayings from this period (Manju-ji goroku) show the Japanese character that Rinzai Zen was assuming. At the time the Tendai monks of Mount Hiei, who were not at all happy about Nampo's unadulterated style of Zen, prevented him from taking over Kagen-ji, which the former emperor Go-Uda had erected for him. Nampo moved to Kamakura, where for a short time he directed Shōkan-ji. Shūhō followed him. At last he was called to take over as abbot of Kenchō-ji.[141] For exactly one year Nampo occupied the highest office of the nation's most venerable Zen temple. As he predicted, he died on the twenty-ninth day of the twelfth month—one year to the day after he had been enthroned as abbot. According to tradition, he stated at the installation ceremony, "On the twenty-ninth day of the twelfth month of next year, my going will be going to nowhere."[142] Before he died he composed these parting verses:

I rebuke the wind and revile the rain,
I do not know the Buddhas and patriarchs;
My single activity turns in the twinkling of an eye,
Swifter even than a lightning flash.[143]

While Nampo was certainly well-known and respected during his lifetime, he owes his prominent place in the history of Japanese Zen in no small measure to that incomparable table that presents him as the real patriarch of Japanese Rinzai Zen. The name of the first disciple to appear on the table is Shūhō Myōchō. The subsequent history of Rinzai Zen in Japan would show how important it was that this ingenious disciple, after growing dissatisfied with the guidance he was receiving in Zen meditation from his master, Kōhō Kennichi,[144] entrusted himself wholeheartedly to Nampo, went on to attain enlightenment under him, and became his Dharma heir. It is because of Shūhō, the founding abbot of Daitoku-ji in Kyoto, that the name of Nampo—or Daiō Kokushi as he is usually called, abbreviating his full posthumous title of Enzū Daiō Kokushi—is closely associated with Daitoku-ji, where his tomb is located. By imperial order his ashes were actually housed in Ryōshō-ji, which had been built especially for this purpose,[145] but to this day, National Teacher Daiō is revered in the monastery of Daitoku-ji.

The founding of Daitoku-ji, which was consecrated in 1327, dates from the Kamakura period. Kanzan Egen (1277–1360), Shūhō's disciple, became the first abbot of the Myōshin-ji, which was completed ten years later. The Daiō line formed by Nampo's disciples developed into the Daitoku-ji-ha and the Myōshin-ji-ha, both of which are still influential today, and bring us to the next period. Before the end of the Kamakura period, the implantation of the Rinzai school in Japan was complete.

NOTES

1.   The story of Bodhidharma's passage to Japan and his meeting with Prince Shōtoku (572–621) in the twenty-first year of the reign of Emperor Suiko (ruled 593–628) is legendary. Kinomiya Yasuhiko describes the sources and contents of the legend in his book on Eisai, *Eisai Zenji*, pp. 10ff.

2.   According to Gundert, Dōshō was the first Japanese monk of importance (*Japanische Religionsgeschichte*, p. 36). He is renowned as the first known meditation teacher in Japan (Miura and Sasaki, *Zen Dust*, p. 17) and as such stands at the beginning of the pre-history of the Zen movement in Japan.

3.   M. Eder, *Geschichte der japanischen Religion*, vol. 2, p. 5. Cf. Kinomiya, *Eisai Zenji*, p. 15.

4.   On Tao-hsüan Lü-shih see *Zen Dust*, pp. 17–18. Cf. Ui, *Zenshūshi* I, pp. 307–308.

5.   Gundert provides the most important dates, events, and writings of Saichō (*Japanische Religionsgeschichte*, pp. 54ff). All works on Japanese Buddhism and relevant lexicons treat this famous monk from the Heian period (794–1192).

6.   See Kinomiya, *Eisai Zenji*, pp. 17–18.

7.   Ibid.

8.   It is not clear whether Kūkai (774–835), the founder of Shingon Buddhism, had contact with the Zen school during his stay in China, but we may suppose that he knew of it. In later years a place for meditation would be established on Mount Kōya. See Kinomiya, *Eisai Zenji*, pp. 17ff.

9.   I-k'ung was the first to introduce the Zen of the Sixth Patriarch, Hui-neng, into Japan. See *Zen Dust*, p. 295. On the invitation of I-k'ung to Japan see Y. H. Ku, *History of Zen*, p. 156. Cf. Kinomiya, *Eisai Zenji*, pp. 21–22.

10.   See *Zen Dust*, p. 295; Ku, *History of Zen*, pp. 156–57.

11.   The dating of the Kamakura period varies. If one takes the decisive defeat of the Taira clan at Dan no Ura as its beginning, it begins as early as 1185. In 1192 Minamoto Yoritomo was ceremoniously introduced into the service of the shōgun.

12.   Apparently Kakua was the first Japanese Buddhist monk to have traveled to China with the express purpose of searching for Zen. See M. Collcutt, *Five Mountains*, p. 38. The anecdote is mentioned in M. and A. Matsunaga, *Foundation of Japanese Buddhism*, vol. 2, p. 187. See also Ku, *History of Zen*, p. 160, and *Zengaku daijiten*, vol. 1, p. 149.

13.   See the brief biographies in *Zen Dust*, pp. 195–96 and *Zengaku daijiten*, vol. 1, p. 82 b,c.

14.   See the brief biography in *Zengaku daijiten*, vol. 2, p. 1008; cf. vol. 1, p. 149. See also Washio Junkei, *Nihon zenshūshi no kenkyū*, pp. 106–121); Ōkubo Dōshū, *Dōgen Zenji-den no kenkyū*, pp. 406–68; Kinomiya Yasuhiko, *Eisai Zenji*, p. 25.

15. Ed. by Ishii Shūdō in *Kanazawa bunko shiryō zensho*, vol. 1, pp. 174–220.

16. Above all see Ishii Shūdō, "Busshō Tokkō to Nihon Daruma-shū," *Kanazawa bunko kenkyū* 222, 223 (1984); Nakao Ryōshin, "Dainichi Nōnin no zen," *Shūgaku kenkyū* 26 (1984): 221–35, and "Nōnin botsugo no Daruma-shū," *Shūgaku kenkyū* 27 (1985): 209–21; Funaoka Makoto, "Nihon zenshūshi ni okeru Daruma-shū no ichi," *Shūgaku kenkyū* 26 (1984): 103–108; Niikura Kazufumi, "Dōgen no Daruma-shū hihan," *Indogaku bukkyōgaku kenkyū* 32 (1984): 124–25. See also the summary article in English by Bernard Faure, "The Daruma-shū, Dōgen, and Sōtō Zen," MN 42.1 (1987): 25–55.

17. *Dainihon bukkyō zensho*, 63, p. 273. For a brief life of Mangen Shiban, see *Zengaku daijiten*, vol. 1, p. 460b.

18. See Funaoka, "Nihon zenshūshi ni okeru Daruma-shū no ichi," p. 105.

19. *Ibid.* Cf. B. Faure, "The Daruma-shū, Dōgen, and Sōtō Zen," p. 29 and n. 13. The Daruma school is also mentioned in the Japanese literature of the day, for example by Kamo no Chōmei in the *Mumyōshō* (see Faure, p. 29 and n. 14) and in the *Tengu sōshiki* (see Yanagida Seizan, "Dōgen to Chūgoku bukkyō," *Zen bunka kenkyūsho kiyō* 13 (1984): 15). This latter work, a famous literary work from the end of the Kamakura period (1296), criticizes the Daruma school. Yanagida notes, "The progress of the Daruma school was a social problem already around the end of the Heian period" (p. 15).

20. T.2689, vol. 84. Nōnin and Hōnen were contemporaries and represent the uprising at the start of the Kamakura period.

21. Ōkubo Dōshū, *Dōgen Zenji-den no kenkyū*, p. 408. Cf. Nakao, *Dainichi Nōnin no zen*, p. 222. Nakao discusses the reasons for and against the propriety of the designation, pp. 226–27.

22. T.2543, vol. 80. For an annotated edition with translation into modern Japanese, see Yanagida Seizan, *Chūsei zenka no shisō*, vol. 16 of the collection Nihon Shisō Taikei. I have used this edition in the preparation of the remarks in the text. Furuta Shōkin has edited, translated, and commented on this important text in the first volume of *Nihon no zen-goroku*.

23. T.2543, vol. 80, p. 7c; translation by Yampolsky, cited in Faure, "The Daruma-shū, Dōgen, and Sōtō Zen," p. 39.

24. *Chūsei zenka no shisō*, p. 41; *Nihon no zen-goroku*, p. 173. Yanagida and Furuta both note in their commentaries that the text refers to the Daruma school of Nōnin.

25. In his essay, "Kūbyō no mondai" (*Bukkyō shisō*, pp. 757–98) Yanagida treats interpretations of the key word "emptiness" in Chinese Buddhism (see especially pp. 771ff). In his opinion, Eisai's judgment of Nōnin is not correct, since the attitude of the Daruma school represents the generally held view of early Chinese Zen (p. 775).

26. *Dai-nihon bukkyō zensho*, vol. 62. For a brief biography of Kokan Shiren, see *Zengaku daijiten*, vol. 1; p. 602 b–c. See also Tradition Chart III-C.

27. See Nakao, *Dainichi Nōnin no zen*, pp. 225–26. For these views he relies on Ōkubo Dōshū and Takahashi Shūei, respectively.

28. In his commentary on the *Shōbōgenzō*, Kyōgō, a disciple of Dōgen, lays particular stress on the relationship of the Daruma school to the three treatises of Bodhidharma.

29. See Niikura, *Dōgen no Daruma-shū hihan*, p. 125.

30. On the three treatises, extracted from the six treatises of Bodhidharma (*Shōshitsu rokumon*), see vol. 1, chap. 6, n. 31. Cf. Yanagida, "Dōgen to Chūgoku bukkyō," p. 20, and "Kūbyō no mondai" pp. 780ff.

31.   See for example, *Mumonkan*, case 30. On Ma-tsu, see vol. 1, chap. 9.

32.   See vol. 1, chap. 11.

33.   Like Eisai, Dōgen censures the Daruma school, albeit indirectly. On this point see the following chapter.

34.   B. Faure treats the esoteric element in his study of the Northern school of Chinese Zen. See "The Daruma-shū, Dōgen, and Sōtō Zen," p. 35.

35.   On Ta-hui and his style of Zen, see vol. I, chap. 12.

36.   In his study Ishii investigates the similarities and differences between the style of Zen practiced in the Daruma school and that of Te-kuang. Both stress sitting in meditation and the enlightenment experience, but the Daruma school does not aspire to sudden enlightenment as the *kanna-zen* of Ta-hui does. Ishii also laid out other peculiarities of the Daruma School and arrives at the conclusion that the Zen of the Japanese Daruma school is very different from that of the line of Ta-hui (*Kanazawa bunko shiryō zensho*, 223, p. 13b).

37.   See part 2 of Yanagida Seizan, *Chūsei zenka no shisō, 439*

38.   *Dōgen zenji-den no kenkyū*, p. 410.

39.   See Yanagida Seizan, *Chūsei zenka no shisō*, p. 467.

40.   See Takahashi Shūhei, "Sambō-ji no Daruma shūmon to rokuso fugen shari," *Shūgaku kenkyū* 26 (1984): 116–21. The author, director of the collection, recounts how in 1975 he happened on the occasion of an art exhibit in Nara to find objects from Sambō-ji, seventeen of which he describes. See also the article by Ishikawa Rikisan in the same issue of the journal, "Daruma-shū no sōjōbutsu ni tsuite," pp. 109–15.

41.   See Nakao, "Dainichi Nōnin no zen," p. 229.

42.   See Funaoka, "Nihon zenshūshi ni okeru Daruma-shū no ichi," p. 108.

43.   Nakao, "Dainichi Nōnin no zen," p. 233.

44.   See note 13 and also Collcutt, Matsunaga, Gundert, Eder, and Yampolsky, all of whose works are cited in the foregoing notes. Among the wealth of Japanese materials the following may be singled out: Furuta Shōkin's two essays "Zen no shisōron—Nihonzen" and "Nihon zenshūshi—Rinzaishu" which appear in vol. 4 of a collection of works on Zen entitled *Zen no rekishi—Nihon*; Yanagida Seizan, *Rinzai no kafū*; Ienaga Saburō, et al., eds., *Nihon bukkyōshi II—Chūsei*, the third chapter of which, "Chūsei bukkyō no tenkai" (pp. 153–221), has been edited by Imaeda Aishin and is accordingly cited hereafter as Imaeda II; Imaeda Aishin, *Chūsei zenshūshi no kenkyū* and also his "Kamakura zen no seiritsu" in *Ajia bukkyōshi*, vol. 4, part 2.

The name can also be read (with equal validity) as Yōsai, although Eisai is the usual form of pronunciation.

45.   *Zen Dust*, p. 196. Similarly, Collcutt notes (*Five Mountains*, p. 36) that Myōan Eisai is revered as the founder of the Japanese Rinzai school; see also Yampolsky, *The Zen Master Hakuin*, p. 2.

46.   Eisai, it seems, left Mount Hiei for a period.

47.   Compare the condensed biographical sketch, "Myōan Eisai, Founder of Kennin-ji" in *Nihon bukkyō kiso kōza*, vol. 6, pp. 247ff. The volume falls into two parts, dealing respectively with the Sōtō and Rinzai schools. The latter half has been edited by Nishimura Eshin and Katō Masatoshi.

48.   T. 2543, vol. 80. See note 22. I have used the edition prepared by Yanagida Seizan.

49.   See section 5 of *Kōzen gokokuron* in the edition of Yanagida, p. 54.

50.   *Ibid.*

51.   *Ibid.*, p. 55.

52.   The master speaks of the great Dharma joy that his disciple experienced. No doubt he was pleased with his Japanese students, perhaps also because he shared his esoteric inclinations. See Collcutt, *Five Mountains*, p. 37. See also Yanagida's translation of the rather lengthy text from the fifth section of *Kōzen gokokuron*, pp. 55–56.

53.   See Kinomiya, *Eisai Zenji*, p. 34.

54.   On the following, see Furuta, *Zenshisōshi-ron—Nihon zen*, pp. 71–72.

55.   See *Kōzen gokokuron*, section 9, in Yanagida's edition, p. 89.

56.   According to Furuta, Eisai knew from hearsay that five thousand monks were living in the center at Nālandā (*ibid.*). The figure does not make sense. What is more, the time of Nālandā's flourishing had long since passed.

57.   *Kōzen gokokuron*, section 1, Yanagida edition, p. 11; see also Furuta, *Zenshisōshi-ron—Nihon zen*, p. 72, and also his essay "Eisai ni okeru jikai jiritsu shisō no igi," which includes numerous citations from Eisai's works. The essay is printed in the collection *Nihon bukkyō shisō no shomondai*, pp. 18–35. The disciplined life of the monk that so impressed Eisai in the Chinese Rinzai monasteries reaches back to the T'ang period and is attributed in Zen tradition above all to the efforts of Pai-chang. The earliest available collection of monastic rules for the Zen school, *Zen'on shingi* (Chin., *Ch'an-yüan ch'ing-kuei*), from the Sung period (1103), was brought to Japan by Japanese Zen monks and was influential during the Kamakura period, when the monastic life of Zen was taking shape. Eisai cites from this work. Collcutt (*Five Mountains*, pp. 141ff, 147) gives an overview of the content on the basis of the *Yakuchū zen'on shingi*, an annotated Japanese version prepared by Kagamishima Genryū, Satō Tatsugen, and Kosaka Kiyū.

58.   Section 3, p. 37.

59.   *Ibid.*, p. 38.

60.   Kinomiya lists three temples, *Eisai Zenji*, p. 37. Matsunaga reports on the erection of the temple of Hōon-ji in the province of Chikuzen, *Foundation of Japanese Buddhism*, vol. 2, p. 186.

61.   Cited in Nishimura and Katō, *Nihon bukkyō kiso kōza*, vol. 6, p. 248. Saichō taught Tendai as a four-pronged tradition, *en-mitsu-zen-kai* (teaching-arcanum-Zen-Vinaya). See Matsunaga, *Foundation of Japanese Buddhism*, vol. 2, p. 188. Further details will be provided on this point later.

62.   Kinomiya offers an account of this, *Eisai Zenji*, pp. 38–39.

63.   See note 22 above for further information on this text.

64.   A detailed treatment of the editions of the *Kōzen gokokuron* during the Edo period is given by Yanagida in an appendix to his translation entitled "Problems of the *Kōzen gokokuron*," pp. 439–86. At the time, the learned monk Gitai argued strongly against the authenticity of the text (p. 440). Furuta (*Zen shisōshiron—Nihon zen*, p. 69) finds no basis to doubt the authenticity of the work either, and treats the transmission of the text and the critique of Gitai in the introduction to his translation, pp. 56–60.

65.   This aspect is particularly prominent in section 2 of the text (see Yanagida's edition, p. 13). Furuta proposes, in his introduction to the translation, that the spread of Zen represented "the very protection of the country" (*Zen shisōshiron—Nihon zen*, pp. 54ff). All Buddhism in Japan has recourse to this salutary effect.

66. *Kōzen gokokuron,* section 9, Yanagida edition, p. 92.

67. *Ibid.,* pp. 92–93.

68. This is treated in section 4, pp. 48ff.

69. Section 6, p. 56; see also section 7, p. 62.

70. *Ibid.,* p. 63.

71. This ends the line of tradition in section 5; see p. 53.

72. This famous and oft-cited saying appears in Furuta, *Zen shisōshiron—Nihon zen,* p. 74, and in Nishimura and Katō, *Nihon bukkyō kiso kōza,* vol. 6, p. 248.

73. The ranking of the Five Mountains of Kamakura and Kyoto was only fixed much later.

74. This appears in the so-called *Miraiki (Annals on the Future),* dated 1197. The text appears in the Yanagida edition on pp. 96 and 97, after the treatise.

75. On this text see *Zen Dust,* p. 196.

76. See *Zen Dust,* p. 197. Regarding the death of Eisai see Nishimura and Katō, *Nihon bukkyō kiso kōza,* vol. 6, p. 249.

77. Eisai maintained strict ties to the imperial household and the shogunate. Matsunaga *(Foundation of Japanese Buddhism,* vol. 2, pp. 190–91) reports the completion of the reconstruction of Tōdai-ji through the efforts of Eisai. With the consecration of Hosshō-ji he is said to have requested of the emperor to be awarded the title of "Great Master" *(daishi).* On the close ties between Eisai and the *bakufu* see Collcutt, *Five Mountains,* p. 309, n. 26. Both reports cast a shadow over the personality of Eisai.

78. For a treatment of Eisai's disciples, see Furuta, *Zen shisōshiron—Nihon zen,* pp. 53ff. See also Kinomiya's two chapters on the Dharma inheritance of Eisai, *Eisai Zenji,* pp. 119–43.

79. The best introduction we have to Myōzen we owe to Dōgen, in whose writings Myōzen appears frequently. See the biographical chapter by Hee-Jin Kim in *Dōgen Kigen: Mystical Realist,* esp. pp. 28ff; and Takashi James Kodera, *Dōgen's Formative Years in China,* pp. 29ff, 36–37, 57–58.

80. *Bendōwa,* Iwanami edition, p. 55, DZZ I, p. 729; English translation by M. Abe and N. Waddell, EB 4.1 (1971): 130. Regarding the editions of the *Shōbōgenzō* see chap. 15.

81. *Shōbōgenzō zuimonki* 5:12; Iwanami edition, vol. 1, pp. 93ff; DZZ II, p. 486. English translation by Reihō Masunaga, *A Primer of Sōtō Zen,* p. 86. On this work see note 19 of chap. 2.

82. *Ibid.* Note how these words express the "longing for the Dharma and journey into the Kingdom of the Sung" in inverse order; cf. the epilogue to vol. 1.

83. *Ibid.* Iwanami edition, pp. 95–96; DZZ II, pp. 486–87; English trans., p. 87.

84. See Ku, *History of Zen,* p. 160; Kinomiya, *Eisai Zenji,* p. 120.

85. See also the section on Minamoto Sanetomo in my essay on the history of Japanese research on the *Man'yōshū,* MN 8 (1952): 67–98. Included are some German translations of the poems of Sanetomo in the *Man'yōshū* style (pp. 78–79).

86. On *Kongōzammai-in* see Kinomiya, *Eisai Zenji,* pp. 125–26. There are several hypotheses regarding its origins.

87. On the foregoing see also the entry on "Gyōyū" in the *Zengaku daijiten,* vol. 1, p. 230.

88. See Ku, *History of Zen*, p. 160, and the entry on "Eichō" in the *Zengaku daijiten*, I, p. 84.

89. Almost all the literature dealing with the history of Japanese Zen Buddhism treats Enni Ben'en. See especially Furuta, *Zen shisōshiron—Nihon zen*, pp. 122–31; Furuta, *Zen no rekishi—Nihon*, pp. 25–34; Imaeda, *Kamakura zen no seiritsu*, pp. 164–75; Imaeda II, pp. 154ff; Nishimura and Katō, *Nihon bukkyō kiso kōza*, vol. 6, pp. 249ff; the entry in the *Zengaku daijiten*, vol. 1, p. 115; Collcutt, *Five Mountains*, pp. 41–48; Matsunaga, *Foundation of Japanese Buddhism*, vol. 2, p. 217.

90. See Imaeda II, pp. 153–54. According to the entry in the *Zengaku daijiten*, Eisai and his disciples are counted among the line of Huang-lung.

91. Compare the remarks on Wu-chun in Brinker, *Die zen-buddhistische Bildnismalerei in China und Japan*, pp. 160ff.

92. *Ibid.*, p. 161.

93. The first two characters come from the names of the famous Nara temples of Tōdai-ji and Kōfuku-ji.

94. Already during Enni's lifetime, Michiie had referred to him as "the venerable Shōichi." A biographical preface that reports his death and assignation of the posthumous title concludes with the words, "As for the title Shōichi, it is said that it was left him by Kujō Michiie." See *Shōichi kana hōgo* (Shigensha edition), p. 410.

95. *Shōichi kokushi goroku*, T. 2544, vol. 80. The "Dharma Sayings of the Zen School" (*Zenmon hōgoshū*) appeared in 1921. S. Yamada and T. Mori drafted a new, improved edition issued by Shigensha of Tokyo in 1973 (reprinted 1977). The text appears on pp. 409–24. On the *Jisshūyōdōki*, see Furuta, *Zen shisōshiron—Nihon zen*, p. 60.

96. *Shōichi kana-hōgo*, in the index of the *Kokushi Shōichi hōgo*, *Zenmon hōgoshū*, p. 411.

97. *Ibid.*

98. *Ibid.*, p. 412.

99. *Ibid.*, p. 413.

100. *Ibid.*, p. 416; cf. pp. 414–15.

101. *Ibid.*

102. *Ibid.*, p. 420.

103. See Imaeda II, pp. 154ff; Matsunaga, *Foundation of Japanese Buddhism*, vol. 2, pp. 217, 324, n. 23.

104. Besides Mujū Dōgyō, Imaeda draws attention to the fourth abbot of Tōfuku-ji, Hakuun Egyō (1228–1297) and Nanzan Shiun (1254–1335). See Imaeda II, pp. 156–57.

105. See *Zen shisōshiron—Nihon zen*, p. 56. Furuta describes the development in two sections entitled respectively "From a Zen dominated by the esoteric tradition (*mikkyō*) to a distinctively Zen school" (pp. 53–66) and "From the blossoming of a distinctively Zen school to independence" (pp. 66–84). The first phase revolved about the central figure of Eisai, while the transition to the second phase, which was supported by the Chinese Zen masters in Kamakura, begins with Enni. For Furuta, Japanese Rinzai Zen only became independent (phase three) when the Japanese masters (Nampo, Shūhō, and Kanzan in the temple monasteries of Daitoku-ji and Myōshin-ji) took over. Furuta points to the process of development of the Japanese Rinzai school in similar fashion in his "The History of the Zen Schools: The Rinzai School." Collcutt also gives three phases

(*Five Mountains*, pp. 28–29). While his first two phases coincide with those of Furuta, the third period, which begins at the end of the Kamakura period, embraces nearly the whole of the Muromachi period and is marked by the institution of the *gozan*. The viewpoint of the two authors is different. I am following Furuta since it is less matters of institutional development that concern me than of the religious development of Rinzai Zen during the Kamakura period.

106. *Ibid.*, p. 60.

107. *Ibid.*

108. See Furuta, *Zensō no shōji*, p. 23; cf. p. 19.

109. A brief biography of Shinchi Kakushin appears in *Zen Dust*, pp. 199–203. See also Collcutt, *Five Mountains*, pp. 48–49; Matsunaga, *Foundation of Japanese Buddhism*, vol. 2, pp. 217–18, 261–62; and my introduction to the German translation of the *Mumonkan*, pp. 23ff.

110. He also compiled rules for the monastic life. His *Hottō kokushi zazengi* was influenced by Dōgen's writings on the practice of Zen. See Collcutt, *Five Mountains*, p. 49.

111. See Collcutt, *Five Mountains*, p. 49. There are still other writings of Kakushin that have been passed down, in particular his Dharma sayings (*Hottō hōgo*). His relations to the many monasteries in the country are in great part inspired by his esoteric inclinations. Compare the information provided in Imaeda II, p. 159.

112. 1326 and 1329. See Gundert, *Bi-yän-lu*, p. 25. Dōgen had already brought a handwritten version of the kōan collection to Japan in 1227. The long hidden manuscript was edited by D. T. Suzuki; see *Zen Dust*, p. 358.

113. The two quotations at the start of this section come from D. T. Suzuki, *Zen and Japanese Culture*, p. 63, and G. B. Sanson, *Japan: A Short Cultural History* (rev. ed.), p. 286. Compare the chapter on "Zen Archery and Swordsmanship" during the Kamakura period in T. Hoover, *Zen Culture*, pp. 57–67.

In his book *Zen and the Ways*, T. Leggett draws attention to the peculiarity of "Kamakura Zen," which possessed numerous purely Japanese kōan even before the leading classical Chinese kōan collections became widespread in Japan. The Japanese kōan were highly treasured and carefully collected; some of these can be found in the little known collection *Shōnankattōroku*. The collection speaks of warrior monks (*nyūdō*) who took up the Buddhist monastic vows without leaving their families. Leggett offers a selection of kōan in English translation (*Zen and the Ways*, pp. 77–113; on the *nyūdō*, see p. 37). Also instructive is the *Zenrin kushū*, an anthology of Zen texts from an earlier period that were gathered during the middle ages but only printed for the first time in 1688. Ruth Fuller Sasaki offers important selections in English translation in *Zen Dust*, pp. 79–122.

114. Bersihand, *Geschichte Japans*, p. 142.

115. On this important Zen monk see Furuta, *Zen shisōshiron—Nihon zen*, p. 62; Imaeda II, pp. 164–65; Ku, *History of Zen*, p. 170.

116. Cited in Furuta, *Zen shisōshiron—Nihon zen*, p. 62. Mūzō studied with Enni Ben'en in his youth. He compiled the *Kōzenki* in 1272 for the imperial household as a defense against the assault of the monks from Mount Hiei. See Imaeda II, p. 164.

117. See Furuta, *Zen shisōshiron—Nihon zen*, p. 62.

118. For biographical data see Imaeda II, pp. 161ff; Collcutt, *Five Mountains*, pp. 65ff; Matsunaga, *Foundation of Japanese Buddhism*, vol. 2, pp. 219–20.

119. For biographical data see Imaeda II, pp. 163–64; Collcutt, *Five Mountains*, pp. 68ff; Matsunaga, *Foundation of Japanese Buddhism*, vol. 2, p. 220.

120. See Imaeda II, pp. 163–64; Collcutt, *Five Mountains*, p. 71.

121. Biographical data can be found in Imaeda II, pp. 164–65; Collcutt, *Five Mountains*, p. 70; and Matsunaga, *Foundation of Japanese Buddhism*, vol. 2, pp. 220–21.

122. See Imaeda II, pp. 165–66; Collcutt, *Five Mountains*, pp. 72–73; and Matsunaga, *Foundation of Japanese Buddhism*, vol. 2, p. 221.

123. See *Zen Buddhism and Japanese Culture*, pp. 40–41. Suzuki remarks that the account of this episode can lay no claim to historicity.

124. During World War II air-force suicide squads were referred to as *kamikaze*.

125. The monastery of Tōkei-ji is counted among the "Five Mountains" of Zen nuns in Kamakura. The nuns of the Rinzai school had also referred to their five main temples in Kamakura and Kyoto as "Five Mountains."

126. See Imaeda II, p. 166; cf. p. 211 and Matsunaga, *Foundation of Japanese Buddhism*, vol. 2, p. 221.

127. Ku offers a list with all the names and dates; see *History of Zen*, pp. 279ff.

128. For biographical details see Imaeda II, pp. 166–67; cf. Collcutt, *Five Mountains*, pp. 73ff, and Matsunaga, *Foundation of Japanese Buddhism*, vol. 2, p. 222.

129. See the entry on the first Chinese Sōtō master in Japan in *Zen Dust*, p. 199. The Japanese reading of the first name differs from author to author. *Zen Dust* and Ui, *Konsaisu bukkyō jiten*, p. 771 read it Tōmei; Imaeda II, p. 167, and Matsunaga, *Foundation of Japanese Buddhism*, vol. 2, p. 260, read Tonmin; Collcutt, *Five Mountains*, p. 74, and Yampolsky, *Zen Master Hakuin*, p. 5, use Tōmyō. These Chinese masters had no relationship to the Japanese Sōtō school (see chap. 3).

130. In addition to the entry in *Zen Dust* referred to in the previous note, see Imaeda II, p. 167 and Matsunaga, *Foundation of Japanese Buddhism*, vol. 2, pp. 260–61.

131. Imaeda II, p. 168. Compare Matsunaga, *Foundation of Japanese Buddhism*, vol. 2, p. 260. Imaeda devotes a section to this school in his *Chūsei zenshūshi no kenkyū*, pp. 483–503.

132. See Collcutt, *Five Mountains*, p. 77.

133. For biographical details see Imaeda II, pp. 169–70. The monastic rules *Taikan shingi* (also pronounced *Daikan shingi*, T. 2577), edited by Ch'ing-cho, belong among the early monastic rules of Zen to appear in Japan. The Chinese Zen masters adopted Chinese models from the Sung period, especially the *Zen'on shingi* (Chin., *Ch'an-yüan ch'ing-kuei*; see note 31 above), *Biyō shingi* (Chin., *Pei-yung ch'ing-kuei*, 1330), and *Kōtei shingi* (Chin., *Chiao-ting ch'ing-kuei*, 1274). See Imaeda Aishin, *Chūsei zenshūshi no kenkyū*, pp. 64–65; Collcutt, *Five Mountains*, pp. 77–78; Matsunaga, *Foundation of Japanese Buddhism*, vol. 2, p. 222. Ch'ing-cho presents a transition from the leading Chinese masters in Kamakura to Japanese Zen.

134. See Matsunaga, *Foundation of Japanese Buddhism*, vol. 2, p. 224. Collcutt, too, maintains that the system of the Five Mountains began with the time of the Hōjō; see *Five Mountains*, p. 109; see also p. 93.

135. Imaeda lists the names of a number of Japanese Zen monks who preferred a life of solitude after their return from China and remained true to unadulterated Zen practice. See Imaeda II, p. 160.

136. See table 10 in *Zen Dust*, pp. 506–507. A brief biography appears on pp. 205–206. See also Matsunaga, *Foundation of Japanese Buddhism*, vol. 2, pp. 221–22. Like Imaeda II, p. 165, the Matsunagas reads his personal name Jōmin, although the usual reading is Jōmyō; see the *Zengaku daijiten*, vol. 2, p. 974.

137. Cited in Furuta, *Zen no rekishi*, p. 34. My not entirely literal translation follows Furuta's paraphrase. Compare the essay on the internal agreement between Hsüeh-t'ang and Nampo (Jpn., *Daiō*), *Zengaku kenkyū* 49 (1959): 40–56.

138. T. 2547, vol. 80. For further information on the collection see *Zen Dust*, p. 206. The temple of Sōfuku-ji can also be read Sūfuku-ji, on which see *Zengaku daijiten*, vol. 1, p. 638.

139. On the following see also Furuta, *Zen no rekishi*, pp. 36ff.

140. See Furuta, *Zen no rekishi*, pp. 38–39. *Zen Dust* is confused in speaking of the stay of Shūhō in the Manju-ji monastery of Kamakura (p. 231), the two Zen temples sharing a common name.

141. See Furuta, *Zen no rekishi*, pp. 39–40. Nampo owed his appointment as abbot of Kenchō-ji above all to his relationship with the earlier abbot of the monastery, Lan-hsi, under whom he had practiced in his youth (see above).

142. Cited in *Zen Dust*, p. 206.

143. *Ibid.*

144. See Imaeda II, p. 211.

145. See the account in *Zen Dust*, p. 206.

2

Dōgen

No other religious personality in the history of Japan has so stirred contemporary interest and admiration as the Zen master Dōgen Kigen (1200–1253). Buddhists—members of the Sōtō school and numerous members from the various other Buddhists schools alike—hold him in reverence. Philosophers are attracted to "the depth and precision of his thought . . . which early on perceived and penetrated what is the starting point for the systematic thought of contemporary philosophy." They regard Dōgen as a "religious person."[1] During the first half of this century in Japan this unique blend of lofty religious achievement and uncommon intellectual gifts awakened a strong interest in this Zen master, whom not a few Japanese take to be one of their strongest and most spirited intellectual figures. At the same time, Dōgen is not without his critics. Researchers are turning up new data that makes a definitive judgment impossible at this time. Yet the two main components of his personality—a religious expression inspired by genuine inner experience and his early contribution to a Japanese philosophy grounded in Mahāyāna Buddhism—assure him an important place in the religious and intellectual history of his country.

LIFE AND WORK

DŌGEN'S YOUTH

Like all Zen masters, Dōgen is known in history by his monastic name.[2] His family is known to have been court nobility but the question of his genealogical origins is rather complex. It may be assumed that his father was Koga (or Minamoto) Michichika (d. 1202), although recent research indicates that it may have been Minamoto Michitomo (1170–1227).[3] His mother came from a highly esteemed aristocratic family.[4] As was the case with all noble families, their talented son was given an exacting literary education. He was a mere four years old when he read his first Chinese poem! Though Chinese was a central part of his continuing education, it does not seem to have had much influence on his later religious development. His works show only slight traces of his earlier study of Chinese literature, which was for him, evidently, more a study of form than of content.

His father (Michichika) died when he was two, his mother when he was seven. Exceptionally sensitive child that he was, this was his first religious shock. Through the pain and loneliness he realized the passing nature of all worldly realities. His biography reports:

> The loss of his beloved mother when he was only seven threw him into deep sorrow. As he watched the clouds of incense rise in the Takao Temple, he understood the coming-to-be and passing away of all things. The longing for enlightenment was awakened in his breast.[5]

His pious mother had called him to her deathbed and urged him to become a monk, to follow the precepts, and to pray faithfully for his dead parents and for the welfare of all living beings. These experiences penetrated his heart indelibly and confirmed his resolve to renounce the world.

After his mother's death, Dōgen moved to the house of an uncle,[6] a powerful nobleman who received the child in the hope that his nephew would become his heir and successor. But shortly before the day on which he was formally to begin his adulthood and his life in the world, the twelve-year-old lad, fully aware of what lay ahead, fled his uncle's house and took refuge with Ryōkan Hōgen, a relative from his mother's side who was pursuing Buddhist studies and the practice of magic in Onjō-ji at the foot of Mount Hiei. This was in the year 1212. When the boy expressed a desire to become a monk, Ryōkan at first refused but finally gave in to youthful persistence. Rather than allowing the boy to stay at Onjō-ji, however, he sent him to the monastery of Senkōbō, where he was warmly received by Abbot Jien. Shortly afterward, the abbot died and Dōgen found himself under the protection of Kōen, the head of the Tendai school,[7] under whom he was ordained a monk one year later. Whether at the same time he also received the bodhisattva precepts on the ordination platform of Enryaku-ji is not known. Many of Dōgen's biographers argue that he did, but we know that according to Tendai tradition one could not be fully made a monk before the age of twenty. His given monastic name was Dōgen, literally, "Foundation of the Way." Only later in life did he also use the name of Kigen. It is, in any case, significant that Dōgen began his Buddhist career as a Tendai monk and remained in this tradition for many years.

In the monastery of Mount Hiei, Dōgen devoted all his energies to the study of the scriptures and to the religious life, but in so doing soon found himself dogged by a painful and apparently insoluble question. He had read: "Both doctrines, the open and the secret, teach the original Buddha nature of all sentient beings. But if that is so, why do all the Buddhas and bodhisattvas arouse the desire for enlightenment? Why do they engage in ascetic practices?" The question of the relation between Buddha nature and enlightenment—or in Mahāyāna terminology (as in the Mahāyāna-śrāddhotpāda Śāstra), between one's original enlightenment and acquired enlightenment—disturbed young Dōgen's inquisitive mind and drove him from his mountain seclusion on Mount Hiei, where no one could give him a satisfying answer.

The precise date of this important event is not clear. Dōgen went back to Onjō-ji (also called Mii-dera), where his uncle was superior. There he posed his question to the well-known monk Kōin (1145–1216). An upright, religious man still searching for truth in his old age, Kōin had not long before burned all his earlier writings and taken up faith in the Buddha Amida. Unable to resolve Dōgen's doubts, Kōin referred him to Eisai, who was held in high regard after his travels to China. It is not certain whether Eisai and Dōgen actually met,[8] but at the time Dōgen would have visited him, Eisai was no longer living in Kennin-ji in Kyoto. Although Dōgen frequently mentions Eisai in his discourses, he never states that they had met. In any event, it is clear that Dōgen considered Eisai a very important Buddhist monk, especially because of his two trips to China.

After traveling through the land and visiting a number of monasteries, Dōgen finally entered the Kennin-ji monastery in 1217 and enrolled in the school of Myōzen, who had succeeded Eisai as superior. Zen at Kennin-ji was mixed with Tendai and Shingon. As it is stated in the chronicles, Myōzen taught "the three religions of open doctrine, secret doctrine, and the mind"—namely, the sūtras, the Tantric rites, and Zen.[9] On Mount Hiei, Dōgen had already immersed himself in the study of the sacred scriptures and became familiar with popular esoteric rites.[10] Myōzen, who was himself committed to Zen, permitted his disciples to practice according to the strict rules of the Rinzai school. Dōgen recognized Myōzen as a genuine master, yet his deep religious desires remained unsatisfied and he longed ever more to go to China, the birthplace of Zen, where able masters of the tradition of the Sixth Patriarch would be able to show him the way to enlightenment. Myōzen, who shared in this dream, not only readily granted his disciple permission to travel, but decided to go with him, after removing some final obstacles. In the spring of 1223, they set out together for the Middle Kingdom.

THE VOYAGE TO CHINA

The fellow-travellers set sail from Hakata and after a difficult crossing landed in a harbor in central China in April. Perhaps because of difficulties with immigration officials, Dōgen remained on the ship for three months and was thus able to take his time adjusting to the new world around him. His first deeper impressions of Chinese Zen came from the head cook of the monastery on Mount A-yü-wang, who most likely sought him out, in order to buy a kind of Japanese mushroom known as *shiitake*. Dōgen implored the worthy monk to stay aboard a while but he declined because he had to return to his work in the monastery. When Dōgen asked what was so pressing about his work, the monk explained that kitchen work was his form of Zen practice. Surprised, Dōgen inquired why in his advanced years he did not prefer to devote himself to meditation and kōan practice. At that the old monk laughed out loud. "My good fellow from a foreign land," he said, "you do not yet know what practice (Chin., *pan-tao*; Jpn., *bendō*) means, nor do you yet understand words and scriptures (Chin., *wen-tzu*; Jpn., *monji*)." Abruptly bidding good-bye he vanished into the dusk. Later that year, Dōgen was to meet the cook a second time when the old man paid him a visit in the monastery on Mount T'ien-t'ung, where Dōgen was living after the summer retreat (Jpn., *geango*). Taking up where they had left off, Dōgen asked him what he meant by "practice" and "words and scriptures." The monk replied, "Words and scriptures are: one, two, three, four, five. Practice means: nothing in the universe is hidden."

Far from being a trivial episode, this meeting with the aged cook had a lasting impact on Dōgen. Fourteen years later he would recount it in his work *The Lesson from the Monk-Cook (Tenzo kyōkun)*,[11] indicating how deeply he had been moved. His biographers see the event as "an extremely important turn"[12] or even "a personal transformation."[13] This old cook—this "man of the Tao"— had shown him how daily work that flows out of enlightenment is actually religious practice and brought him to understand how any activity can be Zen practice. It was an insight that Dōgen would express in many different ways throughout the rest of his life. The cook embodied the living tradition of Chinese Zen from the time of the fourth and fifth patriarchs and Master Pai-chang, which taught that Zen is practiced not only by sitting cross-legged in meditation or reading the sūtras but just as much in daily service to the community.

After Dōgen was finally allowed to disembark, he went at once to the monastery of Ching-te-ssu, located on Mount T'ien-t'ung, where the eminent master Wu-chi Liao-p'ai was in charge and where, according to sources dating from that time, some five hundred monks were quartered. Dōgen zealously took up his own daily practice, deeply impressed by the monastic life of Chinese Zen. He was particularly astonished at the strict discipline of the monks, which had already struck him during his first meeting with the cook from Mount A-yü-wang. He was less happy with his position in the community, since as a young foreigner he was subordinate even to the novices. He protested but to no avail.[14] The complaint seems to have caused something of a stir in the community, but it did not keep Dōgen from continuing his practice faithfully. Yet for all his determination, the experience of enlightenment eluded him.

Historical sources do not tell us just how long Dōgen remained at the monastery on Mount T'ien-t'ung nor whether he left before or after the death of Master Wu-chi near the end of 1224, but it is possible that his departure was occasioned by the master's death. He subsequently visited many Chinese Zen monasteries and became acquainted with different schools and orientations. At that time, the Southern Sung period, there were many masters like Abbot Wu-chi who belonged to the dominant school of Ta-hui, which would also have a marked influence on Dōgen. It is clear from his later writings that Dōgen came to be well versed in kōan. Most probably he was aware of the less fortunate traits of the Ta-hui movement as well, but the harsh criticism he was later to level against Ta-hui stemmed from subsequent experiences.[15]

His pilgrimage to many different monasteries satisfied another of Dōgen's inclinations—his lively interest in the generational lines of Zen. The documents containing the lines of succession had been preserved like precious treasures in the monasteries, and Dōgen studied them carefully. It was an extraordinary privilege for Dōgen, a Japanese Zen disciple whom zeal for the Dharma had driven across the sea, to be allowed to examine these valuable and often esthetically ornate manuscripts. He poured over the testimonies supporting the lists of succession in the three houses of the Yang-ch'i school and the houses of Yün-men and Fa-yen. Dōgen's historical consciousness, one of the hallmarks of his personality, was richly nourished by this travel to China.[16]

A few months later, as he was preparing for the trip home, he made plans to return to Mount T'ien-t'ung. One source has it that it was then that he heard of the death of Wu-chi; disappointed, he was about to board the ship for Japan when an old monk told him that a famous and incomparable master named Ju-ching (Jpn., Nyojō, 1163–1228) had, at the request of the imperial court and the monastic community, been named abbot of Mount T'ien'-t'ung. On 1 May, 1225, Dōgen met his new master for the first time. At once he felt his spirit soar. At last he had found the "authentic teacher" (Jpn., shōshi). Ju-ching received the Japanese novice warmly and readily gave him permission to visit him at any time, regardless of the normal regulations.

T'ien-t'ung Ju-ching was the Dharma heir of Tsu-an Chih-chien of the House of Ts'ao-tung (Jpn., Sōtō), which had lain dormant for a spell but, due mainly to the two great masters Fu-jung Tao-k'ai (1043–1118) and Hung-chih Cheng-chüeh (1091–1157), had been reawakened. During the late Sung period, Ju-ching again brought forth the best of the Ts'ao-tung house. From his two eminent masters he inherited a monastic lifestyle and a great zeal for seated meditation, two characteristics we will meet again in Dōgen. Although Ju-ching's achievements are significant in themselves (he left us a collection of sayings),[17] he is remembered mainly as the "authentic teacher" for whom Dōgen had sought. Ju-ching's personality comes across clearly in the writings of his famous disciple.

An impressive figure of imposing stature, Ju-ching devoted a life of distinguished service to Zen,[18] and even in old age continued to labor energetically. His was a strict ascetic life, simple and unpretentious. He was fond of the crude monastic diet and the rough monk's robes and, because he eyed honors and decorations with enmity, kept aloof from court life. He devoted himself unreservedly to the training of young monks, before whom he combined rigor with geniality. Dōgen tells us how he conducted Zen practice:

> My former teacher Ju-ching, when he was priest of the temple at Mount T'ien-t'ung, would strike the monks with his slipper to keep them from dozing during zazen sessions in the meditation hall and would revile and scold them. Yet the assembled monks were glad to be hit, and praised him for it.
>
> Once, after having delivered a lecture, he said: "I have grown old, retired from the assembly, and now live in a small temple and nourish this old body of mine. Yet, being the teacher to the assembly, I serve as the head priest of this small temple so that I may destroy the delusions of each one of you and teach you the Way. That's why I sometimes use words of rebuke, and I sometimes strike you with my bamboo rod. But I really have no heart for it. Nevertheless, I use these instruction methods standing in the place of the Buddha. Monks, permit this with compassion." When Ju-ching finished, the assembled monks all wept.[19]

As Dōgen tells us, Ju-ching practiced until eleven o'clock in the evening and then arose at three in the morning or earlier in order to resume his practice. He followed this routine every night.[20] In his monastery the monks meditated literally day and night, the aged master setting the example. Striking the drowsy, he would remind them of the hardships endured by people in the world, the dangers faced by soldiers, and the sweat poured out by the peasants. How disgraceful that monks should fall asleep during their sacred pursuits! He would hear nothing of shortening meditation periods, and complained rather that because of old age he was losing strength in his arm and his energies were waning.

It is the time of summer retreat (geango), from mid-April to mid-July, a time conducive to strenuous effort. Dōgen is exerting all his energies to make the most of the opportunity. He hears of the death of his Japanese teacher and friend, Myōzen, who had passed away at the T'ien-t'ung Monastery after a serious illness.[21] Suitable funeral services are held in the temple and Dōgen mourns deeply, but soon afterward is back at his practice. The matchless zeal of this temple is an exception in China at the time. In this atmosphere, Dōgen gives his utmost and soon is ready for the great enlightenment. Once again the monks are seated in midnight meditation. One of them falls asleep. Noticing it, Ju-ching remarks, "In Zen, body and mind are cast off. Why do you sleep?" On hearing this, Dōgen suddenly experiences enlightenment. He rushes to the Dharma hall, lights some incense, and gives thanks to the Buddha. Convinced of the authenticity of Dōgen's enlightenment, Ju-ching rejoices. Dōgen, liberated from all illusion, all passion and attachment to self, exults in the freedom of an enlightened being. From Ju-ching he receives the seal of succession to the patriarchate of the Ts'ao-tung house.

We have no direct testimony, written or oral, from Dōgen himself about his experience of enlightenment. The closest thing is a statement by his disciple Ejō that Gikai, the third abbot of Eihei-ji, has passed down to us: "Concerning the circumstances of the great enlightenment of our deceased master, it took place when he heard the words about the casting off of body and mind."[22] Dōgen says something similar: "When I heard T'ien-t'ung (Ju-ching) speak about the casting off, I fulfilled the way of Buddha."[23] According to the early biographies Kenzeiki and Eihei-ji sanso gyōgōki as well, it was Ju-ching's remark about the casting off of body and mind that sparked enlightenment in Dōgen. Indeed, these words can stand as the motto of Dōgen's experience, inasmuch as they characterize his enlightenment as a total existential experience that shaped his entire life and influenced his religious metaphysics from that point on.[24]

The confirmation of his experience by Master Ju-ching was important for Dōgen, well aware as he was that the seal of succession had placed him in a line of tradition leading back through Hui-neng and the Chinese and Indian patriarchs to Kāśyapa and Śākyamuni. Later during his stay at Mount T'ien-t'ung, Ju-ching presented him with a document verifying that the master had bestowed the title of succession on his disciple Dōgen, a monk from Japan. The solemn event is regarded by adherents of the Sōtō school as the starting point of their school. Nevertheless, the differences between the Chinese House of Ts'ao-tung and the Japanese Sōtō school cannot be overlooked.

During his remaining time on Mount T'ien-t'ung Dōgen devoted himself to postenlightenment practice, the importance of which he would later stress. He realized the need for deepening his experience. Ju-ching offered him the position of assistant in the monastery, but Dōgen turned it down.[25] In 1227, "with empty hands," he began his journey home. Aside from the master's two gifts—the Dharma robe of the old master Fu-jung Tao-k'ai that symbolized his line of tradition and a portrait of Ju-ching that would serve him as a personal memory—he brought back nothing with him to Japan, none of the scriptural scrolls, cultic pictures, art work, or liturgical utensils that Zen monks returning from China usually bore. The great nation of the Sung had fulfilled its promise to him and stilled his longing for the Dharma. The sketchy report on his pilgrimage that he gives us in the *Bendōwa* ends simply: "Ultimately, I went to T'ai-pai peak and engaged in religious practice under the Zen master Ju-ching, until I had resolved the one great matter of Zen practice for my entire life *(isshō sangaku no daiji)*. After that . . . I returned home."[26]

FOUNDATION AND EXPANSION IN JAPAN

From Kennin-ji to Kōshō-ji.   In Japan, Dōgen repaired to Kennin-ji in Kyoto where he laid the bones of his departed travel companion Myōzen to rest. He found the temple in the same disappointing state he had left it when he set out for China. Indeed, in the meantime things had worsened due to the moral degeneration and restlessness of the times. The monks went about securing their livelihood but there was little to be seen in the way of serious religious striving.

Dōgen wished only to devote his life to the realization of the true Dharma and in so doing to help as many others as possible. Thus already in the first year of his stay in Kennin-ji he wrote a brief primer of less than a thousand Chinese characters on the practice of meditation, the *Fukanzazengi (General Teachings for the Promotion of Zazen).*[27] The text opens with the question that had disturbed him during his youth and that he did not let go of for the rest of his life:

> The Way is basically perfect and all-pervading. How could it be contingent upon practice and realization? The Dharma vehicle is free and untrammeled. What need is there for man's concentrated effort?[28]

He does not pursue the question any further, however. His brief instruction was intended for a wider circle and focused on promoting concrete practice.

Dōgen did not feel at home in Kennin-ji. Hostilities plagued him within the monastery and persecution by the monks from Mount Hiei pressed from without. He did not feel called to the role of reformer for a community that had gone to seed. Accordingly, in 1230 he chose to transfer his residence to Fukakusa (in the region of Fushimi near Kyoto). There, in the country temple of An'yō-in, he was able to teach seated meditation and realization of the Buddha nature through meditation to a growing number of listeners. People of all ages, men and women alike, from all social classes, flooded to hear his lectures and practice with him. He turned no one back and instilled in all the confidence that even in the degenerate age of *mappō* people could find peace of heart by attending to the true law of the Buddha. Many earnest pilgrims from the area around Kyoto came to Fukakusa, which became a focal point of Zen practice.

Fleeing from the inconveniences of life in the city Dōgen developed his spiritual strength in the poor country temple. With the impressions of his trip to China still fresh, in 1233 he wrote his first important book, *Bendōwa (Discourse on Practice)*, dealing mainly with practical questions and aimed at instructing and stimulating his growing audience.[29] To the attentive reader the spiritual maturity of the young master shines through. This book of practice, which today forms the first chapter of his great work, the *Shōbōgenzō (The Treasure of the Eye of the True Dharma)*, is an important testament from Dōgen's earlier period and both contains in germ the whole of his written work and offers a relatively easy introduction to it. The main motifs that resound in this youthful work will be taken up later, but it may be helpful here to single out a few points to give a sense of the spiritual atmosphere of his early work.

The book is dominated throughout by a conviction of the incomparable value of seated meditation, or *zazen*. This position of all the Buddhas and patriarchs is the unequaled and irreplaceable gate of entry to enlightenment. Dōgen undertook to communicate this conviction to his hearers. Many were attracted by the openness that he exuded. The practice of *zazen*, as he taught tirelessly, is necessary and beneficial for all, even for the laity and for women. Worldly affairs are not an obstacle, but one must cast all considerations aside. There is no time at which the practice of Zen cannot succeed. Along with his openness, Dōgen possessed a broad spirit of tolerance. He acknowledged that other Buddhist schools, such as the Hokke (Lotus) and Kegon (Hua-yen) traditions, also possessed genuine experience and remarked at one point, "You should know that for a Buddhist it is not a matter of debating the superiority or inferiority of one teaching or another . . .; all we have to know is whether the practice is authentic or not."[30]

The winds of spring blew into the poor surroundings. An'yō-in was half in a state of collapse and no longer suited Dōgen's purposes. After nearly three years a rather large building was erected in the vicinity by the Fujiwara clan on the grounds of Gokuraku-ji, a temple dedicated to the bodhisattva Kannon (Avalokiteśvara). Dōgen resolved to take up residence in this building in 1233 and named the temple precincts Kannondōri-in. At once he began efforts to expand the construction and already in the same year was able to consecrate a Buddha hall. At last he stood on firm ground. On these new premises he would pass the happiest and most fruitful years of his life.

A Brief Climax.   We may refer to the ten years that Dōgen spent in the temple monastery constructed for him as the brief high point of his life. And not without good reason. In the normally longer than average life of a Zen master—not uncommonly they reached the height of their effectiveness at the age of seventy or eighty, even ninety—ten years make but a brief interlude. Moreover, Dōgen did not reach the heights all at once and the descent during his final years was considerable. Nevertheless, in the ten years he was at Kōshō-ji Dōgen undoubtedly completed the best part of his work.

At first, of course, the construction of the temple facilities took a great deal of time. The culmination of the building was neither the Buddha hall nor the Dharma hall but rather a detached monks' hall (sōdō), the heart and center of the Zen temple-complex. It was consecrated in October of 1236, at which time it was named Kōshōhōrin-ji (Kōshō-ji for short). One year later the Dharma hall (hattō) was completed and shortly thereafter an annex (jūundō) was added to the monks' hall. Dōgen's idea of a total Zen center with the three main buildings of a Buddha temple, a Dharma hall, and a monks' hall, had become a reality. The monks' hall was the first of its kind in Japan; the practice and ritual that were carried on there were pure, unadulterated Zen.

Meantime, inner development kept pace with the outer construction. Dōgen was in the prime of his life. In addition to the many capable disciples that came to him, a large number of laity, both men and women, entrusted themselves to his guidance. The size of the complex was sufficient to accommodate a large quantity of religious seekers. The increasing envy and animosity of the Tendai monks were only further proof of the far from trifling importance that was being attributed to Dōgen's Zen movement.

Naturally, the most important thing of all was the recruiting of suitable disciples. There was no lack of young men in the region around Kyoto interested in the new method of mediation, but it was no easy matter to sift out the wheat from the chaff. This only made a second meeting with Ejō, who had already visited Dōgen in Kennin-ji, all the more a joy. On this occasion, in 1234, Ejō took the decisive step and asked to be accepted into the circle of Dōgen's disciples. His loyal assistance was to prove invaluable for Dōgen and his community.

Koun Ejō (1198–1280),[31] a personality of stature, had decided after in-depth study of Buddhism to enter the previously mentioned Japanese Daruma school of Dainichi Nōnin, where he practiced Zen under Nōnin's disciple Kakuan. Ejō was two years Dōgen's senior. When he came to visit Dōgen it was not immediately clear which one of them was to be "junior." But Dōgen's personality was convincing and Ejō decided to enter into his discipleship. The relationship of the master to his first real disciple, whom he named head of the monks' hall in 1236, developed into a warm friendship. Together they discussed future plans, in particular literary ventures.

Dōgen composed the largest and most significant section of the Shōbōgenzō, his magnum opus, written in Japanese, during the ten years he was at Kōshō-ji. Although now comprising a collection of no less than ninety-two books of differing length, the work was not originally conceived as a single whole but brings together a number of individual pieces that in the view of the author form a unity. The books treat a variety of themes and are of varying quality. This latter fact has given cause for controversies that are far from resolved even today.

The short and typical *Bendōwa* book on practice referred to earlier may be taken as the first foundational section of the work, although not included in an early redaction of the *Shōbōgenzō*. In it Dōgen sets out the new style and characteristics of *zazen* meditation and offers a forceful invitation to serious practice. Another important book from this initial period is the collection of sayings, *Shōbōgenzō zuimonki*, composed between 1235 and 1238. Yanagida Seizan writes:

> The *Shōbōgenzō zuimonki* represents Dōgen's collected sayings. The tradition of such *goroku* as the direct transcription of Zen sayings began in Chinese Buddhism. One might say that the achievement of the *Shōbōgenzō zuimonki* symbolizes the era of Kamakura Buddhism.[32]

The import of this literary genre is familiar from Chinese Buddhism. The *goroku* expresses most forcefully the Zen style of a master. In the *Shōbōgenzō zuimonki*, however, we see "the combined work of two hapless masters, Dōgen and Ejō."[33] Ejō was the redactor of the collection but the substance of all its elements was drawn from his master. Through and through, this little book, with its directness, its wealth of anecdotes, its blending of the humorous and the serious with its focus always fixed on what is essential, has the unmistakable flavor of the Zen *goroku* that makes at once demanding and absorbing reading.

The new style represented by this work became the standard in the circle around Dōgen. The transition was not only made at the scribe's desk but was given life and concreteness in the temple halls. Whereas it had long been an unwritten law that the Chinese *kanbun* style be used for official ceremonies and for addresses of the master, Dōgen was the first to use Japanese. The Zen annals relate that the inaugural celebration of Kōshō-ji was the first great ceremony to be performed in the Japanese language.[34]

The books of the *Shōbōgenzō* followed one another in quick succession, each book a self-contained whole. Dōgen took great care in writing the manuscripts, striving for the most effective expression for the matter he was treating. He preferred to speak in the intimate atmosphere of the evening hours. There is a particular charm in the harmony he strikes between his personal words and a stylistically honed presentation. It may be that he read his written manuscript aloud so to heighten the effect.[35]

In any case, the early books of the *Shōbōgenzō* have contributed not a little to his reputation as a thinker and literary figure. In order to fully appreciate this one needs to be conversant with the language. Educated Japanese have corroborated the deep impression that the youthful, fresh, natural, and forceful flow of the young Dōgen's language has made on them. The American Buddhologist Thomas Kasulis singles out Dōgen's deeply moving linguistic skills and his concrete and immediate experience as the two main grounds for the lasting influence of this "incomparable philosopher."[36] A thematic presentation of the content of Dōgen's work will be left for a later section of this chapter, but our biographical sketch cannot fail to point to the extraordinary power of his literary creativity.

An example of Dōgen's linguistic power is to be found in the short masterpiece of 1237, *Ikka myōju*[37] (*One Bright Pearl*), where all of reality, be it great or small, beautiful or ugly, expensive or trifling, is likened to a pearl that shines from its own inner nature. A charming counterpoint is struck in the much later work, *Nyorai zenshin* (*The Whole Body of the Tathāgata*), completed in 1244.[38] As the title suggests, the work speaks of the oneness of the Tathāgata with all of reality. Dōgen sees in everything the living practice of the whole body of the Perfected One.

The book *Raihai tokuzui* (*Attaining the Marrow through Worship*, 1240)[39] brings us to the depth of the Zen movement that had formed about the person of Dōgen. Literally, *tokuzui* means "to attain the marrow." The title alludes to a famous episode, practiced as a kōan, of the Bodhidharma legend.[40] The departing patriarch, who dispenses his gifts to his disciples in accord with the level of development of each, says to his successor Hui-k'o, "You have attained the marrow"—that is, the inner core of the spiritual transmission. In the *Raihai tokuzui* Dōgen shows that the essence of the Dharma surpasses all differences. Nuns who have reached enlightenment attest to the fact that the Zen way is open to all, men and women, monks and laity. This broad conception dominated the Zen circle of Kōshō-ji. Unfortunately, Dōgen's outlook narrowed in his later years, during which he increasingly came to regard the monastic life as indispensible to enlightenment. This is a serious weak point in the late Dōgen, who was no longer able to bring his original conviction of the possibility of the achievement of full enlightenment for all into harmony with his view of the monastic way as the fundamental form of the Buddhist life. The *Raihai tokuzui* bears witness to the high esteem in which Dōgen held women and remains an important document for the place of women in Zen Buddhism.

The work he did in Kōshō-ji shows Dōgen at the peak of his life. Toward the end of the decade we see signs of a change in the making. The monastic community went through a remarkable period of expansion with the entry of a group of monks from the Japanese Daruma school, who came to Dōgen under the leadership of Ekan (d. 1251). Increase signifies enrichment but can also prove a burden. Moreover, dark clouds of enmity were gathering over Kyoto.

The Journey to Echizen.   In July of 1243, not unprepared and without hesitating, Dōgen left Kōshō-ji in Uji with his community in order to take up the residence in the region of Echizen, on the inhospitable northern coast of Japan, at the invitation of his friend and disciple Hatano Yoshishige. There the wealthy landowner generously offered him a large plot of land and an ample work force. The resolve and speed with which he carried out the move were remarkable. Japanese historians are agreed that there is no fully convincing explanation of what motives prompted this action.[41] Dōgen's successful work in the region of the capital had previously been a thorn in the side of the Tendai monks on Mount Hiei. Even in his immediate surroundings there was no lack of antagonistic neighbors who wanted to do away with the new Zen center. Dōgen did not work only for the common people but carried on friendly relations with the nobility and the military. He was successful and had earned general recognition. Why the sudden departure?

The most plausible explanation seems to be that of the distinguished Japanese Zen historian Furuta Shōkin, who considers the question in the light of the overall situation of the Zen movement in the country, particular in Kyoto and surrounding areas.[42] After the death of Eisai, Rinzai Zen secured a strong foothold in Kamakura and Kyoto, as well as on the southern island of Kyūshū. The current was running against Dōgen. The pressure turned into a threat after the return of Enni Ben'en from China in July of 1241. Through his imposing personality this Rinzai master quickly won a following and spread his influence. The monastery of Tōfuku-ji was built for him not far from Dōgen's center. This aggravated matters for Dōgen. Should he take up the struggle with his powerful rival or should he withdraw to the countryside? Compelled by outer circumstances, he gave way. One may call it as well a defeat as a renunciation.

Other circumstances strengthened him in his resolve. The monks of the Daruma school who had joined Dōgen had lived before in the Tendai monastery of Hajaku-ji not far from the estate of Hatano Yoshishige. Many of them came originally from the region. Their encouragement must have had something to do with the transfer. Later idealized descriptions of the Sōtō school recall the admonition that Master Ju-ching had given to his disciple at his departure: that after returning to his country he should shun large cities, dwell deep in the mountains and valleys, and realize his inner nature.

In any case, Dōgen's retreat to the country marks a turning-point in his life. In Echizen he had first of all to put up with the small country temple of Kippō-ji. It goes without saying that he was not troubled by poverty and want. However, he fell into a depression that had been building up through the external pressures and animosities of the dark times he was going through. The year that Dōgen spent in Kippō-ji marked a low point of his life and a break in the quality of his literary pursuits as well. It is not that there are no valuable passages in the late books of the *Shōbōgenzō*, but the downturn is undeniable.[43]

Critique of Lin-chi and the House of Rinzai.   Dōgen's depression vented itself in a surfeit of literary productions. During the one lean year of his stay at Kippō-ji he composed almost twenty books of the *Shōbōgenzō*. The rigorous critique of Rinzai Zen that comes out in these books represents a marked departure from his earlier views. Already near the end of his time at Kōshō-ji he complained that "from ancient times to the present, few have understood *zazen*,"[44] and singled out the Rinzai monks of his time for reproof. Signs of his dislike of the Rinzai school increased, showing up after 1243 in several books of the *Shōbōgenzō*.

Dōgen had a solid understanding of the House of Rinzai. In his youth he had lived with Myōzen in Kennin-ji, and during the course of his quest for the right master in China he met Rinzai monks at every step. As he recounted in the autobiographical section of his *Bendōwa*, "in the empire of the great Sung, only the Lin-chi school is found throughout the country." Dōgen also noted the Five Houses, each in its own way, "are all reducible to the one Buddha-mind seal."[45] The weaknesses of Chinese Zen did not escape his notice, but the admiration he brought back to Japan for what he had seen in China was unbounded. On important points his standpoint differed from the dominant Rinzai line of the Sung period, namely from the style of Ta-hui Tsung-kao (1089–1163), but in the early books of the Shōbōgenzō Ta-hui is mentioned favorably. The Shōbōgenzō zuimonki accords him high recognition.[46]

Dōgen's attacks against Ta-hui begin after his move to Echizen. In his Sesshin sesshō (Explaining Mind, Explaining Nature, 1243) he launches a confrontation that flows over from the issues into a personal affront. Ta-hui's promotion of the emptying and quieting of mental activity are said to accord ill with the doctrine of the Buddha nature. Ta-hui "did not yet know the fine writings of the Buddhas and patriarchs, nor had he heard of the splendor of the gems of the Buddhas and patriarchs," with the result that "he had a one-sided view of the Buddha-Dharma."[47]

The Jishōzammai (The Samādhi of Self-Enlightenment), which Dōgen presented to his disciples at the beginning of the following year in Kippō-ji, contains lengthy passages aimed against Ta-hui. The books as such treats the transmission of mind in the proper generational succession. He cites classical examples from early Buddhism—Śākyamuni's transmission of the Buddha mind to Mahākāśyapa and the scene from the Bodhidharma legend in which Hui-k'o severs his arm—in order to clarify the necessity of the master-disciple relationship.[48] "Yet foolish people, when hearing of self-awakening and self-enlightenment think that it is sufficient to study by themselves without receiving the transmission from a master. This is a grave error."[49] Dōgen was convinced that the great way of the Buddhas and patriarchs was not accessible without proper succession and inheritance.

The example of Ta-hui, who did not receive the seal of enlightenment from any of the masters he approached, is offered by way of warning.[50] Dōgen reports three such attempts. The first master he approached taught the way of enlightenment basing himself on the writings of Yün-men. Failing to attain certification from him, Ta-hui next turned to Tao-wei (Jpn., Dōbi), a master of the Chinese Ts'ao-tung school. Here, Ta-hui's request for certification of enlightenment was rather direct and the master refused, admonishing him to further practice. Undaunted, Ta-hui went to yet a third master, a monk by the name of Chan-t'ang Wen-chun (Jpn., Tandō Bunjun, 1061–1115) of the Huang-lung line of the Rinzai school. He spent a longer time with the master and had kōan-type conversations with him. Before he could confirm his disciple's enlightenment, Wen-chun took fatally ill. According to Dōgen's report, Tai-hui finally repaired to the highly reputed master Yüan-wu K'o-ch'in (1063–1135), under whom he gained no new insight. Dōgen deviates here from the historical course of events. In the collection of sayings of Ta-hui there is also a detailed description of the enlightenment of Ta-hui.[51]

Dōgen attributes Ta-hui's failure to a lack of serious practice and of genuine understanding of the Buddha way. The great doubt did not awaken in him nor did he experience the liberation of the dropping off of body and mind, yet still he had the arrogance to seek certification of Dharma succession. "He was not able to grasp the Buddha-Dharma."[52] Dōgen extended his critique in excessively sharp terms to the followers and disciples of Ta-hui. This merits mention because it includes Te-kuang, the Chinese master who certified the enlightenment experience of Dainichi Nōnin, the founder of the Japanese Daruma school.[53] It may be that Dōgen intended his harsh judgment of Ta-hui to express to those among his disciples who had previously belonged to the Daruma school his basic disgust for that style of Zen and to wipe away any trace of dependence on Ta-hui they still carried with them. This may also have had a part to play in the strong invective he aimed at the adherents of the Rinzai school.

Ta-hui is frequently mentioned unfavorably in the final books of *Shōbōgenzō*. In the *Ōsakusendaba* (*The King's Wish*, 1245), Dōgen cited Master Ju-ching's view that (in contrast to the widespread view) Hung-chih Cheng-chüeh, the protagonist of the Ts'ao-tung school, showed himself superior to Ta-hui in the famous controversy between *kanna-zen* and *mokushō-zen*.[54] He does not, however, pronounce on this confrontation that was so critical for the relationship between Rinzai and Sōtō Zen. In the *Jinshin inga* (*Belief in Causality*, 1225) he tosses out some statements of Ta-hui that misinterpret the Buddhist karmic law of cause-and-effect and show a tendency to naturalism.[55]

The discord with Rinzai Zen that Dōgen carried with him at the time of his departure from the capital for Echizen manifested itself in its fullest and sharpest form in the critique of Ta-hui. Although Dōgen had not met the master personally, the Rinzai monks who set the tempo at the time of his travels in China came from the line of Ta-hui. In Kyoto, representatives of this line, known in Japan as "Daie (i.e., Ta-hui) Zen," caused him much trouble. Moreover, the monks of the Daruma school in his community were connected with the line of Tai-hui through their generational line of succession. This makes it clear that Dōgen's most extensive and abrasive criticisms against Rinzai Zen were directed against this master, who, whatever one may think of his particular style, did not compare unfavorably with his contemporaries in Sung China and gave no cause for damaging reproof. Ta-hui is the only Rinzai figure whom Dōgen takes up and mentions by name.

Dōgen's critique of Lin-chi himself at no time calls into question the integrity of the eminent master. The young Dōgen harbored high esteem for Lin-chi. In his early works one finds not so much as a word of objection. For Dōgen, Lin-chi stood squarely in the best tradition of Chinese Zen, "a kind of Ma-tsu" who preserved the style of Pai-chang.[56] In the main portion of his work Dōgen mentions that "Huang-po's staff and Lin-chi's shout are inaccessible to reason."[57]

His familiarity with the Chinese master rises to the heights of praise in his book on continued practice, *Gyōji* (1242). In this important text a panorama of the great generation of Chinese Zen during the golden age of the T'ang era unfolds. Lin-chi appears not merely as a typical embodiment of classical Zen but as its very summit. In a lengthy section, Dōgen attributes to Lin-chi, the Dharma heir of Huango-po, the spirit of a serious and pure practice, and extols his enlightenment:

> Lin-chi and Te-shan are mentioned as the heroes of the patriarchate. But how can Te-shan be compared to Lin-chi? Truly there is none other in the

lot of them like Lin-chi. And the excellent ones of that time by far surpassed those of today.[58]

Dōgen's change of heart came shortly before his departure from Kōshō-ji. It expressed itself in a comparison that makes Lin-chi the inferior of classical masters like Chao-chou[59] and Huang-po[60] and ranks him beneath Hsüeh-tou Chin-chien,[61] the teacher of Ju-ching, who is also raised above Lin-chi.[62] Lin-chi and Te-shan—the two masters are named together in Zen literature—neither possess the ability of Tung-shan to transcend the Buddha[63] nor know the Dharma sermon by non-sentient beings as the Buddhas and patriarchs do.[64] Still sharper in tone is the sarcastic remark that if those who give a wrong answer to a question were to be reborn as foxes, masters like Lin-chi and Te-shan as well as their followers would have met this fate.[65]

Such comparisons and terse remarks show the animosity Dōgen bore Lin-chi after leaving the capital. Passages in the *Kembutsu* (*Seeing Buddha*, 1243) shed light on the deeper reasons for his outlook:

> Recently in the great Sung dynasty of China there are many who call themselves "Zen masters." They do not know the length and breadth of the Buddha-Dharma. They have heard and seen but little. They memorize two or three sayings of Lin-chi and Yün-men and think that this is the whole of the way of the Buddha-Dharma. If the Dharma of the Buddha could be condensed in two or three sayings of Lin-chi and Yün-men, it would not have been transmitted to the present day. One can hardly say that Lin-chi and Yün-men are the Venerable Ones of the Buddha-Dharma.[66]

Dōgen carries on with his reproof of the Rinzai disciples of the time for indiscriminately slandering the sūtras and abandoning practice. "They count among the non-believers; they are not the children and grandchildren of the Buddhas and patriarchs."[67]

The passage articulates important aspects of Dōgen's critique of Rinzai. The reference to "two or three sayings" of the Chinese masters refers to the dialectical formulas that for Dōgen do not express the true Buddha-Dharma. Intellectual games all too quickly land Zen in the realms of rational conceptuality. In the *Butsudō* (*The Buddha Way*, 1243) and *Bukkyō* (*The Buddhist Sūtras*, 1243), he expressly rejects such formulas, not only those of Lin-chi—namely, *shiryōken* (the fourfold alternative), *shishōyō* (the fourfold before and after of light and action), *sangen* (the three mysteries), *sanyō* (the three essential principles), and *sanku* (the three statements)—but also the *goi* (five ranks) of the House of Ts'ao-tung.[68] "The way of Śākyamuni," he explains in the *Butsudō*, "does not consist of such small matters."[69]

In the *Bukkyō*, Dōgen recounts that his master Ju-ching had always laughed about formulas and weaves into the text comments sharply critical of Lin-chi. He heaps praise on Huang-po, whom he places higher than Ma-tsu and Pai-chang. He continues:

Lin-chi did not possess such excellent powers of mind. Why? Because he did not speak what he had heard, not even in his dreams. He seems to have understood many things but forgotten one, to have attained one thing but forgotten many. He found the taste of the Way in formulas like *shiryōken* and so forth; how can they be made into a guide to the Dharma?[70]

In the view of Yanagida Seizan, Dōgen's critique of Lin-chi peaks in the *Bukkyō*.[71] If Lin-chi, for want of higher capacity for the Dharma, lags behind his predecessors, this also reflects on his qualification as a Zen master. This oft-repeated claim, climaxing in the passages cited, bespeaks an unblunted critique but does not touch on Lin-chi's personal integrity or contradict Dōgen's previously announced esteem. Yanagida concludes that "the point of Dōgen's critique does not for all its force touch the person of Lin-chi," and indeed "if Lin-chi were pulled into the times of Dōgen and allowed to speak, the manner of expression of the two figures, would at bottom be surprisingly the same."[72]

Dōgen's critique of Lin-chi was aimed principally at the patriarch of the House of Rinzai. The passage cited above from the *Kembutsu* closes with a strong attack against Lin-chi's followers. In a number of books written at different periods of his life Dōgen laments the decline of original Zen, to which he wished to return. Typical is the general complaint he voices in the *Shisho* (*The Genealogical Records*, 1241) which points out abuses and thrashes them roundly.[73] Dōgen rebukes all disciples of Zen who have not remained true to the demands of their calling, singling out the widespread following of the House of Rinzai as particularly responsible for the increasing signs of degeneration. His bitter complaints applied specifically to the Rinzai disciples who had harassed him during his stay in Kōshō-ji. His invectives against decadent monks often extend beyond reasonable limits and smack of a bitterness unbecoming a Zen master. The most bothersome text stems from the year of his stay in Kippō-ji.[74]

Affiliation with the House of Ts'ao-tung.   The departure for Echizen necessitated a reduction in the size of Dōgen's community. In Kōshō-ji there had been many local inhabitants and Buddhists from the capital who had come to listen to the master. Only the narrower circle of monks accompanied him to his isolation in the mountains. New followers emerged from among the country folk, but it was Dōgen's intention to concentrate life henceforth on the community of monks. The monastic ideal proper to the religion of Śākyamuni from the time of early Buddhism was well suited to Dōgen's deepest inclinations. Body and soul he was a "monastic father." The overemphasis on monasticism in later years brought with it wide-reaching changes. Mention has already been made of the restriction of the immediate attainment of salvation to monks, an important point that touches the core of Mahāyāna.

Along with this went a new awareness of affiliation with the House of Ts'ao-tung. Dōgen was fundamentally opposed to the idea of "schools" and "houses" within Buddhism. The very idea of a "Zen sect," the young Dōgen notes in the *Bendōwa*, stemmed from a misunderstanding.[75] The term arose in China; it was unknown in India. Unaware of the transmission of Bodhidharma "unthinking laymen spoke loosely of a 'zazen sect.' "[76] For Dōgen, the true Dharma of the Buddha is the only touchstone. Did this basic position conform to his growing emphasis that the true Dharma subsists only in the line of generation from Tung-shan and Ju-ching? Dōgen's most important remarks on this difficult question are to be found in the Butsudō.

In this work Dōgen appeals to his conviction that the only true transmission of the Dharma in Buddhism consists of what Śākyamuni taught and passed on to his disciples. This is why he rejected the word "sect." In later ages people ignorant of "the Eye and Treasury of the True Law" and the "serene mind of nirvāṇa" adopted on their own the false designation of "Zen sect." They began to call patriarchs "Zen patriarchs" and masters "Zen masters."[77]

> It never happened that the Buddhas and patriarchs used the term "Zen sect." One must know that "Zen sect" is the term of Māra. Those who use the devil's word belong to the devil; they are not the descendants of the Buddhas and patriarchs.[78]

Dōgen goes on to apply this thesis to the history and current situation within Zen. Like Śākyamuni, Bodhidharma, the first Chinese patriarch, did not speak of a Zen sect, nor did any of the next five patriarchs use the term. In dealing with their followers, the important masters of the golden age of the T'ang period remained true to the transmission of early Buddhism. Then came false associates who brought the expression with them, as if there were a Dharma of the "Zen sect" parallel to the Dharma of the Buddhas and patriarchs. This claim leads one astray of the Buddhist way.[79]

This position lays the ground for Dōgen's confrontation with the subsequent history of Zen, which, toward the end of the T'ang period and throughout the period of the Five Dynasties, distinguished "Five Houses" within Zen Buddhism. He notes that his master Ju-ching had laid bare the false development and branded it a deviation from tradition that falsified the essence of Buddhism. He enumerates the Five Houses and then notes: "This is not the Buddha-Dharma; this is not the way of patriarchs."[80]

Dōgen reserves high praise for his master Ju-ching, who was unfortunately very little known and not given due recognition at the time. "Unfortunately, in the great kingdom of Sung they think that my late teacher was just another senior monk. . . . Some considered him equal to Lin-chi and Te-shan, but it must be said that they had never seen my late teacher, nor had they ever met Lin-chi.[81] Further praise is scattered throughout the book. Although Ju-ching appears but rarely in Dōgen's early work, he is cited abundantly in the later writings. This reappraisal would seem to be another sign of the change that resulted after Dōgen's departure for Echizen. Yanagida Seizan accords great significance to the arrival of the collected sayings (goroku) of Ju-ching,[82] which fell into Dōgen's hands in August of 1242. In Yanagida's view he was disappointed—to the point of anger—at this mediocre work and took it out on the Chinese disciples, to whom he ascribed an inferior transmission of the sayings of Ju-ching, sayings that had once moved him so deeply and that he had idealized in memory and drawn inspiration from for long years. This in turn led him to esteem his Chinese master all the more and to appeal continually to his superior wisdom. At the same time, it strengthened Dōgen's awareness of belonging to Ju-ching's line.

Appealing to his master, then, Dōgen dismisses the characterization of the Five Houses that had earlier been a normal part of his descriptions of the history of Chinese Zen. Henceforth they are viewed as a sign of degeneration, the result of a lack of understanding of the Buddha-Dharma, "the confused state of society"[83] The founders of the Five Houses, all reputed masters of the T'ang period, were not conscious of this designation, which began only with their disciples in subsequent generations, particularly in the Zen chronicles of the Sung period.[84]

The repudiation of the term "Zen sect" is one of the principal themes of the Butsudō book of the Shōbōgenzō. But there is another motif that surfaces in passages on the transmission of the Dharma in the line of Ch'ing-yüan Hsing-ssu, a line carried on through his heir Shih-tou and then through Tung-shan and Ju-ching up to Dōgen himself. Dōgen openly assigns a place of preeminence to this line of tradition over others, particularly over the line of Lin-chi. He elevates the place of Shih-t'ou (posthumously known as Great Master Wu-chi). Shih-t'ou, the successor of Ch'ing-yüan, was "the true disciple of the high patriarch Ch'ing-yüan and the only one to receive his inner teaching. He was ordained by Ts'ao-hsi (Hui-neng), the ancient Buddha. . . . The right transmission was passed to him alone."[85] This confirms his remark that "the Eye and Treasury of the True Law of the ancient Buddha was rightly transmitted only to the patriarch Ch'ing-yüan." Confirming this statement, Dōgen states in the same book:

> The great master Tung-shan, the fourth Dharma-heir after Ch'ing-yüan, rightly transmitted the Treasure of the Eye of the True Dharma and opened the eye for the Marvelous Mind of nirvāṇa. There is no other transmission, no other school.[86]

None of the disciples spoke of a "Tung-shan sect" or a "Ts'ao-tung (Sōtō) sect." The construction of the name Sōtō by combining glyphs from the two names is a later device that originated with ignorant disciples, "drifting clouds blocking the bright sun" even though things are clear.[87]

The Butsudō reveals the problem that the late Dōgen had with branch forms of Zen Buddhism. On the one hand, he repudiates every form sectarianism. He is convinced that there are no "sects," "schools," or "houses" in Buddhism, but only one Buddha-Dharma and one Buddha way, the transmission of which Śākyamuni entrusted to his disciples. On the other hand, the tradition in which he stands is narrowed to the line that leads from the Sixth Patriarch through Shih-tou and Tung-shan to his own master Ju-ching. Clearly an opposition is being set up between the general Buddhist tradition, which knows no boundaries, and the emphasis on one particular line that surpasses the others. Already in the early books of the Shōbōgenzō Dōgen speaks of this line. For example, in the Busso (Buddhas and Patriarchs, 1241) he enumerates the names,[88] and in the

Shisho he speaks warmly of "our Tung-shan discipleship" *(waga Tōzan monka)* and tells of the certificate of succession that Ch'ing-yüan received from Hui-neng, inscribed in the blood of the two patriarchs.[89] According to the *Ji-shōzammai (The Samādhi of Self-Enlightenment)*, this line of transmission of the Dharma is known only to the followers of Tung-shan.[90]

The interpretation of these apparently contradictory texts lands us in difficulties. The undeniable narrowing of Dōgen's perspective is a weakness occasioned by the deep depression that came with his move to Echizen. His repudiation of the designation "sect" remained unchanged. We should remember that this designation, as well as the notions of orthodoxy and heterodoxy, are alien to the Far East. In the Western languages in which they originated the words refer to particular contents.[91] The idea of a generational line of succession is central to Zen Buddhism. For Dōgen's strong sensitivity to tradition the line of Dharma inheritance based on the master-disciple relationship was of decisive importance. This point is mentioned expressly also in the *Butsudō*. The great masters of golden antiquity did not speak of houses much less of sects in Zen but are bound to their ancestors and one another through a complex network of connections among succeeding generations of disciples. This view of tradition is irrevocably valuable. The narrowing, which would seem to have come mainly from frictions with contemporary Rinzai followers, belongs to a later development of Zen Buddhism and is to be regretted as a misunderstanding of the actual facts and the interference of personal emotions. Dōgen retired to his monastic community in Eihei-ji without making it into a "sect." He and his monks influenced one another in the solitude of the cloister. The community belonged to the line of tradition of Ts'ao-tung (Sōtō) Zen.

Dōgen and the Daruma School.   The monks of the Japanese Daruma school of Dainichi Nōnin no doubt had an impact on the development of Sōtō Zen in Japan, negligible during Dōgen's lifetime but highly successful after his death. Dōgen's first contact with the Darmua school was through the disciple Ejō who provided him with valuable service. The monks from the Daruma school who later, in 1241, affixed themselves to Dōgen's community under the leadership of Ekan strengthened his resolve to move to Echizen and were extremely helpful in their home environment.

Dōgen does not mention the name of the Japanese Daruma school in his writings, but in several early books of the *Shōbōgenzō* we find remarks showing his attitude to this branch of Japanese Zen. Question sixteen and its corresponding answer in the *Bendōwa* is to be read, it would seem, in relation to this school. The interlocutor suggests that theoretical knowledge of the identity of mind and Buddha is sufficient: "Is there, then, really any need to trouble oneself with negotiating the Way in *zazen*?" Dōgen replies:

> Understand that the Buddha-Dharma consists, above all, in practice, quitting the view that differentiates between self and others. If the way were attained by knowing that "self is Buddha," Śākyamuni long ago would not have undergone the hardships he did in guiding others to enlightenment.

He goes on to illustrate with an example and concludes:

> It is clear one cannot realize the Buddha-Dharma by understanding that one's self is Buddha.[92]

Like Eisai, Dōgen underscores the importance of observing the precepts and practicing zealously in order to reach the goal of the way of Zen. The neglect of these conditions was the main reproach leveled against Nōnin and his school. In his *Jōtōshōgakuron* Nōnin gives the well known Zen axiom "our mind is Buddha" (*jishin sokubutsu* or *zeshin sokubutsu*) a free interpretation injurious to the precepts and practice of Zen. We may assume that Dōgen was familiar with Nōnin's writing. Whether the *Sokushin zebutsu* (*This Mind is Buddha*, 1239) is directed against the false interpretation of the expression by Nōnin cannot be determined with certainty. Dōgen's warning against false understanding is worth noting. In his view "when foolish people hear the words, 'the mind is the Buddha,' they think that the rational knowing of sentient beings who have not yet awakened to the *bodhi*-mind are Buddha. This is because they have not met a true teacher."[93] Mere rational knowledge is futile; experience can only be gained through the practice of sitting in meditation (*zazen*):

> "The mind is the Buddha" refers to all the Buddhas who have awakened the mind, devoted themselves to ascetic practice, and attained enlightenment and nirvāṇa. If awakening, practice, enlightenment, and nirvāṇa are lacking, one cannot say "the mind is the Buddha."[94]

If one lines up the relevant passages from the Daruma school, Dōgen's position toward them is critical. This in no sense denies the possibility that he was influenced by those holding opposing views, which is a common enough event in the history of ideas. His listeners in the cloistered isolation of Echizen, as historians have argued, provoked not a few of his sayings. It was his task to free his disciples from the Daruma school as much as possible of their former views and customs.[95] It may be that this element had a role to play in his critique of Rinzai Zen. Nōnin, the founder of the Japanese Daruma school, had himself been accredited in the Rinzai line by procuring a certificate of enlightenment from the Chinese master Te-kuang, one of the disciples of Ta-hui from the Yang-chi'i line. Accordingly, his disciples belonged to the generational line of Rinzai. Perhaps Dōgen's forceful attacks against this powerful school prejudiced his disciples from the Daruma school against the Rinzai tradition.

The *Menju* (*Face-to-Face Transmission*, 1243) implicitly rebukes Nōnin insofar as it stresses the indispensable necessity of a direct, one-to-one, relationship between master and disciple, a relationship that Nōnin forsook. Given this lack, Dōgen could not have recognized Dainichi Nōnin as an authentic Zen master. While we cannot find a statement to this effect in his writings, the standpoint of the master can be known through his disciples. In the *Menju*, Dōgen portrays in strong terms the inner relationship he had with his master Ju-ching during his stay in China and runs the head of the Daruma school effectively out of the picture.[96]

The mutual influence between master and monks in Eihei-ji is difficult to pinpoint. We do not even know the numerical composition of the community. The names of eight monks from the Daruma school—actually, a considerable number—have been handed down. Yet it is in no sense certain that they formed a group or shared common views. Ejō, we may surmise, followed Dōgen entirely. The other monks of the Daruma school, in transferring their allegiance to his discipleship, were also convinced of the trustworthiness of their chosen master. Still, a few—above all Ekan (d. 1251), who held succession in the Daruma school, and Gikai, whom we shall treat later—held fast to their bonds to the Daruma school, perhaps with Dōgen's knowledge and consent. He gave the disciples of the Daruma school, particularly Ejō and Gikai, important tasks in the administration of the temple. During the last years of his life the master no longer possessed the requisite strength to monitor closely all the activities of the monastery. But he did watch over the monastic ideal with an excessive care. The zealous practice of seated meditation remained central and the daily order was regulated down to the smallest details. Dōgen did not take over the style of the Daruma school in the life he decreed for the cloister.

FINAL YEARS AND DEATH

The most important external event of Dōgen's final years was the erection and consecration of a new monastery, for which the lay disciple Hatano Yoshishige had provided a splendid piece of land. Construction began immediately after the arrival of Dōgen and within two years after the move to Echizen the new buildings, at first called Daibutsu-ji, were open. In June of 1244 Dōgen left the country temple of Kippō-ji; in the following month the great hall of Daibutsu-ji was dedicated. Two years later the complex was renamed Eihei-ji, the "Temple of Eternal Peace," a name that will forever be linked to the memory of Master Dōgen and stand as a worthy tribute to him.

Although Dōgen was only to return to Eihei-ji for a few brief final years, it was for him a fitting crown to his life's work. For it was there, in the vast temple complex, that his dream of an authentic monastic community finally came to life. While he busied himself with the development of rules and rituals, his fame was spreading far and wide. The shōgun Hōjō Tokiyori invited him to his residence in Kamakura, and in the winter of 1247–1248, Dōgen accepted. In no time, however, he was happily back in his mountain solitude. By that time his health, which had always been rather fragile, was a cause of grave concern. Frequently he remained confined to his room. Inspired by the sūtra of the last doctrines proclaimed by the Buddha, he wrote the final book of the Shōbōgenzō, The Eight Virtues a Bodhisattva Should Attain (Hachidainingaku). At the insistence of his friends he accompanied his trusted disciple Ejō to Kyoto to seek medical care, but his illness, apparently pulmonary, was already in an advanced stage. Dōgen passed away on 28 August, 1253.

Like a dark cloud, the painful awareness of the transitoriness of all things had overshadowed all of Dōgen's life. Nature and poetry calmed his spirits. He had the gift of expressing rich and pure human sentiments in Chinese and Japanese verse. Two Japanese poems written shortly before his death breathe this spirit. Nature, though subject to change and death, is beautiful even in its decay when transfigured by the mind. Like the dew, the world and its people pass away and yet are mirrored for a moment in the mind like a drop of dew that reflects the moon before it evaporates into the air. His parting verses read:

Asahi matsu	On leaf and grass
kusa-ha no tsuyu no	Awaiting the morning sun
hodo naki ni	The dew melts quickly away.
isogi na tachi so	Haste thee not, O autumn wind
nobe no akikaze	Who dost now stir in the fields!
Yo no naka wa	To what indeed shall I liken
nani ni tatoen	The world and human life?
mizutori no	Ah, the shadow of the moon,
hashi furu tsuyu ni	When it touches in a dewdrop
yadoru tsukikage	The beak of the waterfowl.[97]

THE *SHŌBŌGENZŌ*

In his master work, the *Shōbōgenzō*, Dōgen left posterity a literary work of exceptional quality and unique importance. It is without equal in the whole of Zen literature. The best way to appreciate the work would no doubt be to sit down and carefully read through one chapter after the other. But given its size and the difficulty of its language and content, that would take one the better part of a lifetime. Alternatively, one might find it instructive to page through the entire work, skimming a section here and there, noting the chapter titles, taking note of the quotations from the Chinese, and as far as possible trying to get the main idea of each of its books. In so doing one cannot fail to be surprised at how in all books of the *Shōbōgenzō* Dōgen has the same thing in mind: to see all things "as the Buddha did" (*butsu no kata yori*),[98] an accomplishment actualized in *zazen*. From this Buddha view every aspect of life is seen—from the ordinary things of everyday life to Zen practice to the nature that envelops the Zen monastery to the teachings of the Buddha, the rituals, and finally, absolute reality itself.

A standard edition of the collected works of Dōgen[99] contains the *Shōbōgenzō* in the first of two large volumes. It begins with the "old manuscript" (*kyūsō*) of seventy-five books, followed by the twelve books of the "new manuscript" (*shinsō*), and ends with an appendix of five books also composed by Dōgen— ninety-two books in all. Dōgen intended the work to reach one hundred books and hoped to work through the entire manuscript once more for a final revision. He was able to do this for only the twelve books of the "new manuscript" before ill health forced him to quit. This means that seventy-five books remain in their original condition, partially corrected but not finished as the author had intended. In addition to the five books that make up the appendix of the standard edition, Dōgen had more than enough material to reach one hundred books had his health not failed him.

How did the seventy-five, twelve, and five books, respectively, come to be written? How much do we know about the master's way of working? The *Shōbōgenzō* that we possess in the standard edition of Dōgen's works has been composed in the Japanese style with Chinese quotations scattered here and there, in some sections profusely, in the course of the Japanese text. The text has been called *Kana-shōbōgenzō* for its use of the Japanese syllabary. We now know that in addition to the *Kana-shōbōgenzō* (or *Keji-shōbōgenzō*) there is a *Kambun-shōbōgenzō* (or *Shinji-shōbōgenzō*), still existent, which was the basis for the work written in the Japanese style (*wabuntai*).[100] The *Kambun-shōbōgenzō* resembles a collection of three hundred cases (*sambyakusoku*) in the kōan style, which has also been preserved.[101] Dōgen gathered this material during his stay in China and particularly emphasized the discourses of Ju-ching in his collection. He found important passages in the wealth of Chinese Zen literature of the Sung period.[102] His examples show a preference for episodes and sayings of the T'ang masters. The title *Shōbōgenzō* was not his own. The expression *shōbō* (literally, "the true Dharma"), a translation of the early Sanskrit Buddhist term *saddharma*, points to the essence of the Buddha way that Dōgen strove to realize in his life. Recognizing no other goal for Buddhists, he was obliged to reject narrow structures like "Zen sects" within Buddhism. Like the word *shōbō*, the compound *Shōbōgenzō* is also to be found in the Chinese Buddhism of the Sung period.[103] In his discourses of the first years of his activity in Japan, Dōgen drew mainly from this material, which he gathered together in 1235 in a collection entitled *Shōbōgenzō sambyakusoku*. While there are grounds for seeing *Kambun-shōbōgenzō* as the basis for the Japanese work, questions still remain regarding the relationship of the two works. Dōgen research is faced here with an important historical and philosophical task yet to be carried out.[104]

The Japanese *Shōbōgenzō* shows a fluency of style of unmistakable uniqueness. Dōgen's thought is branded with his own language. Even when he takes over expressions from colloquial Chinese of the Sung period, he renders them in Japanese constructions suited to his own style. He labored for special effects through the repetition of certain expressions and a liberality of grammar and syntax. In contrast both with the usage of his time and contemporary Japanese, Dōgen's language needs to be interpreted. Sometimes he will adopt a number of different expressions to communicate nuances, thus opening the way to a variety of interpretations. Dōgen's language and style pose obstacles of every sort to his translators. Not uncommonly, English and German translators simply throw up their hands on certain expressions and declare them "untranslatable."[105]

The riches of the *Shōbōgenzō* offer a perspective on the world of Dōgen— a world that we will later try to understand more fully. The formal aspect of the work is expressed in the Chinese character *gen* ("eye") that appears in the title. It is this character that makes the title difficult to translate—or in the opinion of Ōhashi and Brockard, outright "untranslatable."[106] Wilhelm Gundert paraphrases the title as a whole as "The Fullness of the Vision of Truth," and then simply translates the four characters one after the other, "Truth-Law-Eye-Treasure," adding the clarification: "all the precious things that fill the eye which beholds the real, true law of Buddha."[107] Tsujimura Kōichi concludes that the title *Shōbōgenzō* means "the eye of the authentic law (subjective and objective genitive) that contains in its vision the all—that is, everything in the entire world.[108] Clearly, the "eye" constitutes the central element in this difficult but rich combination of words. It is the eye of enlightenment, the Buddha eye that does not distinguish between objects but is pure seeing. For this seeing, all reality is Buddha or Buddha nature or Buddha mind, indissolubly one with the seeing eye itself. It is toward this insight into reality that the reader is constantly being led. Therein lies the formal unity of the work.

The title of one of the chapters of the *Shōbōgenzō* reads "Only between a Buddha and a Buddha" *(Yuibutsu yobutsu)*, meaning that "only between a Buddha and a Buddha is the true Dharma transmitted." The term "true Dharma," the first word of the title *Shōbōgenzō*, is a favorite expression in Buddhism for the Buddha-Dharma. The notion of Dharma is broad and manifold. In the Mahāyāna world of Dōgen it signifies the Buddha as the essence of all reality, including all of Buddhism with its two vehicles and variety of schools. Looking at Buddhism from the standpoint of the true Dharma, Dōgen was able to transcend the common differentiations. His higher viewpoint helped him to affirm all the holy scriptures and rites, even though he sometimes judged them negatively and took issue with them. His last word, spoken from the perspective of true Dharma, is a transcendental Yes.

This perspective, which grew out of Dōgen's own enlightenment, opened up into a universality that both embraces and surpasses all other realms of Buddhism. In his work Dōgen seeks to deal with the totality of the real and speaks continually of the realm of being, without limits. His open-minded spirit sought to penetrate intellectually the Whole that he had experienced personally. Metaphysical concerns are evident in many of the books of the *Shōbōgenzō*.[109] He addresses the realm of the Absolute. Being and time, affirmation and negation, duration and becoming—he is familiar with the fundamental categories of ontology. For this reason his writings on Buddhism and the history of religion have excited the interest of Western philosophers. His thought has been compared to that of Heidegger. Whatever the value of such comparisons, Dōgen is through and through Buddhist and at the same time a full-fledged speculative mind.

The writings of Dōgen are read today in university seminars as well as in monastic schools. In addition to the extensive literature of Buddhist commentaries,[110] above all from the pen of monks of the Sōtō school, there is another no less important body of literature, namely the commentaries, often connected with the translations of Western authors,[111] which turn to Dōgen's work out of philosophical or religious concerns. The scholarly scrimmage is in full swing today. The clarification of the historical origins of the work contribute much to our understanding of the widely divergent books. In presenting the course of

Dōgen's life, it has often been possible to refer to the books of the *Shōbōgenzō*
as a result of just such scholarly pursuit. Next we turn to the characteristic traits
of Dōgen's thought and religious way.

ESSENTIAL CHARACTERISTICS

ZAZEN

Dōgen's name is linked above all to the practice of *zazen*, which for Dōgen was
the practice. Not only did he give himself over to this practice with consummate
devotion, but he praised its merits over all else and taught his disciples the
proper form of sitting cross-legged in meditation, seeing *zazen* as the realization
and fulfillment of the whole law of the Buddha. His approach is known in Buddhism as the religion of "*zazen* alone" (*shikan taza*) and is said to represent a
return to the pure transmission of the Buddhas and patriarchs and thence to
the true Dharma of Śakyamuni himself. Nothing was as odious to Dōgen as the
sectarian divisions in Buddhism and within the Zen school itself, the disastrous
results of which (weakening of the mind, alienation and stubbornness, animosities
and jealousy) he had witnessed with his own eyes in Sung China. From his
master Ju-ching he took over a critical attitude to the historical development
of Zen during the Sung period. He considers the extreme rejection of the Buddha's
words in the sūtras as a mistake. Bound to no school, Zen was for him "the way
of all the Buddhas and patriarchs."[112] It is something of an irony of history that
the Sōtō Zen that he planted in Japan has developed into one of the best organized, strongest Japanese Zen schools.

   Zazen is meditation performed sitting upright with legs crossed. Dōgen found
this form of meditation as part of hallowed Buddhist tradition. Sitting meditation
provided the basis for the various types of concentration in early Indian and
Mahāyāna Buddhism. The example of Bodhidharma, the founder of Chinese
Zen who sat meditating in front of a wall for nine years, inspired his disciples
to strive for perfection in seated meditation. In his early treatise entitled *Fukanzazengi*, Dōgen describes the correct posture for sitting in meditation and
gives specific instructions for proper practice:

   If you wish to attain enlightenment, begin at once to practice *zazen*. For
   this meditation you need a quiet room; food and drink should be taken in
   moderation. Free yourself from all attachments and bring to rest the ten
   thousand things. Think not of good or evil; judge not on right or wrong;
   maintain the flow of mind, will, and consciousness; bring to an end all
   desire, all concepts and judgments!

   To sit properly, first lay down a thick pillow and on top of this a second
   (round) one. One may sit either in the full or half cross-legged position.
   In the full position one places the right foot on the left thigh and the left
   foot on the right thigh. In the half position, only the left foot is placed
   upon the right thigh. Robe and belt should be worn loosely, but in order.
   The right hand rests on the left foot, while the back of the left hand rests

on the palm of the right. The two thumbs are placed in juxtaposition. Let the body be kept upright, leaning neither to the left nor to the right, neither forward nor backward. Ears and shoulders, nose and navel must be aligned to one another. The tongue is to be kept against the palate, lips and teeth firmly closed, while the eyes should always be left open.

Now that the bodily position is in order, regulate your breathing. If a wish arises, take note of it and then dismiss it! If you practice in this way for a long time, you will forget all attachments and concentration will come naturally. That is the art of *zazen*. *Zazen* is the Dharma gate of great rest and joy.[113]

The final word in this instruction, whose Chinese compound expresses repose and delight, is especially important for Dōgen. *Zazen* is an easy way to enlightenment, not in the sense of the pious invocation of the name of Amida Buddha but because it is a natural position for one to assume. An Indian Mahāyāna text already stated that

among all the manners of sitting, the full cross-legged position is the most restful and does not tire. Though the hands and feet are thereby disciplined, consciousness is not dissipated. Of the four positions which the body can assume, this is the most restful.[114]

In postured sitting the body finds itself in a state of relaxed attention in which senses and mind remain awake and yet are fully relaxed. The room is kept in subdued daylight, bright sunlight being just as detrimental to concentration as sleep-inducing darkness. A monk walks through the hall continuously dealing sharp blows to awaken and encourage those who grow drowsy. The disciple sits upright as a candle, with eyes open and body at attention, fully in control of the senses and yet not unnaturally straining.

For the body to relax in restful attention, proper breathing is essential. Breathing, which carries the organism's life activities, is the basis for rest and movement of body and spirit. It is no less important for *zazen* if one is to attain the completely restful mobility that comes from an unconscious center. When the breath flows uniformly through the body tension is dissolved. Accordingly, after taking their place on the pillow and settling their bodies into the proper upright position, practitioners must breathe deeply and regularly until the body finds its natural rhythm and the organism rests in equilibrium. This does not mean that *zazen* is a breathing exercise similar to the practice of Indian Yoga, which seeks to drive the breath, as the last vital movement, from consciousness. For *zazen*, the purpose of regulating one's breath is not to eradicate it from consciousness but to put the organism in a completely rested state of equilibrium. Ancient Indian anthropological and anatomical notions of the mind lying a hand's breadth below the navel in the abode of one's true center of being play a role in this understanding of controlled breathing.

Dōgen never tired of teaching proper sitting. In spoken and written word he gave detailed instructions concerning the correct posture and bearing for meditation. In keeping with Indian tradition, he understood bodily posture in a religious sense and attributed supernatural powers to it. He once considered the question why the recitation of the sūtras and the invocation of the name of Amida are not the most appropriate means to salvation. To the question, "But to sit idly, doing nothing—how can that be of help in gaining *satori?*" he replies:

> By picturing . . . the unsurpassed, great Dharma and the *samādhi* of the Buddhas as sitting idly and doing nothing, you malign the Great Vehicle. . . . Thankfully, Buddhas are already sitting serenely in self-joyous *samādhi (jijuyū-zammai)*. Does this not constitute extensive merit?[115]

Sitting in meditation is the most powerful of all the bodily positions (*prabhāva*) praised in the sūtras. The full cross-legged position is also known as the "seat of conquest of the devil," since the heart of the wicked one is saddened and frightened by seeing someone seated in this way.

Concerning the mental attitude one should have in *zazen*, the long quotation with which we began admonishes one to free oneself from all attachments and "bring to an end all desire, all concepts and judgments!" The *rufubon* version adds the sentence: "Do not strive to be a Buddha!" The purposelessness that Dōgen so stresses is not hard to understand if one realizes that enlightenment is already present in *zazen* itself. Why should one nurture desires or dream about the future when in the very moment of sitting in meditation one already has everything? Dōgen, of course, knew the experience of enlightenment well, but he also knew that it is no different from practice itself. He chides the unlearned who so wait for the big experience that they miss the present moment. Nothing is more detrimental than the conscious intent to attain Buddhahood through practice.

We read too, Dōgen's practical instructions on how conscious mental activities are to be brought to rest. First, thoughts spontaneously arising are to be brought into the light of consciousness and noted so that they may then be dismissed. Drowsiness and distractions are eliminated from the beginning. Disciples reach the state of concentration in which they are aware of both their thinking and their nonthinking and yet cling to neither. In the *Zazenshin* Dōgen explains a conversation recounted in the Chinese Zen chronicles:

> As the great master Yüeh-shan Hung-tao sat quietly, a monk asked him: "Of what does one think while sitting?" The master replied: "One thinks of not-thinking." To this the monk replied: "How does one think of not-thinking?" The master: "Without thinking."[116]

The final "without thinking" (*hi-shiryō*) transcends both thinking (*shiryō*) and not-thinking (*fu-shiryō*). The master concretely shows the way of negation, which, bound to concentration in completely unmoved sitting, brings about, or more correctly is, realization. In this state one can know "without touching things," that is, without making things into objects in one's consciousness. In this way, things are known as they are—not as objects in relation to the subject, but in their emptiness.

In Dōgen's directives concerning the physical bearing and psychological processes of Zen one finds deep insights into the unity of body and mind in the human being. In a discourse from the *Zuimonki* he discusses whether "the Way is attained through the mind or through the body."[117] The Buddhism of the sūtras solves the problem by pointing to the identity of body and mind. Dōgen was not happy with this explanation since it fails to bring out clearly the role that the body has to play. He was convinced that the way of the Buddha cannot be followed only with the mind—not even if one were to ponder the Buddha-Dharma for ten thousand *kalpas* or through thousands of rebirths.

> Therefore, if you cast aside completely the thoughts and concepts of the mind and concentrate on *zazen* alone (*shikan taza*), you attain to an intimacy with the Way. The attainment of the Way is truly accomplished with the body. For this reason I urge you to concentrate on *zazen*.[118]

By no means does Dōgen wish to deny the unity of body and mind, only to insist that a theoretical knowledge of this unity is not enough. One must realize it in *zazen*.

In the *Bendōwa* Dōgen emphasizes that "the Buddha-Dharma from the first preaches that body and mind are not two, that substance and form are not two."[119] Immutability and transience are both predicated of mind and body in the same way. Like substance and form, mind and body are inseparable. When the body assumes the Buddha form in upright, motionless sitting, the mind becomes the dwelling place of Buddha. The posture of sitting cross-legged, which allows the blood to flow freely through the body and which clams inner feelings—especially of anger, resentment and egoism—while collecting and emptying the mind, is not a mere precondition for enlightenment. It *is* enlightenment itself, for enlightenment is the state of the entire person, which in *zazen* is the state of Buddha. As an expression of the Buddha nature, sitting in meditation is an eminently religious act beyond price.

For Dōgen the practice of *zazen* is permeated with high ethical concern. He sought to instill in his disciples the taste for the ascetic life that had inspired him from early youth. In speaking to wider audiences he stressed the ethical value of practice. In his simple writings for the common people the ethical tones are clear. His book on life and death (*Shōji*)[120] closes with these words, which contain the essence of his practical wisdom and which counsel:

> There is an easy way to become a Buddha: refraining from all evils, not clinging to birth and death, working in deep compassion for all sentient beings, respecting those over you and pitying those below you, without any detesting or desiring, worrying or lamentation—this is what is called Buddha. Do not search beyond it.[121]

RELIGIOUS METAPHYSIS

The Unity of Practice and Enlightenment.   For Dōgen, as for all great religious leaders, religious practice took precedence over all else. *Zazen* alone sufficed. At the same time, he was a thinker who probed the depths of reality and lived from an understanding of ultimate things. The key to his exclusive emphasis on *zazen* is to be found in his understanding of the identity of *zazen* and enlightenment, an understanding that springs in turn from his metaphysical speculations on the Buddha nature. Original enlightenment—that is, innate Buddha nature—is the *a priori* basis of all practice; practice is identical with the sole, ever-unfolding reality of enlightenment. Dōgen elaborates:

> In the Buddha-Dharma, practice and realization are identical. Because one's present practice is practice in realization, one's initial negotiation of the Way in itself is the whole of original realization. Thus, even while one is directed to practice, he is told not to ancitipate realization apart from practice, because practice points directly to original realization. As it is already realization in practice, realization is endless; as it is practice in realization, practice is beginningless.[122]

The unity of practice and enlightenment excludes all duality, especially that of means and end. This means that practice should not be construed as a means to a future enlightenment. This form of Zen, the so-called Zen of expectation (*taigo-zen*), is explicitly rejected by Dōgen. The Mahāyāna distinction between "original enlightenment" and "acquired enlightenment" is helpful for understanding what he has in mind here. Original enlightenment makes practice possible, in fact necessary, since without it, and without the enlightenment gained in it, one's Buddha nature would not become manifest. Although practice and enlightenment are identical, the distinction between them, like the distinction between original and acquired enlightenment, is significant. When practiced by an enlightened being, *zazen* is the self-development of original enlightenment. Zen disciples who comprehend this do not seek an absolute outside of themselves; they do not gaze upward toward some supreme being or seek to bring the eternal down to earth. Rather, they seek in themselves the Buddha nature that is the ground of their very being. "Learn the backward step that turns your light inward to illuminate your self," admonishes Dōgen. Then "body and mind of themselves will drop away, and your original face will be manifest."[123]

The Doctrine of the Buddha Nature.   Dōgen's thought finds its focal point in his teaching on the universal Buddha nature, which in a unique way unites the religious drive with philosophical speculation. One can look on the doctrine of the Buddha nature within all sentient beings and in the whole of reality as a philosophical statement—that is, as a conceptual formulation for the absoluteness of the really real. Yet the teaching of the Buddha nature, the central doctrine of Mahāyāna Buddhism, is religiously inspired. Indeed, nowhere else do we so clearly encounter the religious character of Mahāyāna philosophy than in this notion. Dōgen's religious devotion embraced belief in the Buddha nature and his philosophical mind penetrated its content. Here above all we see the special quality of his metaphysical powers at work.[124]

The *Buddha Nature*, one of the most important chapters of the *Shōbōgenzō*, takes its starting point from a statement of the Buddha in the *Nirvāṇa Sūtra* that, rendered literally from the Chinese, reads: "All sentient beings without exception have the Buddha nature. Tathāgata abides forever without change." For Dōgen, this statement contains the whole of the Buddha's teachings. But in his Japanese translation, Dōgen renders the sentence differently, to read that all sentient beings without exception *are* the Buddha nature. The meaning of the statement has shifted and the Buddha nature is extended to include all beings, so that "*whole being* is the Buddha-nature; I call one integral entity of whole being 'sentient beings'."[125] It is worth recalling that the original reason for limiting Buddha nature to sentient beings was rooted in the soteriological character of the term "Buddha nature." According to Mahāyāna thought, Buddha nature achieves its full meaning in the attainment of Buddhahood, the goal of the way of salvation. If the attainment of salvation is limited to sentient beings, then naturally Buddha nature will be predicated only of sentient beings. Long before Dōgen, the question had been disputed of whether inanimate beings can attain Buddhahood. In Dōgen's doctrine of oneness all modes of being are fundamentally on the same level:

> Hence, all mind is sentient being: sentient beings are all being Buddha nature. Grass and trees, states and lands, are mind. Because they are mind, they are sentient beings. Because they are sentient beings, they are being Buddha nature. Heavenly bodies are mind. Because they are mind, they are sentient beings. Because they are sentient beings, they are being Buddha nature.[126]

The soteriological dimension of Buddhist doctrine is present in Dōgen, but there salvation is made to embrace all of reality, the entire cosmos.

The second limit assigned to Buddha nature by standard Mahāyāna teaching, especially in Yogācāra philosophy, derives from the movement from potentiality to act. Sentient beings possess Buddha nature as a seed or embryo that is destined to become the fullness of Buddhahood. Buddhahood contains the whole, but only potentially. Rejecting this limitation of being, Dōgen writes:

> A certain group think the Buddha nature is like the seeds of grasses and plants; when this receives the Dharma rain and is nourished by it, sprouts shoot forth, branches and leaves and flowers and fruits appear, and these fruits have seeds within them.
>
> This view is the mind-bred judgment of unenlightened men. Even though you might hold such a view, you still should penetrate in practice to the truth that seed and flower and fruit are each, one after another, the unbared [Buddha] mind itself. In fruits there are seeds. Though the seeds are not visible, roots, stem, and the rest of the plant grow out. Though they are

not brought together [from elsewhere], still the twigs and branches multiply, the trunk thickens, by themselves. It is not a question of something in the tree or something outside the tree It is always so, at any time of the past or present. Therefore, even though men may accept the unenlightened view, root, stem, branch, and leaf are still, without differentiation, produced and live the same life and die the same death and are Buddha-nature as the same *whole being*.[127]

Dōgen is convinced that all beings, just as they are, are always and ever Buddha nature.

Dōgen expressly warns against viewing the Buddha nature as a substantial core in all things, a view found in Indian philosophy but inappropriate to Buddhism. Dōgen himself explains this notion in several books, most extensively in the *Sokushin zebutsu*, where he notes that Buddha nature, as the core of all things, is often called Tao or mind-nature or simply spiritual knowledge. According to this view, which Dōgen rejects as false, mind-nature is given the characteristics of an absolute essence. In this view, all things arise and pass away in dependence on spiritual knowledge. Having no reality, the phenomenal world prevents one from seeing absolute essence, and only the enlightened one sees through the plurality of the phenomenal world to their essential nature. In the final part of his description, Dōgen depicts the way of salvation in Indian philosophy:

> One calls it spiritual knowledge or true self, the ground of enlightenment or original nature or original substance. To grasp original nature in this way means to return to permanence. One who has done so is called "a great one returned." Thereafter, one no longer moves in the circle of rebirth, having entered the ocean of no-birth and no-death. There is no other true reality.[128]

In his book on practice (*Bendōwa*) Dōgen declares this a "false, non-Buddhist view" that it would be foolish to adopt as one's own.[129] In the book on Buddha nature (*Busshō*) he examines the relation of his viewpoint to the understanding of the self in Indian philosophy. Many people misunderstand Buddha nature and affirm a substantial ego because "they have not encountered their true self; they have not met with an authentic Buddhist teacher."[130] For his part, Dōgen firmly rejects any identification of Buddha nature with an eternal, substantial self.

If all being is Buddha nature, so are the ephemeral phenomena of the changing world, all changes of consciousness, and all defilements. Everything that exists is Buddha nature without substance or form, whole and undivided, neither subject nor object.

> Buddha nature is always *whole being*, because *whole being* is the Buddha nature. *Whole being* does not mean a vast number of miscellaneous things, and it does not mean an undifferentiated, uniform oneness. It is the raising of a balled fist, so it is not large or small.[131]

In the *Busshō* Dōgen develops his doctrine of the Buddha nature in three terms: "the being of Buddha nature" (*u-busshō*), the "no-Buddha-nature" (*mu-busshō*), and the "the impermanence of the Buddha nature" (*mujō-busshō*). Some commentators have seen a threefold dialectic here, but one can speak of dialectics in Dōgen only in a very loose and general sense. The three terms stand alongside each other, each embracing the whole and giving it a definitive expression. The being or existentiality of the Buddha nature is maintained from beginning to end. For Dōgen, Buddha nature is first, last, and always concrete existence—a "this."

In the fourth section of the book, the "being of Buddha nature" is contrasted with "no-Buddha-nature." This section contains comments on a discussion between the Fourth Patriarch and the Fifth Patriarch, focused on the "name":

> The patriarch asked him, "What is your name?" The boy replied, "There is a name, but it is not an ordinary name." The master said, "What name is it?" "It is Buddha nature," said the boy. [132]

Thus Buddha nature is a "what," a concrete, real being. And yet the being of Buddha nature is not anything that can be expressed fully in words. For this reason, Dōgen describes it with negative expressions. Just as the name *Buddha nature* is an uncommon one, so too the Buddha nature cannot be seen with the eyes nor heard with the ears; it is formless, "neither large nor small, neither broad nor narrow." Perhaps the deepest insight into the positive content of the Buddha nature is found in the profound words appearing in the seventh section of the book and attributed to the great Indian patriarch Nāgārjuna: "The meaning of the Buddha nature is vast emptiness, open, clear and bright." [133]

The conversation between the two patriarchs that we are using as our point of reference represents the first important step in determining that the name is a "what" and that it is called "Buddha nature." That statement implies an ontological realism that needs further explanation. To make sure that no limitations are placed on this "what" or on the "being" of Buddha nature, the Fourth Patriarch now turns to its negative aspects as the conversation continues:

> The patriarch said, "You have no Buddha nature." The boy replied, "You say no [Buddha nature] because Buddha nature is emptiness." [134]

In his commentary on this conversation, Dōgen explains the meaning of affirmation and negation, both of which are absolutely necessary. The name is the Buddha nature. The affirmation contained in Dōgen's typical expression "It is Buddha nature" (*ze busshō*) does not exhaust the Buddha nature, which cannot be contained in any "it." Dōgen therefore resorts to a negative statement aimed at transcending all limitation: "no-Buddha-nature." [135] Dōgen showers praise on the Fourth Patriarch, who, according to tradition, was the first to introduce the *via negativa* into Chinese Zen:

> Thus the utterance "no-Buddha-nature" is something that reverberates far beyond the patriarchal chambers of the Fourth Patriarch. It was seen and

heard in Huang-mei, circulated freely in Chao-chou, and was exalted in Ta-kuei.[136]

The passage highlights some of the main milestones of the negative way in Chinese Zen Buddhism. The fourth and the fifth patriarchs resided in Huang-mei; Chao-chou is the name of the master who appears in the first kōan of the *Mumonkan* in the celebrated case of the nothingness (Chin., *wu;* Jpn., *mu*) of a dog's Buddha nature; and Mount Ta-Kuei was the site of the activity of a certain Kuei-shan, about whom we will have more to say later.

The word *empty* that appears in the final response of the conversation is fundamental. Dōgen adds some important clarifications of the relationship between nothingness and emptiness (*śūnyatā*), the key concept in the philosophy of the Middle Way (*mādhyamika*):

> Emptiness is not "no." [But] in uttering "Buddha-nature-emptiness," one says "no." One does not say, "half a pound," or "eight ounces." One does not say emptiness, because it is emptiness. One does not say no, because it is no. One says no because it is Buddha-nature-emptiness.
>
> Thus, each piece of no is a touchstone to articular emptiness; emptiness is the power articulating no.[137]

Far from being a tautology, this statement expresses a relationship moving in the direction of a final identity. At the end of this section of the book, Dōgen lines up all three statements: "Buddha-nature-no" (*busshō-mu*), "Buddha-nature-emptiness" (*busshō-kū*), and "Buddha-nature-being" (*busshō-u*). Each of the three from its own perspective expresses one and the same Buddha nature.[138]

Dōgen goes on to articulate the "no-Buddha-nature" in sharp relief and then to locate it alongside the "being-Buddha-nature." Next he comments on a conversation between the fifth and the sixth patriarchs from the Zen chronicles. Asked by the Fifth Patriarch where he had come from, the Sixth Patriarch answers, "I am a man of Ling-nan," and adds that he has come to become a Buddha. The Fifth Patriarch responds: "People of Ling-nan have no Buddha nature. How could you attain Buddhahood?" Dōgen's subtle explanation follows:

> This utterance does not mean that people of Ling-nan have no Buddha nature, or that they do have a Buddha nature; he means, "man of Ling-nan, you are no-Buddha-nature."[139]

Just as he had done with the axiom from the *Nirvāṇa Sūtra*, with which the book on the Buddha nature began, Dōgen alters the sentence structure here and reads the character "to have" as "to be." Having or "not having" the Buddha nature is not the point. Both of these notions contain limits that have to be transcended. The "no-Buddha-nature" transcends "having" and "not having."

In so speaking, Dōgen articulates further the dynamism of Buddha nature. He explains that one does not have the Buddha nature by acquiring it; rather, it is already there in the acquisition. "The Buddha nature is always manifest simultaneously with the attainment of Buddhahood." This immediacy of having and acquiring the Buddha nature indicates, as Waddell and Abe note,[140] the "dynamic oneness" of both, a unity that transcends all conceptualization. Dōgen himself explains the matter in reference to the conversation between the Fifth and Sixth Patriarch cited above:

> You should know, the very uttering and hearing of "no-Buddha-nature" was itself his immediate passage to Buddha-attainment. Since it was, right at the very time of "no-Buddha-nature" he became a Buddha. To have not yet experienced or articulated "no-Buddha-nature" is to have not yet attained Buddhahood.[141]

He further strengthens his argument by referring to the origins of the transmission of mind in Zen. In the following passage, being-Buddha-nature (u-busshō) and no-Buddha-nature (mu-busshō) are juxtaposed:

> Buddhas such as Kāśyapa Buddha and Śākyamuni Buddha . . . have the capacity when they attain Buddhahood and preach the Dharma to articulate the utterance "whole-being-Buddha-nature" (shitsuu-busshō). So how could the being of whole being not succeed to the nothingness of absolute nothingness (mu-mu)? Therefore, the words "no-Buddha-nature" reverberate far from the chambers of the fourth and fifth patriarchs.[142]

The starting point for the ninth section is taken from the statement of Kuei-shan: "All sentient beings have no Buddha nature."[143] This seems to be in direct contradiction to the statement of Hsi-an at the beginning of the eighth section: "All sentient beings have the Buddha nature."[144] In a citation from the Nirvāṇa Sūtra, this positive statement is also attributed to Śākyamuni. Dōgen therefore compares Hsi-an and Śākyamuni to "two men holding up one staff."

> Now Ta-kuei is different. With him, "one staff swallows up both men." Of course, the National Teacher (Yen-kuan) was a child of Ma-tsu. Ta-kuei was his grandchild. Nevertheless, in the way of his Dharma grandfather, the Dharma grandson Ta-kuei proves to be an old graybeard, and in the way of his Dharma father, the Dharma son Yen-kuan is still a callow youth.
>
> The truth of Ta-kuei's words is the truth of "all sentient beings have no Buddha nature."[145]

The superiority of the negative way is given clear expression:

> The words have and have not are totally different in principle. Doubts will understandably arise as to which utterance is correct. However, in the Buddha Way, "all sentient beings have no Buddha nature" alone is preeminent.[146]

This does not imply however that affirmations lose their value. As already pointed out, affirmations can still make declarations in a limited sense, which is not the case with transcendental negation. After some consideration, Dōgen comes to the conclusion that all verbal statements are inadequate. He quotes Pai-chang:

> To preach that sentient beings have Buddha nature is to disparage Buddha, Dharma, and saṅgha. To preach that sentient beings have no Buddha nature is also to disparage Buddha, Dharma, and saṅgha.

Dōgen explains:

> Therefore, whether it is "have Buddha nature" or "have no Buddha nature," both end up disparaging the Three Treasures. . . . Despite such disparagement, however, you cannot go without making an utterance.[147]

For the rational intellect, there is no way out of this kōan-like bottleneck, but in enlightenment the Buddha nature is experienced in all its ineffability.

Dōgen's metaphysics also includes the world of becoming. An essential element of the Buddha nature is the "impermanence of the Buddha nature" (mujō-busshō). The sixth section of the Busshō opens with these words:

> The Sixth Patriarch taught his disciple Hsing-ch'ang: "Impermanence is in itself Buddha nature. Permanence is, as such, the (dualistic) mind that discriminates all dharmas, good or bad."[148]

This statement from the chronicles contradicts the common view that the Buddha nature is permanent, the ground of the mind, while the activities of the mind are changing. Dōgen explains it this way: "The preaching, practicing, and realization of impermanence by the impermanent themselves all must be impermanent."[149] He takes seriously the Mahāyāna axiom about the identity of saṃsāra and nirvāṇa. "There is no permanence apart from impermanence. The world of becoming, with all its phenomena, is the Buddha nature." This holds true even of the enlightened ones themselves:

> The "permanent" saint is impermanent; the "permanent" unenlightened man is impermanent. Were saints and ignorant men permanently so, that would not be the Buddha-nature.[150]

Holding such views, Dōgen stands opposed to non-Buddhists and Buddhists of the Hīnayāna tradition, as well as to many Mahāyāna schools. His concern is to reveal the Buddha nature in all of reality, and that includes the ever-changing psychological and physical world. He writes:

> Therefore, the very impermanency of grass and tree, thicket and forest, is the Buddha nature. The very impermanency of men and things, body and mind, is the Buddha nature. Nature and lands, mountains and rivers, are impermanent because they are Buddha nature. Supreme and complete enlightenment, because it is the Buddha nature, is impermanent. Great Nirvāṇa, because it is impermanent, is the Buddha nature.[151]

This equivalence is carried through radically, necessitating some clarification of the second part of the Sixth Patriarch's statement mentioned above. Dōgen explicitly rejects the views of the Chinese Zen master Ta-hui (1089–1163) on the nature of mind (shinshō). Distinguishing between the essence and the function

of the mind, Ta-hui proposed a "pure and calm mind-nature." This turns enlightenment into a static condition. Dōgen undertakes a detailed criticism of
this viewpoint,[152] arguing that there is no such thing as an unmoved center of
the mind but that all beings are impermanent and are the Buddha nature.

The quintessence of Dōgen's metaphysics, including his teaching on the
Buddha nature, is contained in the short but difficult book known as the Genjōkōan, even though the expression "Buddha nature" itself is not found there.
The fruit of his intense intellectual efforts at the beginning of his teaching career
as a master, this book remained to the end his deepest work, containing all that
he sought to communicate.[153] The gateway to the book consists of four sentences
that, in the view of many commentators, form its foundation. Together they
express a manifold understanding of reality—that is to say, the reality of the
Buddha nature.

The first sentence asserts:

> When all dharmas are the Buddha-Dharma, there is illusion and enlight-
> enment, practice, birth, death, Buddhas, and sentient beings.

This statement corresponds to the claim about "being-Buddha-nature" developed
in the Busshō book.

The second sentence is expressed in negative terms:

> When myriad dharmas are without self, there is no illusion or enlightenment,
> no Buddhas or sentient beings, no generation or extinction.

Reality is "no-Buddha-nature" (mu-busshō).

The third statement takes up from the first, but articulates the transcendental
character of reality:

> The Buddha Way is originally beyond fullness and lack, and for this reason
> there is generation and extinction, illusion and enlightenment, sentient
> beings and Buddhas.

The fourth sentence turns to the impermanent world of becoming in which
we live and in whose impermanence we participate:

> In spite of this, flowers fall always amid our grudging, and weeds flourish
> in our chagrin.[154]

The constant change that surrounds us in the world of becoming—as well as
our sadness and our anger—are actually the "impermanence of the Buddha nature" (mujō-busshō).

The full perspective of Dōgen's metaphysics is present in all the books of
the Shōbōgenzō. We may cite yet another climactic passage from the Genjōkōan:

> To learn the Buddha Way is to learn one's own self. To learn one's
> self is to forget one's self. To forget one's self is to be confimed by all
> dharmas. To be confirmed by all dharmas is to effect the casting off of one's
> own body and mind and the bodies and minds of others as well. All traces

of enlightenment [then] disappear, and this traceless enlightenment is continued on and on endlessly.[155]

Given the identity of Buddha and the self, to learn the way of Buddha and to learn the self are really the same thing. To forget the self is to make way for enlightenment, which Dōgen therefore could characterize as the dropping off of body and mind. The ten thousand things, the cosmos, also have a role to play in bringing about the state of enlightenment. And once this state is fully realized, there is no trace of consciousness and knowledge, nor any clinging to enlightenment. The experience pervades everything and is lived out in everyday life.

Mention of the cosmos leads to a consideration of nature, which, like the cosmos, is essentially the Buddha nature. Dōgen's love of nature, which rests on a metaphysical foundation, is evident in many parts of the Shōbōgenzō and has inspired many of his Japanese songs (waka). Here we can touch no more than the fringes of his poetic accomplishments. To study his relationship to nature one needs not only to keep his metaphysics in mind but to appreciate his sense of the symbolic character of things (water, mountains, flowers, the moon) and the sensorial power of his poetry, which has earned Zen Master Dōgen a place in Japanese literature.

Being-Time (Uji).   An essential element in Dōgen's metaphysics is his unique notion of time, which surfaces in several of the books of the Shōbōgenzō, including the Busshō and Genjōkōan. One book, entitled Uji (Being-Time) is dedicated especially to the topic.[156] Prefacing this short but difficult text are eight lines (hakku) portraying the reality of all being in its inexhaustible diversity and its dynamic becoming. Mountain heights and ocean depths, mythical figures as well as ordinary objects found in Zen monasteries, the decorations of temple buildings and gardens, together with the people who move about in them—all are "being-time." All the activities and qualities that appear in the never-ending flow of becoming are being-time. All reality, characterized by its dynamic and cosmic qualities and marked by its identity with continuing, is being-time. The self, one with the world and with the Buddha, is also being-time.

After introducing his subject, Dōgen gives us a clear and straightforward statement of the identity of being and time: " 'The time being' means time, just as it is, is being, and being is all time."[157] This statement is then taken up and elaborated for different perspectives. He tells his disciples that they must learn to see the "glorious golden radiance" of time

> in the twelve hours of your day. . . . Although you have never measured the length or brevity of the twelve hours, their swiftness or slowness, you still call them the twelve hours. . . . Even though you don't come to have doubts about them, that is not to say you know them. . . . Still, the doubts themselves are, after all, none other than time.[158]

The identity of being and time entails the unbreakable bond between space and time. Things, as they exist in space, are time. Even wondrous, superhuman things like the demons (*asura*) or the bodies of the Buddha are time; and since time is not an abstract concept, the twelve hours of the day are also time. Because time is in motion, the unenlightened try to understand time in terms of its orientation to the future or its traces from the past. Spring and autumn point in a fixed direction and leave a visible trail behind them, there is no way really to doubt the passage of time. Yet doubting itself is one of the ever-changing processes of the psyche and thus is also time.

The self unfolded in full array is the whole world. All the things of the world are being-time and do not obstruct one another any more than one time gets in the way of another:

> Because of this, there is an arising of mind at the same time, and it is the arising of time of the same mind. So it is with practice and attainment of the Way, too. We set our self out in array and we see that. Such is the fundamental reason of the Way: that our self is time.[159]

The unfolding of the self corresponds to the unfolding of being in the manifold diversity of things, which is identical with the unfolding of the one time within the present moment. Given the unity of reality, the self and time are interwoven in the interpenetration of all things. This simultaneity of all things in the now, this radical totality of reality, is what one aims at in practice and experiences in enlightenment.

In a lengthy section, Dōgen takes up the erroneous views of unenlightened persons who think that time flows in a movement from the past through the present and into the future. After having climbed a mountain or forded a stream, such people think that the mountain and the stream are behind them and belong to the past. It is as if a man thought that

> while the river and mountain may still exist I have now passed them by and I, at the present time, reside in a fine vermilion palace. To him, the mountain and river and I are as far distant as heaven from earth.[160]

But this is not the way things are at all. What we call yesterday and tomorrow are really the one time. Time is only the one moment, "the absolute presence, in which all that is present or absent is as such present."[161] The mistake that unenlightened people make is to understand things and times and the self (of persons) as separate. Reality is a whole. Ignorant of the oneness of reality, the unenlightened follow their discriminating intellects and separate being and time, while reality displays itself—in the cosmos, in time, and in the self—to be a whole. Whenever I really grasp a concrete moment, be it in the things of the world or in the passing of time or in relation to the self, I come in touch with the whole of reality:

> The essential point is: every entire being in the entire world is, each time, an (independent) time. . . . Inasmuch as they are being-time, they are my being-time. Being-time has the virtue of seriatim passage: it passes from today to tomorrow, passes from today to yesterday, passes from yesterday

to today, passes from today to today, passes from tomorrow to tomorrow. This is because passing seriatim is a virtue of time. . . . As self and other are both times, practice and realization are time; entering the mud, entering the water, is equally time . . .

While the unenlightened man . . . learns that this tie, this being, is not the Dharma, he reckons the sixteen-foot golden Buddha body is not himself. His attempts to escape, saying "I am not the sixteen-foot golden Buddha body," are, as such, portions of being-time too. It is the "Look! Look!" of "those who haven't yet confirmed this."[162]

Not only flying ahead but also lagging behind is a quality of time. The unenlightened who imagine that time is only a flowing from the past into the future do not understand this. Wishing to spare disciples the same error, Dōgen admonishes them to "Look! Look!" at those who have not yet understood—a phrase that appears on exceptional occasions in the Record of Lin-chi.[163]

The reality of being-time embraces all being and all time, both what passes and what tarries, both the provisional phenomena arising according to the chain of causation and the self. For the enlightened and the unenlightened alike, there is but one and the same reality. The one Dharma contains all the errors of the persons; to escape its reality is simply impossible.

For Dōgen, being-time, or the whole reality, is dynamic, in constant movement. Dwelling in their Dharma positions (jūhōi), things and points in time come and go, "ascending and descending up and down."[164] In the Genjōkōan, Dōgen states that one cannot say that death becomes life or that life becomes death, since "Life is a stage of time, and death is a stage of time, like, for example, winter and spring,"[165] In the Uji we read:

> The times before and after one immediately manifests the blunder are both, together with it, dwelling positions of being-time. The sharp, vital quick itself of dharmas dwelling in their Dharma positions is being-time (uji).[166]

Dōgen goes on to point out that persons notice only the passing of time, without realizing that time has not yet come; they see only the coming and going. Like all reality, being-time is essentially impenetrable.

Faith.   There are few key concepts of Mahāyāna Buddhism that appear in Mahāyāna texts as frequently and with so many different nuances as the word faith (Skt., śraddhā; Chin., hsin; Jpn., shin). The same holds true in Dōgen's writings. Faith is among the essential elements in his religious metaphysics and occupies a well-defined place in it, though there are many passages in which the term is used in a more general sense. In order to appreciate the basic meaning of faith for Dōgen, we need to return to the essential unity he posits between practice and enlightenment. In the passage cited above, enlightenment (or realization) is said to have no end and practice no beginning because it is grounded in original enlightenment. The same can be said of faith. Like practice, faith is grounded in original enlightenment and therefore participates in the simultaneity of practice and enlightenment. Dōgen explains this in his important work, Advice on *Studying the Way (Gakudōyōjinshū)*,[167] which like the *Bendōwa* book of the *Shōbōgenzō*, is an introduction to the essentials of his thought. In this book, he speaks of the Buddha Way. A way must be walked; the Buddha Way must be practiced. But the Buddha Way must also be believed. Dōgen writes:

> Those who would practice the Way should first of all believe in it. Those who believe in the Way should believe that they have been in the Way from the very beginning, subject to neither delusion, illusive thoughts, and confused ideas nor increase, decrease, and mistaken understanding. Engendering belief like this, clarify the Way and practice it accordingly—this is the essence of studying the Way.[168]

Immediately thereafter he adds:

> In general, there are only a very few who believe they are in the Way. If only you believe that you are truly in the Way you will naturally be able to understand both how it functions as well as the true meaning of delusion and enlightenment. Make an attempt at cutting off the function of discriminating consciousness; then, suddenly, you will have almost realized the Way.

The faith that Dōgen is speaking about here is not directed toward a specific object either outside or within the self; it is, rather, a basic sensitivity that arises concomitantly with practice and enlightenment. In another passage, Dōgen speaks about the roots of faith:

> One must know that the roots of faith do not grow in one's self, or in others, or in one's own efforts. . . . One can talk about faith when the entire body becomes faith *(unshin-jishin)*. Faith necessarily grows together with the Buddha-fruit. If the Buddha-fruit is not there, faith will not appear. . . . Where faith appears, there appear also Buddhas and patriarchs. *(sanjūshichihon bodaibumpō)*.[169]

The Buddha-fruit is enlightenment. In this text, too, faith appears as a fundamental element. In the *Bendōwa* book, as in so many of his works, Dōgen praises faith without clarifying its nature or origin. He writes:

> The spiritual realm of buddhas is totally incomprehensible. It is not to be reached by the workings of the mind; still less can it be known by a man of disbelief or inferior intelligence. Only a person of great capacity based on right faith is able to enter here. Even were a person of disbelief given teachings of it, he would find it difficult to receive them. Even on Vulture Peak there were some the Buddha allowed to leave. If right faith arises in your mind, you should practice religious discipline and study under a master. If it does not arise, you should cease for a while, and regret the fact of not receiving the benefits of the Dharma from the past.[170]

The connection between faith and original enlightenment is not expressly stated here. Dōgen asserts that faith arises in the mind, but he does not say how this comes about. If faith is to be found in original enlightenment, then one cannot really speak of its arising.

Dōgen's religious metaphysics is central to his spirituality—a spirituality marked by faith, commitment, trust, devotion, and participation in a community of Buddha-disciples. It is a spirituality rooted in monasticism.

Monasticism. Buddhism began as a monastic religion, and this aspect came to the fore in Mahāyāna Buddhism during the middle ages. Through and through Dōgen thought of himself as a monk and many of his works were signed "Dōgen the Monk" (Dōgen *shamon*). He lived the monastic life more totally than any of the other great Japanese Buddhist reformers of his time. Indeed, no small part of his work as a reformer was aimed at renewing the monastic orders in Japanese Buddhism.

Entrance into Monastic Life. The path of a Buddhist monk begins with embracing homelessness. Like many young Japanese of his day, Dōgen was barely out of childhood when he entered the monastic life. During the first years of his difficult search, he was conscious of his duties as a monk even if he did not clearly realize the full implications of the life he had chosen. Immediately after arriving in China, we recall, he was deeply impressed by the old monk-cook who found fulfillment in his daily monastic chores. During visits to various Chinese monasteries, he was repeatedly amazed at the strict observance he found there. It was this kind of monastic life that he hoped to cultivate when he returned to Japan, and the more he dedicated himself to the formation of his disciples, the more this hope became his life's mission. Many of his works are wholly or in part concerned with promoting the monastic life.

We may begin by mentioning two books of the *Shōbōgenzō* whose titles refer to entering the monastic life.[171] The short book *Shukke* opens with a lengthy passage from the *Ch'an-yüan ch'ing-kuei* (Jpn., *Zen'on shingi*) by the Chinese Zen master Chang-lu Tsung-i which begins:

> All the Buddhas of the past, present, and future taught home departure and achievement of the Way. All the twenty-eight Indian patriarch and the six Chinese patriarchs who have transmitted the seal of the Buddha-mind were *śramanas*.

In his commentary, Dōgen stresses the remark that "all of the Buddhas and Patriarchs have attained the Way by renouncing the world and receiving the precepts." This rule of life endures in Buddhism up to the present.[172]

Receiving the precepts and entering into homelessness are fundamental to the monastic state. In Buddhism there are two kinds of precepts: in the "Small Vehicle," there are the "precepts of the hearer" (*śrāvaka*), and in the "Great Vehicle," the "precepts of the bodhisattva." It is not enough for Zen disciples to commit themselves to observing the precepts of hearers, as commendable as this is. As the passage from the *Ch'an-yüan ch'ing-kuei* states: "If you have already received the Hīnayāna precepts, strive to receive the precepts of the bodhisattva. This is the way to progress in the Dharma." Dōgen himself dedicates an entire chapter to the subject of receiving the bodhisattva precepts[173] in which he explains the sixteen precepts: the three refuges (to the Buddha, the Dharma, and the saṅgha), the three "pure precepts" (to commit no evil, to do good, and to benefit all sentient beings), and the ten great precepts (which include the five foundational injunctions of Buddhist morality against killing, stealing, improper sexual relations, lying, and drinking intoxicating beverages, and five other norms governing monastic life).

The receiving of the precepts is carried out in a ritual ceremony in which the disciples prostrate themselves devoutly three times and promise to observe the relevant precepts. Dōgen provides a detailed description. We should note here that the observance of Buddhist morality is an integral part of all forms of Zen Buddhism. According to Dōgen, the choice of the monastic life is to be recommended even if a monk or a nun does not fully observe all the precepts. He appeals to a saying of an ancient master: "Even though a monk breaks the ten grave prohibitions, he is superior to a lay person who observes the five lay precepts." Dōgen notes that the sūtras promote ordination, and goes on to stress the point that commitment to the Buddha in the monastic life and taking the precepts constitute a path that surpasses all others.[174]

Such statements may appear somewhat offensive at first glance. The impression is somewhat mitigated if one keeps in mind the notions of karma and rebirth that are part and parcel of Buddhist ethics and also influenced Dōgen. Human life is not a one-time matter; it is caught in a cycle of rebirths that can be broken in enlightenment. In the same context Dōgen recounts traditional stories of people who had led sinful lives entering the monastic life in a later reincarnation and, after further failures, finally attained salvation. We might recognize familiar psychological processes in such stories and feel that we understand them better today, but Dōgen's thoroughly ethical concerns remain beyond doubt. In the same book, Dōgen reminds his monks of the words of Buddha, "A monk should do no wrong. If he does he is not worthy of being called a monk," and comments:

> The original nature of a monk is to have compassion for all sentient beings as if they were his own children. That is to say, he should do no wrong and, by his actions, should live up to his word. If he does this, the resulting merit will be great indeed.[175]

Although Dōgen did not look down on the laity and allowed lay men and women to attend his lectures, he clearly preferred the monastic life. While both laity and monastics can attain salvation, the former do so with difficulty, the latter easily. Since the laity have to work for a living, if they devote themselves exclusively to the way and the Dharma they neglect their family responsibilities, and if they see only to their household duties, they cannot pursue the way; they cannot do both at the same time. It is much easier for the monks. Free from worldly responsibilities, worries, and distractions, they can dedicate themselves to the way of the Buddha. Such reflections form the beginning of his book *Merits of Renouncing the World (Shukke kudoku).*[176] Dōgen not only attributes superiority to the monastic life but transcendent value as well:

Coming into contact with the teachings of the buddhas and entering
the monkhood is an extremely fortunate occurrence. One should not enter
the monkhood for self and what is possessed by self, nor for the sake of
one's body or mind. It is neither our body nor our mind that becomes a
monk. This is the teaching of all the Buddhas, the eternal Way of all the
Buddhas. Because it is the eternal Way of all the buddhas it is beyond self
and what is possessed by self, beyond body and mind, and beyond the three
delusive worlds.

It is for these reasons that entrance into the monkhood is the highest
teaching of Buddhism. It is beyond "sudden" or "gradual," "eternal" or
"temporary," "coming" or "going," "stationary" or "moving," "wide" or
"narrow," "large" or "small," and "doing" or "non-doing." There has never
been a patriarch who has directly transmitted the true Law who has not
entered the monkhood and received the precepts.[177]

With its lineup of negations, this passage harkens back to the *prajñāpāramitā*
sūtras. For someone as committed to tradition as Dōgen was, monasticism, Buddhahood, and the transmission of the Dharma formed a close-knit unity, and
since this unity was lived in the Zen monasteries, they are to have a privileged
place within Buddhism. The last lines of the book swell almost hymn-like:

The correct transmission [of the fact] that all the Buddhas in the three
stages of time have realized enlightenment after having entered the monkhood is the most exalted teaching of all. There has never been a Buddha
in the three stages of time who failed to enter the monkhook. This is because
entering the monkhood is the true Law, the excellent mind of enlightenment, and the supreme *bodhi*-wisdom, which the Buddhas and patriarchs
have correctly transmitted.[178]

Rules for Monastic Life.   The external structures of Buddhist monasticism came
from the Indian motherland. As Buddhism spread through the regions of East
Asia, it changed as it adapted to new customs and climates. In China, the first
Zen disciples lived mainly in monasteries of the strict Vinaya school (Jpn., *risshū*).
We have already studied the development of community living at the time of
the Fourth and Fifth Chinese Patriarchs, as well as the contributions of Pai-
chang to the formation of an independent Zen monasticism. Through his own
experience during his years in China, Dōgen became well acquainted with monastic living. The Zen monasticism that he promoted in Japan bears the clear
stamp of his experience and personality. He strengthened the ancient discipline,
clarifying its contemporary meaning and incorporating new features into it. As
we have already noted, he attributed a unique significance to the monastic life.
His appreciation for concrete details was extraordinary. A young monk who
entrusted himself to Dōgen's direction was required from the very first day to
observe a long list of rules, all of which, the master assured him, flowed from
the basic practice of Zen and guaranteed the efficacy of that practice. Upon
entering the monastery, the monk was given three things: a haircut, a set of
monastic robes, and a begging bowl. As Dōgen explains:

In order to receive the precepts of home departure, you must supply your-selves with the three robes, bowl, eating utensils, cushion, and new un-derclothes. If you do not have new underclothes you may use some that have been washed, but when you enter the place where you are going to receive the precepts, you must not use someone else's robes and bowl.[179]

Three symbolic gestures inaugurate the young aspirant into the life of the monastery. The bald head, shorn of its natural adornment, symbolizes renun-ciation of the world; the begging bowl witnesses to a life of poverty; while the robes mark an individual as a member of a community of monks. Zen monastic dress is made up of different robes. The most notable is the *kesa* (Skt., *kaṣāya*), which is worn somewhat like a tunic or sash. According to tradition it originated with the Buddha and signifies enlightenment. As Dōgen explains in the *Merits of Wearing the Kesa (Kesa kudoku)*, all the Buddhas and patriarchs wore this robe, which symbolizes the Dharma.[180] Śākyamuni gave it to Mahākāśyapa, who was succeeded by the twenty-seven Indian patriarchs up to Bodhidharma, who brought the robe to China, where the Sixth Patriarch, Hui-neng, eventually received it. Dōgen refers to this Zen tradition because his disciples need to know that they are part of an orthodox line of tradition, even though in later times it was not limited to one particular line. The enlightenment robe became part of a ritual investiture undergone by every monk in a Zen monastery. Dōgen speaks with deep reverence of the power of the robe, specifying the kind of material to be used, what color it can be, and what different styles are permitted for different situations (robes worn for garden or field work are styled differently from those used during liturgies).

The ceremony of investiture with the *kesa* is replete with expressions of respect. The monk must always remember that it is Śākyamuni himself who bestows the robe. The act of bathing is practically a cultic act, using incense, flowers, and prostrations. The famous *kaṣāya* verse is recited:

How wondrous this deliverance robe is,
Like a field bestowing unlimited happiness!
Now we unfold the Tathāgata's teachings,
Making a vow to save all sentient beings.[181]

Concluding the chapter, Dōgen narrates a personal experience from his stay in China. He once sat next to a Chinese monk who every morning paid homage to the *kesa* by placing it on his head, folding his hands, and reciting the *kaṣāya* verses. Dōgen recalls: "At that time I was filled with the deepest emotion and joy that I had ever experienced. Unknowingly, I shed so many tears of gratitude that my collar became wet." It was then that he formed his resolve to return to Japan and bring his people the true Dharma so that his fellow countrymen might have the opportunity to experience the Law that had been correctly transmitted together with the *kesa*. He also describes two Korean monks who demonstrated great knowledge of the sūtras but who had neither *kesa* nor begging bowls: "How tragic it is to be a monk in name but not in reality!"[182] Characteristically, Dōgen attributes this to the fact that they came from a small, remote country.

The direct connection between daily life and enlightenment flows from the unity between practice and enlightenment, insofar as practice *is* everyday life and work: ". . . The everyday life of the Buddhas and patriarchs is nothing but drinking tea and eating rice." With these words Dōgen closes his book on everyday life *(Kajō)*.[183] The ordinary things that make up the everyday world represent life at its fullest—practice is enlightenment. This central rule of Zen informs the various particular rules. A few of them especially stressed by Dōgen may be mentioned here.

Consider, for example, the mealtime prescriptions so important in every Zen monastery. Dōgen lays them out in elaborate detail in one of his six main books of rules *(Eihei shingi)*.[184] For Dōgen himself they are not details. Each and every one of the minutiae of monastic life is important; each part contains the whole. In his volume on table manners, *Fushukuhanpō*,[185] a variety of directives are given that, when carried out, amount to a kind of spiritual drama. When monks sit down to table together something essential and spiritual is taking place. The book opens with a reminder about the relationship between meals and the Dharma. The common meal is a manifestation of all things, including the Dharma and enlightenment. Mutual courtesy and regard require that the monks avoid bumping into each other and that they eat neither too quickly nor too slowly.

As early Zen masters report, the begging bowl can serve as an eating bowl. Like meals in general, the bowl from which rice is eaten is deeply significant. Dōgen appeals to his master Ju-ching to tell the story of the great Pai-chang, who, when asked for an example of something that was truly worthy of wonder and praise, answered, "sitting alone in *zazen* on the top of Mount Ta-hsing." Dōgen comments that it is no less worthy of wonder and praise to "eat rice from one's begging bowl." "To do *zazen* on the top of Mount Ta-hsing" is the same as drinking tea or eating rice. Dōgen continues: "The function of the begging bowl is to eat rice. The function of eating rice is the begging bowl." One who has eaten enough of it knows what rice is.

> What is this begging bowl? I do not think that it is just something made of wood. Nor is it something made of black lacquer, nor something made of stone. It has no bottom and no opening. It can swallow the universe in a single mouthful and the whole universe receives it with folded hands.[186]

The begging bowl, which in later monastic practice did become an eating bowl, was thus elevated to a higher, wondrous realm in line with the metaphysical import that Dōgen's spirituality attributed to mealtimes. Dōgen also gave clear directives for washing the eating utensils, a fact that brings us to a second important area of monastic life, the rules for bathing and cleanliness, the subject of two books in the *Shōbōgenzō*.[187] Dōgen's directives here, as with those for food and sustenance, are replete with metaphysical remarks. Bodily cleanliness is a sign of the mind's inner purity—that is, of emptiness. The "washing of the mind" takes place when it is emptied of concepts and images.

Some of the ancient Indian traditions concerning cleansing and bathing were transmitted to China and passed on there. According to a directive from the Buddha himself, the purification of body and mind calls for a threefold ceremonial bathing and censing.[188] After the entire body is bathed in water fresh robes are put on, a small amount of incense is kindled, and the smoke made to waft through the clothes and the *zazen* seat. This procedure is repeated, in exactly the same order, three times. Then one pays homage to the image of Buddha, recites some sūtra verses, and, after a final washing of the feet, returns to the practice of *zazen*.

> In the Buddha-Dharma the way of purification is clearly fixed: washing the body and washing the mind, washing the feet and washing the face, washing the eyes and washing the mouth, washing the two parts used for elimination, washing the hands, washing the begging bowl, washing the *kesa,* washing the head. All these are the true method of all the Buddhas and patriarchs of the three times.[189]

While in China, Dōgen not only took an interest in current customs observed at Zen monasteries but also acquired a sound knowledge of monastic architecture. The monastery of Eihei-ji was constructed on the Chinese model; as we know from Dōgen's detailed specifications, even the latrines (*tōsu*) were built in Chinese style. "Dōgen's descriptions of the proper etiquette and attitude of mind to be observed while using this building . . . echoes the descriptions given in earlier Chinese codes."[190] In Dōgen's monastery there was also a special bathhouse (*goka* or *kōka*) annexed to the monks' hall. The master even directed his monks to clean their teeth every morning with a special wooden pick (*yōji*)— a practice that had been in vogue in India but fell out of use in China—and provided two verses that the monks may recite while cleaning their teeth, one of the verses assuring them that with strong teeth they can chew-up all illusions.[191]

Dōgen's rule books cover all aspects of life in the monastery, each treating a particular topic, as we saw in the *Fushukuhanpō's* treatment of mealtimes. The *Shuryōshingi* contains rules for the reading room (*shuryō*) or monastery library, so important for the intellectual well-being of the monks. While reading was forbidden in the monks' hall, which was reserved exclusively for the practice of sitting meditation, the monks were able to study Buddhist scriptures in the reading room. The code known as the *Bendōhō (Forms of Practice)* offers concrete directives for practice during the different periods of the day as well as guidelines for community life. Another code, the *Taitaiko-goge-jarihō,* provides younger monks with rules for treating aged members of the community.

Proper order is important for maintaining a harmonious communal life among the monks. The various offices and positions designed for this purpose are treated in the *Chiji shingi.* Monks who hold office are instructed to carry out their duties conscientiously and not to look upon it as a disadvantage when these duties require them to take up worldly tasks that might distract them from the spiritual life. Dōgen provides abundant examples of monks who underwent enlightenment experiences while faithfully carrying out their duties. In his monastery there were only six offices: *tsūsu* and *kansu* for monastery business, *fūsu* for financial matters, *ino* for the supervision of the monks, *tenzo* for the kitchen, and *shissui* for maintenance of the buildings. Each of the offices is described and practical guidelines given for carrying them out.

Only cooks are given an additional book all their own. I have already mentioned the *Tenzo kyōkun*,[192] which merits special attention for the deep insight it provides into Dōgen's understanding of monasticism. The cook carries out a simple daily job that is crucial for the physical well-being of all the monks. But Dōgen's prescriptions are not a cookbook or a manual on hygiene. In his daily work for the community the cook, if his service is rooted in enlightenment, represents the ideal for all the other monks. Though he is conscious of his own liberation, the cook does not distinguish himself from the other monks but joins them in their *zazen* and other practices. Unceasingly he remembers that "a few vegetables can nourish the Buddha-sprigs and enable the buds of the Buddha Way to blossom."[193] Fully detached from his work, he lives in constant contact with the Absolute, which for Dōgen is the aim of all monasticism. This is why he devoted so much energy to the formulation and development of a well-regulated monastic life. Nowhere were his hopes more clearly expressed than in his book for the monastery cook, a work which echoes his very first experience of Zen in China when he met the old cook.

Spirituality and Devotion.   The two words in this subtitle overlap. Spirituality is the broader notion, embracing the overall spiritual attitude of religious persons in their relations to the world and to others, as well as their virtues, their goals, and a disposition we may call devotion. In the preceding discussion, we have already had a great deal to say about Dōgen's spirituality. The *Zuimonki*, a precious little volume that contains events, stories, and talks from Dōgen's lifetime, is a rich source of insight into Dōgen's spirituality. Indeed, as we have already attempted to do, one could select passages from this book to construct a representative picture of Dōgen's spirituality. Relying on the *Zuimonki* we have looked at attitudes that for Dōgen are essential for the practice of *zazen*: poverty, detachment, simplicity, goodness, inner freedom, fidelity to tradition, obedience to one's master, and a sense of community.[194] In this section of our somewhat lengthy, but still inadequate, chapter on Dōgen we shall look especially at his devotion. This will also provide an opportunity to examine a few problems regarding our study and knowledge of Dōgen.

It is hard to miss Dōgen's deep-seated and reverent sense of devotion, which, in its varieties of expression, does not look very different from what we find among the pious faithful in other Mahāyāna schools. "Taking refuge in the Three Jewels" (Skt., *triratna*; Jpn., *sambō*), the basic practice in all Buddhist devotion and the title of one of the books of the *Shōbōgenzō*, provides the foundation for Dōgen's own devotional attitudes.

. . . Veneration of the Buddha, the Law, and the Buddhist community is the essence of the correct transmission of the Buddhas and patriarchs in both Indian and China. Without taking refuge in the Three Jewels it is impossible to reverently venerate them. Without reverently venerating them it is impossible to take refuge in them. The merit of having taken refuge in the Three Jewels inevitably appears when there is spiritual communion with the Buddha.[195]

Such devotion grows beyond the cycle of rebirths to the highest enlightenment and calls for "the pure essence of faith." With hands folded in *gasshō* and head bowed, one recites the formula of refuge in the Three Jewels.

Dōgen comments on the meaning of the Sino-Japanese compound *ki-e*, which means "taking refuge." *Ki* signifies "to throw oneself," like a child throwing itself into the arms of its parent; *e* signifies "to rely upon," as a nation is dependent on its regent. The formula encapsulates the Buddhist way of salvation. Buddha is the great teacher, the Dharma (teaching) is the dependable means of salvation, and the community consists of treasured friends ever ready to help. To ground his explanation, Dōgen first of all appeals to the *Lotus Sūtra*, which he calls "the king of the sūtras." Compared with this sūtra, "all the other sūtras are merely its servants." They represent "provisional teachings of the Buddha and therefore do not express his real intention." This sūtra held a prominent place in Dōgen's spiritual life, for he immersed himself in the study of this text during his early years on Mount Hiei. We may suppose that his own inclinations were nurtured by the sūtra's strong emotional tones. The *Lotus Sūtra* shows how "the merit of the Three Jewels is truly of unsurpassed value."[196]

Because the Buddhas belong to "the realm of the Three Jewels,"[197] they are worthy of honor. Throughout his writings, Dōgen shows the greatest respect for the Buddhas and the patriarchs and calls upon his disciples to do likewise. He makes use of many traditional examples and stories drawn not only from historical tradition but also from legends and mythical accounts. Numerous stories dealing with reports of reincarnations make up an extensive part of his instructional writings.

In a book of the *Shōbōgenzō* entitled *Veneration of the Buddhas (Kuyōshobutsu)*,[198] Dōgen spells out the motives for honoring the Buddhas and details how one goes about doing so. The first and foremost motive is the example of Śākyamuni himself, who in his former life as a bodhisattva showed great reverence toward all previous Buddhas. On matters of Buddhology Dōgen was cautious, not wishing to get embroiled in questions about whether past Buddhas existed without beginning. For him it was clear that a Buddha has no real need of the gifts offered him: "Even though our offerings be gold, silver, incense, or flowers, they are of no use to the Buddhas. The reason why the Buddhas accept them is simply that out of their great compassion they wish to increase the merits of all beings."[199]

In the *Nirvāṇa Sūtra* and the *Lotus Sūtra* Dōgen finds moving passages on honoring the Buddhas. In the latter we read for example: "If someone respectfully makes reverential offerings of flowers, incense, banners, or canopies to the stūpas, statues, and portraits of the Buddha, he will eventually realize the Way . . .[200] Among the ten ways of venerating a Buddha that Dōgen enumerates and explains, he gives special attention to the stūpa devotions. Because they contain the relics of the Buddha, the stūpas can be viewed as representations of the Buddha. Three poetic passages on the merits of stūpa devotion proclaim that the clay from which the stūpa is made, the act of prostration before a stūpa, or the gifts laid before a stūpa are all more valuable than a great mound of gold. In each passage, however, the importance of an inward sense of devotion is stressed. It is worth noting that the tenth form of venerating the Buddha consists of one's own practice of the Way. Devotion flows into praxis, namely the discipline of zazen.

Commenting on the story of the Chinese Zen master Tan-hsia, who burned a wooden image of Buddha as his disciple watched in astonishment, Dōgen points out that the meaning is not a literal one.[201] Zen does not advocate or practice iconoclasm. The meaning of the story is clearly that Zen disciples should not cling even to so esteemed an object as an image of the Buddha. In the same context, Dōgen tells the story of a monk who was chided by his master for carrying around a box with a golden Buddha image and relics. "Open your box and look inside" shouted the master as the disciple was reluctantly about to leave. Inside a poisonous snake lay coiled.[202] Impediments arise not only from dependency but also from monotonous routine. We have seen how much Dōgen stressed the importance of inner disposition for proper devotion; personal sincerity and effort were his constant concerns.

Like images, statues, and reliquaries, sūtras are also worthy of devotion, for they too belong to the "realm of the Three Jewels." As Dōgen explains in the *Nyorai zenshin (The Whole Body of the Tathāgata)*,[203] the deeper meaning of the sūtras is to be found in their being the body of the Perfected One. The sūtras are the whole body of the Tathāgata.

> This being so, the sūtra is the whole being of the Tathāgata. Paying homage to the sūtra is paying homage to the Tathāgata. Coming into contact with the sūtra is meeting the Tathāgata. The sūtra is the Buddha's relic. This being so, the relics are the sūtra. Even though you may understand that this sūtra is the relics of the Buddha, if you do not know that the relics are the sutra, it cannot be said that you know the Buddha Way yet.

It is precisely this direct link between the sūtras and the Perfected One that make the sūtras a treasure beyond price. Like the stūpas and images of Buddha, the sūtras bring to awareness the all-penetrating presence of the Buddha reality. Insofar as they are the whole body of the Perfected One, they are specially qualified to foster a devotional attitude. Clearly Dōgen's disciples learned from their master the greatest respect for the sūtras.

Dōgen's religious devotion, which has been presented in some detail because of its importance for the total picture of his personality, always remained within the context of Mahāyāna Buddhism. Though temperamentally more devout than other Zen masters, his worldview is that of the great Mahāyāna sūtras. Mahāyāna

Buddhism itself is an example of how a distinct religiosity can be combined with a cosmotheistic view of the universe. The whole of reality—the One and the Whole—that the human individual identifies with is also experienced as superior and transcendent. The negativity in the conception of this reality only confirms this. The world of Buddhas and bodhisattvas, even if it is ultimately absorbed in emptiness, stirs devotion in the here and now. Dōgen opened himself to the essential elements of Mahāyāna religiosity and allowed them to penetrate his entire being.

The way in which Dōgen, so untypical of Zen masters, praises the glory and holiness of the Buddha reality and commits himself to it has given rise to some controversy. The clearest textual evidence for this is found in the *Shōji*, referred to earlier.[204] Although the authenticity of this book has been questioned in the past, scholars today are generally agreed that it is the authentic work of Dōgen. Certain questions regarding the transmission of the text are fairly easily resolved[205] and certain pecularities of the style can be accounted for. Most of the other books of the *Shōbōgenzō* were directed at his disciples, but the *Shōji* seems to have been written for a lay person, for whom the colorful, vigorous, and easily comprehensible style would provide direct access to the content of Dharma words (*hōgo*).[206]

The question of life and death is an important theme in Buddhism but not in the leitmotifs of Dōgen's metaphysics. Besides the *Shōji*, only one other text gives central consideration to the question, the short *Zenki*. The title is difficult to translate, but means something like "total dynamism."[207] On the basis of the Mahāyāna doctrine of the identity of saṃsāra and nirvāṇa, Dōgen argues in the *Shōji* for the identity of life and death. The key statement reads as follows:

> Just understand that birth and death itself is nirvāṇa, and you will neither hate one as being birth and death, nor cherish the other as being nirvāṇa. Only then can you be free of birth and death.[208]

The *Bendōwa* makes the point similarly:

> . . . You must realize birth and death is in and of itself nirvāṇa. Buddhism has never spoken of nirvāṇa apart from birth and death.[209]

The *Zenki* stresses that both life and death manifest the complete dynamism that transcends the duality of life and death.

Dōgen's teaching on life and death is part of the seamless garment of his overall metaphysics. In identifying life and death with the life of Buddha, the *Shōji* accords with the way the identification of the Buddha with saṃsāra and nirvāṇa illustrates the general Mahāyāna doctrine of the oneness of reality. We repeat the relevant passage because, together with the immediately following sentences, it forms an important element of Dōgen's devotionalism:

> This present birth and death itself is the life of the Buddha (*on inochi*). If you attempt to reject it with distaste, you are losing thereby the life of the Buddha. If you abide in it, attaching to birth and death, you also lose

the life of the Buddha, and leave yourself with [only] the appearance of Buddha. You only attain the mind of the Buddha when there is no hating [of birth and death] and no desiring [of nirvāṇa]. But do not try to gauge it with your mind or speak it with words.[210]

Dōgen is referring to the Buddha when he uses the honorific prefix *on*, employed in Japanese when speaking to a person of high standing. It shows both respect and intimacy. Without pressing the point of linguistic too much, it is worth noting that the Zen master adopts the style of the Dharma word to bring out both the eminence of the Buddha as well as his familiarity. In the following sentences the passage rises to a crescendo:

When you simply release and forget both your body and your mind and throw yourself into the house of the Buddha, and when functioning comes from the direction of the Buddha and you go in accord with it, then with no strength needed and no thought expended, freed from birth and death, you become the Buddha. Then there can be no obstacle in any man's mind.[211]

This passage is often cited to demonstrate Dōgen's proximity to Pure Land Buddhism. To be sure, the style does evoke Amida peitism. How we are to understand the implied metaphysics depends on our interpretation of the words "life of the Buddha." Certainly a Buddha working from without makes no sense in the context of Dōgen's teachings. Abe and Waddell note that "in the context of Dōgen's thought as a whole, it would perhaps be preferable to understand it in the sense of 'Buddha Nature' or 'Original Face.' "[212] Kawamura, who proposes a similar interpretation in his essay on the *Shōji*, suggests that what Dōgen has in mind is the life and death of the existential subject who has been transformed by the life of the Buddha.[213] The life of the Buddha is the same as original enlightenment, which is identical with the self. The object of the injunction to "release and forget" (Jpn., *hanachi-wasureru*) is the empirical, discriminating ego, while "throwing oneself into" (*nageireru*) the house of the Buddha implies an original enlightenment identical with the Buddha nature. The Japanese scholar Itō—with whom Kawamura disagrees—reads an "immanent mystical vision" into the passage and speaks here of a "pantheistic Buddha" (*hanshinbutsu*).[214] Interpretations of this sort, insofar as they lack consistency with the whole of Dōgen's metaphysics and especially with his view of the Buddha nature, must remain doubtful.

For our purposes, the *Shōji* is helpful not for its implied metaphysic but for the way it expresses Dōgen's devotion. To appreciate this properly we must refer again to the role of faith in his spirituality. As we pointed out in the previous section on Dōgen's metaphysics, faith, as the root of the spiritual life, is grounded in original enlightenment. This notion of faith is evident in the two books of the *Shōbōgenzō* that deal with the awakening of the *bodhi* mind. According to the book on *Arousing the Supreme Mind* (*Hotsumujōshin*), the entire devotional life flows from the *bodhi* mind. Dōgen explains that it is the sitting like a Buddha and making an effort like a Buddha that is called "arousing the thought of enlightenment."

The conditions for arousing the thought of enlightenment do not come from outside. It is the enlightened mind that arouses the thought of enlightenment. The meaning of this phrase, "it is the enlightened mind that arouses the thought of enlightenment" is that one makes a Buddha with a blade of grass, one makes a sūtra scroll with a rootless tree, one honors the Buddha with a grain of sand, one honors the Buddha with the water in which rice has been soaked. One offers a handful of food to living creatures and one presents five flowers to the Tathāgata; this is arousing the thought of enlightenment.

Not only that, but knowing that one's home is not really one's home, abandoning home and going away from home, entering the mountains and practicing the Buddha's Way, practicing with faith [in the teacher] or practicing according to the Dharma [as found in the scriptures] is also arousing the thought of enlightenment. It is making the image of a Buddha, making a stūpa, reading the sūtras, being mindful of the Buddha, preaching the Dharma for living beings, visiting a true teacher and asking questions, and sitting cross-legged and doing zazen. It is also bowing to the Buddha, Dharma, and saṅgha, and it is reciting, "I take refuge in the Buddha."[215]

Dōgen gives still other examples of "the awakening of the bodhi mind within the awakening of the bodhi mind."[216] All of Buddhist devotion, especially throwing oneself into the house of the Buddha described in the Shōji, takes place within the awakening of the bodhi mind.

The bodhi mind is something that neither existed from the beginning nor arose recently, It is neither one nor many, neither free not fixed. It neither exists within us nor extends throughout the universe. It is far from such differences as before and after, being and nonbeing. It is neither the essence of one's self nor of others' selves, nor of both. It does not arise spontaneously but accrues when there is a spiritual communion between sentient beings and the Buddha. We neither receive it from the Buddhas or bodhisattvas nor produce it through our own ability, for as has been stated, it arises not spontantously but only when we have a spiritual communion with the Buddha.[217]

The many negations in this passage should not obscure its positive content. Dōgen distinguishes the bodhi mind not only from the discriminating intellect but also from enlightenment; it is for him only the first step on the path to enlightenment. There is an evident relationship between the bodhi mind and faith, both of which are indispensable driving forces for progress along the religious path. Francis Cook treats this in the two introductory chapters of his book on Zen practice. Faith, he writes there, is "not simply one important element among others; it is the indispensable prerequisite"[218] for attaining the goal. In his view, awakening the bodhi mind requires that one has "a faith that the Dharma has the potential of restoring clarity, sanity, contentment, and supreme goodness to our everyday, ordinary lives."[219] Faith and the awakening of the *bodhi* mind lead one into the Dharma realm and at the same time furnish the key to that fullness of benefits that culminates in enlightenment. Dōgen considered this decisive step to be extremely important. Introducing the categories of *jiriki* ("self-power") and *tariki* ("Other-power") is of no help here since they imply polarity rather than complementarity in religious life. Although Dōgen neither defined nor even clearly described faith and the awakening of the *bodhi* mind, they are the source of devotion as he understood and practiced it.

The awakening of the *bodhi* mind is bound up with the bodhisattva ideal in the Mahāyāna tradition, just as faith is a help in practicing the way of the bodhisattvas:

> Those who have awakened the *bodhi* mind constantly endeavor in body, word, and mind to arouse this mind in all sentient beings and lead them to the Way.[220]

The book on the *Awakening of the Bodhi Mind* extolls this attitude repeatedly and expressly, deploring the idea that it is better first to save oneself and only then to help others cross over to the other shore of enlightenment: "A bodhisattva always protects the *bodhi* mind."[221] Dōgen warned his disciples against the danger of falling asleep on the way and losing the *bodhi* mind.

By way of conclusion to these reflections on Dōgen's spirituality and devotion, I would like to recall the words of Nakamura Hajime: "Japanese Buddhism is, above all, a Buddhism centering around faith. The Japanese emphasize purity of faith. Even the Zen sect, in which faith is comparatively less esteemed, exhibits this trend in Japan."[222] Dōgen (perhaps together with Shinran and Nichiren) embodies as few others the Japanese Buddhist religiosity[223] that is acknowledged to have come to full flower during the Kamakura period.

ZEN MASTER AND RELIGIOUS THINKER

It is not possible, given the current state of research, to give a definitive evaluation of Dōgen as a person. In the course of the foregoing account of his work as a Zen master and his performance as a religious thinker, I have tried to portray the distinctive cast of his personality. Japanese historians prize his accomplishments as a Zen master because of their importance for the religious renewal of Buddhism during the troubled state of *mappō* that marked the Kamakura period. For the most part modern historiography gives first place in its assessment, rightly or wrongly, to visible results. In his popular but painstakingly written little book, Imaeda offers some thought-provoking statistics.[224] Basing his claim on an overall picture of the factual results, he writes that through Dōgen's efforts countless monks and laity were led to Buddhism, noting Dōgen had accepted more than three hundred monks into the monastic life and that more than seven hundred of his disciples had taken up the bodhisattva precepts under his direction. Clearly this shows the significance of Dōgen's work for the rising tide of people from all walks of life drawn to the gates of Kyoto to practice Zen. Later, the military regime would call him to Kamakura from his retreat in Echizen.

Dōgen stands as the "master of *zazen*" *par excellence*. It is not as if he was the first to have taught sitting cross-legged in meditation and to have stressed its significance for the way of Zen, even though his "*zazen* only" (*shikan taza*) was seen as a novelty by his contemporaries. His message, like that of Shinran and Nichiren, had a radical accent, and yet he was not able to accept the former radical claim of Zen to be a special tradition outside the scriptures (*kyōge betsuden*). He established profound inner bonds with the *Lotus Sūtra* and other Mayāyāna texts based on his experience as a young Tendai monk on Mount Hiei. The words of the Buddha recorded in the sūtras remained close to his heart to the end, yet his radical interpretations gave a new and rousing resonance to many scriptural passages.

Zen masters are often idealized in historical records. This is no less true of Dōgen. I have tried not to gloss over weaknesses of his that appear in the sources. If his integrity as an individual stands above reproof, his critique of Lin-chi and his house, both because of the volume of his judgments and their sharpness, lay bare a flaw of temper. Displays of emotion are too obvious in his work to gainsay. Pressing ahead in our exploration of Dōgen's character, we exposed an apparently unresolvable contradiction in Dōgen's attitude: on the one side we saw his awareness of the universal, true Dharma of the Buddha as the only goal of Buddhism; on the other, we saw a family loyalty that paid high tribute to the House of Ts'ao-tung.

Weaknesses in Dōgen's written work point to a weakness in leadership as the master advanced in age. Together with the increasing domination of his monastic inclinations we also see evidence of a lack of character provoked by an unhappy physical condition during the final years of his life. No longer the master leading his disciples with a strong, sure hand, Dōgen was unable to leave behind a life work equal to the challenge of the unavoidable tempests that all human achievements forment in later times. Already in the generation after him a catastrophe set in that was only set aright after a long interval.[225] Dōgen is not the only Zen master to have suffered this fate.

The assessment of Dōgen's artistic and intellectual achievement is extremely important for the overall evaluation of his personality. The Dōgen renaissance began in our own century when ranking Japanese scholars independent of the Sōtō school discovered extraordinary spiritual qualities in his work. Many of his texts are not simple instructions for an audience but pieces ranking as literature in their own right. Is there an originality to be seen in the creative powers of the author of the *Shōbōgenzō*?

Zen scholarship today is still faced with the task of providing a satisfactory answer to this question. A decision needs to be made between the artistic value of his power of expression and the depth of his intellectual insight. Mention has been made of his powerful and moving language when speaking of his activities in Kōshō-ji. Hee-Jin Kim's treatment of Dōgen's "creative expressions" provides an important impetus for further work in this area.[226] Indeed, as not a few publications have shown, interest in this approach has awakened among a considerable number of scholars. That language and expression excite human creativity hardly needs repeating in the intellectual climate of our times. If Dōgen succeeded in expressing the thought of China and India in a genuinely Japanese idiom, the achievement merits recognition.

Strictly speaking, intellectual originality is a rarity. New perspectives, the discovery of connections, paradigm shifts, and changes of accent for the most part satisfy our claims to a writer's originality. In the case of Dōgen we cannot but assert that his thought moved within Buddhist horizons. The great Mahāyāna sūtras as well as the Chinese collections and chronicles formed the background and driving force of his work. From these sources he drew insight and inspiration. His work excites the impression of a powerful reflection distilled into new modes of thought with the aid of his linguistic skills.

I have the impression myself that his comprehensive book on the Buddha nature (Busshō), which I have had occasion to read with Japanese students in a philosophical seminar, is one of Dōgen's well-balanced and mature works. Turning to this book after reading some of his shorter pieces, we wanted to soar high with the master and follow him to the depths, and so to get a sense of a skillfully constructed whole. In no small way the students confirmed me in my happy conviction that we were encountering a truly significant production of the human spirit.[227] It is incumbent on Dōgen studies that the master's work be researched and assessed in all its parts that it might take a lasting place in the universe of human knowledge.

Dōgen is a towering figure in Japanese Buddhism. He has entered into other cultural circles as few other Japanese intellectuals. May we not count him among the constructive spirits of humanity?

NOTES

1.   Tanabe Hajime, Shōbōgenzō no tetsugaku shikan, vol. 5 of his Collected Works, pp. 451ff, as cited in the foreword to Masunaga Reihō, Eihei-Shōbōgenzō—Dōgen no shūkyō, p. 3. Tanabe belongs to the Kyoto school of philosophy. His fascination with Dōgen seems to have been inspired by Watsuji Tetsurō, whose noted essay "Shamon Dōgen," composed in 1926, can be found in a larger work, Nihon seishinshi kenkyū.

2.   The basic work for the biography of Dōgen is the Denkōroku (T. 2585, vol. 82) of Keizan Jōkin (1268–1325), dated 1300. The original manuscript has been lost and the oldest extant copy dates from the year 1430. This work, which originated within the Sōtō school, is historically reliable only in a restricted sense. The same holds true of eight more extensive biographical works (reaching up to 1753) presented and discussed by T. James Kodera in his book, Dōgen's Formative Years in China, pp. 7–13. From the wealth of material a rather standardized account of his life has emerged that leaves a number of questions unanswered. In addition to a discussion on the sources, the work of Kodera has two biographical chapters that treat the course of his life, including his stay in China. Hee-Jin Kim's Dōgen Kigen: Mystical Realist includes a lengthy chapter on

the life of Dōgen (pp. 13–61). Important modern Japanese books include the following: Ōkubo Dōshū, *Dōgen Zenji-den no kenkyū* (rev. ed., 1966); Nakaseko Shōdō, *Dōgen Zenji-den kenkyū* (1979); Imaeda Aishin, "Dōgen no shōgai," in *Dōgen no shōgai to shisō,* pp. 40–109. Additional sketches of the life of Dōgen are to be found in the introductory material to annotated Japanese editions of the *Shōbōgenzō.* Regarding the biographical material in the text, see especially Ōkubo and Masunaga.

3.   Nakaseko arrives at this conclusion in his *Dōgen Zenji-den kenkyū.* He first establishes that the oldest sources do not mention Dōgen's father by name, and from there undertakes a thorough examination of the data, giving particularly extended treatment of the long dominant view that his father was Michichika, opting in the end for the view that his father was Minamoto Michitomo (see pp. 49–58). Kodera treats the genealogy in detail on the grounds of its traditional composition, according to which Minamoto Michichika was Dōgen's real father, whereas Minamoto Michitomo is regarded as his foster-father or stepfather (pp. 17ff). My presentation agrees with this view. Nakaseko's research commands attention, and yet a corresponding presentation of Dōgen's early years on the basis of his findings has yet to be forthcoming. He himself offers only research on particular details.

4.   The background of his mother is completely uncertain. The oldest sources do not touch on the question. Nakaseko considers several possibilities as to the identity of her mother. The question is complicated by several concubines and numerous marital separations at the time. See Nakaseko, *Dōgen Zenji-den kenkyū,* pp. 58–65. According to a simple and traditional explanation, his mother was Ishi, a daughter of Matsudono (also Kujō) Motofusa (1144–1230), who belonged to a branch of the Fujiwara family. Compare Kodera, *Dōgen's Formative Years in China,* pp. 20ff.

5.   Cited in Masunaga, *Eihei-Shōbōgenzō—Dōgen no shūkyō,* p. 7. The place is mentioned in the early source, *Kenzeiki* (named after its compiler, Kenzei, the fourteenth abbot of Eihei-ji). The earliest extant edition of this work is dated 1589, though Kenzei himself lived about a century before that. See Kodera, *Dōgen's Formative Years in China,* pp. 9ff.

6.   It is hard to establish who this uncle or relative was. I leave the question moot here. The story of Dōgen's childhood is marked by unhappy but not entirely clear family circumstances, which may have heightened his sense of the transitoriness of this world.

7.   Kōen ranks as the seventieth abbot in the Tendai sect. He is the successor of Jitsuen and later studied under Jien. See Kodera, *Dōgen's Formative Years in China,* p. 146, n. 62.

8.   According to the exhaustive treatment in the biography, the question remains inconclusive. Kodera draws upon early sources to conclude that it is most unlikely that Dōgen could have met with Eisai (*ibid.,* pp. 27ff). Masunaga cites grounds for and against, deciding that the meeting did actually take place (*Eihei-Shōbōgenzō—Dōgen no shūkyō,* pp. 16ff). Nakaseko's researches lead him to the conclusion that "it is hard to suppose" that the two could have met (*Dōgen Zenji-den kenkyū,* p. 157).

9.   See Masunaga, *Eihei-Shōbōgenzō,* p. 22, who draws on the text of the *Eihei kōroku* for this questionable statement.

10.   On Myōzen, see the section on Eisai's disciples in chap. 14.

11.   The text is found in *Dōgen Zenji zenshū,* vol. 2, pp. 295–303. The meeting with the cook appears on pp. 298–99. This standard edition of Dōgen, edited by Ōkubo Dōshū, (2 vols.; Tokyo, 1969–1976) will be cited hereafter as DZZ I and II. The text of the

Tenzo kyōkun is written in Chinese characters. Japanese authors paraphrased the text. In the foregoing I have adhered to the Japanese versions. Recently, an English translation of Dōgen's text, with a commentary by Uchiyama Kōshō, appeared under the title *Refining Your Life: From the Zen Kitchen to Enlightenment* (New York, 1983).

12. Imaeda, "Dōgen no shōgai," p. 49.

13. Masunaga, *Dōgen Zenji-den kenkyū*, p. 30.

14. The point was made by the authorities of the monastery that other Japanese monks as well, such as Saichō, Kūkai, and Eisai, had been ranked beneath the novices. Since Dōgen did not give in, the matter was brought before the authorities of the Five Mountains. It is hardly likely that Dōgen appealed to the Chinese emperor, as some biographers report. See Kodera, *Dōgen's Formative Years in China*, pp. 39–42.

15. A great deal of criticism of the Rinzai school and its representative Ta-hui is contained in Dōgen writings. This critique may have been influenced in part by Ju-ching.

16. In one passage Kodera describes in detail the documents and their inspection by Dōgen; *Dōgen's Formative Years in China*, pp. 42–47.

17. *Nyojō Oshō goroku* (or *Tendō Nyojō Zenji goroku*), T. 2002, vol. 48.

18. After roaming from one monastery to another for more than twenty years, he was invested as abbot of three great monasteries, the last of which was Ching-tz'u-ssu in Hang-chou, one of the Five Mountains.

19. The *Shōbōgenzō zuimonki* stems from brief occasional talks and instructions given by Dōgen recorded by the disciple Ejō between 1235 and 1237. The text was first printed in 1651. The monk Menzan Zuihō (1683–1769) prepared an improved edition known as the *rufubon* which appeared in 1769. The booklet enjoyed great esteem, as the great number of modern editions shows. The English translation of Masunaga Reihō, *A Primer of Sōtō Zen: A Translation of Dōgen's Shōbōgenzō Zuimonki*, relies on the Iwanami edition of the *rufubon* by Watsuji Tetsurō. The quotations in the text are drawn from this edition (hereafter referred to simply as Masunaga), as well as from the standard DZZ. For the passage quoted, see Iwanami edition I, p. 6; (Masunaga, I, p. 7), DZZ II, p. 452.

20. Compare *Zuimonki*, Iwanami edition II, 19; Masunaga II, 25, DZZ II, p. 457. Particular details in the text are taken from the *Zuimonki*.

21. On Myōzen's death see the previous chapter.

22. *Eihei shitsuchū monjo*, DZZ II, p. 503.

23. See *Dōgen Oshō kōroku*, vol. 2, in DZZ II, p. 34.

24. Kodera draws attention to a difficulty (*Dōgen's Formative Years in China*, pp. 106–107). In Ju-ching's collected sayings the expression "casting off of body and mind" does not appear, though another expression of four characters appears once, "casting off of the dust of the mind." Both expressions are read the same in their Japanese pronunciation *shinjin datsuraku*. The Chinese pronunciations, however, differ. The "casting off of body and mind" is read *shen-hsin t'o-lo* and the "casting off of the dust of the mind" is read *hsin-chen t'o-lo*. The difference in meaning is considerable. While the casting off of body and mind signifies a total existential experience, the metaphor of the dust suggests the image of a mirror, which reminds one of the unsatisfactory enlightenment verses of Shen-hsiu that are recorded in the *Sūtra of the Sixth Patriarch*. As I learned from an expert of the Sōtō school, it may have to do with a slip of the pen of a Chinese monk. The problem remains unresolved. In any case, the phrase "casting off of body and mind" has become part of the history of Dōgen's experience of enlightenment.

25.   See *Zuimonki*, Iwanami edition VI, p. 1 (Masunaga VI, p. 1), DDZ II, p. 419.

26.   *Shōbōgenzō bendōwa*, DZZ I, p. 729. English translation, EB 4.1 (1971): 130. See note 29 on the *Bendōwa*, book.

27.   DZZ II, pp. 3–6, 519–22. Cf. the essay on the *Fukanzazengi* by Suzuki Kakuzen in a study of Dōgen's writings that appeared as vol. 3 of the *Dōgen Kōza, Dōgen no chosaku* (Tokyo, 1980), pp. 189–215. Text-critical researches are also included. I have prepared a German translation in MN 14 (1958): 429–36. English translations include those by Norman Waddell and Abe Masao in EB 6.2 (1973): 115–28 and Francis Dojun Cook, *How to Raise an Ox: Zen Practice as Taught in Zen Master Dōgen's Shōbōgenzō*, pp. 95–99. The literary genre of the *Zazengi (Manual of Zazen Practice)* existed already long before Dōgen's time. Waddell and Abe speak in their introduction to the English edition of two or more texts circulating in China. Lan-hsi, founding abbot of Kenchō-ji in Kamakura (see chap. 1), edited a *Zazenron*. An instruction of Zen practice in the rule of Pai-chang (720–814) is especially important for the history of Zen (on Pai-chang see vol. 1 of the present work, especially pp. 170–172. The 1103 text of the *Zen'on shingi* (Chin., *Ch'an-yüan ch'ing kuei*) of Chang-lu Tsung-i, from the House of Yün-men, had a direct influence on Dōgen's text. Dōgen reported Tsung-i's differences from Pai-chang. See Waddell and Abe's introductory comments, pp. 115ff. The *Zazengi* and *Zazenshin* books of the *Shōbōgenzō* also treat *zazen*. The *Hōkyōki*, the diary Dōgen kept during his stay in China, also contains advice on *zazen*. This work has been translated several times into English; see N. Waddell, EB 10.2 (1977): 102–39 and 11.1 (1978): 66–84. See also the richly annotated edition of Kodera in *Dōgen's Formative Years in China*. Kodera edited the text in Chinese characters.

28.   English translation, EB 6.2 (1973): 115.

29.   DZZ I, pp. 729–63. The fine English translation by N. Waddell and Abe Masao can be found in EB 4.1 (1971): 124–57. The *Bendōwa* composed in Fukakusa in 1231, was first taken up in an edition of the *Shōbōgenzō* compiled into eighty-four volumes (later expanded to eighty-nine volumes) by the Sōtō monk Manzan Dōhaku (1635–1714). Later it appeared in the chronologically arranged and at the time standard Eiheiji edition (see note 99 below), in which it was placed first. Regarding a recently uncovered text dated 1515, which relies on the manuscript from 1332, see Waddell and Abe's introductory remarks to their English translation (p. 126).

Waddell and Abe render the title *Bendōwa* literally as *Discourse on Negotiating the Way*. In his translation of the *Gyōji* book, Francis Dojun Cook translates *bendō*, as well as similar expressions of Dōgen's, as "practice" (*How to Raise an Ox*, pp. 175–203). John C. Maraldo, in an essay on "The Hermeneutics of Practice in Dōgen and Francis of Assisi," shows that praxis in Dōgen does not stand in opposition to theory but signifies a particular form of performance. See EB 14.2 (1981): 22–44.

30.   DZZ I, p. 734. English translation by Waddell and Abe, EB 4.1 (1971): 140.

31.   See the brief biography in *Zengaku daijiten* I, p. 328.

32.   *Dōgen to chūgoku bukkyō*, p. 76, n. 19. See also his treatment of the *Shōbōgenzō zuimonki*, where he argues that the work breathes with the idealism of the young Dōgen and forms a transition to the Japanese style of speech.

33.   *Dōgen to chūgoku bukkyō*, p. 76.

34.   *Dōgen to chūgoku bukkyō*, p. 82.

35.   *Dōgen to chūgoku bukkyō*, pp. 81–82.

36.   See his essay, "The Incomparable Philosopher: Dōgen on How to Read the *Shō-bōgenzō*," in William LaFleur, ed., *Dōgen Studies* (Honolulu, 1985), pp. 84–85. See also Hee-Jin Kim, *Dōgen Kigen: Mystical Realist*, pp. 96–126. Dōgen's power of expression should not be overlooked as an element reinforcing his originality.

37.   DZZ I, pp. 59–63.

38.   DZZ I, pp. 536–38.

39.   DZZ I, pp. 246–57.

40.   See vol. 1, p. 93.

41.   See Yanagida Seizan, "Dōgen to Rinzai," *Risō* 513 (1976): 75.

42.   *Nihon bukkyō shisōshi no shomondai*, pp. 145–61.

43.   In his essay "Recarving the Dragon: History and Dogma in the Study of Dōgen" (W. LaFleur, ed., *Dōgen Studies* [Honolulu, 1985], pp. 21–53), Carl Bielefeldt describes the phases of Dōgen depth. In his view the decline begins around 1240–1241 (p. 29).

44.   *Zazenshin (Admonitions for Zazen, 1242)*, DZZ I, p. 96.

45.   DZZ I, p. 730; English translation, Waddell and Abe, EB 4.1 (1971): 132–33.

46.   DZZ II, pp. 489–90.

47.   DZZ I, p. 359.

48.   DZZ I, pp. 552, 554.

49.   DZZ I, p. 555. Regarding the translation of the difficult terms *kenshō* ("fine writings") and *reppeki* ("splendor of the gems"), see Kim, *Dōgen Kigen: Mystical Realist*, p. 153.

50.   DZZ, I, pp. 556ff.

51.   Cited in *Zen Dust*, p. 163–64.

52.   DZZ I, p. 557.

53.   See chap. 14 above.

54.   DZZ I, p. 595. On this controversy during the Sung period see vol. 1, pp. 256–261. Dōgen had high esteem for Hung-chih and cited him frequently in the *Zazenshin* book (see DDZ I, pp. 97–98).

55.   See DZZ I, p. 680. Imaeda Aishin treats Dōgen's critique of Ta-hui exhaustively in his presentation, *Dōgen: Zazen hitosuji no shamon* (Tokyo, 1976), and expresses his astonishment at "the harshness he feels to be unwonted" (p. 135).

56.   DZZ I, p. 126–27.

57.   DZZ I, p. 260. Cited from the *Sansuikyō* book (*The Sūtra of the Mountains and Waters*, 1240). This short text stands as a testimony to Dōgen's love of nature and his power of expression.

58.   DZZ I, p. 136.

59.   See the *Kattō* book (*Spiritual Entanglement*, 1243), DZZ I, p. 355.

60.   In the *Bukkyō* book (*The Buddhist Sūtras*, 1243), DZZ I, p. 409.

61.   In the *Mitsugo* book (*Secret Teaching*, 1243), DZZ I, p. 396.

62.   Cf. DZZ I, pp. 380, 409, 413.

63.   In the *Butsukōjōji* (*Continuous Development beyond Buddha*, 1242), DDZ I, p. 225.

64.   In the *Mujōseppō* (*Proclamation of the Law by Non-Sentient Beings*, 1243), DZZ I, p. 404.

65. In the *Daishugyō* (*Great Ascetical Practice*, 1244), DZZ I, pp. 545–46.

66. DZZ I, p. 486.

67. DZZ I, p. 486.

68 DZZ I, pp. 381, 409.

69. DZZ I, p. 381. Dōgen also carps at Lin-chi's use of the term "true human without rank." See DZZ I, p. 362.

70. DZZ I, p. 410.

71. See his *Dōgen to Rinzai*, p. 86.

72. See his *Dōgen to Rinzai*, p. 74.

73. DZZ I, p. 341. The text mentions explicitly the disciples of the schools of Lin-chi, Yün-men, and Tung-shan.

74. DZZ I, pp. 511–12.

75. I have generally translated the Chinese glyph *tsung* (in its Japanese reading, *shū* or *sō*) as "school," since the term "sect" has an unclear and typically Western meaning. The Chinese character means literally "ancestors." The *Dictionnaire Française de la Langue Chinoise* (Taipei, 1976) gives "sect" or "school" as a sixth meaning (p. 992). I use the term "sect" in the text because in this connection it seems to accord with ordinary usage.

76. DZZ I, p. 736; English translation, EB 4.2(1971):143.

77. DZZ I, p. 376.

78. DZZ I, p. 377.

79. See DZZ I, p. 378.

80. DZZ I, p. 380.

81. DZZ I, p. 380.

82. On the following see Yanagida, *Dōgen to Rinzai*, pp. 81–82. Cf. the monograph on Ju-ching by Kagamishima Genryū, *Tendō Nyojō Zenji no kenkyū* (Tokyo, 1983), which treats the collected sayings of Ju-ching on pp. 25–60.

83. DZZ I, p. 382.

84. Dōgen reads much into the fact that Lin-chi did not use terms like "house," "school," and "sect." See DZZ I, p. 384.

85. DZZ I, p. 379.

86. DZZ I, p. 386.

87. DZZ I, p. 386.

88. DZZ I, pp. 454ff.

89. DZZ I, p.345.

90. DZZ I, p. 559.

91. Bielefeldt uncovers a problem here: "We must expect Dōgen to reject as heterodox all Ch'an masters falling outside his own tradition. In fact, he does not." See his "Recarving the Dragon," p. 33. B. Faure correctly points to an uncritical bias that historians tend to fall into regarding words like "sect," "tradition," and "orthodoxy." See his "The Daruma-shū, Dōgen, and Sōtō Zen," MN 42.1 (1987): 52.

92. DZZ I, pp. 742ff; English translation, EB 4.1(1971): 51–52.

93. DZZ I, p. 42.

94. DZZ I, p. 45.

95.   Yanagida often points to this aspect; see for example *Dōgen to Rinzai*, p. 86; *Dōgen to chūgoku bukkyō*, p. 49. See also Imaeda, "Dōgen no shōgai," p. 136.

96.   DZZ I, pp. 446–53.

97.   Cited in Masunaga, *Eihei-Shōbōgenzō—Dōgen no shūkyō*, pp. 97–98.

98.   See the entire essay of Kawamura Kōdō on the *Shōbōgenzō* in *Dōgen no chosaku* (see note 27), pp. 1–73. The quotation appears on p. 58.

99.   The DZZ. The edition begins with the seventy-five old pieces ordered according to content by Dōgen, and is followed by the twelve and five books. Of nearly equal value is the ninety-five-volume edition of Kōzen (1627–1693), arranged in chronological order. It was first issued in 1690 as the Eihei-ji edition and has been reprinted numerous times since until the appearance of a three-volume edition edited by Etō Sokuō (Tokyo: Iwanami Bunko, 1939–1943). This Eihei-ji edition was prohibited during the second half of the Edo period because of the appearances of divergent versions, but was widely used nonetheless. In 1796 the fiftieth abbot of Eihei-ji, Gentō Sokuchū (1729–1807) succeeded in obtaining permission to print the work and made preparations for a new printing. When it was completed in 1811, a few books were not included. Only during the Meiji period, in 1906, did the authoritative edition appear in its complete form; it is known as the Daihonzan-Eihei-ji edition. Also deserving of mention are two early editions, one of seventy-five books overseen by Ejō (1198–1280) and Sen'e (n. d.) and annotated by Kyōgō (n. d.), and another edition of sixty books attributed to Giun (1253–1333), the fifth abbot of Eihei-ji but in any case compiled by Ejō (see Kawamura Kōdō's exhaustive study, *Shōbōgenzō no seiritsushiteki kenkyū* [Tokyo, 1986], pp. 449–61). The edition of Taiyō Bonsei in eighty-four books dates from the year 1419. Besides the details presented in Kawamura's essay (see note 98), see *Zen Dust*, pp. 396–97; and my comments on the transmission of the text of the *Shōbōgenzō* in the introduction to a German translation of the *Genjōkōan*, MN 15 (1959–60): 217ff.

100.   On the two versions of the *Shōbōgenzō*, different in aim and execution, see the detailed treatment of Kawamura, *Shōbōgenzō no seiritsushiteki kenkyū*. See also the section devoted to this subject in Yanagida Seizan's *Dōgen to chūgoku bukkyō*, pp. 97–126.

101.   See *Shōbōgenzō sambyakusoku*, 3 volumes, DZZ II, pp. 201–52.

102.   Some one-hundred cases of the *Shōbōgenzō sambyakusoku* correspond to passages of the *Wanshi kōroku* of Hung-chih Cheng-chüeh (1091–1157) of the Ts-ao-tung line. See Yanagida, *Dōgen to chūgoku bukkyō*, p. 102.

103.   Ta-hui Tsung-kao completed a different collection of Dōgen's work at the age of 59. It appears that he chose the title in memory of an admonition of Lin-chi not to forget the *Shōbōgenzō*. See Yanagida, *Dōgen to chūgoku bukkyō*, pp. 102, 110. Dōgen recalls this saying of Lin-chin in the *Butsudō*, DZZ I, p. 384.

104.   Yanagida characterizes the study of the *Kambun-shōbōgenzō* as indispensable for the study of Dōgen. "This is easily said," he writes, "but quick results are hardly to be expected. It is taxing work that one cannot undertake on one's own. It requires a group effort from the start by a team of scholars of different specializations" (*Dōgen to chūgoku bukkyō*, p. 125).

105.   See Ryōsuke Ōhashi and Hans Brockard in "Das Buch Genjōkōan aus dem Buch *Shōbōgenzō* von Dōgen: Übersetzung und Erläuterungen," *Philosophisches Jahrbuch* 83 (1976): 402–15, citation on p. 405. In their translation of the *Genjōkōan*, Waddell and Abe find that "the words themselves are impossible to give adequate English translation" (EB 5.2

[1972]: 130). They do argue, however, that literally the term *genjō* can mean "becoming manifest" or "immediately manifesting." "Dōgen uses the term *kōan*," they go on, "differently from the traditional Rinzai Zen meaning of a 'problem' given by a Zen master to a practicer to lead him to self-awakening. According to the earliest existing commentary on the *Shōbōgenzō*, by Kyōgō [see note 99], the *kō* of *kōan* means sameness or ultimate equality that is beyond equality and inequality, and *an* refers to 'keeping to one's sphere.' . . . Accordingly, the term *genjōkōan* points to ultimate reality in which all things are distinctively individual, and yet equal in the presence of their suchness." In similar fashion, Akizuki Ryōmin explains in his introductory work, *Dōgen nyūmon* (Tokyo, 1970): "*Kō* means likeness. To make what is unlike like is called *kō*. *An* signifies the preservation of its portion (i.e., difference). The preservation of the portion is called *an*." *Kōan* therefore means the simultaneous recognition of likeness and difference, or the oneness of the absolute and the phenomenal (see pp. 186–87).

106.   The same holds for the title of the *Genjōkōan* (see note 105).

107.   *Bi-yüan-lu* II, p. 311.

108.   "Dōgen's Lehre von Sein-Zeit" (a translation of the *Uji* book of the *Shōbōgenzō*) in *Festschrift Medard Boss*, p. 173. Miura and Sasaki translate the general title as "Treasury of the True Dharma Eye." See *Zen Dust*, p. 198.

109.   See for example the *Genjōkōan, Busshō, Uji*, and *Kokū* volumes.

110.   The earliest commentary on the *Shōbōgenzō*, edited by Kyōgō, who had already known Dōgen personally, was completed in 1308. More than four centuries went by before another commentary, the *Shōbōgenzō benchū* by Tenkei Senson (d. 1735), appeared. The work, completed in 1730, was only printed in 1881. In Chinese there appeared a fourteen-volume work, *Shōbōgenzō kyakutai ichijisan* (abbreviated as *Sanchū* or *Sanbon*), by Katsudō Honkō (completed 1712, printed 1812). Menzan Zuihō (d. 1769) wrote an encyclopedia on Dōgen's work entitled *Shōbōgenzō shōtenroku;* whether he authored another work, *Shōbōgenzō monge*, transcribed by his disciple Fuzan Genshutsu (during the An'ei period, 1772–1781) is uncertain. The importance of this latter work is due in part to its sharp critique of the commentary of Tenkei Denson, against which Banjin Dōtan (d. 1775) expressly aimed his own commentary, *Shōbōgenzō benbenchū* (1766). There followed several other commentaries. The final commentary of the Edo period was the *Shōbōgenzō naippō* by Fuyō Rōran (d. 1805). The lectures of the important Sōtō master of the Meiji period, Nishiari Bokuzan (d. 1910), were written down by his disciple Tomiyama Soei and issued as *Shōbōgenzō keiteki*. At the beginning of the twentieth century the two Zen scholars Jimbō Nyoten and Andō Bun'ei produced the standard work *Shōbōgenzō chūkai* (1913–1914). The eight-volume collection *Shōbōgenzō shisōtaikei* by Okada Gihō, the former president of Komazawa University, represents an important commentary on Dōgen's work. See the detailed account of commentaries on the *Shōbōgenzō* in the introduction to my translation of the *Genjōkōan* in MN 15 (1960): 219–22.

111.   We may begin by noting the well annotated translations of Norman Waddell and Abe Masao that have appeared in the pages of *The Eastern Buddhist* as follows: *Bendōwa* 4.1 (1971): 124–57; *Ikka myōju* 4.2 (1971): 108–18; *Zenki* and *Shōji* 5.1 (1972): 70–80; *Genjōkōan* 5.2 (1972): 129–40; *Sammai-ō-zammai* 7.1 (1974): 118–23; and *Busshō* 8.2 (1975): 94–112, 9.1 (1976): 87–105, 9.2 (1976): 71–87. See also Waddell's translation of the *Uji*, EB 12.1 (1979): 114–29. An unannotated English translation of the entire work was published by Kōsen Nishiyama and John Stevens in three volumes (Sendai, 1975—1983). As stated in a translator's note, the translation makes no claim to be literal but "intends to be a combination of translation, commentary, and paraphrase" (xxii).

Yūhō Yokoi (with Daizen Victoria) has published *Master Dōgen: An Introduction with Selected Writings* (Tokyo, 1976), which contains the *Fukanzazengi* and *Gakudōyōjinshū* as well as the twelve books of the so-called "new manuscript" (*shinsō*, see note 99 above and accompanying text). The English translation of the seventy-five books of the "old manuscript" and the five books of the appendix (see note 99), which Yokoi Yūhō brought out in five volumes in 1986, unfortunately does not measure up to the quality of the earlier work. Francis Dojun Cook has translated the *Keisei sanshoku, Hotsu mujōshin, Shukke, Raihai tokuzui, Shunjū, Shinjin inga, Nyorai zenshin, Gyōji,* and *Kajō* books in his *How to Raise an Ox.* Only two books (*Genjōkōan* and *Uji*) have been published in German (see notes 105 and 108). Hoang-Thi-Bich has published a study of the *Gakudōyōjinshū*, with translation, in French (Paris, 1973).

112. DZZ I, p. 377.

113. The *Fukanzazengi* exists in two versions. An early text of 1227 is available in Dōgen's own hand and dated 1233. In a second text (called *rufubon*) further changes are introduced by Dōgen. This latter text is more mature and expressive. The confrontation with Tsung-i (see note 27 above) is further developed. The translation given here—based on an earlier German translation in MN 14 (1958): 431–32—was made from a holograph of the early text, whereas the English translations of Waddell and Abe, Yūhō Yokoi, and F. D. Cook present the text of the *rufubon.* Suzuki Kakuzen compares the condition of the two texts in his essay (see note 27). The standard edition uses the holograph text, DZZ II, pp. 3–6, and gathers together material related to textual changes in an explanatory appendix, pp. 519–22.

114. *Ta-chih-tu lun* (Jpn., *Daichidoron*), book 7. (This work, a commentary on the *Mahāprajñāpāramitā Sūtra,* is inextant in Sanskrit.) See also *Bendōwa,* DZZ I, pp. 736–37. As to why sitting is preeminent among the four positions (walking, standing, sitting, lying), Dōgen relies on Buddhist tradition.

115. *Bendōwa,* DZZ I, p. 733. On the notion of *jijuyū-zammai,* see the explanation of Waddell and Abe, EB 4.1 (1971): 128–29; translation, *ibid.,* p. 138.

116. DZZ I, p. 96. This kōan also appears in *Dōgen Oshō kōroku* (or *Eihei kōroku*), a voluminous text consisting mainly of a collection of the sayings of Dōgen; see DZZ II, pp. 7–200, and the kōan in the fifth collection, p. 88. On the *Eihei kōroku* see the essay by Sakai Tokugen in *Dōgen no chosaku,* pp. 75–117. Dōgen finds in the kōan the essence of Zen. The unmoving posture of sitting cross-legged (in the kōan *gotsu-gotchi, gotsu* means literally "upright, soaring upwards alone") is the proper Dharma position. The differentiation of the meaning between the two expressions *fu-shiryō* and *hi-shiryō* is virtually impossible to render in Western languages. Linguistically, both contain a negation. Etō Tarō translates *fu-shiryō* as the "unthinkable" or "that which cannot be thought" (in the negative sense), while *hi-shiryō* in his view, which he bases on old commentaries, means simply "the beyond." See his essay on Dōgen's philosophy and Heidegger in the Japanese journal *Risō* 349 (1962): 2. Japanese commentators stress that *hi-shiryō* points to the final sense of reality. T. Sakai writes: "This *hi* is not a negation . . . but expresses a reality that transcends all things human" (*Dōgen no chosaku,* p. 107).

In a section of his book *Zen Action/Zen Person* entitled "Thinking, Not-Thinking, Without-Thinking" (pp. 71–77), T. Kasulis offers three explanations of the terms, first with reference to Takahashi Masanobu, according to which not-thinking is a denial of thinking and without-thinking a going beyond thinking and not-thinking. As he illustrates with a quotation from a commentary on Dōgen by Terada Tōru and Mizuno Yaoko, "without-thinking" comes close to the notion of "emptiness," or *śūnyatā.* This explanation is, as already noted, common in Dōgen literature. I have followed it above. A second explanation according to Akiyama Hanji assumes "a dialectical relation between the three terms." "Without-thinking" sublates thinking and not-thinking and is that which binds the two together. Akiyama's studies on Dōgen bring the dialectical aspect—in the Western philosophical sense—to bear, a view not without its critics today, particularly in the Sōtō school. Dōgen's thought no doubt contains a dialectical moment as do the kōan, but does not for that reason admit of being forced into a dialectical philosophy like that of Hegel, for instance. Kasulis concludes with a third explanation, which does not exclude the first, that includes a longer and attentive treatment of the relation of the three terms to states of consciousness. Without-thinking too, even though it "circumvents all objectification," is in his view also a mode of consciousness, and indeed "a nonconceptual or prereflective mode of consciousness." The states of consciousness described by Kasulis seem to approach closer to "objectless meditation" as described in the text of the present work.

117.   DZZ II, p. 458. English translation, Masunaga, A *Primer of Sōtō Zen*, p. 47.

118.   A *Primer of Sōtō Zen*, p. 47.

119.   DZZ I, p. 740. English translation, EB 4.1 (1970): 146–47; see also note 80.

120.   DZZ I, p. 778–79. On the *Shōji*, see notes 204–206 below and the accompanying text.

121.   DZZ I, p. 779; English translation, EB 5.1. (1972): 80. In the text, which is mainly an expression of the Buddhist ethic of compassion, there are echoes of the Confucian norms of "above" and "below."

122.   *Bendōwa*, DZZ I, p. 737; English translation, EB 4.1 (1970): p. 143. See "Indivisibility of Practice and Enlightenment" in R. K. Heinemann, *Der Weg des Übens im ostasiatischen Mahāyāna: Grundformen seiner Zeitrelation zum Übungsziel in der Entwicklung bis Dōgen* (Wiesbaden, 1979), pp. 147–49. The linguistic studies of Heinemann are helpful for the reading of Dōgen (see the four entries in OE, 15.1 and 2, 16.2 and 18.1.

123.   *Fukanzazengi*, DZZ II, p. 3; English translation, EB 6.2 (1973): 123.

124.   Compare the essay by Abe Masao, "Dōgen on Buddha Nature" in EB 4.1 (1971): 28–71, and my essay "Die religiöse Metaphysik des japanischen Zen-Meisters Dōgen," *Saeculum* 12 (1961): 205–36. In the standard edition, the book on the Buddha nature appears in DZZ I, pp. 14–35.

125.   DZZ I, p. 14.

126.   DZZ I, p. 27; English translation, EB 9.2 (1976): 72.

127.   DZZ I, p. 16; English translation, EB 8.2 (1975): 102.

128.   *Sokushin zebutsu (This Mind is Buddha)*, DZZ I, p. 43.

129.   DZZ I, p. 739; English translation, EB 4.1 (1971): 146.

130.   DZZ I, p. 15; English translation, EB 8.2 (1975): 100.

131.   DZZ I, p. 15; English translation, EB 8.2 (1975): 102.

132.   DZZ I, p. 17; English translation, EB 8.2 (1975): 108.

133.   DZZ I, p. 22; English translation, EB 9.1 (1976): 94.

134.   DZZ I, p. 18; English translation, EB 8.2 (1975): 108.

135.   DZZ I, p. 18; English translation, EB 8.2 (1975): 108.

136.   DZZ I, p. 19; English translation, EB 8.2 (1975): 111.

137.   DZZ I, p. 18; English translation, EB 8.2 (1975): 111.

138.   DZZ I, p. 18; English translation, EB 8.2 (1975): 111.

139.   DZZ I, p. 198; English translation, EB 9.1 (1976): 87.

140.   See the note 5 in the second part of the translation in EB 9.1 (1976): 88.

141.   DZZ I, p. 20; English translation, EB 9.1 (1976): 89.

142.   DZZ I, p. 20; English translation, EB 9.1 (1976): 90.

143.   DZZ I, p. 27; English translation, EB 9.2 (1976): 73.

144.   DZZ I, p. 27; English translation, EB 9.2 (1976): 73.

145.   DZZ I, p. 28; English translation, EB 9.2 (1976): 74.

146.   DZZ I, p. 28; English translation, EB 9.2 (1976): 74.

147.   DZZ I, p. 28; English translation, EB 9.2 (1976): 75–76.

148.   DZZ I, p. 21; English translation, EB 9.1 (1976): 91.

149.   DZZ I, p. 21; English translation, EB 9.1 (1976): 91.

150.   DZZ I, p. 21; English translation, EB 9.1 (1976): 92.

151.   DZZ I, p. 21; English translation, EB 9.1 (1976): 93.

152.   *Sesshin sesshō*, DZZ I, pp. 358–59. On this see Hee-Jin Kim, *Dōgen Kigen*, pp. 153–54.

153.   According to the colophon it was edited in 1233 and after later revision and improvement was placed by Dōgen at the head of the seventy-five books he singled out shortly before his death (see note 99). This permits us to conclude, as Abe and Waddell do in the introduction to their English translation, that he himself considered the text "an essential way into his religious world of thought" (EB 5.2 [1972]: 129ff). See also the introduction to my German rendition in MN 15 (1959–60): 219ff.

154.   DZZ I, p. 7; English translation, EB 5.2 (1972): 133.

155.   DZZ I, pp. 7–8; English translation, EB 5.2 (1972): 134–35. There follow two sentences that round off the text: "The very moment one begins to seek the Dharma he becomes far removed from its environs. When the Dharma has been rightly transmitted to one, he is at once the person of his original part." T. Kasulis analyzes the text in his section on "Dōgen on the Self," *Zen Action/Zen Person*, pp. 87–93. He translates the final word, *honbunnin*, as "the primordial person," Kasulis sets Dōgen's "primordial person" alongside Rinzai's "true person of no status" *(mui shinnin)*. On this see vol. 1 of the present work, p. 191–197. The comparison between the anthropology of Rinzai and Dōgen needs to be pursued further. In a book entitled *Rinzai to Dōgen* published in 1971, Masutani Fumio puts the psychological aspect in the foreground. Dōgen showed a strong interest in the great Chinese master, whom he "considers, expounds, and criticizes" in fourty-six places in the *Shōbōbenzō* (Masutani, pp. 20–21). Masutani dates the change of attitude to the year 1243, the year in which Dōgen first judged Lin-chi critically. He sees in this shift "an altogether clear mirroring of the intellectual development of Dōgen" (p. 30). The psychological difference between the two masters is clear to see. But Yanagida rightly notes that the two were "in fundamental agreement" (p. 75) since they shared common roots in the Mahāyāna understanding of the world and human nature. Yanagida further takes up the question in a contribution to vol. 6 of the collection *Kōza Dōgen*, *Bukkyōgaku to Dōgen* in the literary form of a fictional dialog between Rinzai and Dōgen (pp. 104–30).

156.   DZZ I, pp. 189–94. See the English translation by Norman Waddell in EB 12.1 (1979): 114–29; German translation by Kōichi Tsujimura in *Festschrift Medard Boss*, pp. 172–201.

157. DZZ I, p. 189; English translation, EB 12.1 (1979), p. 16.

158. DZZ I, pp. 189–90; English translation, EB 12.1 (1979), p. 117. This passage recalls Augustine's profound reflections on time in the *Confessions*.

159. DZZ I, p. 190; English translation, EB 12.1 (1979), pp. 117–18.

160. *Ibid.*

161. Tsujimura translation (note 156), p. 188, note 23.

162. DZZ I, p. 191; English translation, EB 12.1 (1979), pp. 120–21.

163. See the section "The True Human Without Rank" in vol. 1 of the present work, pp. 191–197.

164. DZZ I, p. 191; English translation, EB 12.1 (1979): 121–22.

165. DZZ I, p. 8; English translation, EB 5.2 (1972): 136.

166. DZZ I, p. 191–92; English translation, EB 12.1 (1979): 122. The expression *kappatsu patsuji*, which Abe and Waddell translate simply as "sharp, vital, quick," uses onomatopoeia to liken the living origination of the Dharma to the flopping about of a fish. It appears in the *Discourses of Lin-chi*. See vol. 1 of the present book, chap. 10, notes 53 and 54.

167. The full title is *Eihei shoso gakudōyōjinshū*, DZZ II, pp. 253–60. In addition to an English translation by Yūhō Yokoi, there is a French translation by Hoang-Thi-Bich (see note 111 above).

168. DZZ II, p. 260; English translation, Yokoi, *Zen Master Dōgen*, p. 57. Compare Etō Sokuō, *Shūso to shite no Dōgen Zenji*, pp. 223ff.

169. DZZ I, p. 507.

170. DZZ I, p. 733; English translation, EB 4.1 (1971): 138.

171. *Shukke*, DZZ I, pp. 597–99; *Shukke kudoku*, DZZ I, pp. 603–17. *Shukke* describes both leaving home (the literal sense of the characters) as well as the monk who sets off in homelessness; *kudoku* means merit.

172. DZZ I, p. 597; English translation, Cook, *How to Raise an Ox*, p. 127. In the order of the monk's life Dōgen relies on the Chinese model. Like Eisai he cites from the earliest complete Chinese monastic rules, the *Ch'an-yüan ch'ing-kuei*, which he ascribes to Pai-chang. See Collcutt, *Five Mountains*, p. 149.

173. *Jukai*, DZZ I, pp. 619–22.

174. *Shukke kudoku*, DZZ I, p. 608; English translation, Yokoi, *Zen Master Dōgen*, p. 75.

175. DZZ I, pp. 611; English translation, Yokoi, *Zen Master Dōgen*, p. 77.

176. Cf. DZZ I, p. 603; English translation, Yokoi, *Zen Master Dōgen*, p. 69.

177. DZZ I, pp. 612–613; English translation, Yokoi, *Zen Master Dōgen*, p. 78.

178. DZZ I, p. 617; English translation, Yokoi, *Zen Master Dōgen*, p. 83.

179. *Shukke*, DZZ I, p. 597; English translation, Cook, *How to Raise an Ox*, pp. 127–28.

180. DZZ I, pp. 623–44. The robe was called a Dharma robe (*ehō*) and also a "robe of liberation" (*gedatsufuku*) by Dōgen.

181. DZZ I, p. 638; English translation, Yokoi, *Zen Master Dōgen*, p. 102 (translation adjusted).

182. DZZ I, pp. 642–43; English translation, Yokoi, *Zen Master Dōgen*, pp. 105–106.

183. DZZ I, p. 501; English translation, Cook, *How to Raise an Ox*, p. 210.

184. The standard edition of Ōkubo Dōshū presents twelve texts under the title *Shingi*; see DZZ II, pp. 293–367.

185. DZZ II, pp. 348–58.

186. DZZ I, pp. 499–500. In the text Dōgen calls his master Ju-ching "the old Buddha." One of the books of the *Shōbōgenzō* also treats the begging bowl, *hou*, DZZ I, pp. 565–67; English translation, Cook, *How to Raise an Ox*, p. 207.

187. The two books are the *Senmen (Washing the Face)* and its appendix, *Senmen betsubon*, DZZ I, pp. 424–45, and the *Senjō (Rules for the Lavatory)*, DZZ I, pp. 464–74. Hee-Jin Kim gives extensive treatment to the important role of purification in Dōgen's monastic asceticism; see *Dōgen Kigen*, pp. 234ff.

188. *Senmen*, DZZ I, p. 426.

189. DZZ I, pp. 426–27.

190. M. Collcutt, *Five Mountains*, p. 205.

191. See Kim, *Dōgen Kigen*, p. 236.

192. DZZ II, pp. 295–303.

193. DZZ II, p. 300.

194. Compare the section "Zazen as the Focus of a Buddhist Spirituality" in my *Zen Enlightenment*, pp. 95–101.

195. DZZ I, pp. 667–75; quotation on p. 667; English translation, Yokoi, *Zen Master Dōgen*, p. 128.

196. DZZ I, pp. 669; English translation, Yokio, *Zen Master Dōgen*, pp. 129–30.

197. *Shōbōgenzō zuimonki*, DZZ II, p. 428; Masunaga, *A Primer of Sōtō Zen*, p. 5.

198. DZZ I, pp. 652–66.

199. DZZ I, pp. 656–57; English translation, Yokoi, *Zen Master Dōgen*, p. 118.

200. DZZ I, pp. 658–59; English translation, Yokoi, *Zen Master Dōgen*, p. 119.

201. The story is related in book 14 of the Zen chronicle *Keitoku dentōroku* and has found its way into common Zen tradition. Generalizations in Western literature, above all deductions, are often unwarranted.

202. *Shōbōgenzō zuimonki*, DZZ II, p. 428; Masunaga, *A Primer of Sōtō Zen*, p. 5.

203. DZZ I, pp. 537; English translation, Cook, *How to Raise an Ox*, p. 173. See Cook's chapter on the scriptures (pp. 63–71). He finds not only a reverence for the written word in Dōgen but even thinks that in Dōgen's view "reading the sūtra is an important condition for our attainment of *satori*" (p.69).

204. DZZ I, pp. 778–79; English translation Waddell and Abe, EB 5.1 (1972): 70–80.

205. Waddell and Abe draw attention to certain difficulties related to authenticity, arguing that the authenticity of the text was acknowledged at the time by the majority of Japanese scholars (EB 5.1 [1972]: 72). A detailed study on this question by Kawamura Kōdō, under the title *Shōbōgenzōkenkyū josetsu*, treats the authenticity and the content of the *Shōji* in separate sections. Kawamura takes issue with the scholar Itō Yūten, who offers critical grounds internal and external to the Sōtō sect (to which he belongs) against authenticity. His researches appear in Komazawa University's *Journal of the Faculty of Buddhism* 23 (1965): 109–25 and 24 (1966): 52–72.

206. Kawamura stresses that the *Shōji* is not a secret text, even though it was long stored with arcane materials in the monastery of Eihei-ji. In his view it was composed for Buddhist laity but because of the distinctness of its style was not transmitted with other books of the *Shōbōgenzō* (ibid., 23: 112, 116, 117).

207. DZZ I, pp. 202–205. Waddell and Abe write: "The word *zenki*, which we have translated here as 'total dynamic working' and also 'total dynamism,' lacks any truly satisfactory English equivalent." EB 5.1 (1972): 71.

208. DZZ I, p. 778; English translation, Waddell and Abe, EB 5.1 (1972): 79.

209. DZZ I, p. 740; English translation, Waddell and Abe, EB 4.1 (1971): 147. Compare the entire section on the answer to the tenth question.

210. DZZ I, pp. 778–79; English translation, Waddell and Abe, EB 5.1 (1972): 79.

211. DZZ I, pp. 778–79; English translation, Waddell and Abe, EB 5.1 (1972): 79. One notes the use of the passive mood in this passage, which defies literal translation. Akiyama Hanji takes it into account in his explanation of Dōgen's form of faith to conclude: "If I am not mistaken, faith is wrought by the Buddha." See *Dōgen no kenkyū* (Nagoya, 1965), p. 324. Akiyama's studies are perhaps the first impressive work on Dōgen after his rediscovery in Japan by Watsuji Tetsurō, whose famous essay "Shamon Dōgen" first appeared in 1926. Akiyama gives a comprehensive presentation in the third volume of the five-volume popular *Dōgen-Zen* (Tokyo, 1961), which was produced with the assistance of Watsuji. Akiyama's volume treats Dōgen idea of the human.

212. From the commentary to the English translation, EB 5.1 (1972): 80.

213. On the following see also the second part of his *Shōbōgenzō kenkyū josetsu*, no. 24, pp. 66ff.

214. *Shōbōgenzō kenkyū josetsu*, no. 24, pp. 65, 68.

215. DZZ I, pp. 525–26; English translation, Cook, *How to Raise an Ox*, pp. 116–17.

216. DZZ I, pp. 525–26; English translation, Cook, *How to Raise an Ox*, pp. 116–17.

217. *Hotsu bodaishin*, DZZ I, pp. 645–46; Yokoi, *Zen Master Dōgen*, p. 107.

218. See the chapters "The Importance of Faith" and "Arousing the Thought of Enlightenment" in Cook, *How to Raise an Ox*, pp. 19–32 and 33–47. The quotation appears on p. 25.

219. Cook, *How to Raise an Ox*, pp. 34–35. Cook stresses emphatically that "Dōgen's Zen is a Buddhism of faith" and calls on Japanese scholars like Akiyama Hanji and Okada Gihō for support (p. 26). One cannot but agree with his characterization of faith as "faith in the Buddha." Cook concludes: "One must also have faith in the teachings of Buddhism, but are these not merely verbal expressions of the Buddha mind. Also, and most important of all, one must have faith in one's own intrinsic Buddha nature, for Zen teaches that all things are the Buddha" (pp. 21–22).

220. DZZ I, p. 646; English translation, Yokoi, *Zen Master Dōgen*, p. 107.

221. DZZ I, p. 650; English translation, Yokoi, *Zen Master Dōgen*, p. 111.

222. H. Nakamura, *Ways of Thinking of Eastern Peoples*, p. 485. Nakamura states earlier that "Dōgen does emphasize the significance of faith just as do the partisans of Pure Land Buddhism." In his view, Dōgen's idea is that "rather than achieve enlightenment through one's ascetic practices, one should, in the final analysis, have absolute devotion to the Buddha as an ideal person and *be saved by him*" (p. 457). In Dōgen one finds unmistakable steps in the direction of the personal.

223.   Two books are often cited together as literary representatives of the Kamakura period: the *Shōbōgenzō zuimonki* of Dōgen and the *Tan'ishō* of Shinran. Nichiren, the militant prophet, left behind a legacy of correspondence that shows his religious depth as well.

224.   See Imaeda Aishin, *Dōgen: zazen hitosuji no shamon*, p. 173.

225.   Critics have pointed out that Dōgen's main work, the *Shōbōgenzō*, lay for approximately four centuries virtually unnoticed in the storehouse of Eihei-ji. At first, difficulties within the Sōtō school, which shall be taken up in the next chapter, may have suffocated interest in his written legacy. Then again, perhaps the preference of the Japanese middle ages for arcane literary and religious traditions had a role to play. Finally, the predominance of Chinese *kambun* that Neo-Confucianism inspired in the modern period must have had an additional impact on the work, which was written in the Japanese *kana* script.

226.   See Kim, *Dōgen Kigen: Mystical Realist*, pp. 96–126, where the point is explained amply.

227.   Abe Masao, a pioneer of Dōgen research known for his first-rate translation of several of the books of the *Shōbōgenzō*, shared my early fascination with Dōgen and encouraged me in my work. Abe also shared with me at the outset an unclouded appreciation of his thought. He described Dōgen as "one of the most outstanding and unique Buddhists in the history of Japanese Buddhism," adding that his speculative and philosophical nature makes him unique in the history of Japanese Buddhism. Regarding his powers of expression, Abe saw him as endowed with keen linguistic sensibility and a philosophical mind, concluding that "his main work [*Shōbōgenzō*], . . . perhaps unsurpassable in its philosophical speculation, is a monumental document in Japanese intellectual history." See EB 4.1 (1971): 28–29. I suppose that like me, Abe would qualify these remarks today, without minimizing the significance of Dōgen.

The renowned Japanese philosopher, Nishitani Keiji, whose work has recently begun to attract attention in Western intellectual circles, displays high regard for Dōgen as a religious thinker and as a representative of Buddhist philosophy. See his *Religion and Nothingness* (Berkeley, 1982), esp. pp. 178–81, 184–93, 196, 198–99, 261–62, and 264.

3

The Sōtō School after Dōgen

DŌGEN AND HIS DISCIPLES

One of the main reasons the Zen that Dōgen brought to Japan from China had such a difficult time establishing itself as an independent religious community in Japan concerns his disciples. Although the great Zen master and thinker was spiritual guide to countless serious religious seekers and abbot of a flourishing monastic community, he cannot be considered the founder of an independent religious movement. As noted in the previous chapter, he himself rejected all talk of sects or schools in order to concentrate totally on preaching the "Buddhism of the authentic Dharma" (shōbō no bukkyō).

Be that as it may, the school that honors him as its founder came to be called the "Sōtō school," or more precisely, the "Japanese Sōtō school" to distinguish it from the Chinese Sōtō school that developed from one of the Five Houses. The Chinese House of Ts'ao-tung (Jpn., Sōtō) took the first character of its name from Ts'ao-shan Pen-chi (Jpn., Sōzan Honjaku, 840–901), while the line of Ju-ching, to which Dōgen belonged, traced its origins to Yün-chü Tao-ying (Jpn., Ungo Dōyō, d. 902), the Dharma brother of Ts'ao-shan. The first character in its name, Sō, was drawn from the first character in the name of the seat of the Sixth Patriarch, that is Ts'ao-hsi (Jpn., Sōkei) in Kuang-tung;[1] the second character tō was the same in the Japanese and Chinese name. Japanese authors avoid using the term Sōtō Zen to refer to Dōgen, preferring to speak of the movement originating from him as "Dōgen-Zen."[2]

In order to gain a proper understanding of the origins and development of the Sōtō school one must take into consideration the decisive influence of Dōgen's disciples.[3] Already during the early stages of his activity in Kyoto and its neighboring areas, Dōgen attracted many friends and followers. Like all great Zen masters, he was driven by the zeal of the bodhisattva mind to save all sentient beings wandering in the transient world of suffering and was indeed able to lead many along the way of liberation and enlightenment. But he had no interest in numbers. Just as he himself aspired to what was highest, what he prized most in his followers was the quality of their efforts, which he found to cut across the lines of social class. The circle of disciples that formed around Dōgen included high class and low, young and old, men and women, laity and monks. His largest group of followers gathered around him during his years at Kōshō-ji near Kyoto. It was a time when Dōgen's penetrating intellect was best balanced by a gentle and sensitive heart open to all. Later his idealism turned to the rigors of monastic discipline. During the last decades of his life, in the rural solitude of Echizen, he was primarily a teacher and a master for his monastic community. Under his direction, the monastery at Eihei-ji became a center of Buddhist monasticism. In this sense, developments in his personality were mirrored in the circle of disciples, composed of widely divergent elements, that formed around him.

After his return from China, Dōgen remained for a time at Kennin-ji in Kyoto, with which he had been familiar from his younger days. Most of the people who came to him for spiritual direction there were women. Curiously one of his lay pupils was a certain Myōchi, the mother of a pious woman devoted heart and soul to the Buddha-Dharma, who was to give birth to Keizan, the patriarch of the Sōtō school in its fourth generation.[4] It was at this time, too, that he first met Koun Ejō (1198–1280), the first member of the Japanese Daruma school to come to Dōgen (1229). We will have more to say about this encounter in a section devoted to Ejō. Dōgen received his visitor cordially but was not able to accept him as a disciple since the conditions that he deemed necessary for a genuine practice of Zen were not present at Kennin-ji.

Things changed when Dōgen moved to Fukakusa near Kyoto, where in 1236 he established the monastery of Kōshō-ji, including a monks' hall. Here Ejō ranked first among the disciples. The difference in age between the two friends is noteworthy. Ejō was fifty-four, two years older than his master, at the time of Dōgen's death. Although they belonged to the same generation, Ejō succeeded Dōgen as patriarch of the second generation. The third generation was made up of disciples who had all had both Dōgen and Ejō as master and superior, a circumstance that turned out to be important for the early history of the Japanese Sōtō school.

There is no need to offer a comprehensive list of Dōgen's disciples.[5] Especially important for the development of the Sōtō community were the members of the Japanese Daruma school of Dainichi Nōnin, who, after the example and probably the encouragement of their colleague Ejō, joined Dōgen's Zen community in 1241. Their leader was Ekan, a serious and reliable devotee of the Dharma whom Dōgen regarded highly and whom he later appointed "Monk of the First Seat" at Eihei-ji. Ekan was most likely older that the other disciples who came to Dōgen from the Daruma school. The date of his birth is unknown, but we do know that he died during Dōgen's lifetime without really having been able to adjust to Dōgen's special style of Zen.[6]

Accompanying Ekan to Kōshō-ji were Tettsū Gikai (1219–1309), Gien (d. 1314), Gijun (n. d.), Kangan Giin (1217–1300), and other members of the Daruma school who decided to follow in the footsteps of so many of their confreres. The influx of such a strong and well-formed group certainly exercised a marked influence on Dōgen's community. This influence became evident only toward the end of Ejō's life and during the third generation, as we shall see when we examine the role of Gikai, the Third Patriarch of the school. Gien, the fourth abbot of Eihei-ji, was also to be a central figure in the dramatic events of those days.

Kangan Giin, of imperial blood, deserves special note.[7] He was still a boy when he set out on his spiritual quest, receiving his first ordination at sixteen and devoting himself thereafter to the study of the sūtras. Eventually he turned to Zen. The widespread view that he had also been a member of the Daruma school is not definite. He set out on a trip to China in 1242, but upon hearing news of Dōgen's death turned back to pay the master his last respects.

During a second trip to China (1264–1267) Giin showed some of Dōgen's writings to Chinese friends of Zen who praised them highly. Giin later founded the monastery of Daiji-ji in the region of Higo (Kumamoto, Kyūshū), where he combined Zen meditation with other Buddhist practices. While this resulted in some weakening of the pure Zen spirit, his life's work is an example of how Dōgen's influence was spreading throughout the country.

It was after being deeply moved by one of Dōgen's lectures that Sen'e (n. d.), a learned monk from Mount Hiei, converted to Zen and went on to offer the master valuable literary assistance.[8] After Dōgen's death he edited a number of volumes of the *Eihei kōroku*, but is best remembered for being the first to produce a commentary on the seventy-five volumes of the *Shōbōgenzō* based on lectures he delivered at Yōkō-ji, a monastery he had founded in the vicinity of Kyoto. His disciple Kyōgō (n. d.) produced a commentary on Sen'e's ten volumes in a sixty-volume work known as the *Shōbōgenzō goshō*.[9] Although the writings of Sen'e and his followers clearly reflected the spirit of Dōgen's Zen, they too broke from the circle of disciples at Eihei-ji after Dōgen's death.

Among the many other disciples of Dōgen renowned for their special gifts we may mention Gishin (n. d.), who never held any position of importance in the community and left behind no special name, and Kakubutsu (n. d) of whom we know only that he held a second position to Ejō for a while.[10]

A story connected with the name of the talented monk Gemmyō (n. d.) shows that things at Eihei-ji were not all ideal.[11] Dōgen had just returned from Kamakura where, at the invitation of the shōgun Tokiyori, he had passed what turned out to be a rather unhappy winter (1247–48). Dōgen was not able to adjust to the military regimen and his conversations with Tokiyori were not particularly harmonious. To assuage the master's unpleasant memories, the shōgun presented him at the time of his return to Eihei-ji with a piece of land to expand the monastery's holdings. When Dōgen unconditionally re-jected the offer, the business-minded young disciple Gemmyō was upset. Hold-ing high the certificate of the grant, Gemmyō demonstrated his willingness to accept the additional property. Disgusted by such a display of greed, Dōgen promptly expelled Gemmyō from the community and dismissed him from the monastery.

The story is yet another example of Dōgen's upright character. His noble personality stood beyond reproach. Still, limitations and shadows surfaced during the later years. Not all the disciples were happy with him; many felt frustrated, others were simply not up to the rigors of monastic life. More significantly, the times were changing in many ways and were making new demands on the religious community. Only some two decades after Dōgen's death did these new demands come to full expression.

KOUN EJŌ

Dōgen was succeeded by Koun Ejō (1198–1280).[12] Having lived in intimate harmony with Dōgen for nearly twenty years, he occupies a place alongside his master. Nevertheless, his own personality played a unique and important historical role, forming a bridge between Dōgen-Zen and the Japanese Sōtō Zen school, which actually fell apart in the course of its initial formation. Many factors were at work in this turn of events and not everything should be blamed on Ejō. Still, his own temperament and behavior were an essential part of many of the unfortunate developments.

YOUTH AND FIRST STEPS

The sources tell us little of Ejō's childhood and youth. As a member of one of the Fujiwara families, he was educated in Kyoto with a solid grounding in Buddhism, as befitted his aristocratic background. When still a boy, he was turned over to a teacher on Mount Hiei for further formation. The literature highlights two dates during this stay at the center of Tendai Buddhism: 1215, when he was ordained a monk, and 1218, when he received the bodhisattva precepts on the ordination platform of Enryaku-ji. At the time it was not uncommon to send lads of seven or eight years old to the monastery for an education. Ejō served under the well-respected and pious Dharma master Ennō. We do not know how long he was with Ennō before being ordained, but it may have been as long as ten years.[13] His biographer points out different motives for Ejō's final decision to become a monk: the general mood of the times, the totally Buddhist milieu of his education, the death of a number of his relatives, and especially, the inclinations and longings of his own deeply religious nature.[14] Far from being a purely external ritual, the ordination ceremony was for him a sign of a life's commitment. It is possible that he was also influenced by nagging feelings of guilt, as is indicated in the following verses that he is supposed to have penned on his own portrait:

> Weighted down with karma and a despicable character,
> By far the first among humans in sinfulness,
> Barefoot he learned to walk.
> Before he wore out his sandals, he saw his original self.

Although the guilt feelings expressed in these lines—reminiscent of Shinran—are overcome in the moment of beholding his original self, it is likely that they continued to oppress Ejō throughout his life. His guilt may even hold the key to his inner development.[15] The fact that he was so deeply moved by religious rituals may have resulted from the tension he experienced between his high ideals and his sentiments of unworthiness.

Historical accounts vary in details but are all agreed that during his time on Mount Hiei Ejō committed himself to an extensive study of Buddhism that included not only the Buddhism of the Nara period but also the public and secret teachings of Tendai and probably also the esoteric Shingon doctrines.

Weary of traditional forms of Buddhism, he searched for a more existential version of Buddha's teachings and while still at Mount Hiei turned to the study of Pure Land Buddhism. In Keizan's *Denkōroku,* the author's pious mother admonishes her son to persevere as a monk, not to content himself with the kind of learning that seeks after one's own honor and gain but to don the rob of the monk and— if this is the correct interpretation of the text—to practice the *nembutsu,* thinking devoutly of Amida Buddha. Most likely these maternal words were directed to Ejō, who visited her in 1219, the year after he had received the bodhisattva precepts on Mount Hiei. It is possible that his meeting with Keizan's mother was the reason he did not return to Mount Hiei but decided instead to study Pure Land Buddhism under the head of the Seizan line of the Jōdo school, Zen'ebō Shōkū (1171–1247), who practiced the continual recitation of the *nembutsu* at Ōjō-in in Kyoto. But Ejō grew dissatisfied with Amida Buddhism and in 1222 or 1223 turned his religious search in the direction of the Zen of the Japanese Daruma school.[16]

At the time, the school was located in Tōnomine (in the area around Nara).[17] There Kakuan (d. 1234?) and his disciples had retreated, apparently to avoid the enmity of the monks on Mount Hiei. Ejō was bound to Kakuan through personal contacts. A zealous seeker of the true way, he hoped to fulfill his heart's desire in the Daruma school. He had already heard so much about this Zen community and now at last he was in a position to solicit admission.

As noted in the previous chapter, the Daruma school took as its axiom the words that have echoed within all Zen schools since the time of the Sixth Patriarch: "Look into your own nature and become Buddha" (*kenshō jōbutsu*). Its program of study revolved about the *Shuryōgon-gyō* (*Śuraṃgama Sūtra*) and the *Engaku-gyō* (possibly apocryphal).[18] Kakuan selected passages from these sūtras for the lectures with which he prepared his monks for meditation. One of the parables from the *Shuryōgon-gyō* led Ejō to his first Zen experience, a "look within" (Jpn., *seigo*) bringing clarity and great peace. The text speaks of an emptiness of consciousness that effects liberation from sinful karma and from impurities. At last Ejō was free from his inner oppression. Continuing with his practice, he penetrated the mystery of seeing into one's own nature and of becoming a Buddha until at last he came to experience the maternal womb of the Perfected One. This, he felt, was an experience comparable to the wonderful enlightenment (*myōkaku*) of Śākyamuni. He devoted all his energies to practicing in Kakuan's school and according to one chronicle "stood out among the hundreds of Kakuan's students and was praised by all."[19]

"Hundreds of students" may be an exaggeration. The *Denkōroku* tells simply of more than thirty pupils who committed themselves to the direction of Kakuan at the Tōnomine center.[20] Around 1228 the Daruma school suffered a severe blow when bands from Kōfuku-ji in Nara burned down the buildings at Tōnomine. The disciples scattered. Some of them headed with Ekan to Hajaku-ji in Echizen, which had been set up for Zen practice. Among this group were Gikai, Gien, Gijun, Giin, and others who later were to join Dōgen.

Ejō's visit to Dōgen at Kennin-ji in Kyoto took place not long after the

Tōnomine center had gone up in flames, around 1228 or 1229. There is no cause to speculate about the motives for his visit. News of Dōgen's return from China and his enthusiastic efforts for the spread of Zen had also reached Ejō. He heard of the extraordinary impact of the young master's first written work, which, as stated in its title, insisted on the practice of *zazen*. But when Ejō stood knocking at the door of the hermitage inside the monastery grounds of Kennin-ji where Dōgen lived and practiced, little did he know that it was to be the most important and far-reaching act of his life.

The fullest and most reliable account of this first meeting of Dōgen and Ejō is found in the *Denkōroku*.[21] His experience made Ejō aware of himself and gave him a sense of a new inner strength. He also knew that his own extended process of serious discipline had something to do with it. He had indeed appropriated the approach of the Daruma school, "to see into one's own nature and acquire spiritual knowledge" *(kenshō reichi)*. The two monks spoke of all these things during the first two or three days of what the *Denkōroku* calls the first round of their conversation. Ejō was delighted and felt himself confirmed when Dōgen recognized the authenticity of his experience. Such agreement fortified the hope of an even deeper mutual understanding.

Ejō was not as pleased with the conversations of the following days. He was astonished at the new and original perspectives Dōgen kept introducing into their discussion. Eventually they found themselves in a spirited disagreement—a "Dharma struggle" *(hōsen)*—in which Dōgen's superior insight shone forth. Deeply impressed, Ejō bowed to his superior. Conscious of his own immaturity, he resolved to return to the search for full enlightenment and asked to be received among Dōgen's disciples. At this first meeting, as mentioned, his request was turned down. Dōgen voiced his refusal in a remarkably friendly, even trusting manner, telling Ejō that he should come back once a suitable place for Zen practice had been found. Dōgen then went on to explain his dream of spreading the true Dharma throughout Japan. Evidently impressed by the young disciple, Dōgen recognized in him a companion for his life's work.

Other, briefer accounts of this first meeting between Dōgen and Ejō differ slightly.[22] For example, Ejō is said to have withdrawn after Dōgen did not acknowledge his practice and experience in the Daruma school. Or he is reported to have courteously taken leave of Dōgen and gone on a pilgrimage, realizing that the right time had not yet come. A number of versions state that it was only during his second visit that Ejō committed himself to the master. One thing remains constant in all the accounts: Dōgen's superiority.

Ejō had found the "true teacher" who would show him the way of "the authentic tradition of the Buddha-Dharma." Once admitted to the circle of Dōgen's disciples, he at last felt secure. It is not clear precisely when this took place. As the *Denkōroku* puts it, he "waited, following the command of the master, until the time was right."[23] Reports that he waited four to five years are not reliable. Neither is it likely that he wandered around the land from monastery to monastery. Quite possibly he returned to the mountains region of Tōnomine to live in a small settlement with his former master Kakuan.[24] In any case, wherever he was, he tried to keep well informed of events and changes in the life of Dōgen.

Not long after the meeting with Ejō, Dōgen decided to leave Kennin-ji to distance himself from the animosity of the monks of Mount Hiei. In 1230 he took refuge in the modest estate of An'yo-in in Fukakusa. There he led a quiet life, dedicated entirely to practice. It was during this period that he wrote his important work on practice, Bendōwa, in which he adopts the device of questions and answers, most likely inspired by his conversations with Ejō.[25] His next move was to Kannondōri-in, which, after expansion, became the Zen monastery of Kōshōhōrin-ji. After its consecration in early 1233, Dōgen once again devoted himself fully to the propagation of Zen and the true Dharma.

Since Ejō certainly was aware of all these developments, why did he not immediately join the master in his new and promising location? According to his biographer, Ejō was held back by his concern for Kakuan, who had taken sick after the destruction of his Daruma school in Tōnomine and was in need of Ejō's help. This is supported by a report in the biography of Nōnin, the founder of the Daruma school, according to which Kakuan entrusted Nōnin's literary works to Ejō shortly before passing away and urged him to join Dōgen after he had died. The date of his death given in this not entirely reliable account is fall of 1234. In winter of the same year, Ejō left to join Dōgen's disciples.

DŌGEN'S DISCIPLE AND FRIEND
According to the Denkōroku, Dōgen "joyfully" welcomed Ejō into the community of Kōshōji. Day by day Ejō's appreciation of his new master's personal qualities grew as they "discussed by day and by night the way of the patriarchs."[26] One year later, Dōgen added a third ordination to the two basic ordinations that Ejō had received on Mount Hiei—this one for the "Dharma of the precepts of the true tradition of the Buddhas and the patriarchs."[27] This confirmed Ejō's reception into the Zen tradition of the line of Ju-ching, who had conferred this same ordination on Dōgen before he returned from China to Japan. The ceremony resembled the one by which Bodhidharma had transmitted the Zen patriarchate to Hui-k'o. Ejō was overjoyed at the demonstration of his master's trust in him.

The first three years in Kōshō-ji marked the climax of Ejō's life. He had been ordained on 15 August 1235; in winter of that same year the planning and building of a monks' hall (sōdō) began, with Ejō playing an enthusiastic role in the project. Dedicated in October 1236, the new building permitted an even stricter program of formation for the monks. An integral part of this formation were the kōan that Dōgen had brought back from China. Ejō was one of the first to experience personally just how helpful this strenuous exercise in the monks' hall could be. As the master was presenting to his disciples the classical kōan of the Chinese tradition, Ejō attained his great enlightenment. His experience was triggered by a question that a monk posed to Master Shih-shuang (986–1039): "How is it that one hair digs many ditches?"[28] Stunned by the words, Ejō reverenced the Buddha and hastened to Dōgen, who confirmed the authenticity of his experience with the words, "It has dug perfectly." Explanations of this famous kōan tell us that the hair symbolizes the Absolute, while the many ditches represent the myriad things of the transient world. It is one of the many images that enable one to experience the unity of reality in the immediate Now.

For Ejō the time spent with Dōgen in Kōshō-ji (1234–1243) was a period of spiritual maturation and intellectual broadening. Since the day of his great enlightenment (probably mid-November of 1236), he was considered Dōgen's Dharma heir and successor, as is evident in several historical sources for this period. The *Denkōroku* stresses his privileged position among the disciples and his familiarity with Dōgen. He alone could hear things that others could not, and he was privy to anything said to anyone else. While he assumed various important positions in the monastery, he was always in service of the master, a service marked by extraordinary confidentiality and intimacy. "Throughout the day, he was inseparable from the master, like a trailing shadow," says the *Denkōroku.*

The Japanese sources do not supply the date on which Ejō succeeded Dōgen in the patriarchate, an unfortunate lacuna in the historiography of the Sōtō school. Dairyō Gumon (?–1687), the thirty-second abbot of Eihei-ji, was the first to give 18 November 1236 as the date for this historical event.[29] Gumon's description could well be accurate: on the evening of this day, Ejō betook himself to the cell of Master Dōgen and received from him the document that confirmed him as the Second Patriarch of the Japanese Sōtō school and the fifty-second Zen Patriarch after Śākyamuni. In December of that same year Ejō was named "monk of the first seat" (*shuso*) for Kōshō-ji.

During this period (1235–1237) Ejō compiled the *Shōbōgenzō zuimonki*. It should be remembered that all the lectures and events recorded in the work were filtered through the soul of the disciple. If we have claimed that the essential elements of Dōgen's spirituality can be found in the *Zuimonki*, we should also add that the work represents a harmony between the spiritualities of Ejō and Dōgen.

Another event from this busy period of Ejō's life bears mention: the serious illness of his mother.[30] His close ties to his mother, so evident during his vocational quest, surfaced again clearly in the many signs of childlike love he showed her at the time of her illness (probably 1235). Her condition worsened during the period of the monks' winter *sesshin* at Kōshō-ji (October to January). The monastic rule allowed monks to take two three-day vacations from the monastery at the end of such a period of intense practice. Ejō used his six days to visit his dying mother. In exact observance of the rule, he returned to the monastery when the six days were over. No sooner was he back then a messenger reported that his mother's condition had taken a turn for the worse. Soon afterward, a second messenger brought the news that her end was approaching and that she wished to see her son. The entire community unanimously urged him to go. But Ejō, who knew and shared Dōgen's viewpoint, would not allow human feelings to override the monastic rule. To the assembled community of fellow monks he explained that it would be a gross violation of filial love and not at all beneficial to his mother's welfare if he disregarded the rule; for a monk, the Buddha Way is always the final norm.

Ejō was in his mid-forties in July of 1243 when Dōgen and his monks set out for Echizen.[31] Gijun remained in Kōshō-ji while Ejō and the others from the Daruma school who had been with Dōgen since 1241 accompanied the master. Their first stop along the way was the small temple of Kippō-ji, which served Dōgen as a home base when he went to preach in nearby Yamashibu. Throughout the transition, Ejō continued to devote himself to the personal service of the master. He also busied himself copying and editing the books of the Shōbōgenzō, a project that had already occupied him during the final years at Kōshōji. He also helped with the preparations for the construction of the new monastery of Daibutsu-ji under the spirited supervision of their benefactor and friend Hatano Yoshishige. Already in July of 1244 the monks were able to begin using the Dharma hall (hattō) and the monks' hall. In June of 1246 the monastery was renamed Eihei-ji, the "Temple of Eternal Peace."[32]

With the move to the new monastery, Ejō's responsibilities changed. He remained the master's closest friend and servant, but as Dōgen gave more and more attention to the training of the monks and continued his energetic work for the spread of the Dharma and Zen meditation among the laity, Ejō found that he had to bear more of the burden of caring for the internal life of the monastery, cultic services, and religious affairs. When Ejō asked the master why he was allowing all this to happen, Dōgen told him that he was hoping that the Dharma would long endure on this location. "I may be younger than you," he is supposed to have said, "but my life will be shorter than yours. . . . You will surpass me in years and live a longer life. . . . For this reason I have intentionally turned over to your care the entire good order of the monastery and the future development of the school."[33] It is doubtful that the confusing events after his death corresponded to Dōgen's hopes for the future.

With Dōgen directing his attention mainly to the formation of his monks, his written work at Eihei-ji took a new direction. His conferences had to be preserved for a collection of sayings called the Eihei goroku. At the same time, important sections of the monastic rule (Eihei shingi) were taking shape, as was the Bendōhō, which also contained instructions for practice and for the religious life of the monks. While other disciples such as Sen'e and Gien helped with this work, the main responsibility was Ejō's.

Ejō accompanied Dōgen on his trip to Kamakura and was with him during the six months he spent in the capital of the military regime (1247–1248). After they returned to Eihei-ji, Dōgen's life took its final sharp turn. He had always shown a sincere regard for the laity and dedicated much time to their spiritual welfare, but during his last years he focused all his energies on the spiritual progress of his monks. He spent long hours with them in meditation and delivered innumerable sermons and exhortations. He tightened the rule and sharpened the rigor of monastic life. All of this, together with the events of those days,

Ejō was to record in writing. Even when Dōgen's new stringencies regarding monastic asceticism might have seemed to go too far, Ejō continued to regard his master with unswerving respect.

In autumn of 1252 there were clear indications that Dōgen's health was failing. The master was seen less often in the monks hall; in his farewell discourses he was delivering the final book of the *Shōbōgenzō*, the *Hachidainingaku* (*The Eight Virtues a Bodhisattva Should Attain*). His illness growing progressively worse, and on 8 July 1253, in a moving conversation at which Ejō was present, he turned over the governance of Eihei-ji to his disciple Tettsū Gikai. On 14 July he formally passed on the succession to Ejō and made him the gift of a priestly robe he himself had made. At the urging of his friend Hatano Yoshishige he left Eihei-ji on 5 August and on 28 August 1253, a few days after he had arrived in Kyoto, he died.

After the official mourning ceremonies were concluded, Ejō occupied himself for a time with pious duties toward his deceased master. He had a pagoda built in the area around Eihei-ji. While going through Dōgen's things he was deeply moved to come upon a manuscript entitled *Hōkyōki*, which the master has written during his stay with Master Ju-ching in China. Determined to follow faithfully in the footsteps of his great and esteemed predecessor, Ejō began a new and demanding chapter of his life as the second abbot of Eihei-ji.

THE SECOND ABBOT OF EIHEI-JI

The last part of Ejō's life falls into three clearly distinguishable periods: first, his time as superior of Eihei-ji (1253–1267), then his five years in seclusion (1267–1272) after turning over the powers of office to his successor, and finally his last years as director of the monastery complex (1272–1280). Ejō's tenure as abbot was marked by simplicity and order. One of the concerns closest to his heart was the proper preservation of Dōgen's works. With established rituals and the regular practice of meditation, the routine of the monastery moved along smoothly but fell more and more in a rut. Ejō did not command the authority of his master Dōgen. He lacked leadership, particularly where the monks from the Daruma school, who had known him as a disciple of Ekan, were concerned. Failures of discipline were to pave the way for the coming unrest.[34]

Disturbances arose under Ejō because of Tettsū Gikai, Dōgen's third successor and the central figure in the "dispute over the third-generation successor" (*sandai sōron*), a cloud that also hung over Dōgen's final days. What transpired between Ejō and Gikai during the first year after the master's death constitutes the background and the beginning—really the first phase—of this dramatic conflict.[35]

Almost immediately after Ejō became abbot he had to face the question of his successor. Tettsū Gikai (1219–1309), an exceptional and richly gifted monk, seemed to be the only choice. Moreover, his age placed him in the following generation.[36] Born in the land of Echizen, he was still a boy when he received his first monastic ordination in the Hajaku-ji monastery under Ekan, then leader of the Japanese Daruma school. The following year he went to Mount

Hiei, where he took on the obligations of the precepts and began his studies of Buddhism, especially Tendai. At the suggestion of Ekan he also studied Pure Land Buddhism, esoteric teachings (mikkyō), and meditation. Later, with a group of colleagues from the Daruma school, he followed Ekan to Dōgen's monastery, where he practiced and worked zealously. Dōgen had high hopes for the young monk and assigned him to such important positions as cook and manager. During his last days at Eihei-ji the master extended to Gikai a special confidence.[37] In the meeting of 8 July 1253, as already mentioned, he entrusted him with the future of the monastery. Moved to tears, Gikai confessed: "In everything, I will never act contrary to your wishes." Even the master could not hold back his tears. Before he left for Kyoto, Dōgen once again conferred the governance of Eihei-ji on Gikai, urging him at the same time to exercise discretion toward the other disciples, who perhaps would not properly understand his words. Gikai accompanied his departing master on part of his journey and then returned to the monastery.

As the sole witness to Dōgen's extraordinary gesture of confidence toward Gikai, Ejō himself felt that the question of his successor was already determined.[38] His unconditional devotion to his departed master not only helped him keep a clear head regarding the master's intentions for him, it also gave Dōgen's wishes a power that went beyond the grave. At the same time, Ejō could not close his eyes to certain weaknesses in the spirit and character of Gikai. Two shortcomings in particular stood out. As a product of the Daruma school, Gikai tried to introduce into authentic Dōgen-Zen certain key elements from his earlier school that were incompatible with Zen. Dōgen himself had pointed out another weakness, which he hoped would gradually be overcome, when he observed that Gikai still lacked "the heart of an aged mother" (rōbashin). This expression, so beloved by Zen followers especially when applied to aging masters, points to "sympathetic empathy" (jihi), that remarkable mixture of coarseness and unlimited compassion that the masters, each in his own style, embody. In Gikai's case it is not clear just what Dōgen had in mind; perhaps he noticed a certain edge to his disciple's character that came out in his dealings with fellow monks.

In spite of everything, Ejō took the decisive steps to make Gikai his successor.[39] In December of 1255 he showed him the documents and the robe of the Dharma heir, and during the first days of January bestowed on him, without written confirmation, the insignia of the patriarchal office. On another January evening he took Gikai aside to explain further essential points, especially the unity of practice and teaching that constitutes the foundation of Dōgen-Zen. Dōgen had firmly condemned the false view that there is another spiritual principle besides practice. Knowing full well that such a viewpoint had its sympathizers among the monks, Ejō directly asked Gikai what he thought about this matter. At first Gikai expressed a certain understanding for the sympathizers, but eventually, convinced by Ejō's insistence, agreed on all points. Ejō's reservations were relieved. A striking change is supposed to have come over Gikai's countenance. A critical reading of the account leaves one with an undefinable sense of uneasiness. Even the account of Gikai's enlightenment experience that follows is not fully convincing. Upon hearing the famous words of Dōgen, "Body and mind are cast off," Gikai experienced something. When Ejō questioned him about what had happened, he responded with the story of the beardless barbarian from the West, the fourth case of the *Mumonkan*. [40]

There are small discrepancies in the historical reports of Gikai's succession. Pleased that his weighty responsibility had been completed successfully, happily Ejō resumed direction of the monastery. He had avoided the great sin of "cutting off the Buddha seed." [41] With youthful enthusiasm Gikai committed himself to working for the welfare of the monastery until Ejō sent him on a pilgrimage to different Zen monasteries throughout the land to gather knowledge that would help him understand and carry out his mission at Eihei-ji. Gikai visited four of the most important Zen monasteries of the time: Kennin-ji and Tōfuku-ji in Kyoto, and Jufuku-ji and Kenchō-ji in Kamakura. His zeal drove him further still, and in 1259 he set out for the land of the Sung, where he devoted himself to intensive study in Chinese Rinzai monasteries. Blessed with a talent for practical things, he was able to make drawings of architectural plans, interior designs, and cultic articles. [42] He also brought back to Japan valuable copies of Zen writings, monastic rules, and collections of sayings of the masters.

The year of Gikai's return to Japan in 1262 marked a turning point in the history of the Eihei-ji monastery and in the development of the Sōtō school. Gikai had undertaken his journey with the full consent, indeed the encouragement, of his abbot Ejō. Following what he felt were the wishes of Dōgen, Ejō himself was busy completing the building plans of Eihei-ji and making necessary adaptations to the changing times. Apparently for these reasons, when Gikai returned, Ejō gave him free hand in directing construction and expansion of the physical plant and in making adjustments in the daily life of the monastery. This is why historians mark 1262 as the beginning of the first stage in the "dispute over the third-generation successor." [43] Five years later, Ejō decided to step down as abbot. It is hard to suppose that health was his only, or even his main reason for retiring, since immediately after he left office his health improved. [44] At the same time, we cannot simply place the blame on Gikai, for it seems that his resistance to becoming abbot was honest. The divisions that were evidently developing within the monastic community were making Ejō's job as abbot increasingly difficult.

For five years Ejō remained in the "rank of the east-chamber" (*tōdōi*), a designation for retired superiors. He lived in a small settlement not far from Eihei-ji and gave himself over totally to meditation and study. Monks from the monastery visited him regularly to express their enduring friendship and confidence. Dōgen's disciples, especially those who had come from the Daruma school, had, after the master's early death, become Ejō's disciples. Among his visitors were Bussō (d. 1282) and Dōson (d. 1289), both of whom had attained enlightenment under his direction.

Back at the monastery, things were not going well for Gikai. In order to escape the determined opposition of a large group of monks, he built a small temple at the foot of the mountain for his old mother, whom he was trying to care for. Meanwhile, despite Ejō's advanced age, the monks had asked him to come back and assume leadership of the monastery. When he did so in 1272, the first stage of the "dispute over the third-generation successor" came to an end.

It is fairly easy to give reasons why Gikai's attempts to reform the Eihei-ji monastery failed. The monks—or at least a good number of them—thought that he was abandoning the foundations that Dōgen had laid. Whereas Dōgen's principal concerns had been with the inner life, Gikai seemed more taken up with externals, neglecting the monastic ideals of poverty and simplicity that had always guided Dōgen. Instead of these ideals, the monks saw grandiose building projects and new shrines with artistic images of Buddha. And when Gikai introduced Shingon rituals into the liturgies, they felt he was directly contradicting what the master had expressly taught. Recognizing that his new style was meeting widespread opposition, Gikai preferred to step down rather than be the cause of open rebellion.

Ejō's last years passed without incident. He tried to cultivate a better understanding of Gikai, to temper the emotions of his opponents, and restore harmony to community life. Deeply pained by this internal dissension, he sought reconciliation and appeasement. This was one of the motives behind a work he completed in 1278 entitled *Kōmyōzōzammai*,[45] in which he quotes copiously from the great Mahāyāna sūtras—especially the *Mahāvairocana Sūtra*, the *Avatamsaka Sūtra*, and the *Saddharmapundarīka Sūtra*—as well as from the words of the early Chinese Zen masters and the "golden words" of Śākyamuni. His aim in the work was to make Dōgen's authentic tradition of the Buddha-Dharma more accessible to a larger audience. It was at this time that he described himself as a great sinner in the verses, quoted above, that he wrote on a self-portrait. He signed the painting, "Ejō in the second generation of Eihei-ji."

Ejō worked zealously up until just a few months before his death. In April, 1280, it was evident that he was ailing. Feeling his end to be near, he issued a final directive that no pagoda was to be built in his memory; rather, true servant that he was, he wanted to be buried next to the pagoda of his master. His farewell verses are a blend of a sense of sinfulness and a trusting resignation. To the end, he was tormented by the fear that he had not passed on Dōgen's heritage untarnished. Sadly, his final days were marked by tragedy. The apparently implacable unrest that was breaking out among the monks he attributed to his sinful karma. With his thoughts set on Master Dōgen, he died peacefully.

THE DISPUTE OVER THE THIRD-GENERATION SUCCESSOR

The heated controversy about succession that marked the beginnings of the Sōtō school of Japan and led to splinterings and divisions is a bitter historical reality for Sōtō Buddhism. It is difficult to form a clear picture of just what happened, mainly because the controversy was played out inside the monastic community at Eihei-ji between opposing parties of the same school. To this day, there are varying opinions about the motives and causes at work in the conflict and a historical consensus is yet to emerge.

Kagamishima Genryū, currently president of the Sōtō Buddhist Komazawa University, presents three current explanations. The first takes into account the juridical dispute between the two rivals Gikai and Gien. Gikai based his claim on the fact that the Dharma (succession in the line of Dōgen) had been transmitted to him by Ejō, while Gien had received from Dōgen only the precepts like the other disciples. In this scheme Gikai figures as a *dempō no deshi* ("disciple to whom the Dharma is transmitted") while Gien remains a *denkai no deshi* ("disciple who received the precepts"). Against this, Gien disputed the validity of the transmission of succession in the line of Dōgen to Gikai, who had already been installed by Ekan, head of the Dharma school, as heir in this Rinzai-line school. A second explanation stylizes the opposition between the conservative strain of Gien and the progressive strain of Gikai into an antinomy that takes the form of a dilemma: on the one hand, unworldliness, and a necessary foresaking of popularity; on the other, an openness to the common people and a renunciation of the purity of the Zen transmission. After the death of Dōgen, as those who hold this view insist, it was inevitable that this dilemma would rise to the surface, and in fact it took place in the dispute over succession in the third generation. A third explanation has the strife developing between parties within the monastic community, which Gikai and Gien in any case served as leaders. It has to do not with a basic opposition but with an insignificant squabble.[46]

Each of these explanations has a kernel of truth to them and are not necessarily mutually exclusive. The first is directly concerned with the right of succession. Gikai had been made successor in Eihei-ji by Ejō with the presentation of a document. In addition, he possessed the certificate of succession to the branch line of the Japanese Daruma school that he had been given by Ekan before the latter's death. Ekan, Kakuan's Dharma heir, had established the school in Hajaku-ji in Echizen prior to transferring to the discipleship of Dōgen's temple. Thus Gikai disposed of two roles, properly founded but contradictory and finally irreconcilable, to which Gien, as an elder disciple of Ejō from the Daruma school, protested. The protest was all the more justified in that the certificates proceeded from two different houses of Zen (namely, the House of Ts'ao-tung and the House of Lin-chi). This added complication festered during the struggles over succession and was only resolved after the death of the two protagonists.[47]

As Kagamishima notes, Gikai and Gien represented opposing orientations that only hardened further as the confrontation developed. After the death of Ejō things settled down somewhat. After leaving Eihei-ji, Gikai spent eight years in the surrounding area, apparently keeping up relations with the community of monks, particularly with Ejō. In deference to the expressed wish of Ejō shortly before passing away, he resumed the direction of the monastery after the death of the second abbot of Eihei-ji. He was well aware of his precarious situation and exercised the powers of his office with great caution, knowing only too well the different factions within the community.

As it happened, Gikai's second term of office coincided with the most severe national crisis Japan faced prior to the Meiji Restoration. After the rather fortunate repulsion of the first Mongol invasion in 1274, the Inner Asian hoards returned with a formidable naval fleet in 1281. The menace not only stirred up nationalist feelings within the old schools of traditional Buddhism, it also made the magical rituals of esoteric Buddhism—of Shingon and Tendai as well as of Shugendō—especially attractive to both nobility and commoners. Commands went out to all the Buddhist temples and Shinto shrines throughout the land to offer up rituals and prayers for the repulsion of the Mongol threat. In these circumstances Gikai and his followers in Eihei-ji felt encouraged, more than ever, to make room for esoteric rituals.

This fit in well with Gikai's own esoteric leanings even as it accommodated the mood of the times. Gikai, as had Eisai before him, had already gained a considerable understanding of esoteric rites from his time on Mount Hiei. There he learned not only Tendai rites (taimitsu) but also esoteric elements having to do with meditation. Dainichi Nōnin, striving to appropriate Zen meditation, may have come into contact with esoteric elements of the Northern school of Chinese Ch'an on Mount Hiei and may have used them in the formation of the Japanese Daruma school. If so, this would make a relationship possible between the esoteric practices that enjoyed such popularity in the Daurma school and those of the Northern school of Chinese Ch'an.[48] That Buddhist esoteric tradition (mikkyō) was in full bloom during Japan's middle ages explains its spread and diversification in the later Sōtō school. In any case, esoteric rites had an important role to play in the reform that Gikai initiated in Eihei-ji. It was precisely this dimension of his reform movement that aroused such strong antipathy from his opponents.[49]

But all this brought the divisions already existing in the monastery to an even greater intensity. Opposition to Gikai increased among the disciples who appealed to a certain Jakuen for support.[50] Jakuen, whose Chinese name was Chi-yüan (1207–1299), had been with Dōgen during his discipleship under Ju-ching. As a Dharma brother, Jakuen had accompanied Dōgen on his return to Japan and for some time had lived with him and Ejō at Eihei-ji. In 1261 he left the monastery and established the small temple of Hōkyō-ji in the not too distant region of Fukui. There he and his disciples, among them Gien, practiced a pure Zen strictly according to Chinese style. Although Jakuen apparently did not become involved in the conflict about the succession, his disciples proved to be fierce opponents of the esoteric rituals that Gikai was practicing. The conflict came to a head when violent fighting broke out within the monastic community, forcing Gikai into an untenable position. In disgrace Gikai was obliged to leave the monastery—fleeing freely or forcefully banished—where he had been the superior for seven years. His patron Hatano Tokimitsu tried once more to bring him back, but without success. His place was taken by Gien, one of the disciples from the Japanese Daurma school, who was designated by his supporters as the third abbot in order to show that they never recognized the legitimacy of Gikai. Thus did the controversy that was to give this period its name take shape. Who was to be recognized as the third abbot of Eihei-ji, Gikai or Gien?

Gien's tenure as abbot was not a very happy one. Tensions within the community did not fade away easily. When a fire destroyed part of the monastery buildings in 1297, efforts to rebuild lagged, mainly because Hatano, the patron of the temple, had withdrawn his support. In these circumstances, many monks left the monastery to seek more satisfying surroundings elsewhere. Even Gien himself, during his later years, retreated to a nearby hermitage.

Gikai's twilight years were happier. With the help of Chōkai, a member of the Fujiwara clan and a former friend and disciple from earlier years at the Japanese Daruma school, he moved around 1292 to the Shingon monastery of Daijō-ji in Kaga (district of Ishikawa). There, thanks to good relations with Shingon, he was able to convert the temple into a Zen monastery. After its dedication in 1293 Gikai set about trying to develop a monastic community truly adapted to the needs of the times. While the heart of the monastic practice was Zen mediation, there was also a considerable mixture of Shingon elements, which once again precipitated further crises. In any event, this monastery laid the foundations for the medieval, popular Sōtō school of Japan. Gikai died at Daijō-ji in 1309 at the ripe old age of 91.

Even after the death of Gikai and Gien, the echoes of their conflict (1314–1317) resounded again when it came time to erect a memorial stone at Eihei-ji. Their disciples could not agree about which of the three rivals should bear the title of third abbot.[51] At loggerheads, they turned to the military regime at Kamakura for a decision, but this was no to avail. Finally, they decided to lay two stones, one with Gikai's name, the other with Gien's, while Kakuen of Hōkyō-ji was listed as the third successor in the chronicles of Eihei-ji. In the lists of abbots of Eihei-ji, Gikai and Gien are usually given as the third and fourth abbots after Dōgen and Ejō, followed by Giun as the fifth abbot (1253–1333).[52]

Giun was born of court nobility. After becoming a monk in Kyoto, he turned to Zen and spent more than twenty years as a disciple of Jakuen in Hōkyō-ji. Giun's grasp of Zen deepened under the strict direction of this Chinese master, and he was eventually designated Dharma heir, succeeding Jakuen in 1299. Meanwhile, when Gien died in 1314, Hatano, Eihei-ji's patron who was then in charge of reconstruction, prevailed upon Giun to become abbot at the monastery. As one of the most respected spiritual personalities of the time, he was soon able to win the support of influential circles, and the ruined temple buildings were soon rebuilt. His preparation of a sixty-volume edition of the Shōbōgenzō, testify to his intellectual qualities. The cultivation of the tradition of the founder, Dōgen, remained the particular task of Eihei-ji.

That the conflict over the third-generation successor came to a peaceful end was due in no small part to the great personalities of Giun and Keizan. Keizan, of whom we shall have more to say in the following pages, never broke completely with Eihei-ji and the monks living there who had belonged to Dōgen's community. Although a disciple of Gikai, he had received the bodhisattva precepts in Eihei-ji. Despite the fact that he allowed Gikai to name him Dharma heir to two lines, it is uncertain how much he felt himself a part of the Daruma school. He had no personal aquaintance with any important monk of this school apart from Gikai. The influence of the Daruma school on Keizan, and through him on the Sōtō school, is difficult to assess. In order to put an end once and for all to the entanglements, towards the end of his life, in 1323, Keizan constructed a memorial hall in the area of Yōkō-ji, which he had converted into a Zen temple. The hall was named "Peak of the Five Elders" (gorōhō) after masters Ju-ching, Dōgen, Ejō, Gikai, and Keizan. There he had enshrined in a stone box the certificates of succession, relics, and insignia of the various lines. The hall was considered both a repository for venerable memorabilia and a memorial. With one final symbolic stroke Keizan closed the chapter on the unedifying struggles over succession. In following generations nothing more was to be heard of the Japanese Daruma school in the Sōtō school.[53] In the school numerous currents flow together as into a reservoir.

The effects of the strife over succession lingered in the Sōtō school long afterward. This should give us cause to reflect. The confrontation was not just a matter of personal opposition. In the dynamics of the conflict we witness an explosive tension rooted in the very heart of Zen and destined to appear repeatedly throughout its history. Given its preoccupation with penetrating to the depths, Zen appears to be elitist; at the same time, it is unable to forego an openness to the common people, mainly because it is essentially bound by the bodhisattva ideal of the Mahāyāna tradition to work for the salvation of all sentient beings. Although it is precisely this tension that so contributes to the religious inspiration and power of Zen's great figures, one must contend with the human imperfections that, despite long practice and deep experiences, are also part of Zen. Every religion can look to only a few, happy instances in which there has been a truly harmonious melding of lofty personal qualities and spiritual depth (especially as embodied in the monastic life) on the one hand, and extensive work among the common people and the masses on the other. The conflict and torment over the third successor provided the Sōtō school with a needed warning as it continued its way through history.

KEIZAN JŌKIN

The further lines that developed within the Sōtō school did not all grow out of the dispute over the third-generation successor. In addition to the two opposing camps within the Eihei-ji community, there were a number of other divisions among Dōgen's disciples. The state of affairs after the conflict over the succession was indeed complex, but we can distinguish five overlapping lines defined in terms of either organizational or doctrinal differences:

1. The Eihei-ji line, centered in the headquarters established by its founder, was led by the fifth abbot, Giun, and his successors, all of whom belonged to the Jakuen line for the next twenty generations.

2. The line of Sen'e and his disciple Kyōgō[54] was extremely important for preserving the speculative and literary works of Dōgen. After Ejō, Sen'e was Dōgen's most prominent disciple. His good relations with Mount Hiei account for his being able to found the Yōkō-ji monastery near Kyoto, where, with his disciple Kyōgō, he devoted himself to important academic pursuits.[55] Besides publishing the first commentary on the Shōbōgenzō, Sen'e and Kyōgō were instrumental in clarifying the distinctive features of Dōgen-Zen in comparison with the Rinzai school and to the Chinese Zen of the Sung period. Though biographical data on this line is scant, we do know that the Yōkō-ji monastery suffered an early demise (before the middle of the fourteenth century); yet all subsequent interpretations of Dōgen refer back to the commentaries of this line.

3. The Jakuen line traces its lineage through its founder directly back to the Zen of the Sung period. Numerically not very strong, it lent support to the conservative Eihei-ji line insofar as Giun, the fifth abbot of Eihei-ji, was also a disciple of Jakuen. There was a clear overlapping between these two schools, especially in spiritual matters. Perhaps it was Jakuen's enduring bonds with the Rinzai Zen of the Sung period that prevented him from truly appreciating Dōgen's uniqueness, despite his own closeness to the master. Jakuen's strong influence emerges in the Chinese flavor of Giun's sixty-volume commentary on Dōgen's works, which makes it clearly distinguishable from the interpretations of Sen'e and Kyōgō.[56]

4. The Kangan Giin line, centered in the Daiji-ji monastery in Kumamoto (Kyūshū), is also called the "line of the Imperial Dharma" (hōkōha) because of Giin's family ties with the imperial court. Integrating elements from the old schools of Tendai and Shingon, as well as Rinzai, this line flourished in the third generation under Kezō Gidon, whose disciples went on to form thirteen different lines.

5. The fifth line was first formed by Tettsū Gikai in Daijō-ji in the province of Kaga, and under Keizan Jōkin (1268–1325) became the most important organization of the Sōtō school. It originated the nationwide Sōtō movement during the middle ages.

Born in the province of Echizen, Keizan Jōkin is remembered in the Sōtō school alongside the "high patriarch" (kōso), Dōgen, as the "great patriarch" (taiso). The story of his life and work is woven with legend, an indication of the popular esteem he enjoyed as a religious leader.[57] Like Hakuin, his spirituality was strongly influenced by his mother, who—the story goes—before he was born vowed to the bodhisattva Kannon, to whom she was fervently devoted, to consecrate her son to the Buddha. The pious woman filled her young son's fertile imagination, as he stood before an image of the bodhisattva, with stories of how those who reverenced Kannon would be richly rewarded. Early on his mother brought him to be educated by the Zen monks of Eihei-ji. He was only twelve when he received his first monastic ordination from Ejō shortly before the master died (1280). When Ejō looked upon this young boy so fervently committing himself to the precepts of Buddha, he is said to have prophetically foreseen a source of hope for the then beleagured Sōtō school.

Keizan remained in Eihei-ji under Gikai's direction until he was seventeen, at which time he set out on a pilgrimage to visit monasteries and well-known masters across the country. Legend tells us that he was once so angered by an immoral monk he encountered that he raised his staff in the air to pummel the unworthy creature when he suddenly remembered his mother's admonition to temper his impetuosity and to imitate the gentle Kannon. He was of a mystical temperament and had frequent visions from which he drew the strength to carry on.

Keizan's pilgrimage, which spanned the years from 1285 to 1288, prepared him for his life's work. With a free spirit that found good everywhere, he was able to acquire a broad knowledge of Buddhist teaching and practice. Though he sought out people of different views he was especially interested in Zen meditation, to which he had committed himself under the stern direction of Jakuen. In Kyoto he visited the two Rinzai masters Tōzan Tanshō (1231–1291) and Hakuun Egyō (1228–1297), disciples and successors of Enni Ben'en (1202–1280) as abbots of Tōfuku-ji in the second and fourth generations. Like Gikai, these two masters freely mixed their Zen practice with elements of Shingon. Keizan took advantage of a visit to Mount Hiei to study the teachings of Tendai. He also spent time with and was deeply impressed by the originality of Master Shinchi Kakushin (also known as Muhon Kakushin, 1207–1298), the most illustrious expert on the Mumonkan kōan collection. Before concluding his journey, he returned once again to Jakuen. It is impossible to know fully the effects of this pilgrimage on Keizan. Hakuun Egyō and Shinchi Kakushin were strongly bound to Shingon, while Tōzan Tanshō was devoted to Amida. The broad range of Buddhist religiosity that he learned from this journey would later bear fruit in the variety of activities he would soon be undertaking.

In 1294, after returning to Daijō-ji, Keizan experienced his great enlightenment. Gikai had presented his pupil with the nineteenth case of the Mumonkan when Keizan felt his mind's eye open. In the dialogue that constitutes the kōan, the disciple Chao-chou asks his master Nan-chü'an about the Way and receives this answer: "The ordinary mind is the Way." As Keizan tried to show the ordinary mind to Gikai, a kōan-like scene unfolded, with the master giving his pupil a slap on the face. Soon afterward, convinced that his disciple has attained a high degree of enlightenment, Gikai made Keizan his Dharma heir and appointed him the founding abbot of Jōman-ji in the province of Awa. The following year Keizan visited the esteemed Eihei-ji monastery, where he received the bodhisattva precepts from Gien. Thereafter he traveled southward and visited Daiji-ji in Kyūshū. On his return he stopped in Kyoto and there met for the first time Gasan Jōseki, who was to become his disciple and successor. When Keizan was about thirty years old and intensely busy instructing disciples and laity at Jōman-ji monastery, he was summoned by the aging Gikai to return to

Daijō-ji. There, in the year 1300, he began work on his major literary achievement, the *Denkōroku*. In 1303 Gikai retired as abbot of Daijō-ji and Keizan assumed the post.

Under Keizan's direction, the monastery of Daijō-ji developed into one of the most important centers of Buddhism in the northeastern provinces. As the number of disciples increased, the monastery's renown spread throughout the land. Keizan presented the books of his *Denkōroku*[58] to his disciples. Like the early Zen chronicles, the books begin with the transmission of Śākyamuni's mind to Kāśyapa and then list first the Indian and then the Chinese patriarchs up to Ju-ching, with Dōgen listed as the fifty-first patriarch. The work closes with the book on Ejō. Keizan's much loved *Notebook on Zen Practice (Zazen yōjinki)*[59] originated during his work at Daijō-ji. The book follows Dōgen's directions and encourages the disciples to practice zealously, explaining that *zazen* is concerned mainly with a basic attitude. It begins:

> *Zazen* clears the mind immediately and lets one dwell in one's true realm. This is called showing one's original face or revealing the light of one's original state. Body and mind are cast off, apart from whether one is sitting or lying down. Therefore one thinks neither of good nor of evil—transcending both the sacred and the profane, rising above delusion and enlightenment—and leaves the realm of sentient beings and Buddhas.[60]

Keizan provides a convincing description of the quiet style of Zen:

> The mind, originally marvelous, clear, and bright, suddenly emerges, and the original light shines fully at last. . . . All Buddhas appear in this world because of the one great thing, in order to show all sentient beings the wisdom of the Buddha and to lead them to enlightenment. This is a wonderful art of stillness and purity called *zazen*. It is the self-joyous *samādhi* (*jijuyū-zammai*) or the kingly *samādhi* (*sammai-ō-zammai*).[61]

Basing himself on the classical teaching on enlightenment, Keizan develops his advice on how to go about practice; he can be very concrete, as shown in the following:

> Great Buddha festivals and massive constructions are very good things, but if you concentrate entirely on *zazen*, you should avoid them . . .
>
> Do not practice *zazen* where it is extremely light or extremely dark, extremely cold or extremely hot, or near pleasure-seekers and public women. You can stay in the meditation hall with a good master, deep in the mountains and secluded valleys. Green waters and verdant mountains are the place for walking in meditation;[62] by the streams and under the trees are places to clear the mind. Do not forget the sight of impermanence,[63] which encourages the mind to seek the Way.
>
> The mat should be spread thickly; *zazen* is a comfortable way of sitting. The place of practice should be clean. If incense is always burned and flowers are offered, the good gods who protect the Dharma and the Buddhas

and bodhisattvas will cast their shadows and watch guard. If you put images of Buddhas, bodhisattvas, and arhats there, no devil or demon can trouble you.

Always dwelling in great compassion, dedicate the boundless merits of sitting in meditation to all sentient beings! Do not let pride, conceit, and feelings of superiority arise! They are the manner of unbelievers and the unenlightened. Vow to cut off the passions and acquire *bodhi!* Sitting only in *zazen* and doing nothing else—this is the essential art of *zazen.*

Always wash your eyes and feet; your body and mind should be calm, your behavior well-ordered. Cast away worldly feelings and do not attach yourselves to feelings of the Way.[64]

Keizan treats in detail all the bodily and psychological aspects of Zen meditation and has much to say about bodily posture and breathing. Drowsiness can be fought off by moving the body and walking around. A definite mental attitude is also of great help. He offers encouragement:

. . . By various means avoid sleep! The matter of life and death is great, impermanence moves swiftly. How can you sleep, when the eye of the Way is not yet cleared?[65]

If sleepiness is due to bad karma, then the meditator should pray: "May Buddhas and patriarchs in their great compassion remove the pain of my heavy darkness!"[66]

Keizan used the practice of kōan as an aid for concentrating during meditation. If one is beset with distractions, he suggests concentrating on a kōan, and offers two possibilities from the *Mumonkan:* case 1, dealing with the Buddha nature of a dog, and case 37, "The Oak Tree in the Garden." He also cites a kōan question from a Zen chronicle.[67]

Keizan's *Notebook on Zen Practice* has been highly regarded throughout the history of Zen and is still used today in Sōtō temples as a basic text for learning how to mediatate. Though close to Dōgen, there are also echoes of elements of the Chinese Zen of the Sung period that Dōgen had criticized. The following passage, which summarizes Keizan's point of view, is the book's climax:

Cast off mind, intention, and consciousness; stop recollection, imagination, and vision; do not intend to become a Buddha, do not judge about right and wrong! Use time to the utmost, as if you had to save your head from burning! The Perfected One sitting upright and Bodhidharma wall-gazing in the temple of Shao-lin concentrated on *zazen* and did nothing else. Shih-shuang Ch'ing-chu sat like a withered tree, Ju-ching warned not to sleep while sitting. He said that without burning incense, paying veneration, reciting the *nembutsu*, practicing *sange*, reading the sūtras, or performing rites, you can attain enlightenment by only sitting in *zazen.*[68]

These short sentences describe the *zazen* of classical tradition. Bodhidharma and a famous Zen master of the T'ang period (Shih-shuang Ch'ing-chu) are referred to. The image of fire threatening one's head is an allusion to kōan literature, while the name of Ju-ching recalls Dōgen's great experience of enlightenment. In the last sentence, Keizan affirms Ju-ching's and Dōgen's insistence on "*zazen* only" (*shikan taza*) to the exclusion of all other practices of Buddhist piety.

In his *Notebook for Zen Practice*, as in the *Denkōroku*, Keizan shows himself to be a learned and trustworthy Zen master belonging to the tradition of authentic Zen. We need to keep this in mind as we turn to consider Keizan's typical but syncretistic way of adapting to other forms of Buddhism.

Keizan administered Daijō-ji for nearly a decade (1303–1311), first during the lifetime of Gikai and then by himself. During these years he added to his literary works the *Shinjin meinentei*[69] and the *Sankon zazensetsu*,[70] both very much in the spirit of authentic Zen tradition. Energetic by nature, he tried to take a active part in the life of the people, which in turn brought him to the conviction that it was necessary to adapt Zen to the spirit of the times and to integrate it with other forms of Buddhist life, especially those of esoteric Buddhism. Gikai had already prompted him in this direction, and the experiences gained during his pilgrimage had prepared him for it. He saw nothing preventing the realization of his ideas and considered the northeastern provinces especially receptive to what he had in mind. Turning over the direction of Daijō-ji to his disciple Meihō Sotetsu (1277–1350), he went on to found Jōjū-ji, where he soon appointed his disciple Mugai Chikyō (d. 1351) abbot.

Keizan maintained good relations with many different abbots and with their help was able to promote the rapid growth of Sōtō Zen. The monasteries of Yōkō-ji and Sōji-ji, both in the region of Noto, became centers for his activity. He enlarged the Shingon temple of Yōkō-ji, turning it into a Zen monastery, and worked there for a number of years. His most important institutional achievement came toward the end of his life. Thanks to his friendly relations with the Vinaya master (Jpn., *risshi*) Jōken, he inherited the Shingon temple of Shogaku-ji in 1322, renamed it Sōji-ji, and turned it into the main temple of the Sōtō school. Emperor Go-Daigo elevated it to the rank of a "great head temple" (*daihonzan*), on the same level as Eihei-ji. Soon afterward, Keizan appointed his able disciple Gasan Jōseki (1275–1365) to take his place as abbot of Sōji-ji so that he could spend his final days in his beloved Yōkō-ji. Shortly before he died, he wrote the book of rules for monastic living known as the *Keizan shingi*.[71] His remains were divided among the temples of Daijō-ji, Yōkō-ji, and Sōji-ji and reverently laid to rest.

At the end of Kamakura period, the Sōtō school had crystallized around three centers: the original foundation of Eihei-ji, the Daijō-ji monastery with Master Meihō as abbot, and the two temples of Yōkō-ji and Sōji-ji, both under the direction of Gasan. The real axis of the movement was clearly with Gasan, in that the influence of Sōji-ji not only equalled but came to surpass that of Eihei-ji. During the second half of the middle ages, the movement of Sōtō Zen among the common people originated from Sōji-ji. Eventually the two monasteries ironed out apparent rivalries and formed one centralized Sōtō school.

We are left with the question of how to evaluate this development of Sōtō Zen that Gikai began and Keizan brought to fruition. For the most part, contemporary Sōtō scholars consider the evident changes in the style of Dōgen's school to be the ineluctable result of institutionalization.

When an institution takes shape, the school of the patriarchs undergoes change. This is its unavoidable fate and part of the process of adapting to the needs of the times and of society. One must ask, however, whether such change actually served as a form of "skillful means" (Jpn., hōben) to further the spread of doctrine and the advancement of the community, or whether under the pressure of democratization it led to another school that was totally different from the style of Zen Master Dōgen. No doubt experts will answer this question differently; what is clear is that Zen Master Keizan himself firmly believed that he was preserving the style of Dōgen's school.[72]

What prevailed in fact was a widespread mixture of Zen with elements of esoteric Buddhism. In leading Sōtō monasteries one could find next to the hall of Zen mediation a cultic hall where mainly Shingon rituals were carried out. Burial services were prominent, though incantations and petitionary prayers (kaji-kitō) for one's earthly well-being were also part of the daily cult. Relatively few of the monks practiced regular mediation, and still the communities had a strong sense of belonging to Zen Buddhism. Just as throughout their lives Keizan and Gikai considered themselves to be disciples of Dōgen, so do Sōtō monks up to the present feel themselves bound to the practice of meditation. At no time has there been a dearth of individuals having extraordinary enlightenment experiences through meditation. The line that took shape during the third and fourth generations after Dōgen endured through the history of Sōtō Zen. The historically significant developments in the Sōtō school have their roots in Dōgen and Keizan, and, as we shall see in the next section of the book, in Gasan as well.

NOTES

1. See Takeuchi Michio, Nihon no zen, pp. 166–67. Cf. vol. 1, part 2, chap. 7.

2. Nihon no zen, pp. 167ff. Imaeda Aishin calls the way of Zen directly descending from Dōgen "the Zen of pure Dharma" (shōbō-zen); see Nihon bukkyōshi, vol. 2, p. 200.

3. On the following see Azuma Ryūshin, "Dōgen to sono montei," in Kōza Dōgen, vol. 1, Dōgen no shōgai to shisō, pp. 169–222.

4. The tradition regarding this woman mixes legendary elements; Azuma, "Dōgen to sono montei," pp. 177–78.

5. The names (including those of disciples in the broadest sense of the term) are given by Azuma; "Dōgen to sono montei," pp. 177–78.

6. This is Azuma's judgment; "Dōgen to sono montei," p. 188.

7. Azuma doubts the affiliation of Kangan Giin to the Daruma school ("Dōgen to sono montei," pp. 191–92). See Y. H. Ku, History of Zen, pp. 243–44, who also offers the line of disciples through eighteen generations (pp. 261–62).

8.   Azuma, "Dōgen to sono montei," pp. 197ff.

9.   On this commentary to the Shōbōgenzō see Zen Dust, p. 396.

10.   See Azuma, "Dōgen to sono montei," pp. 208–09.

11.   Ibid., pp. 213–14. Takeuchi reports on the episode, Nihon no zen, p. 175.

12.   Helpful for the study of Ejō is Takeuchi Michio's recent biography, Eihei niso Koun Ejō Zenji-den. Compare the collection of essays edited by the staff of Eihei-ji under the title Ejō Zenji kenkyū. In his studies on Dōgen's disciples Azuma devoted a lengthy section to Ejō ("Dōgen to sono montei," pp. 183–86). See also the entry on Ejō in Zengaku daijiten I, p. 98.

13.   Cf. Takeuchi, Eihei niso Koun Ejō Zenji-den, p. 40.

14.   See Takeuchi's presentation, ibid., especially pp. 48–49.

15.   This is the view of Takeuchi who sets the verses at the outset of his biography, ibid., p. 3, and continually returns to this psychological finding.

16.   See the section on this school in chap. 1.

17.   On this ancient Buddhist temple city, see Zengaku daijiten II, p. 938.

18.   Takeuchi bases his account of Ejō's practice at Tōnomine under the direction of Kakuan on source materials; see Eihei niso Kuon Ejō Zenji-den, pp. 76–80. For the two sūtras, see the catalog Nj. no 446 (Shuryōgon-gyō) T. 945 and Nj. no. 1629 (Engaku-gyō or Engaku-kyō), T. 842. According to the edition of the catalog compiled by Paul Demiéville, Hubert Durt, and Anna Seidel on the editing of the Sino-Japanese Buddhist canon, (Répertoire du Canon Bouddhique Sino-Japonais [Paris, 1978]) Taishō shinshū daizōkyō, the Shuryōgon-gyō is in part apocryphal (p. 86), and the Engaku-gyō entirely apocryphal (p. 78). Despite their popularity at the time, Dōgen did not like these two sūtras.

19.   Cited in Takeuchi, Eihei niso Kuon Ejō Zenji-den, p. 84.

20.   By Keizan Jōkin in 2 volumes, T. 2585; it ends with a biography of Ejō. The place is given in T. 82. 409a, where there is also a treatment on the practice of Ejō in Tōnomine. On the compilation of the work, see Zen Dust, p. 354.

21.   T. 82. 409b. Takeuchi analyzes this report, Eihei niso Koun Ejō Zenji-den, pp. 97ff. The expression reichi (spiritual knowledge) is put in the mouth of the nonbeliever Śrenika in the Bendōwa and then repudiated. See the answer to question 10 in DZZ I, p. 739.

22.   See Takeuchi, Eihei niso Koun Ejō Zenji-den, pp. 95–96.

23.   Shimei ni shitagaite toki wo matsu, T. 82. 409b.

24.   This is the conjecture of Takeuchi, Eihei niso Koun Ejō Zenji-den, p. 107. Where there are lacunae in the sources, Takeuchi fills out the picture with conjecture.

25.   This seems particularly evident in the answer to question 10, where he refers back to the notion of reichi (as well as the compound kenshō reichi). See the details provided by Takeuchi. Eihei niso Koun Ejō Zenji-den, pp. 99–103.

26.   On the following, Takeuchi, Eihei niso Koun Ejō Zenji-den, p. 109.

27.   T. 82. 409b.

28.   Kōan 85 in the first volume of the collection Shōbōgenzō sambyakusoku, DZZ II, pp. 201–52, especially p. 215. On Ejō's enlightenment experience cf. Takeuchi, Eihei niso Koun Ejō Zenji-den, pp. 141–48, and Thomas Cleary, Timeless Spring: A Sōtō Zen Anthology, p. 107. Takeuchi brings out all the reports from the source materials and argues that Ejō found in the experience the solution to the inner contradiction rooted in his consciousness of sin.

29. See Takeuchi, *Eihei niso Koun Ejō Zenji-den*, pp. 152ff, 156. For the metaphor of shadow and figure in the *Denkōroku*, see T. 82. 409c.

30. Takeuchi, *Eihei niso Koun Ejō Zenji-den*, pp. 169–82 for a detailed description of the incident.

31. On this, see the section on the description of Dōgen's life in the previous chapter.

32. The name stems from the name of the period in which Buddhism first found entry into China under Emperor Ming of the Later Han period. This was in the year 67, or year 10 of the Eihei period. With the arrival of Buddhism, according to the pious belief of its adherents, "eternal peace" came to eastern Asia.

33. Cited in Takeuchi, *Koun Ejō Zenji-den*, pp. 216–17. Compare the text in the *Denkōroku*, T. 82. 409c.

34. Ōkubo Dōchū compares the precarious situation at the time the cloister was under Ejo's direction to the period when Dōgen's community was in full bloom. See his *Dōgen Zenji-den no kenkyū*, p. 429.

35. See Takeuchi, *Nihon no zen*, p. 184.

36. On the course of his life, see Azuma, "Dōgen to sono montei," pp. 189ff; Takeuchi, *Koun Ejō Zenji-den*, pp. 243–44.

37. On the following see Takeuchi, *Koun Ejō Zenji-den*, pp. 244ff.

38. Takeuchi draws attention expressly to the weaknesses of Gikai referred to in the text; *Koun Ejō Zenji-den*, p. 246.

39. On the following, Takeuchi, *Koun Ejō Zenji-den*, pp. 247–55. He cites the relevant passages from the conversation between Ejō and Gikai.

40. Ejō recognized the enlightenment of Gikai; Takeuchi, *Koun Ejō Zenji-den*, pp. 254–55.

41. See quotation, Takeuchi, *Koun Ejō Zenji-den*, p. 258.

42. The oldest plan of construction, probably prepared by Gikai, is preserved in Kanazawa. See Collcutt, *Five Mountains*, p. 174.

43. In addition to Takeuchi (see note 35 above), see for example the section on the Sōtō school in vol. 6 of the collection *Nihon bukkyō kiso kōza*, p. 93.

44. Takeuchi also thinks that the sickness was nothing serious to worry about; *Koun Ejō Zenji-den*, pp. 266–67.

45. T. no 2590, vol. 82. 453a–460a. Compare the studies on the quotation in *Kōmyōzōzammai* by Ishii Shūdō in *Ejō Zenji kenkyū* (see note 12 above), pp. 145–74. Ishii also takes up the question of the purity of the text (about which doubts have arisen), claiming Ejō as the original author (p. 167). At the conclusion of his study he presents a tabular alignment of the quotations (pp. 169–74). It is surprising that Ejō, in his detailed knowledge of Buddhism as testified to in the quotations, had left behind the *Kōmyōzō-zammai* as his only written work, besides the *Shōbōgenzō zuimonki*. The explanation lies in the fact that he concentrated entirely on the literary work of his master before and after the death of Dōgen. In the *Kōmyōzōzammai* important Dōgen-like expressions come up, like *shikan taza* (T. 82. 454a, b), *shushō* (p. 455c), and *myōshu honshō* ("wondrous practice—original enlightenment," p. 457b), but one misses a statement on the relationship between practice and enlightenment so characteristic of Dōgen's doctrine (Ishii, p. 164).

46.   The résumé follows the presentation of Kagamishima in his introductory essay on the Sōtō school, "Nihon zenshūshi: Sōtōshū," which appeared in vol. 4 of an eight-volume work on Zen, *Zen no rekishi: Nihon* (Tokyo, 1967), pp. 98–100.

47.   See Ōkubo's presentation of the conflict over succession in the third generation, *Dōgen Zenji-den no kenkyū*, pp. 430–446. It is clear from the outset that Ōkubo cannot bring himself to condone the "impossible" situation of Gikai from the standpoint of contemporary Sōtō Zen. He accuses Gikai of inconsistency in continuing to maintain his interests in the branch line of the Daruma school even after assuming succession in Eihei-ji. See especially pp. 442, 443, 445–46. On this point see also Yanagida, *Dōgen to chūgoku bukkyō*, p. 41.

48.   See B. Faure, "The Daruma-shū, Dōgen, and Sōtō Zen," MN 42.1 (1987): 35.

49.   Among the reforms that Gikai effected in Eihei-ji, Takeuchi mentions the introduction of esoteric ceremonies *(mikkyōteki gyōji)*; *Koun Ejō Zenji-den*, p. 269. In his book *Nihon no zen*, he gives as the third of six essential characteristic marks of Dōgen-Zen Dōgen's repudiation of all syncretism, namely of animistic folk beliefs, of esoteric, magical prayer *(mikkyōteki kitōgyōji)*, and *mappō* belief (p. 178). Imaeda stresses, on the basis of Dōgen's writings, particularly the *Bendōwa*, that Dōgen rejected all admixture of Shingon and Tendai as well as of Amida Buddhism; *Nihon bukkyōshi*, vol. 2, pp. 198–99, 200.

50.   Takeuchi judges adherents to the opposition group sharply and thinks that many of them had become adherents of Jakuen (*Eihei niso Koun Ejō Zenji-den*, p. 290). On Jakuen, see Azuma, "Dōgen to sono montei," pp. 199–200. In an appendix to his monograph on Ejō, Takeuchi described a visit to the monastery of Hōkyō-ji, where traces of the Chinese style remain. Takeuchi was particularly impressed by the peculiar temple gate *(sanmon)*, a masterpiece of Chinese architecture.

51.   Takeuchi refers to this incident as the third phase of the strife over succession in the third generation. See *Eihei niso Koun Ejō Zenji-den*, p. 288; *Nihon no zen*, p. 184.

52.   See the article on Guin in the *Zengaku daijiten* vol. 1, p. 192. Furuta Shōkin relates remarkable elements in his life in a chapter on this important personality in *Zensō no shōji*, pp. 142–49.

53.   Ōkubo Dōshū remarks: "With that the Daruma school was finally dissolved" (*Dōgen Zenji-den no kenkyū*, p. 444). On the *gorōhō* see Takeuchi, *Sōtōshū kyōdanshi*, pp. 77–78. The entry on *gorōhō* in the *Zengaku daijiten* (vol. 1, p. 362) points to the relationship to Ju-ching stressed through the memorial hall.

54.   On Sen'e and Kyōgō, see the section on Dōgen's disciples with which this chapter opens.

55.   Cf. Kagamishima, *Zen no rekishi: Nihon*, pp. 101–102.

56.   As restorer of Eihei-ji, Giun performed a great service for Dōgen-Zen. His edition of the *Shōbōgenzō* in sixty volumes availed itself of a certain freedom toward Dōgen's work. Kagamishima attributes the fact that the books in which Dōgen criticized other Buddhist schools, in particular Rinzai Zen, were left out to the fact that Giun came from the circle of Jakuen's disciples. "Nihon zenshūshi: Sōtōshū," pp. 105–106. Giun belongs to the most important Zen masters, and left behind him a collection of sayings known as the *Giun goroku* (T. 2591).

57.   See the entry on Keizan Jōkin in the *Zengaku daijiten* I, p. 536. On the occasion of the 650th anniversary, a massive volume was published, *Keizan Zenji kenkyū*, edited by the Association for Publications Commemorating Zen Master Keizan (Tokyo, 1974). It included a comprehensive bibliography of Japanese works on Keizan compiled by Azuma

Ryūshin (pp. 1135–82), editor-in-chief of the collection. For the legendary elements in Keizan's life, compare the preface to my German translation of the Zazenyōjinki, MN 13 (1958): 330–31; T. 2586, vol. 82. 412a–414b. There are two English translations: Reihō Matsunaga, "Zazenyōjinki: Points to Watch in Zazen" in The Sōtō Approach to Zen (Tokyo, 1958), pp. 106–24, and "Keizan Jōkin's Zazen Yōjinki," in Thomas Cleary, Timeless Spring: A Sōtō Anthology (Tokyo, 1980), pp. 112–25. The two translation, neither of them quite literal, differ from one another; both have been consulted for the English rendition given in the text.

58.   See note 20 above.

59.   T. 2586, vol. 82. 412a–414b.

60.   T 82. 412a.

61.   T 82. 412a.

62.   Meditation in the cross-legged position is broken periodically by the practice of walking around, known as kinhin. One walks through the meditation hall or cross the veranda in short, quick steps.

63.   The vision of transitoriness, which Dōgen also stressed again and again, embraces reflection on passing away in death and on the continued dying through becoming.

64.   T. 82. 413a, b.

65.   T. 82. 414a.

66.   T. 82. 414a.

67.   T. 82. 414a.

68.   T. 82. 413c.

69.   T. no. 2587, vol. 82. 414b–422a.

70.   The brief text is found in a book compiled for cultic practice, the Sōtōshū nikka seiten, pp. 69–72. Some of the Dharma sayings of Keizan are contained in the collection of Dharma sayings of the Sōtō school known as the Zenmon hōgoshū, pp. 501–505.

71.   T. no. 2589, vol. 82. 423c–451.

72.   Kagamishima, Zen no rekishi: Nihon, p. 109.

SECTION 2

Expansion and Achievements to the End of the Middle Ages

It was for the most part during the years of Japanese history known as the Kamakura period (1185–1333) that Zen took root in Japan. The collapse of the military might of the Hōjō regency brought far-reaching political and social changes that also affected the religious communities. As the nation's center shifted to the old capital of Kyoto, the aborted attempt at a coup by the *tennō* Go-Daigo split the imperial house for a half a century into a northern and southern dynasty (1333–1392).[1] Even though this event is no more than a passing episode in the wide course of Japanese history, it has remained latent in the depths of Japan's identity. The restoration of imperial power through Go-Daigo during the Kemmu era—the so-called Kemmu Restoration—lasted only two years (1334–1336). The emperor was forced to bow to the military might of the Ashikaga, who were related to the earlier samurai house of Minamoto. The emperor fled south to Yoshino, where death awaited him in 1392 and where his successors remained, without real power, until the third Ashikaga shōgun, Yoshimitsu, would succeed in bringing the two lines of the dynasty back together again. When Go-Komatsu Tennō was installed as emperor in 1392, he was instructed to make sure that after him the northern and southern lines would take turns in imperial succession—an ideal that in the circumstances soon proved impossible. With the northern line controlling the succession, the shōguns from the Ashikaga clan retained power until the end of the Muromachi period (1573).[2]

It is possible to understand how the Zen schools could enjoy the enduring good graces of the different rulers only by taking note of the tremendous growth of Buddhist influence during the feudal period of Japan's middle ages. While there are no precise statistics,[3] Buddhist monks and monasteries numbered in the thousands and enjoyed the widespread devotion of the populace; Buddhism won over the popular mind and heart mainly by taking on elements of the indigenous Shinto religion. During the Kamakura period, when the richest religious growth in all of Japan's history took place, Buddhism flourished in the form of three renewal movements: Amida piety, the Nichiren tradition, and Zen. Zen's unique contributions to this period of growth lay in the realms of intellectual stimulation, religious interiorization, and cultural refinement. More than the other two religious movements of the Kamakura period, Zen was able to penetrate the whole of national life, especially after Kyoto had once again become the nation's center. The Zen temples in this metropolis found themselves at the cross-currents of the nation's political, social, and intellectual life. The temples that grew up in Kyoto during the second half of the Kamakura period, together with the Zen centers that were established under the aegis of the Ashikaga shōguns, represent both the climax of the history of Japanese Zen and at the same time the beginnings of its secularization and decline. This entire development is focused in the system of the "Five Mountains" (gozan) of the Rinzai school.[4]

NOTES

1.   This span of time, the Nambokuchō, or "Southern and Northern Dynasties," does not represent a particular epoch in Japan's history inasmsuch as the Ashikaga lords came into power soon after the outset of the period.

2.   The Muromachi period is variously reckoned: from 1392 to 1573 if the time of the split between the northern and southern dynasties (known either as the Nambokuchō or as the Yoshino period) is considered an independent era (1333–1392), or from 1338 to 1573 if the period is made to begin with the installation of the Ashikaga lord Takauji as shōgun.

3.   See Collcutt, *Five Mountains,* pp. 10–11. Collcutt cites some statistics drawn from Japanese literature on the subject.

4.   Also *gozan-sōrin,* in contrast to the *Rinka* monasteries; on this latter see chap. 5.

4

The Five Mountains
of the Rinzai School

THE ESTABLISHMENT AND REINFORCEMENT OF THE SYSTEM

The Rinzai school, or at least a rather considerable and influential part, was officially institutionalized by the state in the form of a three-tiered system composed of the "Five Mountains" (gozan), the "Ten Temples" (jissetsu), and a number of larger temples (shozan). The system, which corresponded to a Chinese hierarchical model (wu-shan, shih-ch'a, chia-ch'a),[1] was established in Japan during the Kamakura period when the most famous Zen temples of Kyoto were known as the Five Mountains: Kenchō-ji, Engaku-ji, Jufuku-ji, Jōmyō-ji, and Jōchi-ji.[2] It was worked out fully during the following period under Emperor Go-Daigo and especially under the rule of the Ashikaga shōgun. When the powers of state moved to Kyoto, the list had to be reformulated and throughout the first decades of this period was repeatedly revised.[3] A list drawn up during the time of Emperor Go-Daigo (1334–1336) shows trends current at the time. First on the list was the Nanzen-ji temple, closely tied to the imperial court and the government, followed by two Zen temples of the capital city, Tōfuku-ji and Kennin-ji, with the Kamakura temples of Kenchō-ji and Engaku-ji, once the heart of the Zen movement, in last place.[4] This ranking was subsequently changed many times. In a list dated 1341, the two monasteries of both central cities were placed along side each other—Kenchō-ji next to Nanzen-ji, and Engaku-ji next to Tenryū-ji; Jufuku-ji (Kamakura) occupied third place, while the two oldest Zen temples of the capital, Kennin-ji and Tōfuku-ji, were listed last. A final arrangement was made during the reign of the third Ashikaga shōgun, Yoshimitsu (1358–1408). It is composed of two lists, each with five temples from Kyoto and Kamakura respectively, lined up alonside each other and both beneath Nanzen-ji, which is entitled "the first Zen temple in the land." The parallel listing reads as follows:

KYOTO	KAMAKURA
Tenryū-ji—Kenchō-ji	
Shōkoku-ji—Engaku-ji	
Kennin-ji—Jufuku-ji	
Tōfuku-ji—Jōchi-ji	
Manju-ji—Jōmyō-ji	

The Kamakura temples occupy a subordinate position. Leading the Kyoto list are the two temples from the line of the national master Musō: Tenryū-ji and Shōkoku-ji. The place of Tōfuku-ji, the central temple of Enni Ben'en's line, does not reflect its numerical strength or the important influence it enjoyed among the masses. Manju-ji, like the final three Kamakura temples, was never as important as the other temples.

The second tier of the overall system was made up of the Ten Temples. These were large, influential temple complexes in cities or in rural areas that, like the Five Mountains, enjoyed both general esteem and privilege, and were at the disposal of the military government for financial assistance and general services. The figure ten, though it provided limits, was never strictly interpreted, while a large number of Zen centers belonging to the "great temples," enjoyed the protection of and support of the shōgun. The system assured mutual benefits for all involved.

The entire system was under state control and supervised by a bureaucracy specially created for the purpose.[5] The first Ashikaga shōgun, Takauji (1305–1358), a rather rough warrior, left this part of his government to his more culturally inclined brother Tadayoshi (1306–1352), who established a special office for Zen and Vinaya monasteries (zenritsugata). The civil officials appointed to this office (zenritsugata no tōnin) were men favorably disposed toward Zen and interested in what the monasteries could contribute to the cultural life of the land. They assured a harmonious relationship between the Zen temples of the gozan system and the military government until the third shōgun Yoshimitsu turned over this office completely to Zen monks in 1379. Imitating the Chinese model, Yoshimitsu established the office of sōroku (Chin., seng-lu) and gave it full jurisdiction over all the temples and monks belonging to the gozan system. Musō's disciple Shun'oku Myōha, who enjoyed the great favor of the shōgun, was selected as the first sōroku. Toward the end of his life Yoshimitsu built the branch temple of Rokuon-in on the grounds of the Shōkoku-ji monastery; its superior was Zekkai Chūshin (1336–1405), who succeeded Shun'oku in the office of sōroku. In its heyday, the broadly extended gozan system was headquartered in this minor temple.

Based in the two main cities of Kyoto and Kamakura, the gozan system extended its influence throughout the country. In 1338, at the suggestion of Musō, the shōgun Takauji and his brother Tadayoshi ordered the construction of "temples for the national pacification" (ankokuji) and "pagodas for the welfare of sentient beings" (rishōtō) across the country to commemorate those who had fallen in the battles of Emperor Go-Daigo against the Hōjō during the Genkō era (1331–1333). One temple and one pagoda were built in each of sixty-six regions and two islands. The temples were associated with the Zen temples of the gozan system under the protection of the bakufu government and the local magistrates (shugo), while the pagodas—except for those belonging to the Ashi-kaga clan, which had special connections to Shingon, Tendai, and Ritsu (Vinaya) temples—were made gozan property. Although the system was fashioned after the Chinese model of the Sung period,[6] they may to some extent be considered a continuation of the provincial temples (kokubunji) of the Nara period. The organization was soon forgotten after the death of the shōgun Takauji, but this broad network of government-controlled temples was always readily available when it was needed. The Zen temples in the provinces, like the entire *gozan* system, served as a means of strengthening the political and economic power of the central government.

The shōgun made ample use of the *gozan* monks for their political purposes. Highly educated and with excellent social skills, the monks were ideally suited for diplomatic missions, and with their popular and highly respected spiritual image they were effective means for quelling unruly elements among the populace.[7] The monks demonstrated their ability in economic matters as well. It is reported that at the suggestion of the national teacher Musō, the shōgun put a monk in charge of a ship dispatched to China in 1342 to secure financial resources. This mission was occasioned by a lack of funds for the construction of a memorial temple for the deceased Emperor Go-Daigo. Without funding it appeared that the building known as Tenryū-ji would not be completed. From this mission, it is said, commercial negotiations began with China that eventually developed, under the supervision of the business-minded monks, into a flourishing exchange. That first voyage is known in Japanese history as the *Tenryū-ji bune,* "the ship of Tenryū-ji."

The organization of the *gozan* temples of the Rinzai school made immeasurable contributions to the political, social, and economic power of the state apparatus. In this chapter we will focus on the spiritual values that the temples and monks contributed, while their cultural artistic contributions will be examined in the chapter 6.

NATIONAL TEACHER MUSŌ

The most famous Buddhist monk of this period is National Teacher Musō (1275–1351) whose name first rose to ascendancy during the bloody, war-torn period of division within the imperial house and went on to shine brilliantly for more than a century.[8] His person is linked with the two principal temples of the capital, Tenryū-ji and Shōkoku-ji, but he is best known by his title Musō Kokushi, which was given to him during his lifetime (1335) by Emperor Go-Daigo. Seven emperors bestowed on him the unique title of "National Teacher" (*kokushi*),[9] which is why he appears in the historical records as the "teacher of seven emperors." He was instrumental in helping Chinese Zen, which Japanese disciples had practiced and appropriated over the course of a century, to develop in Kyoto into a constitutive element of Japanese culture, despite the confusion and suffering of the times. One of the most prominent spiritual figures of his day, National Teacher Musō took full part in both the agonizing struggles and the glory of this epoch. His incomparable fame won him both friends and enemies. His was a personality full of contradictions and insoluble enigmas around whom judgments continue to differ widely even today. Unlike any other figure of Zen history, Musō is surrounded by mystery and darkness.

A PATH TO ENLIGHTENMENT WITHOUT A MASTER

The chronicle of Musō's life composed by his diciple Shun'oku Myōha (1311–1388) offers a brief summary of his origins: "The family of the master was born to the clan of Gen-ji (Minamoto) in Ise; he was the nephew in the ninth generation of Emperor Uda."[10] Early on, legends began to gather around this celebrated man, making up for historical gaps. The chronicle, for example, does not give a place of birth, but two different birthplaces are mentioned in the records of the lines of Tenryū-ji and Shōkoku-ji, both of which honor him as their founding abbot. Little is known of his father except that he was of noble stock; there is equally little to report of his mother. The boy was four years old when the family moved from the Ise (present day Mie prefecture) to Kai (Yamanashi prefecture), an unexplained incident in his mother's family occasioning the move. The mother died in their new home. We have no information about how the child reacted emotionally to the tragic turn of events, but we have no grounds for supposing that he was driven to the monastic life out of grief over his mother's death.

The family was closely bound to the province of Kai, where the Takeda family, a branch of the Genji (Minamoto) clan, were wealthy and powerful landowners.[11] The Nikaidō and Sasaki families also excercised great influence in this province. Musō's second mother probably came from the Nikaidō clan. We are certain that the Shingon monk, Kūa Daitoku, was a friend of his father and was related to the Takedas.[12] It is possible that one of the reasons why the family moved to Kai was to entrust their son's education to this monk, it being the custom at the time for young boys from the nobility to become monks at a very early age. We may further assume that the nobleman Kūa was held in high regard as a monk on Mount Hiei, a prominent Shingon center in eastern Japan (present-day Yamanashi region) during the middle ages.

The almost ten years that Musō spent as a disciple in the Shingon monastery must have left deep traces. The province of Kai remained home for him and he always felt drawn to its quiet, dark mountains. There he was able to study to his heart's content first the complex doctrines of Tendai and the deep secrets of *mikkyō* and then the learning and wisdom of China. His docile spirit drank in the rich world of the maṇḍala as well as the exuberant rituals and deep symbolism of Shingon. He interrupted his studies in 1292 to travel to Nara where, at the age of seventeen, he received his monastic ordination on the platform of Tōdai-ji. This official, ceremonial inauguration into the monastic state strengthened his religious resolve, and he decided now to concentrate exclusively on the study of Buddhism. His life as a Shingon monk was exemplary, combining a deep religiosity with a broad, lively, and artistic sensitivity for nature and the cosmos.

Already during the following year, Musō's life was to take the momentous turn from Shingon to Zen. The motivation for his conversion was somewhat different from what had prompted monks one hundred years earlier to leave Mount Hiei in search of the authentic Dharma or travel to China in order to bring back to Japan the true Buddhism of authentic Zen. The time of heroic

Zen was over. It was personal experience that brought Musō to Zen, in particular, the death of his Shingon teacher. It had been a painful death, one that shocked Musō into realizing that the problem of life and death—*the* problem of human existence—cannot be solved through learning alone. He cleaned the space around him, committed himself to silence, and began a hundred-day period of prayer before the image of the Buddha. Before the hundred days were over he experienced a liberating dream. Two famous Zen monks of the T'ang period appeared to him—Su-shan Kuang-jen (Jpn., Sozan Kōnin, 837–923), who was a disciple of Tung-shan Liang-chieh (Jpn., Tōzan Ryōkai), and Shih-t'ou Hsi-ch'ien (Jpn., Sekitō Kisen, 700–790)—the one in the form of a Shingon monk and the other as the reincarnation of Bodhidharma. "Dreams are a conversation with one's true self,"[13] bringing to light the images and desires of one's unconscious. Given the proximity and the close relations between Mount Hiei and Kamakura, the young Musō was almost certainly acquainted with the Chinese Zen of the Kamakura temples. Through the dream he felt himself drawn by an extraordinary longing toward the world of Zen Buddhism. Was it the pull of his karma he felt in his attraction to the black-clad Zen monks? He took his dream with the utmost seriousness. By taking the first graphs of the two T'ang masters' names, he formed *Soseki*, the name he felt himself destined to assume and which he used from this point on. The "dream window" (Jpn., *musō*) had opened and had shown Musō Soseki the path to enlightenment.[14]

Upon leaving the Shingon temple, Musō set out directly, perhaps on the advice of Kūa, to Shinchi Kakushin (1207–1298), who, though a Shingon monk, had turned to the Zen way of enlightenment and traveled to China, where he attained certain enlightenment experiences under Master Wu-men Hui-k'ai (Jpn., Mumon Ekai).[15] The aging monk, beloved by everyone, went about his work in the monastery of Kōkoku-ji in Yura (present-day Wakayama prefecture). But Musō never arrived at Shinchi's temple. Instead, he was detained in Kyoto, where he gathered much useful information about Zen. He had been told that in order to study Zen properly one had to experience life in one of the great Zen monasteries. Accordingly, he practiced for some time in Kennin-ji with Muin Emban (1230–1307),[16] a disciple of Lan-hsi Tao-lung (1213–1278), who had studied in China under Chung-feng Ming-pen (Jpn., Chūhō Myōhon, 1263–1323). He then left Kyoto for Kamakura, where he devoted himself to the practice of Zen meditation under well-known masters in various of the prominent Zen temples.[17] Soon thereafter he returned to Kennin-ji in Kyoto, but did not stay for long. Once he heard that the well-known Chinese Zen master I-shan I-ning (Jpn., Issan Ichinei, 1247–1317) had arrived in Kamakura, he left to seek him out. This was in the year 1299.[18]

After passing the required examination, Musō was accepted into the circle of I-shan's disciples. In his lectures, the Chinese master sought to guide his Japanese students into the depths of Chinese learning. Musō was disappointed and found that even this profound, extraordinary learning did not satisfy his inner longing. In the *Seizan yawa*[19] Musō refers to his experiences during his long stay with I-shan. He opened his mind to the teachings of the Chinese master, practiced *zazen* in his free time, and read the collections of sayings of the masters. I-shan, Musō notes there, was in charge of Kenchō-ji and Engaku-ji at the same time. During his years with the master, he studied his lessons every morning and evening, and mastered the style of the Five Houses. But when he looked back over everything he had done, his heart remained as restless as before:

> I had thrown away the knowledge of Buddhism for the knowledge of Zen. The content was different, but the standpoint of knowing was the same. To pass one's time in this way, is it not to darken the light of the mind?[20]

The knowledge of Zen that the learned I-shan offered was not able to provide Musō what he had sought in vain on Mount Heien.

Once again Musō took to the road, heading north, where he pitched tent amid the paradisal beauty of Matsushima. By chance, he had the opportunity to attend a number of introductory lectures on Tendai meditation given by a learned Tendai monk. Meantime, he persevered, still without guidance, in his practice of Zen meditation. One night he had an experience that rewarded his persistence. He had an insight into the differences among Buddhist teachings. Still, self-reflection helped him not to confuse the intuitive knowledge he had gained in meditation from the Zen enlightenment that he was seeking.

While in Matsushima word reached him about Kōhō Kennichi (1241–1316), a disciple of the Chinese master Wu-hsüeh Tsu-yüan and abbot of Engaku-ji. A son of Emperor Go-Saga, Kennichi was said to have lived for some thirty years in the monastery of Ungan-ji in Nasu, which was close to the Shingon temple of Chōraku-ji, which had cultivated good relations with Mount Hiei. Determined to meet Kennichi, Musō set out for Nasu but was disheartened to learn that Kennichi had recently left the monastery and was now residing in Kamakura. A problem with his foot made further travel impossible, and so Musō spent the winter in Ungan-ji. In the new year he set off for Kamakura, where he first visited his teacher I-shan I-ning. His hopes rekindled when he was admitted amicably to the abbot's chamber, but the two were not able to reach a deep, mutual understanding. Once again discouraged, Musō left the temple.[21]

During his time in Kamakura (1303) Musō managed to visit Kōhō Kennichi, who had since become abbot of Manju-ji. This was the first direct encounter between the two and turned out to be uneventful. Not even their common interest in the esoteric teachings of Shingon sparked any important exchange. Musō's close bonds with Shingon were rooted mainly in his youthful experiences on Mount Hiei.[22] Later, Kennichi did confirm Musō's enlightenment and this placed him in the ranks of Kennichi's disciples. But what the disciple received from his master was more in the line of inspiration than clear direction. Musō followed a solitary path to the goal of enlightenment, without a master.

More than simple wanderlust drove Musō to a second journey to northern Japan. Like all genuine Zen disciples, he was a seeker of the Way who treasured solitude above all else. Oppressed by the busy, worldly, and greedy atmosphere of the capital cities of Kyoto and Kamakura, he preferred rural living, where people were straightforward and life was simpler. And so he traveled to the northern part of Japan's main island, to Shiratori (in the region of Iwate), where he found a friendly reception.[23] As a disciple of the great Chinese Zen master I-shan I-ning, he was admired by all. Young men flocked to him for guidance, and soon plans were being made to provide him with a temple and school. Musō himself could not come to a decision whether to stay or not. The following spring he again bid farewell and set out for the south, to Hitachi (Ibaraki prefecture), where he stayed for almost a year. From there he traveled on to Usuba, the site of his great enlightenment.

The chronicles report that when Musō arrived in Usuba from the north in 1305, he was warmly welcomed by a lay benefactor, "his first patron" (Jpn., dannotsu; Skt., dānapati),[24] who offered him repose and invited him to spend time in an uninhabited hermitage where he might find peace and quiet. Musō turned down the offer, claiming that he had some pressing questions that he had to lay before Master Kennichi. But before he left, and in spite of his initial refusal, he did spend some time in the hermitage of Usuba, where he went on a kind of "private retreat" (doku-sesshin).[25]

On a warm May evening, he was enjoying the cool shade of a tree in front of the garden. Time passed, and before he knew it darkness fell under a starless, moonless sky. Tired, Musō stumbled along the way back to the hermitage to continue his meditation. Thinking to lean against a wall where there was none, he lost his balance and fell. At that moment, with a loud clamor, the wall of darkness disintegrated. It was as if the world had collapsed in on itself. Nothing any longer separated one thing from another. As Musō stood up, he felt an extraordinary strength course through his every fiber. Around him he felt the freshness of morning air. The verses commemorating this enlightenment read as follows:

> For many years I dug the earth and searched for the blue heaven,
> And how often, how often did my heart grow heavier and heavier.
> One night, in the dark, I took stone and brick,
> And mindlessly struck the bones of the empty heavens.[26]

It is not likely that Musō wrote these beautiful verses (four lines of seven glyphs each) immediately after his experience. The description of his experience is similar to that of the T'ang-period Chinese master Hsiang-yen Chih-hsien (Jpn., Kyōgen Chikan), a disciple of Kuei-shan Ling-yu (Jpn., Isan Reiyū, 771–853).[27] Musō remained in Usuba for a few months and then, in October, bade farewell to his friendly benefactor and set out for Kamakura to tell Master Kennichi of his great experience. Deeply impressed by Musō's enlightenment verses, Kennichi did not hesitate to bestow on him the seal of a Zen master (inka). These events are described in detail in the chronicle. After a long and mutually satisfying discussion, Musō suddenly gathered his things and set out again on his journey.

BETWEEN HERMITAGES AND TEMPLES

The next phase of Musō Soseki's life is a patchwork of pressing projects and long stretches of solitude—excessive activity joined to an extraordinary love of quiet and remoteness. His life moved back and forth between hermitage and temple. Hirata Kōji, present abbot of Tenryū-ji and a successor of Musō, has studied this monk who sought after solitude and yet lived in many of the great temples, whose "two-tracked personality" could not resolve the contradiction between "his desire to be famous and his longing to be alone." He concludes that the key to the "irony of Musō's life" rests in the "extraordinary gentleness of his being."[28] Hirata's perspective is helpful when we find ourselves perplexed by the many stages and events that crowd the course of Musō's life.

Musō's sudden, almost impetuous, departure from Kamakura comes as something of a surprise. After his master Kennichi had so warmly accepted him and designated him as his Dharma heir, the path was open to a glorious career in the second capital of the nation. Perhaps it was precisely the prospect of a leading position in one of Kamakura's most prominent temples that sent him, precipitously, on his journey. He was disgusted with the worldly turmoil that embroiled the *gozan* centers. Perhaps, too, his keen political sense, which later was to demonstrate itself in his ability to assess changing political situations, already foresaw the coming downfall of the Hōjō clan and the end of the military regime in Kamakura. Hirata, whose work I have used extensively here, thinks that one of the ingredients in the contradictory personality of the National Teacher may have been a latent, though always limited, desire for fame. Even if present, such ambitions were never really very significant. More determinative, at least in Musō's decision to leave Kamakura, was his love for his home. He returned to Kai to complete his spiritual journey where it had begun.

Back home, Musō took things slowly. The twenty years that passed after his great experience form a rather uniform flow of events. Relatives and friends welcomed him home warmly. Thanks to a benefactor, he came into possession of a small temple called Jōko-ji, the first of the many temples that he was to found. In his home area, he could not really free himself from the influence of the esoteric Buddhism (*mikkyō*) he had studied so deeply in the dark mountains of Hiei. Jōko-ji became a center for the practice of both Zen and Shingon.[29] Also in his home territory, on an upper course of the river Fuefuki, he established the "Hermitage of the Dragon Mountain" (Ryūzan-an, also known as the "Hermitage of the Hidden Mountain").[30] There he spent many years of meditation, immersed in the quiet of the mountain landscape, until his wanderlust once again stirred and led him across stream and mountain into the land of Mino (in the district of Gifu). Close to "Tiger Mountain" (named after a mountain in China) he established the "Tiger Hermitage" (Kokei-an) in 1313, a temple that monks of his line were later to develop into a leading center of the Rinzai school.[31] It was there that he received word of the death of his master Kennichi, in whose honor he composed a ritual memorial text. Despite his remote location he had many visitors. Soon even Kokei-an was unable to provide him with the solitude that he needed, and in 1317 he decided to leave his beloved hermitage for another on the northern mountain bordering the city of Kyoto.

At this time Kakukai, the widow of the shōgun Hōjō Sadatoki (1270–1311), let it be known that she desired Musō to follow the wishes of his dead master Kōhō Kennichi and become his successor in Kamakura. When the news reached Musō he fled to Tosa on the island of Shikoku, where he lived for some time in a small hermitage (Kyūkō-an). The determined woman sent emissaries throughout the land to look for him, warning that anyone giving him hiding would face punishment. In order not to cause problems for anyone else, Musō surrendered. Back in Kamakura, however, he managed to escape the office that was awaiting him. He retreated to a hermitage called Hakusen-an in Tōtōmi (Shizuoka prefecture), and soon afterwards moved to another nearby retreat in Shimōsa (Chiba prefecture) called Taikō-an.

We have named six hermitages in which Musō spent longer or shorter periods of time during the twenty years after his great experience. After listing these six locations, Yanagida Seizan makes an insightful comparison between the National Teacher Musō and the Chinese Zen master Chung-feng Ming-pen (Jpn., Chūhō Myōhon).[32] Both masters are known for their unusual love of solitude. Chung-feng, one of the greatest figures at the beginning of the Yüan period (1271–1368), was called by his contemporaries "the old Buddha south of the sea," alluding to the Zen movement of Ma-tsu during the T'ang period (618–907).[33] When as a young man he was appointed to succeed the abbot of the monastery on Mount T'ien-mu, Chung-feng temporarily fled the busy life of the monastery and boarded a boat that took him on a journey over lakes and rivers to the solitude he sought. Musō found a spiritual brother in this highly revered master. Through the Japanese disciples who were then studying on Mount T'ien-mu in China a genuine relationship developed between the two, even though they never actually met. The Chinese master had special praise for one of Musō's poems that a Japanese disciple had brought. We may conclude that Musō was familiar with one of the superb portraits of Chung-feng that made their way to Japan.[34] According to Yanagida, all the portraits of Chung-feng emphasized his overpowering physical build,[35] giving him a corporeal appearance that matched his spiritual energy. Little wonder, then, that Musō found in Chung-feng both his own reflection and a model for all Zen masters.

Musō's life was to take a sharp turn when Emperor Go-Daigo called him to become abbot of the Zen monastery of Nanzen-ji in Kyoto in 1325. In vain he sought to evade the honor, but even the last *shikken*, Hōjō Takatoki (1303–1333), under whose authority Musō came, urged him to comply with the imperial wish. And so it was that after years of solitude, Musō Soseki stepped before the public eye as abbot of the most prominent Zen temple in the nation. His assumption of the post was not without its critics. The retired emperor Hanazono (1297–1348), who himself was then living in seclusion, contrasted him with Shūhō Myōchō (known also by his title Daitō Kokushi), who had just completed plans for the foundation of Daitoku-ji.[36] Unlike this authentic Zen master, the

Emperor claimed, the learned Zen monk newly arrived from the east had not yet gotten beyond the verbal content of the teachings. This criticism was directed at Musō's Zen style, about which we will have more to say below. We can imagine how deeply hurt Musō must have been upon receiving this imperial censure.

The move to Kyoto spread the National Teacher's fame even more. With his noble lineage and polished social grace, he won over both the politically powerful and the spiritually influential. But his tenure as abbot of Nanzen-ji lasted only a year; his resignation was in all probability due to the restless mood of the times. Emperor Go-Daigo was looking for a way to seize and wield more of the power that was his due. The time had already come, he felt, to topple the rule of the Hōjō. In such circumstances, Musō thought it best to leave the capital city of Kyoto, and so by autumn of 1326 he was once again on the road. In Ise he built Zennō-ji; in Kamakura he lived, at the behest of the shōgun, in Jōchi-ji, in order to oversee the speedy construction of the Zuisen-ji monastery on the eastern border of the city, a place of exceptional natural beauty that to this day redounds to the honor of Musō's name.

In 1329, after his resistance had proved in vain, Musō was transferred to Engaku-ji to become abbot of the community. Though he once again remained in this post for only a year he succeeded in launching a general reform of this seriously corrupt monastery.[37] The following year he was supposed to take over the direction of Kenchō-ji, but he successfully resisted and withdrew to his homeland in Kai, where with the help of a member of the Nikaidō family he established the monastery of Erin-ji in 1330, near which he resumed a hermit's existence.

Meantime, the conflict between Emperor Go-Daigo and the Kamakura *bakufu* had reached the boiling point. It was only resolved in May of 1333, when the fugitive emperor was permitted to leave his island prison of Chiburi and return to Kyoto. Ashikaga Takauji, the commander of one of the *bakufu* armies that was supposed to overrun Kyoto, defected to the emperor, while Nitta Yoshisada marched on Kamakura, surrounded the entire city, and conquered it. Hōjō Takatoki, together with his loyal followers, committed suicide by *seppuku*, ending the rule of the Hōjō *shikken* in Kamakura.[38]

Back in Kyoto, Emperor Go-Daigo immediately summoned Musō Soseki to the capital. Acquiescing to the Emperor's order, Musō soon found himself quite at ease in his new situation. As an expression of his gratitude, the emperor allowed him to build the temple of Rinsen-ji for his residence, just south of the imperial summer palace (*rikyū*) of Kameyama. On the eastern mountain, Musō built a pagoda that came to be a landmark for this part of the city. Seeking to solidify his position of power in Kyoto, Go-Daigo drew up a code of law during the short period of the Kemmu Restoration (1334–1336) and ruled with the help of the court nobility. To Ashikaga Takauji, without whose assistance he would not have regained power, the emperor bestowed powers of counsel but not of governance. Little did he realize that the dissatisfaction of this mighty samurai was growing day by day.

For a second time Musō Soseki was appointed abbot of Nanzen-ji. Well aware of the precariousness of the situation, the clever master took care to maintain proper relations with the imperial court at the same time as he sought to expand his circle of friends. In particular, he cultivated the favor of the rising star in the Ashikaga clan, Takauji. It was a time of tensions, rivalries, and intrigues, and to Musō's watchful eye the situation was clearly worsening. Before the catastrophe could break loose, he left Nanzen-ji and withdrew from the central location to Rinsen-ji. As already mentioned, Emperor Go-Daigo fled to Yoshino in the south and the dynasty was split into a southern and a northern line. When Ashikaga Takauji was appointed shōgun in 1338 by Kōmyō, the emperor of the Northern dynasty, the Ashikaga period (also known as the Muromachi period) began.

The eventful year of 1339 marked the beginning of a new period in Musō's life. The most significant political event was the death of Emperor Go-Daigo. Musō had foreseen the death in a dream, which he reported to his disciples, in which Go-Daigo was wandering around the chambers of the Kameyama Rikyū as a Buddhist monk—a clear sign that he was soon to leave this world. In the summer of that same year, Musō was commissioned to reform the unruly monastery of Saihō-ji, located south of the summer palace. The temple traced its origins to the Nara period, when it was built under the eminent monk Gyōgi (670–749) who had received the title *bosatsu* (bodhisattva) from the pious Buddhist emperor Shōmu. During the Kamakura period the Jōdo school had also been located there. Musō transformed Saihō-ji into a center for Zen practice; more importantly, he built there the highly popular Moss Garden, which provided the temple with its popular name, Koke-dera—"Moss Temple." It was to provide him a great deal of solace in his final days.

Before he left Rinsen-ji, Musō wrote two important works, the *Rinsen kakun*, a local rule for Rinsen-ji, and the *San'e-in yuikai* (or *ikai*), a legacy of admonitions for the disciples of San'e-in, a small branch temple of Rinsen-ji (1339). A later work, the *Saihō yuikai* (1345), also provided directives for the ever increasing number of his disciples.

A collection of guidelines for monasteries and monks, the *Rinsen kakun*[39] is similar to the Chinese writings of the same genre during the Sung period. It shows Musō to be a consciously responsible and strict Zen master who insisted that his disciples practice meditation faithfully and lead a well-regulated monastic life. Resembling above all the *Genjū shingi* (*Huan-chu ch'ing-kuei*), a monastic rule book compiled by Chung-feng Ming-pen in 1317, the work gives us a glimpse into the daily life in a Zen monastery of the time. Warning against a dangerous emphasis on ceremonies, Musō prescribes four hours of *zazen* a day (with some exceptions). He has high praise for the early Zen disciples who practiced constantly without a daily order. Later it would become part of the rule that monks meditate four hours a day. For Musō it was a source of sorrow and shame that so many people should be calling for shorter periods of meditation. The house rules of Rinsen-ji made it a point deliberately to follow the lines of the early

Buddhist *sangha* and to prescribe punishments for those who broke the rules or caused unrest.

In the important work, *San'e-in yuikai*, written in the form of a testament twelve years before his death, Musō distinguishes three classes of disciples:

> I have three kinds of disciples. The first group is made up of students who energetically try to remove all attachments and concentrate on seeking after the self. The middle group are those whose practice is not pure and who are distracted by intellectual pursuits. The bottom group is made up of those who cloud their own minds and only lick the spittle of the Buddhas and patriarchs. As for those who shave their heads and poison their minds with foreign literature, aspiring to be authors, they are lay people with shaven heads, not even worthy to be placed below the lowest group. Even less worth of being called monks are those who indulge in lavish meals, long hours of sleep, and unbridled pleasures . . .[40]

The end of the passage makes it clear that even the middle group would not qualify as Musō's disciples. He defends the strictness of the ancients and their concern with cultivating a communal life built on goodwill.

Yanagida sees in Musō's testament a picture of the master's true personality, a man who cannot be classified properly either as a successful proselytizer of the Ashikaga clan or as a "worldly Zen monk who knew how to make the most of confused times."[41] Yanagida finds in the work traces of "the unspeakable loneliness" of the master who suffered greatly under the unseemly events of the day. This whole period of Japanese history needs closer analysis. It would be superficial, and unjust, to disregard Musō's constant efforts at meditation and reconciliation and to present him only as a politician playing off both sides of the conflict against each other.

Emperor Go-Daigo died in August 1339, and in October Musō conducted memorial services for him. He also urged the shōgun Takauji to convert the imperial summer palace, Kameyama Rikyū, into a Zen temple and to dedicate it to the memory of the deceased *tennō*. Takauji agreed. Construction of the famous monastery of Tenryū-ji began during the eventful year of 1339, and the main building was completed the following year. Subsequently, the temple was renamed Ryakuō Shishō Zen-ji. But after Tadayoshi, the shōgun's younger brother, had a dream in which a golden dragon came up from the river in the south and climbed over the temple, its name was changed to Tenryū Shishō-zenji (shortened to Tenryū-ji, "Temple of the Heavenly Dragon"). When the Tendai monks from Enryaku-ji heard that the retired emperor of the Northern dynasty, Kōgon, was going to take part in the dedication ceremonies in 1344, they protested and prevented his attending. The temple was considered a symbol of atonement for the injustice that the Ashikaga shōgun Takauji had done to Go-Daigo, a matter over which Musō himself might also have harbored some guilt feelings. At the dedication ceremonies, prayers were offered for all those who had died, both friends and enemies, since the outbreak of the conflict during the Genkō period.

As a leading personality of the early Ashikaga period, Musō used his influence to complete (in 1342) the organization of Ankoku-ji and Rishō-tō referred to earlier. During this same year, in a lavish ceremony, the two emperors of the Northern dynasty—the retired Kōgon and the reigning Kōmyō—received the Buddhist precepts at the hands of Musō.[42] It was in the same year, it will be remembered, that the *Tenryūji-bune* set sail for China to secure the financial means necessary for completing the construction of Tenryū-ji.

Musō did not lose his yearning for solitude. After the Dharma hall was finished in 1345 and the temple complex of Tenryū-ji could thus be considered complete, he resigned his position as abbot, turned over the office to his disciple Mukyoku Shigen (1282–1359), and withdrew to the hermitage of Ungo-an. Assisted by his young student Zekkai Chūshin (1336–1405), he spent his few remaining years pursuing his two great loves, contemplation and art.

For several months during 1351, the last year of Musō Soseki's life, the capital city of Kyoto became the arena of combat between followers of the Southern and Northern dynasties. At the same time, tensions between the two Ashikaga brothers, Takauji and Tadayoshi, which had been stewing for a long time, erupted into open conflict. Musō tried in vain to quell the fraternal feud.[43] Before he died he turned his attentions once again to Tenryū-ji. In January, he told his disciples:

> Perhaps this year I will die. Tenryū-ji was built as a center of practice to commemorate the death of Emperor Go-Daigo. The thirteenth anniversary of his demise is approaching and still the monks' hall is not finished. If I don't finish it now, who will?[44]

Work on the monks' hall began in April; on 20 July it was dedicated. On the sixteenth day of the following month, according to Buddhist custom, the thirteenth anniversary of Emperor Go-Daigo's death was celebrated. The day after the celebration Musō withdrew exhausted to the San'e-in, close to Rinsen-ji, where emperors Kōgon and Kōmyō both visited him during the first part of September for what was to be the last time.

Before his death on 30 September, 1351, Musō composed farewell verses that virtually defy translation. The final lines of one of his poems direct the attention of his remaining disciples to the present moment. In his daily life Musō revealed everything; nothing remained to be explained:

> In the world of the truly pure, there is no separation.
> Why wait again for another time?
> The tradition of Vulture Peak has arrived.
> The authority of the Dharma needs no one.

The verses with which he took his leave of this world (*jisei*) resemble a *kikan-kōan* (see below) that dissolves all bonds:

> With one stroke I erase my delay in the transient world.
> What does this mean?—Yāsa.[45]

Both poems are typical of the Zen style of master Musō Soseki.

CHARACTER AND ZEN STYLE

There is no mold for Zen masters, no ideal type that fits all. This is evident in the many fine portraits of Zen masters that famous artists have left us, for despite the common traits in their depiction, they also highlight the uniqueness and individuality of each. The portrait of Musō Kokushi is particularly different from the others[46] and leaves an unforgettable impression on the beholder: the long face with its fine, almost feminine features, the light growth of hair on his cheeks, the small but strong head, certainly the most impressive part—in all, a slender, upright figure that conveys the presence of a master. The seriousness on his countenance shows that he knows suffering, while his open, gentle eyes communicate trust. Would it ever be possible to penetrate the essence of this man?

We have already seen glimpses of master Musō's inscrutable character. Abbot Hirata provided us earlier with a clue to the master's personality when he claimed that Musō's basic quality was his extraordinary gentleness. Gentleness, which in personal relations means goodness, is related to tolerance, adaptability, and an all-embracing intellectual openness. But Musō's life also shows us perseverance in the midst of difficulties, a practical approach to problems, and a realistic sense of judgment. A modern biography of the man would have to show how all these characteristics harmoniously worked together.[47] For the time being, we have bracketed Musō's artistic accomplishments, since Zen art during the Muromachi period deserves its own chapter. Our present analysis of his Zen style, however, does lead us to one further and fundamental trait: his leanings toward scholarship and learning.

Reflecting his own personality, Musō Soseki's unique style of Zen sought a broad synthesis of opposing elements within Zen practice. As he understood it, practice should include both the use of Kōan and the study of Buddhist doctrine. His writings reveal how he thought these two elements could be joined.

Musō's Zen style may be characterized in terms of the tension between two terms, richi and kikan. Richi means academic learning, in particular as related to the Buddhist sūtras, while kikan signifies the kōan method of direct experience. Musō combined the two without preference, avoiding either an exclusive love of richi that rejects kikan or a bias for kikan that ignored richi. Because of the influence of Chinese Zen masters of the Rinzai school who had come to Japan and were active mainly in Kamakura, the kōan method had assumed a certain priority in the Zen practice of the time. This explains the background to a question that one of Musō's disciples posed to him:

> Why is it that although the master belongs to the Rinzai school he does not follow its method, preferring to give lectures on the sūtras?[48]

Musō answers that it is important to adapt to one's situation or interlocutor, humbly adding that he himself is still a little cook and not really able to carry out that task. He then sharply criticizes the way his contemporaries were more concerned about imitating the external practices of the ancients than imitating their virtues.

Unable to detect any fundamental or insoluble contradiction between the teachings of the sūtras and the kōan, he questioned current distinctions: "To explain the sūtras is to speak of Zen."[49] In his *Seizan yawa*, although he does not treat the matter systematically, Musō does mention the terms *richi* and *kikan:*

> The ancients maintain that before Ma-tsu and Pai-chang there was much *richi* (teaching) and no *kikan* (kōan). After Ma-tsu and Pai-chang there was much *kikan* and little *richi*. What does this mean? Did the early Buddhist learned ones make use of much teaching because they had no mind for Zen? Or do contemporary learned ones restrict their practice to the kōan because, unlike the ancients, they have no mind for teaching?[50]

In his major work, *Muchū-mondō*,[51] Musō takes the question up at length. Referring to the same historical background as in the previous passage, he finds a resolution of the tension in the provisional character of "means." In Buddhist terminology, both practices belong to the category of "skillful means" (Skt., *upāya*; Jpn., *hōben*):

> Concerning the Real, the door of the Dharma is found neither in what is called *richi*, nor in what is called *kikan*. But if one opens the door of means to show the meaning of a school, one will call *richi* what the sages expounded vigorously with arguments; *kikan*, the use of staff and shouting (*bōkatsu*); and kōan, *kikan* that goes beyond reason. All these are means that one can call *shōgyoku*.[52]

Musō found the term *shōgyoku* in the Zen literature of China. According to tradition, when the famous master Wu-tsu Fa-yen (Jpn., Goso Hōen) was asked by an official to explain the Zen style of his house, he recited some verses from a Chinese song in which the term *hsiao-yü* (Jpn., *shōgyoku*) appear. In the song, a lady uses the name *shōgyoku* apparently to call her servant but actually to attract the attention of her lover who is waiting outside. Wu-tsu uses the verses as a kōan. The term *shōgyoku* (literally, "little jewel") is not itself important. The name is only a means or tool, no more than a help for the disciple to attain enlightenment. The verses can also be understood as applying directly to the lover. The noble lady calls her servant, but really means her lover. Like Wu-tsu's disciples Yen-wu K'o-ch'in (Jpn., Engo Kokugon) and Ta-hui Tsung-kao (Jpn., Daie Sōkō), Musō found the story a fitting expression of the provisional usefulness of all things: anything can serve as a sign of the Real. He interpreted these verses broadly and often mentioned the term *shōgyoku* in his writings, thus giving the story a well-known place in Zen literature.

In the passage cited above, *shōgyoku* symbolizes skillful means, or *hōben*. In Zen practice, everything but the "one great thing" (*ichidaiji*)[53]—namely, en-lightenment—is *hōben*. The skillful use of means entails adapting them to changing individuals and circumstances. Musō expressly states that kōan are a means, and as such cannot be considered absolutely necessary:

Those of extraordinary abilities do not necessarily need kōan; such people do not fall into silence but always carry on their search. In my school, they are the searchers of the Way.[54]

Musō is alluding here to a danger against which kōan serve as a protection. Constantly thinking of a kōan keeps the mind alert. In the *Muchū-mondō*, the question of the need for kōan is treated in connection with the problem of doubt. The question is stated as follows:

Must beginners in practice necessarily first make use of kōan or are kōan like branches and leaves? Which of these two views is correct?

The answer:

This question is the same as that of doubt and non-doubt. Sometimes it is necessary to give a kōan and demand that it be studied; other times it is better to remove it. For the master, everything is a means. There is no hard and fast rule for this issue.[55]

Doubt is the core of the kōan. As Musō states in the previous chapter of the work, it is as impossible to pin down rules for the use of doubt and non-doubt as it is to predict which way the spark from a flintstone will fly or a flash of lightening will strike.

When one has a clearheaded master, there is no problem in making use of doubt and non-doubt. But when clarity is lacking, doubt and non-doubt can darken the eyes of the student.[56]

The origins of kōan make clear that they are means. In the early days, neither the method of kōan nor that of doubt existed. The help of kōan became necessary only for later generations of practitioners because of their bad karma and negligence in diligently following the Way.

Small-minded people have little imagination and are caught in boredom. Out of pity for such people, Yüan-wu and Ta-hui introduced the practice of kōan . . . . Yet because even kōan do not suffice for some, Master Chung-feng discovered the means of the "ball of the great doubt" in order to enliven their practice.[57]

Just as Zen embraces the whole of life, so can all the events and activities of everyday life serve as a means for practice. In no way is Zen practice limited to seated meditation. Musō warns against restricting practice to certain times such as the "four times for *zazen*" (*shiji zazen*) customarily observed in Zen monasteries. For those who have understood what it is all about, at no moment of the day is one away from practice or free from the need to struggle, alert and attentive to the Real. Musō uses a Zen term that he learned from the Chinese masters to refer to the internal energy that moves one to Zen practice: *kufū* (Chin., *kung-fu*). By means of *kufū*, the practice of Zen covers the entire day.

It is said that there are some people who practice *kufū* in all things and others who do everything with *kufū*. What is the difference between the two?[58]

Musō uses this question to deliver some important instructions. The Chinese word *kung-fu* belongs to popular usage and corresponds roughly to the Japanese term *itoma* (leisure), which originally connoted activities of all kinds including the work of farmers, carpenters, and so forth. In everything they do, disciples of the Way should be totally devoted to the Dharma—they should practice *kufū*. "For those who practice essential *kufū*, there is no difference between 'within all things' and 'within *kufū*.' " For such people, everything is *kufū*, and vice-versa.

> Those who are really imbued with the spirit of the way do not waste time. Whether eating or drinking, whether putting on their clothes or reading the sūtras or chanting, even when going to the toilet, in all activities and at all places, in greeting the crowd or in talking, they never forget essential *kufū*.[59]

As this passage makes clear, Zen does not distinguish between daily life and practice in the Zen hall. Everything is practice. "According to a true principle of Mahāyāna, there is no separation between the law of Buddha and the law of the world."[60] The unity of these two laws, which is a favorite theme of Japanese Zen, flows from the spirit of Mahāyāna, and it is this spirit that informs Musō's Zen style. Indeed, this spirit informs all of his personality—as is so movingly evident in the words about the "little jewels" with which these comments open.

Tradition has it that Musō spoke the following words shortly before he died: "Everything that I have said up to now, even though it avoids the eyes of the interlocutor and is of little value, is only a means that one can call *shōgyoku*."[61] The statement applies to his whole life. According to Yanagida, Musō considered

> all the words of the Buddha and the many means (*hōben*) of the patriarchs to be *shōgyoku*. Also his own sermons, as well as all the activities of his life were means that can be called *shōgyoku*. . . . All the *mikkyō* of his early years, all the Zen and Pure Land, the law of the king and the law of Buddha, Kamakura and Kyoto—all, in the same fashion, were *shōgyoku*.[62]

Musō also considered his own views to be a means, marked by the same provisional quality as all the things of life. This is one of the fundamental notions of the Mahāyāna worldview, stemming from the Buddhist conviction of the transitoriness of all things. Musō was aware of this universal impermanence, that every "yesterday" disappears and no "today" endures.

> The breath of life eventually takes leave of all of us; whether we are young or old, if we live we must die. The number of the dead grows; the blossoms of the flowers fade; the leaves of the trees fall. Things are like foam in a dream. As fish gather in tiny pools of water, so life moves on as the days

pass by. Parents and children, husbands and wives who passed their lives together, do not remain together. What use is high standing or wealth? Red cheeks in the morning, dead bones in the evening. Not to trust in the things of this perishing world but to enter upon the way of Buddha— thus will one stir up the mind that seeks the way and believes in the exalted Dharma.[63]

This awareness of the provisional nature of all means is every bit as radical as the experience of impermanence and leads to the same total renunciation of fame and fortune. In these temporary means Musō could find "small jewels," and this imbued his whole bearing with a warm humanity that opened hearts and doors wherever he went. His adaptability was praised by all; indeed, many felt that he sometimes extended his intelligence and goodness too far.

As a Zen master he was broad-minded toward other forms of Buddhism, maintaining good relations with Amida Buddhists and even practicing Shingon rituals himself. In his view, it was not right to pass judgment on the different schools of Buddhism. Just as different people have different tastes, so do the upright searchers of the way select the Dharma school that best suits their nature. "The Buddha taught all his doctrines in order to save all sentient beings."[64] Musō kept up his magnanimous, tolerant attitude energetically. His tolerance— which occasioned accusations of syncretism—was grounded in an awareness of the provisional nature of all means.

Musō Soseki is one of the most important personalities in the history of medieval Japanese Zen Buddhism. With his extraordinary artistic talents he was a pioneer in many areas of Japanese Zen art. We will have more to say on this point later. It is significant not only that his accomplishments earned him admiration but that his artistic gifts flowed from the very core of a personality deeply inspired by the beautiful.[65] His spirituality combined enlightened wisdom with a creative, aesthetic sensitivity that formed an unbroken whole with the open, magnanimous tolerance of his personality. National Teacher Musō represents an enduring embodiment of the most important qualities of a Japanese Zen master. The reason for his continued resistance to travel to China and dissuasion of his disciples from doing so was that he was able to realize his Buddhist ideals in his own homeland. His roots sink deeply into the soul of Japan; in the middle of the fourteenth century his figure graced the capital city of Kyoto, with its elevated spirituality, its cultural harmony, and its creative artistry, in a unique manner.

The two principal disciples of Musō Soseki were Mukyoku Shigen (1282–1359), his first successor at the Tenryū-ji monastery, and Shun'oku Myōha (1311–1388), who gained prominence as the first abbot of Shōkoku-ji (founded in 1384). Shun'oku was Musō's nephew and the closest of his disciples. He is known for having assembled the literary works of the master, and especially for the compilation of the *Seizan yawa* and the chronological table *Musō nempu* (1353). Among Musō's numerous disciples we may also mention Seizan Jiei (1302–1369), Ryūshū Shūtaku (1308–1388), Gidō Shūshin (1325–1388), who for some years taught Zen to the shōgun Ashikaga Yoshimitsu, and Zekkai Chūshin (1336–1405), who during a trip to China in 1368 was received by the reigning emperor of the Ming dynasty. These disciples belong to the period of the Five Mountains. From the rich and varied panorama of this period we can consider only a few of the major elements and events.

THE MOVEMENT OF THE FIVE MOUNTAINS DURING THE MUROMACHI PERIOD

One does not have to study the history of Zen very long before coming to the evident and paradoxical insight that this "special tradition outside the sūtras and independent of word and scriptures" produced an incredible richness of literary works. In China and Japan there arose an abundance of Zen religious literature of overwhelming quantity and a variety of literary forms and powerful themes. Especially innovative in the movement of the Five Mountains was the fact that it cultivated a secular literature that eventually earned recognition.[66] Zen works, originally of a religious nature, earned a respected place as secular art within Japanese literature.

The heart of the *gozan* movement lay in its literary work; however, the historical and philosophical productions, as well as the intellectual and cultural achievements of this period, molded as they were by China, were centered in the movement of the Five Mountains, or the "literature of the Five Mountains" (*gozan bungaku*), or, as it was more broadly described, the "culture of the Five Mountains" (*gozan bunka*), since nearly all the representatives of the movement resided in the Zen monasteries belonging to the *gozan* system as described earlier. However, the leading pesonality of the era, Musō Soseki, is usually not mentioned in works dealing primarily with *gozan* literature, mainly because he transcended purely literary accomplishments. Musō's significance goes beyond any expertise in Chinese literature and its religious roots reach beneath the whole of the intellectual life. A man of unusual intellectual independence, Musō was an exception for his age. Although he followed the social customs of the times and maintained close relations with the imperial court and with the bureaucracy established by the Ashikaga lords, he was a universal master who refused to be swayed by social pressures. His life was an example of the freedom that comes from enlightened wisdom. Like few other Japanese Zen masters of this early period, he embodied the special quality of Japanese identity at a time when the *gozan* movement was looking back into the past and bringing Chinese influence to a new and powerful revival.

BEGINNINGS AND EARLY PERIOD

Scholars who have researched the origins of the *gozan* movement trace Japanese poetry and learning of the time back to two prominent Chinese figures whose influence is hard to overstate: I-shan I-ning and Ku-lin Ch'ing-mao (Jpn., Kurin Seimu, 1262–1317).[67] The two differed considerably in the way their lives unfolded and in the influence they exercised on their disciples, yet both enjoyed a great influence on not a few of Japan's *gozan* poets. I-shan I-ning, whose literary style reflects the Zen of the Southern Sung dynasty, arrived in Japan during the early Yüan period (1299). Though active in the main temples of Kamakura, Kenchō-ji, and Engaku-ji, his life's work climaxed in the Nanzen-ji temple in Kyoto. His Zen style shows clear traces of secular coloring; for him, art is primary, poetry has its own meaning, and religion holds a subordinate place. As a young man he entered the school of masters of the Ta-hui line, whose interest in art and whose style of the Chinese Southern Sung period he brought to Japan.[68] His pedagogical skills surpassed his artistic creativity and enabled him to exercise a deep-reaching influence on a large number of Japanese students. He is known as "the patriarch of *gozan* literature in Japan."[69]

Such influential poets as Kokan Shiren (1278–1346) and Sesson Yūbai (1290–1346) were among I-shan's students. Kokan Shiren belonged to the Shō-ichi line.[70] No sooner had I-shan arrived in Japan than Kokan sought out the famous Chinese master to study literature with him. Kokan's own poetic talents soon became evident. He became the Dharma heir of Tōzan Tanshō (1231–1291),[71] Enni's most famous student, and went on to earn wide acclaim as the abbot of Nanzen-ji and Kenchō-ji. His influence was to extend over future generations, principally because his literary school, which was located primarily in Tōfuku-ji and was the oldest such school of the *gozan* period,[72] prospered and attracted a steady influx of students. A good number of Kokan's and his students' works are still extant. While the main representatives of the *gozan* movement are found in the two lines of Musō and Shōichi, most of the literati were from the Musō line.

Not only did Sesson Yūbai[73] study literature under I-shan I-ning, he also became his Zen disciple and eventually his Dharma heir. He went to China in 1306 and studied under the other most influential teacher of the *gozan* movement, Ku-lin Ch'ing-mao, who touched him deeply. His exceptional talents were soon recognized among the Chinese; a group of students formed around him and he was made an abbot of a monastery and given a honorific title. Though he also had to endure hardships during his twenty years in China, he succeeded in appropriating the spirit of this new epoch. Back in Japan, he lived in a number of different monasteries before assuming the office of abbot in the influential temples of Engaku-ji and Nanzen-ji. A man of broad education and solid character, Sesson held fast to the strict way of life of the Rinzai school, practicing *zazen* regularly and delighting in silence. Within the *gozan* movement he represented the serious, religious style of *geju* literature, which he had learned from Ku-lin. While Kokan Shiren remained within the tradition of the Southern Sung dynasty, Sesson Yūbai and his followers brought the *gozan* movement into its period of greatest growth and literary productivity.

The second dominant figure of the Japanese *gozan* movement was the Chinese Zen master Ku-lin Ch'ing-mao,[74] who never set foot on Japanese soil and yet stands second to none in his influence on Japanese Zen of the Muromachi period. As a member of a branch of the Yang-ch'i line of the Rinzai school, he was one of the most prominent names in Chinese Zen of the time. During the early Yüan period his school inaugurated a new phase in Zen literature.[75] Contrary to the secular tendencies of the Sung period, he grounded his strict Zen style in the literary forms dear to Zen—collections of sayings (goroku), dialogues (mondō), and kōan. Although the composition of his verses—called geju[76]—was not much different from that of other Chinese poetry its contents drew predominantly on Buddhist themes. Without in any way neglecting the beauty of form, Ku-lin included many powerful, Zen-like sayings. On account of this, his works mark a clear enrichment of Zen literature. His personality attracted not only Chinese but many Japanese disciples, who brought his style to full fruition during this early period of the gozan movement. "Ku-lin's influence on the Japanese gozan movement, which he exercised through the style of his geju works, is incomparable."[77] This assessment, given by one of the foremost experts in Gozan literature, is corroborated by the many accomplished writers of the time who directly or indirectly stand in relation to master Ku-lin.

It was an epoch-making event when three of Ku-lin's chief Chinese disciples—Ch'ing-cho Cheng-ch'eng (Jpn., Seisetsu Shōchō, 1274–1339), Ming-chi Ch'u-chün (Jpn., Minki Soshun, 1262–1336), and Chu-hsien Fan-hsien (Jpn., Jikusen Bonsen, 1292–1348)—arrived in Japan.[78] Since these masters had already made friends with many Japanese disciples in China, they were given a warm reception. Responding to an invitation from Japan, Ching-cho Cheng-ch'eng made his journey in 1326 with a group of Japanese disciples: Jakushitsu Genkō (1290–1367), Kosen Ingen (1295–1374), and Sekishitsu Zenkyū (1294–1389).[79] He visited the main temples of Kamakura and Kyoto, established the monastery of Kaizen-ji in Shinano, became abbot of Nanzen-ji, and in general did much to adapt the Chinese monastic rule to Japanese circumstances.[80] When guiding his students he made great use of the Chinese classics and followed the lines of Ku-lin in promoting the gozan literature of Japan.

Three years after Ch'ing-cho's arrival, the masters Ming-chi and Chu-hsien[81] appeared in Japan accompanied by a number of Japanese disciples, among whom were Sesson Yūbai and Getsurin Dōkyō (1293–1351). Both masters attracted considerable followings and did important work. Through his patron, Emperor Go-Daigo, Ming-chi became abbot of Nanzen-ji, while Chu-hsien, with his disciples, contributed greatly to the publication and distribution of gozan literature.

The long list of more or less significant representatives of gozan literature[82] from this and the next two generations attests to the popularity this literature enjoyed during the fourteenth century. Extending almost up to the end of the fourteenth century, the first period of the gozan movement has also been called the period of the Kitayama culture, after the location of the residence of Yoshimitsu, the third shōgun of the Ashikaga clan (1358–1408, ruled 1367–1395).[83] It is marked by the influence of the courtly nobility, by the support that Zen received from the warrior class, and by the widespread practice of the mikkyō rituals. Despite the bureaucratic rigidity that set in after the organizational measures of the Ashikaga shōgun, and despite the strong influence of the aristocracy and esoteric practices, the gozan monasteries of this period maintained their Zen character. Serious Zen meditation and kōan practice were combined with efforts to promote a knowledge of Chinese culture. Though the lifestyle of Yoshimitsu showed an unrivaled extravagance, it was not decadent.

THE BEGINNINGS OF THE SECOND PERIOD

Toward the end of the fourteenth century, the Rinzai school of Zen, and especially the *gozan* movement, entered a new phase. The confusion preceding the dissolution of the Yüan dynasty in China continued through the accession of the Ming lords and was to last well into the new period, one effect being the decrease in communication between China and Japan. The last of the Chinese Zen masters came to Japan in 1351, and only a few Japanese disciples were to travel to the kingdom of the Ming. Left to themselves, the Japanese first grew slack in Zen practice and then their interest in Chinese intellectual culture, which was growing more and more worldly, cooled.

Signs of an imminent change were evident already by the middle of the fourteenth century. An incident that took place in 1367, in which Tendai and Zen monks engaged in hand-to-hand combat in front of the main gate of Nanzen-ji, led to the weakening of the Zen institution.[84] Musō's disciple, Shun'oku Myōha, the leader of the Musō school, was banished from Kyoto in 1371 by the powerful Hosokawa Yoriyuki, the teacher of the Ashikaga shōgun Yoshimitsu (who had not yet come of age), but shortly afterward Shun'oku was readmitted to the capital by Shiba Yoshimasa. Shun'oku[85] came to enjoy the great favor of Yoshimitsu, who in the meantime had been installed as shōgun. Yoshimitsu entrusted him with the construction of Shōkoku-ji and later appointed him its second abbot, the honor of founding abbot having gone to the deceased Musō Soseki. Shun'oku was also appointed *sōroku*, the highest official of the *gozan* system. A dependable Zen monk, he also showed considerable intellectual and poetic gifts. His greatest services lay in overseeing the publication of the ever-growing *gozan* literature. While his accomplishments marked an external high point in the Gozan movement, they also signalled its decline.

Hardly any other event captures the shift in Zen culture better than the split between Musō's two disciples Gidō Shūshin and Zekkai Chūshin.[86] Besides receiving the Dharma from the same master, they also followed the same program in their study of classical Chinese literature. Their education began under Ryūzan Tokken (1284–1358),[87] who had mastered the authentic *geju* style in China under Ku-lin. As abbot of Kennin-ji, Nanzen-ji, and Tenryū-ji, Ryūzan exercised direct influence on the three disciples Chūgan Engetsu (1300–1375), Gidō Shūshin, and Zekkai Chūshin. Chūgan, who was the oldest of the three, also incorporated influences from Ku-lin and I-shan I-ning (by way of Kokan Shiren) and became the most influential teacher of the subsequent generation, communicating authentic Zen to many of his contemporaries, including the two other mentioned disciples of Musō, in artistic form. His work was molded by the spirit and style of the Ku-lin school. He also deserves credit for trying to promote the acceptance and observance of the monastic rule that at this time came to Japan from China—the *Chokushū Hyakujō shingi* (*Chih-hsiu Po-chang ch'ing kuei*).[88]

Correctly, and yet with some reservations, Musō's disciples Gidō and Zekkai can be called the two pillars of the *gozan* movement. Gidō Shūshin (1325–1388)[89] promoted a Zen style tightly bound to *zazen* and kōan practice and to the *geju* poetry that had brought the *gozan* movement to its full flowering during the early Muromachi period. Together with his disciples and friends, he stands at the apex of the *gozan* movement, which at that time had solid institutional support from the Ashikaga shogunate. It seems, however, that already early on Gidō sensed a shiver in the timbers. With considerable success he warned and urged his disciples to remain true to the simple monastic way of life, and he insisted on limitations to their literary pursuits.[90] The seriousness of his religious convictions earned him the respect of the shōgun Yoshimitsu, who called him to Kyoto from Kamakura after twenty years in the eastern regions in order to instruct him in Zen practice. Gidō also instructed the emperor in the wisdom of China, especially Confucianism, which he set forth in its traditional and modern interpretations. With full confidence in his teacher, the emperor grew to be a zealous practitioner of Zen meditation. Gidō's growing influence came to an end only with his death.[91]

Zekkai Chūshin (1336–1405),[92] the youngest of Musō's three principal disciples, brought the new literary style of the Gozan movement to full form. Like Gidō, he came from the island of Shikoku in the area of Kōchi prefecture, went to Kyoto as a young boy, received the tonsure at Tenryū-ji when only fourteen years old, and had the privilege of assisting his sick master Musō for an entire year before he died. As a novice he practiced *zazen* earnestly and seems to have attained certain enlightenment experiences. After three years he was sent to Kennin-ji (1353), where Ryūzan was abbot. Gidō was among the monks with whom Zekkai went about his daily practice. During this stay at Kennin-ji, he received from Ryūzan and Gidō an excellent foundation in the *geju* style of the Ku-lin school. In 1364 Ryūzan would become abbot of Nanzen-ji, but during the ten years that Zekkai spent at Kennin-ji he became acquainted with some of the most prominent Zen personalities of the time. After a short stay in eastern Japan he finally fulfilled his long cherished desire to travel to China.

His ten-year stay (1368–1378) in the Middle Kingdom was a turning point in his life. After some delays he finally found a friendly reception—and his own master—in Chi-t'an Tsung-le, who was a disciple of the famous poet-monk Hsiao-yin Ta-hsin. The literary style practiced in his temple was essentially different from anything Zekkai had known. Mainly under Hsiao-yin Ta-hsin's inspiration, the literary movement of the end of the Yüan period (which, as we already mentioned, carried on the tradition of the Sung period to which I-shan I-ning belonged) had reached new heights that went well beyond Ku-lin and his disciples. Liberated from Zen and Buddhist expressions, this new style was, first of all, completely secularized. Its second chief characteristic was a purely artistic form called *shiroku-benrei-bun*,[93] in which alternating lines of four and six characters were rhythmically combined. Like many of his contemporaries, Zekkai was excited about this new device and energetically tried to put it to practice. During his ten years in China he also visited other monasteries where pupils of Hsiao-yin were furthering their master's literary form.

There is no need to detail all the events of Zekkai's eventful life after he returned from China. His biographer describes the joy he felt when after thirteen years of separation he arrived in Kyoto and embraced his old friend Gidō. With Gidō's help, he was appointed abbot of Erin-ji in Kai, where he stayed for three years until the repeated invitations of the shōgun Yoshimitsu brought him back to Kyoto. The shōgun offered him a number of high offices, but a disagreement between the two soon arose and Zekkai was banned from the capital in 1384. Repenting of his rash action, Yoshimitsu had Gidō write Zekkai and call him back to Kyoto in 1386. Zekkai was head of Tōji-ji[94] from 1386 to 1391. During that period Gidō died, leaving him the sole surviving disciple of the National Teacher Musō and the recognized leader of the *gozan* movement. Soon thereafter, in 1392, Yoshimitsu appointed Zekkai abbot of Shōkoku-ji, whose sub-temple Rokuon-in had been the traditional residence of the *sōroku*. In time Zekkai would also occupy this highest office of the *gozan* system. Twice he withdrew from the office of abbot at Shōkoku-ji, but each time he was reinstated almost immediately.[95] He enjoyed the continued good graces of Yoshimitsu, who for the master's sake temporarily placed Shōkoku-ji at the top of the list of the Five Temples, immediately above Tenryū-ji. Zekkai died before Yoshimitsu and ended his glorious career laden with the honors of the shogunate.

Zekkai's role in the *gozan* movement lay mainly in the decisive influence he had on the development of its literary arts. Especially important is the contrast between his leadership and the extended leadership of Gidō Shūshin. In old age, Gidō must have suffered a great deal from the change of course that Zekkai had introduced, but these differences never broke into an open dispute. This was due as much to the even, peace-loving character of Gidō as to the abiding respect that Zekkai had for his older companion. In his practical decisions Zekkai followed the advice and directions of his elder, a practice that is deeply rooted in Asian sentiments.[96]

While Musō Soseki had remained thoroughly Japanese, well protected as he was in the atmosphere of Japan, his disciples succumbed to the influence of China. This is even more the case with Zekkai than with Gidō, for Zekkai passionately devoted himself as a true poet to the new poetic style that the Chinese artist Hsiao-yin had created and that he had learned from Hisao-yin's disciple, Chi-t'an. His works were thoroughly cast in a Chinese mold and easily fit into the Chinese character of the court of the Ashikaga shōgun Yoshimitsu, who went so far as to dress according to Chinese fashions.[97] In this sense, life-style and artistic taste were in full accord. The shift to the second period of the *gozan* movement took place without any rupture with the first period, despite the considerable differences between the two.

DECLINE DURING THE SECOND PERIOD

The decline of the *gozan* movement during its second period was brought on primarily by two factors: the close ties between the movement and the Ashikaga shogunate, whose misfortunes were bound to affect the *gozan* movement, and the increasing secularization in the Zen monasteries. The Ashikaga period came to the height of its power during the reign of the third shōgun, Yoshimitsu, who showed an evident and personal favoritism to the Zen monks of the Rinzai school active under his protection in the capital city of Kyoto. After his retirement the shōgun formally became a Zen Buddhist and for some time submitted himself to Zen practice. But in his own religious convictions it seems that he never moved very much beyond the medieval mentality of popular Buddhism. It was to him that the institution of the Five Mountains owed the privileged place it held for a long time in civil and political matters, and in return the monks provided political assistance to the shōgun, especially by using their knowledge of the Chinese language and culture to promote good relations with China. Through their unconditional support of the shōgunal government the gozan monks enjoyed numerous favors as well as the regard of the people—but only as long as the shogunate could keep a tight hold over the nation.

During the fifteenth century this hold began to loosen. Yoshimitsu's successor, Yoshimochi (1386–1428, reigned 1395–1423), still retained enough authority to maintain control and carried on his predecessor's favors toward Zen. But during his reign an unrest spread throughout the land that in coming decades was to mean considerable loss of power. Local lords carried on bloody battles against the central regime unchecked. It was only after strenuous effort and heavy military action that the rebellion of the Kamakura branch of the Ashikaga clan was brought under control. The main family was victorious, but not long afterward, in 1441, the murder of shōgun Yoshinari, one of Yoshimitsu's sons, reminded both the government and the people of how precarious and dangerous the times were. By the middle of the century the rule of the Ashikaga, though still in command, had weakened and begun its downward spiral. The shogunate's ill fortunes were bound to have their effects on the gozan movement.

The secularization of the monks was another factor in the decline of the gozan monasteries. During the movement's first period, literary concerns, which formed the heart of the gozan movement, had religious content and were tightly bound with the spiritual strivings of the monks. But with the adoption of a profane literary style, a fundamental change set in that led, at first slowly but then every more precipitously, to a total secularization. During the first generation after Zekkai the representatives of the movement were all qualified literati of great reputation. Donchū Dōhō (1365–1409)[98] a Dharma disciple of Kūkoku Myōō (1328–1407),[99] who had received the Dharma from Musō's first disciple Mukyoku Shigen and served as abbot in the Shōkoku-ji and Tenryū-ji monasteries, was a member, like so many of his contemporaries, of Zekkai's school and imbibed his literary style. Another highly gifted student of Zekkai, Ishō Tokugan (dates unknown),[100] who was head of Tenryū-ji and Nanzen-ji, counted among his students two of the leading representatives of the gozan movement during the middle of the fifteen century: Zuikei Shūhō (1391–1473) and Kisei Reigen (1403–1488).[101] The Shōichi line was also represented by a number of monks who could trace their connections back to the abbot of Tōfuku-ji, Mugan Sōō (d. 1374);[102] among them the most notable was Giyō Hōshū (1361–1424), whom Zen literature of the time describes as "a man of the Way without equal."

It was Giyō who introduced the shōgun Yoshimochi to the Zen community.[103] He also served as abbot of Tōfuku-ji and Nanzen-ji

During the first half of the fifteenth century Musō's exemplary disciple Gidō was not entirely forgotten. Although a number of Zen monks recalled his memory with a kind of sad devotion, the literary style of the time was totally determined by the secular methods of *shiroku-bun,* and the *gozan* masters were more literati than monks, and more often academicians than poets. They pursued literature for the sake of literature, which eventually had a negative impact on their work. Convention became more important than artistic creativity; verbal structures that were hardly comprehensible were simply passed on; no one dared to change fixed forms.

Learning played an important role in the Gozan monasteries, Chinese classics and history being the favored areas of study. Texts were learned by heart and then commented on in Japanese. The monasteries became centers of scholastic formation, open to both Zen students and laity, and were highly regarded as means of fostering general education. Indeed, the contribution of Zen monks to the education of the nation should not go unmentioned. The Ashikaga school (Ashikaga Gakkō), founded by the Ashikaga family in 1190, experienced a vital renewal after 1400, due both to the patronage of Uesugi Norizane and above all to the experienced direction of the Zen monks.[104] For some time this school remained the only place where one could receive an education in the Chinese classics. On the other end of the educational spectrum, Buddhist priests, mainly Zen monks, conducted their temple schools and cared for the simple people, teaching their children to read and write and explaining for all the principles of Confucian ethics. The oft-cited close bonds between Confucian ethics and Zen Buddhism were tied firmly during the *gozan* period.[105]

After the middle of the fifteenth century, the political and cultural decline accelerated. Under Yoshimasa (1435–1490, ruled 1449–1474), the last significant shōgun from the Ashikaga clan, the Ōnin War (1467–1477) sealed the fate of the shogunate. When Yoshimasa ascended the throne, he looked out over a nation torn apart by division and confusion. But since the young ruler was more interested in the beauty of art than in the government of the nation, the situation deteriorated until the country was engulfed in the worst of all the medieval civil wars, dubbed the Ōnin War *(Ōnin no ran)* after the name of the era in which the turmoil began (1467–1469). It was fought over the right of succession to the shogunate. In 1464 the childless Yoshimasa had promised the throne to his monk brother, who forthwith abandoned his monastic life and took the name Yoshimi. A year later, however, a son was born to Yoshimasa. Naturally, the father wished his son to be his successor, and it was at this time that the problems began. The powers that be took sides and embarked on a war that would last for ten years and leave Kyoto in ashes. The war finally came to an end not because of the superior gains of either side but simply because both sides were worn out from the fighting. During the conflict Yoshimasa withdrew from the government to make way for his son, Yoshihisa, in 1474; after Yoshihisa's death in 1489 Yoshimasa bestowed the succession on Yoshitane, a son of Yoshimi, with whom he had been reconciled. Enmities between the aristocratic families continued after the war, leading historians to call the following century the "age of the Warring States" (*sengoku-jidai*) (1478–1577 or 1490–1600).

The effects of the civil wars, especially the Ōnin War, on culture and art were devastating. Most of the temples in the capital fell to the flames, including all of the Five Temples except Tōfuku-ji. Nonetheless, there was one final outburst of *gozan* art. During the Ōnin War, Yoshimasa, probably inspired by the Temple of the Golden Pavilion (Kinkaku-ji) built by his predecessor, Yoshimitsu, in 1397, drew up plans to construct a sister structure. The result was the Temple of the Silver Pavilion (Ginkaku-ji), built between 1482 and 1483, a monument to the extravagance of Yoshimasa and his determination to enjoy the arts. Because of its location on Higashiyama in the eastern side of the city, the term *Higashiyama culture* has been given to this period of refined aestheticism. Though this culture was destined for a rapid demise, it has an irreplaceable place in the history of Japanese art. The determinative role here was played by the Zen monks of the Five Mountains.

The most prominent of the Zen monks of this period was Ōsen Keizan (1429–1493), of the line of Gidō and Ganchū, who exercised great authority as abbot of Shōkoku-ji and Nanzen-ji and as holder of the office of *sōroku*.[106] Through his disciples, the *gozan* movement was carried on into the next century, its main remaining purpose being the transmission of Chinese culture. In the *gozan* monasteries, popular Buddhism, including the practice of the *nembutsu*, blended with Chinese science and art, as well as with basic elements of Japanese culture. Not limited to literary and academic activities, the process of secularization also pervaded daily life in the monasteries, expressing itself in empty pomp, rivalries, ambition, the cooling of monastic fervor, and other signs of corruption. This led many serious Zen disciples to abandon the *gozan* monasteries in order to find stricter forms of practice with other masters. It is superfluous to list the details of this widespread decline.

Zen historians have often been critical of the *gozan* movement. The article in the *Zengaku daijiten* on *gozan* literature, which calls this period "the golden age in the history of Chinese literature in Japan," comes to this conclusion:

> From the perspective of the original Zen school, *gozan* literature must be called a defective product; still, it occupies a permanent and important place in the history of Japanese literature and played a key role in the formation and development of Chinese culture [in Japan].[107]

This is not the only possible verdict on the matter. An authentic form of Zen was still dominant during the first period of the *gozan* movement; it was only during the second period that secular Chinese literature began to color the spirit of Zen. Moreover, the movement's contribution to the overall educational level of the nation remains a positive one. Nevertheless, it is true that the *gozan* movement, like the Ashikaga shogunate that patronized it, ended in failure. It was the stream of tradition flowing outside the movement of the Five Mountains that carried Zen forward into Japanese history, as we shall see in the next chapter.

NOTES

1. Collcutt, *Five Mountains*, pp. 109ff. On the following see chapter 3 of Collcutt's book, pp. 91–129. The title *kanji* ("official monasteries"), which the temples of the *gozan* system use, describes their adherence to the state. Such official temples in China were open to monks from all Buddhist schools (pp. 29, 112). This was not the case in Japan, but a trace of this openness can be seen in the fact that any monk of a monastery belonging to the *gozan* could be made abbot. Outstanding monks were often placed one after the other as administrators of different *gozan* monasteries. Distinct from monasteries of the regime of the Five Mountains (*gozan no kanji*), whose members could come "from all over" (*jippō jūji sei*), in many Rinka (rural) monasteries the principle of "succession in one line" (*ichiryū sōjō sei*) was in effect. Regarding the system of succession dominant in Zen monasteries during the middle ages (*jūji seido*), see Imaeda Aishin's detailed presentation in his "*Chūsei zenshūshi no kenkyū,* pp. 367–407. The arrangement often underwent modifications of minor or major importance.

2. See chapter 14 above, note 134 and the accompanying text.

3. See the tables in Collcutt, *Five Mountains*, p. 110.

4. Collcutt accords Daitoku-ji first position in the ranking of the *gozan* monasteries under Go-Daigo (*Five Mountains*, p. 110). This temple was later assigned to the category of the Ten Temples (*jissetsu*) and was eventually excluded entirely from the system (pp. 111–12).

5. Collcutt, *Five Mountains*, pp. 117–23.

6. See *Nihon bukkyōshi* II, pp. 173ff.

7. For two examples, see Collcutt, *Five Mountains*, p. 124.

8. Some years ago Oskar Benl introduced Musō Soseki early on to the German-speaking public in his essay "Musō Kokushi (1275–1351): Ein japanischer Zen-Meister," OE 2 (1955): 86–108. The notes include some bibliographical references. There is a sizeable literature on National Teacher Musō in Japanese. Outstanding is Yanagida Seizan's introduction to the edition and modern Japanese translation of Musō's collected sayings, *Musō Kokushi goroku* (T. 2555, vol. 80), pp. 7–128. Further, see the essay on Musō by Hirata Kōji in vol. 4 of the collection of historical works, *Zen*, pp. 233–48. See also the monograph by Tamamura Takeji, *Musō Kokushi* (Tokyo, 1958) and the entries in the *Zengaku daijiten* II, pp. 771, and EJ, vol. 5, p. 287b. A report on the monastery of Tenryū-ji has been published by Nara Mototatsuya in the collection *Temples and Shrines* (Kyoto, 1978).

9. See the list of the seven titles in Benl, "Musō Kokushi," p. 92, note 29. Cf. Hirata, p. 238.

10. *Musō Kokushi nenpu* (or *Musō shōgaku nenpu*), in the collection of Japanese historical sources, *Zoku gunshoruiju*, vol. 9.

11. On Musō's relationship to the province of Kai, see the detailed account in Yanagida, *Musō Kokushi goroku*, pp. 58ff, 68ff.

12. Yanagida, *Musō Kokushi goroku*, p. 69.

13. Yanagida, *Musō Kokushi goroku*, p. 76.

14. Musō gave the name to himself. Yanagida gives an impressive description of how Musō was born as a Zen monk from the dream (*Musō Kokushi goroku*, pp. 72ff).

15. On Shinchi Kakushin see pp. 29–31 in the text above.

16. See the brief biography in *Zengaku daijiten* I, p. 116.

17. Benl mentions the names of Mukyū Tokusen, Chidon Kūshō, and Tōkei Tokugo, all students of Lan-hsi Tao-lung; see "Musō Kokushi," p. 89.

18. On I-shan I-ning, see pp. 169–70 above.

19. Compiled by the disciple Shun'oku Myōha, edited and annotated by Yanagida Seizan in the collected sayings of Musō. Yanagida compares the text strewn with light pieces (anecdotes, quotations, and so forth) to the *Shōbōgenzō zuimonki,* edited by Dōgen's disciple Ejō, and also to Shinran's *Tan'ishō* (written by the disciple Yuien); see p. 240.

20. *Seizan yawa,* in Yanagida's edition of the collected sayings, pp. 249–50.

21. Hirata presents a differing picture of the sequences of events that are repeated here in the order given them by Yanagida (*Musō Kokushi goroku,* p. 81). According to Hirata, the enlightenment follows immediately after Musō's second stay with I-shan. He ascribes the falling out with I-shan to the difficulty of understanding a foreign master (p. 235).

22. Alicia and Daigan Matsunaga (*Foundation of Japanese Buddhism,* vol. 2, p. 229) ascribe Musō's inclinations to the esoteric largely to the influence of Kōhō Kennichi. On close inspection it appears that a strict master-disciple relationship did not form between the two. Kennichi did not exert any noteworthy influence on Musō.

23. On the following, see Yanagida, *Musō Kokushi goroku,* pp. 81–82.

24. *Musō Kokushi goroku* p. 83. Yanagida describes the enlightenment process, pp. 83–86.

25. See Hirata, *Zen,* vol. 4, p. 235. Yanagida uses the expression *mushi dokugo,* meaning "enlightenment by oneself, without a master" (p. 384).

26. See the enlightenment verses in Chinese and Japanese translation in Yanagida, *Musō Kokushi goroku,* p. 305. An easily understandable paraphrase is given in Hirata, *Zen,* vol. 4, p. 235.

27. *Keitoku dentōroku,* book 2. See Chang Chung-yuan, *Original Teachings of Ch'an Buddhism,* pp. 219–26. On the enlightenment experience, see p. 220 (suddenness and resolution through a noise).

28. See Hirata, *Zen,* vol. 4, p. 236.

29. Yanagida, *Musō Kokushi goroku,* p. 89.

30. Yanagida, *Musō Kokushi goroku,* p. 384; cf. p. 89.

31. On this see *Zengaku daijiten* I p. 337. Cf. Yanagida, *Musō Kokushi goroku,* p. 89.

32. See the section in Yanagida, *Musō Kokushi goroku,* pp. 91–94; H. Brinker, *Die zen-buddhistische Bildnismalerei in China und Japan,* pp. 163–66 (with reproductions); and the brief biography in *Zen Dust,* pp. 150–51.

33. See chapter 9 on the Zen movement after Hui-neng in vol. 1 of the present work, where the famous passage from the *Keitoku dentōroku* is cited on p. 161 and note 30.

34. In particular, the portrait in Sembutsu-ji, which for a time had been in Nanzen-ji; on the portrait, see Brinker, *Die zen-buddhistische Bildnismalerei in China und Japan,* p. 165.

35. Yanagida, *Musō Kokushi goroku,* p. 93.

36. Cf. Yanagida, *Musō Kokushi goroku,* p. 385.

37. Hirata, *Zen,* vol. 4, p. 236. Hirata does not go any further in his description of the conditions, but there are also other Japanese historians who report on abuses in Engaku-ji, even though from the outset it had been administered by Zen masters of high standing.

38.   The events are reported in relevant historical studies of Japan.

39.   Although Musō had never visited China, he was familiar with monastic rules of the Zen schools during the Sung period. He cites the rule book *Biyō shingi* (Chin., *Pei-yung ch'ing-kuei*). Collcutt has offered a completed English translation of Musō's *Rinsen kakun* in his book *Five Mountains*. Although the thirty-two articles of the text do not in his view admit of any logical ordering, he has arranged them in categories dealing with the monastery, the community, and the monastic life. See the section "The Rinsen-ji Code," pp. 149–65.

40.   Cited in Yanagida, *Musō Kokushi goroku*, p. 39.

41.   *Musō Kokushi goroku*, p. 40. The entire passage, which Yanagida has written in an emotional style, is direction against modern misinterpretations of Musō.

42.   A proof of the Buddhist piety of the two men is that they did not thereby become Zen monks. Only a few persons in political life practiced Zen expressly.

43.   Tadayoshi apparently came to his end by poisoning.

44.   Cited in Hirata, *Zen*, vol. 4, pp. 237–38. In Japan, particular years are singled out for commemoration, among them the seventh and thirteenth years.

45.   The verse of the farewell poem and funeral song are cited in Yanagida, *Musō Kokushi goroku*, p. 125. He does not render them into modern Japanese but adds an explanation. The translation offered here attempts to incorporate the clarifications brought forth there. On the *kikan-kōan*, see *Zen Dust*, pp. 49ff.

46.   Brinker presents six pictures of Musō Soseki, which he explain in detail. See *Die zen-buddhistische Bildnismalerei in China und Japan*, pp. 166–69 and the tables on pp. 107–112.

47.   The explanation of Yanagida offers remarkable comments on Musō's personality. See his introduction to Musō's collected sayings (cf. note 8 above).

48.   *Seizan yawa*, cited in Yanagida, *Musō Kokushi goroku*, p. 242.

49.   Yanagida, *Musō Kokushi goroku*, p. 244.

50.   Yanagida, *Musō Kokushi goroku*, pp. 247–48.

51.   In the collection *Zengaku taikei (sorokubu)*. Parts of this work appear in the section on "Buddhism" in vol. 9 of the *Nihon tetsugaku shisō zensho*, pp. 213–55. For translations in this chapter, compare Benl, "Musō Kokushi," pp. 97–106.

52.   *Muchū-mondō*, chap. 81. Compare with the explanation of the *shōgyoku* in the following section in Yanagida, *Musō Kokushi goroku*, pp. 117–20.

53.   The expression is often used in Musō, for example in the *Muchū-mondō*, in *Nihon tetsugaku shisō zensho*, vol. 9, p. 223, and in the *Seizan yawa*.

54.   *Seizan yawa*, in Yanagida, *Musō Kokushi goroku*, pp. 268–69.

55.   Chap. 54, *Nihon tetsugaku shisō zensho*, pp. 219–20.

56.   *Muchū-mondō*, chap. 53, p. 219.

57.   *Muchū-mondō*, chap. 55, p. 221.

58.   *Muchū-mondō*, chap. 56, p. 222.

59.   *Muchū-mondō*, chap. 56, pp. 223–24.

60.   *Muchū-mondō*, chap. 57, p. 224.

61.   Yanagida, *Musō kokushi goroku*, p. 117.

62.   Yanagida, *Musō kokushi goroku*, p. 122.

63.   In the text "Twenty-Three Questions and Answers" of the National Teacher Musō, no. 1.

64.   *Muchū-mondō*, chap. 90, p. 246.

65.   *Muchū-mondō*, chap. 57. Benl has translated the entirety of this important chapter, a justification of the aesthetic world view of Musō; see "Musō Kokushi," pp. 103–106.

66.   There are a number of works in ths history of Japanese literature that treat the *gozan* literature. On their importance in Zen Buddhism see the entry "Gozan bungaku" in the *Zengaku daijiten* I, p. 341. Cf. also G. B. Sansom, *Japan: A Short Cultural History*, pp. 371ff, 378ff.

67.   Tamamura Takeji, in his remarkable introduction to the volume on the monk-poets of the Five Mountains (*Gozan shisō*) in the Japanese collected Zen sayings (*Nihon no zen-goroku*, vol. 8), places of Ku-lin Ching-mao and I-shan I-ning at the beginning. See pp. 29–30.

68.   Tamamura treats I-shan's affiliation with the Zen of the Southern Sung period, the style of which is different from that of the early Yüan period. *Nihon no zen-goroku*, vol. 8, pp. 34ff.

69.   Tamamura calls I-shan the "patriarch of the literature of the Japanese forest of Zen, namely of *gozan* literature," *Nihon no zen-goroku*, vol. 8, p. 31.

70.   Imaeda Aishin treats both in Imaeda II, p. 184; on the literary performance of Kokan Shiren, see Tamamura, *Nihon no zen-goroku*, vol. 8, pp. 150–55. A brief biography appears in the *Zengaku daijiten* I, p. 602.

71.   See the brief biography that appears in the *Zengaku daijiten* II, p. 837.

72.   Tamamura, *Nihon no zen-goroku*, vol. 8, p. 36.

73.   On Sesson Yūbai, see Tamamura, *Nihon no zen-goroku*, vol. 8, pp. 155–164; see the brief biography in the *Zengaku daijiten* II, p. 1245.

74.   Tamamura, *Nihon no zen-goroku*, vol. 8, pp. 38–41; see the brief biography in the *Zengaku daijiten* II, p. 649.

75.   On his school, Kongō dōka, see the entry in *Zengaku daijiten* I, pp. 365–66. Cf Imaeda II, pp. 168ff.

76.   See the entry on geju (Skt., *gāthā*) in *Zengaku daijiten* I, p. 269. On its literary significance see Tamamura, *Nihon no zen-goroku*, vol. 8, pp. 38ff.

77.   Tamamura, *Nihon no zen-goroku*, vol. 8, p. 41.

78.   Tamamura, *Nihon no zen-goruku*, vol. 8, p. 45.

79.   Imaeda II, pp. 185, 170–71.

80.   See note 133 to chap. 1 and its corresponding text above.

81.   Tamamura, *Nihon no zen-goroku*, vol. 8, pp. 48–49; Imaeda II, pp. 170–71.

82.   For example in Tamamura, *Nihon no zen-goroku*, vol. 8, pp. 49–50; Imaeda II, p. 170.

83.   On the following, see also the appraisal of this first period by Imaeda in the section "From the North Mountain to the East Mountain," Imaeda II, pp. 187–88.

84.   On the background, as well as the events preceding and following this unusual incident, see Collcutt, *Five Mountains*, pp. 120ff.

85.   On Shun'oku Myōha, see Imaeda II, pp. 181–82; cf. Tamamura, *Nihon no zen-goroku*, vol. 8, p. 58; Collcutt, *Five Mountains*, p. 111.

86.   Light is shed on the phenomenon by Tamamura in his sections on Gidō Shūshin (*Nihon no zengoroku*, vol. 8, pp. 76–105) and Zekkai Chūshin (pp. 105–26). Tamamura takes it as of central importance in the development of the *gozan* movement.

87.   On Ryūzan Tokken see Imaeda II, pp. 184–85; Tamamura, *Nihon no zen-goroku*, vol. 8, p. 58.

88.   Chūgan Engetsu is the only Japanese disciple to have received the seal of enlightenment in China from Master Tung-yang Te-hui, the compiler of the monastic rule, *Chokushū Hyakujō shingi* (Chin., *Chih-hsiu Pai-chang ch'ing kuei*, T. 2025). He could not have been familiar with the rule in China because he had already returned to Japan in 1332, well before its compilation, dated 1336. The text was probably brought over to Japan in 1350 and in 1356, fully twenty years after its compilation, published by the Zen monk Kokyō Myōsen (d. 1360), a Japanese Dharma heir of Ch'ing-cho Cheng-ch'eng (Jpn., Seisetsu Shōchō). Chūgan Engetsu and his co-disciple Gidō Shūshin propagated these rules, well suited to the requirements of the *gozan* monasteries of the time, which, as Imaeda notes, "not only contained in good order the kernel of all rules up to that time but also many Buddhist ceremonies and incantations beloved by the aristocracy" (p. 69). In the title of the text the name of Pai-chang appears. Thus this comprehensive monastic rule can be seen as greatly expanded version of the original "pure rule of Pai-chang" (*hyakujō shingi, pai-chang ch'ing kuei*). Nonetheless, we lack any material to substantiate such a relationship. The sources provide no information on the origins of the well known rule attributed to Pai-chang. It is indeed uncertain whether Pai-chang's rule had been available in a complete edition, nor do we know when this text, if it ever existed, was lost. On the foregoing see Imaeda Aishin, *Chūsei zenshūshi no kenkyū*, pp. 56–72, especially pp. 67ff; Collcutt, *Five Mountains*, pp. 135ff. A brief biography of Chūgan Engetsu appears in the *Zengaku daijiten* I, p. 110; cf. Imaeda II, p. 186–87.

89.   Besides the relevant section in Tamamura (note 86), see Imaeda II, p. 183, and the short biography in *Zengaku daijiten* I, p. 487.

90.   Collcutt relies on Gidō's diary (*Five Mountains*, p. 100). G. Sansom also relies on this "valuable historical document" in the detailed treatment he devotes to Gidō; see *A History of Japan 1334–1615*, pp. 161–66.

91.   On the foregoing see Sansom, *A History of Japan*, pp. 163ff. Gidō was first entrusted with the running of Kennin-ji in Kyoto and then Tōji-ji by the shōgun Yoshimitsu; not long after the death of the shōgun he was elevated to the highest order as abbot of Nanzen-ji. On the activity of Gidō in Kamakura, where he held important offices, see Tamamura, *Nihon no zengoroku*, vol. 8, pp. 82ff.

92.   See Imaeda II, pp. 183–84; Tamamura, *Nihon no zen-goroku* 8, pp. 105–26. See also the short biography in *Zengaku daijiten*, pp. 854–55.

93.   See *Chūgokugakugei daijiten* (Tokyo, 1959), pp. 423–27; cf. Tamamura, *Nihon no zengoroku*, vol. 8, pp. 59ff.

94.   The temple served as the memorial temple of the Ashikaga family; see Collcutt, *Five Mountains*, p. 106.

95.   The temple was destroyed by fire in 1394, after which Zekkai made efforts for its reconstruction and was for the third time called on to be its abbot. See Tamamura, *Nihon no zen-goroku*, vol. 8, p. 113.

96.   Tamamura (*Nihon no zen-goroku*, vol. 8, p. 117) compares Gidō and Zekkai to two wings, each of which was greatly necessary for the movement to stay in flight.

97.   See Sansom *Japan: A Short Cultural History*, p. 379.

98.   See Imaeda II, p. 188, and the brief biography in *Zengaku daijiten* II, p. 940.

99.   See Imaeda II, p. 188, and the brief biography in *Zengaku daijiten* II, p. 1187.

100.   See Imaeda II, p. 188, and the brief biography in *Zengaku daijiten* II, p. 947.

101.   See Imaeda II, p. 191, and the brief biography in *Zengaku daijiten* I, p. 494, II, p. 1303.

102.   See Imaeda II, p. 187, and the brief biography in *Zengaku daijiten* II, p. 760.

103.   See Imaeda II, p. 188, and the brief biography in *Zengaku daijiten* II, p. 1131.

104.   See the section on education during the Muromachi period in Sansom, *A History of Japan*, 1334–1615, p. 373.

105.   Sansom stresses, in contrast to critical appraisals, that "the attempt of Zen scholars in Japan as in China to harmonize Zen principles with the Confucianism of Sung thinkers is a sign of vitality in sharp contrast to the sleepy contentment of some of the older sects of Buddhism." (*A History of Japan*, p. 160).

106.   See Imaeda II, pp. 192–93; see the short biography in *Zengaku daijiten* I, p. 259.

107.   *Zengaku daijiten* I, p. 341.

5

The Rinka Monasteries

The *gozan* temples, and the entire system that grew up around them, can rightly be regarded as representative of Japanese Zen during the Muromachi period. This is especially true since the Five Temples of Kyoto and Kamakura, which for the most part are all still well preserved, remain for modern Japanese a powerful reminder of the might and the beauty of Zen during Japan's middle ages. Yet although the central significance of the *gozan* movement cannot be questioned, the movement by itself does not give us a complete picture of this period of Zen history; it was a part of a much larger picture. The other side of the picture, the so-called Rinka monasteries, also deserves our attention.

According to Nakamura Hajime, the distinguishing characteristic of the Rinka monasteries is that they were "the large temples of the Zen school in rural areas, in contrast to the so-called Sōrin temples of the Zen school of Kyoto, Kamakura, and so forth, which were found in urban centers."[1] The two distinguishing features of the Rinka monasteries, then, are their detachment from the *gozan* temples and their rural location. More concretely, Japanese historians list under Rinka monasteries the foundations of the Sōtō school with its center in Eihei-ji, those of the Daiō line centered in Daitoku-ji, and the monasteries of the Myōshin-ji and Genjū lines.[2] Unlike the *gozan* system, the Rinka monasteries did not form a well-organized institution and loosely included numerous Zen monasteries in rural areas as well.

In the Chinese Zen literature of the Sung period, the terms *sōrin* and *rinka* signify Zen monasteries and Zen communities respectively. The striking metaphor of a "forest" of Zen disciples—as in the expression *zenrin* meaning "Zen-forest"— was very popular. Both images, *rinka* (sometimes read *ringe*) meaning "under the forest" or "under the thicket," and *sōrin* meaning "lavish undergrowth," belong to the same root metaphor. During the Muromachi period in Japan the two expressions were contrasted. "There was in the Zen school," Tamamura Takeji tells us, "a group that resented the control of the *bakufu;* they lived mainly in the countryside and devoted themselves industriously to purely religious activities. To distinguish this group from the *gozan* line, they were called Rinka."[3] The Rinka monasteries were also called Sanrin (literally, "mountain forest"), whereas *gozan* institutions were sometimes referred to as *gozan-sōrin.*

DAITOKU-JI AND ITS FOUNDER

The history of the Rinzai line that is centered in Daitoku-ji predates the founding of the monastery. This line is known in Japanese Zen history as the Ō-tō-kan line, after the names of the three prominent masters who founded it: Nampo

Jōmyō (titled Daiō Kokushi, 1235–1308), Shūhō Myōchō (titled Daitō Kokushi, 1282–1338), and Kanzan Egen (1277–1360).[4] Nampo belongs to the
Kamakura period. We discussed him and his unique place in the history of Japanese Zen in our chapter on the implantation of Rinzai Zen in Japan, above.
During his eight-year stay in China he studied only the most authentic Zen and
then brought it back to Japan, where he spent decades teaching it to his disciples,
among whom there were individuals of extraordinary quality. We mention him
here because as the master of Shūhō Myōchō, the founder of Daitoku-ji, he
represents the beginning of the most influential Rinzai line in all of Japanese
Zen history.

Legends surround the figure of Nampo's famous chief disciple, Shūhō Myōchō.[5] Born in the province of Harima, not far from modern Osaka, he was
credited with extraordinary deeds and words while still a boy; it is said he was
only ten years old when he grew tired of child's play and became disgusted with
the things of the world. He was turned over to a Vinaya master for his further
education. He dedicated himself forthwith to the study of Buddhist teachings,
but even this did not satisfy him. And so, still a youngster, he began to practice
meditation. Burning with the desire to follow the way, he soon set out on a
pilgrimage to various monasteries and hermitages.

He was twenty-two when he knocked on the monastery door of Manju-ji
in Kamakura and begged Master Kōhō Kennichi for admission. The doors opened
and Shūhō began his monastic life. His faithful practice soon brought him to
an initial experience of enlightenment that was verified by Kennichi. Around
this time he heard that Nampo Jōmyō had arrived in Kyoto, summoned there
in 1304 by the retired emperor Go-Uda. Nampo was well-known for his rigid
practice and Shūhō felt called to follow his direction. When Nampo set out for
Kamakura to assume the office of abbot at Kenchō-ji, Shūhō followed; Shūhō
was to be at Nampo's side during the most important months of his life.

Ten days after arriving in Kamakura, Shūhō experienced his great enlightenment. He had been working with the kōan of Yün-men's barrier. As his biography reports, he suddenly smashed through the barrier and at that moment
he found himself in a state in which all opposites were harmonized. His body
covered in sweat, he hastened to his master's quarters. Hearing of his experience,
the master spoke: "Last night in my dreams I saw Yün-men enter my room.
Now today you have passed through the barrier. You must be a second Yün-
men."

The next day, Shūhō brought the master two stanzas of poetry:

Having once penetrated the cloud barrier,
The living road opens out north, east, south, and west.
In the evening resting, in the morning roaming, neither host nor guest.
At every step the pure wind rises

Having penetrated the cloud barrier, there is no old road,
The azure heaven and the bright sun, these are my native place.
The wheel of free activity constantly changing is difficult to reach.
Even the golden-hued monk [Kāśyapa] bows respectfully and return.

Having read the poem, the master wrote in the margin:

> You have already cast away brightness and joined yourself to darkness. I
> am not like you. Now that my line has reached you, it is firmly established.
> But for twenty years you must ripen your spiritual understanding.[6]

To confirm his experience, the master bestowed on his disciple a ceremonial
robe (kesa).

After Nampo Jōmyō's death, Shūhō returned to Kyoto, where he dedicated
himself to postenlightenment practice, the importance of which his own experience had confirmed. He lived in a hermitage close to Ungo-ji on the East
Mountain, where day and night he pondered the Zen way transmitted by the
patriarchs. His biography reports that he was oblivious of hunger and cold as
he guided a growing number of followers along the way. Utterly dedicated to
Zen tradition, as the chronicles tells us, he copied all thirty volumes of the
Keitoku dentōroku in a period of only forty days.

There is a famous legend about his stay with the beggars of the Gojō bridge
in Kyoto. Stories of this unusual beggar spread among the monks and even
reached the imperial palace. A certain high official—some sources say it was
Emperor Hanazono himself—decided to find out the truth about this much-
discussed beggar. He brought a basket of makuwa melons, much loved by Shūhō,
showed them to the beggars, and said: "I will give a melon to anyone who can
step up to them without using his feet." No one moved. Then Shūhō stepped
forward and said: "Give one to me without using your hands!" His bright eyes
gave him away. Hakuin has painted an ink drawing of National Master Daitō
as a beggar, with his straw mat and hat and a begging bowl in his left hand,
and over the picture he inscribed four verses describing this story. Tradition has
it that Shūhō was immediately taken to the imperial palace, where he was given
monastic robes.

Emperor Hanazono delighted in conversing with the famous monk. According to tradition, he once asked the master, who was sitting in front of him
clad in his monastic habit:

> "Is it not a matter of unthinkability that the Buddha-Dharma should
> face the Royal Dharma on the same level?"
> Daitō replies, "Is it not a matter of unthinkability that the Royal Dharma
> should face the Buddha-Dharma on the same level?"[7]

The answer was as sharp as it was deep, and the emperor was satisfied.

More reliable is the report that in 1315 Shūhō built a hermitage in the
district of Murasakino, in the northwest of Kyoto, and named it Daitoku ("Great
Virtue"). His reputation in the capital was growing, and his conversations with
Emperor Go-Daigo in the palace became more and more cordial. In 1324 the
emperor gave him a rather extensive piece of land to a large monastery, and
under the direction of a Tendai monk (who, after a religious discussion, became
especially devoted to Shūhō) a circle of friends and benefactors developed to
support the project. In February of 1327, in the presence of the two emperors—
the retired Hanazono and the reigning Go-Daigo—the festive dedication of the

monastery took place.[8] During the ceremonies Shūhō spoke special words of gratitude for his deceased master, Daiō Kokushi.

Emperor Go-Daigo continued to shower Shūhō with favors. On three different occasions Shūhō was obliged to turn down the emperor's offer to make him abbot of Nanzen-ji.[9] Shūhō spent most of the following period at Daitoku-ji, interrupted only by a visit of one hundred days in 1331 to visit Sōfuku-ji in Kyūshū, a temple built in memory of Daiō Kokushi. The clearest expression of the Emperor's goodwill came in 1333, when he raised Daitoku-ji to the rank of first monastery of the country and then placed it alongside Nanzen-ji at the head of the list of *gozan* monasteries in the following year. At the same time, Daitoku-ji was granted the privilege of selecting its abbots exclusively from the generational line of its own disciples, a departure from the regulations of the *gozan* system.[10] When Emperor Go-Daigo was forced to leave the capital and the Ashikaga assumed full power, Daitoku-ji was reduced to the rank of one of the Ten Temples (*jissetsu*), and in 1431 freely withdrew from the *gozan* system.

The monastery of Daitoku-ji and its abbot enjoyed the full favor of the emperor and the people. The retired emperor Hanazono, who chose Shūhō as his private teacher, granted the master the title of Kōzen Daitō Kokushi, while the ruling Emperor honored him with the title of Kōshō Shōtō Kokushi. In the historical records, he is referred to as Daitō Kokushi.

Details of the Zen style practiced in Daitoku-ji are found in the instructions that Daitō set down in writing. He instructs beginners to

> practice only *zazen*, in full or half lotus position, with your eyes half-opened. In this posture, look upon the original countenance that you had before you were born of your mother and father! Before you were born of your mother and father means before your mother and father themselves were born, before heaven was separated from earth, before I took on human form. Your original countenance must be seen. In its original countenance a thing has neither color nor form, like formless emptiness. Thus the Buddha has taught: "Buddha body and Dharma body are like emptiness; Buddha body and Dharma body are your original countenance."[11]

Daitō explains that no written character can express one's original countenance. One may call it "Buddha nature" or "True Buddha." "When the Exalted One had endured six years of sitting meditation on Vulture Peak, in his enlightened state he looked upon the morning star and beheld his original countenance."[12] Daitō offers other examples of enlightenment from the early Zen chronicles, which he knew very well. He reached back to the Zen of the Patriarchs, to the "six gates" of Boddhidharma (which have since been shown to be apocryphal[13]), to Hui-neng's *Platform Sūtra*, and to works from the T'ang period. In his well-known work, *Dharma Words in Kana (Kana-hōgo)* he shows himself to be a classical Zen master, tracing the origins of the Zen tradition transmitted to him by the Chinese masters of the Sung period, especially by Hsü-t'ang Chih-yü and by Ta-hui Tsung-kao and his school. His practice centered on seated meditation (*zazen*), kōan practice (which he considered requisite for any authentic exploration into the self), and the experience of enlightenment.

Daitō's parting advice, composed two years before he died, is well-known. Rooted in the marrow of Zen tradition, this text bared what was closest to the master's heart. To this day, with some stylistic changes, it graces almost every Zen hall of the Rinzai school. What follows is a somewhat free rendition:

> After this old monk dies, let the temples flourish, let the portraits of Buddha and the sūtra scrolls be encased in gold, let disciples in great numbers assemble to read the sūtras and recite the incantations, to sit in meditation at night and to content themselves with one meal by day, let them observe the rule and follow the Way. If they do not hold dear to their hearts the wonderful way of the Buddhas and the partriarchs that no scriptures contain, they will not be able to cut through the knots of karma, the true style will fall asunder, and they will be numbered among Māra's tribe. Although much time has passed since the old monk's departure from the world, one should not call them his grandchildren.
>
> But if there is one who spends his days out in the field, under a straw roof, eating his damp vegetables and roots from a wobbly kettle, if such a one is in exclusive pursuit of the self, he will meet the old monk face to face day after day and become a person of deep gratitude.[14]

The old monk is, of course, the National Master Daitō himself. This text bears literary resemblances to early Chinese Zen literature. The rejection of all external pomp contrasts sharply with the secular leanings of the middle ages in Japan, while the unique diction, relentless and pressing, reminds one of Lin-chi's (Rinzai's) talks. Like the great Chinese master, Daitō was not one for half-measures. Disciples have to turn inward completely in order to search for the self; they must expend every effort in pursuit of enlightenment—as Lin-chi so graphically put it, they must embrace authentic homelessness.

Daitō insisted on strict observance of the monastic rule. The rigor of the directives he laid down for his monasteries is somewhat surprising. The daily order contains three periods for the recitation of sūtras and liturgies, four periods for zazen, as in the early Buddhist rules, and only two meals, in the morning and at noon. Despite his careful regard for older customs, Daitō took into consideration the rigors of the Japanese climate and allowed an additional light meal in the evening, which is still known in Zen monasteries today as the "medicinal stone" (yakuseki).[15] Students who are not yet permitted to join the meditation periods (shami) are to devote their study sessions only to the Buddhist canon. In the observance of these external rules, however, Daitō always left room for inner freedom among his disciples.[16]

Daitō was only fifty-five when he contracted a fatal illness. He turned the direction of the monastery over to his chief disciple Tettō Gikō (1295–1369); before dying he gave clear instructions to Tettō not to build a pagoda in his honor. As befits a Zen master, he wished to die while sitting in meditation, but injury to his foot prevented him from assuming a full lotus position. As he felt the hour of death approaching, he took his place on the abbot's cushion, and with a mighty effort placed his left leg over the right. His bone broke, and blood could be seen on his robe. In this perfect lotus position he penned his farewell poem, which is difficult to render in translation. Roughly put, it goes like this:

> I have cut off Buddhas and patriarchs;
> The blown hair [sword] is always burnished;
> When the wheel of free activity turns,
> The empty void gnashes its teeth.[17]

The Chinese master Ch'ing-chŏ Cheng-ch'eng (Seisetsu Shōchō, 1274–1339), who at the time of Daitō's death was abbot of Nanzen-ji, is said to have been amazed at this farewell poem. "I would not have thought," he confessed, "that there could be such a clear-visioned master in Japan. I am saddened not to have met him during his lifetime." With Daitō, the process of transplanting Zen from China is complete; the Japanese masters have themselves equaled the heights of their Chinese prototypes.

Prominent among Daitō's disciples were Tettō Gikō, his successor at Daitoku-ji, and Kanzan Egen, the founder of Myōshin-ji. Tettō was from Izumo and studied at Kennin-ji, where he grew dissatisfied with the gozan style and turned to Daitō. He lived many long years with the master in close spiritual communion. A copy of the the Rinzairoku written in his own hand testifies to his closeness to Daitō and his devotion to the school's founder. He met with great success at the second abbot of Daitoku-ji and was succeeded by his disciple Gongai Sōchū (1315–1390), and then in the next generation by Kasō Sōdon (1352–1428). By the end of the fourteenth century, however, Daitoku-ji, like almost all the monasteries in the capital, was falling into decline.

In its intellectual and cultural splendor, Daitoku-ji ranks among the great Zen temples of this period. Virtually all the Zen arts found a home within its walls, as did numerous Zen painters. Daitō himself numbers among the foremost calligraphers of Japanese Zen. We will have more to say about the gardens of Daitoku-ji. Toward the end of the middle ages, Daitoku-ji also became the center of the tea ceremony.

KANZAN EGEN AND THE MYŌSHIN-JI LINE

The unity that binds the Ō-tō-kan masters is based not only on their master-disciple relationships but more particularly on the normative role that this three-starred constellation played in the history of Japanese Zen. Although the National Master Daitō, the founder of Daitoku-ji, surpassed both his predecessor Nampo Jōmyō and his successor Kanzan Egen, all three of them together laid the foundations and set the directions for the future of Rinzai Zen in Japan.

At first glance, it would seem that Kanzan Egen[18] was the least significant of the three, yet it was his line that was primarily responsible for both the future fame and the endurance of the Rinzai school. Born in Shinano (in the province of Nagano), the talented young boy was brought by his father to his uncle Gekkoku Sōchū in Kamakura, where his education as a monk began. He had the good fortune to be able to spend a year under the direction of Nampo (Daiō Kokushi) in Kenchō-ji, but after the master's death in 1308 he returned to his homeland in Shinano (exact details are missing), where for some time he led the rigorous life of a hermit. Once when visiting in nearby Kamakura, he happened to hear about the work of the renowned Shūhō Myōchō (Daitō Kokushi) in Kyoto. Immediately he set out for the capital and soon found himself among the disciples of the abbot of Daitoku-ji.

Having received from Shūhō the case of "Yün-men's Barrier" as his assigned Kōan, Kanzan spent two years working with it before discovering the solution. To express his joy over his disciple's enlightenment, Master Shūhō composed the following verses:

Where the Way stands closed and difficult to follow,
Cold clouds constantly embrace the green peaks.
The one character "barrier" of Yün-men hides the deed.
The one with right vision sees further than ten thousand miles.[19]

As a confirmation of Kanzan's enlightenment, the poem is signed by Shūhō and dated mid-spring 1329. Kanzan was over fifty years old when the doors of enlightenment were opened for him.

Following the advice of his master, Kanzan left the following year for the mountain solitude of Ibuka (in the province of Gifu), where he lived for eight years with farmers, helping them tend their cattle and fields. He spent the nights sitting on a stone in deep meditation. Well aware of the enlightened mind of his disciples, Master Shūhō recommended him to his benefactor and friend, Emperor Hanazono, who at the time was hoping to transform his country estate on the western edge of Kyoto into a temple where he could carry out his Buddhist studies and meditation. At the recommendation of his master, Egen complied with the request of the emperor and assumed the direction of the newly renamed Myōshin-ji.[20] He was installed in the post in 1342.

At first, Myōshin-ji was a rather unpretentious foundation.[21] Under a leaky roof that offered little protection during the rainy season, Kanzan led a simple, rigorous life with a handful of disciples. National Master Musō told of how on a visit he once paid the community the monks had to run to a nearby store in order to offer him a few bean cakes. The master was greatly impressed by their spirit of poverty. When he returned he is said to have told his disciples that a great future for Japanese Zen was taking shape in Myōshin-ji.

"Shūhō left the temple to Daitoku-ji, but the school to Myōshin-ji."[22] This terse statement by a monk of that time describes the situation succinctly. Through the rigorous Zen style that Egen promoted in his monastery, he passed on the authentic spirit of Rinzai to succeeding generations. There was nothing superfluous in the entire house; Kanzan was continually demanding that his disciples push themselves to their limits. Following traditional Rinzai customs, he made use of both staff and shouting. One of the few Kōan that he assigned was: "For Egen here there is no birth-and-death."[23] Only those with the firmest resolve could persevere under such rigors. Many left this monastery that lay people came to call the "crown of the nation's Dharma caves."

With sincere gratitude, Kanzan Egen, the "patriarch of hidden virtues" (intoku no soshi),[24] attributed his own achievements to his two predecessors, the National Masters Daiō and Daitō. If he ever forgot these two masters, he once confessed, he would not deserve to have grandchildren. As he felt death approaching, he gave his robe to his sole Dharma heir Juō Sōhitsu (1296–1390), decked himself out in traveling attire, and died near "wind and pond."[25] Muin Sōin (1326–1410), the third successor at Myōshin-ji, came from the gozan line, of which he had been a member for some time with Kaō Sōnen (d. 1345) at Kennin-ji. He became a disciple of Juō Sōhitsu and later his successor. He was influenced considerably by gozan art. After his term as abbot, the influence of Myōshin-ji began to wane. One of the subsequent abbots, Setsudō Sōboku,[26] was a close friend of the rebellious Ōuchi Yoshihiro (1356–1399), who incurred the wrath of Ashikaga Yoskimitsu. After the rebellion of the great family of Ōuchi was quelled in 1399, Myōshin-ji was obliged to make heavy restitution. The temple grounds were confiscated and the monastery, which had been a branch temple of the Daitoku-ji line, was renamed and made a branch of Nanzen-ji.

Myōshin-ji's recovery from this devastating blow was slow. A clear turn for the better came in 1432, when some of the Myōshin-ji monks were allowed to return to the monastery. Subsequently the abbot, Myōkō Sōei, who was related to the imperial house, began a restoration that his successor Nippō Sōshun (1368–1448),[27] from the Musō line, brought to completion. The next abbot, Giten Genshō (1393–1462), confirmed the full recognition and influence of all the Rinka monasteries.

A new period of growth for Myōshin-ji began under the leadership of the renowned abbot Sekkō Sōshin (1408–1486), who, after the devastations of the Ōnin period, restored order to the monastery's internal and economic life and succeeded in getting back all the monastic properties. Among his disciples, the best known are the so-called "Four Wise Men": Tokuhō Zenketsu (1419–1506), Keisen Sōryū, Gokei Sōton, and Tōyō Eichō (1429–1504). Toward the end of the middle ages, the Myōshin-ji line had surpassed that of Daitoku-ji and had a firm hold on first place in the Rinzai school. The great expansion that followed, however, brought with it a drastic dilution of Zen with popular beliefs."[28] But despite the overall decadence that had set in, the branch-lines of Myōshin-ji kept on producing personalities of prominence. This was especially true of the line of Tōyō Eichō, which produced Hakuin Ekaku (1685–1768), Rinzai's most famous master and the father of modern Japanese Zen.

IKKYŪ SŌJUN

HISTORICAL BACKGROUND

The Muromachi period was a time of flourishing growth for the Japanese Zen movement. After overcoming great initial difficulties, Zen had struck deep roots in Japan, thanks above all to the role played by the great Zen temples of Kyoto. Further details on this period will help us understand it more clearly.

The ruling powers of the Muromachi period were partial to Zen monasteries, favoring them over all other Buddhist foundations. This should not blind us to the weaknesses of the Rinzai school, which were apparent in the *gozan* as well as in the Rinka monasteries. A rise all too readily leads to a fall. While the *gozan* monasteries, as state institutions, occupied a position of prominence, the Rinka monasteries also enjoyed the unrestricted graces of the imperial court, as is clearly shown in the founding of the Daitoku-ji monastery. Shūhō, the founding abbot of Daitoku-ji, was among those considered for the office of abbot of Nanzen-ji, the first temple of the capital day. Daitoku-ji received a lower ranking in the *gozan* system and later withdrew from the system entirely. Myōshin-ji, a branch foundation of Daitoku-ji, was counted among the most important temples of the capital.

Ikkyū[29] is a dominant figure within the Daitoku-ji line; he was already an old man when he took up the post of superior of its main temple. His life is a series of puzzles, and not of few of the controversies he stirred up have yet to be resolved. New interpretations of his life and work have recently been advanced and perhaps can clear up some of the main issues. These difficulties do not result merely from the uncertainty of historical data; Ikkyū himself was a highly gifted, eccentric, and traumatized personality about whom the modern sciences of genetics, medicine, and psychology no doubt have much to say. We still do not have a complete and satisfying biography of this figure who was so important for the medieval history of Japanese Zen. What follows is only a sketch of his life and activities.

EARLY DEVELOPMENT

Little is known of Ikkyū's childhood.[30] His mother was most likely a lady of the southern court of Emperor Go-Komatsu, of the line of Fujiwara. She was dismissed from the court during pregnancy and ended up leading an impoverished life in a dilapidated house in Saga, a suburb of Kyoto. Ikkyū was only five when he was entrusted to a nearby local temple. There he used his exceptional talents to acqure a solid knowledge of Chinese history and literature. He especially enjoyed poetry and music. With his monk-teacher, he read the *Vimalakīrti Sūtra*. At the age of thirty he joined the *gozan* school to study under the poet-monk Botetsu of Kennin-ji, and soon mastered the Chinese poetic form of four seven-syllable lines. The direction of his life became clear. "The opening of Ikkyū's literary eyes," writes Yanagida, "determined his entire life."[31] His early poems already show great talent. Echoing through his poetry is the tragedy of his mother, which instilled in him a deep concern for the plight of women. The impermanence of this world also deeply affected him and led him to criticize the superficial religiosity that he witnessed all around him. He was disgusted by the worldly, ambitious monks of Kennin-ji. During these early years, the dominant motifs of his poetry and activity took shape.

After some four years, he left Kennin-ji and joined the simple, friendly, hermit-monk Ken'ō, of the Myōshin-ji line; in the small temple of Saikin-ji they led a quiet, austere life. Here, too, Ikkyū practiced *zazen*. His efforts seem to have born good results, but Ken'ō could not verify his enlightenment since his own had never been verified. Ken'ō died at an early age and Ikkyū was overwhelmed by loneliness, despair, and a disgust for life.

The following year, however, he finally found a suitable Zen master in Kasō Sōdon (1352–1428), whom he joined in a small hermitage in Katada on Lake Biwa. Kasō was abbot of Daitoku-ji, but preferred living in these meager quarters attached to the monastery. For nine years Ikkyū lived with this serious-minded ascetic, who spared no pains in directing his young disciple. While Ikkyū gladly bore his master's rigorous discipline, he was distressed by the constant tensions between himself and Kasō's older disciple Yōsō Sōi (1379–1458). The animosity between the two grew and endured until Yōsō's death. In both their personalities and in their views of authentic Zen, they were stark opposites.[32]

Under Kasō, Ikkyū had a Zen experience while practicing the kōan of Tung-shan's sixty blows (case 15 of the *Mumonkan*). It was on this occasion in 1418 that the master is said to have given him the name Ikkyū. Some two years later, suddenly startled by the cawing of a crow, he experienced his great enlightenment. The verses that he composed on this occasion are contained in the collection of his poetry:

> Violent wrath and passions linger in my heart
> For twenty years which is this moment.
> A crow laughs, as an arhat from this dusty world.
> What means the beautiful face singing in the sunshine?[33]

Confirming the authenticity of his disciple's experience, Kasō immediately bestowed on him his certificate of enlightenment *(inka)*. But Ikkyū was reluctant to accept it; indeed, he is said to have thrown it into the fire. His resistance seems to have had a deeper cause: he was so utterly convinced of the experiential character of enlightenment that he would countenance no second opinions on its authenticity. Exercising his powers as a master to the full, he did not hesitate to disregard established Zen conventions entirely. Nonetheless, he remained with Kasō until his master's death. At the time, he was only thirty-three and a new chapter in his life was to about to begin.

WAYS TO THE PEOPLE

While the implantation of Zen in Japan depended to a great extent on the ready reception it found among the samurai, its subsequent development was marked by a reaching out to the masses. Large portions of the population were attracted by the role Ikkyū was playing in the realm of art and culture. During the latter half of the Muromachi period he was the most popular figure in Japanese Buddhism.

Though he could have claimed the privileges of an enlightened Zen master, Ikkyū chose the life of a wandering monk instead, a way of life befitting one in search of the true way. His wanderings lasted for about thirty years. Rather than spend much time in Zen monasteries, he lived primarily among the people, making friends with all classes of society—with the nobility and knights as well as with merchants, artisans, and farmers, with authors, tea-masters and artists, as well as with prostitutes, whose simplicity he held in high regard. He moved mainly between Kyoto, Osaka, and the flourishing commercial city of Sakai, which he had known already during his student days at Saikin-ji on Lake Biwa, when he traveled to the growing city to find support for his small, poverty-stricken community.

Ikkyū went far, perhaps too far, in his efforts to reach the people.[34] He had little regard for monastic rules and even broke basic laws of Buddhism, eating fish and meat, loving saké and women. An enemy of all narrowness and hypocrisy, he fostered a naturalistic religiosity that was close to the people's own religion. If he complained about degeneracy among the monks, it was only to exert himself all the more on behalf of lay Buddhism. He writes:

> Formerly, those who were religiously inclined entered the temples, but now they all shun them. The priests are devoid of wisdom; they find zazen boring. They don't concentrate on their kōan and are interested only in temple furniture. Their Zen meditation is a mere matter of appearance; they are smug and wear their robes proudly but are only ordinary people in priestly garments. Indeed, their robes are merely ropes binding them, their surplices like rods torturing them.[35]

These last words mirror the current image of hell, which in any case Ikkyū regarded with skepticism.

Since his childhood, Ikkyū had been moved by the impermanence of all things and taught indifference toward life and death. On New Year's Day he paraded through the streets of Sakai carrying a bamboo rod to which he had affixed his treatise "Skeletons." To the questions of the astounded onlookers he replied, with an untranslatable play on words, that only the skull is a happy omen. Only those who, like the skull, had come to terms with death can be happy.[36]

He sharply challenged the ideas of the afterlife cherished by Amida believers. The paradise expected by the pious is more fleeting than a stream of water rushing by:

> If one purifies the ground of one's own mind and beholds one's own nature, there remains no Pure Land for which to hope, no hell to fear, no passions to overcome, no duality of good and evil. One is free from the cycle of rebirths. One will be born in every life as one's mind wishes.[37]

From such a view of enlightenment, Ikkyū drew practical conclusions. He discarded old customs and mocked the superstitious practice of kindling lights on the feast of the dead and of making food offerings to the deceased and reciting the sūtras. Rain and dew, the sacrificial gifts of the universe; the moon dispensing light; the breeze rustling in the pine trees; the gurgling of waters in the fountains: these are the true reading of the sūtras. In a Japanese song he sings: "Bring melons and eggplants as a sacrifice, or the water of the Kamo River!"

Ikkyū referred to himself as the "son of the errant cloud."[38] There was much in him that was eccentric, but he also possessed a high-minded liberality and a laughter bordering on tears so characteristic of popular humor. Both the pride of the aristocracy and the destitution of the poor aroused his anger, which he expressed in biting irony. Numerous anecdotes about him have come down to us. Once when he was begging, dressed in old clothes, he was given a half-penny at the door of a wealthy landlord. He later visited the same house dressed in the violet garb of his office. He was received in an inner room and offered a sumptuous meal. He then rose from the table, took off his robe, and placed it before the food, declaring that the festive meal belonged not to him but only to his robe.

His originality, his independent thinking, and his compassion endeared him to the people. He must be counted among the outstanding Zen monks of the Japanese middle ages. His puns and songs live to this day. His most salient virtue is his honesty, which is expressed in the following verses:

Hetsuraite	Though servility
tanoshiki yori mo	May bring pleasure, rather
hetsurawade	Without falsehood and deception
mazushiki mi koso	Would I dwell in poverty, with
kokoro yasukere	My heart cradled in peace.

FINAL YEARS

The final period in Ikkyū's life began in 1456, when in his sixtieth year he restored the monastery of Myōshō-ji, which had been built in memory of the National Master Daitō. His disciples had a hermitage built there for him called Shūon-an, which then became the name of the entire complex.[39] This was the first time after the death of his master Kasō that Ikkyū actually resided in a monastery, gathered disciples, and became the center of a monastic community.

In old age Ikkyū enjoyed the well-deserved esteem of all. Amid the terrible sufferings the population endured as a result of the disturbances continually plaguing the capital city, Ikkyū's bodhisattva vow showed itself in a spirit of selflessness and readiness to help. Even among his fellow monks, whom he had antagonized and alienated through his excessive attacks on their style of life, he won growing recognition. With the help of friends he was able to restore the buildings of Daitoku-ji that had been destroyed by fire. Toward the end of his life he was elevated to the post of abbot at Daitoku-ji, but he preferred to continue living in his beloved Shūon-an hermitage, where he died in 1481 at the ripe old age of eighty-seven. Like no other Zen master of the middle ages, Ikkyū's figure has remained popular in Japan until today. Both history and legend have contributed to keeping his memory alive. His versatile and highly regarded artistic talents formed part of the high point that Zen art reached during the Muromachi period.

THE GENJŪ LINE

Because they trace their origins to Nampo Jōmyō (Daiō Kokushi), the most important of the Rinka lines, centered in Daitoku-ji and Myōshin-ji in Kyoto, belonged to the Daiō line. This line flourished during the Muromachi period and later spread throughout the rural provinces of Japan. Of crucial importance in this expansion were the four disciples of the Kanzan line mentioned earlier, a line that had begun to thrive again after having experienced some difficult times.

The Genjū line,[40] a second Rinka line of less intellectual significance, also had an important role to play in Zen history, mainly through the fostering of contacts between the rural monasteries. This line took shape at the end of the Kamakura period as more and more Japanese Zen monks took to visiting the famous Chinese master Chung-feng Ming-pen (1263–1323),[41] who during the Yüan period (1260–1368) in China worked to restore Rinzai Zen. Master Chung-feng Ming-pen traced his lineage back to Hui-neng's disciple Nan-yüeh Huai-jang (677–744). He loved quiet and seclusion and practiced a rigorous Zen, all of which earned him a good name. When he turned down the invitation of Emperor Jen-tsung (ruled 1312–1320) of the Yüan dynasty to come to the imperial court, he was given the title Fo-tz'u Yüan-chao Kuang-hui Ch'an-shih (Jpn., Butsu-ji Enshō Kōe Zenji). There formed around Ming-pen a circle of disciples from lower and upper classes, including a number of Japanese who were greatly devoted to him and who brought his line back to Japan.

Tradition records the names of a large number of Japanese disciples who studied under Ming-pen on Mount T'ien-mu.[42] From the main temple of Kōgen-ji in Tamba (Kyōto prefecture), under the direction of Abbot Onkei Soyū but without forming a distinctive school, they spread throughout all the provinces of the land. Kosen Ingen (1295–1374), one of Ming-pen's most important disciples, maintained relations with the Ashikaga clan and with the *gozan* temples. The tolerance of these Genjū disciples helped foster good relations among different monasteries and monks throughout the country. One of the factors that made this possible was the monks' acceptance of devotion to Amida, which Ming-pen himself had practiced.

In the seventh generation, an important new development began under Ichige Sekiyu (1447–1507),[43] a disciple of Genshitsu Sekkei in the generational line of Onkei. To combat his own doubts he turned to esoteric traditions, which he passed on as part of the Zen of the Genjū line, which had already been mixed with elements of Pure Land Buddhism. He was well received in numerous Rinzai monasteries, where he would present certificates of enlightenment without obliging monks to renounce affiliation with their current school or generational line. With his pleasant personality he met with great success and so helped reunite the different Rinzai groups that toward end of the middle ages had been greatly divided. The unification of the Rinzai school fostered by the Genjū line became the springboard to a new era.

RURAL RINZAI MONASTERIES

For a long time after its arrival from China, the Rinzai school in Japan was located mainly in Kyoto and Kamakura. There, with the assistance of the state, the *gozan* system developed and the distinction between *gozan* and Rinka monasteries appeared. As Zen spread throughout the rural areas, large temples grew up outside the central cities; these temples, mainly because of their distinguished abbots, grew in influence.

THE HOTTŌ-LINE: BASSUI (KŌGAKU-JI)

We have already mentioned the Hottō line as one of the earliest important Rinzai lines directly related neither to Kyoto nor Kamakura; its master Shinchi Kakushin (also Muhon Kakushin, 1207–1298) ranks among the pioneers of Zen Buddhism. In the third generation after Kakushin, Jiun Myōi (1273–1345)[44] and Bassui Tokushō (1327–1387),[45] both disciples of Kakushin's Dharma heir Kohō Kakumyō (1271–1361), worked successfully in the remote provinces; Myōi resided in Kokutai-ji in Etchū (Toyama prefecture) and Bassui (Yamanashi prefecture) was abbot of Kōgaku-ji in Kai.

A first-rate Zen master, Bassui in many ways anticipates the perfection of Zen that Hakuin was to realize. The starting point for his approach was that same gnawing doubt that was to become the keystone of Hakuin's teachings and the hallmark of authentic Zen practice. Bassui already detected such doubt in early Chinese Zen. His own first encounter with it came when he was six years old; a Zen monk was conducting the memorial ceremonies for the third anniversary of his father's death when the young boy looked at the offerings and asked the monk: "My father is dead and no more has a form. How, then, can he come and eat these gifts." The monk answered, "Even when this appearance-body dies, the soul still comes to receive them."[46] Concluding that his body housed a soul, the boy began to ponder what kind of form the soul might have. Years later, as an old man, Bassui indicated that this had not been a passing childhood question; he wrote to a hermit friend:

> As a little boy, I confronted the doubt: after the body departs, how does one answer the question about the identity of the "I." Many years went by after I began to struggle with this doubt. Because it became more painful, I decided to become a monk, and then faced the great vow: if I become a monk, I cannot search after the Way only for myself. Only after seeking to save all sentiment beings can I experience the great Dharma of all Buddhas and attain enlightenment. So [I decided that] I would not study the teachings of Buddha nor would I learn the rituals of the Buddha house until I had resolved this doubt.[47]

The basic motivation of Bassui's life appears in this text: doubt is the driving force for his denial of the world and his bodhisattva desire to work for the salvation of all sentient beings. Never was he really free of doubt, but like Hakuin was plagued by a hellish anxiety. Only rarely did meditation provide him with some modicum of relief. Meantime, he had reached an age when he was expected to devote himself seriously to secular studies. Urged to do so, he answered: "If I am really intelligent, I should the more give myself to the proper study of the teaching on liberation (nirvāṇa). What good is there in pursuing worldly studies?"[48] He was twenty-eight when he entered monastic life, taking the tonsure but not the monastic habit. He embarked on a pilgrimage throughout the country and practiced assiduously, but could not make the final breakthrough to enlightenment.

Bassui was searching for experienced Zen masters when a Zen friend of his, Tokukei Jisha (a disciple of Lan-hsi Tao-lung, who had come to a physical awareness of the futility of mountain asceticism), referred him to Kohō Kakumyō, a disciple of Kaskushin, who was living at Unju-ji in Izumo. Kohō presented Bassui with the kōan about Chao-chou's "Nothing" (mu) and received the amazing answer: "It is fully announced by mountains and rivers, the great earth, grasses and trees."[49] With Kohō, Bassui attained the great enlightenment and received from him the name Bassui (literally, "high above the average").[50] But a close relationship between master and disciple was not to arise, since Bassui departed after only sixty days. Though he bore Kohō the greatest gratitude, it is not certain just how much he allowed himself to be influenced by this widely experienced disciple of Muhon Kakushin. Under Kakushin's direction, Kohō had looked deeply into esoteric Buddhist teachings; he had also known Dōgen, from whom he received the bodhisattva vows. In China during the Yüan period, he had visited the great Chung-feng Ming-pen, and he maintained friendly relations with the important Sōtō master Keizan Jōkin (1268–1325). Undoubtedly, Bassui's meeting with Kohō Kakumyō constitutes one of the most decisive and fruitful events of his life. He continued his pilgrimage to other famous Zen masters before finally settling down in Kai, where friends had the monastery of Kōgaku-ji[51] built for him. There a large number of followers, monks and lay people alike, gathered to profit from his direction.

The kōan-like doubt that dogged Bassui might be formulated in these terms: What is the mind in me? how can I attain clarity concerning the mind? This problem permeates all his writings. The first of his Dharma sayings sheds light on his view of this kōan-question. It reads:

> Those who wish to break the cycle of rebirth must know the way of becoming a Buddha. The way of becoming a Buddha is the way of enlightenment of the mind. Before one's father and mother were born and before one's own body was formed, one's own mind existed unchanged until now, as the ground of all sentient beings. This is also called one's original countenance. This mind is pure from the beginning. When the body is born, it is without the form of life, and when the body dies, it is without the form of death. Neither does it have the form of man or woman, of good

or evil. Because there is nothing to which it can be compared, it is called Buddha nature. From this mind there arise ten thousand images, like waves on a vast great sea or forms reflected in a mirror.[52]

This passage clearly expresses the basic teaching of Mahāyāna that Zen practice seeks to realize in enlightenment. Bassui goes on to stress the kōan-like quality of this effort, noting that asleep or awake, in all one does, one should never lose sight of this doubt. The depth of one's desire for enlightenment is measured by one's doubt. Bassui uses different terms for this constant effort: "ascetic practice" (shugyō), searching (kufū), determination (kokorozashi), "the way's mind" or "the heart seeking the way" (dōshin). Like Hakuin he had a clear insight into the inner relation between doubt and enlightenment; indeed, he anticipated Hakuin's expression of the unconditional relationship between the two almost literally: "When doubt is strong enough, so will enlightenment be strong enough."[53]

Any comparison of Bassui and Hakuin cannot fail to mention the popularity of the two masters. The vow mentioned in Bassui's letter refers to the Bodhisattva resolve to work for the salvation of all sentient beings. If for a time he was worried that this vow might obstruct his striving along the way toward enlightenment, he eventually came to realize that the two tasks form a single whole. After his enlightenment, he exchanged his beloved solitude in nature for a genuine concern for his disciples. His writings, all of them composed in the easily understood Japanese kana style, grew out of this concern. He addresses monks and lay people alike. The way of living in the world has its merits just as the observation of the precepts of the Buddha law does. He encourages everyone to use the kōan of their own mind and to strive for enlightenment.

If you see this kōan, then the diamond king gives you his precious sword with which you can cut through all the things that come up in your mind. When the things of this world approach, cut through the things of this world. When the things of Buddha approach, cut through the things of Buddha. When illusions approach, cut through the illusions—including enlightenment, Buddha, and Māra—cut them away![54]

The radicalness of Bassui's admonitions reminds one of Lin-chi's famous saying about killing the Buddha and the patriarchs. Bassui's diction was probably influenced by the great founder of his school, but the unique, personal qualities of his style are expressed in the large number of letters that give voice to his care and concern for individuals. Whether writing to monks or laity, a large community or individuals, he delivers basically the same message. In picturesque images, he tries to bring his followers closer to enlightenment, which he frequently compares to waking from a dream:

If, for example, you are dreaming that you are lost outside and cannot find the way home, even if you ask for help or pray to God or to the Buddha, still you cannot find your way home. But if you wake from your dream, you find yourself in your original place . . . .[55]

If you practice this kōan so intensively that you forget all the things of this world, then you will indeed attain enlightenment. It is like a sleeping person who awakens from a dream. Then there is no doubt, and in that moment, flowers bloom on dried-up trees and flames come forth from the ice. At that moment, the things of Buddha and the things of this world, the myriad things good and bad—everything is like a dream of last night. Only the Buddha of one's original nature appears.[56]

Bassui's stylistic gifts, his moving imagery and similes, made him a popular author of the first water. His stirring language heightened the urgency of his admonitions. His ability to find the right word for any situation comes through. He comforts a dying person by pointing to the emptiness of all things, the unreality of sickness, and the transcendence of the Buddha nature over all pain and passion:

The Buddha nature of your mind was neither born nor does it die, it is neither being nor non-being, neither emptiness nor form. It experiences neither pleasure nor pain. If you desire to know what it is that now feels the pain of sickness, and if you meditate on what the mind is that experiences the pain of this sickness, and beyond this one thought you do not think, desire, know, or ask anything; if your mind evaporates like a cloud in the ether and comes to naught, then the way of rebirth is cut off and the instant of immediate release has come.[57]

GETTAN (DAIMYŌ-JI)

A contemporary of Bassui, Gettan Sōkō (1326–1389)[58] may not have had Bassui's intellectual stature but he did share his full-hearted devotion to the people. Gettan entered monastic life at an early age and went on to study under a number of prominent masters, including Kosen Ingen, Musō Soseki, and for some time, Kohō Kakumyō. He received the seal of enlightenment from Daichū Sōshin, a representative of one of the Myōshin-ji lines. After an eventful life and residence in several different temples, he founded the monastery of Daimyō-ji in Tajima (in the region of Hyōgo), where his labors bore much fruit.

Gettan's Dharma sayings, collected by his disciples, are directed primarily to the laity, who he was convinced would profit greatly from the practice of Zen and would even attain enlightenment from it. Indeed, he felt that if lay people devoted themselves heart and soul to their practice they would have even greater success than the monks, who often depended too much on study and the guidance of a highly qualified master. Despite this strong emphasis on educating the laity, Gettan's Dharma sayings in no way oppose higher levels of monastic instruction.

When the occasion presented itself, Gettan did not hesitate to explain the fundamental notions of Zen to a lay woman, a devout Buddhist who adhered to the external formalities of her religion and to the popular concepts of Buddha lands, heavens, and hells. He taught her about the Buddha nature as mind free of all duality, especially of any distinction between illusions and enlightenment. He writes:

My mind is Buddha. Through thousands of births and ten-thousands of *kalpas* it exists forever without illusion. And if there is no illusion, then there is no Dharma to be grasped in enlightenment. If there is no illusion and no enlightenment, then the mind is not originally subjected to the cycle of birth and death. For this reason, when it arrives there is no place where it arrives; and when it departs, there is no place from where it leaves; and when it remains, there is no place where it stays. The mind of the three times [past, present, future] is incomprehensible and all things are equally free. There is no ignorance to be overcome, no passions to be cut off. And since there is neither good nor evil, neither is there any heaven or hell. Because there is no true or false, there is no Buddha world and no world of dust.[59]

Gettan appeals to the *Lotus Sūtra* for support. Unborn and indestructible, the mind is originally Buddha. Free of all duality, it knows no distinction between male and female. At the end of his letter, Gettan speaks again of the original purity of the mind and of the "power of faith" that leads to becoming a Buddha.

In his letter to the lay woman, Gettan does not speak of Zen practice. Instead he concentrates on the basic Buddhist mentality that every Zen disciple tries to realize. Indeed, the main theme of all of his letters is that in the practice of *zazen* and in the use of kōan, the Zen practitioner should forget the self and seek the mind.

In the practice of *zazen* one must concentrate on a single thing from the very beginning, namely, on the illumination of the Buddha's Dharma, and clear the mind of all else. If the mind applies its every energy to this end it will forget itself; when nothing remains but the posture and movement of the body in *zazen,* the moment of illumination will arrive without one's desiring it, as suddenly as if one had awakened from a dream. At that moment all attachment to concepts will disappear—concepts of being and of nonbeing, of becoming and of passing away—and the way of escape into living freedom will be opened.

Beginners, who know nothing of any of this, think that enlightenment comes when one's mental attitude changes and one sees into nothingness (*mu*) and emptiness (*kū*). They will falsely suppose that they have achieved clarity quickly on their own without a true master. And because of their elated attitude of mind, much harm will come in the end.[60]

Lay men and woman who are not looking for anything special or striving for enlightenment but simply forget themselves, live Zen in their everyday lives. This is the kind of spirituality that Gettan tries to teach his lay disciples. In the everyday things of life one can combine the law of the Buddha and the law of the world. In a letter to a sick friend he first lays out some fundamental principles, as is his wont, and then urges his friend to hold fast to his faith and to abandon himself without further thought to his painful reality. In this way, the sick person will escape the cycle of birth and death and will attain Buddhahood.[61] In the figure of Gettan we see reflected the great good accomplished by a Rinzai master who truly lives with and for the people.

JAKUSHITSU (EIGEN-JI)

Founded in 1361, shortly after the beginning of the Muromachi period, Eigen-ji has had a checkered history. This typical example of the Rinka monastery of the Rinzai school still stands today. Its location outside the capital of Kyoto belongs to that special monastic milieu "under the forest" (rinka) that produced the simplicity so characteristic of rural Zen. Ensconced amid mountains and streams, birds and trees, the monks could look on nature as their home.

In Eigen-ji the memory of its founder Jakushitsu Genkō (1290–1367)[62] was kept alive not only in the beautiful memorial the monks constructed for him but in the way they have preserved down through the centuries the spirit of this sensitive, highly poetic individual who lived an authentic Zen by combining a strict sense of responsibility with an inner love of nature. He wrote many poems, some of which represent the rich popular heritage that has survived to this day.

Jakushitsu embodied the spirit of Rinka Zen in his own person. "The man of Rinka Zen," writes a contemporary Zen poet, "wanders, flute in hand, through mountain paths, seeking shelter in small temples, in Zen retreats, hermitages, and straw huts."[63] This lifestyle reflected Jakushitsu's personality and heart's desire. He walked the way of a wandering pilgrim faithfully until just a few years before his death, when he took up residence at Eigen-ji, a monastery built for him in Ōmi (Shiga prefecture). For his own part, he made no claims on the temple and left behind no treatises and but few exhortations. For him, Zen was primarily a matter of the personal experience of the greatness of human life in the midst of its impermanence. He was convinced that the one central task of the Zen follower was to grasp the meaning of birth and death. Still, he spoke little on these matters, preferring the forest solitude where he found so many mute symbols of the transiency of life.

Jakushitsu Genkō is one of the most important representatives of Zen Buddhism of his time and one of the clearest incarnations of the Rinka ideal. But because he did not come from a background at all conducive to monasticism he had to go through a considerable process of personal evolution before finding his way. Born in Mimasaka (in the region of Okayama), he seems to have been related on his father's side to the extensive Fujiwara family. As a child he was lively but at the same time docile and intelligent, and of a sensitive and rather delicate personality. When he was twelve his parents entrusted him to the care of the monks of Tōfuku-ji in Kyoto, not because the boy had expressed any desire or shown any sign of religious leanings, but simply in order to give the sound education that at the time Buddhist monasteries were best equipped to provide.

Though he began as a student, before two years had passed Jakushitsu underwent a conversion. It happened during a stay in the country, when a Zen monk on his way home from the eastern part of the country stopped at the

monastery and impressed the young man profoundly by his deep spirit of recollection. Realizing that erudition and knowledge of the scriptures were not
enough, Jakushitsu decided to become a monk. A fellow monk who was also
dissatisfied with the academic life at Tōfuku-ji told him about the Zen master
Yakuō Tokken (1245–1320),[64] an eminent student of Lan-hsi Tao-lung, then
abbot of a small monastery in Kamakura that had been founded by Lan-hsi.
Determined to become disciples under the master and to learn authentic Zen,
the two young men set off in 1305 and soon thereafter were accepted as disciples
of Tokken. When Yakuō was appointed abbot of Kennin-ji in Kyoto the following
year, Jakushitsu accompanied him, continuing the practice of Zen under his
guidance and helping the master when he fell seriously ill. One day, in the year
1306, he asked the master for a "final word" (matsugo; the term has a double
meaning, implying either the last words of a dying master or a verbal device for
the attainment of enlightenment). Without answering, the master slapped his
disciple in the face. With that slap, Jakushitsu was enlightened.

On the advice of his master, Jakushitsu spent several months studying the
Buddhist monastic rule under the Vinaya master Eun in 1309, after which he
returned to Yakuō. Over the next decade, he spent a number of years with
different Chinese Zen masters in Japan, offering them friendly and valuable
assistance. He first served Tung-ming Hui-jih (1272–1340), a representative of
the Chinese Ts'ao-tung school who joined the Rinzai school in Japan, in Kenchō-
ji. From there he went to Tung-li Hung-hui, who had also shifted from Ts'ao-
tung Zen to Japanese Rinzai. But Jakushitsu was most influenced by a two-year
stay with I-shan I-ning, the abbot of Nanzen-ji. A noted author in his own
right, I-shan expressed great praise for a poem Jakushitsu had written at the age
of seventeen, "Bodhidharma in the Snow." With the devoted interest of the
master in his talents, Jakushitsu went on to become one of the most prominent
Zen poets of the time. His poems combine rich and profound feeling with extraordinary creativity. In the judgment of his translator and editor, Iriya Yoshitaka, Jakushitsu's "exceptional and superb works" surpass even those of the well-
known contemporary gozan poet Chūgan Engetsu (1300–1375), whose poems
are impeccable in form but lack the depth of poetic feeling.[65] Jakushitsu's poems
make up the greater part of his collected sayings.

Another turning point in Jakushitsu's life came during a trip he made to
China with a group of fellow Zen monks after his the death of his master Yakuō.
His primary and most pressing goal was to visit Chung-feng Ming-pen, the
Chinese master who had been so friendly to the Japanese. Jakushitsu presented
himself not as a guest but as a disciple in need of direction. His expectations
were not disappointed. The great Chinese master's influence was to remain with
him for the rest of his life. What Jakushitsu was later to pass on to his disciples
was but an echo of the pure Zen he had learned from Ming-pen.

The devotion to Amida that had become part of the practice of Chinese
Zen masters toward the end of the Sung and the beginning of the Yüan period
did not in any way jeopardize the central place reserved for the practice of the
kōan. It should be remembered that, like all Buddhas, Buddha Amitābha (Jpn.,

Amida) was revered by pious Buddhists. Jakushitsu's collection of sayings contains a section of special praise for the Buddhas. In two poems that deal with Amida, Jakushitsu explicitly states that the Pure Land is to be sought not in the Western Paradise but in one's own mind. The following passage from Jakushitsu's Dharma sayings should be read in this sense:

> The *nembutsu* seeks to break out of the cycle of birth and death; Zen practice seeks to clarify one's original nature. Never has it been said that those who have grasped the original nature in enlightenment did not also escape the cycle of birth and death, nor that those who have escaped the cycle of birth and death have lost their original nature. Therefore, even though the *nembutsu* and Zen are different in name, in essence they are the same.[66]

Both the *nembutsu* and Zen practice share a common foundation in the Mahāyāna sūtras. Correctly understood, this allows for the parallel practice of both Buddhist ways. Jakushitsu's Zen, like that of Ming-pen, is rooted in the tradition of the Sixth Patriarch, Hui-neng. The expression "union of Zen and Pure Land," which is often used in relation to both masters, does not indicate "as one might conclude from the expression, communion or synthetic unity."[67]

Jakushitsu's stay in China lasted six years, from 1320 to 1326. After a year as a student with Ming-pen on Mount T'ien-mu, he travelled throughout the Middle Kingdom visiting famous temples, meeting with experienced masters, and in general trying to learn the ways of China. We have the names of many of the Chinese sites he visited.[68] He enjoyed his journeys and was greatly enriched by them. Moreover, many of his poems describe the unique beauty of the Chinese landscape.

Back in Japan, Jakushitsu continued the itinerant life for some twenty-five years, traveling through the southwestern part of the country, mainly in the areas of Bizen and Bitchū (in the region of Okayama) and in Bingo (in the region of Hiroshima). On occasion he also passed through his home area of Mimasaka. His biography lists the names of many of the rural temples he visited, but provides few details. The monk-poet loved the simple life of the rural monasteries, immersing himself in the solitude of nature and finding deep satisfaction in repose on a mountain slope or next to a country brook. He emanated an aura that attracted many like-minded individuals to Zen.

Jakushitsu's itinerant life came to an end in 1350, when he took leave of the areas of Bizen, Bitchū, and Bingo and set out for the northeast. For about three years (around 1352) he stayed at Tōzen-ji in Mino (in the prefecture of Gifu) and then sojourned to Shizuoka and Kai (Yamanashi prefecture). As he moved westward he came to the area of Ōmi (Shiga prefecture), where the ruling lord (*shugo*), Sasaki Ujiyori (1326–1370), took a strong liking to him. When Sasaki had the temple of Eigen-ji built for him in 1361, the old master, though not at all pleased at the prospect of abandoning his unencumbered pilgrim's existence, bowed to the wishes of his friend and settled down there. As time went on his work as abbot took on growing importance; during his first year in office some two thousand visitors are said to have passed through the monastery. Jakushitsu's detachment from the dignity of his office became evident five years later in 1366, when he retired to make place for his principle disciple Miten Eishaku.[69] He had previously turned down offers to preside over the two famous *gozan* temples Tenryū-ji in Kyoto and Kenchō-ji in Kamakura. Earlier, the two small temples of Chōshō-ji (Kamakura) and Manju-ji (in the district of Bungo, present-day Ōita prefecture) had tried in vain to persuade him to accept the post of abbot. Jakushitsu declined these offers with deep feeling and conviction.

Although Jakushitsu's name is not as well known as the famous contemporary masters of the large cities, he ranks among the most important Zen figures of this period. The life he led for decades as a poor, solitary, wandering monk made him a kind of ideal Buddhist not uncommon during these early times. His last will and testament gives clear expression to the total detachment that characterized his life. In it he requests that after his death all the lands of Kumahara that had been given to the monastery should be returned to the donors and the temple buildings should be given back to the village of Takano, unless people preferred to use them as practice centers for Zen monks.[70] His genuine Zen spirit was evident in his consistency of lifestyle, above all in his disdain for the pomp and circumstance of ornate temple buildings, his reluctance to accept positions of honor, and his renunciation of all material goods.

Many of the rural Rinzai monasteries belonged in spirit to the Rinka institutions. Among them is Hōkō-ji in the district of Shizuoka, founded in 1384 by Mumon Gensen (1323–1390),[71] a master from the Daiō line, and Buttsū-ji in Aki (in the region of Hiroshima), founded in 1399 by Guchū Shūkyū (1323–1409).[72] During the Muromachi period both monasteries carried on independently, but were later incorporated into the *gozan* as a result of regulations issued by the Tokugawa government. After Hakuin's reform of Rinzai Zen, the Hōkō-ji and the Buttsū-ji lines would take on added importance.

The Rinka monasteries kept the tradition of the patriarchs alive in the Rinzai school. Today, all Rinzai monasteries, including the *gozan* temples, are governed by abbots who trace their lineage back to the three great figures of the Daiō line, who in turn belong to the Rinka movement: Nampo Jōmyō, Shūhō Myōchō, and Kanzan Egen. During the middle ages there were two ways to determine succession in the Rinzai school—by transmission of the office by the abbot of the temple and by transmission of the mind of enlightenment. In the first instance, it was not necessary for the new abbot to have been a disciple of his predecessor; new candidates could come "from all over"[73] (meaning, of course, from monasteries throughout the *gozan* system) and could be invited to the temple from outside, according to the "Dharma of the temple building" (Jpn., *garanhō*). Succession through transmission of mind (*busshinhō*), which was urged by the defenders of the "teaching on succession in the one line," was based on the seal of enlightenment (*inka*) that the master bestowed on his disciple. This was the form used in the Rinka monasteries, and through it nearly all the prominent personalities of the Rinzai school could trace their lineage back to the Daiō line of Nampo Jōmyō. This is the line that would lead to Hakuin. All contemporary Japanese Rinzai abbots belong genealogically to the line of Hakuin and are conscious of the fact that it is through him that they belong to the authentic tradition of the Zen of the Patriarchs extending back to Bodhidharma.

THE EXPANSION OF THE SŌTŌ SCHOOL

Our presentation of the Sōtō school in chapter 3 went as far as the end of the Kamakura period, concluding with a treatment of Keizan Jōkin, the second Sōtō patriarch. Seen from the viewpoint of the history of Sōtō Zen, the developments going on within Sōtō school spread across the country during the Nambokuchō and Muromachi periods. Although the school continued to follow the direction given by Keizan, a number of new elements merit our consideration.

THE TWO PRINCIPAL DISCIPLES OF KEIZAN

The most distinctive figure of this period is Gasan Jōseki[74] (1275–1365) from the district of Noto (present day Ishikawa prefecture). He entered monastic life in 1290 as a young boy and took up the study of Tendai on Mount Hiei. His conversion to Zen was occasioned by a meeting with Master Keizan in 1297. Two years later he joined the Daijō-ji community, whose abbot, Tettsū Gikai, thought so highly of his chief disciple Keizan that he put him in charge of the novices. In directing his students Keizan made extensive use of kōan, an intimate knowledge of which he had gained from his friend Shinchi Kakushin, who had brought the kōan collection known as the *Mumonkan* to Japan. Taking up the practice of both *zazen* and kōan, Gasan soon attained the great enlightenment and received the Dharma seal (*inka*) from Keizan. The master then sent his disciple on a journey across the land so that he might make acquaintance with other Zen masters of the time. During his travels Gasan spent some time with Kyōō Unryō (1267–1341), the Dharma brother of Keizan and later abbot of Daijō-ji. Upon his return, Keizan appointed him and his fellow monk Meihō Sotetsu[75] (1277–1350) as his successors.

Meihō Sotetsu was made head of Yōkō-ji in Noto, a temple that Keizan had converted from a Shingon to a Zen temple in 1325; in nearby Etchū he established the temple of Kōzen-ji. At Yōkō-ji the practice of alternating abbots was introduced for the first time, though only briefly. At first, Meihō's line grew quickly in the Hokuriku region (embracing the prefectures of Fukui, Ishikawa, Toyama, and Niigata) and surpassed all the other Sōtō lines, but this period of rapid growth did not last long. In 1337 he was appointed abbot of Daijō-ji (in Kaga). His fame spread and soon he was able to count many important figures among his disciples, figures such as the poet-monk Daichi Sokei (1290–1366), to whom he entrusted his Dharma sayings (*kana-hōgo*).[76] Daichi spent some eleven years in China during the Yüan period; there his literary works drew much enthusiastic attention. After returning to Japan he founded Gidai-ji in Kaga and went on to become abbot of Kōfuku-ji in Higo (Kyūshū).

The name of Meihō never become as widely known in Japanese history as that of Gasan. Indeed, after Dōgen and Keizan, Gasan is the third most influential figure in Japanese Sōtō Zen. Nearly all of the innovations that he introduced into the Sōtō school took place in Sōji-ji. He was absent from the monastery only briefly, when he took on the direction of Yōkō-ji in 1340. Under his direction, Sōji-ji, which had become a Sōtō center under Keizan, grew to even greater prominence. During the forty years in which he presided over its community (1324–1363), a large number of gifted disciples gathered around the famous master. Animated by a genuine love of humanity, Gasan made efforts to bring education to the impoverished rural population and to instill in his disciples a social consciousness that Buddhists would call a bodhisattva heart, thus carrying on the tradition that his master Keizan had implanted in the Sōtō school.

GASAN AND THE FIVE RANKS

With Gasan, the doctrine of the Five Ranks became part of the heritage of Sōtō Zen.[77] Just how this remarkable innovation came about is not entirely clear. Certainly Dōgen and those of his disciples who had visited China and spent time practicing and studying in Chinese Zen monasteries knew of the formula. Dōgen had expressly rejected it, as he did all academic and special forms, convinced as he was that such techniques were not in conformity with the one Buddha-Dharma of the founder Śākyamuni.[78]

Gasan was the first Japanese Sōtō master to give the Five Ranks a central place in his teaching. He had found the formula in the Chinese work *Jen-t'ien yen-mu* (Jpn., *Ninden gammoku*, first published in Japan in 1303[79]), which is basically a compendium on the Five Houses. Its third book, dealing with the House of Ts'ao-tung, treats the Five Ranks in great detail, and includes excerpts from Chinese commentaries, particularly the commentaries of the Rinzai masters Fen-yang Shan-chao (947–1024) and Shih-shuang Ch'u-yüan (986–1039), as well as of Chüeh-fan Hui-hung (1071–1128), who was part of the Ōryō (Chin., Huang-lung) line of Rinzai Zen.[80] Fen-yang was the first to introduce this doctrine, which originated in the House of Ts'ao-tung, into the Rinzai school, and his disciple Shih-shuang carried on the task of teaching the doctrine's full meaning to Rinzai students.

Dialectical in structure, the formula of the Five Ranks admits of a variety of explanations and uses. Inspired by Chinese tradition, especially by the ancient *Book of Changes (I-ching)*, it is a precise and direct expression of the metaphysics of the Kegon (Hua-yen) school. Its dialectical formulations make for ready use as a kōan. Although Gasan had been carefully trained in the use of kōan, he showed little interest in the practice. In the Five Ranks, however, he found an adequate expression of the Mahāyāna worldview of Zen. Following the interpretation of Chi-yin Hui-hung, he changed the terms (which Chi-yin had already altered considerably) in order to facilitate the realization of the Buddha-Dharma within the phenomenal world. As a Japanese author of the Sōtō school sees it, "Under Gasan, the Sōtō Zen of China took on a Japanese form."[81]

In Japanese Sōtō Zen the contents of the doctrine of the Five Ranks are summarized as the "teaching of the Five Ranks of Tung-shan" (*Tōjō goisetsu*).[82] Essential to understanding this doctrine is the five-stanza formula that has been attributed to Tung-shan and that the young Ts'ao-shan calls more simply the "manifestation of the mystery of the Five Ranks" (Jpn., *goi kenketsu;* Chin., *wu-wei hsien-chüeh*). There is also the formula of the "five ranks of merit" (Jpn., *kōkun goi;* Chin., *kung-hsün wu wei*). Japanese interpreters interpret the former as a theoretical statement of a doctrine that finds a practical application in the latter. Far from remaining only on the metaphysical level, the teaching on the Five Ranks can be applied to everyday life.

In the fourth generations after Gasan the teaching of the Five Ranks was taken up intensively by two Sōtō masters, Ketsudō Nōshō (1355–1427) and Nan'ei Kenshū (1387–1460). A disciple of Baizan Mompon, who was connected with Gasan through his own master, Taigen Sōshin (d. 1370), Ketsudō Nōshō was abbot of Kōun-ji in Echigo, where he taught his students a somewhat simplified version of the "manifestation of the mystery of the Five Ranks." These lectures formed the basis for the three-volume work, *Tōjō ungetsuroku*,[83] edited by his disciple Nan'ei Kenshū. In his short treatise *Henshō goi zusetsu kitsunan*, Nan'ei criticizes his contemporary Mujin Shōtō[84] of the Rinzai school for showing excessive dependence on the *Book of Changes* in his *Henshō goi zusetsu*. In their own interpretations of the doctrine of the Five Ranks, Ketsudō and Nan'ei rely primarily on the Chinese Rinzai master Shih-shuang Ch'u-yüan.[85]

Since the time of Gasan Jōseki, the Five Ranks have played an important role in Sōtō Zen, providing the speculative content capable of responding to the intellectual needs of Sōtō followers. At times, the Five Ranks took precedence over Dōgen's masterpiece, the *Shōbōgenzō*. In the Sōtō monasteries a rich literature attempts to explain the Five Ranks[86]—a task that was never really carried out to anyone's full satisfaction. In any case, the formulas of the Five Ranks occupy a firm place in the teachings of the Japanese Sōtō school.

THE INFLUENCE OF SŌJI-JI

As we saw in the preceding chapter, the dispute over the third-generation successor at Eihei-ji ended in divisions. Dōgen's disciple Gien remained at Eihei-ji, while Tettsū Gikai, Eihei-ji's first designated abbot, went to the Shingon temple of Daijō-ji, which he converted into a Zen monastery. His disciple and follower Keizan Jōkin, also a member of the Daijō-ji community, established two other Zen monasteries, Yōkō-ji, previously a Shingon temple, and Sōji-ji, formerly a Vinaya monastery in Sagami (Kanagawa prefecture). While Meihō Sotetsu assumed the leadership of Yōkō-ji and Daijō-ji, the abbot's position at Sōji-ji went to Gasan Jōseki, a man of exceptional intellectual qualities and abundant energy who attracted many gifted disciples. Among these large numbers of followers, twenty-five received special recognition, five of whom were called "wise" (Jpn., *gotetsu*). These students were to spread the influence of Sōji-ji throughout the land.[87]

What made Sōji-ji organizationally unique and increased its influence was the periodic change in the office of abbot—an ordinance that Gasan had introduced before his death.[88] Though other monasteries followed this same organizational structures, Sōji-ji illustrated how advantageous it could be. It was a model that combined the advantages of strict centralized governance with the possibility of broad expansion. The five chief disciples each had a hermitage or small residence within the temple area.[89] Assuming the honors of the abbot's position, they felt the responsibility of working all the more industriously for the spread of the Sōtō way throughout the vast realms of rural Japan and were honored for the rural temples they founded. The local nobility and samurai, in these rural areas eagerly welcomed and helped promote the successful operation of this system, which was so well adapted to the conditions of medieval feudal society.

Taigen Sōshin (d. 1370) headed the first of Sōji-ji's five lines; before retiring as abbot, Gasan had appointed him to be the first administrator of the temple complex in 1324. As the third Sōtō abbot of Sōji-ji, Sōshin followed his master in using the teachings on the Five Ranks as the center of his own method and in explaining it to the inner core of his circle of disciples. Clearly influenced by the spirituality of the Sung period, he made use of metaphors such as that of lord and vassals or of the levels of merit in order to clarify the Sōtō teachings for both his disciples and laity. Of all the lines, his enjoyed the broadest expansion, with the major portion of its more than one hundred establishments located in middle and eastern Japan. Sōshin later lived in Yōkō-ji, and during the final years of his life founded the temple of Budda-ji in Kaga.

Tsūgen Jakurei (1322–1391) is the best known of the five chief disciples of Gasan.[90] Highly gifted, he read the Buddhist sūtras as a young boy and at seventeen decided to be a monk. He took his first steps in the monastic life in his native Kyūshū, but soon traveled north to present himself before the doors of Daijō-ji in Kaga, where Meihō Sotetsu received him warmly. Tsūgen, a determined searcher of the Way, carried on his practice continually by day and by night and elicited the admiration and wonder not only of his fellow monks but also of the surrounding population. After more than ten years at Daijō-ji, he moved to Sōji-ji in 1352, hoping that Gasan's direction would bring his progress along the path of enlightenment to completion. In 1356 he had an experience of the great enlightenment at Sōji-ji. His conversation with his master, which he wrote down while the intensity of the experience was still fresh, has been preserved in tradition.[91]

Jakurei's efforts to propagate Sōtō Zen in no way lagged behind those of his older colleague Sōshin. He founded a number of central temples, which then gave rise to branch temples. At the request of the local lord Hosokawa Yoriyuki (1329–1392), he assumed the direction of Yōtaku-ji in Tamba. Known for the wisdom and rigor of his direction, he attracted many disciples, the most notable of whom was his Dharma heir Ryōan Emyō (1337–1411), who, after being abbot of Sōji-ji and Yōtaku-ji, opened the well-known Saijō-ji monastery in Sagami.[92]

Together with other respected disciples of the Gasan line, Jakurei called a conference at the line's headquarters in Sōji-ji (where he was abbot three times) to discuss organizational issues. He was indeed one of the most influential Sōtō masters of his times and made great contributions to the spread of the Sōtō school and to the promotion and strengthening of monastic discipline throughout Sōtō monasteries. The lines of these first two disciples of Gasan were active mainly in the Hokuriku territories and Shin'etsu, as well as in the lands of Tōkaidō.

Mutan Sokan[93] (d. 1387) spent most of his life in the areas of Echizen, Noto, and Iwami, where he founded numerous monasteries. His first and second generation disciples upheld the dominant influence of the Sōtō school in northern Japan (Tōhoku). The line of Daitetsu Sōrei (1333–1408) of Hizen established a great number of monasteries, Sōrei himself founding Myōōkyō-ji in Mino and Rissen-ji in Etchū. The fifth of Gasan's chief disciples, Jippō Ryōshū (1318–1405), was an extraordinarily gifted and educated individual. It is said that he made up his mind to follow the Zen way when he first saw the famous ten oxherding pictures. He stayed with Gasan for some ten years, providing the master with valuable personal service. He did much to promote the development of Sōtō Zen in the region of San'yō, particularly through founding the Eishō-ji in Bitchū. The disciples who carried on his line were active throughout the country.

These last three disciples of Gasan followed the example of Taigen Sōshin and Tsūgen Jakurei in giving great attention to the organizational development of the Sōji-ji headquarters. They took part in the conference of 1370 and succeeded each other as abbots, Mutan Sokan as the seventh abbot, Daitetsu Sōrei as the eighth, and Jippō Ryōshū as the ninth abbot of Sōji-ji.

The first and second generation disciples that carried on the five primary lines of Sōji-ji covered the entire country with their temples. Among the most effective workers were the twenty-five chief disciples of Gasan mentioned above. We should at least list some of the rural temples of the Sōtō movement that came to prominence at this time. Gasan's disciple Mutei Ryōshō (1312–1361)[94] founded Shōbō-ji (Iwate prefecture), the first major Sōtō monastery in northern Japan, which was known for its large community of both monks and laity. His second and third generation successors, Gessen Ryōin (1319–1400) and Dōsō Dōai (d. 1379), made significant contributions to the strengthening of the Sōtō community. Under their guidance, Shōbō-ji came to be elevated to the third main temple of the Sōtō school in Japan. Another of Gasan's disciples, Gennō Shinshō (1329–1400), made his way into the remote area of San'in and there established Taikyū-ji (in the district of Tottori), which then gave rise to smaller branch temples. In Hyūga (Kyūshū) the disciple Mugai Enshō founded Kōtoku-ji.[95]

This expansion of the Sōtō school throughout the rural areas of the country was centered in Sōji-ji and came to be named after its two most prominent abbots, Keizan and Gasan.[96] Known for its openness to other Buddhist schools and for its popular appeal, it stood in a certain opposition to Eihei-ji but without causing a lasting rift between the two monasteries. How much did the Sōtō Zen of the Keizan-Gasan lines preserve the authentic heritage of Dōgen? A look at developments at Eihei-ji after the successional disputes can help answer that question.

THE RESTORATION OF EIHEI-JI

After the heads of the two rival parties, Tettsū Gikai and Gien, left Eihei-ji, a small circle of disciples carried on the tradition of Dōgen. The fifth abbot of Eihei-ji, Giun (1253–1333) was highly regarded and encouraged his disciples to preserve the spirit of Dōgen by keeping faithful to regular Zen meditation and a strict monastic discipline. This does not mean that under Giun monastic practice once again flourished at Eihei-ji. Although his successor, the sixth abbot Donki,[97] was able to complete reconstruction after a fire, he was not able to attract many new members for the community. He devoted much of his energy—as did the ninth abbot, Sōgo (1342–1406)[98]—to preserving the literary works of Dōgen. In the shadow of the many large and flourishing temples of the Keizan-Gasan line, the quiet monastery of Eihei-ji led a rather unassuming existence. For a long time, relations between the two monasteries, Eihei-ji and Sōji-ji, were broken off. The lowest point of Eihei-ji's decline came in 1473, during the civil war of the Ōnin period, when soldiers burned the monastery to the ground. The remains presented a sad and desolate picture.

Help was to come from the outside—from the powerful Keizan-Gasan line, which in the end was not able to forget its founder Dōgen and the monastery he himself had established. Don'ei Eō (1424–1504), a master from the line of Tsūgen Jakurei, visited the ruins of the venerable monastery with a group of like-minded colleagues and began the work of rebuilding,[99] thus establishing a bridge that would reunite the two groups. From this point on, more and more followers of the Keizan-Gasan line visited Eihei-ji and began to reside there. A new period of growth began, encouraged by honors and support from high places. In 1507 Emperor Go-Kashiwara granted the monastery the title of "First Practice Center of Japanese Sōtō Zen," and shortly thereafter Emperor Go-Nara added the title "First Transcendent Practice Center."[100] And so Eihei-ji was raised to a rank equal to that of the Rinzai temple of Nanzen-ji and became the headquarters of Sōtō Zen in Japan, to which all other Sōtō institutions—including Sōji-ji, Yōkō-ji, Daijō-ji, and Yōtaku-ji—were subordinate. The masters of Eihei-ji were accorded great honors; at civil ceremonies they wore the purple robes bestowed by the imperial court. The reunion of the Sōtō schools had begun, and by the beginning of the Edo period the reunification was complete. Smaller rivalries between the two centers of Eihei-ji and Sōji-ji could no longer disturb the new-found peace.

The restoration of Eihei-ji during the second half of the Muromachi period and the transitional years before the advent of the modern age marked the completion of developments within the Sōtō school, developments that historians assess differently. Complex as they are, these developments cannot be judged quickly in either positive or negative terms. At the same time that the Sōtō school was developing into a popular religion, it tried to preserve the central importance of Zen meditation. This polarity, sometimes spoken of as a transition from Dōgen Zen to Sōtō Zen, is what concerns us here. The phrase directs attention back to Dōgen, whose imposing figure hovered over this development even when Sōtō monks were well aware that they were, to some degree, departing from the spirit of their founder. Such situations are not uncommon in the history of religions when followers find it impossible to follow, to its last detail, the example of a creative and genius founder.

In Dōgen's case, the impossibility was rooted first and foremost in the way he had united his practice of "zazen alone" (shikan taza) with metaphysical speculations that grew out of Mahāyāna tradition and his own extraordinary intellect. His followers had to content themselves mainly with exploring and editing the literary works of their master. There were, therefore, very concrete reasons for the softening of the founder's message that set in soon after his death. Dōgen's insistence on strict adherence to tradition and to monastic practice naturally placed limitations on any kind of open evolution toward new possibilities. Particular events after his death are open to varying judgments. Certainly the dispute over succession was unhappy; and yet important Sōtō masters of the third and fourth generations like Keizan and Gasan opened up new horizons. Keizan made certain syncretistic concessions toward elements from Buddhist traditions that were not entirely foreign to Zen Buddhism; in doing so, he made Zen more available to the general public. Keizan's heart's desire was to effect a harmonious unity of Buddhist popular piety and its esoteric rituals with the serious practice of Zen meditation. This could not be accomplished, however, without compromise. Pursuing the path that Keizan had pioneered, Gasan and his disciples made substantial breakthroughs in spreading Sōtō Zen throughout the rural population. Gasan was much more a Zen master of deep intellectual ambition that he was a popular preacher. For instance, it was he who took up the doctrine of the Five Ranks. Although this placed him in opposition of Dōgen, it did much to benefit Sōtō Zen. His organizational achievements lent durability to his undertakings. As a result, the Sōtō movement experienced a new spring. Under his numerous disciples the transition from Dōgen-Zen to Sōtō Zen was completed.

The entire life of the rural population was permeated by the religiosity of Sōtō Zen. The monks took as their main task responsiveness to the religious needs and desires of the peasant population. Together with the people they prayed for the prosperity of the nation and its princes, for protection against the elements and against war and fire, for rain and a bountiful harvest, for their children and good health. For all these ends the old schools of Buddhism provided an abundance of appropriate formulae, combining prayers of thanksgiving and petition with magic rituals, suited to the changing seasons of the year. The Sōtō monks were most at home with the funeral services, which were so important for the people and whose effectiveness seemed to be measured by their elaborate ceremony.

Another bond of solidarity between the Sōtō monks and the people was the monks' willingness to join the people in strenuous work in the fields. The monks were always ready to help with social projects such as building bridges, irrigating rice fields, draining swamps. In this they were being faithful to their Buddhist heritage, for the bodhisattva ideal had always been proven in concrete acts of service.

For all its popularity among ordinary rural people, Sōtō Zen never lost its roots in Zen meditation. For the monks who had practiced from their early years, daily labor, whether in the temple or in the fields, was a continuation of Zen meditation. To them, everything was *zazen*, and their persistent hope was to bring all the people in the areas surrounding their monasteries to see the value of Zen meditation. To do this, Zen associations (*zazenkai*) were begun in the various temples. These clubs enabled *zazen* to grow into a popular community activity. The traditional Buddhist periods of practice (*ango*)[101] before summer and winter were devoted primarily to meditation. Also quite popular then, as it still is today, was the winter practice known as *rōhachi-sesshin*, which took place from 1 to 18 December in remembrance of Śāyamuni's enlightenment; during this *sesshin* zealous students sat in meditation almost uninterruptedly in the hope of experiencing enlightenment. Lay people could participate in all these meditation sessions, and indeed were encouraged to do so.

By the end of the period, many differing elements had been integrated into Sōtō Zen. *Zazen*—the all-inclusive, foundational practice of Dōgen Zen and the heart of his heritage—remained the primary form of practice. The use of kōan receded somewhat, though it still formed a definite part of the overall Sōtō movement. As always, there were enlightened Sōtō masters who passed on the great experience. In addition to these essential Zen elements, a unique Sōtō style, clearly distinct from the Rinzai school, arose during the middle ages. Despite recurring tensions, neither school ever seriously claimed that the other did not belong to the Zen tradition or had lost its Zen identity. But there is no gainsaying the clear differences between them. The distinctive style of Sōtō was treated in the previous section of this chapter; the character of the powerful Rinzai school was most visible in the Five Mountains movement, with its great monasteries of Kyoto and Kamakura. It should be pointed out that the differences between the schools were not the extension of the controversies between the "Zen of silent illumination" (*mokushō-zen*) and the "Zen of seeing into the kōan" (*kanna-zen*) in Sung-period China. Rather, they resulted from the different ways in which each Chinese school adapted to the ways of Japan. In the following chapter on the Zen art of the Rinzai school during the middle ages, the specific values of Rinzai Zen will be in greater evidence.

NOTES

1.   *Bukkyōgo daijiten*, vol. 2, p. 1430. Cf. the entries on *rinka* and *sōrin* in *Zengaku daijiten* II, pp. 757 and 1291.

2.   Imaeda II, p. 173.

3.   In the introduction to the *gozan* monk-poets in *Nihon no zen-goroku*, vol. 8, p. 15. Cf. Imaeda Aishin, *Chūsei zenshūshi no kenyū*, pp. 389ff.

4. The first two characters are taken from the masters' titles, while the third is from the original name.

5. Zen Dust offers a particularly detailed account of Shūhō Myōchō (pp. 231–34) and Daitoku-ji (p. 234). See also the essay by Ogisu Jundō in Kōza zen, vol. 4, Zen no rekishi: Nihon, pp. 203–32, the final section of which treats Kanzen Egen; and the introduction to the collection of sayings, Daitō Kokushi goroku (T. no. 2566) in Nihon no zen-goroku, vol. 6, by Hirano Sōjō, pp. 9–66; cf. Imaeda II, pp. 210–14.

6. Cited in Ogisu, Zen no rekishi: Nihon, p. 213; the English translation comes from Zen Dust, p. 232. According to Miura and Sasaki, the Daitō Kokushi goroku is "the most important of all the early Japanese Zen goroku" (Zen Dust, p. 388).

7. Cited by D. T. Suzuki in The Essence of Buddhism: Imperial Lectures, first printed in London in 1947 and reprinted in a collection of Suzuki's works edited by B. Phillips, The Essentials of Zen Buddhism (New York, 1962), p. 393.

8. Ogisu gives 1326 as the date for the completion of the Dharma hall (hattō), and 1325 for the religious conversation he had with Gen'e. See Zen no rekishi: Nihon, p. 217.

9. Ogisu's account does not include a date (Zen no rekishi: Nihon, p. 217).

10. Cf. Collcutt, Five Mountains, pp. 29–30, 291.

11. From the Dharma sayings (kana-hōgo) contained in the collection of sayings, Zemmon hōgoshū, vol. 2, pp. 512–13.

12. Zemmon hōgoshū, vol. 2, pp. 512–13.

13. See Daitō Kokushi goroku, which include several quotations from Bodhidharma, pp. 513ff. On Bodhidharma's "six gates" see Zen Dust, pp. 398–99.

14. Cited in Ogisu, Zen no rekishi: Nihon, p. 219. Ogisu offers a free translation into modern Japanese of the text compiled in 1335, which Hirano also cites and comments on in his introduction to Daitō's collected sayings.

15. See also the explanation in the Japanese-English Buddhist Dictionary, p. 329.

16. Hirano cites the exchange of a monk with Daitō, from which he concludes that Daitō had not proscribed the use of alcoholic drink. See his introduction to Zen no rekishi: Nihon, p. 65.

17. Hirano finds this verse difficult to understand and offers no explanation (Zemmon hōgoshū, vol. 2, pp. 40–41). Ogisu skips over it without comment (Zen no rekishi: Nihon, p. 221). The English translation in the text is taken from Zen Dust, p. 234.

18. See the brief biography in Zen Dust, pp. 324–27; Ogisu, Zen no rekishi: Nihon, pp. 223–28; Takeuchi Michio, Nihon no zen, pp. 252ff.

19. Cited in Ogisu, Zen no rekishi: Nihon, p. 225.

20. The full name of the monastery is Shōbōzan Myōshin-ji (Temple of the Wonderful Mind of the Mountain of the Right Dharma); see Ogisu, Zen no rekishi: Nihon, p. 226, and Zen Dust, pp. 217–18, 326.

21. Ogisu depicts the situation cautiously, as well as the visit of Musō; Zen no rekishi: Nihon, pp. 226ff, 229–30.

22. Cited in Imaeda II, p. 215.

23. Cited in Zen Dust, p. 326. There is also recounted the occasion on which Yin-yüan Lung-ch'i, the Chinese founder of the Japanese Ōbaku school, some centuries later asked about the collected sayings of the founder of the temple on the occasion of a visit to Myōshin-ji, only to be told that it did not exist. He is reported to have said that this kōan was worth more than ten thousand volumes of sayings.

24.   This is the view of Ogisu, *Zen no rekishi: Nihon*, p. 231.

25.   See the account of his death in *Zen Dust*, p. 326.

26.   See Imaeda II, p. 216; Collcutt, *Five Mountains*, p. 128. According to Tamamura Takeji, the fifth abbot of Myōshin-ji resigned his office as a favor to Setsudō Sōboku. Yet the line of tradition is not certain. See the article, "Shoki Myōshin-ji shi no nisan giten," in *Nihon zenshūshi ronshū*, vol. 2, part 2 (Kyoto, 1981), pp. 274, 276.

27.   See Sugawara Tōzen's essay on the re-establishment of Myōshin-ji by Master Nippō, in his collection *Nihon zenmon iketsu-den*, vol. 9 of the series *Zen*, pp. 165–67. Cf. Imaeda, *Chūsei zenshūshi no kenkyū*, pp. 200–201.

28.   Collcutt, *Five Mountains*, p 129.

29.   Worth singling out from the wealth of material in Ikkyū is the work of Yanagida Seizan, *Ikkyū: Kyōunshū no sekai*, and the introduction by Katō Shūichi to the collection of poems, *Kyōunshū*, edited and annotated by Yanagida; in English, see John Carter Covell in collaboration with Sobin Yamada, *Unraveling Zen's Red Thread: Ikkyū's Controversial Way*. In addition, there has recently appeared a collection *Nihon meisō ronshū*, vol. 10 of which contains nine essays devoted to Ikkyū (pp. 8–274).

30.   In Japanese historiography Ikkyū stands throughout as the illegitimate son of the emperor Go-Komatsu (ruled 1392–1412, died 1433); there is no agreement regarding his mother. His provenance and earliest years are not completely clear.

31.   *Ikkyū: Kyōunshū no sekai*, p. 16.

32.   Yōsō died as abbot of Daitoku-ji. He was a competent administrator lacking a sense for Zen, and seems to have made a business of the sale of enlightenment certificates (*inka*).

33.   In the Japanese edition of the poetic collection (see note 29), no. 8, p. 67. The edition includes the Chinese text, a translation into modern Japanese, and explanatory notes. An English translation of the poem appears in Covell and Yamada, *Unraveling Zen's Red Thread*, p. 41. A selection of Ikkyū's poems appeared in German translation in "Im Garten der schönen Shin: Die Lästerlichen Gedichte des japanischen Zen-Meisters Verrückte Wolke," translation with an introduction and commentary of Shūichi Katō and Eva Thom.

34.   This is the judgment of Furuta Shōkin in his essay, "Nihon-zen no hattatsu," in vol. 2 of *Gendai zen kōza*, p. 68.

35.   In the text of the "Gaikotsu" ("Skeletons") in *Zenmon hōgoshū*, vol. 1, pp. 231–32. See the English translation of R. H. Blyth reprint from *The Eastern Buddhist* in *The Buddha Eye*, ed. by Frederick Franck (New York: Crossroad, 1982), pp. 75–85; quotation on p. 82.

36.   The incident is not historically certain. Another episode, his parading through the city with a wooden sword, has been estalished in art. Contemporary monks, Ikkyū thought, no longer care to wield the sword of the mind but are satisfied with the simple substitute of a wooden sword.

37.   Cited by Ichikawa Hakugen in his essay on Ikkyū in *Gendai bukkyō kōza*, vol. 5, p. 182.

38.   A collection of his poems is known by this name. He also used the pen names "Blind Ass" (Katsuro) and "Sleeping-room" (Mukei).

39.   See Covell and Yamada, *Unraveling Zen's Red Thread*, pp. 124–25.

40.   Imaeda II, pp. 219ff; Takeuchi, *Nihon no zen*, pp. 254ff; Imaeda Aishin, *Chūsei zenshūshi no kenkyū*, p. 217. The line is named by Imaeda after the Japanese reading of the name of the Chinese masters Ming-pen in the detailed table of the Japanese lines during the middle ages.

41.   A brief biography appears in *Zen Dust*, pp. 150–51; on his writings see pp. 411–12; on his portrait see vol. 1 of this work, p. 282.

42.   Imaeda II, p. 219.

43.   Imaeda II, p. 220. There further representatives of the Genjū line, who drew very near to the *gozan* line, are given. On Ichige Sekiyu, see Imaeda, *Chūsei zenshūshi no kenkyū*, p. 510; Imaeda, *Zenshū no rekishi*, pp. 210ff.

44.   On the Hottō line and its development, see Imaeda, *Zenshū no rekishi*, pp. 34–37; Imaeda II, pp. 158–59. See the brief biography of Jiun Myōi in *Zengaku daijiten* II, p. 1186; cf. *Nihon bukkyō kiso kōza* 6, p. 262. The Hottō line, as well as the Genjū line, are taken together with other Rinzai lines in the *gozan* schools. See Imaeda, *Chūsei zenshūshi no kenkyū*, p. 139; cf. Tamamura Takeji's introduction to *Nihon no zen-goroku*, vol. 8, pp. 14–15.

45.   See the brief biography in *Zengaku daijiten* II, p. 950. See also the essay on Bassui by Miwa Tōgai in *Zen* IV, *Zen no rekishi: Nihon*, pp. 351–60; see also *Nihon bukkyō kiso kōza* 6, pp. 260ff, 278; Imaeda II, p. 159. Furuta treats Bassui in *Nihon-zen no hattatsu*, pp. 64ff. Philip Kapleau has published a translation of passages of Bassui's Dharma sayings and letters, with introduction, in his book, *The Three Pillars of Zen* (Tokyo, 1965), pp. 155–86. A covenient Japanese edition of Bassui's works appears as vol 11 of *Nihon no zen-goroku*, edited, introduced, and annotated by Furuta Shōkin. The Dharma sayings of Bassui (*Bassui kana hōgo*) are cited in the text here according to the edition in vol. 1 of the *Zenmon hōgoshū*, pp. 41–74.

46.   See Miwa, *Zen* IV, *Zen no rekishi: Nihon*, pp. 351–52. Miwa uses the modern Japanese word *reikon* for what is translated here as "soul."

47.   *Zenmon hōgoshū* I, pp. 64–65.

48.   Miwa, *Zen no rekishi: Nihon*, p. 352.

49.   Miwa, *Zen no rekishi: Nihon*, p. 355.

50.   See Kapleau, *Three Pillars of Zen*, p. 158. Kapleau relates the description of Bassui's enlightenment experience by one of his biographers, p. 157.

51.   Bassui favored the name Kōgaku-an, namely "the hermitage facing the mountain [Fuji]." Kapleau, *The Three Pillars of Zen*, p. 157.

52.   *Zenmon hōgoshū* I, p. 43.

53.   Bassui carries on: "It is just as when the bottom of a bucket is struck and all the water spills out, or when blossoms suddenly open on a withered tree." *Zenmon hōgoshū* I, p. 46.

54.   *Zenmon hōgoshū* I, p. 68.

55.   *Zenmon hōgoshū* I, p. 45.

56.   *Zenmon hōgoshū* I, p. 69.

57.   *Zenmon hōgoshū* I, pp. 58–59.

58.   See the brief biography in *Zengaku daijiten* II, p. 725. His Dharma sayings (*Gettan kana hōgo*) are included in the same valume as those of Bassui, *Zenmon hōgoshū* I, pp. 171–210.

59.   *Zenmon hōgoshū* I, pp. 185–86.

60.   *Zenmon hōgoshū* I, p. 193.

61.   *Zenmon hōgoshū* I, p. 208.

62.   See the brief biography in *Zengaku daijiten* I, p. 280. See Imaeda, *Zenshū no rekishi,* pp. 44–45; Imaeda II, p. 185. The collections of Jakushitsu's sayings (*Jakushitsu-roku*) has been edited and introduced by Iriya Yoshitaka in *Nihon no zen-goroku,* vol. 10. On the monastery of Eigen-ji and its history, see *Nihon bukkyō kiso kōza,* vol. 6, p. 281.

63.   See Namimoto Sakaichi, "Rinka no zensha Jakushitsu Genkō," *Daihōrin* 1, 1982, pp. 60–65; the quotation appears on p. 62.

64.   Imaeda, *Zenshū no rekishi,* p. 43; Imaeda II, pp. 162–63. As a disciple of Yakuō Tokken, the Dharma heir of Lan-hsi Tao-lung, founder of Kenchō-ji in Kamakura and of the Daikaku line, Jakushitsu belongs, according to the generational line, also to this branch of Rinzai Zen, but his style of life and the monastery of Eigen-ji that he founded bear the unmistakeable Rinka character.

65.   *Nihon no zen-goroku,* vol. 10, pp. 290–91. Iriya devoted a postscript to the literary achievement of Jakushitsu.

66.   *Jakushitsuroku,* p. 250.

67.   Iriya Yoshitake, postscript to the *Jakushitsuroku,* p. 294.

68.   *Jakushitsuroku,* p. 24. The introduction contains several pecularities from the life of Jakushitsu.

69.   See the chronology (*nenpu*) in *Nihon no zen-goroku,* vol. 10, p. 303. Compare this section with the data in the chronology.

70.   Iriya, *Jakushitsuroku,* pp. 43–44.

71.   *Zengaku daijiten* I, p. 290. On the history of the monastery of Hōkō, see *Nihon bukkyō kiso kōza,* vol. 6, p. 280.

72.   *Zengaku daijiten* I, p. 481; on the moanstery of Buttsū-ji, see *Nihon bukkyō kiso kōza,* vol. 6, p. 281.

73.   See ch. 4. note 1.

74.   See the brief biography in *Zengaku daijiten* I, p. 563. All the standard works on the history of Japanese Zen give attention to Gasan. Takeuchi Michio, who belongs to the Sōtō tradition, treats him in detail in his *Nihon no zen,* pp. 199–204, and *Sōtōshū kyōdanshi,* especially pp. 78, 81–89; see also Kagamishima Genryū, *Zen* IV, *Zen no rekishi: Nihon,* pp. 109–14, and the essay in the same volume by Sahashi Hōryū, pp. 193–201. A brief text of the Dharma sayings of Gasan (*Gasan Oshō hōgo*) is given in *Zenmon sōtō hōgo zenshū* I, pp. 51–55.

75.   See the brief biography in *Zengaku daijiten* II, p. 774; see also Takeuchi's two works (note 74), pp. 293–94 and p. 81 respectively; Kagamishima, *Zen* IV, *Zen no rekishi: Nihon,* pp. 109–10; Imaeda, II, pp. 202–205.

76.   Kagamishima, *Zen* IV, *Zen no rekishi: Nihon,* p. 110; Imaeda II, p. 204; Takeuchi *Sōtōshū kyōdanshi,* p. 93; and *Nihon no zen-goroku,* vol. 9, ed. by Mizuno Mihoko.

77.   On the Five Ranks see Vol. 1 of the present work, pp. 222–30.

78.   Dōgen writes on Tung-shan and the Five Ranks in the *Shunjū* of the *Shōbōgenzō,* DZZ I, pp. 327–30. Dōgen "rejected the existence of the Five Houses and recommended the single and complete Buddha-Dharma that surpasses the Five Houses." See Sahashi, *Zen no rekishi: Nihon,* p. 199. On Dōgen's rejection of the Five Ranks and his repudiation of every sort of syncretism, see Takeuchi, *Sōtōshū kyōdanshi,* pp. 82–83.

79. Zen Dust, p. 365. On the Ninden gammoku, see vol. 1 of the present work, p. 214.

80. See the short biography in Zengaku daijiten I, p. 95.

81. Takeuchi, Sōtōshū kyōdanshi, p. 83. Takeuchi ascribed to Gasan the "foundation of Japanese Sōtō Zen." Kagamishima writes: "The science of the Sōtō school of the late middle ages unfolded with the Five Ranks as its center" (Zen no rekishi: Nihon, p. 112). Hui-hung changed, as Verdu notes, the term kenchūshi to henchūshi (Dialectic Aspects in Buddhist Thought, p. 134). For a biography of Hui-hung, see Zengaku daijiten I, p. 95.

82. According to the Zengaku daijiten, tōjō signifies "the religious view brought out by Tung-shan" (II, p. 927). See Takeuchi, Sōtōshū kyōdanshi, pp. 26–27, 30.

83. Cf. the biography of Nan'ei Kenshū in Zengaku daijiten I, p. 286.

84 See the brief biography in Zengaku daijiten I, p. 572.

85. Kagamishima, Zen no rekishi: Nihon, p. 113.

86. See the titles in Zengaku daijiten I, pp. 301–302; II, pp. 927–28. See also Zen Dust on the Five Houses, pp. 426–32.

87. On the "five wise disciples" see the detailed treatment in Takeuchi, Nihon no zen, pp. 276–87, and Sōtōshū kyōdanshi, pp. 83–84. See also Imaeda, Zenshū no rekishi, pp. 169ff; Kagamishima, Zen no rekishi: Nihon, p. 110.

88. See Takeuchi, Nihon no zen, pp. 272, 275; see also Sōtōshū kyōdanshi, pp. 83–84.

89. Takeuchi gives the names of the five hermitages in Nihon no zen, p. 272.

90. On Tsūgen Jakurei and his line see the detailed treatment in Imaeda, Zenshō no rekishi, pp. 172–76. For his collected sayings, see T. No. 2592.

91. See Takeuchi, Nihon no zen, pp. 279ff.

92. The site of this famous temple had formerly been used for the practice of Shugendō; see Imaeda II, p. 205.

93. See the brief biography in Zengaku daijiten II, p. 760. Imaeda refers in his place to the third of the "five wise disciples" as Mugai. See Zen no rekishi, p. 170.

94. On the following see also Takeuchi, Nihon no zen, pp. 287–88; Nihon bukkyō kiso kōza, vol. 6, pp. 133–34; Imaeda II, p. 204.

95. See Takeuchi, Nihon no zen, pp. 274, 322; and Imaeda II, pp. 204–205.

96. This movement can be best called the Keizan-Gasan line. It included also the temples of Daijō-ji and Yōkō-ji, which did not depend on Sōji-ji but were related to Keizan. In this way it is possible to reckon the Kangan line, the influence of which spread from its center, Daiji-ji in Kyūshū, outward into the country. See Imaeda, Zen no rekishi, pp. 177–78; Takeuchi, Sōtōshū kyōdanshi, pp. 102ff.

97. A brief biography appears in Zengaku daijiten II, p. 958. On the reconstruction of Eihei-ji, see Imaeda II, pp. 209–10; Imaeda, Zenshū no rekishi, pp. 183–84; Takeuchi, Nihon no zen, pp. 188–89. Eihei-ji was destroyed by fire fourteen times; see Nihon bukkyō kiso kōza, vol. 6, p. 129.

98. See the brief biography in Zengaku daijiten II, p. 725.

99. See the brief biography in Zengaku daijiten I, p. 90. See Takeuchi, Nihon no zen, pp. 290–91, and Sōtōshū kyōdanshi, pp. 101–102.

100. Jpn., Daiichi shusse dōjō; see Takeuchi, Sōtōshū kyōdanshi, p. 102.

101. Skt., vārṣika. The word goes back to ancient Indian Buddhism. The monks spent the rainy season from 15 April until 15 July in seclusion, using it as a time for spiritual and ascetic development.

6

Zen in Art and Culture

Zen occupies a central place in the cultural history of Japan. The period of greatest Zen influence begins with the transplantation of Zen from China at the beginning of the Kamakura period (1185–1333) and extends well into the Tokugawa period (1600–1868). This time-span was preceded by a longer but less clear prehistory, comprising the Nara (710–784) and Heian periods (794–1185), during which Buddhist influences enabled Japan to attain a high level of cultural development. Throughout the Tokugawa period, Buddhist influence was no longer dominant. The modern period dawned as Japan opened its doors to foreign influence and trade at the beginning of the Meiji era. Within the span of Japanese history, the almost half a millennium in which Zen influence was dominant was a time of extraordinary cultural growth. Through it would certainly be an exaggeration to attribute every cultural value in Japan to Zen, it remains true that Zen is the nation's most distinctive cultural achievement. One cannot but agree with the assessment of the historian J. W. Hall that "the fourteenth and fifteenth centuries . . . produced the art forms and clarified the aesthetic values which to this day are most admired by the Japanese."[1]

This brings up the differing influences that Zen culture has had on East Asia's two giants, China and Japan. In China, Zen art and its unique aesthetics represent an important cultural contribution; in Japan, the entire culture is permeated by Zen. The difference between the two is not merely one of quality but of total context. In treating this question in volume 1 of this work, I indicated some of the foremost artistic accomplishments of China, achievements that, despite great efforts, were never equalled in Japan. Nevertheless, for nearly half a millenium, the intellectual and spiritual climate of Japan bore the distinctive mark of Zen. For a long period the Japanese lived in an atmosphere saturated with Zen. This is the topic of the present chapter. Without an overall perspective on Zen culture, it is impossible to fully understand Zen as a religious school. Throughout the entire religious history of humankind, we find few examples of such close bonds between religion and culture.

ARCHITECTURE

The imposing force of Zen culture is seen most clearly in the layout and architecture of its temples. Entering the Zen centers of Kyoto and Kamakura, the visitor today can hardly avoid being impressed by the richness of Zen culture. To list only the most important centers, let alone to attempt to analyze how they reflect the spirituality of Zen, is an impossible task.

THE MONASTERY OF NANZEN-JI

The early Zen temples owe their construction mainly to the generosity of the imperial house and the nobility. A strong cultural and artistic influence emanated from the splendid temple of Nanzen-ji, which had been transformed from an imperial palace on the East Mountain outside of Kyoto at the command of Emperor Kameyama (ruled 1260–1274). Setting aside his imperial responsibilities, the emperor took up residence in some of the palace rooms, but was soon frightened away by what he thought were nocturnal ghosts. He immediately called a famous priest from Tōdai-ji in Nara, who after a ninety-day exorcism was unable to restore tranquility to the palace. Frustrated at the futility of all these imprecations and incantations, the emperor turned to Mukan Fumon (1212–1291), a highly regarded Zen monk from the school of Enni Ben'en who lived at Tōfuku-ji. Mukan arrived with a group of fellow-monks; as all of them sat in silent meditation, not a sound from the spirits could be heard. From that moment on, the palace served as a Zen temple.

Mukan Fumon (who received the title Daimin Kokushi), was first abbot of the newly founded monastery. He had practiced for twelve years in China under a highly qualified master and had received the seal of the Dharma mind. A disciple of National Master Shōichi, he was the master's third-generation successor as abbot of Tōfuku-ji. He died during his first year in office, having been appointed the founding abbot of Nanzen-ji by Emperor Kameyama.

In recognition of the merits of the former emperor Kameyama and perhaps in view of the legends about the monastery's origins, Nanzen-ji was granted the title of "first rank in the realm" (tenka daiichi) in 1334. The monastery's buildings and the art reflected the natural beauty of its surroundings. The temple complex, one of the most grandiose in the capital, contained all the required buildings— a Buddha hall, a Dharma hall, a monk's hall, a temple tower—and many others besides. The buildings, as was so often the case with Zen temples, were damaged by recurring fires. The list of temple fires in Kyoto is almost endless, but the Japanese rarely gave a second thought to reconstructing them, usually according to their original design. The main buildings of Nanzen-ji, as they stand in Kyoto today, date from the beginning of this century. The precious Nikkamon ("Sunflower Gate"), which had been a gift from the imperial house to the first Zen temple in Kyoto, today serves as the Chokushimon ("Gate of the Imperial Messengers").[2]

Two more elements can be added to this brief description of Nanzen-ji, both of them are typical of Japanese Zen temples and indicative of how these temples contributed to Zen culture. Because not a few of the great Zen temples were originally imperial palaces and castles, from the very beginning they were considered among the finest examples of Japanese architecture. With such clear links with the imperial court, their architectural quality was assured. Imperial protection also played a particularly important role in the establishment of Daitoku-ji and Tenryū-ji.

Nanzen-ji is also an example of the sumptuous buildings frequently found in Zen temples. A Zen temple or monastery in Kyoto almost always included a spacious area filled with buildings and gardens. Examples of such temple designs date back to the early period of Japanese Buddhism, indicating that Chinese influence existed from the earliest times. Japanese Zen architecture is clearly dependent on the designs of Chinese Zen monasteries during the Sung period.[3]

TEMPLES FOLLOWING THE CHINESE DESIGN

During their long stays in China during the thirteenth century, leading Zen masters like Eisai, Dōgen, and Enni Ben'en carefully studied the architectural design of the monasteries in which the rigorous life of the Zen monk was carried out. During the T'ang period in China (618–907), a Buddhist temple architecture had developed that served as the basic design for Zen temples and their grounds during the Sung period, especially for the monasteries of the Five Mountains. The first of these mountains, Ching-shan (Jpn., Kinzan), with the monastery of Hsing-sheng-wan-shou-ssu (Jpn., Kōshōmanju-ji), became the normative model for many other temples. Making up the other mountains were Pei-shan (Jpn., Hokuzan), with the temple of Ching-te-ling-yin-ssu (Jpn., Keitoku-reiin-ji); T'ai-po-shan (Jpn., Taihakuzan), with the temple of T'ien-t'ung-ching-te ch'an-ssu (Jpn., Tendō-keitoku-zenji); Nan-shan (Jpn., Nanzan), with the temple of Ching-tz'u-pao-en-kuang-hsiao-ssu (Jpn., Jōjihōonkōkō-ji); and A-yü-wang-shan (Jpn., Aikuōzan), with the temple of Kuan-li-ssu (Jpn., Kōri-ji).[4] The layout of the temple of Mount Ching has never been discovered.[5] The layout of T'ien-t'ung and Pei are of special significance in that traces of their influence can be found in numerous Zen temples of Japan.

Not only did the Japanese Zen monks bring back architectural plans from China, they also succeeded in making friends with Chinese artisans and convincing them to make the trip to Japan.[6] In this way, the Zen temples that were constructed during the thirteenth century in Japan were under both the theoretical and practical influence of China.

Among the medieval Zen temples of Japan, Kenchō-ji (Kamakura) and Tōfuku-ji (Kyoto) are perhaps the most significant from an architectural point of view. One of the oldest architectural plans discovered in a Japanese Zen monastery supplies us today with valuable information on the similar layout used for both temples.[7] Friendly relations existed between the temples, so that when fire devastated many of the buildings at Tōfuku-ji in 1319, Kenchō-ji responded by supplying a copy of the general design that had been used for its own construction. With the help of this design, Tōfuku-ji was carefully restored to its former glory. Again, around the beginning of the fifteenth century, a fire razed Kenchō-ji to the ground, destroying in the process the documents containing the temple's original design. With the help of earlier copies, the monks of Kenchō-ji immediately set about reconstruction, though only partially reproducing the original design. The overall style used at Kenchō-ji in Kamakura can be considered the original model for all medieval Japanese Zen temples. It is in the actual layout of the Tōfuku-ji complex, however, that we find an incomparable expression of the charm of a medieval Zen temple. An enchanting clarity hovers over the entire complex, which still contains some of the original buildings from the Kamakura period. It represents the classical style of a "seven-hall monastery" (shichidō-garan).[8]

The ground plan of Kenchō-ji and Tōfuku-ji was modeled after the imposing Chinese temple structures of T'ien-t'ung-shan.[9] Although the layout of Japanese temples corresponds basically to that of their Chinese prototypes, there are some small differences. The size of the buildings varies from temple to temple. In the Buddha halls of Zen temples the primary cultic object is an image of the historical Buddha, Śākyamuni, at the moment of his enlightenment; other figures, also objects of devotion, usually accompany the image of Buddha. One enters the temple area through the "Mountain Gate,"[10] symbolizing the purging of desires and conceptual thinking as one enters the realm of empiness, and then mounts directly toward the Buddha hall. Reverencing of the Buddha image must be

Figure 1: *Typical "Seven-hall Monastery" Layout*

Key: 1. Mountain Gate (*sammon*); 2. Buddha Hall (*butsuden*); 3. Dharma Hall (*hattō*);
4. Latrine (*tōsu*); 5. Bath (*yokushitsu*); 6. Monks' Hall (*sōdō*); 7. Kitchen (*kuri*).

Figure 2: *The "seven halls" in analogy to the human body*

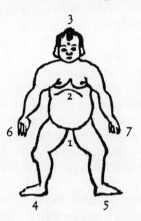

preceded by cleansing and purgative exercises. In these rituals washing and the purging of bodily impurities are necessary, for which purpose two wooden buildings, on the right and left, are located between the gate and the Buddha hall. Two other buildings, the monks' hall of meditation (*sōdō*) and the kitchen and storehouse (*kuri*), are located a little behind the Buddha hall. The seventh building is the Dharma hall (*hattō*), in which an enlightened monk lectures on the holy scriptures. This hall is situated on the central ascending axis, and constitutes the focal point of the entire complex. Given differences in size and adornment, the arrangement of the buildings can also differ. In earlier temples, for instance, the monks' hall, the Dharma hall, and the Mountain Gate occupied places of greater importance. In Tōfuku-ji, the layout of the buildings takes on a clear analogy to the human body. A few of the buildings of this monastery have somehow escaped the ravages of frequent fires and today are designated as national "cultural treasures," giving us a rare insight into ancient architectural skills.[11]

The classical layout of the seven halls is often somewhat difficult to detect because of the many secondary buildings scattered around the temple area. One of the most prominent of such additions is the abbot's residence (Chin., *fang-chang*; Jpn., *hōjō*); often consisting of three buildings, with garden and pond, it is a noteworthy addition to the overall beauty of the temple complex.

KINKAKU-JI AND GINKAKU-JI

The grandoise buildings of the Golden Pavilion (Kinkaku-ji) and the Silver Pavilion (Ginkaku-ji), which the Ashikaga shōguns built in the metropolitan center during the Muromachi period, mark a high point in the development of Zen architecture. Both works of art were inspired by the spirit of National Teacher Musō and were closely associated with his name, though at the time of their construction he had long since departed this life. Built by Yoshimitsu (ruled 1367–1395) as a retirement residence in 1397, the Golden Pavilion occupied a large expanse of land owned by the emperor on North Mountain (Kitayama), on the outskirts of Kyoto. With its three-storied, tapered structure, the building resembles a pagoda. Its name comes from the gold-covered roof of the third floor, which served as a shrine for relics.[12] After Musō Kokushi's death, the Golden Pavilion became the Zen monastery of Rokuon-ji, dedicated to the memory of its founder. The buildings were constructed in the Japanese style (wayō), which was a blending of the Chinese style of the Sung period (karayō) with older elements of Chinese architecture.[13] The Japanese once again proved their masterful skills of restoration in 1950 when, with their usual care and precision, they entirely rebuilt this "landmark of Zen taste"[14] after it had burned down. Yoshimitsu's long rule embodied the summit of Zen culture during the Muromachi period; given the geographical location of his residence, history has designated this era as that of the "culture of the Northern Mountain" (Kitayama-bunka).

Following the example of his great ancestor, Ashikaga Yoshimasa (ruled 1443–1473) built an extravagant palace on East Mountain (Higashiyama) during a time of excruciating need, as thousands of his subjects were perishing from famine, fire, and sword. After his death in 1490, the palace was transformed into the Zen temple of Jishō-ji, also dedicated to Musō Kokushi as its founder, even though the master had not been its first abbot. The residence there known as Tōgudō,[15] to which the shōgun retired in seclusion to pursue his aesthetic interests, houses the oldest existing tea room, whose measurements of four-and-a-half mats (koma) became the standard for all tea rooms. Only a few steps from this house Yoshimasa built the two-story Silver Pavilion. Its construction was to take longer than expected. Begun in 1473, the structure was fully finished three years after Yoshimasa's death. Although the shōgun's own artistic tastes bordered on the extravagant, during the time of the "East Mountain culture" (Higashiyama-bunka, named after his residence) Zen aesthetics reached its climax. Still, experts in the history of art and culture offer differing evaluations of the significance of Higashiyama-bunka.

EIHEI-JI

Given the conditions of the times, the Rinzai school could boast of a far greater number of impressive temple buildings during the Muromachi period. A description of the temple complexes already referred to would take us far beyond the scope of this book, but one of the most imposing of Zen temples during the medieval period of Japan was the monastery of Eihei-ji, founded by Dōgen and today the headquarters of the Sōtō school. The entrance gate is preceded by a gate for the imperial messenger (chokushimon). The path to the three main buildings ascends along a stone path among towering cedars and then up rock stairs. The multi-storied Buddha hall overlooks the entire complex, but the focal point is the Dharma hall. On completion of the monks' hall, the source of the monastery's spiritual energy, Dōgen is said to have exclaimed in joy: "Now this mountain has a monks' hall—the first we have heard of [in Japan], the first we have seen, and the first in which we have sat."[16]

GARDEN ART

Japanese architecture—and this is particularly so in the case of Zen temples—builds into nature and forms an incomparably beautiful whole with mountains and valleys, hills, lakes, and streams.[17] Gardens have been a part of Japanese art since its beginning. This, too, was inspired by China, a nation whose beautifully landscaped gardens have merited it the epithet "mother of gardens." Japan eagerly followed China's example. Even prior to the Nara period, as the chronicles report, there were well-tended, enchanting gardens. The Heian period boasts broad, lavish gardens, with smiling people happily exploring the small pathways and well-dressed, festive parties in small boats moving across ponds and under arched bridges; an elegant nobility populated these gardens. Under the influence of Zen, garden art took on a new development toward a more spiritualized love of nature; for Zen, the garden became a symbol of the cosmos.

LANDSCAPE GARDENS

The gardens of National Teacher Musō, among the oldest still in existence, belong to the most beautiful achievements of Japan's art of gardening. Their style represents the transition from the landscape gardens of the Heian period to the stone gardens of the later Muromachi period. Rather than simply to imitate nature, Musō sought to imbue nature with new meaning and spirit and to present it as part of the overall beauty of the world. He designed or remodeled the gardens of Saihō-ji (c. 1339) and of Tenryū-ji (c. 1343), drawing on examples from the Heian period to create the new and impressive style of Zen gardening.

The garden of Saihō-ji, an old temple dedicated to Amida Buddha and situated on the western end of Kyoto, was rebuilt by Master Musō and transformed into a Zen temple. Today it is one of the best known and most beautiful gardens in the capital. There were formerly two paradise-gardens, which Musō changed into what is today a symbolic representation of Zen's ideal land as described in the *Hekiganroku*. Because of the more than twenty varieties of moss found within the garden precincts, this temple came to be know popularly as the "Moss Temple" (Koke-dera).

The garden is divided into two parts separated from each other by a gate. Steps carved out of the natural rock ascend to the higher part of the grounds. In the lower section, a landscaped garden extends around a "Golden Pond," which is laid out in the shape of the Sino-Japanese glyph for heart. Such heart-shaped ponds *(shinji-ike)* are found throughout the country, and although there are no historical grounds for doing so, are often attributed to Musō Kokushi. The paths stretching around the pond beckon the visitor to follow and enjoy the enchanting views that the garden offers everywhere. The Moss Garden of Saihō-ji is a "garden for walking" *(kaiyūshiki teien)*, in contrast to many Zen gardens that are intended to be viewed from without, as for example, from the veranda of the abbot's residence. The pond is marked by larger island-like rocks that provide a dynamic quality even in this quiet part of the garden.

The higher level of the garden is very different, containing a stone garden in the *kare-sansui* style. *Sansui* (literally, "mountain and water") usually has the simple meaning of "landscape," while *kare* signifies "dry." The combination of mountain (implying "rock" or "stone") and water points to the foundational polarity of hard and soft, man and woman, and in general *yin* and *yang* within the ancient Chinese worldview. The quality of hardness introduces a paradox that can be traced back to Taoism; after it was taken up and perfected by Zen this paradox came to express its very essence. Already in the *Sakuteiki*,[18] an esoteric book on garden art from the Heian period, the *kare-sansui* style is mentioned. We can assume that its roots lie in Taoist symbolism. An amazing aspect of these dry gardens is the way they can create an enchanting impression of watercourses or waterfalls without using a drop of water, as seen in the upper level of the Saihō-ji garden. In the center of this level, large boulders grow amid artfully arranged stone-constellations. Constituting the northern part of the garden, the upper level, with its hard, angular stones stands in sharp contrast to the blooming trees and soft moss paths that surround the Golden Pond on the lower level. For the Zen monk, this garden illustrates the two opposing aspects of reality, which can be experienced in the amenities of a harmonious life or in the raw, ascetical climate of Zen practice. In the silence of these stone gardens one senses the lasting power of committed practice. A well-rounded stone (*zazen-seki*) invites one to seated meditation. Here, within nature, the monk finds a spiritual home.

The garden in the middle of Tenryū-ji, like the Moss Garden of Saihō-ji, was not the original creation of Musō, though the important changes that he brought to its original layout have given it its present-day form. This landscape garden, offering no possibilities for strolling around, is meant to be viewed from the temple veranda. Set within a glorious landscape of wooded hills and near and distant hills, the garden is dominated in the background by the mighty Arashiyama ("Storm Mountain"). The spontaneity of nature joins with symbolism. At the outer reaches there is the suggestion of a waterfall, though there is no real water. At the center is a lake, fed by natural springs and shaped like the glyph for "heart." The pure, transparent water in the lake signifies the mind of the person as it ought to be and, in enlightenment, indeed is. In the middle of the lake, there is an "isle of paradise." Groups of stones depict turtles and storks, animals that are believed to be omens of good fortune. A bridge rests on stones rising above the water; they are spaced at intervals corresponding to the numbers 3, 5, and 7, which according to Chinese belief signifies the perfect form of human life. An indescribable stillness reigns over the garden. The many insoluble difficulties that beset human life are here symbolized by the spring (a figure taken from the Chinese artistic tradition); as the water wells up from the ground to rise in the lake, so the human spirit draws strength from the tranquility of nature. The white sand at the border of the pond has the same cleansing power for the mind as the pure water. From this purity springs the triumphant courage displayed by the young carp when in the spring it leaps upward against the waterfall, a figure familiar to the Japanese from the popular festival of the carp streamers (*koi-nobori*).

The gardens that form part of the two pavilions of Kinkaku-ji and Ginkaku-ji also contributed greatly to the beauty of the capital. The garden of the Golden Pavilion, completed in 1397, proved that Yoshimitsu, a great lover and expert in the arts, was also a garden architect in his own right. Although inspired by the Saihō-ji garden, which he greatly esteemed and loved, his own garden was a spiritually independent creation. Moreover, in his case he had an original garden with pond that could be reworked. He transformed the pond by adding a number of enchanting little islands and planting carefully selected trees all around. Blending in with the overpowering beauty of the surrounding landscape, the garden offers, from within the pavilion, a view that reaches out and loses itself in the panoramic distance. It has been called one of the finest Zen landscape gardens ever created.[19]

Ashikaga Yoshimasa shared his predecessor Yoshimitsu's admiration for the garden of Saihō-ji. In fashioning a garden for his Silver Pavilion, he too was strongly influenced by Musō's work. Under the shōgun's direction, a garden with both higher and lower levels took shape, with a rather large pond enhanced by schools of lotus flowers and small bridges connecting scattered islands. Massive, angular borders constitute an exact imitation of the famous Saihō-ji garden.[20] Frequently damaged throughout the centuries, the garden of the Silver Pavilion has often had to be repaired and expanded. Two later additions are especially striking. The "sea of silver sand" (ginshadan), a flat expanse of white sand, represents a Chinese lake. The raked white sand symbolizes waves that during the night reflect the silver moon. Also noteworthy is the flattened mound of sand (kōgetsudai) that leads one to meditate on the moon or on the nocturnal play of the moonlight.

The numerous landscape gardens in Zen style that sprang up throughout the country from the Muromachi period on give witness to the Zen monks' love of nature and their ability to see the whole of the cosmos in a single piece of nature and all of reality in each natural symbol. "The fundamental thing about Japanese gardens. . . . is the fact that the art was definitely used in China and Japan to express the highest truths of religion and philosophy."[21] Like the meditation hall and the Buddha shrine, the garden formed part of the essence of a Zen temple and enabled it to carry out its religious purpose.

STONE GARDENS

Symbols play an important role in Japanese Zen gardens. The symbol-laden stone or dry gardens in the kare-sansui style flourished around the end of the Muromachi period. Without use of color or decoration and with few symbols, these gardens capture the entire cosmos on a little piece of earth. Stones and boulders represent mountains or islands, and instead of water, plains of moss or sand symbolize the endless sea. This kind of a garden is like a kōan, providing the viewer with both a question and a task: What does it mean? In the final analysis, it means of course the Buddha, whose body makes up the whole of nature.

In the garden of Shinju-an, which was a branch temple built in honor of the Zen master Ikkyū in the area around Daitoku-ji and that tradition says was designed by the tea master Murata Jukō (1423–1502),[22] the ground surface is made up of a single expanse of moss, incredibly soft, quiet, and shimmering. Unusually shaped natural rocks, arranged in the 7-5-3 series, give the impression of power and security. To view this garden purifies the heart, pacifies the mind, and directs the eye inward.

This style of garden, distinguished by its angular, sharply rising, and unusually shaped rocks, is found in many temples—as for instance, the branch temples of Taizō-in and Reiun-in in Myōshin-ji and the abbot's residence of Konchi-in in Nanzen-ji, as well as in many rural temples. The harsh discipline of these gardens is meant to promote the concentration of mind necessary for meditation.

The stone gardens of Ryōan-ji and Daisen-in, a branch temple of Daitoku-ji, are recognized as outstanding works of art. The temple of Daisen-in was built by the Zen monk Kogaku and is supposed to have been completed in 1513. The garden probably was finished around the same time. Nature in all its grandeur and multiplicity of forms is here compressed into a tiny space. Two upright rocks at one end of the expanse attract the visitor's gaze like two towering mountain peaks. Around the rocks are scattered stones of different sizes, washed by the furrowed white sand. A boulder in the form of a boat adds to the impression of water all around. Strewn over the sand surface, broad flat stones represent bridges and riverbanks. A trace of sand suggests a river. In this simple way, the manifoldness of the world with its ten thousand things is set forth symbolically. Perspective is achieved through variation in size. The garden is like an ink painting, which with a few strokes of the brush can present the viewer with a beautifully rich scene.

The most famous of all Zen gardens is the level stone garden adjoining the Ryōan-ji temple in Kyoto. The garden is rectangular in form, measuring about 31 by 14 meters, and is enclosed by a low earthen wall. One's gaze naturally rises beyond the wall, where an adjoining pine forest and distant hills and mountains provide a harmonious view. The garden consists of nothing but sand and fifteen natural stones arranged in five groups surrounded by a meager growth of moss. The sand symbolizes water, the stones signify mountains or islands, while the moss suggests a forest. The surface consists of coarse snow-white sand. There is neither path nor stepping-stone, since no foot falls upon it. Void of all animal life and nearly all vegetation, this stone garden is a symbol of the pure mind purged of all forms—of nothingness or of what Meister Eckhart calls the "desert of the godhead." At the same time, this strikingly barren desert garden is mysteriously animated from within. The stones are alive. With their curious forms, they bring an uncanny movement into the sand waste that, to anyone quietly and perseveringly taking in its lengthwise view from the temple veranda, seems to reach out into infinity. In full sunlight the rising flood of light blinds the eye, but when the silver moon glides over the white sand, the mind of the contemplative pilgrim is carried to the world beyond, where there are no opposites and the nothingness of pure divinity dwells in impenetrable light. In popular usage the garden at Ryōan-ji is called the "Garden of the Wading Tiger," because these living stones resemble the heads and backs of tiger cubs whom the mother tiger is leading through the ford of a stream. This interpretation, of course, does not correspond to the intent of the artist, who in his work visualized above all the effect of the flat surface, succeeding thereby in combining the greatest abstraction with concrete reality. With the simplest of means he evoked an inexhaustible depth of spiritual meaning. The overall impression of this "Garden of Emptiness" is more powerful and deep than the lavish paintings of the Daisen-in garden.

The gardens of Daisen-in and Ryōan-ji, the two towering peaks in the history of Zen garden art, have often been attributed, with greater or lesser probability, to the famous painter Sōami (1472–1525); in both cases, however, the historical data are uncertain. The great Sesshū is also said to have designed gardens, among them the garden of Jōei-ji in Yamaguchi.[23] This linking of gardens with famous painters is significant in that it points up the relationship between garden architecture and ink painting. Like the powerfully drawn lines and points of an ink painting, the plain, harsh, monochromatic stone gardens are expressions of the enlightened mind.

THE TEA GARDEN

The tea garden is another form of Zen art which we shall only touch on fleetingly here,[24] though in what follows we will have more to say about the tea ceremony (chanoyu). Part of Japan's tea culture, the tea garden was the bridge on which Japan's garden art moved from the religiously inspired Zen garden to the secularization that was evident during the Edo period in the summer villas of Katsura Rikyū and Shūgaku-in.

Consisting mainly of a path surrounded by trees and thick shrubbery leading to the tea room, the tea garden (roji) is a modest facet of the tea ceremony. According to the principle of asymmetry, the stepping stones (tobi-ishi) are irregularly arranged to form a path by which the guest strolls past a stone lantern (ishi-dōrō) and a jet of water from a bamboo pipe on the way to the tea room. In front of the entrance there is a stone water basin (tsukubai) and ladle for guests to rinse their mouths with. The walk through a tea garden is intended to foster recollection and inner peace.

A predecessor of the tea room—or perhaps the very first one—is found in Tōgudō at the Silver Pavilion. It seems most likely that the shōgun Ashikaga Yoshimasa and his friends, under the direction of the tea master Murata Shukō, performed the tea ritual here. During the sixteenth century, when the tea ceremony reached the height of its popularity, tea rooms and gardens sprang up throughout the land. Sen no Rikyū, a counselor to the two rulers Oda Nobunaga (1534–1582) and Toyotomi Hideyoshi (1536–1598), perfected the art of the tea ceremony and fostered the development of tea gardens.

The tea garden was loved and appreciated everywhere. Rikyū's tea garden in the sukiya style reflected the artistic tastes of the times and influenced the expansive design of many other gardens, such as the gardens of the grandiose villas of Katsura Rikyū[25] and Shūgaku-in, attributed to the artistic talents of Kobori Enshū (1579–1647) and his school, which had close ties with Zen. Both gardens are graced with tea houses and tea gardens. At the beginning of the modern period, Zen culture had found an entry into the world of secular art.

CALLIGRAPHY

Calligraphy is considerably older than the Zen movement itself. During the Eastern Chin dynasty in China (317–420), it reached a height of achievement that was to become normative for all subsequent development. The two prominent figures of this time are Wang Hsi-chih (Jpn., Ō Gishi, 307–365) and his son Wang Hsien-chih (Jpn., Ō Kenshi, 344–388).[26] During the Sung period both these masters were studied intensively and their works were analyzed in both original (whenever possible) and copied versions. Among the calligraphers of the Sung period who both studied the past and created their own works, was a Zen poet named Huang T'ing-chien (Jpn., Kō Teiken, 1045–1105), who had practiced Zen meditation under the master Hui-t'ang Tsu-hsin (Jpn., Maidō Soshin, 1025–1100) and attained enlightenment. Huang T'ing-chien seems to have been one of the first persons consciously to realize the relation between the art of writing and Zen. The connection dawned on him when he noticed the difference enlightenment had made for the way he used his brush. After enlightenment, his writing took on an inner vitality.

Huang T'ing-chien had a deep influence on the calligraphy of those dedicated Japanese Zen monks whose esteem for China was focused especially on Chinese calligraphic achievements.[27] One of the Japanese most indebted to Huang T'ing-chien and to the influence he exercised was Shūhō Myōchō (Daitō Kokushi). Even before him, Eisai, who was the first to bring Rinzai Zen from the continent, had introduced Chinese works of calligraphy to Japan. It can be shown that the Japanese calligrapher Shunjō (1166–1227) was influenced by Huang T'ing-chien. Enni Ben'en also brought Chinese works of calligraphy to Japan. With calligraphy flourishing in China during the Sung period,[28] the Chinese masters who came to Japan proved themselves to be capable teachers of this art form—among them Lan-hsi Tao-lung and especially the eminent artist I-shan I-ning. Musō Soseki, an accomplished and well rounded artist, was also an excellent calligrapher. The most significant calligrapher during the late Muromachi period was Ikkyū Sōjun, an artist of eccentric originality who considered himself the artistic progeny of the Chinese Zen master Hsü-t'ang Chih-yü (Jpn., Kidō Chigu, 1185–1269). Among the Japanese gozan scholars who counted the famous writing-artist Ku-lin Ch'ing-mao (1262–1329) in their genealogy, the conservative Zekkai Chūshin (1336–1405) is the most prominent calligrapher. Perhaps because his penetrating metaphysical insights were so imposing, it is often forgotten that Dōgen was a calligrapher whose brush produced some impressive works of art. His school promoted the art of calligraphy and bore considerable artistic fruit. It is clear, then, that in medieval Japanese Zen, the art of calligraphy attained a high degree of perfection. During the modern period, the founders of the Ōbaku school (see below) brought the contemporary Chinese style of calligraphy to Japan. The Japanese monks Hakuin Ekaku (1685–1768), Sengai Gibon (1751–1837), and Ryōkan (1758–1831)—about whom we will have more to say below—left posterity impressive works of calligraphy.

The uniqueness of Chinese logographs has given calligraphy a significant place within East Asian art. One can find in China and Japan highly-prized works of calligraphic art that are not at all related to Zen Buddhism.[29] Nevertheless, it must be acknowledged that the bonds between Zen and the art of calligraphy are rooted in a deep, natural relationship. With their ink brushes, Zen practitioners are able to give unique expression to their inner experience. Enlightenment and the creative power that it taps find spontaneous expression in Zen calligraphy, which first and foremost is an expressive art form. The preferred name for this art form during Japan's medieval period was shojutsu, the "art of writing."[30] Only later, probably during the second half of the Edo period (1603–1867) and under some Confucian influence, did the term "way of writing" (shodō) come into vogue, as it became clear that writing can be a form of meditation practice. Since the Meiji period (1868–1912), the "way of writing" has also become more and more popular as a pedagogical tool, widely used today in Japan's educational system. Although the term shodō ("way of writing"), together with the more common shohō ("method of writing") is found earlier in China, we should look upon shodō as a new development; today it is popularly considered to be a way of expressing one's total humanity. As we shall see, the same would apply to other "ways" (dō) that are related to Zen.

If, as Dietrich Seckel observes, calligraphy is the most highly regarded art-form in East Asia,[31] this is due in no small part to the power of its symbolism. In his studies of the suggestive impact of ink drawing, Seckel has discovered that "the clear, sharp, lines moving back and forth from outside to inside allow for a very precise form of drawing."[32] The art-loving amateur, who finds himself unable to explain the mystery of the ink line, senses the incredible power of this art form, which is an "altogether direct, 'graphological' expression of the creative personality."[33] Enlightened Zen masters grasp spontaneously that "the ink line serves as a decisively important medium for overcoming opposing distinctions. It would have been difficult for Zen to find another artistic medium by which to express itself so directly and perfectly."[34] One can grasp this best by absorbing some of the extremely simple, meaningful characters that have been so masterfully painted—for instance, the character for "heart" or "nothingness" or an ink-drawn circle. Such graphs and circles can serve as "utterly valid and direct artistic expressions of religious insights."[35] The relation between ink drawings and creative personalities[36] constitutes the incomparable value of ink drawing, which is closely linked with calligraphy. A much loved piece of decorative art tokonoma) in tea rooms is a "roll with poem and picture" (shiga-jiku),[37] on which characters are usually written vertically. Such a piece is often called an "ink trace" (bokuseki) and is understood as a trace of the enlightened mind.

PAINTING

Painting represents the highest form of Zen art. Landscape paintings, inspired by the religious world view of Zen, are the most abiding contribution of Zen to the fine arts. In Japan, ink drawing (suibokuga) found its true home in the Zen temples, where painter-monks (gasō) expressed their enlightenment in their brushwork.

During the Muromachi period, Japanese ink-painting carried on the Chinese Zen art of the Sung period.[38] Japanese Zen painters took up themes that had been well developed in China: Zen stories and parables or paradoxical sayings (zenkizu or zenkiga), portraits of arhats, patriarchs, masters (all called chinsō), and the theme in which Japanese artists excelled—landscapes. Purely religious themes of Buddhism, as well, appear in all phases of Japanese Zen painting: the founder Śākyamuni, bodhisattvas (especially Avalokiteśvara [Kannon] and Mañjuśrī [Monju]), and most frequently, the Chinese Zen patriarch Bodhidharma.

Darkness clouds the beginnings of Zen ink-painting in Japan. Only a few of the many painters and paintings of this early period can be determined with certainty. The real pioneers of this new art form were the two Zen monks Mokuan (d. ca. 1345) and Kaō (d. 1345), about whose lives we know relatively little. A dedicated monk and gifted artist, Mokuan traveled to China in his old age, where he remained until his death, having found both a new home and widespread esteem. One of his best known works is the painting of "The Four Sleepers" picturing the two vagabonds Han-shan (Jpn., Kanzan) and Shih-te (Jpn., Jittoku) together with master Feng-kan (Jpn., Bukan) and a tiger he had tamed.[39]

Having entered monastic life at a young age, Kaō travelled to China toward the end of the Kamakura period; there he made impressive progress in the art of ink painting. Some time after he had returned to Japan, he was appointed abbot of Nanzen-ji. His favorite theme was the pair of vagabonds Han-shan and Shih-te. Among the few paintings of his that are preserved, there is his humorous presentation of Han-shan, hands swimming in enormous sleeves and scrubby head held high, looking out on the world with a friendly grin, well aware of the impermanence of it all.[40]

Zen portraiture is inspired both by the school's strong sense of tradition and by the devotion that Zen disciples felt toward their masters. The large number of portraits makes clear the close bonds between Zen monks and their teachers as well as the importance that Zen has always attributed to personalities of great experience.[41]

From the extensive collection of portraits, whose authors often remain anonymous, three paintings illustrating the three phases of medieval Japanese Zen history may be singled out for mention. After his death, Enni Ben'en, the founding abbot of Tōfuku-ji, was honored by numerous portraits, most of them by unknown disciples. A later painting of him by the prominent Japanese Zen artist Kichizan Minchō (also called Chō Densu, 1350–1431) is counted among the most beautiful classical Zen portraits.[42] There is something touching about the figure of the white-haired master—a spirit-filled, almost unassuming ascetic—sitting majestically on his abbot's chair; it is a painting done with warm, reverential feeling. Minchō, a painter-monk of Tōfuku-ji, is one of the earlier artistic personalities of the Muromachi period.

Musō Soseki, one of the foremost Zen masters at the beginning of the Muromachi period, was also a frequent subject of paintings by his disciples, among which one of the best known was done by Mutō Shūi in the middle of the fourteenth century.[43] The fine, aristocratic qualities of this venerable monk give expression to the depths of his enlightened mind. To this day, he is broadly remembered and revered in Japan.

For different reasons, the same can be said of the more earthy Ikkyū. Portraits of him outnumber those of all other masters; almost all of these paintings present him as a relatively young rustic in his fifties, poised in some kind of unconventional, sluggish bearing. Two of the paintings were by his disciple Bokkei (1394–1473), both done around the same time (1452 and 1453), but each from a different perspective.[44] The bald-headed, beardless monk of the first painting was transformed within the space of a year into the scrubby haired, unkempt old eccentric Ikkyū. While many portraits show Ikkyū on the abbot's seat (isu-zō), in only one is he wearing ritual robes. The best known painting of Ikkyū in advanced years is the work of his disciple Bokusai (1412?–1492), an excellent painter who has also given us a sketched portrait that most likely preceded the final work.[45] The sketch is the most impressive picture of the master that we have. Brinker appropriately describes it thus: "From the corner of his eyes, with a penetrating, critically searching, indeed challenging look, the subject stares back at the viewer; this highly unusual form for a Zen portrait creates a lively, intense, and direct communication between the subject of the painting and the viewer."[46]

With its beginnings in the Kamakura period, Japanese Zen painting freely developed in the Zen temples of Kyoto during the Muromachi period, inspired and influenced by Chinese ink-drawing of the Sung period. Tōfuku-ji and Daitoku-ji were important centers of this development, as can be seen in the work of the previously mentioned masters, Minchō[47] and Bokusai. Three generations of Ami were active in the service of the Ashikaga shogunate: Nōami (also called Shinnō, 1397–1471), Geiami (also called Shingei, 1431–1485), and Sōami (d. 1525). Geiami's student Shōkei, who was also called Kei Shoki because of his office as secretary (shoki) at Kenchō-ji in Kamakura, was one of the leading Zen painters in Japan's eastern, or Kantō, region. Sōami, the most important of the Ami, whom we already met in our section on garden art, numbers among the best ink painters of his time. His favorite theme was the rainy, overcast landscapes of Kyoto.

Around the middle of the Muromachi period the shōgun Yoshimitsu founded an artist's studio on the Chinese model and placed it under the direction of the painter-monk Josetsu (fl. c. 1400–1413). Little is known concerning the person and work of Josetsu. His masterful artistry is evident in his painting "Catching a Catfish with a Gourd," which joins the two themes of Zen parables and landscapes.[48] The meaning of the parable is that it is just as difficult to attain en-lightenment as it is to catch a smooth, slippery catfish with a gourd bottle. Josetsu's student Shūbun (d. between 1444 and 1448) carried on and made ink painting more widely known and regarded. After studying in Korea he worked in Japan mainly in the Southern Sung style of the masters Ma Yüan and Hsia Kuei (both from the beginning of the thirteenth century). Ma Yüan is known for his so-called "one-corner" style, which left the entire page empty except for one corner. An example of this style is "A Fisherman," one of the greatest artistic symbols of all time of the grandeur and loneliness of human existence.[49] Shūbun produced a large number of excellent landscape paintings, which were highly acclaimed for so well expressing Japanese feelings for nature. He was an artist of extraordinary originality. With his successor, Sōtan (1413–1481), how-ever, the Ma-Hsia style (so-called after its Chinese originators) fell victim to the lethargy of routine.

Sesshū Tōyō (1420–1506), who probably began his artistic career under the direction of Shūbun and belonged for a while to the studio in Shōkoku-ji, claims a unique place in the history of Japanese art. His fame exceeds that of all his contemporaries. Among both Japanese and Western art historians he is regarded as the greatest of all Japanese ink-painters, perhaps the greatest painter in the entire history of Japanese painting";[50] he has been called the most powerful of all Japan's artists.[51] Both his life and his art are informed by Zen. Born in Bitchū (Okayama prefecture), he was only twelve when he joined a small Buddhist monastery near his home. His Zen training took place at Shōkoku-ji in Kyoto, where he was held in high esteem as a monk and painter. Although his artistic development was greatly influenced by a stay in Ming-dynasty China (1467–1469), upon returning to Japan, he made no secret of his disappointment with the Chinese painters whom he had come to know. In his estimation, Josetsu and Shūbun were every bit as accomplished as the Chinese masters. Still, while in China he did learn a great deal about technique and style. He mastered the brush movement technique developed in Chinese ink drawing as well as the *shin* style of angular lines and sharp contures represented by the 'Northern' Sung school (with Ma Yüan and Hsia Kuei and their successors), together with the *sō* style of soft tones through "broken ink" (*haboku*) or "sprayed ink" (*hatsuboku*).

Upon returning from China, he first took to traveling, frequently changing his residence and regularly avoiding the capital city, which at that time lay in ruins. He left the artist's studio to others and is said to have recommended Kanō Masanobu (1434–1530) to be Sōtan's successor. He himself finally settled down in the quiet hermitage of Unkoku-an, near Yamaguchi, where his artistic gifts reached their highest development and maturity. In his old age he created the masterpieces that give enduring expression to his Zen spirit. Because it does not allow for any subsequent correction, the technique of ink painting demands the kind of mental control that a Zen disciple acquires through rigorous practice. Every brush stroke remains as it is: beginning delicately, it moves boldly across the white paper and then fades out or ends abruptly. The certainty and vigor of Sesshū's brush are unexcelled.

Among his many works are some that clearly show his ability to paint human beings. He was seventy-six years old when he painted "Hui-k'o Cuts off His Arm."[52] Despite the tension of the moment depicted, both patriarchs are made duly to maintain their venerable, collected bearing. In its *shin* style, the painting proves Sesshū's ability to capture individuals.[53] But his landscape paintings show his greatest talent. His exuberant, many-leveled ink-painting, "The Four Seasons,"[54] peers into the very mystery of nature. The sharply angular lines in *shin* style and the delicate, partially colored washes express the artist's conception of how nature changes through the seasons. This picture has been called the foremost expression of Japanese ink painting, though a later picture of the aged Sesshū in the *sō* style, "Landscape in the Broken Ink Style,"[55] is for many the crowning point of his work and the most perfect Japanese landscape painting.

The life and feeling that breathe within Sesshū's paintings of nature are evidence of his Zen spirituality. As the body of Buddha, nature is in a constant process of growth; therefore anyone who seeks to present nature from within has to enter into this process. This is precisely what Sesshū sought to do in his ink paintings; he excells all others in his ability to see into the changing seasons and into the exuberance of plant life.

Although Sesshū did not found a school, he did inspire the work of many young artists of his time. Shūgetsu, who studied under him around 1490 and then undertook a journey to China in 1496, came under the influence of the Chinese painters of the Ming period and made use of ink and colors.[56] The painter-monk Sesson Shūkei (1504–1589),[57] who lived in the province of northern Japan, bore a great devotion to Sesshū and sought to imitate the style of the great master. A highly talented painter himself, Sesson mastered both the *shin* and the *sō* styles. His work, "Boat on a Windy Sea," is among the masterpieces of Japanese ink painting.[58] He stands as the last of the great Zen ink painters of the Muromachi period.

Toward the end of the epoch, although genuine Zen painting still had its devotees, decorative painting came to attract more of the popular attention. In this regard, the Kanō family, famous for its many artists, excelled.[59] Kanō Masanobu (1434–1530), who was the first of the family to become director of the Academy of Art in Shōkoku-ji, bore some affinity to Zen. His paintings, however, show a clear preference for secular tastes. His son Motonobu (1476–1559) painted with both ink and light colors. In his paintings he came close to the *yamato-e* and ended up blending into the Tosa school. The further development of painting during the Muromachi period illustrates the growing secularization of Japanese culture. The temples, which as potent spiritual centers of inner renewal had a refined and religiously inspired culture radiated throughout the nation, degenerated and stagnated spiritually. Only during the Edo period, after a long period of dormancy, was Zen ink painting brought back to life. The outstanding figures at the time were Hakuin Ekaku (1685–1768) and Sengai Gibon (1751–1837).

THE SPREAD OF TEA CULTURE

In this closing chapter on the influence of Zen on the culture of the Muromachi period, we have studied the arts up to the point where, as a new epoch dawned, they adapted to new currents and underwent a profound transformation. During this transitional period, the second half of the sixteenth century, tea culture[60] reached its highpoint. After attaining the heights of its development under Sen no Rikyū, tea culture continued to flourish well into the Edo period.

Originally an integral part of monastic life in Zen temples, tea culture loosened its monastic bonds and began to bring a Zen influence to the bourgeois social classes that were forming as medieval feudalism dissolved. Besides giving birth to a new social structure, this period of transition also saw the first contacts between Japan and Europe and between Far Eastern spirituality and Christianity. Though fundamentally informed by the aesthetic of the transitional period, tea culture entered the modern period without any essential changes; this enabled it to spread broadly throughout the country and to occupy to this day a unique place in Japanese cultural history.

CHANOYU

Many a non-participating observer has marveled at the sense of close community that forms among practitioners of Zen meditation who have spent a week of silently sitting next to each other. At the end of a practice period (sesshin) everyone feels the bonds of friendship and continues long afterward to speak of their Zen friends, with whom, actually, they had very little direct exchange. No doubt, they mean and feel what they say. The tea ceremony, with its silent ritual, works in much the same way and creates deeps bonds of community. "Tea friends" (in Japanese, chajin, "tea people") who come together to perform this detailed and highly ritualized ceremony and who sip the green, aromatic drink from individually made tea bowls, find themselves linked by solemn yet happy bonds. Although the stillness of a Zen monastery dominates the simple, meticulously clean tea room, the solitude is mixed with the sense of being together with like-minded friends.

Okakura, in his classic The Book of Tea, which at the beginning of this century first made known this form of Asian spirituality to the West, states that the tea ceremony is "a cult founded on the adoration of the beautiful among the sordid facts of everyday existence."[61] The Zen master and philosopher Hisamatsu Shin'ichi calls the "way of tea" a "unique, integrated, Zen cultural expression" and sees it as "the creation of Japanese layman's Zen."[62]

Descriptions of the tea ceremony explain all the necessary utensils: the portable table (daisu), the water kettle (kama), the water pot (mizusashi), the tea can (ha-ire), the tea spoon (chashaku), the tea cloth (chakin), the ladle (hishaku), and the center of everything—the tea bowl (chawan). We have already described the tea garden (roji); the tea room can be a separate space in a house (kakoi) or a straw-covered hut (sukiya). The ideal space is a room the size of four-and-a-half mats. Because of its ceremonial character, the entire ritual has been called in the West the tea ceremony—a word that, unlike the term cult, does not really express devotion. While Zen itself stresses the identity of the sacred and the profane, in the tea ceremony one encounters not the sacred but a spirituality in the midst of what is radically profane.

A number of internal characteristics of the chanoyu should be mentioned.

The tea master is the host who greets his invited guests (always five) individually, shows them to their places, and then serves them. The master prepares the tea separately for each guest, pours it into a previously designated cup, and then slides the cup over the straw mat so that the guest, who has just tasted some sweet rice cake, can take it in both hands and, slurping lightly, drink the tea in three swallows. The host follows this same procedure for the next guest, and in this silent, extended, slow-moving ceremony, all the guests drink their tea. Breaking the atmosphere of silence, the host then begins a conversation that has for its object the teacup, the other utensils, and perhaps the paintings, the calligraphy, or the flower arrangement that decorate the tea room. Nothing from the outside is admitted into this select circle, for it is strictly forbidden "to discuss worldly matters either inside or in front of the tea room."[63] This Zen-like spiritual-aesthetic atmosphere, nourished by both silence and words, con-stitutes the essence of chanoyu.

THE JAPANESE TEA MASTER

Tea was known in Japan already during the Nara period, but it was during the Heian period that tea-drinking became widespread among the nobility and monks. After this rather fashionable flourishing, the custom fell out of use until Eisai brought Zen and tea seeds to Japan, encouraged the planting of tea, and explained all the health benefits that tea drinking could bring. During the four-teenth century, the enjoyment of tea once again flourished; tea societies were formed among the nobility and a competitive game (mono-awase) popular during the Heian period took on new life as a tea contest (tōcha). These forerunners of the tea ceremony developed within a social context, and when combined with festive meals and baths, often sank to the level of debauchery. In contrast to such corruptions, chanoyu arose during the fifteenth century; its inspiration was the spirit of Zen.

The first two names associated with these beginnings were Nōami (1397–1471) and Murata Jukō (1423–1502). An artist in the service of the shōgun Ashikaga Yoshinori, Nōami made the first real contributions to the development of the tea ceremony. He moved the tea room from the elegant, usually two-storied tea pavilion (chatei) to a residence done in shoin-zukuri style and made use of the portable table (daisu) and simple tea utensils that were also used in the Zen temple. Because of him the tea ceremony came to occupy an important place in the shōgun's court; beginning with Ashikaga Yoshimasa the tea ceremony became the focus of social life. An expert in Chinese art, Nōami was the curator of the shōgun's art collection, which he catalogued and described in the Kundaikan sōchōki. Nōami's son, Geiami, was less gifted than his father and died at a rel-atively early age. It remained to Nōami's grandson Sōami to carry on the work; he published a second edition of the Kundaikan souchōki in 1511. It appears that the highly artistic Sōami was closely tied to his grandfather and made significant contributions to the development of tea culture. One of Nōami's disciples, Ki-tamuki Dōchin, maintained close relations to the famous tea masters Jōō and Sen no Rikyū.

Murata Shukō, the founder of Zen's art of tea, came from Nara. The son of a Buddhist priest, he entered the local Shōmyō-ji monastery at an early age but returned to the world when he was twenty-four and lived for a long time with a merchant family who gave him the name Murata. In Nara he made the acquaintance of Nōami, who had fled to this rural provincial town to escape the bustle of the capital. His relationship with the famous master became the decisive factor in his decision to undertake a trip to Kyoto, where he became the disciple of the renowned Zen master Ikkyū Sōjun. Ikkyū taught him to appreciate both Zen meditation and the way of the arts and enabled him to understand the bonds between Zen and tea. Through Sōami, the master found access to the shōgun Yoshimasa, whose good graces he soon won through his services and even more so through his artistic talents.

Yoshimasa built a painter's hermitage called Shukō-an, where, in quiet solitude, the master devoted himself to the art of tea. Adorning the hermitage was the calligraphy of the famous Chinese Zen master Yüan-wu K'o-ch'in (1063–1135), which Ikkyū had given him instead of a seal of enlightenment. From that time, tea masters have taken delight in decorating their tea rooms with calligraphy hangings (bokuseki). In his self-sought solitude, Shukō came to realize something that became an enduring dictum: "Zen and tea have the same taste" (zen-cha ichi-mi). Carefully studying the Chinese literature on tea, he then sought to adapt it to Japanese ways. While Dōgen had incorporated Chinese directives for tea drinking among monks into his rule, Eihei shingi, Shukō was intent on working out a synthesis between Chinese tradition and Japanese lifestyle. He is said to be the first to have listed the four principles of the way of tea—harmony (Jpn., wa), reverence (kei), purity (sei), and tranquillity (jaku)—which became the pillars of the fully formed culture of tea. He inspired a large number of followers to take up the art of tea.

Takeno Jōō (1502–1558), the second great Japanese tea master, came from a merchant family of the port city of Sakai near Osaka. His father, a leather dealer, rejoiced in his son's poetic inclinations. First he studied poetry with Sanjōnishi Sanetaka (1455–1537), then chanoyu with two of Shukō's pupils, Jūshiya Sōgo and Sōchin. Jōō brought to fruition the more popular concerns that Shukō had initiated, and chanoyu soon became the favorite artistic pursuit of all ages and walks of life. The performances of the tea ceremony that Jōō conducted and in which he gave special attention to appropriate, artistic utensils, were highly regarded and attracted many. Sakai became a gathering place for devoted students of tea culture. Through his fine and clearly defined tastes, Jōō contributed greatly to the development of chanoyu and helped make it part of popular culture.

Sen no Rikyū (also called Sōeki Rikyū, 1521–1591), Japan's greatest tea master and one of its eminent artistic figures, also came from Sakai. His father, a fishmonger, introduced his son to the circle of the city's tea devotees. Rikyū first studied with Nōami's disciple Kitamuki Dōchin from the Higashiyama school, who eventually sent him to Jōō. Thanks to these early experiences Rikyū was able to join the elegant, noble style of the Higashiyama with the more common, bourgeois tastes of the tea circles of Sakai—a union that raised both styles to higher levels.

Rikyū's ideal was to be as simple and natural as possible. So he was not satisfied with moving the tea room from the pavilion to an ordinary residence (the *shoin-zukuri* style). For him, the ideal place for *chanoyu* was a peasant's straw hut (*sōan*) or a hermit's hut. Among those practicing the art of tea there should be no social classes. To make this clear he did away with the special entrance for dignitaries (*kinjin-guchi*) and required all guests to bend down and enter, almost on their knees, through the lower door (*nijiri-guchi*). This is how he understood the spirit of *wabi*, that extreme form of need or poverty—a virtue that, as the poet Rilke notes, glows from within. In his simple setting in the provincial city of Sakai, Rikyū devoted himself wholeheartedly to *chanoyu* and brought it to the heights of its development.

Rikyū was well into middle-age when the military commander Oda Nobunaga (1534–1582), a lover of the tea-ceremony, called him and other tea masters to Kyoto. After Nobunaga's death, his successor Toyotomi Hideyoshi (1536–1598) appointed Rikyū to be both his tea master and eventually his counselor, and bestowed many other honors on the master. It was the zenith of Rikyū's life. That a tea master of such humble origins could, through his artistic achievements, ascend to a position of such national influence was not only an extraordinary event but a clear indication of the aesthetic sensitivities of the Japanese and of the great value that they attributed to art, especially to the art of tea. As Fujiwara Teika (1162–1241) once set the tone for poetry during the Heian period, so did Sen no Rikyū become the recognized arbiter for all questions of good taste in the tea ceremony. The general esteem that he enjoyed, however, also brought him political influence that eventually was to spell his undoing.

One of the most memorable events of Rikyū's time at the court was the invitation of the military dictator Hideyoshi, an event that brought together nearly eight hundred tea devotees from all social classes at Kitano near Kyoto in the autumn of 1587. Because of an insurrection in Higo (Kyūshū), the ceremonies had to be prematurely terminated. But the triumphal gathering was also darkened in another way. Hideyoshi, who considered himself somewhat of an expert in *chanoyu*, felt that Sen no Rikyū, his great tea master, had upstaged him. The dictator's displeasure hung over the gathering like an evil spirit. Would there be unhappy consequences?[64]

Sen no Rikyū's tragic end came in less than three years. Much has been written about the causes of his undoing. Japanese historians give different reasons for the growing rift between the two men, whose personalities were quite incompatible to begin with. Hideyoshi preferred splendor, as evidenced by his intense building projects, especially his Momoyama Palace.[65] Besides the clear differences in their tastes regarding the tea ceremony, there were also various expressions of rivalry, for example, when Sen no Rikyū had a wooden statue of himself set up on the upper level of the entrance gate of Daitoku-ji. Had the statue not been removed immediately, Hideyoshi would have been required to pass under the statue of his subject when visiting the temple. Such circumstances, however, do not explain Hideyoshi's command that Sen no Rikyū commit ritual suicide. The tea master was no doubt involved in many of the political intrigues of those days. The reason for his sudden demise is probably to be sought in simply an unlucky constellation of political events.[66] To this day, no one has come up with a coherent explanation. On February 28, 1591, Sen no Rikyū called together his tea-friends to perform *chanoyu* for the last time. He left behind two farewell poems, in Chinese and in Japanese, both of which make use of Buddhism to express his readiness to depart.

His sudden death was a hard blow for tea devotees (*chajin*) in the capital, but his numerous students from all social classes committed themselves to carrying on Sen no Rikyū's style of tea culture. Among those followers there were a number of talented men from his native Sakai who are well known in the literature of tea. We may mention for example Nambō Sōkei, the author of the *Nambōroku*, and Yamanoue Sōji (1544–1590), whose pupils edited the work *Yamanoue Sōji-ki*. Tsuda Sōkyū (d. 1591), also from Sakai, had participated in the great tea assembly at Kitano. For a number of different reasons which we shall examine below, it is significant that among the so-called "seven wise men of Rikyū"—noblemen who formed the inner circle of Rikyū's friends[67]—five were Christians. To the present day, the Rikyū style of the tea ceremony is practiced in Kyoto (Omote-senke and Ura-senke).

THE CHRISTIAN DAIMYŌ AND THE WAY OF TEA

The flowering of the way of tea during the Eiroku (1558–1570), Genki (1570–1573), and Tenshō (1573–1592) periods coincided with the early stages of Christian missionary efforts in Japan. So far we have traced the development of the Zen arts from Japan's medieval period to this time of transition that prepared for the modern age. The encounter of Japan with the West and with Christianity, one of the significant elements in the beginnings of the modern age, will occupy us in the following chapter. But since the art of tea belongs to the medieval Zen arts, it seems fitting here to look into the attitudes of the early Japanese Christians toward Japan's tea culture. Here the historical interweaving of events assumes a particular importance.

In Japanese history books, the period we are here dealing with is the time of civil war known as the "period of the warring states" (*sengoku jidai*).[68] For the people, it was a time of widespread confusion and great need. The darkness began to recede somewhat with the appearance of the mighty military leaders Oda Nobunaga and Toyotomi Hideyoshi, both of whom were declared devotees of the art of tea. Many of the early Japanese Christians also learned the way of tea. On the guest lists of many tea societies of the time we find not a few names of Christians, who were happy to carry out the wishes of their missionaries that they adapt to local customs.

Much more than a local custom, the way of tea touches the very soul of Japan. We can glean some idea of how these early Christians experienced and understood the way of tea from the detailed description of *chanoyu* in the writings of the Portugese priest João Rodrigues (1561–1633).[69] As one of the foremost scholars of his works states:

For not only does he he reveal an unrivaled knowledge of the Japanese way of life, but he also shows himself at his most fascinating when, alone among the European observers of his time, he delves into Oriental aesthetic values and canons of taste, displaying a mastery that has astonished modern Japanese readers.[70]

Very much at home in the atmosphere of the tea centers of Kyoto and Sakai, Rodrigues grasped the religious background of the tea ceremony and found in its meaning and values an extension of the religious ideals of Zen into the secular, artistic world. The following lengthy passage from his book enables us to appreciate his deep understanding, the nuances of his evaluations, and some of the unavoidable difficulties of comprehension:

> This art of *suki*, then, is a kind of solitary religion instituted by those who were supreme therein to encourage good customs and moderation in everything concerning the devotees of this art. This is in imitation of the solitary philosophers of the *Zenshū* sect who swell in their retreats in the wilderness. Their vocation is not to philosophize with the help of books and treatises written by illustrious masters and philosophers as do the members of the other sects of the Indian gymnosophists. Instead, they give themselves up to contemplating the things of nature, despising and abandoning worldly things; they mortify their passions by certain enigmatic and figurative meditations and considerations which guide them on their way at the beginning. Thus, from what they see in things themselves they attain by their own efforts to a knowledge of the First Cause; their soul and intellect put aside everything evil and imperfect until they reach the natural perfection and being of the First Cause.
>
> So the vocation of these philosophers is not to content or dispute with another with arguments, but they leave everything to the contemplation of each one so that by himself he may attain the goal by using these principles, and thus they do not teach disciples. So those belonging to this sect are of a resolute and determined character, without any slackness, indolence, mediocrity, or effeminacy. As regards the care of their own persons, they do without a great number of things that they regard as superfluous and unnecessary. They believe that the chief thing in keeping with a hermitage is frugality and moderation, with much quietness, peace of mind, and exterior modesty, or, to describe it better, complete hypocrisy, after the fashion of the Stoics who maintained that perfect men neither felt nor had any passions.
>
> . . . Although they imitate the *Zenshū* sect in this art, they do not practice any superstition, cult, or special ceremony related to religion; for they have taken none of this from the sect, but imitate it merely as regards its eremitical seclusion and withdrawal from all dealings in social matters, its resolution and alertness of mind in everything, and its lack of tepidity, sluggishness, softness, and effeminacy . . .[71]

Rodrigues blends many particulars into this overall picture. He praises purity, simplicity, interpersonal harmony, naturalness—all of which are attitudes taken from the four basic principles of the way of tea and that together make up that human quality that distinguishes the tea ceremony in its original rustic form. He writes: "Everything artificial, refined, and pretty must be avoided, for anything not made according to nature causes tedium and boredom in the long run."[72] From Rodrigues' exposition, which contains precise names of places and persons, it is clear that he was well acquainted with members of the tea circles of his day. He makes special mention of Takayama Ukon (d. 1615),[73] one of Rikyū's seven wise men and a Christian daimyō who, though not the most powerful of the princely friends of tea, exercised a strong influence within Rikyū's tea circle. Personally attractive and well educated, he numbers among the prominent personalities of his time. He enjoyed the favor of Hideyoshi and held the important fief of Takatsuki, in the heartland of Japan between Kyoto and Osaka. In their letters, the missionaries spoke of him with lavish praise. One letter ends with the following words:

> Justus Ukondono (the name they gave him) is a rare phenomenon. He increases daily in virtue and the perfection of life . . . His life makes such an impression on the unbelievers that they generally love and esteem him. Hideyoshi likewise speaks often of him and says that no one else can equal his attainments. He loves and esteems him greatly, and counts him among his closest confidants and protégés.[74]

By combining the military (bu) and the cultural (bun) Takayama Ukon embodied the Japanese ideal of knighthood. He was a multifaceted artist, mastering the various forms of Japanese poetry—the song (waka), the linked verse (renga), and the epigram (haiku). Above all, he was distinguished in the art of tea. Rikyū valued him more than any of his pupils, especially for his strength of character. Sent by Hideyoshi, Rikyū sought to convince him to renounce his new religion, but Ukon placed his faith above tea and power. His friendship with Rikyū survived his fall from Hideyoshi's grace. Later, in times of difficulty, he sought out his beloved tea master in secrecy, and was kindly received by him.[75] Ukon reached the height of his artistry in the years of his exile. In Kanazawa he became the center of a circle of tea friends, to which belonged also the powerful prince Maeda Toshie and his son, Toshinaga. The spirit of the art of tea—characterized by the qualities of harmony, reverence, purity, and tranquillity—found in Ukon its Christian transfiguration.

Among the other Christian lords in Rikyū's tea circle, Gamō Ujisato (1557–1596), a famous commander and favorite of Hideyoshi from the old nobility, was the most prominent. In addition to the tea ceremony, he was well versed in the composition of poetry and in garden design. He had studied Buddhism and Confucianism at the Zuiryū-ji temple, a Zen center in Gifu, and was later won to the Christian faith by Ukon.

The three remaining Christians among the "seven wise men"—Oda Yūraku (or Urakusai), Seta Kamon, and Shibayama Kenmotsu—are not as well known as the others and enjoy a more limited fame in the history of tea. Oda Yūraku (1547–1621), a younger brother of Oda Nobunaga, was baptized during his tea studies with Sen no Rikyū. He wrote his Christian name, Juan, in Chinese characters, which were read *Jōan* in Japanese and which he used to name the tea room that he founded. Seta Kamon was rather unique in his practice of the way of tea and attracted much attention because of his out-of-the-ordinary tastes in the utensils used in the tea ceremony. About Shibayama Kenmotsu not much more is known than that he was of the court nobility.[76]

The most influential personality among the nobles who became pupils of Sen no Rikyū was Hosokawa Sansai, who is better known by his princely name, Hosokawa Tadaoki (1564–1645). His family has given a series of illustrious names to Japanese history. His father, Fujitaka, who was also known under the pen name of Yūsai, was renowned as both poet and warrior. His school of poetics, which was the transitional bridge to the modern age, had as its most illustrious pupil a Christian named Peter Kinoshita Katsutoshi (or Chōshōshi, 1570–1650). Tadaoki was deeply attached to Ukon and often engaged him in long conversations about the new religion. Through Ukon's influence, his high-minded wife, Gracia, became a Christian. A Zen Buddhist and highly gifted, she had many objections that first had to be answered before she was baptized in a secret rite. In loyalty to his house, Tadaoki cultivated the virtues of the knight and the artist. He himself never became a Christian. After the early and tragic death of his heroic wife, he bequeathed rich gifts to the church of Osaka and himself partook in the liturgy of Christian burial.

The name of Araki Murashige (d. 1585), the daimyō of Settsu, occupies an unclear place in the given list of the "seven wise men." Because of his traitorous conniving and the enmity he bore toward Takayama Ukon, he really did not fit into the circle, but his early death, before that of Sen no Rikyū, surrounded this figure with some uncertainty. After Sen no Rikyū's death, the leading position in the circle of his disciples went to his best pupil, Furuta Oribe (1544–1615), a knight who had a lower social ranking than the daimyō but a high reputation in tea circles. Oribe later founded his own school (Oribe-ryū), which departed from the school of Rikyū, and went on to play an important role in tea ceramics. Because of his connections with the Toyotomi clan, he was obliged to commit suicide in 1615 under the rule of the Tokugawa.

The presence of so many Christian tea masters and pupils among the followers of the classical way of tea presents us with a fascinating picture that should not be overlooked. In a unique way it brings together a number of different factors. Under the great tea masters Murata Shukō, Takeno Jōō, and Sen no Rikyū, *chanoyu* reached the epitome of its development. Inspired by the spirit of Zen, these three masters, together with the artists from the Ami family, were Zen Buddhist laymen who pursued their own inclinations without the restrictions of monastic rules and so enabled the way of tea to develop in full freedom. This period of growth lasted for some decades; during ensuing centuries, however, it lost its creative energy and, on the profane level, eventually sank to a form of cultural conversation. The Christians who took up the way of tea, however, were dealing with the classical core of the art of tea that had been developed by religiously minded lay persons. This explains both the Christians' spontaneous enthusiasm for this highly significant phenomenon—the spiritual value of which took strong hold of them—as well as their unencumbered participation in the tea ceremony. The history of Japanese culture owes the most detailed and reliable description of classical *chanoyu* to the sympathetic pen of the Portuguese missionary and tea devotee, João Rodrigues.

TEA CERAMICS

In order to bring the experience of Zen into everyday life, the art of tea draws one closer to the everyday things of life. This accounts for its affinities with pottery and explains why tea masters attribute great importance to ceramics. Among the objects of the ceremony, the tea bowl, which is a work of ceramic art par excellence, is the heart of the art of tea. This is not to deny the importance of the other objects used in the ceremony. The bearing of the tea masters as they prepare the tea illustrates clearly their inner rapport with the objects that are so readily and helpfully at hand. In the aesthetics of tea one can see a certain parallel to social relations among humans. Dietrich Seckel presents an engaging description of the relation between the tea utensils and the social phenomenon of *chanoyu*. Every object (tea canister, tea bowl, water pot, and so forth) is made individually, never mass-produced. As "individuals" or "personalities," therefore, the objects are often given names. With other utensils, which are also considered to be "personalities," they form a group (namely a whole assembly of functionally related utensils) and encounter each other harmoniously on the same level, as is the case with the *chajin*. [77]

Originally a form of popular handicraft, tea ceramics developed as tea drinking grew in popularity. Zen masters, among them Dōgen, showed an early and lively interest in the utensils of tea drinking. Dōgen's potter accompanied him to China, where he stayed for six years before he returned to Japan and set up a kiln in Seto. Though the art of tea ceramics went on to enjoy some limited success, it was not before the middle of the sixteenth century, in connection with the ritual of *chanoyu*, that it really began to flourish. Japanese tea masters placed great value on the development of the art of Japanese pottery, while they also had high regard for the earlier and abundant forms of Chinese ceramics.

Although Shukō, the first of the great Japanese tea masters, had in his possession a precious piece of Chinese ceramics in the Temmoku (Chin., T'ienmu) style from the Sung period, he recommended that for the tea ceremony Japanese pottery from Bizen (in the prefecture of Okayama), Ise (Mie), and Shigaraki (Shiga) be used. [78] Jōō (d. 1558) made the same recommendations, reserving his preferences for the Temmoku cups of Seto that, under Chinese influence, were produced with great artistry in Mino (Gifu) and represent the first glazed ware of truly native origin. [79] The Japanese tea masters often went back to the older works from Seto and from earlier ovens, [80] finding in their utter simplicity a way of approaching the ideals of *wabi*.

Sen no Rikyū met an artist named Chōjirō (1512–1592), probably Korean, in Kyoto and with his help brought Japanese tea ceramics to the apex of its development. Chōjirō was able to meet the great tea master's wishes for simple, monochromatic bowls that would show both breadth and depth. The artist created the Raku-ware that represents the most illustrious achievements of Japanese ceramics during the Muromachi period.

During his campaign in Korea in 1592 and 1593, Hideyoshi observed the work of the famous Korean ceramists and later arranged for the settlement of Korean potters in Japan. The center of Korean ceramics in Japan was Karatsu, on the island of Kyūshū.

Many different styles of tea ceramics developed during the seventeenth century. The splendid green-glazed bowls of the Oribe style can be traced back to Furuta Oribe, the first disciple of Sen no Rikyū, who himself turned out to be a rather unconventional master. Owing much of his artistic accomplishments to his master, Oribe could not, however, maintain the high level of spiritual inspiration in the master's art of tea. The reason seems to be that he was not able to match his master's discipline and depth in Zen experience. Unfortunately, there is not space within the modest scope of this volume to pursue all the movements and accomplished artists in tea ceramics of this period. But we must at least mention the name of the leading tea master and universal artist, Kobori Enshū, whose greatest claim to fame was the masterful design of the Katsura villa. Although the arts, in their different forms, produced many other noteworthy creations, there was a drastic decline during the seventeenth century. Spreading secularization did not leave sufficient room for religiously rooted creative energies. In what follows we shall speak about individual representatives of other art forms.

RELATED ARTS

Certainly, Zen art is far from representative of the whole of Japan's great artistic achievements. At the same time, since the Muromachi period, Zen aesthetics have penetrated broad areas of Japanese culture. Noh, (Jpn. nō), which embraces all areas of Japanese art, was also influenced by Zen. Thomas Immoos offers an excellent description of Noh from its origins to its present-day enactment on the stage:

> Japan's classical drama was born from the cultic dance. In early times, the gods or ancestral spirits, in whose honor and before whose temple or grave the celebration took place, revealed themselves in the shaman who was marked out from the community by mask and costume. For this reason, the structure of most Noh dramas reaches its high point in the dance. The story preceding the drama serves mainly to set up the dramatic context in which the dance can be performed and the powerful manifestation of the gods can take place.
>
> In the interplay of word, music, and dance there takes shape a total work of art that enchants the senses and moves the soul with deep emotions such as marvel at the great deeds and virtues of the heroes, distress over the impermanence of all that is earthly, and reverence before the manifestation of divine powers. The events of the nation's myths and history

pass imposingly before one's eyes. The divine appears as something utterly near to the human, as the spirit of trees, rivers, mountains—as heavenly beings who nourish familiarity with the earth.[81]

This description does not contradict the conclusion that Immoos draws a few lines later: "The Noh drama originated in the fourteenth century through a constellation of foreign influences working in conjunction with primitive Japanese dramatic traditions."[82] The real originators of Noh were Kan'ami (1333–1384) and his son Zeami (1363–1443), who at the time of the Ashikaga shogunate took the *sangaku* ("music for distraction") and *sarugaku* ("monkey music")— popular peasant plays and mythical dances—and developed them into the highly refined dramatic art form of the Noh. Older elements, including Shinto dances, were preserved but were blended with the refined and sober *yūgen* style that derived from Zen. For this reason Hisamatsu Shin'ichi can speak of Noh as an "aspect of Zen Culture." He illustrates the "Zen roots" that he finds in Noh by a comparison between the slow, solemn entrance of the hero of the Noh play and the famous ink painting "Śākyamuni Returning from the Mountains."[83]

Zeami Motokiyo stands as the dominant figure in the art of Noh. As actor, director, and poet he was the delight of large audiences. Although the plays written by him are fewer than had been previously thought, his engaging compositions belong to the best of Noh poetry. Just as significant are his treatises on how to perform Noh drama and on its underlying aesthetic theory. All his writings reflect a Zen aesthetic sensitivity that he had acquired under the direction of the Ashikaga shōgun Yoshimitsu. Well versed in Zen, he loved austere gestures, innuendos, symbolism, as well as sudden surprises. Noh dramas contains little external action; rather, they look inward and bring passion and feeling to the surface only in subdued tones. From Zen, Zeami had learned that the deepest and most intimate movements of the human spirit are beyond words. Although Western audiences do not have easy access to such a different world of theater, they are fascinated by this manner of gently implying unspoken and unspeakable feelings.

An original, powerful creation of the Japanese spirit, Noh theater has enjoyed—although not always in a pure and elevated form—a steady popularity that has endured up to modern times.

Like Noh theater, the Japanese art of flower arrangement[84] cannot, strictly speaking, be called a Zen art. But just as the Noh dances were rooted in indigenous, archaic customs, so the art of flower arrangement reaches back to the flower offerings that the early Japanese (like most early cultures) customarily offered to their gods. During the seventh century, flower offering was a general practice in Japanese Buddhism, especially among the devotees of Amida, who loved to use flowers as a reminder of the Paradise in the West. During the Heian period, flower contests formed part of the widespread *awase*.

But flower-arrangement as an art first developed during the fourteenth century, promoted mainly by the nature and art lover, the shōgun Ashikaga Yoshimitsu. Already in the early *rikka* (or *tatebana*, "standing flowers") style, a cosmic content is evident in the sense that in arranging flowers one feels oneself part of the cosmos. The artistic experts and counselors of the Ashikaga shōguns—especially Nōami, Geiami, and Sōami—were all well acquainted with the art of flower arrangement. For the most famous flower master of those days, Ikenobō Sen'ō (1483–1543), nothing was more important that to effect an arrangement that would best enable the beauty of the flowers to be felt.

Differing from such highly artistic endeavors, the tea master Sen no Rikyū created a form of flower arrangement that was closer to the naturalness and simplicity of the *wabi* style. A chosen branch of blossoms, placed in a simple ceramic or bamboo vase in a recess in the wall (*tokonoma*), were sufficient as a floral decoration. Two branches could also be used, but without trying to achieve an artistic arrangement. This new approach was called the *nage-ire* ("thrown flowers") style or *cha-bana* ("tea flowers"). Flowers in a tea room were not supposed to look different from flowers outside in nature. Later, tastes returned to a single-colored *rikka* style (*isshiki rikka*). This relation to the way of tea allowed for Zen aesthetics to influence the art of flower arrangement. The close bonds between tea and *ikebana* lasted up to the end of the seventeenth century. A real art of the people, *ikebana* continued to develop along a variety of paths and today is a common part of women's education.

As we have tried to show, during the second half of the middle ages in Japan a profound and wide-ranging Zen culture developed; in many instances, its artistic expressions were called "ways" (Jpn., *dō*).[85] In East Asia, the word *way* has a broad conotation that is correspondingly difficult to understand. Art and culture are, to some extent, "ways." The "ways" crisscross in political and social life. The metaphysical searchings of the mind, together with the religious-mystical experiences of the heart, lead to the original way, to the Tao, the basis and goal of all ways.

If the word *way* opens upon immeasurable horizons, we have to keep the rich variety of its meanings in mind when we apply it to the area of art, for there too we can find no definition that will cover the whole. Depending on the area that one is considering, the word *way* will take on different nuances. In many cases, the Zen arts can be called "ways" because they give convincing and moving expression to Zen itself. And they become more genuine ways as they creatively touch the core of Zen ever anew. So the areas that we have studied—architecture, garden design, calligraphy, painting—we can call "ways" mainly because of their power of artistic expression.

In the case of the way of tea, another factor comes into play. This art form, which touches the deepest part of the person, awakens in the "tea person" the form of the way of tea, which is neither a simple expression of the way of tea nor a searching for the way of tea; it is, rather, the ideal embodiment of the essence of the way of tea.

Certainly the element of seeking, of reaching for a higher level of perfection, has to be found in every human art. And yet the intention to strive for a goal, which is clearly felt in the word "way," is played down in the Zen forms of art that we have been looking at. To understand the Zen arts as ways to attain enlightenment misses their essential point. The attempt to regard all the nuances contained or implied in the word "way," together with the word's unavoidable surplus of meaning, would more likely lead to a deeper understanding of the Zen realization contained in each art form.

This chapter requires some justification. Does not the whole realm of art go beyond the manageable scope of a study of religious history? Or does the history of Japanese Zen Buddhism present us with an exceptional situation? A comparison with Chinese Zen would provide a first clue to answering these questions and shed greater light on the love of beauty that is so evident in the tradition and history of the Japanese people. Soon after Zen was implanted in Japan, it was the element of beauty in Zen that became decisively important for the Japanese. This early development reached its epitome during the Muromachi period. But any study of Zen needs to bear in mind all the changes and readjustments that took place in this thoroughly Buddhist school. In addition, the special quality of aesthetic sensitivity that was nourished by Mahāyāna and especially by Zen must be considered.

The rich and broad variety of artistic achievements of the Zen movement required that our presentation in this chapter be limited. But a simple enumeration of Zen's different artistic expressions would not have sufficed. Given the impossibility of a complete treatment of this topic, I decided to focus on individual expressions of the originality and power of Zen art. The reader is left with the task of using the references to the rich, sometimes superb, literature on the subject in order to follows one's own interests and explore this area more amply. If these pages seemed to play down the religious element, it was only so that the chapter could better make its fitting and modest contribution to the overall development of this volume. Such a reduction of Zen to "profane" life is really part of the essence of Zen, in which saṃsāra and nirvāṇa are "not two."

In any case, the broad cultural influence of Zen on the different levels of Japan's population merits special attention. The Zen school in China, despite its syncretistic mixing with other forms of Buddhist religiosity, was not able to attain a similar level of popularity. That Japanese Zen Buddhism has continued to maintain such popular roots remains an important phenomenon for historians of religion.

NOTES

1. J. W. Hall, *Japan: From Prehistory to Modern Times*, p. 113.

2. See R. A. B. Ponsonby-Fane, *Kyoto: The Old Capital of Japan*, p. 155.

3. See T. Hoover, *Zen Culture* (London, 1978), pp. 75ff, 131–45; cf. JH, 746–47.

4. Martin Collcutt treats the Five Mountains in China at several places in his book, *Five Mountains: The Rinzai Zen Monastic Institution in Medieval Japan*. Collcutt is particularly concerned with the transmission of the ground plans of the temples, pp. 172–82. See the list of the five Chinese mountains in Mochizuki, *Bukkyō daijiten*, vol. 2, pp. 1182–83; *Zengaku daijiten* I, p. 340.

5.   See Collcutt, *Five Mountains*, p. 175.

6.   *Five Mountains*, pp. 173–74.

7.   On the following, see *Five Mountains*, pp. 177–78.

8.   The drawings the follow are, as in the earlier edition of my *The History of Zen*, based on those of H. Yokoyama, "Zenshū no schichidō garan," ZB 2.4 (1956): 40–45. The number seven, according to many explanations, represents the completeness of a temple complex.

9.   See Collcutt, *Five Mountains*, pp. 177, 179; for the photographs of the ground plans of T'ien-t'ung-shan and Kenchō-ji, see pp. 176 and 179.

10.   According to the presentation of Ponsonby-Fane (*Kyoto*, p. 153), the *sammon* of Tōfuku-ji stems apparently from the Muromachi period and tradition dates it in the Katei era (1235–1238). In 1585 it collapsed, but was immediately rebuilt by Hideyoshi. From the Katei era only the *yokushitsu* and *tōsu* are available. The Zen hall was erected during the Kenchō era (1249–1256), and the sūtra storehouse during the Tenju era (1375–1381). During the Tokugawa period the buildings were submitted to a basic restoration.

11.   The *yokushitsu* and *tōsu* survive to this day. Some of the buildings of Tōfuku-ji burned down in a fire in 1907.

12.   See JH, p. 747. Hoover refers to the room as a "meditation chapel," *Zen Culture*, p. 76.

13.   On the Chinese *karayō* style, see JH, p. 745.

14.   Hoover, *Die Kultur des Zen*, p. 86.

15.   The work of construction shows the start of the *shoin* style, named after the study room, whose design can be found in JH, p. 751.

16.   Cited in Collcutt, *Five Mountains*, p. 214.

17.   Among the wealth of literature on Japanese Zen art, deserving of mention in the first place is Shin'ichi Hisamatsu's *Zen and the Fine Arts*. The book contains not only an excellent selection of illustrations from various cultural realms (painting, calligraphy, gardening, tea ceremony) and descriptive art tables, but also a metaphysically anchored introduction to Zen art and Zen aesthetics. In a general vein we may mention Hugo Munsterberg, *Zen-Kunst*, and also the English books of the same author, *Zen and Oriental Art*, *The Art of Japan: An Illustrated History* (Tokyo, 1957), and *Dictionary of Chinese and Japanese Art*; Dietrich Seckel, *The Art of Buddhism* and *Buddhistische Kunst Ostasiens*; Thomas Hoover, *Zen Culture*; Otto Kümmel, *Die Kunst Ostasiens*; Curt Glaser, *Die Kunst Ostasiens*. An overview can be found in a chapter entitled "Das Gesicht des Künstlers" in Hans Schwalbe, *Acht Gesichter Japans im Spiegel der Gegenwart*. Besides numerous Japanese publications, the theme of the Zen garden is treated especially in Masao Hayakawa, *The Garden Art of Japan*; Samuel Newsom, *A Thousand Years of Japanese Gardens*; Irmtraud Schaarschmidt-Richter, *Der japanische Garten*; Tsuyoshi Tamura, *Art of the Landscape Garden in Japan*; Loraine E. Kuck, *One Hundred Years of Kyoto Gardens*; and David H. Engel, *Japanese Gardens for Today*. See also Thomas Immoos and Erwin Halpern, *Japan: Tempel, Gärten und Paläste*. See the entries in JH and KWJ. Much material on gardens, painting, and the tea ceremony is also offered in *Zen at Daitokuji*, ed. by Jon Covell and Yamada Sōbin. See also *Pageant of Japanese Art*, vol. 6, *Architecture and Gardens*.

18.   On the text of the *Sakuteiki*, see JH, p. 775. *Sansui* (mountains and waters) are, as Seckel stresses, "not arbitrarily chosen to represent the whole of nature, but symbolize

the two basic powers of world and life according to the ancient Chinese Taoist notions of *yang* and *yin* . . ." (*Buddhistische Kunst Ostasiens*, p. 268, note 171).

19. Hoover, *Zen Culture*, p. 99.

20. See Hayakawa, *The Garden Art of Japan*, p. 69, and plate 59 on the same page.

21. Langdon Warner, *The Enduring Art of Japan*, p. 96. Warner shows in his profound and sensible details on the Japanese garden their "high philosophical truths."

22. The attribution of the work to Murata Shukō is, as Hayakawa sees it (*The Garden Art of Japan*, p. 92), uncertain. Hayakawa describes the garden that he found at the eastern side of the abbot's lodgings (pp. 92ff) and offers an impressive reproduction (plate 39). The dating of the gardens is in many cases not reliable. Only rarely can we rule out the existence of later modifications.

23. On the gardens in Jōei-ji, see *The Garden Art of Japan*, pp. 76, 85. Sesshū is said to have designed some ten gardens, but that they are his original work is in no case certain. The garden in Jōei-ji (a lawn around a pond beset with impressive stones) is well maintained; see the reproduction in plates 37 and 63.

24. Compare the relevant literature on the art of the Zen garden (note 17). Tamura offers the model of a tea garden (*Art of the Landscape Garden in Japan*, p. 58), which he then describes, and also the reproduction of the Myōki-an garden (plate 19), whose creation is attributed to Sen no Rikyū. Munsterberg presents four plates of famous tea gardens, two from Kohō-an in Daitoku-ji, the reproduction of a tea garden of the provincial city of Matsue, and a plate of the famous tea house of Shōkin-tei in the Katsura villa in Kyoto, with the garden path leading up to it (*Zen-Kunst*, pp. 44–47, 123–26).

25. See the impressive collection of photographs entitled *Katsura*, text by Akira Naitō, photography by Takechi Nishikawa (Tokyo, 1977); see also *Imperial Gardens of Japan*, text by Teiji Itoh and photography by Takeji Iwamiya.

26. On the following see also Lothar Ledderrose, *Mi·Fu and the Classical Tradition of Chinese Calligraphy*.

27. See the articles on calligraphy by R. Goepper (JH, pp. 788–794) and the art of writing by Irmtraud Schaarschmidt-Richter (KWZ, pp. 395–400). See also Yujiro Nakata, *The Art of Japanese Calligraphy*; Ōmori Sōgen and Terayama Katsujō, *Tesshū to shodō*; and Terayama Tanchū (or Katsujō), *Hitsu zendō*.

28. Cf. Hisamatsu, *Zen and the Fine Arts*, p. 23.

29. Certain Japanese emperors were excellent calligraphers; see JH, p. 790.

30. On current linguistic usage in Japan, I have Prof. Terayama to thank for his valuable assistance.

31. *Buddhistische Kunst Ostasiens*, p. 158.

32. *Buddhistische Kunst Ostasiens*, p. 250.

33. *Buddhistische Kunst Ostasiens*, p. 251.

34. *Buddhistische Kunst Ostasiens*, p. 252.

35. *Buddhistische Kunst Ostasiens*, p. 242.

36. *Buddhistische Kunst Ostasiens*, p. 252.

37. Cf. JH, pp. 790, 839.

38. See the listing of literature in vol. 1 of the present work, chap. 13, note 66, and the above mentioned detailed works of Hisamatsu Shin'ichi and Hugo Munsterberg (note 17), as well as vol. 2 of *Pageant of Japanese Art* and Hiroshi Kanazawa, *Japanese Ink Painting: Early Zen Masterpieces*.

39.   For a reproduction, see plate 20 in Y. Awakawa, *Zen Painting*.

40.   See the reproduction in Kanazawa, *Japanese Ink Painting*, table 30, p. 61; a somewhat different version of Han-shan is given in Awakawa, *Zen Painting*, table 19. There is some uncertainy concerning the identity of the painter Kaō, on which see Awakawa, p. 177, and Kanazawa, p. 148.

41.   See the citations from H. Brinker, *Die zen-buddhistische Bildnismalerei in China und Japan von den Anfängen bis zum Ende des 16. Jahrhunderts*, in vol. 1 of the present work, chap. 13, note 84ff.

42.   Reproduction in Brinker, *Die zen-buddhistische Bildnismalerei in China und Japan*, plate 55. Cf. the description and evaluation of the picture on p. 123.

43.   *Die zen-buddhistische Bildnismalerei in China und Japan*, plate 111. On Mutō Shūi and his work, see pp. 34–35.

44.   *Die zen-buddhistische Bildnismalerei in China und Japan*, plates 115 and 116. An anonymous picture (plate 113) represents the master five years earlier seated in the abbot's seat in a half-lotus position. On Bokkei, see pp. 37ff.

45.   A portrait sketch is included in Brinker, *Die zen-buddhistische Bildnismalerei in China und Japan*, plate 7, the reproduction on plate 121, and commentary on pp. 39 and 174–75.

46.   *Die zen-buddhistische Bildnismalerei in China und Japan*, p. 175.

47.   In addition to the portrait of Shōichi Kokushi, "of particular importance are the pictures of the 500 Rakan by Minchō" (Seckel, *Buddhistische Kunst Ostasiens*, p. 237).

48.   Plate 28 in Awakawa, *Zen Painting*. Cf. Munsterberg, *Zen and Oriental Art*, pp. 78–79; Hoover, *Zen Culture*, p. 124.

49.   See the reproduction in D. T. Suzuki, *Zen and Japanese Culture* (New York, 1959), plate V after p. 168.

50.   Munsterberg, *Dictionary of Chinese and Japanese Art*, p. 259.

51.   Kümmel, *Die Kunst Ostasiens*, p. 43.

52.   Plate 40 in Awakawa, *Zen Painting*; Munsterberg, *Zen and Oriental Art*, plate 19, p. 81; Seckel, *Buddhistische Kunst Ostasiens*, plate 35 in the appendix.

53.   Sesshū's self portraits are characteristic, even though they are available only in copies, two of which appear in Brinker, *Die zen-buddhistische Bildnismalerei in China und Japan*, plates 20 and 21; see the explanation on pp. 80–81.

54.   A reproduction of the winter landscape is to be found in Hoover, *Zen Culture*, p. 127.

55.   Awakawa, *Zen Painting*, plate 41; Munsterberg, *Zen and Oriental Art*, plate 20, p. 82; Hoover, *Zen Culture*, p. 129.

56.   Munsterberg finds "little of the spiritual quality associated with the greatest masters of Japanese *suiboku*" in Shūgetsu. See *Dictionary of Chinese and Japanese Art*, p. 275. Cf. Brinker, *Die zen-buddhistische Bildnismalerei in China und Japan*, pp. 198–99.

57.   See the brief biography in Awakawa, *Zen Painting*, p. 180; Munsterberg, *Dictionary of Chinese and Japanese Art*, p. 259.

58.   In Awakawa, *Zen Painting*, plate 42.

59.   The Kanō became the official painters of the shōgun; see Hoover, *Die Kultur des Zen*, p. 138; JH, p. 841; KWJ, p. 262.

60.   The majority of the works so far on Japanese art contained also sections on the tea ceremony. Kakuzo Okakura's famous *The Book of Tea* appeared in 1906. Horst Hammitzsch

published Chadō—Der Teeweg: Eine Einführung in den Geist der japanischen Lehre vom Tee. D. T. Suzuki devoted two chapters of his book Zen and Japanese Culture to the tea ceremony. See also Rand Castile, The Way of Tea; Tatsusaburo Hayashiya, Masao Nakamura, and Seizo Hayashiya, Japanese Arts and the Tea Ceremony, as well as the article on the tea ceremony in JH and KWJ. See vol. 8 of the collected works of Furuta Shōkin, Zencha no sekai. On Sen no Rikyū see the comprehensive work by Origuchi Sutemi, Rikyū no cha, vol. 7 of his collected works.

61. Okakura, The Book of Tea, p. 3.

62. Zen and the Fine Arts, p. 25.

63. One of the seven tea rules of Rikyū, cited in Hammitzsch, Chadō—Der Teeweg, p. 100.

64. The presentation follows the work referred to earlier, Japanese Arts and the Tea Ceremony, p. 30. Bersihand describes the event completely differently in his Geschichte Japans, p. 220; similarly, G. B. Sansom offers another account in Japan: A Short Cultural History, p. 438. Japanese authors are to be preferred here. The number of visitors is placed at around eight hundred.

65. On the architectural accomplishments of Hideyoshi, see Bersihand, Geschichte Japans, pp. 218–19; Sansom, pp. 436–37.

66. On the involvements of Sen no Rikyū in the political arena, see Beatrice M. Bodart, "Tea and Counsel: The Political Role of Sen Rikyū," MN 32.1 (1977): 49–74.

67. Kataoka Yakichi refers to the chajin daikeifu and gives the following seven names: Oda Yūraku (or Urakusai), Hosokawa Sansai, Gamō Hida, Araki Settsu, Seta Kamon, Shibayama Kenmotsu, Takayama Ukon. See Johannes Laures, Takayama Ukon und die Anfänge der Kirche in Japan, p. 48.

68. The period of time stretches from about the Ōnin War (1467–1477) until the middle of the sixteenth century.

69. The Portugese manuscript of his work on Japanese culture in two books has been translated and edited by Michael Cooper as This Island of Japan. The four chapters on the chanoyu were translated into Spanish by J. L. Alvarez-Taladriz as Arte del cha. See the comprehensive work by Michael Cooper, Rodrigues the Interpreter: An Early Jesuit in Japan and China.

70. Cooper, Rodrigues the Interpreter, p. 309.

71. Cooper, This Island of Japan, pp. 272–73.

72. Cooper, This Island of Japan, p. 285.

73. On Takayama Ukon, see Laures, Takayama Ukon und die Anfänge der Kirche in Japan; Diego Pacheco, "Fate of a Christian Daimyō," Great Historical Figures of Japan, pp. 174–83.

74. Cited in Laures, Takayama Ukon und die Anfänge der Kirche in Japan, pp. 177–78. The words with which the great Japanese Buddhist scholar Masaharu Anesaki praises Takayama Ukon show the high esteem in which he holds him. Anesaki writes: "The stories of Justo Takayama Ukon's life illustrate a happy union of the valor of a Japanese warrior and the fidelity of an ardent Catholic. His brilliant military achievements, his moral integrity and deliberateness in critical moments, his dauntless spirit combined with meek soul, his earnest zeal in piety expressed in his generosity and charity, all this should be noted as a fruit of Kirishitan missions." History of Japanese Religions, p. 243, note.

75. See Laures, Takayama Ukon und die Anfänge der Kirche in Japan, p. 310; cf. Kataoka Yakichi, "Takayama Ukon, MN 1 (1938): 451–64.

76. Nishimura Tei has written extensively on Christians belonging to the tea circle in his *Kirishitan to chadō*. On Gamō Ujisato, see p. 159; on Seta Kamon, pp. 136–37; on Shibayama Kenmotsu, p. 95.

77. "Soziale und religiöse Aspekte der japanischen Teekeramik," NOAG 126 (1979): 24. Seckel returns to touch on this theme frequently in his comments; see especially pp. 26, 31. He speaks of the history of tea utensils on pp. 27–28. On Japanese ceramics see especially *Japanese Arts and the Tea Ceremony*; JH, pp. 798–99; and KWJ, pp. 200–203.

78. *Japanese Arts and the Tea Ceremony*, p. 54.

79. Hoover, *Zen Culture*, p. 190.

80. Seto has the first of the "six old ovens" (*rikkoyō*); the five others are in Tokoname, Echizen, Shigaraki, Takikui, and Imbe; see JH, p. 798.

81. *Japan, Tempel, Gärten, und Paläste*, p. 78; on Noh drama, see Thomas Immoos and Fred Mayer, *Japanisches Theater*, and the relevant entries in JH and KWJ.

82. *Japan, Tempel, Gärten, und Paläste*, p. 78.

83. See Hisamatsu, *Zen and the Fine Arts*, pp. 100, 101. Donald Keene comments in his essay on Zeami: "I doubt that Japanese poetry can be more powerful. Zeami ranks as one of the greatest Japanese poets as well as the greatest dramatist and the greatest critic of the theatre." *Some Japanese Portraits*, p. 42.

84. In addition to the entries in JH and KWJ, see Hoover, *Zen Culture*, pp. 213–18. The Zen-related art of the *haiku* will be treated later in connection with the great Japanese poet of the Edo period Matsuo Bashō (1644–1694).

85. See Horst Hammitzsch, "Zum Begriff 'Weg' im Rahmen der japanischen Künste," NOAG 82 (1957).

The Zen Movement during the Modern Period

7

The Beginnings of Japan's Modern Period

Japan's modern period may be said to have begun with the coming to power of the Tokugawa, which took place either in 1600, when the decisive battle of Sekigahara was fought, or in 1603, when Ieyasu was officially installed in the office of shōgun. These are the dates given by historians concerned with political events. For students of religion and of the history of ideas, things are not so simple. For them, Japan's modern period is rooted in a total process of secularization that swept the country during the second half of the sixteenth century. A number of dates from this period stand out: 1560 or 1568, two eventful years in the career of Lord Oda Nobunaga (1534–1582), whose leading role in the nation's unification was confirmed in 1573 with the abdication of Yoshiaki, the last of the Ashikaga shōguns;[1] or again, one or two decades earlier, when the first Europeans arrived in Japan, the Portuguese merchants in 1543 and Francis Xavier in 1549.

Without having to fix a particular year, we can say that Japan entered the modern period around the middle of the sixteenth century. The "period of the warring states" (sengoku jidai), which began with the turmoil of the Ōnin War (1467–1477), had led to the definitive collapse of the Ashikaga shogunate. The central government was not toppled by a revolution; indeed, it continued to exist, at least in name. But during the sengoku period a radical decentralization took place, partitioning the entire country into numerous regions ruled over, for the most part, by feudal lords. These sengoku-daimyō, who were either descendants of old noble families or generals who had gained power through the constantly recurring wars, ruled over large and small regions with virtually unlimited authority. On the one hand, this partitioning of the land was certainly a sign of political and social degeneration. But on the other, it became the occasion for a national renewal. Whether through decisions made on the battlefield or through treaties and alliances, the number of the warring daimyō began to decrease. The sengoku jidai led to the period of the three great "ones": Oda Nobunaga, Toyotomi Hideyoshi (1536–1598), and Tokugawa Ieyasu (1542–1616).

THE PERIODS OF AZUCHI (1568–1582)
AND MOMOYAMA (1582–1600)[2]

One after the other, these three men led the nation toward a new secular order. They had two main concerns: the political concern with bringing about national unity, and the intellectual and cultural concern with fostering a process of secularization. Both interests flowed together in the concrete events of the times and created a whole new context for Buddhism. In the midst of rapidly growing secularization, Japanese Buddhism lost the leading role it had played during the medieval period. Gone was the age when government circles, both imperial and military, recognized the spiritual authority of Buddhism and demonstrated their loyalty to the Buddhist clergy by granting special honors; gone was the age when the people, with unquestioning faith, sought their welfare and salvation in the numerous Buddhist or variously amalgamated Shinto and Buddhist temples scattered throughout the land. Despite the tensions and rivalries among the various Buddhist schools, Buddhists abbots had held positions of high authority and shared great political power as counselors and admonitors for whomever happened to be in the ruling office. The old schools of Tendai and Shingon, even though they suffered terrible losses in spiritual prestige and witnessed the continuing corruption of their monks, remained influential and respected institutions well into the fifteenth century. Because of its extremely beneficial relationships with the Ashikaga shōguns, the Rinzai school of Zen had become almost a state religion. All of this changed after the Ōnin War, when weak descendants of the Ashikaga clan, while still bearing the title of shōgun, did not have the wherewithal to exercise their office properly. Blow by blow, Buddhism suffered painful losses and watched as its position of prominence slipped away. Only the Zen school was able to maintain its special place, as we shall see. Naturally, all of this was not without its impact on the common people; Buddhism became primarily a popular religion, without any claims of spiritual leadership or of significant influence among the educated classes.

This general decline of Buddhism during the *sengoku* period was completed under Oda Nobunaga, who, from the middle of the sixteenth century, carried out a ruthless and determined drive to strip Buddhism of the power it had enjoyed up to that time. During this period, too, the highly secularized temples had at their disposition various forms of military might that, like the feudal lords, they mustered for bloody battle. Resolved finally to crush the Buddhist power that for so long had been a thorn in his side, Nobunaga conducted well-planned attacks on Buddhist centers of influence as he went about his campaigns against insubordinate feudal lords. His harshest decree against the Buddhists came in 1571, when he issued orders to burn down all the Tendai temples on Mount Hiei. The fires raged for days; some three thousand buildings went up in flames and thousands of monks lost their lives. The situation was not quite as bad on Mount Kōya, headquarters of the Shingon school, where the monks submitted after some limited encounters but without bloodshed. Only the Shingon temple of Negorō-ji in the district of Kii (present-day Wakayama prefecture) stubbornly resisted and in 1585 was set in flames by Hideyoshi. Groups of resistant Amida devotees called *ikkōshū* were scattered throughout the country and cost the emperor prolonged and heavy battles. Nobunaga had to destroy their support bases in the provinces before he could make an effective move against the bastions and trenches of their headquarters at Ishiyama in Osaka. The siege lasted more than ten years before the monks submitted to a compromise. The monastic buildings were burned down and the group's headquarters moved temporarily to

Nakajima in Settsu. Finally, the community of Amidists reassembled at the completed Hongan-ji complex in Kyoto, which since the seventeenth century has served as the center of the Amida movement.[3]

Nobunaga carried out what proved to be the most significant military measures against the Buddhists. By force and by treaty he surrounded himself with a considerable number of feudal lords throughout the provinces. The new times were symbolized by Nobunaga's Azuchi Castle on Lake Biwa, constructed between 1576 and 1579. Built on rock, the castle was surrounded by stone walls and was fitted out with a citadel armed with firepower and ready for war. Before Nobunaga himself could make use of it, he was murdered by his traitorous general Akechi Mitsuhide (1526–1582).

With Buddhist political power effectively broken, Nobunaga's successor, Hideyoshi, could steer a milder course. The temples on Mount Hiei were rebuilt, and Hideyoshi gave the Amida faithful land in Kyoto for the construction of the Hongan-ji complex. A few hard battles had still to be fought against powerful daimyō in the provinces before Hideyoshi could consolidate his centralized control over the entire country. But with his new title of imperial ruler (kampaku), he was the nation's recognized head. A lover of pomp and festivity, Hideyoshi began construction on Osaka Castle in 1583 (completed only some three years later) and the splendid castles of Jurakudai in Kyoto (1586) and Momoyama ("Palace of Peach Mountain") in Fushimi (1594). The nation had finally recovered from the devastation of the sengoku period. Once again the arts flourished. During Hideyoshi's reign the important achievements of Momoyama culture were able to take place.

In this context, we can again focus our attention on the Zen school. While even Nobunaga granted special favors to Zen, Hideyoshi found himself indebted to Zen in his efforts to raise the cultural level of the country. In the previous chapter I made frequent mention of the art of the Momoyama period. Even though Zen had lost all political influence at this time, it made important and constructive contributions to the artistic and educational development of the new epoch. The Zen arts that had flourished during the Japanese middle ages were, in general, highly regarded and continued to influence further developments well into the modern period; to some extent these influences persist to the present day. In treating the Five Mountains we also spoke of the efforts of the Zen monks to promote study and popular education. The movement of the Five Mountains, the last part of which was dominated by a swing toward secularization, contributed greatly to the spread of Chinese learning throughout the country. Upon returning from China in 1473, Keian Genju (1427–1508), a later representative of the gozan movement, accepted an invitation from the Shimazu lords to come to Satsuma (Kagoshima) and lecture on the Neo-Confucian philosophy of Chu Hsi.[4] As part of these efforts, Genju also established a school (Satsuma gakuha) where monks and laity together could deepen their appreciation of Chinese philosophy. The esteemed Shimazu Nisshinsai (1492–1568) belonged to this school.[5] Similar efforts were carried in other provinces. Among the most notable of them was the Ashikaga Gakkō, which was run by Zen monks somewhat like a modern high school and exercised widespread influence. During the Momoyama period Chinese learning again became popular, thanks mainly to Hideyoshi and his determination to promote popular education. The Neo-Confucian worldview came to dominate attitudes during the Tokugawa period. From their temples, the Zen monks also worked to promote education; indeed, their temple schools, as well as those of other Buddhist communities and similar private institutions, became the forerunners of the later elementary schools. It comes as no surprise, therefore, that when the Europeans came in the sixteenth century, they should have been struck by Japan's high general level of education.[6]

That Zen was the only Buddhist school that at the beginning of the modern period had not lost its good standing in Japanese society was due mainly to its clear contributions to the promotion of the arts and sciences. True, the religious content of the Zen spirit of the great Chinese masters of the T'ang and Sung periods had undergone no small loss in the process of its widespread secularization. We have already pointed out the need for a carefully balanced assessment of this process.[7] The deeply human element of Zen made an adaptation to changing times possible. Perhaps we may even find in Zen itself a subtle forecast of the modern period.

THE FIRST ENCOUNTERS BETWEEN ZEN AND CHRISTIANITY

Zen's first encounter with Europeans and their reaction to the event is more than a matter of mere historical interest. The brief period of Christian evangelization in Japan, from the middle of the sixteenth to the early seventeenth century, provides us with a wealth of useful material for supplementing our knowledge of Zen. The European missionaries recognized in Zen the most significant school of Japanese Buddhism, unrivaled in vitality and influence. As religious persons who had made the proclamation of the Christian message their life goal, the missionaries manifested great interest in the religions they encountered in Japan. At the same time they were the children of their age, which, despite the Renaissance and humanism, was still a long ways from the spirit of tolerance. "The sixteenth century in Europe was the belligerent age of advancing conquistadores, the age of religious wars and religious intolerance."[8] In particular the sons of the Iberian peninsula, which supplied the majority of the missionaries to Japan, were little inclined to compromise themselves by recognizing other religions. In spite of this, however, we are indebted to them for various impartial descriptions of the wisdom and virtue of Buddhism, especially of several distinguished Zen masters.

Two circumstances seriously impaired the encounter between Zen and Christianity at the dawn of the modern period. In the first place, as the Muromachi period drew to a close, Zen found itself in a largely secularized setting. Not only was the religious element stifled by the cultural and artistic elements, but as a result of the unremitting political and social confusion, monastic life in many temples had been corrupted by spiritual laxity and moral degeneracy.[9]

On the other hand, the brief period of undisturbed evangelization provided little opportunity for Christianity to come to full development. Our knowledge of the deeper penetration of Christianity into Japanese culture at that time is limited. The chief historical sources for the period are the detailed letters and reports of the missionaries. The Japanese counterperspective is scarcely available.

FRIENDLY AND HOSTILE CONTACTS

On 5 November, 1549, Francis Xavier wrote in his first long letter from Japan to his brethren in Goa:

> I have spoken often with some of the most learned monks, especially with one who is held in high esteem here by everyone, as much for his knowledge, conduct, and dignity, as for his great age of eighty years. His name is Ninshitsu, which in Japanese means "heart of truth." He is among them as a bishop, and if he measured up to his name he would be blessed. In the many conversations I had with him, I found him doubtful and uncertain as to whether our soul is immortal or whether it perishes with the body. Sometimes he would say "Yes," but again, he would say "No." I fear that the other learned monks are like him. But it is a marvel how good a friend this Ninshitsu is to me.[10]

Ninshitsu, who was abbot of the Zen temple Fukushō-ji, founded in Kagoshima in 1394, was one of the most highly esteemed men of the city. His intimate friendship with the first Christian missionary to Japan testifies as much to his sincerity as to the candor and humanity of his friend. The disciples of Ninshitsu related many details of this friendship after his death. In a stroll through the temple grounds the two friends came across monks seated in meditation. Deeply impressed by the modesty, the concentration, and the repose they displayed, Xavier asked the abbot, "What are these monks doing?" The abbot laughed and said, "Some are calculating the contributions received from their followers during the past months. Others are thinking about how they might get better clothing and personal care. Still others are thinking of vacation and pastimes. In short, no one is thinking of anything important."[11] On another occasion, Xavier asked his Buddhist friend,

> "Which period in life do you regard as better, youth or the old age in which you now find yourself?" After a moment's reflection, Ninshitsu replied, "Youth." When questioned as to the reason for this preference, he answered that then the body is still free from sickness and infirmity, and one still has the liberty to do what one desires. To this the Father replied, "If you see a ship which has sailed out of harbor and must of necessity, therefore, enter another, at what point would the passengers experience the greater happiness: when they are still in mid-ocean and exposed to wind, waves, and storm, or when they approach the harbor and already cross the bar, there to rest from past shipwreck and storm?" Thereupon Ninshitsu said, "Father, I understand full well. Of course, I know that the view of the

harbor is more pleasing to those who have begun to enter it. But since it is not yet clear to me, and I have not yet decided which is the better harbor, I do not know where or how I should put to shore."[12]

The metaphorical language of Xavier is a good approximation of the Buddhist style. Quite effortlessly the great apostle found his way into the heart of his Oriental friend.[13]

With Francis Xavier, Ōtomo Yoshishige (also Sōrin, 1530–1587), the daimyō of Bungo (Ōita prefecture)—next to Takayama Ukon, the most important of the Japanese Christians of the sixteenth century—took the first steps in his ten-year journey toward the Christian faith. Yoshishige's meeting with this holy man, who was as imposing as he was loving, became the most decisive event in his life. An expert in the art of tea and a collector of exquisite tea utensils, Yoshishige was also a religious person and sincere seeker after the truth; for a while he had been taken by worldly honors and the pleasures of the senses, but found no lasting satisfaction in these things. In addition to his concerns about the government, it was mainly his attachment to Zen that kept him from becoming a Christian. Until he reached certainty from his own experience, he could not make up his mind. For this reason he summoned a famous Zen master to his new residence in Usuki where he had a splendid temple built. Under the direction of this master he committed himself zealously to Zen practice and urged that his son Chikaie enter a Buddhist monastery. The young prince, however, had no intention of becoming a monk. Showing his strong character, which was a frequent cause of grief to his father, he became interested in the new padres and began his study of Christian doctrine; eventually, with the approval and presence of his father, he was baptized. Shortly afterward, in 1578, Yoshishige also reached a decision and became a Christian. In their letters, the missionaries described these dramatic events at the court of Bungo, which were also recorded in the Japanese chronicles of the Ōtomo clan.[14]

Ninshitsu was not the only Zen monk with whom Xavier made intimate acquaintance during his brief stay in Japan from 1549 to 1551. The missionaries whom he left behind in Japan as heirs of his spirit and work followed his example and sought friendly contacts with Buddhist monks. The abbot of the Zen monastery of Nanrin-ji, a disciple of Ninshitsu, befriended Brother Almeida, but because of his high position could not bring himself to an open profession of the Christian faith.[15] It was otherwise with a monk at Daitoku-ji:

He was an old man, almost eighty years of age who, because of his age and uncouth manners, lived alone in a house in Miyako. He was of a generous nature and inclined to works of charity and compassion. Arriving at the simple house [of Father Vilela] he began asking the usual questions that most people ask out of sheer curiosity. . . . After the Father had replied to his inquiries, he in turn asked the old man whether he would like to hear something of the law that he preached. The old man answered laughingly that he already knew the things of salvation and only wished to hear of the strange things in India and Europe. . . . And since he took pity on the Father, he returned the next day and brought a small gift of food, attractively and well prepared. While he was in the house they closed the door since the boys in the street persisted in mischievous pranks and threw stones at him. The Father expressed his gratitude and then immediately spoke to his guest of God, the rational soul, and of eternal life. In this way [the old monk's] interest was awakened and he began to listen. Our message aroused in him the greatest admiration and amazement, and since he listened further to our preaching, the good old man received holy baptism and was given thereby the name of Fabio Meison . . .

This upright and amiable old man pitied the Father, whom he saw drinking cold wine out of a silver cup at the early morning Mass. He therefore offered to send him a clean teakettle with a small copper stove. This, he said, "will serve him on the altar, both to keep his hands warm and to warm the wine that he has to drink. For to drink cold wine in the morning would certainly harm his health."[16]

It caused a great sensation in the capital when the Zen master Kesshu, whose enlightenment had been confirmed by two outstanding authorities of his school, was converted. The verses he composed on his enlightenment are as follows:

Ah, dry tree, who hath planted thee?
Whose beginning is nothing and shall return to nothing.
My heart possesses neither being nor non-being.
It neither comes nor goes nor subsists.

This monk, too, first came to the missionary's house out of mere curiosity. Yet soon he listened "with great interest and great satisfaction to the preaching. Finally he became a Christian and a very good one at that."[17]

Yengennan, an eminent monk from the Zen temple of Kennin-ji, showed himself to be an unselfish benefactor. He freely offered to obtain an audience with the shōgun for Father Vilela, and then protected him on the way from the impudent tricks of the street boys and showed him into the palace. As they went along, "the monk who . . . was well known throughout the city suffered more than the priest, since he could not calm the disturbance made by the rabble as they saw them pass." Later he was again helpful in arranging a second visit with the shōgun to obtain permission for them to preach in the city.[18]

The history of the Christian mission reports numerous other meetings with Buddhist monks, among whom there were certainly a number of Zen monks. Often mere politeness or curiosity incited such visits, while in other instances there was also the desire for an exchange of opinions and intellectual broadening. In all cases these friendly contacts bore good fruits, and despite darkening clouds that already foretold the coming storm, the mission visitator Valignano recommended polite and amiable association with the Buddhist monks.[19] From the early days of the mission, however, friction and enmity began to arise. In his first letter from Kagoshima, Francis Xavier speaks already of the possibility of persecution. In Kyoto monks often came in the guise of courtiers to probe into the life and teachings of the missionaries. The enmity heightened in time, and when overly zealous adherents on both sides began setting one another's churches and temples to the torch, the period of friendly accord came to an end. Still, even during the time of persecution, there were good relations between individual missionaries or Christian believers and Zen disciples.

DOCTRINAL DISPUTES

Francis Xavier regarded Japanese people as "the best that we have yet discovered,"[20] and was especially appreciative of the intellectual abilities of the Japanese. He writes that they have "a very sharp mind and respond to reason,"[21] and had a similar high opinion of their "universities." Even someone like Father Cosme de Torres, a man "distinguished in talent and knowledge,"[22] he did not regard competent to partake in the disputations to be held at the universities. Instead, he appealed to Ignatius of Loyola to send "well-experienced men" personally approved by the General Superior of the Jesuit order.[23] Xavier left Father de Torres in charge of the work that he had begun in Yamaguchi. For his part, Torres also praised the reasoning power of the Japanese. His own unshakable confidence in the power of reason was surpassed only by his patience and zeal. Day and night he received visitors eager to learn and disputed with them about religious matters. "Ever since Father Master Francis arrived in this city, which is now more than five months ago, there has never been a day in which from early morning until deep into the night there have not been priests and Laity here to ask all sorts of questions . . ."[24] Detailed reports on these disputations in Yamaguchi give a picture of vigorous intellectual exchange.[25]

In these encounters with Buddhism the major issues were the existence of a creator God and an immortal soul. Zen adherents denied the existence of the soul with particular vigor and thus became known among the missionaries as those who deny the soul. Torres found various approaches to the question among them:

> Some claim that there is no soul, so that when a person dies, everything dies. For they hold that that which is created out of nothing returns to nothing . . . But there are others who say that the soul has always existed, and that when the body dies, just as the four elements return to their original state, so too does the soul return to the condition that it had before it animated a body. There are still others who say that after the death of a body, the soul in turn inhabits another body. In this fashion souls are perpetually born and die.[26]

The first viewpoint represents the Buddhist denial of the substantial soul. In the second we find, somewhat imprecisely expressed, the basic thesis of Mahāyāna, while in the third case we have the Indian doctrine of rebirth. Schooled as he was in European logic, Father Torres could not harmonize these contradictory notions, but could only conclude that the Zen school had various "species" of doctrines.

In the records of the disputations made by the Spanish Brother Fernández—whose good command of Japanese qualified him to serve as interpreter—questions and answers of all sorts are mentioned. All the fundamental problems of religion come up for discussions: the existence and attributes of God, the immortality of the soul, the difference between humans and animals, the presence of evil in the world, the existence of the devil, the mercy of God, and redemption. Above all, the missionaries sought "to maintain clearly that there is a principle (principio) that gives to all things their beginning (principio).[27] The adherents of Zen admitted this, but argued that that principle was nothingness:

> After the great Nothingness has entered existence, it can do nothing than to return to that same Nothingness. . . . This is a principle from which all things proceed, whether human beings, animals, or plants. Every created thing contains this principle in itself, and when humans or animals die, the four elements revert into that which they had been at first, and this principle returns to that which it is. . . . This principle is neither good nor evil. It possesses neither bliss nor pain. It neither dies nor lives, so that it is truly a Nothingness.[28]

Father Torres replies by appealing to the person's natural knowledge of God and insists on the moral law revealed in one's conscience. The nihilistic version of Buddhism recurs in all the disputations of Jesuits with Zen disciples after Torres. The Jesuits theologians were not able to grasp the Mahāyāna philosophy, to which they found no counterpart in European thought as they knew it, and which in any case was difficult for them to comprehend in the complexities of the Japanese language. But with their strong emphasis on morality, they were able to bring some decisive arguments.

Out of these on going doctrinal discussions with the representatives of the Buddhists schools, there arose a need to create adequate polemical tools. This was the century in Europe when the catechisms of Canisius and Bellarmine were enjoying widespread success. Nothing was therefore more natural than the development of a catechism especially adapted to Japan, which as a polemical treatise would present Christian teachings in clear and concise language. The visitator Valignano undertook this work with the help of some capable Japanese who were familiar with Buddhist teachings,[29] but the project proved to be extremely difficult. Valignano complains about the multiplicity of various schools and sects which "treat and argue about these matters so obscurely as to be scarcely intelligible in what they say; they change their view constantly."[30] The catechism mentions none of the schools by name, not even Zen, but the basic attitude of Zen is clearly outlined. The philosophical elaborations are restrained and to the point, but when it comes to the Buddhist distinction between appearance and reality, or between external and internal, Valignano becomes indignant. He rejects the objection that simple people cannot grasp the truth and therefore "they must be soothed by such teaching, just as to stop children from crying they are given little flashy gifts which have no value." "It is the part of a man of probity and good judgment to instruct the lowly and the inexperienced and to guide the erring . . ."[31] Evidently Valignano was not able to grasp what is under consideration here—the Buddhist concept of "skillful means" (Skt., *upāya;* Jpn., *hōben*), which he considered to be contrary to one's obligation to recognize the truth. He had no notion at all of the actual reason for using "skillful means," which is rooted in the Buddhist understanding of sympathetic compassion (Skt., *maitrī-karunā;* Jpn., *jihi*) according to which religion out of compassion must adapt its teaching to the hearers' level of understanding.

The Christian missionaries understood the Buddhist Dharma to be a religion of denial and so committed themselves to proving Buddhism, especially Zen, to be false. This effort was greatly helped by the Japanese Jesuit Brother Fabian, who probably spent his early days in a Zen monastery before becoming a Christian at the age of seventeen.[32] When the brother in one of his writings cites the verses

> The true law of the law—no law,
> This law—no law—is nonetheless law . . .[33]

he is touching on one of Zen's paradoxes. And when he then refers to the Buddhist objection that "nothingness, which is revealed in Buddha nature, is empty but real,"[34] he comes close to realizing that the nihilistic interpretation of Buddhism is really not accurate. Yet he is not able to carry on the dialogue in a satisfying way, most likely because he lacked the necessary training. But neither did the European missionaries grasp the relationship between the Mahāyāna metaphysics that Zen had adopted and traditional Christian negative theology. Never did they make mention of the early teaching on the incomprehensibility and ineffability of the divine nature; all they could do was resort to the rational arguments they had imbibed during their time of studies. The missionaries recognized the ascetic practices of the monks and spoke with undisguised admiration of the "great meditations" of the Zen disciples, praising their concentration of mind and perfect body control. But because they did not really examine Zen enlightenment, they could not understand the experiential character of the Zen way; all that was left to them was to attack the Zen worldview with their weapons of logic. It is regrettable that the circumstances of the time did not permit the development of better mutual understanding.

CULTURAL ADAPTATION AND INFLUENCE

However inflexible and uncompromising the Jesuit missionaries may have been in doctrinal matters, they were very open and receptive to Japanese culture. It was not merely that it was to their own missionary advantage to accommodate themselves to indigenous customs, but also that they admired the Japanese genius, which for all its strangeness exerted a strong fascination over them. Here, too, it was Francis Xavier who set the tone. After his return to Japan he related with great enthusiasm to his friends in Goa the extraordinary qualities of this newly discovered people. "In their culture, their social usage, and their mores, they surpass the Spaniards so greatly that one must be ashamed to say so."[35] To his successor in Japan, Father Cosme de Torres, he left instructions that in the way of life, "in clothing, eating, and similar matters . . . nothing is be changed, unless a change would contribute to the greater glory of God."[36] And so was laid the basis for a missionary method of cultural adaptation. After some wrestling within the missionary community and various experiments and consultations with Japanese Christians, Valignano worked out amazingly bold applications of the principle of accommodation.[37] Of greatest importance, however, was the acceptance and full training of Japanese candidates for the Society of Jesus. If these young Asiatic Christians were to feel at home in their new way of life, and if some day they were to make their own important contributions, it would not do to tear them out of the community they felt with their own people. Therefore, the way of life in the colleges and houses of the Society had to be assimilated to Japanese customs. For Valignano, in the execution of this missionary method, the example of Zen temples was to play an important role.

The *Instruction Regarding Customs and Lifestyle in Japan* that Valignano left for his missionaries is a unique example of ingenious cultural adaptation. The European *bateren*—as the Fathers were called—must have seemed as remarkable and strange to the Japanese as the wonderland of Japan did to them. They had not come as travelers or explorers but with the purpose of planting the Christian faith in Japanese hearts and of founding the church in Japan. Everything depended on their establishing the dignity of the Christian church in a country in which many other religions had been hospitably accepted and were fructifying the culture. In their dealings with the Japanese, the missionaries were to do their best to win authority and confidence among their guests. Authority and confidence presuppose adaptation to the Japanese mind, and especially the corresponding integration into Japanese society, in which all forms of social usage are precisely regulated according to social rank. A sharp distinction was made between the secular and religious classes. For the missionaries, adaptation to the customs of the Japanese religious class seemed advisable. Valignano chose the Zen school as his model in ceremonial matters, since this one "was considered at the time to be the most important of all religious communities in Japan and was in touch with all classes of Japanese society."[38] The difficulty in practicing this ceremonial pattern lay in the problem of determining a hierarchy within the missionary staff, with corresponding titles and forms of courtesy. Valignano solved this problem by assigning the missionaries to ranks similar to those in the Zen community. The head of the mission for all Japan became equivalent to the abbot of Nanzen-ji, while the heads of the missionary districts of Shimo, Bungo, and Miyaki were accorded the dignity of the abbot in one of the Five Mountains of Kyoto. The priests became the counterparts of the head of a temple (*chōrō* or *tōdō*). The Japanese brothers, who bore a great deal of the actual work of the mission, were placed on the level of the overseer or guide of *zazen* (*shuza*); novices were on the level of treasurers (*zōsu*); and neophytes and catechists were ranked as tonsured novices (*jisha*) in the Zen school.[39] Through this ingenious and bold arrangement of the visitator, the Christian missionaries attained high standing in Japanese society. Naturally, opposition and criticism against this new order of things were not lacking. The chief opponent among the missionaries to this policy of accommodation was Father Cabral, who was removed by Valignano from his position as head of the mission in Japan. Cabral rightly observed that the post of abbot of the Nanzen-ji and other leading temples in Kyoto were usually held by the sons and brothers of Japanese princes, or by other members of the high nobility, and that these titles were bestowed by the emperor.[40] How successful the ranks set up by Valignano were in practice we do not know, but it seems safe to assume that many modifications and exceptions had to be made.

Other instructions also reveal Valignano's sincere effort to adapt to Japanese claims. In every mission house a tea room was to be set up near the entrance, where tea was to be served in Japanese style. Guests of whatever class were to be received in a manner appropriate to their station, so that all of them might acquire sympathy and esteem for the Christian mission. Indeed, the Jesuits have been accused of addressing themselves too exclusively to the upper classes of old Japan, at the expense of the common people. However this may have been, their impact on the upper classes were extraordinary.[41] Numerous daimyō and members of the high nobility as well as samurai and monks became Christians. At times Christianity was in the forefront. Portuguese dress became stylish in the capital and all things European were admired.

This first encounter between Zen and Christianity at the beginning of the modern period witnessed a number of significant steps toward mutual spiritual understanding. Two aspects of this encounter are especially important. Followers of Zen and tea culture provided the Christian mission with many incentives to refine and interiorize—really to "easternize"—its approach. These incentives were well received, even though the seeds that were thus planted did not find a conducive climate in that harsh century of civil and religious wars, and even though they were to be rooted out in the coming storms of persecution. Moreover, Christianity fostered the awareness of personal spirituality. At the end of the feudalistic middle ages of Japan, younger powers were stirring and were announcing the coming of the modern period.[42] The harsh rule of the Tokugawa not only violently oppressed Christianity, it also delayed the advent of the modern period.

THE EDO PERIOD AND ZEN

The house of Tokugawa, although stemming originally from the Minamoto clan, was an insignificant family of knights of modest means. It owes its rise to power, its splendor, and its might to Ieyasu (1543–1616). Born in the little rural town of Okazaki in Mikawa, Ieyasu had a difficult childhood and an eventful youth before joining up with the then rising fortunes of commander Oda Nobunaga in 1561. After Nobunaga's death, Ieyasu cleverly moderated his allegiance and became a subject of the commander's successor, Toyotomi Hideyoshi, whose power he faithfully helped extend and by whom, as a reward, he was made lord over five provinces. The year 1590 became a turning point in the history of Japan. At the behest of Hideyoshi, Ieyasu was asked to exchange his five provinces for another territory in eastern Japan, which was actually larger than his original property. Without any resistance he complied with this order and soon became the most powerful prince in the Kantō region (eastern Japan). He selected the village of Edo, strategically located in the middle of his domain, as his head-quarters and ordered the construction of the mightiest stronghold of Japan—Edo Castle. In an insignificant fishing village close to the ruined castle built by Ōta Dōkan in 1457 the central government of the Tokugawa period took shape; thanks to a long period of peace, it developed into a populous city. The city of Edo, which during the Meiji period (1868–1912) was renamed Tokyo, was to become the capital of the Japanese empire and one of the major metropolitan centers of the world.

The Edo period (1600–1868), which began with Ieyasu's victory at Seki-gahara in 1600, extended over the Tokugawa shogunate (1603–1867). Rooted deeply in Japan's traditions, Tokugawa rule was to see the initial expansion, step by small step, of Japanese influence into the modern world. It was a time full of contradictions and so has been assessed differently by different historians. Many stress its negative aspects: the hard, oppressive rule of a distrustful gov-ernment that had to have everything under its exact control; the rigid division of society into the four classes: samurai (knights), farmers, workers, and mer-chants; the closing of the nation (sakoku) to all foreign influence, together with the persecution of Christians and the expulsion of almost all foreigners; the baku-han system of national government, which combined strict centralization with local autonomy; a constant flood of all kinds of prescriptions, restrictions, and rules. These negative aspects have contributed to the Tokugawa's reputation of having harmed the nation and harassed the people. Yet careful research into the events of this period has also revealed positive aspects. Indeed, in psycho-logical terms, one might say that it was a time when a better future was incu-bating.

Following the course of events, we can first say that to finally free the country from two hundred years of war and turmoil was indeed something pos-itive. After the victory at Sekigahara it took more than a decade for all the military operations to be completed and for the Tokugawa to secure their dom-inance. The last military operation was the taking of Osaka Castle, which, fol-lowing Hideyoshi's defeat at Sekigahara, had been entrusted to his son Hideyori. Realizing that his fate was sealed, Hideyori, together with his mother, threw himself into the flames and his young son was beheaded. The entire nation now lay tightly in the hands of the shōgun Tokugawa Hidetada (1579–1632), Ieyasu's third son, who took office when his father abdicated only two years after having captured the honors of the shogunate. Ieyasu retired to Sumpu Castle in Shizuoka, where he remained till his death in 1616. To the end he kept well informed of, and often contributed to, the affairs of government and important decisions of state, especially in matters of foreign policy.

The Tokugawa shōguns depended mainly on the strength of their own family clan, which consisted in the first place of their extensive properties (tenryō) as well as of the most important cities and economic centers of the nation; in a broader sense, these resources also included a number of fudai-daimyō—the lords who stood with the Tokugawa from the beginning and who in part had received their fiefs from them—together with the so-called *sanke* ("three houses"), the three Tokugawa lines of Owari, Kii, and Mito (located in Aichi, Wakayama, and Ibaraki prefectures respectively), originating from Ieyasu's three sons. As later history was to show, although these resources guaranteed the dominance of the Tokugawa shōguns, they were also quite vulnerable. A number of powerful *tōzama* ("external") *daimyō*, especially those of Satusma (Kagoshima) and Chōshū (Yamaguchi prefecture), who were constant threats to the Tokugawa throughout the entire period, played a crucial role in the eventual downfall of the regime, favoring the imperial house, which had not surrendered and waited resolutely for a restoration of imperial power.

According to the *baku-han* system of the Tokugawa, the central government (*baku*) embodied in the shōgun exercised its rule together with the local power of the daimyō (*han*). The laws established under Ieyasu in 1615 and contained in the two texts, *Laws for the Samurai (Buke shohatto)* and *Legal Directives for the Imperial Court and Nobility (Kinchū narabi ni kuge shohatto)*, were expanded and sharpened by decrees from the subsequent shōguns Hidetada and his son Iemitsu (1604–1651). There were special laws for Buddhist institutions (*Shoshū jiin hatto*) and for Shinto institutions (*Kannushi hatto*), which were under the supervision of state officials who did not hesitate to intervene in the internal affairs of temples and shrines.[43]

Under government control during the Tokugawa period Buddhism became more rigid and less meaningful, but it did survive.[44] State control, on the other hand, also meant state recognition and support. The government subjected all religious bodies to a new and strictly defined organization and in return required them to contribute to the general welfare, as understood by the state. In compliance with the new religious laws, all temples were registered, all Buddhist schools were organized in association with either main temples (*honji* or *honzan*) or branch temples (*matsuji*), and all families were required to register their names with a specific Buddhist sect.

In the first place, "the organization of sects," many of which remain to this day, was established.[45] As Watanabe Shōkō explains in his overview of the organizational development of Japanese Buddhism, the well-known "six sects" of the Nara period (710–794) were not really sects but different schools devoted to the study of certain doctrinal perspectives. During the Heian period (794–1192), the Tendai school contributed to the formation of sects when it requested imperial recognition for its institution; in so doing Tendai became, together with the Shingon school, which had not made such a request, one of the two normative Buddhist schools of the times. During the Kamakura period the number of distinct and apparently independent Buddhist schools increased. It is well known that Dōgen struggled mightily, if not successfully, against the terms Zen *sects* and Zen *schools*. During the troubled times that followed, Buddhist temples established their independence chiefly through the military means they took to protect themselves from external attack. It was only when all of Buddhism had to submit to the state control of the Tokugawa government and when all Japanese were forced to register at a Buddhist temple that the organization of sects was finalized. "During the Edo period," says Watanabe, "the inertia of custom set in."[46]

The registration of temples and of Buddhist monks from all the different sects, together with the inscription of the faithful into the sects, took place at Nanzen-ji[47] under the direction of the Zen monk Sūden (also called Ishin Sūden, 1569–1633) of Konchi-in, who enjoyed the confidence of the shogūn's government. As abbot of Nanzen-ji since 1605, Sūden was appointed by Ieyasu in 1608 to be the successor of his counselor, the Zen monk Saishō Shōtai (1548–1607), and was given the assignment of supervising all Buddhist institutions and of formulating a decree against Christians. Together with the Tendai monk Tenkai (1536–1643), who served the following shōguns Hidetada and Iemitsu, Sūden was the most influential Buddhist of his time; a man of iron will and of inexhaustible energy, he not only subjected all religious bodies to the authoritarian government but also met with great success in matters of foreign policy and commerce. Even in difficult situations, he remained faithful to the shōgun, who rewarded him generously for his services. Sūden was granted the title of National Teacher (Honkō Kokushi) and invested with the purple robes of honor. Despite the high ranking that made him one of the central personalities of his time, he remains a marginal figure in the history of Zen.

The sharply intensified persecution of Christians was carried out together with the sealing off of the nation to all foreign influence, a policy rigorously imposed during the first half of the Edo period.[48] Despite its isolation, the nation did not succumb to spiritual stagnation. Unquestionably, Buddhism had fallen from its position of prominence and through the brutal measures of Nobunaga been stripped entirely of its political power. The strict controls exercised by the Tokugawa government further restricted the influence of the temples. Buddhism accordingly had to cede the position of intellectual dominance it had enjoyed for centuries to Confucianism, which in its Neo-Confucian form became the prevalent worldview of the Tokugawa period. Confucian scholars were well received throughout the nation, especially in the courts of the shōguns and of rural princes. While Japan's intelligentsia pursued Confucian learning, Confucian ethics penetrated popular religiosity and determined the life-style of Japanese society. This was the epitome of Confucian growth and influence, which was to remain strong well into the twentieth century.

While all Buddhist schools were more or less influenced by Confucianism, Zen developed particularly strong bonds with Confucian thought. It was the Zen monks during the Kamakura and Muromachi periods who brought back to Japan from the mother country of China a large body of Confucian ideas and literature, which the monks then propagated staunchly. The intellectual achievements of the *gozan* were strongly influenced by Confucianism. For a long time, there was such a symbiosis between Zen and Confucianism that anyone interested in pursuing Confucian studies would go to a Zen monastery to study. Hence it was particularly painful for Zen when Confucian scholars at the beginning of the Tokugawa period consciously began to remove Confucianism from the embrace of the Zen school. The Zen monks tried to make up for the loss by carrying on their pursuit of Chinese learning. Clear indication that Confucian values were in no way neglected in Zen monasteries can be found in not a few of the foremost Japanese masters whom we shall be meeting below. Although the Zen monks could no longer be considered the main advocates of Confucianism, they continued to preserve and carry on the Confucian heritage among the common people. The restrictive religious policies of the Tokugawa government could not prevent the Zen monasteries from carrying on their efforts to promote the formation and education of their fellow citizens.

The conservative character of the times also permitted, albeit in restricted manner, the development of the Zen arts and of art forms related to Zen. In any case, the contemporary tastes of the developing bourgeois class was moving in another direction, a direction that, in the course of the Edo period and with the help of creative artists, produced a large number of works of high quality. Decorative prints and wood carvings (ukiyoe), kabuki theater and puppet plays, shamisen music and erotic novels (ukiyo-zōshi, literally "sundry stories of the passing world") exemplify the totally secularized "culture of entertainment" that pervaded society.[49] This does not mean that the sources of tradition dried up. New Zen gardens appeared, ink drawing continued, and in particular, Noh drama and the tea ceremony enjoyed undiminished popularity. The poetic form of the haiku continued its serious yet cheerful, profound yet playful, development. The Japanese innate love of nature returned again and again to Zen, whose bitter but cultivated taste of late summer fruits attracted a loyal following as much as did their meditation.[50]

TAKUAN SŌHŌ

The many-sided personality of Takuan Sōhō (1573–1645)[51] heralds a new lifestyle in Zen. Highly talented and distinguished for academic and practical abilities, Sōhō is the preeminent representative of Rinzai Zen at the beginning of the Edo period. His solid formation in Zen practice and experience did not allow his secular pursuits to distract him from the way of Zen. For him, academic study was a matter of necessity, and this included both Buddhist scriptures and Chinese learning. He turned a critical eye on the Neo-Confucianism that became so popular at the beginning of the Tokugawa government. The Japanese call such figures gakusō ("learned monk" or "monastic scholar"), and that he was, so much so that throughout his life the monastic element to all appearances took second place to scholarship. Most of his time was spent outside the monastery pursuing scholarly and artistic interests. He was as much a monk-poet as a monk-scholar. Hundreds of poems witness to his creative mind. He also performed the tea ceremony and practiced calligraphy and ink painting. In the beauty of his calligraphy (bokuseki) his spiritual qualities, his rustic simplicity, and the fullness of his inner strength found an enduring expression.

Even the course of Takuan's life distinguished him from earlier Zen masters. He seems to have avoided virtually all the usual concerns of a Zen master, including the direction of disciples and spiritual guidance. His free way of life enabled him to make extensive friendships with all sorts of people and to become one of the most influential Zen monks of his time. Aside from his writings, he left no concrete memorial to posterity. In Zen history he is an individual whose light spread broadly.

LIFE

Born of a samurai family in the small town of Izushi in Tajima (in the region of Hyōgo) in the very year that the last of the Ashikaga shōguns retired from the scene, Takuan belonged to a new era. During the modern period, his home town of Izushi did not develop into a large city and even today is little known. When he was child, however, it was the site of a castle that served as the residence of a daimyō. Besides the local shrine, there were a number of Buddhist temples that, while they did not provide advanced learning, did offer some limited opportunities for intellectual and cultural pursuits.

Takuan's family were members of Hōnen's school of Pure Land Buddhism (Jōdoshū). In view of the boy's apparent religious inclinations and his academic talents, it was decided to send him to school at the Jōdo temple of Shōnen-ji. As a child he practiced the *nembutsu* devoutly and, according to tradition, copied Amidist sūtras, which was considered a meritorious work. But he did not remain long in the Amida temple; as circumstances permitted, he moved to the larger Zen temple of Sugyō-ji (also called Sōkyō-ji), which offered better educational opportunities. His teachers were Kisen Seidō, and, after his death in 1591, Tōho Sōchū, a disciple of the famous Daitoku-ji master Shun'oku Sōen (1529–1611); after three years in Sugyō-ji, Sōchū took his promising young disciple with him to Kyoto and entrusted him to the direction of Shun'oku in Daitoku-ji, who in turn introduced him to Zen practice. Historians offer different reasons why Takuan did not attain enlightenment under this eminent teacher. It may have been that either the master or the atmosphere of Daitoku-ji were not suitable. At the time Daitoku-ji was the center of tea culture in Kyoto, a monastery taken up with worldly pursuits and imbued with the secular spirit of the age—not exactly the environment in which one could touch the inner core of Zen.

In Daitoku-ji Takuan had received from his master the monastic name of Sōhō. Now he carried on his travels and went to continue his practice with another master, Ittō Shōteki who was also related to Daitoku-ji and who lived a harsh, rigid Zen life in the hermitage of Yōshun-an, near Nansō-ji in the region of Kai (Yamanashi prefecture). Because he was not immediately accepted as a disciple of Shōteki, however, Takuan spent time studying with the Zen scholar and master from the *gozan* movement, Monsai Tōnin, who was living in Daian-ji in Kai and directed a small school (*juku*) where he taught Confucianism, poetry, and calligraphy. Takuan soon distinguished himself among the school's many industrious students and was therefore allowed to take up resident in the temple precincts; after Tōnin's death in 1603 he inherited the master's valuable library. This time of study in Daian-ji turned out to be more than a passing episode in Takuan's life. Once he had drunk deeply of the knowledge offered him, he could never be content to remain simply a member of a monastic community. From that time on, learning became a necessity of nature. He did not, however, neglect to complete his Zen practice. Ittō Shōteki took him on as a disciple and through strenuous practice quickly brought him to his goal. Upon attaining enlightenment in 1604 he received from his master the name of Takuan; in Zen history he is known by the full name of Takuan Sōhō.

Takuan felt at home in the quiet of the countryside. He stayed to the end with his aged master, whose strength was failing quickly. After the master's death in 1606 he was made abbot of the Nansō-ji, a branch temple of Daitoku-ji. During that same year his father died, and a year later, his mother. Now he was completely alone—the "naked monk," as the people once laughingly called him when he hung his only white robe out to dry and had to hide in his room. On this occasion, he gave his hecklers a lesson that well expresses his concept of authentic Zen:

> You call me the "naked monk." I am sorry that you all don't become naked. Aren't you pained that your greedy clinging to things, fame, property, and possessions binds you and that you make no bodily movement? If you become a naked monk like I am, you will feel better. Does not the way of the Buddha call us to practice so that we might become naked? That is what the naked monk is doing his best to realize.[52]

Such freedom from clinging is what makes a Zen monk.

Takuan had spent only three years as abbot of Nansō-ji when Emperor Go-Yōzei (ruled 1587–1611) summoned him to Kyoto to become abbot of Daitoku-ji (1609). He could not refuse this request, but after only three days he renounced his office and returned to Nansō-ji. The time of his quiet life in the country was in any case over; he soon felt called to turn his energies to the events of the time. The war for Osaka Castle (1614–15) sent shock waves all the way to the peaceful land of Kai. Nansō-ji fell prey to the fires of war but thanks to Takuan's efforts was rebuilt soon thereafter, in 1617. Only a year before Takuan had expended similar efforts and assured the restoration of Sugyō-ji, in his native Izushi, which had also suffered the devastations of war.

The reconstruction of Sugyō-ji had been carried out under the protection of and with the help of the local lord, Koide Yoshihide (1586–1668), who showed his special favors to Takuan and appointed him abbot of the newly reconstructed temple. The master was at the height of his physical powers; he loved to roam through the land as much as he loved to be alone. Fleeing the defilements of the world, he sought out rural temples, where he delighted in the beauty of nature and composed poetry. After an extended period of travel he returned to Sugyō-ji and built a small country house close to the temple, devoting his days to meditation, study, and art. He also worked on the text of *The Difference between "Ri" and "Ki"* (*Ri-ki sabetsuron*), which included a discussion of Confucianism. During this time, he also produced a collection of one hundred poems. When once asked whether he enjoyed his solitude, he answered:

I feel no loneliness. When my visitors return home, I think to myself, How quiet, how fascinating! And when the sun sets, my questioners leave me to myself. . . . But I remain in this place not to enjoy peace and quiet but because here I have found a resting place for my mind.[53]

After some years, Takuan was shaken out of his beloved quiet by an unhappy incident that has come to be known in Zen history as "the purple robe event" (shie jiken). What happened is easily told. Among the ordinances for religious bodies contained in the laws of the shogunate government promulgated in 1615 there were special directives for Daitoku-ji and Myōshin-ji, in virtue of the fact that they had special relations with the imperial court. One of this ordinances required that anyone who was called to be abbot of these temples must have practiced Zen for thirty years and mastered the seventeen hundred kōan. An earlier disposition had placed some limitations on the emperor's privilege of bestowing the purple robe on the abbots of these two temples. In the future, such a great favor could not be granted without the approval of the shōgun.

At first these decrees did not occasion any changes in traditional procedures. But in 1627 the Edo government enforced the new requirements, censured their neglect, and began punishing offenders. One can imagine the uproar in the affected temples. Upon hearing the news, Takuan immediately rushed to Daitoku-ji, where the monks were divided and unable to reach accord on what to do. Staunchly protesting the measures taken by the shōgunal government, Takuan drew up a statement of justification (Bemmeiron), which was signed by himself, by the current abbot of the monastery, Gyokushitsu Sōhaku (1572–1641), and by the highly regarded Zen master Kōgetsu Sōgan (1574–1643). The statement was then sent to the shōgunal government in Edo.[54] A thirty-year period of formation, argued Takuan, would rob Zen masters of their best years—time that should be devoted to the guidance of their disciples. And to master seventeen hundred kōan (in the Keitoku dentōroku the number signifies a large quantity) is simply impossible. Evidently, the decree was part of some inveiglements arising from the tense relations between the shōgunal government and the imperial court. In Edo, the reaction to the statement of justification was cold and sharp. The "hawks" (Sūden[55] and Hayashi Razan[56]) demanded stringent punishment for the three signatories (who did not even compose their statement in the official kambun style but used a simple Japanese style mixed with kana.) The "doves" (Tenkai and Yagyū Munenori) pleaded extenuating circumstances. The final verdict was that Takuan and Gyokushitsu be sent into exile, while Kōgetsu, who had recanted, escaped any punishment. The emperor Go-Mizunoo resigned from office.

Takuan calmly accepted his exile to Kaminoyama in Uzen (in the region of Yamagata) and found a friendly reception among the local officials and people. In the hermitage of Shun'u-an built especially for him he was able to pursue his favorite pastimes. After the death of the second shōgun Hidetada in 1632, the exile was revoked and Takuan was allowed to come to Edo. Two years later he was allowed to visit Kyoto,[57] and from there went home to Izushi. Once again he took up residence in Tōenken, but a lengthy retirement was not to be his lot.

Takuan's friendly relations with Yagyū Munenori, the sword master of the third shōgun, Iemitsu, led to an invitation to return to Edo, where once again he came into the shōgun's good graces and trust. Conversations revolved around the two arts that Iemitsu so highly prized—poetry and sword-fighting. Takuan was able to return a number of times to Izushi and Kyoto. In the presence of emperor Go-Mizunoo in Kyoto, who held him in high regard, Takuan delivered his lectures on the *Treatise on the Origins of the Human* (Jpn., *Genninron*; Chin., *Yüan-jen lun*), the famous introduction to Buddhism by the Chinese master Tsung-mi (780–841).

Takuan finally gave in to the shōgun's insistence that he settle in Edo. Since he had had to stay for so long with his friend the sword-master Yagyū Munenori in a villa in Azabu on the periphery of Edo, the shōgun announced in 1638 that he was ready and able to build a temple for him. Construction was completed the following year. Located in Shinagawa close to Edo, the temple was called Tōkai-ji, and Takuan was named founding abbot. Taking advantage of having the master so close, Iemitsu visited him and summoned him to his castle often.[58] Takuan, however, refused to take over Sūden's place in religious politics, pressing rather for the speedy resolution of the dissensions with Daitoku-ji and Myōshin-ji. Eventually in 1641 he succeeded and the two temples were reinstated to their previous privileged positions.[59]

Given Takuan's advancing age, the question of his successor became more pressing, especially since he did not have a large following of disciples. Although Takuan had provided direction for a few disciples during his stay at Nansō-ji, he never really took on longer-termed responsibilities for a Zen hall. He did have friendly relations with the young Zen monk Isshi Monju (1608–1646), who, it seemed, might have become his Dharma heir, especially since Monju had accompanied and assisted him during his exile in Kaminoyama. But their friendship did not last long. Isshi Monju maintained close relations with some circles of the imperial court for whom Takuan, himself a member of a samurai family, did not have a great liking. So the young monk moved to Myōshin-ji, where he became a disciples of Gudō Tōshoku (1577–1661).[60]

Both the emperor and the shōgun pressed for a solution to the problem of a successor, while Takuan himself did not seem to give the matter much concern. He really did not want his own name on the historical lists of Zen masters. During the last years of his life, instead of the usual self-portrait, he had a circle painted, in the middle of which he dabbed a point with his ink brush. When asked for a farewell message, he painted the graph for "dream" and left this last wish:

> Bury my body on the mountain behind the temple, throw some earth on it, and then go away! Read no sūtras! Prepare no sacrificial offerings! Accept no gifts of mourning from the faithful! Put on your monks robes and take

your meals as you do every day! Build no pagoda, make no inscription, erect no monument! Ask for no posthumous name! In the abbot's chambers of the temple, set up no inscription in wood! Write down no life's history with dates![61]

His wishes were only partially carried out. His disciples rejected the lavish funeral ceremonies that Iemitsu wanted to have in Tōkai-ji, as well as the shōgun's plans to erect a pagoda. On the mountain behind the temple a simple monument in the form of a round stone on top of a mound of earth was set up. Only as recent as 1944 did he received the title of National Master.

WRITINGS

Takuan Sōhō's prolific writings have been assembled in the six volumes of his collected works. His most important writings can also be found in modern Japanese in a volume of sayings of Japanese masters.[62] He mastered not only the Chinese *kambun* style but also the more flowing Japanese style of writing, which made many of his works readily available to the general public. His poems comprise several volumes and his letters fill one large volume. Many have marveled at the way these letters reveal his broad learning, his many interests, and his humane concern for the people.[63] Throughout his writings there are many short texts consisting of Dharma sayings. With a clear sense of personal involvement, he writes about the early periods of Zen history—of Śākyamuni, Bodhidharma, the patriarchs, and the great Zen masters of past ages.[64] In their incredible diversity of themes, Takuan's collected works occupy a prominent place in Japanese Zen literature.

Academically, Takuan was mainly concerned with Confucianism, attempting to use his Zen Buddhist perspective to present Neo-Confucian doctrine in a more intelligible form. In this regard, his major work was the *The Difference between "Ri" and "Ki,"* of which two versions, differing in both content and form, exist today.[65] The shorter *kambun* text is earlier. Despite the opposition and conflict indicated in its title, the work clearly tries to foster harmony. Takuan does not polemicize against the Neo-Confucians, unlike many of his Buddhist colleagues of the Edo period, who, we must point out, were often responding to the aggressive challenges of the Confucians. Takuan's aim is rather to smooth over points of opposition and show how the two teachings might be united within Zen metaphysics.

Ri (Chin., *li*) and *ki* (Chin., *ch'i*) are cosmic principles. *Ri* (also called *mukyoku*) is the foundation that evolves and becomes *ki*, or the universe of the myriad things (*taikyoku*). Takuan stresses the return of the *taikyoku* to its final ground in *mukyoku*, which he identifies as the emptiness (Skt., *śūnyatā*; Jpn., *kū*) of Mahāyāna metaphysics. According to Zen teaching, the myriad things of the cosmos are not different from emptiness (*kū*) or from nothingness (*mu*). Takuan sees this is as the implication of the negative formulation—*mukyoku*—of the foundational *ri*. His primary concern is the reconciliation of Confucian and Zen Buddhist thought, and at times even speaks of the unity of Confucianism and Buddhism (jubutsu itchi).

The version of the Ri-ki sabetsuron in Japanese kana is the result of the redacting effort of a group of editors from Daitoku-ji.[66] This version also begins with a detailed analysis of basic Confucian conepts. The central meaning of emptiness is clearly stressed. Takuan writes:

> Between heaven and earth there is something called ri. This ri has no form and is empty. Because it is empty, it cannot be seen with the eyes. People say that emptiness cannot be seen with human eyes.[67]

He then presents the interaction between yin and yang and the five elements: earth, fire, water, metal, and wood. Human energies are also examined. Especially interesting is a long closing section on the meaning of the kami (divine forces) in Shinto.[68] Takuan also speaks of unity in regard to Shinto: "Buddha and the kami are the same reality with different names."[69] There is a luminous, good kami and a dark, evil kami. The traditional talk of the unity of three religions (Confucianism, Buddhism, Taoism) is understood in the Japan of the Edo period to apply to the three religions Confucianism, Buddhism, and Shinto. Taoism is sometimes added as a fourth religion. Very much at home with such viewpoints, Takuan was instrumental in promoting them at the beginning of the Edo period.

He developed his Zen teaching in a work written in Japanese script entitled The Dharma Door of the Peaceful Mind (Jpn., Anjinhōmon),[70] at the beginning of which he cites a saying attributed to Bodhidharma: "Caught in illusions, one turns to objective things." Takuan comments:

> Illusion is far removed from reality and hastens toward deception. True reality is the self. The self is the mind. In the mind, there is the mind in illusion and the mind in truth. The self is the mind in truth. In illusion, one falls into the objective world of the six objects.[71]

Takuan develops this thought with the help of a poem attributed to the Third Patriarch, Seng-ts'an (d. 606), "Words Inscribed on the Believing Mind."[72] Part of the poem reads: "When the one mind does not arise, the myriad things (dharma) are no obstacle./When there is no obstacle, no thing appears./And when no thing appears, there is no mind."[73] As D. T. Suzuki makes clear in his English paraphrase, these verses should not be understood in a nihilistic sense.[74] The key idea of the poem is the unity of nondualistic reality. For the enlightened mind, all duality is overcome. Suzuki expresses the philosophical content of the poem in his free and modern translation of the following verse:

> The object is an object for the subject,
> The subject is a subject for an object:
> Know that the relativity of the two
> Rests ultimately on the oneness of the void.[75]

The Anjinhōmon cites many important Zen axioms and establishes Takuan as a sound scholar of Mahāyāna philosophy. We may note in particular his comments on the nondifferentiated, spontaneous "no-mind," which supplies the foundation for his famous text on Zen and swordsmanship, directed to the master of the sword, Yagyū Munenori. Takuan explains the difference between the existing mind taken up with objects (ushin) and no-mind (mushin):

> The existing mind holds objects in the mind [by knowing them]; no-mind holds no thing in the mind. : . . When things constantly come into the mind and remain, one speaks of the existing mind; when things constantly leave the mind, one speaks of no-mind.[76]

Here the objection may be raised that the enlightened person cannot really enjoy flowers or the moon. Takuan replies:

> When the light of one's own mind shines, then the moon is not the moon, flowers are not flowers. Those who themselves make distinctions make the flowers [into flowers]; those who themselves make distinctions make the moon [into the moon]. In the minds of enlightened people, even when their eyes see flowers, there is no form of flowers; in their minds, even when they see the moon, there is no form of the moon.[77]

The way of acting particular to no-mind is called non-acting (musa).[78] Non-acting is not the action of a subject. Actions of a subject directed toward objects bring about the cycle of rebirths; nonaction, on the other hand, bestows enlightenment.

Like most Japanese Zen Buddhists of the Edo period, Takuan taught a Confucian ethic. He admonishes the four classes of knights, farmers, workers, and merchants to fulfill their duties faithfully and to practice the social virtues. Such an ethic, which avoids extremes, reflects human reason. Especially in his later writings, Takuan supplies abundant proofs for his ethical claims; this was especially necessary insofar as the Confucians used to delight in accusing the Buddhists of being so entangled in deep metaphysical speculations that they had little to say that was meaningful for daily life.

A number of the citations from the Evening Talks at Tōkai-ji (Tōkai yawa),[79] compiled from texts from the master and recollections of his disciples, are distinguished for their accessible, practical reasonability, and for their dependence on Confucian thought. Takuan recommends moderation:

> This passing world is as short as a dream. When at play, a person thinks that it would be good to play all night long. Yet every game has its form and measure. Form and measure change according to the times. Suitable form and measure are desirable, and so are games that correspond to one's own self.[80]

In a longer passage, Takuan distinguishes between rational and nonrational forms of life. Even for the latter there is suffering, for even grasses and trees suffer equally as they fade and decay. All things possess reason, each in its own way. Our mind can distinguish between sensate and nonsensate reason.[81]

Takuan speaks clearly for tolerance and intelligence in religion:

It is not at all a sign of reason when people with the mien of enlightenment make fun of those who practice the *nembutsu* and the invocation of the name. The *nembutsu* and the invocation of the name are like the seeds of the tree of enlightenment. How can one reap fruit if one never sows seeds?[82]

As for the *kami*, Takuan's religious sensibilities made him sensitive to the distinction "between those with and without names." He considers it unjust to honor *kami* with names while neglecting those without names. The honoring of all the *kami* is, in his opinion, "true devotion to God."[83]

For Takuan, human beings are beings to be feared; he makes sweeping criticisms against the merchant mentality and greed, and he chides the rich for their lack of kindness. In many of his comments one can clearly feel a tinge of what is evidently a time-conditioned pessimism, for example, when he argues for the impossibility of leading a normal life in the world while at the same time following the way of Zen. True happiness is to be found in a state of peace, without pain or joy, namely in a state resembling the Buddhist state of nirvāṇa. The virtues are all tied together; it is the task of humans to practice them in harmonious balance.

VIEWS ON SWORDSMANSHIP

A Note on the Relation between Zen and the Military Arts.   Despite the strong and undeniable influence of Zen on the arts, it cannot be said that the military arts of archery and swordsmanship in Japan originated from Zen Buddhism. There are two reasons for offering a few reflections on the relation between Zen and the military arts at this juncture. First, we have arrived at that point in Zen history when the development of the mililtary arts was at its peak—basically during the first half of the Edo period, from the seventeenth to the eighteenth centuries. The second reason lies in the important contribution that Zen master Takuan Sōhō made to the art of swordsmanship. In a number of his writings, Takuan offered penetrating insights into this military art.

Many are surprised that such a peace-loving religion as Buddhism—and Zen indeed reflects this aspect of Buddhism—would give any attention to martial arts such as archery or swordsmanship.[84] Obviously, we find mention of bows and swords quite early in Japanese history. At first used only for hunting, the bow and arrow were quickly converted to military purposes. Already by the sixth century, archery—both on level ground and from horseback—was known in Japan. Equestrian archery (Jpn., *yabusame*) has no relation to Zen. Long before the introduction of Zen meditation, Japanese infantry-archers were probably acquainted with Zen-like—or better, Yoga-like—practices such as breath control. At the time of the Mongol invasions archery proved itself effective in warfare. Besides its military advantages, the artistic aspects of archery continued to grow in general esteem.

During the medieval period, the art of archery grew in popularity thanks to Ogasawara Sadamune (1292–1347), whose name is still known among contemporary devotees of archery. The foremost master of that century, Heki Danjō

Masatsugu (d. 1512), was clearly influenced by the militaristic atmosphere of medieval Japan, by Buddhist physical training, and by Yoga-like techniques, without, however, having any close relations to the Zen that was in flower at the time. After a brilliant career as a master archer, he retired during the twilight of his life to Mount Kōya, where he received the tonsure as a Shingon monk.

Like all aspects of Japan's cultural life during the middle ages, the art of archery also came under the formative influence of Zen Buddhism. Among the many famous master archers of that period, not a few had had Zen experience. They did not, however, form any kind of association. Among the numerous groups of accomplished archers there was evident competition regarding different approaches. Eugen Herrigel has introduced archery as a "way of Zen" to the West.[85] His fascinating account makes a convincing case for the close ties of archery to Zen meditation and especially to kōan practice. His master, Awa Kenzō, was full of the spirit of Zen. The different archery groups in Japan have maintained their independence from the Zen school. Up to the Meiji period, the common expression for archery was kyūjutsu (literally, "art of the bow"). The term kyūdō (literally, "way of the bow") became common only during the Meiji period, probably promoted by Confucians. Swordsmanship grew in popularity as a form of physical training and as a sport in clubs and schools, held in high regard especially because of the way it preserved its Zen-like quality.[86]

Despite the different psychologic structures of the arts of archery and swordsmanship, much of what was already said about the former, especially concerning its history, applies to the latter as well.[87] The "art of the sword" (kenjutsu) also enjoyed widespread popularity during the Edo period, mainly after the introduction of firearms had greatly diminished the military use of swords. Early Japanese history speaks of swords made of both stone and bronze, and indicates how the Japanese, from early on, attributed a kind of sacred quality to swords, surrounding them with a special devotion that indicated the popular esteem for the art of forging swords. It was during the Kamakura period that Zen was first spoken of in relation to swordsmanship, yet, as in the case of archery, the relationship was a loose one. Sword masters were eager to learn from Zen monks their fearless attitude toward life and death and to imbibe their courageous readiness to attack (swordfighting is essentially a matter of attacking). During the middle ages swordfighting came to be surrounded with a ritual that bore many Zen-like characteristics. Many of the medieval sword masters were inspired by the Zen spirit and were well-versed in Zen practice. Prominent among them was Tsukahara Bokuden (1490–1572),[88] who practiced an art of swordsmanship free of rough conflict that he called the school of "winning without hands" (mutekatsu).

During the Edo period, the art of swordsmanship—like the independently popular art of archery—was inspired just as much, if not more, by the prevalent teachings of Confucianism.[89] The martial arts were counted among the spiritually relevant movements that the Tokugawa rulers placed under the direction of Confucianism, without, however, excluding all other influences. The syncretistic spirit of the times favored tolerance, which in the case of swordsmanship allowed for the recognition of elements deriving from Zen meditation, especially self-lessness and purposelessness. To these elements Confucianism added its military ethos and its courage, thus bringing about a harmonious interaction of Zen and Confucian contributions. Following the persecution of Buddhism, however, Confucians voiced strong critical reservations as to the efficacy of Zen training. A representative work of the period advances the thesis that a Zen monk could never really excel in the art of swordsmanship because he lacks Confucian virtues.[90]

At the beginning of the Edo period, Confucian views on the nature of war were given representative expression by the scholar Yamaga Sokō (1622–1685), who perfected the "way of the warrior" (bushidō) that was to become so deeply rooted in the Japanese soul. With his insistence on the necessity of uniting technical, military expertise with the Confucianist worldview, he exercised a considerable influence on the art of swordsmanship and established the happy relationship between bushidō and Confucianism. In the pertinent literature, one finds differing, sometimes opposing, views on its advantages and weaknesses.[91] During the Meiji era the art of swordsmanship was promoted, according to the military spirit of the time, as the "way of the sword."

From this brief overview, it is clear that the military arts of archery and swordsmanship do not belong essentially to the world of Zen, despite certain close relationships.[92] Both arts maintained an independent identity of their own. What is remarkable about the two martial skills is their development into art forms. The first step in this process was to adorn with special ceremony what was basically a simple and practical clash of weaponry. The importation of spiritual significance from Zen, together with the custom of building practice centers for the martial arts close to Zen temples, helped foster the artistic aura that surrounded the discipline. It was above all the Zen master Takuan Sōhō who highlighted the Zen values that can be expressed in swordsmanship. With these preliminary remarks we hope to have placed his contribution to swordsmanship in the broader context of the relationship between the history of Japanese Zen and secular history.

TAKUAN AND YAGYŪ MUNENORI ON SWORDSMANSHIP

As already mentioned, there was an especially good, even friendly, relationship between Takuan Sōhō and Iemitsu's sword master, Yagyū Munenori (1571–1646). The sword master came from a family rich in the traditions of swordsmanship.[93] His father, Yagyū Muneyoshi (1527–1607), originally belonged to the Chūjō-ryū, an earlier school of swordsmanship of the Muromachi period. At a meeting with Kamiizumi Nobutsuna (d. 1577), the founder of the Shin-Kage-ryū, he recognized the superiority of this latter school, and on that basis founded the Shin-Yagyū-ryū. Together with his son Munenori he developed this school into one of the main schools of the Tokugawa period; it still exists today. The meeting between Yagyū Munenori and the famed Zen master Takuan prompted an essential deepening of old relations between the Kage-ryū and Zen. A written account from the pens of both masters has been preserved. We will limit our analysis to the two important texts that Takuan sent to Munenori: the longer letter or treatise on *The Mysteries of the Unmoved Prajñā (Fudōchi-shinmyōroku; prajña* is the Sanskrit word for wisdom or transcendental insight) and the short text of the *Taia Sword (Taiaki).*[94]

Takuan's directives for the proper mental attitude for swordfighting are rooted in his understanding of the nature of Zen. Already at the outset of *The Mysteries of the Unmoved Prajñā* he warns of a disastrous misunderstanding that frequently afflicts beginners in this art—the anxiety, an illusion (Skt., *kleśa*; Jpn., *bonnō*) caused by ignorance (Skt., *avidyā*; Jpn., *mumyō*), of remaining or stopping or getting stuck, which inclines the mind to cling to external things. The damage wrought by this tendency is clear. Swordfighters who direct their attention to the movements of their opponents and then get stuck there are mentally imprisoned. They do not have the freedom from distractions by external things. Takuan is concrete about what he means:

> When you see with a quick glance the sword of your opponent raised to strike, if you think about stopping it with your sword your mind clings to the sword of your opponent, your actions are impeded, and you will be struck by your opponent. Even when you see the sword of your opponent descending you should not fix your mind on it, nor should you think about adjusting the timespan to the blow of your opponent's sword in order to return the blow. Give up all distinctions and plans! As soon as you see the moving sword, take action without even a moment's hesitation, take advantage of your opponent's sword; tear away his raised sword and let it strike your opponent.[95]

In Zen, such conduct is called "grabbing the tip of the spear and turning it, piercing one's opponent."[96]

Most importantly, swordfighters must keep themselves free from all ego-consciousness. The mind is hindered whenever directed to anything outside itself, be it the opponent moving in front of one, or one's own sword, or even the timespan between movements. "In the Buddha-Dharma the mind's grasping is called illusion and the place of its clinging, ignorance."[97]

The introductory section contains the basic and practical advice on how one is to move during swordfighting. In order to move with total freedom, the mind should direct its attention neither to the opponent and his action nor to one's own self. Takuan bases this admonition on the paradoxical nature of the mind:

> All Buddhas possess unmoved *prajñā* (Jpn., *fudōchi*). Unmoved means literally the absence of movement. . . . The absence of movement does not mean the immovability of stones and trees. While the mind freely moves forward and backward, to the left and to the right, in the four and eight heavenly directions, if it clings to nothing, then it is "unmoved *prajñā*."[98]

Takuan is convinced that this teaching on unmoved *prajñā* is the heart of art of swordsmanship. The paradox of *prajñā*—to be simultaneously the unmoved ground and at the same time the potential for movement in all directions—is the secret that the swordfighter must master through persevering, meticulous effort. Fudō (Skt., Acala-vidyārāja), the fearsome Hindu god appropriated by Buddhism, is the symbol of this wisdom, unmoved yet capable of everything. Not to move is as indispensable as the ability to move constantly. What Takuan means when he insists that the swordfighter should not allow even a hair's breadth between movements is illustrated in the image of the ten opponents whom the fighter, blow by blow, overcomes. This is possible only because there are no intervals between blows.

Strangely, the process of practice leads back to where it started. At first, beginners have no notion of how they should handle their swords or their bodies. "When the opponent strikes, they respond instinctively, without thinking."[99] The students learn all kinds of things—how to hold the sword, how to direct the mind. When the opponent attacks, they find themselves unexpectedly hindered. And so they spend days, months, years in ceaseless practice until their minds no longer are aware of how they bear their bodies or their swords. Thus they return to where they began, when they knew nothing and had not learned anything; they realize that beginning and end of their practice are really not that different. Takuan illustrates this with the example of musical tones, from which he makes some practical applications for Buddhist practice:

> What is highest and what is deepest are similar to each other. It is the same with the Buddha-Dharma when what is highest is attained; for those who know neither Buddha nor Dharma, it is without impressive appearance. For this reason, the ignorance and illusion of the beginner's clinging is one with the unmoved *prajñā* of the later phase. The activities of the mind disappear as the mind assumes the place of no-mind (*mushin*) and of non-thinking (*munen*). When the highest perfection is attained, hands, feet, and all bodily members move by themselves, without any intervention of the mind.[100]

Takuan spells out in detail the role of the mind in swordfighting:

> If you direct your mind toward the bodily movements of your opponent, your mind will be taken by the bodily movements of your opponent. If you direct your mind toward your opponent's sword, it will be taken by the sword. If you direct your mind toward trying to strike your opponent, it will be taken by this waiting to strike. If you direct the mind toward your own sword, it will be taken by your sword. If you direct it toward not being struck, it will be taken by the desire not to be struck. If you direct the mind toward the attitude of your opponent, it will be taken by this attitude. In brief, there is nowhere to direct your mind.[101]

Takuan finally offers advice on the difficult question of directing the mind by recommending that it be centered below the navel and not permitted to move outward. This will enable it to follow all the opponent's movements continuously. By pervading the entire body, it can become the movements of hands, feet, eyes, and so forth. The mind should not be tied like a cat but must be able to move freely wherever it wishes.[102]

At the end of his treatise, Takuan adopts two concepts of Buddhist philosophy to express his central teaching on swordsmanship. He takes two contradictory terms, *honshin* (literally, "original mind") and *mōshin* ("deluded mind"), and applies them to swordfighting. While the original mind flows through the entire body, the deluded mind holds to one place. Takuan adds an example:

> The original mind flows like water and does not stay in one spot, while the deluded mind is like ice. You cannot wash your hands and feet with ice. But if you melt the ice and turn it into water, then it can flow everywhere and you can wash your hands and feet and everything with it. When the mind stays in one spot and clings to anything it is like hard ice and cannot be used freely, just as you cannot wash hands and feet with ice. To melt the mind and to let it work, like flowing water, in every part of the body—that is what is meant by "original mind."[103]

Just as hard ice and flowing water are two forms of the same reality, so are the stability and movement of *prajñā* essentially the same. The two concepts of *honshin* and *mōshin* imply essentially the same thing as the paradox that Takuan used to express the heart of his teaching on swordsmanship; it is the paradox of unmoved *prajñā* constantly brimming with movement in a dynamism that finds a particularly clear expression in swordfighting.

The second pair of concepts—*ushin no shin* and *mushin no shin*, the mind of existing mind and the mind of no-mind[104]—do not differ essentially in content from the previous pair of concepts but help bring out more clearly the roots of Takuan's teachings in the Mahāyāna metaphysics of the *prajñāpāramitā* (perfection of wisdom) sūtras. The first notion, *ushin* (the mind of existing mind), corresponds to the "deluded mind" (*mōshin*) that clings to external things, while the second concept, *mushin* (the mind of no-mind), reflects the "original mind" (*honshin*), for as Takuan explains in his *Anjinhōmon*, no-mind does not cling to anything. Knowing no hardening, distinguishing (Jpn., *fumbetsu*; Skt., *vikalpa*), or reflecting, the original mind expands through the entire body and flows like water from one place to the next. No-mind is the enlightened mind, not clinging, "empty," ever flowing, unhindered by hardening or deterioration, in a state of dynamic freedom. Takuan's treatise on swordfighting stands as a lucid statement of his understanding of Zen and of Zen enlightenment as impressively illustrated in the art of swordsmanship.

Takuan's second work on the art of swordsmanship is considerably shorter and full of allegory and symbolism.[105] A famous work of the Chinese master smith Feng Hu-tzu, the Taia sword, whose name the work bears, is here said to belong to everyone and to be perfect in itself. When it shines forth, heavenly beings (*deva*) tremble; when it is undrawn, evil runs rampant. It can both kill and give life. In this work, Takuan emphasizes the unconditional necessity of giving up one's self. One of his sayings is often quoted: "The swordfighter does not fight for victory or defeat." One's purpose is not to kill the opponent with one's sword. For Takuan, swordfighting is an art rooted in the metaphysics of Zen.

The master swordsman Yagyū Munenori was in complete agreement with Takuan's views. Those of his writings that are still preserved[106] follow the same train of thought as that of his revered Zen master. Suzuki gives a detailed paraphrase of Yagyū's writings.[107] In swordfighting as in Zen practice, the mind must be given over to total emptiness. All images and thoughts must be cleared away and self must disappear. Swordfighters, if they have mastered their art, act with subsconscious spontaneity. Yagyū Munenori's Zen viewpoint clearly reflects that of Takuan. With their rich formulations, his works make for powerful and stimulating reading. His strong dependence on Taoist thought is evident. His preference for the philosophy of Lao-tzu and Chuang-tzu, of course, in no way detracts from the Zen quality of his views but roots him, rather, in the original spiritual soil of the Chinese Zen movement.

Yagyū Munenori is indeed the most significant of the sword masters of the Tokugawa period who had close ties to Zen. Less well known is his contemporary Odagiri Ichiun, a pupil of Hariya Sekiun, who was a member of the Shin-Kage-ryū.[108] As one extant manuscript indicates, Ichiun's art of swordsmanship was grounded in Zen and for this reason he can be counted among the most original practitioners of his art. Another important name in the history of Japanese Zen is Miyamoto Musashi (also called Niten, 1584–1645), a famous sword master and all-around artist, especially accomplished in ink painting.[109] Many other Zen influences could be traced in the art of swordsmanship of those times. The reverberations of medieval Zen culture were easy to hear as the Zen movement took its first steps into the modern age.

NOTES

1. In the year 1568 Nobunaga entered the capital city of Kyoto, ostensibly under the protection of the emperor and the shōgun Ashikaga Yoshiaki. The latter gave him the sworn assurance that all matters of the regime would be entrusted to him. When Yoshiaki betrayed this trust, Nobunaga removed him as shōgun.

2. On the political events of the epoch the relevant historical works include J. W. Hall and R. Bersihand; on the Christian mission, see C. R. Boxer, The Christian Century in Japan, 1549–1650.

3. In the school of Pure Land Buddhism the ikkō groups, preceded by the followers of Rennyo (1415–1499), launched a formidable revolt known as the Ikkō-ikki against the feudal lords. Nobunaga succeeded in striking down these militant believers of the Buddha Amida only after hard battles. See J. Kitagawa, Religion in Japanese History, pp. 116–17.

4. See the chapter on Zen and Confucianism in D. T. Suzuki, Zen and Japanese Culture pp. 45–46; cf. G. B. Sansom, Japan: A Short Cultural History, p. 380.

5. Suzuki, Zen and Japanese Culture, pp. 46, 67–68 (note).

6.   See Klaus Luhmer, *Schule und Bildungsreform in Japan*, vol. 1, p. 45; JH, pp. 80–81.

7.   See the discussion at the end of chap. 4 of this book, pp. 174–77.

8.   Introduction to *Geschichte Japans, 1549–1578*, by P. Louis Frois, translated and annotated by G. Schurhammer and E. A. Voretsch (Leipzig, 1926), p. xvii.

9.   The opposition of many Japanese feudal lords, such as Oda Nobunaga, against the Buddhists is based above all on Buddhist monastic participation in political events of the times and on the inclination of Buddhist monks to engage in military activities. Francis Xavier and the Christian missionaries were particularly opposed to the pederasty in Buddhist monasteries; see Georg Schurhammer, *Francis Xavier: His Life, His Times*, vol. 4, *Japan and China 1549–1552* (Rome, 1982), pp. 84–85, 77, 144, 160ff, 305, 309; see also Boxer, *The Christian Century in Japan*, p. 35. See also the extensive history of Japanese Buddhism by Tsuji Zennosuke, *Nihon bukkyōshi*, vol. 5, pp. 335–37.

10.   The passage is to be found in the so-called "great letter" of Francis Xavier from Kagoshima, dated 5 November 1549 but "not written on a single day" (Schurhammer, *Francis Xavier*, vol. 4, p. 80) to his confreres in Goa, in the edition of the letters of Francis Xavier of the Monumenta Historica Societatis Jesu, *Epistolae S. Francis Xavier*, vol. 2, ed. by G. Schurhammer and J. Wicki, pp. 189–90; an account of the contents with lengthy quotations appear in Schurhammer, *Francis Xavier*, vol. 4, pp. 80–97. See the text-critical study of the letter by Schurhammer in GS II, pp. 605–29.

11.   Schurhammer and Voretsch, *Geschichte Japans*, p. 7.

12.   Schurhammer and Voretsch, *Geschichte Japans*, p. 7.

13.   Ninshitsu died in the year 1556. Since 1545 he had been abbot of the monastery of Fukushō-ji, which belonged to the Sōtō sect; nothing is known of his death. See J. Laures, "Notes on the Death of Ninshitsu," MN 8 (1952): 407–11.

14.   Schurhammer reports in detail on the meeting of Ōtomo Yoshishige with Francis Xavier in a section entitled "Bei Otomo Yoshishige, dem Herzog von Bungo (September 1551)," *Francis Xavier*, vol. 4, 246–59. The duke was twenty-two years old at the time, one year before the violent death of his father. He found Xavier extremely sympathetic and "showed him great respect and treated him amicably as a guest." Frois knows of no other Japanese sovereign "who embraced so heartily the law of God and showed such love to the priests and the Portuguese as he" (Schurhammer and Voretsch, *Geschichte Japans*, p. 17). Schurhammer has devoted a study to the relationship between the sovereign of Bungo and the Christian mission, "Ein fürstlicher Gönner des hl. Franz Xavier: Ōtomo Yoshishige, König von Bungo," in his *Gesammelte Studien*, vol. 4 (Rome, 1695), pp. 327–34. He also gives the most important Japanese and European sources on Yoshishige (*Francis Xavier*, vol. 4, pp. 237–38, note 6, among which is included the chronicle written in 1635 by Sugitani Muneshige on the rise and fall of the Ōtomo clan *Ōtomo kōhaiki*), in which the goings-on in the court of Bungo are given a dark interpretation. The passage reads:

> Toward the end of the Genki and at the beginning of the Tenshō era, the Zen master Etsu from Daitoku-ji in Kyoto lived at the court of Bungo. While Prince Sōrin occupied his mind with the study of the kōan, a stranger named "Nowhere" came and caused obstacles to the Dharma of the master. Thereafter the two masters Inga and Jorō came from somewhere. After a short while Inga disappeared. Master Jorō taught Zen for many months and years. Everyone said that Master Ikkyū had been reborn and praised him beyond measure . . .

All things possess the Buddha nature. All seventeen hundred kōan are but different names for the same mind. In this way he taught in a language easy to understand. . . . But in the attempt to grasp clearly the moon of the Absolute, clouds arise and block out the light. Furthermore, there are insolent persons who, on hearing the doctrine that through the exercises the disciple can be likened to the true temple (the Absolute) and that apart from the temple nothing exists, destroy Shinto shrines and Buddhist temples and then decorate their own houses with the spoils they have plundered. What Jorō sets forth they regard as nothing.

Thus does the course of the world go astray. One does not honor the kami [Shinto gods] but follows one's own moods. Whether one regards being or nothingness as the principle of Zen, in our country of the kami, one dare not oppose the will of the kami. Did Sōrin in his study at the temple of Suwa succumb to the view of nothingness? He did not honor the way of the kami. His fame flourished and spread through the nine countries and even to China. Nevertheless, "between the lip and the rim of the cup sways the hand of sinister powers!" The form of the sky fills up and decreases.

While his country sunk deeper and deeper into war, Yoshishige revered Christianity to the end of his life. He received baptism on 28 August 1578 (Schurhammer and Voretsch, *Geschichte Japans*, p. 500).

15.   See Schurhammer and Voretsch, *Geschichte Japans*, pp. 122–23. Frois relies on a letter of the Jesuit brother Luis de Almeida and oral reports of a Japanese interpreter. The abbot of Nanrin-ji named Unshū, a disciple of Ninshitsu and his successor in Fukushō-ji, came to know Francis Xavier through this visit and was deeply impressed by him, although he was not able to understand the preaching for lack of an interpreter. He showed himself overjoyed at the visit of Brother Almeida (1562) and carried on with him numerous religious discussions. At these discussion was accompanied by the seventy-year-old Zen monk Tokuō Shunka, a disciple of Ninshitsu, who was residing in the monastery of Fukushō-ji at the time of the visit of Francis Xavier and who later became abbot of Nanrin-ji. There developed a warm bond between Brother Almeida and the two monks, who willingly listened to his explanations. They "finally asked the brother with hands upraised to baptize them in secret. When Almeida insisted they should openly confess their faith and leave their monastery, they were finally even willing to do this, but they could not be further instructed and baptized because of the sudden departure of the brother." Thus writes Schurhammer (somewhat departing from Frois) on the basis of the available sources; see *Francis Xavier*, vol. 4, p. 76, note 70.

16.   Schurhammer and Voretsch, *Geschichte Japans*, pp. 94–95.

17.   Translated from the Portuguese; Schurhammer and Voretsch, *Geschichte Japans*, p. 100. The name of Kesshu is known only through the Portuguese historical work of Frois. The Japanese translator could not verify him and thus writes his name in the Japanese syllabary.

18.   Schurhammer and Voretsch, *Geschichte Japans*, pp. 87ff; cf. p. 76. The way of writing Yengennan (as the name appears in the Portuguese original) is uncommon. I have not been able to ascertain to what characters the transcription corresponds.

19.   See Josef Franz Schütte, *Valignano's Mission Principles for Japan* (St. Louis, 1985), vol. 1, part 2, p. 204.

20.   See Schurhammer and Wicki, *Epistolae*, p. 186; Schurhammmer, *Francis Xavier*, vol. 4, p. 82.

21. Schurhammer and Wicki, *Epistolae*, p. 259.

22. He is referred to in a letter as *vir tum ingenio tum litteris praeclarus* (*Selectae indiarum epistolae*, 127), cited in G. Schurhammer, *Die Disputationen des P. Cosme de Torres S. J. mit den Buddhisten in Yamaguchi im Jahre 1551*, p. 12.

23. Schurhammer and Wicki, *Epistolae*, p. 288. Compare the translation of the letter, in which Francis Xavier lays the request before the general of the Jesuit order, Ignatius; Schurhammer, *Francis Xavier*, vol. 4, pp. 439–40.

24. Schurhammer, *Disputationen*, p. 52. The quotation comes from a letter of P. Cosme de Torres to his confreres in Valencia, dated 29 September 1551.

25. Schurhammer (*Disputationen*) includes a translation of the three letters of P. Cosme de Torres to the confreres in Valencia and India and to Francis Xavier, as well as a letter of Brother Juan Fernández to Francis. The comprehensive letter of Brother Fernández reports in detail on the debates that took place from 15 to 23 September. Francis Xavier was not on hand, being in Bungo at the time. On the disputations in Yamaguchi, see also Schurhammer and Voretsch, *Geschichte Japans*, pp. 21–26, Schurhammer, *Francis Xavier*, vol. 4, pp. 280–90.

26. From the first letter of Torres, Schurhammer, *Disputationen*, p. 50.

27. Schurhammer, *Disputationen*, p. 67.

28. Schurhammer, *Disputationen*, pp. 66–67.

29. On the origin and content of the Japanese catechism of Valignanos, see Schütte, *Valignano's Mission Principles for Japan*, vol. 1/2, pp. 67–89.

30. As Schütte reports, in the first *concio*, where he raises the questions about the nature of God, the form of participation in his being of created things, and the final goal of human beings, Valignano remarks: "*De his etiam quaestionibus sectae japoniorum et leges aliquid tractant: quae quamvis multae sint, et inter se discrepantes, et tam confuse de hisce rebus agant, et disputent, ut vix percipi, et intelligi queat, quod dicitur, et sententiam subinde varient et mutent . . .*" See *Valignano's Mission Principles for Japan*, vol. 1, part 2, p. 70.

31. Schütte, *Valignano's Mission Principles for Japan*, vol. 1, part 2, p. 80. Schütte also gives this passage in its Latin version; he notes parenthetically that it has to do with the method of *hōben*.

32. Fabian later abandoned his Christian faith, left the Jesuits, and wrote tracts against Christianity. See the report by Anesaki Masaharu, *The Writings of Fabian the Apostate Irman*, pp. 307–10. The Christian apologetical tract *Myōtei mondō* has been translated into French by Pierre Humberclaude, MN 1 (1938): 515–48; 2 (1939): 237–67.

33. Humberclaude, MN 1 (1938): 529.

34. Humberclaude, MN 1 (1938): 530.

35. Cited in G. Schurhammer, "Der hl. Franz Xaver in Japan (1549–1591)," GS 3, p. 600.

36. Schurhammer, "Der hl. Franz Xaver in Japan (1549–1591)," GS 3, p. 592.

37. On the following, see also Schütte, *Valignano's Mission Principles for Japan*, vol. 1, part 2, pp. 197–256.

38. Schütte, *Valignano's Mission Principles for Japan*, vol. 1, part 2, p. 160.

39. On the order of ranking and respective titles, see Schütte, *Valignano's Mission Principles for Japan*, vol. 1, part 2, pp. 161–62; on the *dōjuku*, see pp. 39–41. In Zen monasteries, the *dōjuku* were young people who lived in the monastery with the intention of one day becoming monks. They were so called by the Christian missionaries who lived

together with them. Not a few of them entered the order, while others served the mission as catechists.

40.   Cabral's judgment on the hierarchy of ranks is presented in Schütte, *Valignano's Mission Principles for Japan*, vol. 1, part 2, p. 163; on his dismissal from office, see p. 123.

41.   See the section "The Christian Daimyō and the Way of Tea" in the previous chapter. We may also add here the name of Konishi Yukinaga, who represented the ideal of the new age, combining his Christian faith with feudalistic elements, a typical phenomenon of the sixteenth century. The Konishi family belonged to the merchant class. Yukinaga was adopted by a samurai, undertook a military career and quickly rose to the rank of admiral. He distinguished himself in the field in Korea. His name appears occasionally in the lists of the tea guests of Sen no Rikyū. After the decisive seige of Ieyasu in Sekigahara he had to pay tribute to the underaged son of the dead Hideyoshi with his death. Since as a Christian he could not commit suicide by *harakiri (seppuku)*, he suffered the disgrace of execution at the hand of an executioner. Moved by Konishi Yukinaga, Kuroda Yoshitaka (also called Josui), a man of noble birth who had distinguished himself in military pursuits, took up the Christian faith. He established warm ties with the Christian tea adepts Takayama Ukon and Gamō Ujisato. His religious zeal passed through a crisis and was strengthened in the process. In his old age he found a life of quiet peace through his convictions in the midst of animosities and afflictions. The following remark reflects the spiritual state of resignation and maturity that was the fruit of his Christian faith and adherence to the way of tea: "In this my life I wish for no more than quiet. Gold and silver I do not need; they are for me no more than dirt and stone. Nor do I aspire to any fame in the realm of service to humanity. I have no need of beautiful lodgings and fine clothes. Nor do I want tasty meals in the morning and at night. If only I do not suffer hunger and cold I can manage to live and keep my spirits lively." Cited in Nishimura Tei, *Kirishitan to chadō*, p. 150.

42.   The Japanese historian A. Ebizawa treats the subject in detail in his book *Kindai nippon bunka no tanjō*. The cultural activities of the missionaries, in Ebizawa's view, introduced elements of the modern world into Japan. "Through Portuguese business and the direct traffic with ideas and cultures of the world that came in together with the Christian missionaries, the horizons of Japan were at one stroke opened up into the wider world" (p. 7). Ebizawa gives particular significance to the natural sciences introduced through the mediation of the missionaries (pp. 11, 71–87). He also recounts the episode of how the physician and attendant of Hideyoshi, Seyakuin Zensō, sought for Hideyoshi a certain beautiful woman in the region of Hizen who had struck the heart of his master, who was convalescing in Hakata after the battle against the local lords of Satsuma in Kyūshū. Seyakuin's search was frustrated by the unshakeable opposition of the Christian girls, who refused resolutely the copious signs of affection shown to them. The example of the preservation of womanly virtue Ebizawa takes as a sign of the importance given the person among people of the new era (pp. 22–23).

43.   Relevant works on Japanese history (including Japanese encyclopedias) report on the extent of the controls in connection with the *baku-han* system. The supervision extended as far as the imperial palace. The provisions of the *sankinkōtai*, according to which the daimyō must make obeisance at the court of the shōgun in Edo every two years, kept the local lords in rein (see Hall, *Japan: From Prehistory to Modern Times*, p. 261; see also EJ, vol. 7, pp. 14a, b). For a sociological view of the religious situation, see Robert Bellah, *Tokugawa Religion*.

44.   In his massive history of Japanese Buddhism, the Japanese historian Tsuji Zennosuke treats the particular elements that led to the hardening of Buddhism during the Tokugawa period and ended in "the alienation of the hearts of the people from Buddhism" (*Nihon bukkyōshi*, vol. 3, pp. 1–284; the quotation appears in vol. 4, p. 443).

45.   See Watanabe Shōkō, *Japanese Buddhism: A Critical Appraisal*, p. 90; see also pp. 86–94.

46.   Watanabe, *Japanese Buddhism*, p. 86.

47.   See the brief biographies in EJ, vol. 7, p. 255a, and *Tsuji, Nihon bukkyōshi*, vol. 2, pp. 26–88. Sūden seems to have taken sides against the Christians in the composition of the edict of persecution of 27 January 1614; see Boxer, *The Christian Century in Japan, 1549–1650*, pp. 317–18.

48.   Hideyoshi's first prohibition against Christianity (1587) has long been overlooked and only recently brought again into relief. The foreign missionaries were expelled in 1614. Two years later edicts restricted foreign business to the ports of Nagasaki and Hirado. The Spaniards were banished from Japan in 1624 and the Portuguese in 1639. Persecution of the Christians reached a climax in the third and fourth decades of the seventeenth century. In addition to the duty of registering in a temple of a recognized Buddhist sect, the so-called *tera-uke*, annual renewal of the registration (*shūmon no aratame*) was also required. Suspicions persons were put to the test of treading on sacred images (*fumie*). The number of Chrisitians fell dramatically. After the quelling of the uprising in Shimabara in 1637 and 1638, the remainder went underground. For a total picture, Boxer's *The Christian Century in Japan* remains the standard work; for precise statistics of Christian adherents, see EJ, vol. 1, pp. 307a–308a; on the politics of isolation, see Hall, *Japan* pp. 186–190.

49.   The high flowering of this culture took place in the Genroku era (1688–1705) and the Bunka and Bunsei periods (1804–1829). This bourgeois culture was also known as "the culture of the *chōnin*" (the merchants and city people). See Hall, *Japan*, pp. 228–29.

50.   For examples, see the following chapter.

51.   For a brief biography, see EJ, vol. 7, p. 327b. There is a rich literature in Japanese on Takuan Sōhō. For comprehensive accounts, see Nagata Hōjū in *Kōza zen* vol. 4, *Zen no rekishi: Nihon*, pp. 275–88; Itō Kōan in *Gendai zen kōza* vol. 2, pp. 213–22; Furuta Shōkin, "Takuan Sōhō to sono shoseki ni miru mono," *Zenshisōron: Nihon zen*, pp. 164–70. See also the short book by Matsuda Bugyō, *Takuan* (Tokyo, 1978). The complete works of Takuan appeared in six volumes as *Takuan Oshō zenshū*. The most important of his works have been compiled by Ichikawa Hakugen, with a translation in modern Japanese and commentary, in vol. 13 of the collection *Nihon no zen-goroku*.

52.   Cited in Itō, *Genadai zen kōza*, vol. 2, p. 215.

53.   Cited in Nagata, *Zen no rekishi: Nihon*, p. 279.

54.   Nagata treats the event in detail in *Zen no rekishi: Nihon*, pp. 281–85. See also the introduction by Ichikawa Hakugen to vol. 13 of *Nihon no zen-goroku*, pp. 18ff; and the notice in EJ, vol. 7, p. 89b.

55.   Sūden, who belonged to the community of Nanzen-ji, came forth as the antagonist to Takuan, whose first training in Zen had been gained in Daitoku-ji.

56.   Hayashi Razan (1583–1672), the most important Confucian scholar at the beginning of the Tokugawa period, served the first four Tokugawa shōguns as counselor.

57.   According to the relevant section on Takuan and Iemitsu, edited by Chiba Jōryū in vol. 3 of *Nihon bukkyōshi*, Takuan was at first refused permission to travel to Kyoto (p. 43).

58.   During the seven years that Takuan lived in Tōkai-ji, the shōgun Iemitsu is said to have visited him seventy-five times; see Itō, *Gendai zen kōza*, vol. 2, p. 222.

59.   See Chiba Jōryū, *Nihon bukkyōshi*, vol. 3, pp. 43–44. Takuan's friendly relations with Iemitsu (see Nagata, *Zen no rekishi: Nihon*, p. 285; Itō, *Gendai zen kōza*, vol. 2, p. 221) was strongly criticized in Daitoku-ji circles (see Ichikawa, *Nihon no zen-goroku*, vol. 13, p. 26). There is no denying the fact that Takuan fell under the shadow of the shōgun Iemitsu, whom history has judged harshly. Iemitsu's "self-willed and authoritative character" expressed itself not only in his merciless and cruel persecution of the Christians but also in proceedings against foreign emissaries, whom he had executed. See R. Bersihand, *Geschichte Japans* (Stuttgart, 1963), pp. 242ff; Boxer, *The Christian Century in Japan*, pp. 362ff; further details can be found in G. Sansom, *A History of Japan, 1615–1867*, pp. 25ff, 47, 53, 92.

60.   His criticism of Isshi Monju was not unfounded. See Tsuji, *Nihon bukkyōshi*, vol. 8, part 2, pp. 479–80. Furuta Shōkin devotes an essay to this monk who died at an early age, in which he praises his self-sacrificing contribution and "prominent service," reports his life and enlightment, and draws particular attention to his intimate ties to the abdicated emperor Go-Mizunoo (1596–1680, ruled 1612–1629). See "Takuan Sōhō to sono shoseki ni miru mono," pp. 171–83.

61.   Cited in Nagata, *Zen no rekishi: Nihon*, p. 286; see also *Nihon no zen goroku*, vol. 13, pp. 34–35.

62.   See note 51 above

63.   Tsuji reports on the letters in vol. 4 of his work: "The letters are an inexhaustible delight. In reading and savoring them, one feels that one comes close to the master and is drawn into his influence." Cited in *Nihon no zen goroku*, vol. 13, p. 89.

64.   See particularly, *Takuan Oshō zenshū*, vol. 2, *Hekigan kyūjūge*, text 3.

65.   *Takuan Oshō zenshū*, vol. 1, book 9, pp. 13–25. This version appears in *Nihon no zen-goroku*, vol. 13, pp. 97–118, and the original text in an appendix, pp. 369–74. A second version in *kana* script appears in vol. 2. (Note that each of the books of vols. 1 and 2 begin paginating from p. 1.). The *Ri-ki sabetsuron* appears in vol. 6.

66.   On the *Ri-ki sabetsuron* see the section in the introduction to the *Nihon no zen-goroku*, vol. 13, pp. 37–53.

67.   *Takuan Oshō zenshū*, vol. 2, p. 3.

68.   *Takuan Oshō zenshū*, vol. 2, pp. 20–29.

69.   *Takuan Oshō zenshū*, vol. 2, p. 22.

70.   *Takuan Oshō zenshū*, vol. 2, text 4; *Nihon no zen-goroku*, vol. 13, pp. 112–95.

71.   *Nihon no zen-goroku*, vol. 13, p. 121. The six objects are the six objects of consciousness, namely the five senses and objects of thought.

72.   See vol. 1 of the present work, p. 97–98.

73.   Cited in the introduction to *Nihon no zen-goroku*, vol. 13, p. 54.

74.   Suzuki offers a translation in *Essays I*, pp. 196–201; see also *Manual of Zen Buddhism*, pp. 91–97, and accompanying annotation.

75.   *Essays I*, p. 198; *Manual of Zen Buddhism*, p. 93.

76.   *Nihon no zen-goroku*, vol. 13, p. 128.

77.   *Nihon no zen-goroku*, vol. 13, p. 128.

78.   *Nihon no zen-goroku*, vol. 13, p. 173.

79.   *Takuan Oshō zenshū*, vol. 5, text 1. The *Tōkai yawa* is composed of two books, pp. 1–93 and 1–83 respectively; a selection of the two books is presented in *Nihon no zen-goroku*, vol. 13, pp. 309–66.

80.   Cited in the introduction to Nagata, *Nihon no zen-goroku*, vol. 13, p. 82. This and the following quotations were taken by the compiler from the *Evening Talks* and the related text of the *Reirōshū* (*Takuan Oshō zenshū*, vol. 5, text 2, pp. 1–27).

81.   *Takuan Oshō zenshū*, vol. 1, pp. 82–83.

82.   *Takuan Oshō zenshū*, vol. 1, p. 83.

83.   *Takuan Oshō zenshū*, vol. 1, p. 82.

84.   See the article in EJ on *kyūdō*, vol. 4, p. 340a–b, and on *kendō*, pp. 195b–196b. The former entry mentions, in addition to masters from an earlier age, Honda Tochizane (1837–1917), founder of the Honda school, and describes the weapons (bow and arrow) as well as the ceremony. I am indebted for important details to the *kyūdō* master Morioka Masaaki, who stresses the independence of the art of archery.

85.   See the references to the art of archery and the practice of the kōan in vol. 1, pp. 253–54.

86.   On organizational federations, see the article on *kendō* in the EJ (note 83), where references to relevant Japanese literature are also mentioned.

87.   On the following see also Reinhard Kammer, *Die Kunst der Bergdämonen: Zen-Lehre und Konfuzianismus in der japanischen Schwertkunst*. A condensed edition appeared under the title *Die Kunst, das Schwert zu führen: Zen in der altjapanischen Fechkunst*. Cf. Junzō Sasamori and Gordon Warren, *This is Kendō*.

88.   D. T. Suzuki relates two incidents from the life of Tsukahara Bokuden in *Zen and Japanese Culture*, pp. 74ff.

89.   Kammer translates the Confucian-inspired text *Tengu-geijutsuron* (*Discourse on the Art of the Mountain Demons*) of Shissai Chozan (*Die Kunst der Bergdämonen*). Cf. the book of the famous contemporary Japanese sword-master Ōmori Sōgen, *Ken to zen*. (Toyko, 1977).

90.   See the text translated by Kammer, *Die Kunst der Bergdämonen*, especially pp. 82–86.

91.   See the article on *bushidō* in EJ, vol. 1, pp. 221b–223b. The formation of the "way of the knight" (*bushidō*), founded on Confucian principles current since the middle ages and codified during the Ego period by Yamaga Sokō (1622–1685), made important contributions to Zen. Japanese knights cultivated fearlessness and courage. In the work composed by Yamamoto Tsunetomo in 1716 under the title *Hagakure*, the most important handbook of *bushidō*, the way of overcoming the idea of death and fear of death is taught in a manner clearly influenced by Zen teachings. The system of *bushidō*, in Sansom's view, in many ways took over the role of the traditional martial virtues. As knighthood sank, the masterless samurai not uncommonly became a public nuisance. The famous story of the forty-seven *rōnin*, which also figures in Japanese literature, clarifies the limits of the ethic of *bushidō*. See Sansom, *A History of Japan, 1615–1867*, pp. 495ff.

92.   The sword master and Zen master Ōmori Sōgen was familiar with talk of the "unity of sword and Zen," but stressed rather that the practice of Zen is not necessarily required to achieve mastery of the sword; see Ōmori Sōgen, *Ken to zen*, pp. 1–14.

93.   On the schools of the art of the sword in Japan, see the detailed account in Kammer, *Die Kunst der Bergdämonen*, pp. 143–53. On the following see particularly pp. 148–49. The schools were known as *ryū* (literally, "currents").

94.   Both texts appear in *Takuan Oshō zenshū*, vol. 5, text 4, *Fudōchishinmyōroku*, pp. 1–27; vol. 5, text 5, *Taiaki*, pp. 1–13. Both texts are given in *Nihon no zen-goroku*, vol. 13, pp. 197–238, 241–61. The quotations follow the pagination of the latter. D. T. Suzuki devotes two chapters of his book *Zen and Japanese Culture* to the art of the sword (pp. 87–214). He paraphrases a number of passages of lengthy tracts in English and includes a translation of the *Taiaki*. Suzuki's concern, corresponding to the purpose of Takuan, was to illuminate the relationships of the way of the sword with Zen. Takuan did not practice swordfighting himself. His concern was more with the spiritual dimensions of the discipline. For this reason he no doubt entered deeply into the inner bond of the art of the sword with Zen. Furuta Shōkin writes in an introduction to his modern Japanese translation of the *Fudōchishinmyōroku*: "There are Zen sayings referring to the 'sword that kills' and the 'sword that gives life.' If the sword can cut another person, it is to be feared that in being only a thoughtless cutting it becomes a devil's sword. To transform the sword that kills into a sword that gives life, the 'way of the sword' is needed. Takuan sought out the source of this transformation in order to clarify the fundamental principle of the sword." Cited in *Zenshū kana-hōgo* (Tokyo, 1971), pp. 14–15.

95.   *Nihon no zen-goroku*, vol. 13, pp. 199–200.

96.   *Nihon no zen-goroku*, vol. 13, p. 200.

97.   *Nihon no zen-goroku*, vol. 13, p. 201.

98.   *Nihon no zen-goroku*, vol. 13, pp. 201–202.

99.   *Nihon no zen-goroku*, vol. 13, p. 205.

100.   *Nihon no zen-goroku*, vol. 13, p. 207. The modern Japanese translation introduces the concept of the unconscious, which, given its psychological overtones, does not strike me as particularly felicitous. It is a matter of the essence of mind expressed negatively and articulating the spontaneity of the movements of the unmoved mind.

101.   *Nihon no zen-goroku*, vol. 13, pp. 215–16.

102.   On this section see *Nihon no zen-goroku*, vol. 13, pp. 216, 219.

103.   *Nihon no zen-goroku*, vol. 13, pp. 220–21.

104.   On the following see *Nihon no zen-goroku*, vol. 13, pp. 221ff.

105.   The text appears in *Takuan Oshō zenshū* and in *Nihon no zen-goroku*, (see note 94); for the English translation of Suzuki, see *Zen and Japanese Culture*, pp. 166–68.

106.   The manuscript, completed in 1632, was specified for the son of the author. A number of such secret documents were made accessible to the general public in 1937 by Dr. Fukui Kyūzō. See Suzuki, *Zen and Japanese Culture*, p. 150, n. 12.

107.   Suzuki, *Zen and Japanese Culture*, pp. 151–65. Suzuki explains his paraphrasing in a footnote: "In the following pages I have freely culled passages from Yagyū's text disregarding the divisions, in order to present Yagyū's philosophy of swordplay as I understand it. The original is too long, too full of difficult terminology remote from modern thought, to be rendered into any of the Indo-European languages. Any translation of this sort of literature is inevitably an interpretation largely admixed with the translator's ideas and background. It is chiefly for this reason that I have not attempted to mark off Yagyū's words from mine. They are hopelessly mixed up. I hope that, some day, someone will strive to write specifically about what may be designated as the psychology of Zen applied to various fields of art in its development in the Fear East" (p. 151, n. 13).

108.   Suzuki treats this in *Zen and Japanese Culture,* pp. 168ff.

109.   On the art of the sword of Miyamoto Musashi and his school, Niten-ichi-ryū (also called Nitō-ryū, "the school of the two swords"), see Kammer, *Die Kunst der Bergdämonen,* pp. 151–52; on his merits as a painter, see Y. Awakawa, *Zen Painting,* plates 59 and 60, and p. 179.

8

The Zen Schools during the Tokugawa Period

Firmly imbedded in the legally established religious structure of the new age, the Zen schools led a peaceful, well-regulated existence during the Tokugawa period (1603–1867), unshaken by any major event. During the Muromachi period Zen had demonstrated in its imposing and thoroughly Japanese artistic accomplishments how deeply rooted it was in the soil of Japanese culture. The Chinese influence, which belongs to the essence of Zen and dominated its external forms during the first stage of its implantation in Japan, was gradually integrated into the indigenous culture and ways of thinking. Thanks to the protection of the imperial court and the shōgunal government, Zen monasteries attained a position of prominence within medieval Buddhism. They also enjoyed a favor among the general populace that was to increase during the modern period. In spite of all this, by the end of the medieval period, the two Japanese Zen schools of Rinzai and Sōtō were clearly stagnating—Rinzai because of its dominant attachment to upper-class interest in art and literature, Sōtō because of a general lethargy. Efforts at reform moved forward slowly. Yet there was no lack of extraordinary figures in Zen during the Tokugawa period, only of few of whom we shall focus on here.

THE ŌBAKU SCHOOL

PREPARATIONS AND VOYAGE
The coming of Chinese masters to Japan brought new vitality to Japanese Zen around the middle of the seventeenth century. Preparations for the foundation of a third Zen school in Japan were already laid at the start of the Edo period in the port city of Nagasaki, the only port open to foreigners. Through it poured a stream of Chinese, mainly merchants, but also monks, scholars, and artists. The political turmoil that dominated the end of the Ming period (1368–1644) was in part responsible for this migration, which in its next stage would lead to the founding of the Ōbaku school.[1]

The settlers established three Zen temples in Nagasaki, all of which kept up close relations with Buddhist monasteries on the continent. The Chinese merchant ships carried along new Buddhist writings and works of art. In the three "temples of good fortune" (fukuji) of Nagasaki—Kōfuku-ji (founded in 1620), Fukusai-ji (1628), and Sōfuku-ji (1629)—the Zen monks, under the direction of Chinese abbots, performed somewhat esoteric prayer rituals for safe sea voyages and conducted popular funeral rites; in general, however, they did not introduce any new forms of Buddhism. These monasteries provided important assistance to the Chinese Zen masters who arrived around the middle of the seventeenth century.

The first Chinese master to take up residence in Japan and promote the cause of his school was Tao-che Ch'ao-yüan (Jpn., Dōsha Chōgen)[2] from the Chinese Rinzai tradition to which Yin-yüan Lung-ch'i (Jpn., Ingen Ryūki, 1592–1673) also belonged. Tao-che had studied Zen under a disciple of Fei-yin T'ung-jung (Jpn., Hi'in Tsūyō, 1593–1661),[3] renowned as the editor of the *Gotō gentō* (Chin., *Wu-teng yen-t'ung*) chronicle, and stood in direct Dharma relation to Yin-yüan, who had received the seal of enlightenment at the hands of the same master. A strong and highly gifted individual, Tao-che was not content with the religious routine followed in the Chinese temples of Nagasaki. He tried to teach what he understood to be authentic Zen—that is, a Zen aimed at enlightenment yet containing elements of the *nembutsu* and esoteric tradition. Many Zen monks, especially of the Sōtō school, entrusted themselves to his direction.[4] The most prominent monk from the Rinzai school to study under Tao-che was Bankei Yōtaku (1622–1693). We will have more to say about him and his relations with the Chinese master later. Japanese Zen suffered a great loss when Tao-che returned to China after a mere seven years in Japan (1651–1658). Rivalries with his countryman Yin-yüan and his disciples had prompted him to abandon his mission in Japan.[5] His profound efforts on behalf of Zen were to bear only meager fruit.

The contributions of the Chinese Zen masters to the implantation of Zen in Japan during the Kamakura period and the first half of the Muromachi period maintained their essential Chinese character as they were integrated into the Japanese Zen movement. The second wave of Chinese influence at the beginning of the Edo period culminated in the arrival of Yin-yüan Lung-ch'i[6] and his companions. Despite the extraordinary qualities of this master, who had presided over a large Zen monastery in China and was held in high regard, this second influx did not meet with the same smooth and widespread reception as had the first.

Already during its first days, Yin-yüan's expedition was trailed by foreboding shadows. While the transition of dynasties in China was not the only reason for the move to Japan, it was certainly one of the most important. During his last years in office, Yin-yüan was made to suffer injustices bordering on persecution.[7] The details of his trip are not very clear. In any case, his fellow countrymen in Nagasaki awaited his arrival eagerly and made all due preparations. His disciple I-jan (Jpn., Itsunen, 1601–1668), who had lived in Japan after the fall of the Ming dynasty in 1644, was particularly responsible for making his visit possible.[8] An invitation from the abbot of Kōfuku-ji assured Yin-yüan of a friendly reception at the Chinese colony in Nagasaki. Unperturbed, he set sail with a considerable number of companions, landing in Japan in 1654. Historical sources indicate that the group included twenty disciples, half of whom would return home by the following year, and ten artisans. His favored disciple, Yeh-lan (Jpn., Yaran) was not among them, having perished in a shipwreck after embarking for Japan at the invitation of the abbot of Kōfuku-ji. The master felt the loss deeply. In a letter he compared his fate to that of a father "who must pay off the debts of his child."[9]

THE MONASTERY OF MAMPUKU-JI

When he left his homeland at the advanced age of sixty-two Yin-yüan (Ingen) certainly had no intention of founding a new Zen school in the neighboring country of Japan. The glowing reports he had heard about Japanese Zen may have lifted his drooping spirits and quickened his desire to help the Japanese Zen monks in their own country. There are no indications that he harbored the dream of any greater undertakings. A warm welcome awaited him in Nagasaki; for his first lecture he looked out on a packed audience, including many Buddhist monks and renowned scholars.[10] Though Nagasaki offered only a very limited range of activity, news of his arrival was spreading quickly throughout the land.

In Kyoto a number of eminent Zen monks had read his works and were anxious to meet him. Among them were Ryūkei Shōsen (1602–1670) of Ryōan-ji (later abbot for a time of the large temple complex of Myōshin-ji) and his friend Tokuō Myōshū from nearby Myōshin-ji. From the monk Jikuin, a member of the Myōshin-ji community who happened to be in Nagasaki at the very moment of Yin-yüan's arrival, they received a firsthand report of the initial impressions the Chinese visitor was making. While everyone in Kyoto was waiting to welcome him in Japan's old capital, a Zen monk from Zenrin-ji in Hiroshima brought additional information. His report, still preserved, contains a solid base of fact and a mix of praise and cautionary remarks.[11] The Japanese Zen monks of Nagasaki were not at all happy with the master's Chinese companions. The complaints of the Japanese monks had to do mainly with the way the circle around Yin-yüan unabashedly displayed their Chineseness, presenting a Zen distinctly different from the Zen of the T'ang and Sung periods that had been brought to Japan centuries before by both Chinese masters and gifted and experienced Japanese. The foreignness and what seemed to them the many unsuitable qualities of this new Ming Zen filled them with repugnance and even disdain.[12] This mix of impressions, while not the occasion of any disastrous consequences, is characteristic of the history of the Ōbaku school.

After strenuous efforts, Japanese friends in Kyoto were finally able to open their doors to Yin-yüan, although their further hopes of providing him with an invitation to Myōshin-ji encountered insuperable difficulties. Hearing of the plans of his Kyoto colleagues, the master let it be known that he was in agreement.[13] But it soon became clear that there was a split within the large monastery community of Myōshin-ji regarding the advisability of such a visit. Ryūkei had even hoped that Yin-yüan, as a revered master in the thirty-second generation after Lin-chi, might become abbot of the monastery and be invested with the purple robe. After all, for Ryūkei and his followers, Chinese culture, foreign though it was, had for centuries provided the soil for Japanese Buddhism to grow. Many of the monks in the entourage of the abbot, Gudō Tōshoku (1579–1661), were not at all in agreement, and their position was strengthened by reports coming from Nagasaki. Behind the difference of opinion about Yin-yüan lay a deeper division. One camp within the community of monks was urging a strict observance of rules according to the Chinese model, while the other preferred a spontaneity more clearly suited to the Japanese character.

Meantime, Jikuin did everything possible to advance the cause of Yin-yüan. He gained the ear of Itakura Shigemune (1587–1656), who represented the shogunal government as governor of Kyoto.[14] Despite a certain reserve, the highest counselors in Edo received Jikuin with respect and evident good will, but withheld permission for Yin-yüan to remain in Kyoto. A compromise was finally reached: the Chinese master could stay in the Zen monastery of Fumon-ji in Settsu, a branch temple of Ryōanji, at the invitation of its abbot, Ryūkei.

Jikuin brought Ryūkei's invitation to Yin-yüan, who at first declined. But when leading monks from Nagasaki interceded, he yielded. His reception in Fumon-ji in 1655 was friendly. The governor, Itakura Shigemune, granted the Chinese master an audience and relaxed some of the restrictions that had been placed on his movements about the country, fearing that he might be a spy for his powerful Chinese homeland. Yin-yüan was now permitted to take short trips, to visit Kyoto, to walk through the gateways of the Myōshin-ji, Nanzen-ji, and Tōfuku-ji, and to meet with abbots and monks. He established friendly relations with the retired emperor Go-Mizunoo and representatives of the court nobility.

In 1657 Ryūkei travelled to Edo to promote the cause of his protégé. His request that Yin-yüan be given the purple robe was not granted, but the bakufu did assure the Chinese master of a well-endowed residence in Fumon-ji. A turn of events the following year brought Yin-yüan to Edo, accompanied by Ryūkei and Tokuō. He stayed at Tentaku-ji in Yushima, where he was visited by many prominent figures. The audience granted him by the shōgun Tokugawa Ietsuna (1639–1680) had its desired result. Yin-yüan was overjoyed to have gained the full confidence and friendship of the shōgun. Even the shōgun's government showed its friendliness. For a long time people in Edo had held out the hope of someday meeting the famous Chinese visitor. A particularly close friendship developed between the master and the respected counselor Sakai Tadakatsu (1587–1662), for the thirteenth anniversary of whose departed father Yin-yüan celebrated a commemorative ritual.

Shortly afterward Yin-yüan returned to Fumon-ji. From an exchange of letters with Edo, it is possible to piece together what was going on. As far as we know, Yin-yüan had come to Japan with the intention of helping the Japanese Zen monks, but as he faced mounting difficulties, he found himself more and more making serious plans to return to China. Letters from his master and disciples urged him to come home. When he wrote to his patron Sakai Tadakatsu to explain all of this, Tadakatsu tried to do all he could to keep him in Japan. He even convinced the shōgun to write and urge him, in light of his advanced age and the perils of the voyage, to stay in Japan.[15]

As time passed, the Chinese master grew dissatisfied with the insignificant rural temple of Fumon-ji and it became clear that a more suitable site for the construction of a temple had to be found. A large piece of property was eventually selected in Uji near Kyoto. It belonged to the Konoe family and some centuries earlier had been used by Muin Genkai (d. 1358) of the Genjū line for the construction of a temple that had since fallen into ruin. Construction began in 1661 with the approval of the shogunal government. Within a year the dedication of the Dharma hall was held and the monks took up residence while construction continued. The complex, designed in the Chinese style of the Ming period, was finally completed in 1669. From the very first turn of the spade, Yin-yüan had decided to name the new temple Mampuku-ji and its hilly site Ōbaku-san, after the Chinese temple and region he had left behind in China just a few years previously.[16]

The construction of Mampuku-ji represented at the same time the foundation of the Ōbaku school, but this does not imply that the bakufu wanted a new school. It was rather the case that the government assistance was given in "the context of the renewal of the Rinzai school."[17] Since Yin-yüan belonged to the Rinzai tradition, it would have been easy to include this new temple in the already existing Japanese Rinzai school. For a number of different reasons this did not happen. To begin with, unification into a single community was impeded by the tensions between Yin-yüan and the majority of the monks of the Myōshin-ji community. These tensions grew stronger after the expressions of goodwill shown to Yin-yüan by the shōgun. In addition, Ryūkei had not been well regarded in his home monastery, and the rift only grew wider with the respect he paid Yin-yüan and his move to Mampuku-ji while it was still under construction.

Another problem was Yin-yüan's style of combining esoteric rituals and a blend of Zen and the nembutsu, which he was in no way willing to change or adapt. Despite the easygoing attitude of Japanese Rinzai Zen toward rules, traditions, and the like, the leadership at Myōshin-ji was not prepared to acquiesce to this kind of syncretism. The upshot was that Yin-yüan's monastery of Mampuku-ji became the headquarters of a third Zen school in Japan.

Just as the buildings of Mampuku-ji reflected the Chinese temple architecture of those days, so too did the monastery's overall way of life follow the model of Ming-period Zen. In terms of the monk's religious practices, this meant a considerable increase in the cultic element and a great stress on observance of the rules. For Zen practice in general, seated meditation and practice of kōan are central, while cultic ceremony is of secondary importance. Insofar as the Ōbaku school belonged to the Rinzai tradition, zazen and kōan practice were made part of daily life, but ritual was also accorded a place of considerable importance. Besides the sūtras commonly used in Zen—among which the Heart Sūtra of the Perfection of Wisdom (Prajñāpāramitā) literature held first place— Ōbaku monasteries also made use of sūtras from esoteric and Pure Land Buddhism, as well as esoteric formulae (Skt., mantra, dhāraṇī) that were used for morning and evening services. The monks recited the sūtras to the accompaniment of Chinese musical instruments in the Chinese tones and reading style of the Ming-period Fukien dialect. The invocation of the name of the Buddha Amida (nembutsu) was used in meditation to promote concentration, even though it was not really part of the essential practice of Zen.[18] The same would apply to the numerous pictures of Buddhas, bodhisattvas, and arhats done in Chinese style and scattered throughout the temple with the aim of stirring the devotion of the monks.

The monastic rule followed the rule being observed in Chinese Zen monasteries during the Ming period. The particular redaction of the rule applied by the Ōbaku school (Ōbaku shingi) had been enriched through a number of modifications by Yin-yüan.[19] In order to introduce strict observance of the rule effectively into the monastic way of life, a three-story ordination platform was added to the temple complex.[20] Here, in elaborate ceremony, the young monks received the precepts step by step and pronounced the vows of ordination.

Chinese customs of everyday life, markedly different from those of Japan, were followed in Mampuku-ji. Over the course of the centuries, however, certain adaptations took place. Chinese dress was replaced by the Japanese monastic robe and straw sandals were used in place of Chinese shoes. Table etiquette remained Chinese: the monks ate out of a common bowl, each dipping in with his own utensil.

In the beginning, Mampuku-ji met with great success. Yin-yüan's spirit of initiative and his extraordinary organizational skills made themselves felt throughtout the lavish complex. Nor was it an unfavorable time for such reform. Many Zen monasteries in Japan had collapsed into a state of dormancy, and the call that was going forth from this new monastery met with a correspondingly eager response. As soon as the new buildings had been completed, a community of about one hundred members took shape and a steady influx of novices began. The attraction lay not merely in the exotic nature of the new foundation, though it is hard to rule an element of the fadish in its appeal. Yin-yüan may not be numbered among the great figures of Zen history, but as an important master from Zen's motherland he was bound to have an impact. While his first group of companions were of inferior quality, in time other highly qualified monks arrived to strengthen the new school. Among them were Mu-an Hsing-t'ao (Jpn., Mokuan Shōtō, 1611–1684; arrived in Japan, 1655), Chi-fei Ju-i (Jpn., Sokuhi Nyoichi, 1616–1671; arrived, 1657), and Kao-ch'üan Hsing-tun (Jpn., Kōsen Shōton, 1633–1695; arrived, 1661). Japanese Zen monks who had not found what they were seeking in their own monasteries renewed their study of Zen in Mampuku-ji. Moreover, there was no lack of religiously-minded young men strongly attracted by this serious and remarkable monastery. Thanks to Yin-yüan's efforts at expansion, there were some twenty-four Ōbaku monasteries scattered across the nation at the time of his death. The abbots of Mampuku-ji, who were all Chinese for the first fourteen generations, were committed to preserving the purity of the monastery's Chinese character.[21] After a few decades, however, growth slowed and this third school of Zen took its place behind Rinzai and Sōtō. In the end, it was clear that the Ōbaku school would not really be able to sink deep roots in Japanese soil.

The fate of the Ōbaku school has to be considered in terms of what we now call "religious inculturation." The situation is far too complex to admit of simple answers, but a number of points merit mention. The repeated transplanting of Chinsese Zen to Japan could never have taken place without Zen values being presented in new, up-to-date, and convincing forms. However, in this case, such a transmission did not ultimately occur. The Japanese Zen monks maintained their deep respect for Chinese Ch'an, but could not see anything desirable or enriching in what was brought to them from the motherland. The Chinese masters of the Ōbaku school were not superior to the best of their Japanese contemporaries—as we shall see in the examples that follow—even though they often bore an air of superiority that was offensive to Japanese sensitivities.[22] The personalities of the monks who came to Japan from the China of the declining Ming dynasty were not on a par with their predecessors of earlier centuries. The animosities that broke out between them and their Japanese Zen counterparts were all the more damaging to their image for the lack of a truly great figure among them. This general state of affairs is evident in the polemical writings that appeared after the Ōbaku school's early successes in the attempt to curb further expansion by calling the school to task and criticizing its style.[23]

Without doubt, Japan's high esteem for Chinese culture remained. The extraordinary achievements of the Ōbaku masters in calligraphy and ink painting were met with unqualified and enthusiastic acclaim.[24] But at the same time, the Japanese were not interested in forcing all the details of daily life into a foreign mold, as was the case in the Ōbaku monasteries. For a while, this affected lifestyle might have been accepted and even attractive, but eventually such regimentation proved unbearable. The Japanese rightfully expected greater regard for their own national characteristics.

The new Zen school also promoted a further tightening of the general restrictions that had come into effect with the isolation of the nation from the outside world. To compensate for their seclusion, the leading representatives of Japan's intelligentsia turned to the progressive, rationalistic currents of the day, which embodied a sort of "Enlightenment" and prepared the way for the modern period. Whether Chinese or Japanese in origin, these currents arose from the same psychological need for freedom of thought. Compared to such perspectives, the Ōbaku school seemed a countercurrent representing a revivalist or even reactionary movement. Not surprisingly, after a brief period of growth, the school ground to a halt. A breakthrough to a new consciousness of the tradition of Zen was left for the pioneering leader of modern Zen, Hakuin Ekaku (1685–1768). Drawing deeply on Chinese tradition, Hakuin succeeded in planting a Japanese crown firmly on the head of Chinese Ch'an.

TETSUGEN DŌKŌ

The most famous of the Japanese monks of the Ōbaku school was Tetsugen Dōkō (1630–1682),[25] best known for preparing the *Tetsugen-ban* or *Ōbaku-ban*, a complete edition of all the Buddhist scriptures from all the schools (*Daizōkyō* or *Issaikyō*). This edition was based on the Chinese Buddhist canon of the Ming period and compiled in 6,956 block-printed volumes. Although the personality of the editor has taken second place to his life's work—typical of the Ōbaku school—it is useful to make some brief comment on this important Japanese Ōbaku monk.

Born to a pious Buddhist family in Higo (in the Kumamoto region of Kyū-shū), Tetsugen was given a sound education. When he was six his father taught him one of the three great Amida sūtras, which the alert child was soon able to recite by heart. At his father's direction, six years later, in 1642, he joined the monastic life of Kaiun, the Dharma teacher of the local temple. Tradition has it that already from his early years he was able to sink deeply into meditation and evoke the presence of Amida Buddha in his heart. He devoted ten years to religious studies and practice in the temple.

Tetsugen was sixteen when he heard a lecture by the abbot of Eishō-ji in Kokura, Saigin (1605–1663), on the Mahāyāna treatise, *The Awakening of Faith in Mahāyāna* (Chin., *Ta-sheng ch'i-hsin lun*, Jpn., *Daijō kishinron*). Concerning the following years, there is little reliable biographical data.[26] Most likely he accompanied Saigin, who was a unique and important representative of the True Pure Land school (Jōdo Shinshū), when the latter went to Kyoto in 1647 to care for the education of the young monks of his school. His mother died in 1650, and it is likely that Tetsugen left Kyoto to return home and carry out his filial obligations, after which he resumed his studies in Kyoto, possibly under the direction of Saigin. According to later critics, Saigin taught the doctrine of Pure Land from the Zen perspective of the "self-nature of the one mind." This landed him in a position opposed to orthodox Amida doctrine, which had a learned representative in the figure of Gekkan, who was about the same age as Saigin. Gekkan also came from Kyūshū and presided over a temple there. In 1653 he went to Kyoto, probably out of concern for what Saigin was teaching. Saigin defended himself against Gekkan's attacks by pointing to the richness of Buddhist teachings and drawing on writings other than the Amida sūtras. This and other controversies occupied the Amida monasteries in the capital at the time.

Although Tetsugen was not directly involved in the unhappy events that were bringing unrest to the True Pure Land school, these events seem to have prompted him to take leave of Kyoto in 1655 for Nagasaki. There, in the monastery of Kōfuku-ji, he met the Chinese Zen master Yin-yüan, who had just arrived from China. Regarding the circumstances that moved Tetsugen to shift to Zen, the historical sources are mute. According to the author of the introduction to the *Tetsugen goroku*, the lectures of Saigin on *The Awakening of Faith in Mahāyāna*, which Tetsugen heard soon after leaving home, started him on a path that would end in his acceptance of Zen.[27] In any case, this treatise provided him with insights into Mahāyāna philosophy and important foundational ideas in Zen Buddhism; the confusion reigning within Amida Buddhism provided further stimulus for his move to Zen.

Tetsugen's conversion from Amida Buddhism to Zen did not come about without intense inner struggle. His first stay with Yin-yüan was brief, and before leaving Nagasaki he was given a letter from the master recommending him to his main disciple, Mu-an, who had since arrived from China. But that same year, 1655, Tetsugen followed Yin-yüan to Fumon-ji and only two years later returned to Nagasaki to meet with Mu-an. After returning to Yin-yüan the following year and spending only a short time with him, Tetsugen placed himself once more under the direction of Mu-an in 1659. Although there is little precise information abut his Zen practice during these years, we may suppose that he devoted himself energetically to meditation—without, however, managing to overcome his inner blocks and his painful restlessness. For a time he even considered giving up Zen altogether. Whether his separation from his wife—before his conversion to Zen he was, as a follower of Shinran, married—also contributed to his problems, we do not know. According to a not totally reliable source, she yielded to his resolve and finally became a Buddhist nun.[28]

According to his biographer, the period of oppressive darkness and painful doubt lasted for some five years (1656–1661).[29] Driven by inner necessity, he left Nagasaki in 1661 for the Zen monastery of Tafuku-ji in the region of Bungo, there to attend the lectures of the abbot Kengan on the Mahāyāna sūtra *Shu-ryōgon-gyō* (abbreviated as *Ryōgonkyō*, T. 642).[30] This sūtra, a favorite among adherents of Zen, was given preferential treatment by Tetsugen; of all the texts of the Buddhist canon, this was the one on which he expounded most frequently to his followers.

His first lectures on this sūtra were given in 1663 at the Zenjō-ji monastery near Kumamoto. They met with immediate success. A naturally gifted speaker, Tetsugen used his clearsighted intelligence to deliver his explanations in coherent form and lucid language. From this time on, he would devote himself mainly to delivering talks and lectures. His untiring commitment to lecturing on the Mahāyāna scriptures also provided a good part of the finances necessary for printing the Buddhist canon.

Out of his devotion to the Mahāyāna scriptures Tetsugen soon came to recognize the desirability of having the Buddhist canon, which had appeared in different editions during the Ming period in China, accessible. One year later, in 1664, he is said to have expressed to a small circle of friends for the first time his plan to print the entire canon in Japan. The idea took hold of him and would give him no rest. In summer of the following year he concentrated all his energies to a course on Zen under the guidance of the famous third Chinese master of the Ōbaku school, Chi-fei (Jpn., Sokuhi), but the period was too short to effect a decisive breakthrough. After that he gave himself over entirely to the development of his project.

From 1667 on, Tetsugen lived in the commercial city of Osaka, first in a private residence and later in Zuiryū-ji (1670), which his disciples had built for him and over which he presided as founding abbot. During a lecture to a large audience on *The Treatise on the Awakening of Faith in Mahāyāna* he spoke of his plan; there was a strong echo of support and he received the first financial help in the form of a spontaneous collection. Without any further hesitation, he made known his hopes to the head of the Ōbaku school, Yin-yüan, who immediately gave full consent, composing a poem to mark the occasion and placing all required means at Tetsugen's disposal. One of the fundamental goals of the Ōbaku school was to foster the reading of the sūtras. Already on Mount Huang-po (Ōbaku) in China there had been a printing shop for Buddhist scriptures.

The first step in Kyoto was to set up a house for the printers. Buildings for a central office were erected on a piece of land donated by the abbot within the temple complex of Mampuku-ji. Known as Hōzō-in (or "Hermitage of the Precious Canon"), the center was inaugurated two years later, in 1671. This material aid was surpassed only by the generous cooperation of the Ōbaku monks. The beginning of the undertaking is generally fixed at the time of the abbot's approval, 1669. In 1681, some thirteen years later, the task was completed. From Yinyüan's approval to the steady cooperation of the Ōbaku monks, the entire project was an undertaking of the Ōbaku school.

The need for a good Japanese edition of the Buddhist canon had long been felt.[31] Flawed by numerous printing errors, an edition based on the Chinese text from the Yüan period, prepared by the Tendai monk Tenkai at the request of the shogunal government, was unreliable and scarcely used. Since the T'ang period a number of printed editions of the Buddhist canon had been published in China. Above all, there were Northern and Southern versions dating from the Ming period that served as the foundation for a corrected edition, known in Japanese as the *Manreki-hon*, after the name of the Chinese era (*Wan-li*, 1572–1619) during which it was printed. This was the edition that Tetsugen chose for his printing, adding reading marks (*kunten*) for the Japanese characters. Composed of 6,956 wooden printing plates in 48,275 pages, this edition gave Japanese readers access to the period's best Chinese edition of the Buddhist scriptures. According to modern experts, a Korean edition that had appeared some centuries earlier (first printing around 1082, second corrected edition around 1236–1251) actually excelled all other pre-modern editions; it had been known in Japan, but at the time of Tetsugen Japanese culture was oriented more toward China.[32]

Naturally, Tetsugen and his colleagues were overjoyed at the completion of their project. The Ōbaku edition, which had been made financially possible by the breath of fresh air that had blown in with the Tokugawa period, stood as a first-rank cultural achievement. Numerous copies were scattered throughout the island of Japan and even influenced early European research into Sino-Japanese Buddhism.[33] (Today, the standard Japanese edition, *Taishō shinshū daizōkyō* [Tokyo, 1924–1935], named after the Taishō era [1912–1925], is internationally recognized as normative. While not complete, it is an extensive, well chosen, well ordered, critically edited collection of ninety-eight large volumes.)[34]

Tetsugen died at the age of fifty-two, shortly after completing his major work, his energies prematurely consumed by the constant round of trips and lectures. Like the Ōbaku school of which he was a member, Tetsugen stands in Zen history as a representative of the close bonds between Zen and sūtra teaching (*zenkyō itchi*), which, despite the famous verse attributed to Bodhidharma that speaks of Zen as a "direct transmission of mind to mind, independent of words and letters," had many followers in later centuries throughout all the schools of Asia. Tetsugen's predilection for the sūtras stems from the fact that they had led him to Zen. In all his writings, the influence of the Mahāyāna scriptures is clear. The *Kana-hōgo*,[35] his most important work, is a careful explanation of the *Heart Sūtra* that bears testimony to his deep grasp of the Zen worldview.

As already mentioned, Tetsugen made use of the Zen practices of *zazen* and the kōan. While he did have significant experiences, it is doubtful that he ever made the breakthrough to the great enlightenment.[36] For Mu-an, he was "the monk who lectured on the sūtras." Still, the master bestowed on him his whisk *(hossu)*, a sign that Tetsugen was his Dharma heir.[37] Because Tetsugen did not select any of his disciples to be his own successor, he gave rise to no new Zen line. During the final months of his life, he manifested his religious maturity by gathering together his remaining energies to devote himself whole-heartedly to aiding the victims of a serious famine in the provinces of the Kinki region. He is known as one of the "famous monks" *(meisō)* of Japanese Zen history.

THE RINZAI SCHOOL BEFORE HAKUIN

The Rinzai school was especially affected by the change of events effected by the Tokugawa period, largely because during the Ashikaga era the prominent leaders of the school had played a significant role in shaping government policies concerning religion. The lavish Zen art of the Muromachi period had bedecked the Rinzai monasteries of the capital with an aura of splendor. That period of exuberant growth was clearly over. The Rinzai school was not spared the blows that staggered Buddhism during the fifteenth and sixteenth centuries. At the beginning of the Tokugawa period Rinzai Zen also faced the difficult task of revitalizing itself in the confrontation with the Confucian and Shinto movements of the time. The renewal movements that characterized the intellectual life of the Tokugawa period coalesced in the Kogaku ("ancient learning") school of early Confucian learning and in the Kokugaku ("national learning") school that dominated Shinto; the intent of these movements was to bring about reform by reaching back into the past and drawing on original sources. Although they lacked the powerful regenerative energies of the Renaissance, they did embody and communicate the spirit of the modern period.

Changes were taking place in Zen as well. Important masters awakened a religious vitality, particularly in Rinzai Zen. New creative forces appeared within the Japanese Rinzai school as never before. The primary figures here were Bankei Yōtaku and Hakuin Ekaku, who, together with Dōgen, may be considered the most influential spiritual leaders in all of Japanese Zen.[38] Whereas Dōgen had belonged to the medieval period, Bankei and Hakuin fashioned the Tokugawa period into one of the most fruitful periods that Rinzai Zen would ever know.

The areas in which the Rinzai school were most severely affected by the general decline of Buddhism were the Five Mountains of Kyoto and Kamakura. The *gozan* movement collapsed. Leadership within the Rinzai was held by the line of Nampo (Daiō Kokushi), even though in the course of the Tokugawa period the mother monastery of Daitoku-ji had to yield its leading position to the branch monastery of Myōshin-ji. This process was given a strong impetus by the abbot of Myōshin-ji, Gudō Tōshoku (1579–1661),[39] who some twenty years later worked for the renewal of Japanese Rinzai Zen. As the last great representative of Daitoku-ji, Takuan Sōhō (1573–1645). The effects of Gudō's efforts are the only remaining testimony to the spiritual energy he radiated, since he left behind no writings to reveal the inner core of his personality. Through countless journeys across the land he restored many temples and founded new ones. More importantly, he provided numerous students with reliable guidance along the way of Zen.

Gudō entered monastic life at an early age, passing most of his youth in rural temples and in wandering. Even before he joined the community of Myōshin-ji—where on three separate occasions he would hold the position of abbot—in 1628 he finally attained the great enlightenment. Throughout his adult years he traveled widely, traversing many of Japan's provinces, all the way to the southern island of Kyūshū. During his final years he retired to a small temple in the capital of Kyoto. After his death, his students carried on his spirit by laboring energetically for the renewal of Rinzai Zen. Branch lines developed after him and remained active in the countryside.

In the fourth generation after Gudō, the direct line of Myōshin-ji arrives at the figure of Hakuin, the foremost figure of his age. The two members of this line that link Hakuin with Gudō—Gudō's immediate disciple Shidō Munan (1603–1676) and his disciple in the second generation Dōkyō Etan (1642–1721)—were worthy bearers of the true Zen mind. This lineage roots Hakuin in Gudō. That the old man from the hermitage of Shōju-an—as Etan is known in Zen—could produce a Hakuin was possible, Furuta Shōkin observes, only because of Gudō.[40] From the retired emperor Go-Mizunoo he was to receive the honarary title of Daien Hōkan Kokushi.

The three Rinzai personalities to be treated next all stem from the Myōshin-ji line: Bankei Yōtaku (1622–1693) from a branch line; Shidō Munan (1603–1676), who was Gudō's Dharma heir; and Dōkyō Etan (1642–1721). They prepared the way for Hakuin Ekaku (1685–1768), who outshined them all.

BANKEI YŌTAKU

In D. T. Suzuki's efforts to make Zen known in the West, the principal bearers of his new message were, historically speaking, the Chinese patriarchs and masters of the T'ang period. Readers of his early English works were introduced to Hui-neng and the circles of Ma-tsu, Shih-t'ou and Pai-chang up to Huang-po and Lin-chi. Suzuki's pioneering work on behalf of Japanese Zen is not as well known. Yet even before World War II, his Japanese writings were drawing attention to the extraordinary creativity of Bankei. In the foreword to the volume on Bankei he edited as part of the series of collected sayings of Japanese Zen masters, the Japanese Buddhist scholar Tamaki Kōshirō describes how moved he was when Suzuki introduced him for the first time to Bankei. In his excellent commentary on Bankei's writings, Tamaki demonstrates the authenticity of this first impression.[41]

In his English writings, Suzuki translates only a handful of passages from Bankei's sermons.[42] Only after his death did Suzuki's considerable contributions to the study of Japanese Zen receive greater attention. In the introduction to his English translation of Bankei's sermons, Norman Waddell observes that Suzuki's studies "revealed for the first time in concrete terms the true significance of Bankei's Zen and its high place in the history of Zen thought."[43] Waddell quotes a lengthy passage from Suzuki's Japanese writings that culminates in the recognition that "slightly before Hakuin's time was Bankei, whose 'Unborn Zen' advocated a new and original thought for the first time since Bodhidharma."[44] To be sure, the place that Bankei holds in the history of Zen is an eminent one.

Life. There is much about Bankei that is unusual. To begin with, his birth in a Confucian family was not at all typical of well-known Zen monks, nor was the fact that his father was a lordless samurai warrior *(rōnin)* before becoming a doctor. It was also rather peculiar for a Zen monk to have experienced the great doubt that shakes one to the very depths while studying the *Great Learning* (*Ta-hsüeh;* Jpn., *Daigaku*), one of the Four Books of the Confucian tradition. There he came upon the words, "The Great Wisdom illumines bright virtue" (Jpn., *meitoku*). Simple words, he thought, but what does "bright virtue" mean? At the time he was eleven years old.

A year previously his father had died and his older brother took over head of the household. Bankei himself was greatly devoted to his mother. Many stories about his childhood have been passed down. He himself remarks, for example, that he was a lively, mischievous child. When his brother sent him to the local school in his hometown of Hamada in the region of Harima (today a part of the city of Himeji in Hyōgo prefecture), he was not at all happy. With his mother's permission, he read the *Great Learning* under the direction of a Confucian scholar. At that time, people were content just to be able to read the characters and grasp the sentence structure properly, with little concern for the actual meaning. Bankei's question about the meaning of "bright virtue" caused his teacher no little embarrassment. His mother was not much help either.

A frustrating period of searching began for young Bankei. A Confucian to whom he had turned for help suggested that he go to the Zen monks who concern themselves with such difficult questions about the inner nature of things. But there were no Zen monasteries in his home town or surrounding area. Whenever the opportunity presented itself, he attended lectures and listened to sermons. Again and again he asked his question, never getting a satisfactory answer. In 1635 his quest brought him to the Amida temple of Saihō-ji, where he practiced the invocation of the name *(nembutsu)*, and in 1637 to the Shingon temple of Enyū-ji where the monks engaged in esoteric rituals. In both places he attempted to learn the art of concentration. The Shingon monks tried to convince him to enter their monastery, but their efforts were in vain.

A year later, in 1638, he found his way to the Zen monastery of Zuiō-ji in Akō (also in Harima), where he was warmly received by the abbot, Umpo Zenjō (1568–1653), a disciple of Nankei Sōgaku of the Myōshin-ji line.[45] A man of deep insight, Umpo was quick to recognize the exceptional qualities of his new disciple. Bankei promptly received the tonsure and eagerly took up the practice of Zen. Not much more is known about this first visit of Bankei to Zuiō-ji, except to say that for the time being the young monk no longer felt the need to search elsewhere, but devoted himself to *zazen* as an effective means of concentration.

After about three years he set out on a journey which, through its renunciations and penances, turned into a true pilgrimage. At times he would go for days without food or drink, or spend whole nights in meditation, often sitting on pointed rocks, expending every possible energy to realize his goal. After four years of such strenuous travels (1641–1645), he returned to Zuiō-ji, completely exhausted. He had been able neither to grasp the nature of "bright virtue" nor to find the "good friend" (*zenchishiki* Skt., *kalyāṇamitra*) who would serve him as a guide. He related to Umpo everything that had happened, and embraced wholeheartedly his master's warning against striving too hard or trying to force experience.

For the last stretch of his journey he chose to practice in a dilapidated straw hut close to Kōfuku-ji. With the door shut and with total concentration, he devoted himself to *zazen*. The exacting strain proved too much for his weakened condition; he fell seriously ill and showed no signs of recovery. From Bankei's own description of the symptoms, he seems to have contracted some form of pulmonary disease. A rash broke out on different parts of his body. Years later, in a sermon to the laity, he described what he had been through:

> My utter neglect of health . . . and the years of physical punishment finally took its toll, and came to a head in a serious illness. . . . My condition steadily worsened, I grew weaker and weaker by the day. [Whenever I spat, gouts of bloody sputum as big as thumbheads appeared. Once I spat against a wall and the globules stuck and slid to the ground in bright red beads.] At this time everyone was concerned about my condition and urged me to withdraw and take care of myself. I acquiesced to their judgment. A servant took care of me in my retreat. Finally, my sickness reached its crisis point. For a whole week I was unable to swallow anything except some thin rice broth. My throat could bear no other food. So I was ready to die, and at the time I felt no remorse. There was nothing special left to me. My only thought was that I was going to die without fulfilling my long nourished desire. Then I felt a strange sensation in my throat. I spat against a wall. A mass of black phlegm, large as a soapberry, rolled down the side. . . . Suddenly just at that instant . . . I realized what it was that had escaped me until now: *All things are perfectly resolved in the Unborn.*[46]

After this experience, which took place in 1647, Bankei ate two or three bowls of rice that his servant had prepared for him and quickly regained his strength.

In *Bankei Oshō gyōgōki*, a work written by Bankei's disciple Mōzan Soin after his master's death, Bankei's enlightenment is described in this way:

> One morning he went outside to wash his face. The aroma of the plum blossoms reached his nostrils and his feeling of doubt suddenly left him, like a pail whose bottom has dropped out. Immediately he was healed of his ailment.[47]

The account is poetic, tinted with cliché, and of little historical value. The account from Bankei's sermon, which is based on his own words, is clearly more important.

When Bankei told Umpo of his experience, the master recalled a scene from the Bodhidharma legend. "You have attained Bodhidharma's mark," Umpo said, and encouraged him to seek out prominent Zen masters that his experienced might be validated. Bankei was not able to meet Gudō Tōshoku in Myōshin-ji since the master was in Edo at the time, and none of the masters that he did meet were prepared to recognize his experience as genuine Zen enlightenment.[48] Most likely what held them back were the clear differences between what Bankei reported and what they themselves had experienced or had encountered in their own circles. The ecstatic element that goes with the experience of *satori* seemed to be missing. Bankei's insight was more like a deep experience than enlightenment. In any case, this insight was to become the subject matter of his sermons, on whose formulation we shall have more to say presently. The fact that his contemporaries looked on his message as something new brought Bankei no little grief.

After returning to Zuiō-ji in 1651, news reached Bankei of the arrival of the Chinese Zen master Tao-che Ch'ao-yüan (Jap., Dōsha Chōgen) in Nagasaki. At once he set out for Kōfuku-ji where the master was staying. But Tao-che, too, hesitated to make a judgment. Greatly impressed with the personality of the master, Bankei surrender to his guidance and before long Tao-che was able to certify his disciple's enlightened state of mind.[49] When the master began to write out the certification of enlightenment (*inka*), Bankei tore it from his hands and ripped it up. He had no need of written documents. Tao-che praised this extraordinary disciple before the entire community and posed to him the question of whence the Buddha had descended. Bankei pointed his finger to the heavens and to the earth, and the master was delighted.[50]

Bankei loved and honored Tao-che, but there were limits to his admiration. He regretted his master's abrupt return to China due to pressing circumstances and his early death in 1662. Dark clouds hung over Bankei's memories of Tao-che, who had not, he felt, grasped the full meaning of the unborn Buddha mind. In a later sermon, Bankei remarked that Tao-che had disclosed to him that although he had transcended life and death and was therefore able to witness Bankei's enlightenment, he had not achieved full maturity. This he could have done had he been able to remain in Japan.[51]

Bankei's years as a student came to an end with his stay at Kōfuku-ji under Tao-che's direction. Leaving Nagasaki in 1652, he traveled to the mountain country of Yoshino, where, in simple, often poetic, language, he instructed the peasants on the unborn Buddha mind. His travels took him once again back to Nagaski to see Tao-che, where for the first time he met Yin-yüan, who had just arrived with a group of disciples from China. From the start, Bankei did not get along with him and kept his distance from the Ōbaku school.

Zen history locates Bankei within the Myōshin-ji line of the Rinzai school. A certificate verifying his enlightenment was provided by Bokuō Sogyū, the Dharma heir of Bankei's first Zen teacher, Umpo. It would seem that relations between Bankei and Bokuō were not particularly close; indeed, they had a temporary falling out but were soon reconciled.[52] Bankei's legitimate membership in the Rinzai school needs to be stressed, inasmuch as later generations of Rinzai disciples, spurred on by Hakuin's cutting criticism of Bankei's Zen style, would engage in polemics against him. Bankei's stays at Myōshin-ji were frequent; following the order of the court in 1672 he even donned the abbot's robes for a short time. On that occasion, it is interesting to note, he returned the purple robes that had been offered him and donned the simple black habit of an ordinary monk. For the most part, his relations with Myōshin-ji were rather tenuous.

To try to track Bankei through his decades of travel would be an impossible task. Ryūmon-ji, which his friend Kyōgoku Takatoyo (1655–1694), the lord of Marugame in Sanuki (in the region of Kagawa, Shikoku) had built for him in 1661 in his native town of Hamada, served him as a home base. Gradually the monastery complex expanded. Bankei would return there from his frequent travels to train disciples, preach, and hold training courses.

Among the three monasteries that he founded, Ryūmon-ji is the first and most important. The other two monasteries were Nyohō-ji in Sanuki (Shikoku) and Kōrin-ji in Edo (in the Azabu district of the city). Nyohō-ji was erected in 1669 with the aid of the princely benefactor Katō Yasuoki. Nearby, in surroundings of which he was particularly fond, Bankei had the Ōshiken hermitage built. Refusing to receive visitors, he would spend long hours of contemplation in quiet solitude there. Many of his poems sing of the natural beauty of this beloved spot.

About ten years later, in 1678, at the request of the mother of Kyōgoku Takatoyo, he founded Kōrin-ji, which became a center of much salutary work among the urban population of Edo. Another favorite location for Bankei was Jizō-ji in Kyoto, where he would frequently repair for brief or extended periods of recuperation; the ill-effects of the extreme asceticism he had practiced in his youth remained with Bankei for the rest of his life.

These three major temples, together with his refuge in Kyoto, represent the principal destinations of his many journeys across the land. We should also mention in this connection Fumon-ji in Hirado, which brought him repeatedly to the southern island of Kyūshū. Throughout these travels and during his stays in different temples, Bankei adhered closely to the way of life of a Zen monk. There are many stories—of questionable historicity—illustrating his fidelity to the monastic rule. Over the years, the orbit of his activity widened. In addition to preaching to the common people, he observed the ancient Buddhist practice of offering spiritual retreats during the summer or winter (in India, preferably during the rainy season), called *ango* in Japanese (Skt., *vārṣika*). The list of these retreats, complete with dates, places, and number of participants, paints an impressive picture of the master's ceaseless activity.[53]

This brings us to the final years of Bankei's life, the high point of his work and the real reason for his ensuing fame. Written versions of his Dharma sayings and sermons stem mainly from the year 1690 and the winter of 1690–1691. Now sixty-nine years old, matured by long experience, Bankei preached a moving message about the unborn Buddha mind in a style characteristically his own yet adapted to his audience. One series contains the sermons he gave in a temple of Marugame in Sanuki (Shikoku) on 23, 25, and 26 August, and 1 and 2 September, 1690. In winter of the same year he held a series of sermons in his home monastery of Ryūmon-ji, for which, according to the records, some thirteen hundred people assembled. On this occasion someone committed his words to writing. Besides religiously minded lay people, there were among his audience many Buddhist monks from different schools—Rinzai and Sōtō monks, representatives from the old schools of Ritsu, Shingon, and Tendai, Amida believers, and followers of Nichiren. Bankei had evidently launched a popular movement. His convincing spirituality, combined with his tolerance and genuine friendliness, brought people from different backgrounds to seek him out for personal consultation.

During the last two years of his life he traveled about as usual. Both winters were devoted to practice courses—1691–1692 at Ryūmon-ji and 1692–1693 at Gyokuryū-ji in Mino. From there he set out in February on his last trip, which took him to Nagoya for ten days and then on to Edo. On the return voyage to Ryūmon-ji, in May he became sick and had to interrupt the trip at Hamamatsu. But he was soon back on the road and back at Ryūmon-ji in June. In August he delivered his final sermons for the people. He informed his disciples that he felt his end drawing near. When they requested a farewell poem, he told them that if they would hear his parting words they should listen to his everyday life. He died on 3 September, 1693.

The number of people estimated to have heard the sermons of Bankei is placed at around fifty thousand; he founded or restored some fifty to sixty temples. The title given him three years before his death by Emperor Higashiyama, Butchi Kōsai Zenji, crowns a formidable lifetime of work.

The Experience and Preaching of the Unborn Buddha Mind. Bankei's life and work are characterized by his experience of the unborn Buddha mind. The experience overtook him after long years of hard ascetic practice, bestowing on him powers of penetrating insight. Permeating his being to its very marrow, this experience resolved his doubt and opened up for him a new horizon on reality. Even though he sought out enlightened Zen masters to confirm the authenticity of what he had experienced, Bankei was already convinced of what he had seen—as he described it, "the unborn Buddha mind." The expression as such is rather unusual. Disturbed by the words of a Chinese classic, as we noted above, his doubt focused on the nature of "bright virtue." Over the course of many years of painful searching, the doubt swelled to the proportions of an all-embracing existential question. When Bankei finally came to his liberating vision there were no traces left of the Confucian context that had originated the process. The resolution of his doubt is poetically contained in the altogether Buddhist terminology of the unborn Buddha mind.

How did Bankei come to this formulation? A completely satisfactory answer is not possible. Both parts of the expression derive from Mahāyāna Buddhism, which has much to say about the Buddha mind and the Buddha nature. "Unborn" harkens back to the famous verse of the Pāli Canon that illustrates the absolute quality of reality:

> Monks, there is a not-born, a not-become, a not-made, a not-compounded. Monks, if that unborn, not-become, not-made, not compounded were not, there would be apparent no escape from this here that is born, become, made, compounded.[54]

We may be fairly confident that Bankei was not acquainted with this text. Still, he would have been familiar with the negations in the Mahāyāna Wisdom sūtras. The "Unborn" (Skt., anutpāda; Jpn., fushō) is tied in with the teaching of the Middle Way on the "Undestroyed" (Skt., nirodha; Jpn., fumetsu) in a statement that includes the notion of indestructibility. In his own view, Bankei's experience goes beyond the teaching of the sūtras. As he observes in the course of one of his sermons:

> If you live in the Unborn, then there's no longer any need to speak about "nonextinction" or "undying." It would be a waste of time. So I always talk about the "Unborn," never about the "Undying." There can be no death for what was never born, so if it is unborn, it is obviously undying. . . . You can find the expression "unborn, undying" here and there in the Buddha's sūtras and in the recorded sayings of the Zen masters. But there was never, until now, any proof or confirmation given of the Unborn. People have just known the words "unborn, undying." No one before has ever really understood this matter of the Unborn by confirming it to the marrow of his bones.[55]

For Bankei the expression in the sūtras, "unborn, undying," remains on the conceptual level. To truly know the Unborn, some such experience as he had is necessary. The insight into the Unborn that he attained is not simply the clarification of "unborn" or "undying" (fushō-fumetsu). The Unborn, in which everything comes together in harmony, transcends the meaning of "unborn" as found in the parallel expression "unborn, undying." He thinks he is the first to make this clear.[56]

As Bankei understands it, the Unborn that lies beyond "unborn and undying" belongs to the realm of the Absolute. When he touched this reality with his own experience, he could not announce his message in the words of the sūtras. And yet in Mahāyāna, the Unborn appears in both cultic and meditative expressions, especially in the esoteric school of Shingon, which applies the name unborn to the first vowel, A—the ground and mother of all sounds and all beings—and practices meditation on the unborn A, the so-called ajikan fushō. Bankei, who knocked on many a temple door during the course of his long period of practice, spent some time in the Shingon monastery of Enyū-ji and learned the esoteric rituals practiced there. He surely became acquainted with the popular meditation on the unborn A, and it is in fact very possible that he first encountered the term *unborn* in this Shingon temple and carried it in memory as he continued his voyages. In this regard, a historically reliable episode from the last years of his life recounts that during his stay in Jizō-ji in Kyoto, a dignitary from the Shingon school came to visit him. For his entire life, the learned monk had been a searcher after truth. Though devoted to his own school, the monk also had the highest regard for Zen, was well acquainted with many Zen writings, and maintained contact with Zen masters. He presented himself as an honest inquirer. Bankei spoke to him about the originally unborn Buddha mind. Deeply moved, the Shingon monk confessed that for the first time he really understood what it meant to say that "the sound of A and all *dharmas* are originally unborn." The following day he sent the master a poem on the unborn mind.

Bankei's preaching on the unborn Buddha mind is thus grounded in his own experience. Transcriptions of his talks written down by his audience—all dating from his final years—contain his central ideas in slightly differing formulations. The frequent repetitions of the same ideas, often in the identical words, can only partially be explained by textual tradition. More important is to realize that they can be attributed to Bankei himself, who, as he once confessed, always talked about the same thing in his sermons—namely, what was most important to him. The differing formulations all bring out the mature message of the aging master.

Unremittingly, Bankei tried to make clear that the unborn Buddha mind was innate in people. As he says in a sermon:

> What I say to everyone is that the Buddha mind is innate in them from their parents. Nothing else is innate. This Buddha mind innate from their parents is unborn; it enlightens the mind. All things have their rightful place in the Unborn.

Yet all persons must recognize and decide to give themselves over to the Buddha mind and with their whole beings live according to it.

> Those who opt for the unborn Buddha mind that enlightens the mind remain, from the very moment of this birth on, a living Perfected One (*tathāgata*). Because they are living Buddhas, I call my school the Buddha mind sect.[57]

The same fundamental idea resonates in another text:

> The Unborn that I am talking about is the Buddha mind. The Buddha mind is unborn, and it illumines the mind. In the Unborn everything is properly ordered. Those who carry out all things according to the Unborn find their eyes open to other persons so that they can today behold all other persons as living Buddhas. . . . These people recognize the loftiness of the Buddha mind and are no longer prey to confusion. Because people do not know of the loftiness of the Buddha mind they cause illusions in all things, even in small things, and hence live as unenlightened beings (Jpn., *bombu*; Skt., *pṛthagjana*).[58]

In their urgency, Bankei's sermons are reminiscent of Lin-chi's discourses, though they do not match the intellectual and literary power of the great Chinese master. As Lin-chi had taught his disciples, so did Bankei remind the common people that they are perfected beings and Buddhas, if they could but realize their unborn Buddha mind. His admonitions touched on the realm of the Absolute. But the Unborn is inexpressible, and there were not words for Bankei's school to mediate it.[59] Buddha is a word, a name, but the Unborn is nameless. As he says in one of his sermons:

> The Unborn is the ground of everything; the Unborn is the beginning of everything. Because there is no ground for anything outside of the Unborn and because before the Unborn there was no beginning for anything, the Unborn is the foundation of all Buddhas.[60]

In terms of their content, Bankei's sermons were clearly within the bounds of Mahāyāna teaching, and yet presented his audience with something new and unusual. The gray-haired master could look back at the early years when he first preached the authentic Dharma of the Unborn: "When I was young, there wasn't anyone who really understood me; when they heard me they thought I was an outsider or a Christian. Everyone was afraid to draw close to me. . . ."[61] In time this situation was to turn around completely. Bankei went on to recount how once people had begun to understand and to realize that he was preaching the genuine Dharma of Buddhism, they flocked to him until eventually he scarcely had time for peace and quiet any more.

The older and more mature Bankei grew, the more he became a man of the people. In his sermons he avoided difficult expressions or quotations from the sūtras and the sayings of the masters. In one of his sermons, for example, he provoked the hearts of his hearers with these words: "There is no one among you who does not wish to become a Buddha."[62] He went on to assure them that not a one of them was unenlightened[63] since all possessed the unborn Buddha mind:

> Those who live according to the Buddha mind and do not succumb to illusions have no cause to seek enlightenment outside of themselves. Sit with the Buddha mind, keep company only with the Buddha mind, sleep with the Buddha mind, arise with the Buddha mind, dwell only with the Buddha mind; then in all your daily activities—walking and waiting, sitting and lying down—you will act like a living Buddha. Nothing else remains to be said.[64]

Nothing is more important than to know the Buddha mind. "Whoever does not know the Buddha mind falls into illusions."[65] Bankei made great efforts to aid his hearers with their burden of illusions and passions. A peasant once asked him:

> By nature I am impulsive and easily angered. As a farmer, I am absorbed in my chores and find it difficult to follow the Buddha mind. How can I follow the unborn Buddha-mind?

The master replied:

> Since all people possess the unborn Buddha mind from their birth, you are
> not now seeking for the first time to follow it. If you perform your chores
> with all your energies, you are practicing the unborn mind. Also, if while
> hoeing in the field you speak with the people and hoe at the same time,
> then you hoe while speaking and you speak while hoeing. But if you hoe
> in anger, your anger is an evil work that deserves the punishment of hell,
> and your work is toilsome and painful. But if you hoe without the clouds
> of anger or other passions, your work will be easy and pleasant. It is a work
> of the unborn, unperturbed Buddha mind.[66]

In his talks and answers to questions, Bankei spent a great deal of time
urging and counseling people how to overcome illusions and passions. Understanding well the needs of the common people as he did, Bankei sought to help
them. Accordingly he avoided harshness, explaining to his listeners that a life
lived in harmony with the Buddha mind is easy and open to everyone. Having
experienced in his own body the dangers of excessive asceticism, he pointed
out that it is possible to "fulfill the Dharma in a pleasant setting, on a straw
mat, without unnecessary stress"[67] and so to dwell happily in the unborn Buddha
mind. Concretely he recommends that people

> first tarry for thirty days in the Unborn. Those who are accustomed to live
> for thirty days according to the Unborn will afterwards live spontaneously
> in this same way; indeed they will realize that such a life is necessary, and
> they will feel extraordinarily well in the Unborn.[68]

To a monk who feared that life in the Unborn could lead to laziness he
explained: "Those who do not dwell in the Unborn are busy with many secondary
works; rushing about, they disfigure the Unborn into superfluous things." When
the monk could make no reply, the master admonished him: "Don't waste any
time! Dwell in the Unborn!"[69] Two other monks asked whether dwelling in the
Buddha mind would not lead to distractions, thoughtlessness, and insensitivity.
They too received the simple answer that they must dwell securely in the Buddha
mind.[70]

There was a group of Vinaya monks who felt certain that they would attain
Buddhahood by holding to their resolve to observe the 250 precepts or rules.
Is this good or bad? "Certainly this is good and not at all bad," the master told
them.

> But you can't say it's the best. It's shameful to wear your rules as a badge
> and call yourselves the "Precepts" sect (Risshū), as if you think that's some-
> how superior. . . . The Unborn is the mind of the Buddhas. If you live
> according to it, then from the first there's no distinction between observing
> and not observing. Those are designations that arise after birth. They're
> one or more removes from the place of the Unborn.

With gratitude the Vinaya monks accepted this teaching.[71]

A woman from Izumo was worried that the instructions of the master might be too easy. In his response to her Bankei reiterates his constant admonition not to give in to the passions—whether anger or greed or foolishness—since such failings lead to rebirth in painful forms of existence, even to the depths of hell.[72]

Bankei's Zen teachings have been accused of excessive leniency. He is said to have made things too easy and so to have harmed his students through such a lack of rigor. Two comments are in order here. Unable to forget his bitter bouts with self-tormenting asceticism, Bankei wanted to spare his listeners that experience. A bodhisattva's heart overflowing with compassion not only urged him to preach the Dharma untiringly but also gave him a great understanding of the weaknesses of his listeners. Moreover, one should not overlook the moral content of his preaching, which placed great emphasis on the main Buddhist precepts. In his sermons he continually urges his audience to eradicate egocentric passions and warns those who neglect to do so of resultant punishments in the cycle of rebirths. In this regard, his sermons are no different from those of other Zen masters. But in addition to the morally upright life expected of all, Bankei demands nothing less than solid devotion to the unborn Buddha mind. Particular Zen practices like sitting in meditation (zazen) and the solution of the kōan may be useful, but in his view these were not necessary. This is characteristic of Bankei's Zen style.

Bankei understood Zen history from the perspective of his own experience and this in turn led him to a radical relativization of the usual practices that constituted Zen at that time. The stereotype of this approach had taken shape during the Sung period in China, and after developing into an established method, became a matter of routine in Japan. Bankei measured this system against the standard of his own experience of the unborn Buddha mind and came to the conclusion:

> The unborn Dharma disappeared in both Japan and China and has long since been forgotten. But now it has appeared in the world again.[73]

Or as he expressed it elsewhere:

> Upon reading the latest reports from China, I realized that for some time now persons of the Unborn have disappeared from there; in our days there are no more persons of the Unborn in China.[74]

As Bankei goes on to explain, this has been the situation for some three hundred years, as people have sunk deeper and deeper into doubt until they are no longer able to open their Dharma eyes. "Zazen is another term for the Buddha-mind," explains Bankei.[75] Far from being limited to the Zen hall, zazen is to be carried out in the everyday things of life. Any ordinary experience is zazen as long as it takes place in the Buddha mind. He teaches his disciples:

> Now in zazen, it's a matter of the Buddha mind sitting at rest. It's the Buddha mind doing continuous zazen. Zazen isn't limited to the time you sit. That's why, around here, if people have something to do while they're sitting, they're free to get up and do it. It's up to them, whatever they've

a mind to do. Some of them will do *kinhin* (walking meditation) for one stick of incense. But they can't just continue walking, so then they sit down and for another stick of incense they do *zazen*. They can't be sleeping all the time so they get up. They can't talk constantly, so they stop talking and do some *zazen*. They aren't bound by any set rules.[76]

But to seek directly the experience of enlightenment in one's practice of *zazen* is to go astray. Bankei lays bare this "great error"[77] that has continued unquestioned for three hundred years. This false system is totally incompatible with the teaching of the unborn Buddha mind.

Throughout his life, Bankei almost never took practice of the *kōan* seriously. His repudiation of the method has different explanations. The close, if not indissoluble, bonds between kōan and the Chinese language made access to them difficult and weakened their impact. In his own words:

> Since we [Japanese] aren't very good at Chinese, when we have to use it for such questions and answers, we have trouble expressing ourselves fully and saying just what we want to. But if we use our own everyday language and speak just the way we normally do, there's nothing at all we can't ask about.[78]

His aversion to things Chinese also led him to harbor general reservations about Zen literature. Unlike most of the writings of Japanese Zen masters, which consist of extensive explanations of quotations from the sūtras and sayings of earlier Chinese Zen masters, Bankei speaks to his Japanese hearers in the language of their own milieu. The personal situation of his interlocutor was important for him. Careful to avoid over-generalization, he preached "neither the Buddha-Dharma nor the Zen-Dharma."[79]

Their Chinese linguistic form was not the only reason that Bankei rejected the kōan. He also disliked the artificiality of the practice and considered it unsuitable for disciples of the unborn Buddha mind. Instead of taking up individual kōan, he simply pointed to the unborn Buddha mind. He was not very impressed when someone presented him with the famous, artificially constructed kōan from the *Hekiganroku* (no. 88) concerning the "triple invalid" whose blindness kept him from seeing how the master was frightening him, whose deafness protected him against all noises, and whose muteness kept him from disclosing what he knew. Though a genuine kōan, the example was hypothetical and not a common occurrence. Bankei simply told his questioner that since he was not himself in the situation of the threefold invalid, he was better off trying to get to the bottom of his own self. And with that, he began to teach the unborn Buddha mind.[80] Something similar took place with two other questioners who were unsuccessfully grappling with the first two kōan of the *Mumonkan*— namely, those dealing with the Buddha nature of a dog and the fox of Pai-chang.[81] They, too, were told to turn to the unborn Buddha mind, for "twenty years of practice are not enough to come close to the Unborn."[82]

As we pointed out in volume 1 of this work,[83] D. T. Suzuki took an early interest in the problematic of kōan practice. In his study on Bankei he recognizes the "danger" inherent in what he calls "tendency to formalization":

> The danger that the goods will be sold cheap is something intrinsic to the system. In any construct devised by man a pattern always evolves. When the pattern becomes fixed, the quick of life cannot move within it. . . . Zen ceases to be Zen.[84]

Suzuki rejects what is artificial in the kōan method without ignoring its benefits. The heart of a kōan lies in doubt. The decisive thing is that "the question whose resolution should be prosecuted as a matter of life and death . . . emerge from within oneself."[85]

Bankei was acquainted only too well with doubt himself. Although he approached it first from without when struggling with the words about "bright virtue" that he had met in a Confucian classic, in time he came to know the essence of doubt so deeply that he himself *became* his own existential doubt. The kind of doubt he encountered in people practicing the kōan he rejected as artificial:

> In recent times, wherever you go you find that Zen teachers use "old tools" when they deal with pupils. They seem to think they can't do the job without them. They're unable to teach directly, by thrusting themselves forward and confronting students without their tools. Those eyeless monks with their "tool Zen"—if they don't have their implements to help them, they aren't up to handling people.
>
> What's worse, they tell practitioners that unless they can raise a "great ball of doubt" (*daigidan*) and then break through it, there can't be any progress in Zen. Instead of teaching them to live by the unborn Buddha mind, they start by forcing them to raise this ball of doubt any way they can. People who don't have a doubt are now saddled with one. They've turned their Buddha minds into "balls of doubt." It's absolutely wrong.[86]

Bankei's attitude toward doubt sheds light on his attitude towards the kōan. Remarks in his sermons on kōan occasionally border on the disdainful.[87] Two generations later, Hakuin would respond to these attacks.[88] To illustrate Bankei's balanced judgment and his motives, listen to how he replies to a monk who asks "If that is true, what about all the old kōan? Are they useless and unnecessary?"

> When worthy Zen masters of the past dealt with those who came to him, every word and every movement was appropriate to the moment. It was a matter of responding to their students and their questions face to face. They had no other purpose in mind. Now there's no way for me to tell you whether that was necessary, or helpful, or not. If everyone just stays in the Buddha mind, that's all they have to do—that takes care of everything. Why do you want to go and think up other things to do? There's no need to. Just dwell in the Unborn. You're eager to make this extra work for yourself—but all you're doing is creating illusion. Stop doing that. Stay in

the Unborn. The Unborn and its marvelous illumination are perfectly realized in the Buddha mind.[89]

As these words testify, Bankei had the highest regard for Zen tradition, especially for the early masters of the T'ang period. In his view, the artificiality of the Kōan method marked a departure from this tradition. The overall structure of *zazen-kōan-satori*, in which the first two elements can easily be considered as a means to the attainment of the last, diverges from the original, spontaneous Zen mind. When a monk asked him "Is it good to practice with the goal of *satori* in mind?" Bankei answered: "There is no *satori*. Your mind is the original Buddha. Is there anything lacking in the Buddha mind? Can one attain enlightenment from outside oneself? . . ."[90] Bankei is convinced that no one cannot attain enlightenment since all of us from birth are already possessed of the Buddha mind.

In appealing to this central teaching on the innate Buddha mind that enlightens all minds, Bankei does not intend to deny the significance of the experience of enlightenment, but he does mean to warn against overestimating this experience; hence he urges a proper order to the never-ending process of ascent on the way. Tradition has it that the following conversation took place between Bankei and his disciple Itsuzan Sojin (1655–1734) after the disciple's enlightenment

> Itsuzan: For a long time I have allowed myself to be deceived by the words of the master; now I myself have perceived *satori*; I cannot really explain this state of the mind.
> Bankei: You don't have to say anything. I understand.
> Itsuzan: The master maintains that normally there is no great enlightenment, but from my own experience I now know what it is.
> Bankei: Even when enlightenment is present, it is not good to simply stay with it, for the most important thing comes afterwards. Those who are not of great goodness do not realize the perfect clarity of the Dharma eye.
> Itsuzan: Now I do not have the slightest doubt about the Dharma. No power can add anything to it.
> Bankei: It is easy to reach the stage where there is no longer doubt or questioning. The Dharma is extremely deep; wisdom is extremely deep; the more one enters, the deeper one goes. If therefore throughout my entire life I have never spoken a word of agreement, it is for the sake of my fellow human beings.[91]

Bankei refuses to speak about experiences of enlightenment because they are ineffable and because dwelling on them impedes progress. In his old age he expressed his own progress in the Buddha mind in the following important statement: "Regarding the teachings, there is no difference, but the Dharma eye does become perfectly clear. To penetrate into the great Dharma and to experience the great freedom are as different from each other as are heaven and earth."[92]

· Bankei drew on his own life experience in directing his disciples. The deep experience of the unborn Buddha mind had brought about his youthful conversion, and since that memorable moment he could be counted among the enlightened. Yet over the years his enlightened Dharma eye achieved a clarity that, as noted above, was like a dawn lifting the dark of night. He left behind no detailed description of this important process that had a decisive influence on the way he guided his disciples. For him, sudden experiences took second place to the constant progress that one must make along the way of the Buddha. Regarding the question of whether the perfect clarity of the Dharma eye takes place over a period of time or in an instant, he answered that the Dharma light comes to fullness through ceaseless advance.[93]

Bankei's life in the unborn Buddha mind reached a high level of perfection. For him, the transcendent, absolute reality of the unborn Buddha mind was not an object of metaphysical speculation but a present experience. A conversation he had with a Confucian in the monastery of Kōrin-ji in Edo shows how he could diverge from Mahāyāna philosophy without being untrue to his experience. The Confucian inquired about the relation between the Buddha mind on one hand and birth and the passing of the body on the other. He explained:

This body—born as a temporary composition of earth, water, fire, and air—will eventually corrupt. But the Buddha mind is unborn. When the body returns to earth and ashes, the mind, although it burns, does not burn up. The Buddha mind had taken up temporary residence in the born body—that is, as long as it dwells within the body. And so the mind hears sounds, smells aromas, speaks freely. But when the temporarily composed and born body passes away, the residence of the Buddha mind is destroyed; there is no more walking, hearing, or speaking. Although this body, because it was once formed, comes to birth and passes away, the mind, which from the beginning is the Buddha mind, knows neither birth nor destruction. I have so explained why one can here speak of "unborn" and "undestroyed." Is there any sound proof for this teaching? When Śākyamuni spoke of nirvāṇa (Jpn., nehan) the ne originally meant "unborn" and the han "undestroyed." This is the Unborn.[94]

Bankei's life is full of stories that are still retold but that we cannot include here. He was certainly one of the most popular of all Zen masters. A comparison with other important Zen figures brings out his originality. D. T. Suzuki distinguishes three different kinds of Japanese Zen in the figures of Dōgen, Hakuin, and Bankei. While Dōgen and Hakuin stand out as men of imposing spiritual power, Bankei, in his unassuming ordinariness, has to be looked at more closely before his unique importance becomes evident. In his comparative study, Suzuki makes a remark that can easily be overlooked: "Through the two characters for 'unborn' (fu-shō), Bankei has revealed the universal spiritual significance of Zen experience, without, however, forgetting Zen's intuitive character."[95] The real uniqueness of Bankei's Zen lay in the way he avoided extremes and thereby disclosed an ordinary way open to all—a spiritually that could speak both conceptually and personally to a wide range of people. His strong convictions about a life lived in harmony with the Absolute resonates well with any genuine spiritually. His sincere readiness to help, together with his selfless involvement with others, is the true mark of friends of the Absolute. During his years as a master he proved to be an effective, popular guide and counselor who, without overburdening ordinary people, was able to assist them in the discovery of true happiness. He permitted no extreme experiments within his circle of disciples; for his part, he never had recourse to shouting or striking. The radiant power of his personality, combined with his selfless gentleness, created around him an atmosphere of authentic humanity.

We have given special attention to Bankei because of his significance for contemporary Zen and for its ever increasing diversity of expression. While the distance that separates him from us historically makes for marked differences, Bankei has a important message for our day. For a variety of reasons, often fortuitous, his Zen style did not meet with great success during the Tokugawa period. Outside of Buddhism, he was especially revered by the reform movement known as Shingaku ("School of the Heart"), which found inspiration in his humanism. In our own times, it may well be that a Bankei renaissance would bear many and unexpected fruits.

THE MYŌSHIN-JI LINE

During the Edo period the Rinzai school was represented mainly by the lines of the two great monasteries of the old capital, Daitoku-ji and Myōshin-ji, both of them independent of the Gozan system. Despite the difficult setbacks they had to suffer during the turbulent days at the end of medieval period, they were able to recover to some extent. Daitoku-ji, which tended to embody the material rather than the intellectual achievements of Zen during this period, failed to produce any leading personalities after the death of Takuan Sōhō (1573–1645).

The branch monastery of Myōshin-ji also took quite some time to bring forth influential personalities. It is nonetheless constructive to examine the development of this line, for it was here that modern Japanese Zen Buddhism reached its high point in the towering figure of Master Hakuin. Among the temples in Kyoto at the beginning of the Edo period, Myōshin-ji cast a rather modest figure, though historians tell us that a reform of the monastery had already begun under its ninth abbot, Sekkō Sōshin (1408–1486). His four principal disciples, all of them courageous and successful men, labored relentlessly to rebuild the monastery complex. Two of them, Tokuhō Zenketsu (1419–1506) and Tōyō Eichō (1429–1504), originated flourishing branch lines. Here we shall have to limit ourselves to mentioning some of the most important names, without going into detail about their life and activity.

In the line of Tokuhō, we may mention Daigu Sōchiku[96] (1584–1669), who was born in Mino (Gifu prefecture) and devoted himself untiringly to the reconstruction of ruined temples; Ungo Kiyō[97] (1583–1659), from the island of Shikoku, travelled widely but is best remembered for his work as abbot of the Zen monastery of Zuigan-ji in northern Matsushima; and finally, some two or three generations later, Mujaku Dōchū[98] (1653–1744), who is known for his intellectual and literary work, an impressive collection of which is still preserved today. All of these men occupied at different times the highest office of the Myōshin-ji monastery.[99]

The other side of the Dharma heritage of Myōshin-ji begins with Tōyō Eichō, from whose line Hakuin came. Although this line was later to make a great contribution to the reformation of Zen, we cannot speak of an actual renewal during this period. The rigid routine enveloping the kanna-zen that had been brought from China during the Sung period hampered any kind of breakthrough in this regard. Deprived of their spontaneous power, zazen and the kōan degenerated into mere technique.

Genealogically, Bankei belongs to this line, but in fact he stands apart from it. His was a voice singing extra chorum as he struggled resolutely against the formalism he found on all sides. We have treated him in some detail because of his unique Zen style. Time spent in deeper appreciation of his thought is time well spent.

With Gudō Tōshoku (1579–1661), to whom frequent reference has been made, the Myōshin-ji line was given a breath of fresh air. Although he spent much time traveling, Gudō was a full-time member of the Myōshin-ji monastery, and within it forcefully voiced his conviction that a reform of the Rinzai school was necessary. He himself, however, evidently did not possess sufficient energy to carry out such a reform. Indeed, he was not able to take any decisive steps within his own temple. As has so often been the case in the history of Zen, it was an external stimulus that prompted reform. Gudō's contribution to a new beginning came more from his role as a wandering monk than as an established abbot. Many held out high hopes for Gudō's most gifted disciple, Isshi Monju[100] (1608–1646), but despite his extraordinary achievements these hopes came to naught with his early death. Shidō Munan (1603–1676), whom Gudō visited regularly on his travels and guided along the way of Zen, was to be the precursor of the new age of Rinzai that Hakuin would inaugurate.

HAKUIN'S PRECURSORS AND PREPARATIONS

With Shidō Munan[101] the long-awaited hopes for reform began to take shape. His childhood and youth were markedly different from the usual course of a Zen master's life. The eldest son of the owner of an inn at the outpost of Sekigahara in Mino (Gifu), the young boy showed signs of intellectual vigor combined with religious interests. He took such delight in turning his talents to writing in the Japanese syllabic script (kana) and its artistic cursive style (sōsho) that he became known as "the kana-writing boy" (kanagaki dōji).[102] As the oldest child of a highly respected and well-to-do bourgeois family, he was destined to carry on the family business, though no pressure seems to have been put on him to do so. His religious sensitivities came to the fore when his father decided to take the fourteen-year old along with him on a trip to Kyoto and Osaka.[103] When the boy saw the devastations of the war that had just ended, he was overwhelmed by the suffering state of humanity and recognized the corruptibility of all worldly possessions. He must have felt then a touch of the melancholy that was to accompany him throughout life and that perhaps explains his preference for the somber and solitary life of the hermit. Numerous passages in his writings recall the ancient scriptures of the Pāli Canon, such as the following description, composed "with a sense of deep sympathy," of an old man baring his sorrows and asking for guidance in the way of the Buddha:

> These long autumn nights, I cannot sleep for thinking of things that will never come again, and for hoping for peace in a still uncertain future. Now all my friends have passed away, and the people today with whom I should like to be acquainted look on me as a vile old man. The young ones [finding it unpleasant to be with me] walk out of the room. How miserable is the world of transmigration where I must move constantly between the realms of hell, hungry spirits, beasts, and fighting demons.[104]

On another occasion, a traveling companion with whom he had spent the whole day discussing serious matters groaned when he heard the evening bells toll, "Another day of this miserable life!" Such comments, reminiscent of the early Buddhist "Noble Truth about Suffering," are common in Munan.

We know little of his trip of Kyoto. Evidently he gave himself over to the pursuit of knowledge and learning. It was most likely during this period that he acquired his knowledge of Confucianism and of the teachings and rituals of Shinto that are so evident in his later writings. Nevertheless, his education was fragmented, and although his inclination to Zen grew stronger, he did not take up formal Zen practice. He probably remained in Kyoto for a few years, but we cannot be sure. By the time he returned home he was in his twenties. It was not until 1654, at the advanced age of fifty-one, that he finally abandoned his worldly profession and entered monastic life. His preparation for the religious life had been long, but biographical data is scarce and uncertain, dealing mainly with his interest in Zen.[105]

Munan's spiritual director on the way of Zen was Gudō Tōshoku. We do not know precisely when he first met the renowned Zen master, but it seems their first contact occurred when Munan was still a young man, since Gudō was also from Mino and directed a major temple in the area in addition to holding a number of posts in Kyoto and directing affairs for the Rinzai school in Edo. On his many trips along the Tōkaidō he usually stayed in Sekigahara. There he took a keen interest in the young assistant innkeeper and warm bonds of friendship grew up between them. Again, we have no precise dates when all of this took place, but it would seem that Munan owed his entire Zen formation, from the initial stages right up to enlightenment, to Gudō.

Under Gudō's guidance Munan used as a kōan one of the enlightenment verses of Hui-neng. These verses, it will be remembered, were written for a competition to determine who would succeed the Fifth Patriarch and were posted on the monastery wall. (Legend has it that Hui-neng himself was illiterate and assigned to tread rice in the monastery barn.) The line of the verse that Munan concentrated on read:

From the beginning not one thing exists.[106]

We may suppose that Munan was quite advanced in his practice when the master charged him with the solution of this kōan on nothingness. After many years sitting in meditation, he now wrestled day and night with the kōan, and not without success. The master assured him that he was not far from his goal. Verbally and through the gesture of bestowing on Munan the new name of Kōgai—"beyond time"—Gudō acknowledged the enlightened state of the lay disciple.

All of Munan's biographers relate an episode the historicity of which remains an open question. On one of his visits to the outpost of Sekigahara, Gudō was not able to find his young disciple anywhere and was told that Munan had stepped out. It was at this time that Munan had just taken a fancy to saké; his drinking was upsetting the other members of the household and causing some disturbance in the area. Not at all upset by the situation, Gudō entered the house to await his disciple's return and asked for a bottle of saké to be brought to him. When Munan finally came home he was surprised to meet his master and even more surprised when the master offered him a drink, which of course he accepted. The two Zen friends passed the evening in enjoyable conversation, during which Gudō let his disciple know that he had heard of his recently acquired but unfortunate habit and informed him that the drink they had shared together that night was to be his last. Humiliated but happy, Munan agreed and the following morning accompanied his master not only to the next outpost but, despite all urging to the contrary, all the way to Edo. There he received the tonsure and the monastic robes and joined Gudō's circle of disciples in the monastery of Tōshoku-ji.

This simple story is open to different interpretations. Seen as hagiographical legend, one might say that Munan had invented the event as a way of pointing to the radical change that took place in his life. It is, of course, also possible that during the long periods of waiting at his outpost Munan had yielded to the powers of rice wine. In any case, it is clear that he broke ties with his habitual surroundings and moved to Edo. It was around this time that Gudō gave him the name of Shidō Munan, using characters from the opening verse of the poem Shinjinmei, ascribed to the Third Patriarch, Seng-ts'an: "The Perfect Way (shidō) is not at all difficult (bunan)." The latter compound was transformed into the reading munan for the name. Besides presenting his disciple with a valuable manuscript,[107] Gudō also designated him as his Dharma heir. Gudō did not himself remain long in Edo, taking leave of Munan in what was to be a permanent separation.

Munan's private life had come to an abrupt but belated close. While historical evidence is scarce, we may assume that this lengthy period in Sekigahara was full of hardships and trials. The uncompromising and repeated demands to renounce worldly passions that appear in later sermons suggest a difficult struggle in his own personal past.

In Edo he took up residence in Tōhoku-an, a hermitage in the Asabu district. There he led a rigorously ascetic life and received but few visitors. Dōkyō Etan was the only Dharma heir to whom he granted the seal of enlightenment. He demanded strict practice of all his disciples. An idea of his style of Zen can be found in his writings, especially in the two major treatises *Sokushinki* (*On the Mind,* 1760) and *Jishōki* (*On Self-Nature,* 1672). Neither of these works can rightly be called a masterpiece. His mental acumen was too far removed from that of Hakuin to speak of Munan as a "precursor" of Hakuin. His merit lies rather in the effective manner in which he promoted the reform of the Rinzai school. Above all, his final years exemplified a life of Zen enlightenment and provided his followers with a genuine model.

The programmatic beginning of his *Sokushinki* expresses the core of his Zen experience:

> . . . It is thanks to the teaching of Buddha that [people] can possess the same one mind.
>
> The reason death is abhorred is because it is not known. Men themselves are the Buddha, yet they do not know it. If they know it, they are far from the Buddha mind; if they do not know it, they are deluded. I have composed the following verses:

> When you penetrate the fundamental origin
> You go beyond all phenomena:
> Who knows the realm beyond all words
> Which the Buddhas and patriarchs could not transmit?[108]

Munan speaks often of his experience of the ineffable ground of nothingness. For example, he comments on Chao-chou's answer to the question about the Buddha nature of a dog in the first case of the *Mumonkan:*

> Even though he says "*mu*"
> He throws up a word-barrier;
> Lose consciousness of *mu,*
> And you become one with *mu.*[109]

Mu is the ineffable ground:

> Originally it cannot be taught or learned;
> When you do not know it
> It is unknown;
> When you know it
> It is still unknown.[110]

The aphoristic character of the statements and verses that often follow one another somewhat disjointedly in Munan's works ought not distract us from the unifying source of his Zen experience. For all his dependence on various sources, he is no syncretist. It is his Zen vision that gives everything its value. More particularly, his focal point is the mind. In his own words:

> The wonderful names Buddha, *kami,* the Heavenly Way, bodhisattva, Tathāgata are all different expressions for man's mind.
>
> In mind there is originally not a single thing.

Its function is, above all, compassion, harmony, and artlessness. Before a master, it thinks of faithfulness. Before parents, it thinks of filial piety. Before family or friends, it thinks of the correct relationship. This is the original essence of the mind. It is such a wonderful thing![111]

Munan did not concern himself with metaphysical speculation in order to penetrate to the essence of the original, transcendent Buddha mind or to uncover its associations with all of reality. He writes in a poem:

There are names,
Such as Buddha, God, or Heavenly Way;
But they all point to the mind
Which is nothingness.

Live always
With the mind of total nothingness,
And the evils that come to you
Will dissipate completely.[112]

These passages demonstrate clearly the Buddhist core of Munan's understanding of enlightenment. The structure and internal logic that governs his writings call for a specialized study. For our purposes here it is important to note the urgency with which Munan presses for the proper monastic disposition and a corresponding style of life. He admonishes his disciples forthrightly, "If your practice of Zen cannot be accomplished successfully, you must return to lay life"[113] He knew well what people outside of the monastery expected of a Zen monk. For him the corruption of so many Buddhist priests was the cause of great woe. Again and again he insists on the need to root out all worldly passions. To be a Buddhist priest it is not enough merely to shave one's head:

Even though a man leaves his home and lives simply with his three robes and a bowl on a rock under a tree, he still cannot be called a true Buddhist priest (shukke). Yet if he does wish earnestly to become a true priest, he will realize that he has many desires and is possessed of a body which is endowed with eighty-four thousand evils, of which the cardinal five are sexual desire, cupidity, birth-and-death, jealousy, and desire for fame. These evils are the way of the world. They are by no means easy to overcome. Day and night, by means of enlightenment, you should set yourself to eliminating them one after another, thus purifying yourself. Enlightenment means the original mind.[114]

Munan counsels the practice of zazen and the kōan as a way to wage war against the passions, since these things cultivate peace of mind. His disciples took his advice to heart and within their relatively small community lived a rigorous monastic life aimed solely at attaining enlightenment.

As is the case with most of Munan's life, information about his later work as a monk is scarce. His disciples imitated his lifestyle and he offered words of guidance and inspiration to the faithful who turned to him. In his writings one finds many references to personal dialogues and private instructions. As the circle of his disciples widened, many expressed the desire to have a monastery of their own. The needed assistance was readily available and soon the monastery of Tōhoku-ji (around Shibuya) was completed. Munan resolutely refused the invitation to serve as founding abbot, recommending his disciple Dōkyō Etan for the position. But Dōkyō proved just as adamant in his refusal. In the end, a disciple of Gudō accepted the responsibility. Munan had a hermitage, Shidō-an, constructed in a corner of the temple grounds and there he continued his customary lifestyle. For some time already he had been known as "lord of Shidō-an." The name Shidō, it will be recalled, had been given him by Gudō, and it seems that from quite early on Tōhoku-an came to be known as Shidō-an. Later, in 1673, the hermitage was moved to Koishikawa in another part of Edo. It was there in 1676 that Munan peacefully breathed his last. He was buried in Tōhoku-ji.

Shidō Munan and Dōkyō Etan (1642–1721, also known as Shōju Etan after the hermitage in which he spent the longest period of his life)[115] certainly do not rank among the greatest figures of Japanese Zen. Nonetheless, both are of historical significance in that they set the stage for a reform of Rinzai Zen at a time when Buddhism had sunk to a low level in the secular world. Strengthened by the rigors of monastic practice and firm in their own experiences, theirs was an authentically Zen style of life. Consistent with the severity and single-mindedness of their lives, they rejected all external show and would have nothing to do with the honors and luxury with which high-ranking Buddhist dignitaries of the time, including some Zen abbots, were wont to bedeck themselves. They both lived and died in simple hermitages, Zen monks of no rank.

Of the two, Etan's lifestyle was somehow more extreme and eccentric. They both adhered loyally to the best of the Japanese Rinzai tradition that had begun with Nampo Jōmyō (1235–1309), earned widespread recognition at Daitoku-ji, and in its modern moderate form at Myōshin-ji went on to inspire and direct Rinzai into the modern age. Genealogically, Munan and Etan stem from this line, though they lived in the country at some remove from the old capital city. The new direction they took led the way to Hakuin, the greatest figure within the Japanese Rinzai school.

Etan takes his place between Munan and Hakuin, and the most significant facts about him will be taken up later in the course of our treatment of Hakuin. Here we need only mention the main outlines of his life. Born of the union of a concubine and a samurai in the service of the castle lord of Iiyama in Shinano (Nagano), he received his early education in the royal household. Lord Matsudaira Tadatomo was deeply devoted to Buddhism, and when he received Zen monks would introduce them to his young protégé. There are numerous stories dating from these boyhood years. At fifteen he is said to have experienced enlightenment falling down a set of stairs. Three years later, in 1660, he accompanied the lord of the castle on a trip to Edo, where he visited the hermitage of Munan. So impressed was he by the personality of the master that he immediately became his disciple. One year later Munan commemorated the enlightenment of his young disciple in a poem, bestowing on him the name Etan. On a trip to northeastern Japan Etan visited several monasteries and came to know their abbots. He was particularly moved by lectures he heard on the *Shuryōgon-gyō*,[116] in which the characters for his name, *Shōju* (the Chinese term for *samādhi*), appear.

After returning to Edo, Etan was warmly received by Munan, who had been nurturing the hope that he had finally found a successor. When the question of the appointment of a founding abbot for Tōhoku-ji arose, Munan announced his refusal so that Etan could take his place. When word of this reached Etan, he fled to his home in Shinano and remained there for some time, only returning after another monk had assumed the post. To mature in his enlightenment, he continued his practice of Zen and his service of Munan for a while before returning for an extended stay in his home province. He staunchly opposed the plans of the lord of the castle of Iiyama to construct a temple for him. Once again he fled, this time to the mountains of Shinano, where he took up residence in the hermitage of Shōju-an in the village of Taruzawa.[117]

To his dying day Shōju remained in his hermitage, leading a life of continued practice and ascetic rigor for some forty-five years. His mother, who had left the world to become a Buddhist nun, joined him there, and the two of them outdid each other in their devotion, providing mutual encouragement and security. The model for their hermitage was the ninth-century Chinese Zen master Ch'en Tsun-su (Jpn., Chin Sonshuku), an eccentric disciple of Huang-po whose self-sacrificing care for his aging mother had become something of a model of filial piety in the Zen tradition.[118] One of the best known of the many, often legendary, stories that have been passed down about his hermitage is that in order to protect the village from a pack of wild wolves that had been terrorizing them, Shōju sat in *zazen* for seven nights.

The one notable event that broke the routine of the long years in the hermitage was the visit, in 1708, of Hakuin, who had been introduced to Shōju-an by the disciple Dōju Sōkaku (1679–1730) and who spent eight months there in practice. An amiable master-disciple relationship developed between Shōju and Hakuin, and when it came time to bid his farewell, the old master's warm heart broke through his rough exterior. Shortly before the day of departure he transmitted to his disciple the doctrine of the Five Ranks (*goi*), demonstrating the depth of his learning.

According to tradition, Shōju passed away sitting in *zazen*. His parting verses read:

> In the frantic hurry [of dying]
> It's difficult to utter the last word.
> If I were to speak the wordless word,
> I wouldn't speak, I wouldn't speak.[119]

THE SŌTŌ SCHOOL

THE CONSOLIDATION OF THE ORGANIZATION

The damage that Buddhism had sustained during the last phase of Japan's middle ages and that brought about a notable weakening within all the Buddhist schools also provided the context for the organizational reform that Buddhism so urgently needed as it stepped into the modern age. Because it was able to confront the strict regulations of the government with one of the best corporate organizations within Buddhism at the time, the Sōtō school suffered fewer losses than other Buddhist groups. On the contrary, it secured not a few advantages for its external organization.

Already toward the end of the *sengoku* period, Tokugawa Ieyasu had appointed the highly regarded and well-educated Sōtō monk Hōzan Tōzen (d. 1590)[120] to the office of *sōroku* over four provinces (in imitation of the *gozan* system of Rinzai during the Muromachi period). A number of his disciples also maintained good relations with the Tokugawa government. Within Sōtō, the *sōroku* system spread widely, with the different provincial administrators (*sōroku*) all coming under the spiritual authority of a central administrator (*daisōroku*).

The same rigid organization and centralization that marked the internal politics of the Tokugawa characterized these religious structures. For the Sōtō school, the institutionalization of the most important collection of laws regarding Buddhist bodies (*Shoshū jiin hatto*) brought positive results, despite a few disadvantages. Besides the two main traditional monasteries of Eihei-ji and Sōji-ji, three other temples in eastern Japan (*kansansetsu*) and three temples in Edo (Sōsen-ji, Seishō-ji, Sengaku-ji) came to assume influential roles.

With its ready adaptability to the *bakufu*, the organization of the Sōtō school fit right into the Tokugawa shogunate's system, which was able in turn to make good use of the school's widespread influence over the masses together with its readiness to comply with political structures. Among the special services provided by the Sōtō school was the effort it extended to promote popular education.[121] The many schools attached to Sōtō temples clearly reflected the Confucian concerns of the government, which in 1666 issued guidelines for the education and formation of monks. As part of its efforts to transform Edo into the spiritual and intellectual center of the nation, the *bakufu* extended special support to the Sōtō temples where young monks were receiving what the government considered a proper education (Kichijō-ji, Seishō-ji, Sengaku-ji). According to the *bakufu*, Buddhism should not restrict itself to folk rituals, which were often tainted with magic, but should give solid religious training to monks and future priests serving in the rural temples.

According to the religious laws promulgated at the beginning of the Edo period (1615), equal status was given to the two main temples of Sōtō Zen, Eihei-ji and Sōji-ji, which had been founded by Dōgen and Keizan respectively. Between the two temples there was to be no distinction in rank, authority, ceremonies, or form of dress; all other Sōtō temples were made subordinate to them. These regulations assured proper order and equality within the broad reach of Sōtō institutions. At the same time, changes in hierarchical ranking were not unusual in the Tokugawa government and were enforced to help prevent the formation of political power groups or to keep the influence of religious bodies under control. There is no way of knowing for certain whether such considerations played a role in the changes instituted in the status of the Sōtō school. During the Tenmei era (1781–1788) an imperial decree established the prominence of Eihei-ji as the "general head temple of the Sōtō school."[122] The decree stirred up a great deal of animosity, particularly because many felt that it disregarded the history of Japanese Sōtō Zen. At the same time, the decree was not in keeping with the actual situation of the Sōtō school in Japan during the Edo period. With its 16,179 branch temples, the Sōji-ji line was over ten times larger than the 1,370 establishments of Eihei-ji. The conflicts that broke out and continued unabated between the two centers are recounted by Japanese historians as an unfortunate blemish on the history of Japanese Sōtō Zen.[123] The tension and rivalry were to last well into the next age.

Even where organizational edicts were able to stem widespread abuse, they did not suffice to effect the sort of genuine renewal that would get to the roots of the problems. Only vigorous, prudent, and spiritually gifted individuals could do that—and since the middle of the seventeenth century, more and more such persons were appearing within the Sōtō school. This is not to say that we may liken this period to the flowering that the Japanese Sōtō movement experienced during the thirteenth and fourteenth centuries. Sōtō Zen would not achieve the kind of revival that the ingenious Hakuin made possible for Rinzai.

RESTORATIONAL REFORMS

Prominent among the Sōtō masters of the early Edo period was Man'an Eishu (1591–1654),[124] the Dharma heir in the fourteenth generation after Kangan Giin (thirteenth century). A good friend of Suzuki Shōsan, he sought to raise the Sōtō Zen of this period to a higher level. He succeeded in rebuilding the monastery of Kōshō-ji in Uji. Together with other capable individuals of the period, he was altogether convinced that a general reform was necessary, but he lacked the influence to carry it out. Among his students was Gesshū Sōko (1618–1696), whom we may consider a harbinger of reform within the Sōtō school.[125]

Born in Hizen (Kyūshū), Gesshū first entered a Shingon monastery but soon afterward transferred to Zen and spent time in a number of Zen temples in his home area. After a period with Man'an Eishu, he joined the disciples of Hakuhō Genteki (1594–1670),[126] the abbot of the model Sōtō temple of Daijō-ji, from whom he received the Dharma. He then joined the Chinese masters Tao-che and Yin-yüan, who helped the gifted young disciple channel his energies in the service of Zen. Still, his heart's desire remained fixed on the renewal of his own Japanese school. After further travels, in 1655 he was appointed superior of Chōen-ji in Mikawa, a post he held for more than ten years. In 1680 he took on the more prestigious role of abbot of Daijō-ji. Later he retired to Zenjō-ji in Uji, where he was to spend his declining years in an extended period of peace and quiet. Gesshū remained a loyal source of support to his disciple, friend, and heir, Manzan during the strenuous and trying years in which the latter labored successfully for reform.

Manzan Dōhaku (1636–1714)[127] is the leading personality of Sōtō Zen during the Edo period. In 1642, when he was a mere six years of age, his parents gave permission for him to be turned over to the service of a temple in the region of Bingo (present day Hiroshima). That same year his father died, followed by his mother a few years later. About the same time, the temple's abbot passed away and the new abbot took the young orphan into his ward. Over the following years Manzan followed his teacher on his frequent journeys throughout the country, bringing him to the Tokugawa capital city of Edo in 1651. Over the years, Manzan underwent a number of powerful spiritual experiences, so much so that Gesshū, who first met the young monk in Daijō-ji in 1678, confirmed his state of enlightenment and appointed him Dharma heir. In this way he entered the Sōtō school in the line originating from Keizan's disciple Meihō Sotetsu. Two years later, in 1680, Gesshū resigned as abbot and Manzan took charge of the prominent monastery of Daijō-ji. In no time he was busy with remodeling and enlarging the temple complex. During the twelve years of his tenure as abbot he matured in administrative experience and grew to enjoy the respect and confidence of the fellow members of his school.

To understand Manzan's efforts as a reformer we need look back to the preceding decades, about which in any case we know but little. It is clear that the seriousness with which Manzan took his Zen experience made him suffer all the more under the abuses of the times. In terms of his lofty ideals, the Zen of bygone ages was more representative of what Zen should be. His great respect for the patriarch of his school, Dōgen, led him to return to the master's writings, where he found considerable material on the origins of Zen. According to one testimony still extant, he was reading Dōgen's Shōbōgenzō in 1663 when he came across a passage that for him put the then unhappy state of Zen in clear perspective. In treating the transmission of the mind, Dōgen makes the following critical observation on erroneous developments within the Chinese schools:

> They call themselves grandchildren of Lin-chi, but they are egoistic and dishonest. They study as disciples of a master and ask for his portrait or calligraphy of a Dharma saying, which they then use as proof of succession. They circle about venerable masters like dogs begging for Dharma sayings, portraits, and the like. They accumulate a collection of these things and as they grow older use them to bribe officials to build temples or be appointed superiors, even though they have not attained the right of succession through a Dharma saying or a portrait of a master. Hungry for fame, they pass on the seal of succession to kings, ministers, relatives, and friends without themselves having acquired the Dharma. All they are after is fame. What a sad sight they make! In this wicked age of mappō evil customs like this prevail. Among people like this, none of them so far has ever so much as even seen or heard of the way of the Buddhas and patriarchs in their dreams.[128]

Manzan uncovered the same bad custom that Dōgen had complained about in his time. All too often, succession within Sōtō temples was not determined according to the transmission of mind but by other, dishonest means. After reading the *Shōbōgenzō*, Manzan resolved to devote all his energies to reinstating the old procedure of succession, a project that won the support of his friends. He condensed the goal of his reform efforts in two slogans: "the seal of succession from one master" (*isshi inshō*) and "transmission from master to disciple" (*shishi menju*). This latter was also stated in the form "Dharma transmission from mind to mind" (*menju shihō*). The idea behind the first statement clearly is to abolish the custom of collecting certificates of enlightenment and going around from one master to another. A Zen disciple can properly be the Dharma heir of only one master. The internal master-disciple relationship referred to in the second statement was described by Dōgen in his book *Face-to-face Transmission (Menju)*.[129] Manzan's reform movement had as its goal the return to this custom of the ancients.

In trying to reinstate the spirit of Dōgen into the process of determining temple superiors, Manzan won many respectable temples over to his position but also aroused opposition from within the Sōtō school. Although everyone agreed in principle with the fundamental idea, there were a variety of interpretations.[130] Manzan's ideas were concrete—the transmission of the Dharma is carried out in a ceremony celebrating the master-disciple relationship—and laid stress on external form. Since the medieval period, however, another way of determining succession had taken over. On this understanding, the inheritance of the temple buildings (*garan*) entailed the passing on of the Dharma. This viewpoint was represented by Dokuan Genkō (1630–1698), one of the most highly respected Zen masters of the time and otherwise a good friend of Manzan.[131] A generation later, this same viewpoint found its main defendant in the important scholar Tenkei Denson (1648–1735).

The controversy was influenced by the connections of Gesshū and Manzan with the Ōbaku school, which inspired a revitalization of Zen in general and introduced a modernizing force into Japanese intellectual life, especially into the Sōtō school of Zen. Manzan's opponents aimed their attacks mainly on the modern view that shifted the focus away from the central significance of the Dharma (the object) and toward the human person (the subject)—a view that seems already in evidence in the traditional formula of the "transmission of mind" (*ishin-denshin*).

Against all opposition and in the face of intimidating difficulties, Manzan, with the aid of his like-minded colleague Baiyū Jikushin (1633–1707),[132] succeeded in carrying out his long-cherished and carefully prepared project of reform. In 1700 the two of them presented a petition to the *bakufu* in which they proposed that new laws be issued controlling succession in Zen temples.[133] At first their request was rejected, but after three years of continued efforts it was accepted. Manzan had achieved his goal of the "restoration of antiquity," namely, the traditional manner of succession (*shūtō fukko*). The government entrusted the direction of the Sōtō schools in eastern Japan (Kantō) to Manzan and Baiyū.

Throughout the Edo period, Manzan's represented the dominant position within the Sōtō school. His efforts may be considered a restorative reform insofar as they returned to Dōgen's fundamental ideas and thus effected a revitalization of Japanese Sōtō Zen.

ACADEMIC UNDERTAKINGS

The high regard and concern for Dōgen that characterized the reform efforts of Manzan and his associates made this great patriach of Japanese Sōtō Zen the center of attention. Manzan's primary concern was to appeal to Dōgen's works in order to convince the shogunal government to restore the old customs of succession. At this same time, the monks of Eihei-ji, under the direction of the thirty-fifth abbot, Kōzen (d. 1693), were working on a new edition of the ninety-five books of the Shōbōgenzō, which in fact was only printed a century later (Eiheiji-han, also known as the Kōzen-bon).[134] Here is not the place to examine in detail the intense literary activity that was developing around Dōgen's work.

After Manzan, the most important interpreter of Dōgen's work during the Edo period was Tenkei Denson,[135] the editor of the comprehensive and voluminous commentary known as the Shōbōgenzō benchū. Tenkei came from the province of Kii (in the region of Kumamoto), traveled extensively during his youth, and studied with famous monks, including Tetsugen of the Ōbaku school. He attained his enlightenment experience under the direction of Gohō Kaion of the line of Taigen Sōshin, one of the main disciples of Gasan, who was Keizan's most eminent Dharma heir. Tenkei served as abbot for a number of monasteries, but his heart was in scholarship. Early in his career he withdrew to the Yōshō-an hermitage in Tettsu to dedicate himself to private study.

Although Tenkei agreed with Manzan in his profound respect for Dōgen, he was in clear disagreement with him regarding the question of succession. For him, the significance of the master-disciple relationship took second place to the understanding of the true Dharma given in enlightenment. In his view, what is all important is not one's practice with a master but the attainment of enlightenment, which can take place in any number of different ways. The seal of enlightenment is one's self, and the encounter between the self and its "original face" takes place in enlightenment. The whole universe is the fountainhead of this intuition. Contact with the sun, the moon, and the stars, or with the trees, the grass, and the great wide earth can bring one into touch with the self. And in the self, one comes to grasp the true Dharma. Certainly this can take place through the help of a master, but it is also possible to attain one's original self in the experience. Clearly, Tenkei's interpretation evinces a profound grasp of Zen combined with a metaphysical perspective on what it means to comprehend the essence of reality.[136]

Most of the Sōtō masters of the time sided with Manzan's position. The transmission of mind to mind in the master-disciple relationship is a deeply rooted belief in the Zen tradition. There was one weakness in this belief, however, which in a time of the weakened Dharma was felt in a particularly painful way. Where during the Edo period was it possible to find a sufficient number of genuine, undeluded masters and disciples who could assure the uncontaminated transmission of mind?

Criticisms leveled against Tenkei Denson's interpretation were more philological than metaphysical. As the basis for his commentary, Tenkei had used the sixty-volume edition of the Shōbōgenzō edited by Giun. He was rather free in his use of the text and introduced his own changes, leading the disciples of Manzan to accuse him of arbitrariness.[137] Scholars lined up on both sides of the question.[138] There was no lack of critical replies of Tenkei Denson, one of the most incisive of which was the Shōbōgenzō benbenchū (published in 1766 in two volumes) by Tenkei's contemporary Manjin (or Banjin) Dōtan (1698–1775). Despite these harsh criticisms from his own school, Tenkei Denson remains one of the great scholars of Sōtō Zen during the Edo period.

The most productive scholar of the Sōtō school during the Edo period was Menzan Zuihō (1683–1769),[139] who over the course of his long life engaged in a wide variety of activities. Born in Higo (in the district of Kumamoto), he entered religious life in a Zen temple on the hundredth day after the death of his mother—a decision his father first opposed but later supported wholeheartedly.

The year 1703 is especially important in the history of Japanese Sōtō Zen. In that year, in Edo, Menzan first met Manzan Dōhaku, who had just received the approval of the bakufu government to restore the old process of succession. In adddition to being committed to the same reform, Menzan found himself quite at home in the circle of Manzan's disciples. This brought him face to face with the important decision of whether to remain in the Tokugawa city of Edo, where he had just made the acquaintance of Sonnō Sōeki (1649–1705)[140] and was deeply impressed by him. In 1703 he opted to accompany Sōeki to a monastery in northeastern Japan where authentic Zen was being practiced. During his brief time with the master, Menzan went through some of the most definitive spiritual experiences of his life. Sōeki's premature death in 1705 left Menzan with another difficult decision. In the end he made up his mind to take on one of the most demanding ascetic practices possible: a thousand-day period of strict cloister in the not too distant hermitage of Rōbai-an in Sagami. These three years of intensive solitude had a lasting impact on the rest of his life. It taught him the possibility of combining ascetic monastic practices with academic pursuits. Soon after completing this extraordinary feat, he was called upon to take over the direction of important temples—notably Zenjō-ji in his native district of Higo in Kyūshū, and Kūin-ji in Wakasa (in the region of Fukui), where he remained for about twelve years. During this period he practiced a combination of an active and contemplative life and cultivated his affection for lectures and discourses.

His reputation secured, Menzan began his final and most fruitful phase. After retiring from the office of abbot of Kūin-ji in 1741 to make room for his disciple Katsudō Fukan, he constructed for himself the hermitage of Eifuku-an. Although he continued to lecture widely, most of his energies were devoted to writing. The heart of his literary efforts is found in the eleven volumes of his encyclopedic work, Shōbōgenzō shōtenroku, a comprehensive collection of words, quotations, stylistic forms, and historical information—in a word, a compendium of the philologically and historically important elements—taken from the ninety-five books of Dōgen's principal work. It is said that Menzan already conceived of the idea of such a work at the beginning of his thousand-day period of seclusion. The manuscript, completed in 1759, is a massive achievement that clearly stands as his life's work. This work was written in Chinese, but Menzan also culled difficult Japanese words from the *Shōbōgenzō* and analyzed them in another book called *Shōbōgenzō wagoshō*, completed in 1746. Some years later this book was expanded by the renowned Japanese philologist and Zen master Banzui into the detailed study *Shōbōgenzō wagotei*. The titles of the innumerable works that Menzan produced in his final years are characteristic of his diverse interests, ranging from the *Shōbōgenzō* to a great deal of literature from the early years of the Japanese Sōtō movement. Of particular interest is a collection of sayings of Ju-ching, Dōgen's Chinese master, completed in 1751.

No doubt a complete commentary on the *Shōbōgenzō* from the pen of Menzan would merit careful attention, but unfortunately, it is not certain whether he is really is the author of the *Shōbōgenzō monge*, a detailed and simplified explanation of Dōgen's work attributed to Menzan. While Menzan certainly expounded the *Bendōwa* volume in his lectures, it is scarcely possible that he would have treated all ninety-five books of the *Shōbōgenzō*. The *Shōbōgenzō monge* was written down by Menzan's disciple Fuzan Genshutsu during the An'ei era (1772–1781). For some time now it has been commonly accepted that Genshutsu compiled this two-volume work, written in Japanese, from notes taken from Menzan's lectures. Genshutsu himself expounded all the books of the *Shōbōgenzō* in his own lectures (1755–1756). His explanations, which breathe the spirit of Menzan and make use of the findings of the *Shōbōgenzō shōtenroku*, most likely formed the foundation for the *Shōbōgenzō monge*.

Within the Sōtō school, Menzan remained faithful to his elder Manzan, whom he held in highest esteem. Regarding the central question of the process of determining succession, he opposed the views of Tenkei Denson vigorously. Another of the most controversial issues of the day had to do with the reform of the monastic rule, which Gesshū and Manzan had taken up already at the beginning of the Edo period. Besides appealing to Dōgen, they also displayed an evident sympathy for the Ōbaku school, which enjoyed considerable influence in the early years and stirred the hopes of many reform-minded monks. But enthusiasm for this new arrival from Ming China began to decline and opinion concerning the new practices and customs laid down by the leaders of the Sōtō school remained divided. Menzan himself felt no affinity to Ōbaku and remained faithful to what he thought were the undiluted teachings of Dōgen, devoting his energies entirely to rooting out Ōbaku elements that had crept in. While a unified reform of monastic rules did not come about, efforts in this direction consumed much of the energy of writers of the time.

As already mentioned, Gasan, one of the leaders of the Sōtō school, was particularly interested in the dialectic of the Five Ranks (*goi*). Given the established sense of tradition of Sōtō scholars, they were bound to give great importance to the Five Ranks. Shigetsu E'in (1689–1764),[141] of the line of Gasan, is especially noted for his studies on the Five Ranks. His *Funōgo henshō goisetsu*, a work reflecting the spirit of Dōgen, met with widespread acclaim. Shigetsu may be reckoned among the leading scholars of his time. Menzan also took up the study of the Five Ranks. The numerous studies on the Five Ranks that the Sōtō school produced during the Edo period are of varying quality. From a higher standpoint, Hakuin would bring this Japanese controversy over the Five Ranks to an end, as we shall see in the following chapter.

During the second half of the Edo period, the Sōtō school accomplished much in the way of literary production; we shall not go any further into it here. Suffice it to note that this parallels developments in Japan's wider intellectual history at the time. After a generation of important figures, notably from the two Confucian schools of Chu Hsi (Jpn., Shu Ki) and Wang Yang-ming (Jpn., Ō Yōmei), a kind of positive science began to appear on several fronts. Philological and historical concerns came to the fore and Japanese classical studies emerged after the manner of their Chinese counterpart. The Shingon monk Keichū (1640–1769) was a noted authority on the classical philology of the *Man'yōshū*; Kamo Mabuchi (1697–1769) found the spirit of Yamato in the old language of the *norito* (Shinto prayers) and the *Man'yōshū* poems; the commentary on the *Kojiki* by Motoori Norinaga (1730–1801) was a high-water mark of nativist Japanese scholarship. Under the leadership of Tokugawa Mitsukuni (1628–1700), the Mito school fostered a greater understanding of Japanese history. Countless other names could be mentioned, many of them scholars of mediocre quality. In general, however, the literary efforts of the Sōtō school—and above all the not fully satisfactory "Dōgen Renaissance"—were fitting additions to the overall cultural climate.

POPULAR SECULARITY IN THE MODERN PERIOD

The picture we have painted thus far might give the false impression that the Sōtō school, because of its academic pursuits, had forsaken its popular roots and love of nature during the modern period. This is far from the case. The rigid regulations of the shogunal government promoted monastic life, educational activities, and intellectual growth without in any way jeopardizing the traditional popularity of Sōtō Zen. The school preserved its traits as a movement that avoided large cities and enjoyed widespread popularity in rural areas. During the Edo period its monasteries provided the rural population with many suitable centers for the development of different forms of social life.

Many of the abbots and monks of the Sōtō monasteries were popular figures who preached the message of Buddha in simple, clear language and who could see beyond the lack of deeper religious understanding among the common people. Cultic practices, drawn mainly from esoteric Shingon rituals, enlivened the practice of *zazen*, which was interpreted in the broadest sense as taking place not only in temple buildings but also during work in the fields and at home. Lay believers (*danka*) who belonged to the temple community fulfilled their religious duties in and through their daily work.

The monks not only expounded this broad understanding of Zen practice in sermons; they demonstrated the truth of their religious teachings by taking part in the work of the commoners. They made no distinction between their monastic practices and the performance of useful worldly service. This understanding of the unity between the sacred and the profane, which was rooted in Mahāyāna Buddhism and was accented strongly in Japan, was taken for granted by Sōtō Zen. Sōtō had its own type of secularization, different from the aesthetic and worldly tendencies of Rinzai. The popular secularity of Sōtō established itself within the daily tasks of everyday life.

Suzuki Shōsan.   No one has communicated the heart and soul of this secular religiosity as clearly as the former samurai and Zen monk Suzuki Shōsan (1579–1655).[142] Despite his substantial contributions to the history of Japanese Zen, it is by no means easy to situate this extraordinary personality within Zen history. He remained outside the three official Japanese Zen schools and yet he has always been considered part of Zen. Although he received training in the way of Zen, he could not decide on a master from among his teachers. Nonetheless, he maintained contact with various Zen masters and was especially friendly with Man'an Eishu, at whose suggestion he wrote an exhortation for monks who had strayed from the way.

Born to a samurai family in Okazaki, not far from the castle where Tokugawa Ieyasu was born, he took part in the battle of Sekigahara in 1600 and later distinguished himself in the battle for Osaka Castle (1614–15). After the victorious completion of this last campaign he abandoned his military career and, with the approval of Lord Ieyasu, became a monk. He studied the Vinaya at Hōryū-ji near Nara under the Shingon monk Genshun but did not enter a Zen monastery. Instead, he made his abode in hermitages, teaching disciples and visitors and struggling for an authentic reform of the Buddhist way of life. Although any one of the aspects of Shōsan's life could be examined with profit, we shall focus on his contribution to the modern Buddhist notion of one's calling in life, an idea that has born fruit particularly in Sōtō circles.

Shōsan's understanding of Buddhism is permeated by the spirit of Mahāyāna; he is much more interested in religious practice than in metaphysical propositions about the identity of nirvāṇa and saṃsāra. In his view of Zen, practice is every bit as important as enlightenment. His main concern was that the followers of Sōtō Zen live the spirit of Buddhism and master the life that has been given them in this world. The Buddha-Dharma must be lived concretely, *in the world.* His disciples learned from him what it is to attain peace of mind and to contribute to the proper ordering of society. It is in this sense that we may understand the following exhortation directed to his listeners:

Nowadays people think that the Buddha-Dharma is of no value unless one achieves enlightenment. Not so. The Buddha's teaching requires that we use our mind well and we put it to use here and now. In fact, practice means to apply the mind strenuously. The stronger the mind becomes, the more one is able use it. Those who apply themselves will have great merit;

those who do not have little merit. For example, if one who cannot hold ten thousand stones holds a thousand, such a one is superior to one who holds only a hundred. One gains merit according to the degree of one's effort. When one gains enlightenment one naturally thinks that this truly is the Buddha world. But this is not the case. Those who are of that opinion cannot make free use of it. The Buddha world is a special reality. Do not covet enlightenment but seek merit through good practice.[143]

Clearly, Shōsan respected the Buddha world, but as he states, fully consistent with his practical religious worldview, that world belongs to a "special reality." The same applies, more or less, to enlightenment. He disliked the "expectant Zen" (kitai-zen) that was popular at the time and urged Zen students not to maintain a conscious desire for enlightenment or await it continually. He much preferred the simple Buddhists who went about fulfilling their duties in this world. This practical religiosity made him popular among the common people. He taught them that if, as devout Buddhists, they see their workaday lives as practice and carry out their duties with a joyful heart, they will advance just as if they had been spending their time in Zen meditation. There is, therefore, little difference among the diverse callings in life; they are all meaningful because "all activities are activities of the Buddha. People are to attain Buddhahood through their work. There is no work that is not the activity of the Buddha."[144]

Suzuki Shōsan described the work ethic of Buddhism in his first major work, Banmin tokuyō (Meritorious Way of Life for All).[145] In line with the times, he begins by noting the four classes of society—samurai, farmer, artisan, and merchant. The work of each class is said to be valuable inasmuch as human beings are all endowed with the Buddha nature; therefore every act is the work of the Buddha:

The ascetic practice of the Buddha-Dharma removes all obstacles, eliminates all sufferings, and devotes the mind to the activities of samurai, farmer, artisan, or merchant. Such practice is a treasure of well-being for mind and body.[146]

To the samurai, Shōsan explains that the Dharma of the Buddha and the Dharma of the world are like two wheels of a wagon. Both are necessary to attain Buddhahood. According to the vocational ethic of the samurai, to conquer the fear of death and risk one's life in battle are of the highest value. As foreign as such virtues might seem to us today, they were very real to Shōsan's contemporaries, many of whom had experienced the turmoil of war during the Sengoku period. Moreover, almost three hundred years of the Pax Tokugawa had drawn the warrior class close to the bourgeoisie.

For workers, Shōsan offers advice that has lost none of its timeliness for our own world. A religiously perceptive farmer voiced his concern:

Even though the Great Matter of rebirth is not neglected by us, there is no leisure when we are carrying on our farm work. In the making of a miserable livelihood, this life is spent in vain and it is distressing that suffering will be our lot in future existences. What can we do to attain Buddhahood?

Shōsan answered:

> Working the land is Buddhist practice. If your intention is bad, so will your work be lowly. If you are strong and devout, then yours is the work of a bodhisattva. It is a mistake to long for leisure and ask for happiness in a future life. Those who wish truly to attain Buddhahood will discipline their body and mind. Those who seek after pleasure and ask for happiness in a future life will not achieve Buddhahood in ten thousands *kalpas*. Now as you work with bitter suffering in the extremes of cold and heat, using plow, mattock, and sickle, consider the rank thickets of the passions of this body and mind to be your enemies. Dig them up and cut them down! When one does have leisure, the passions grow in luxuriant thickets in the body. But when you train your body and mind by doing your harsh and toilsome work, then there are no disturbances or troubles in your mind. Why indeed should the farmer who carries on Buddhist practice throughout the four seasons have a desire for any *other* Buddhist practice?[147]

The expression "work of a bodhisattva" that appears here likens the strenuous labor of a farmer to the efforts that the bodhisattva devoted to Buddhahood freely undertakes for the welfare of all sentient beings. When farmers cultivate in their hearts the attitude of a bodhisattva, their work in the fields is said to be in no way inferior to practice in a temple. Hard and painful as their labors are, they are able to bear the same Buddha-fruits as do the efforts of a bodhisattva.[148] This kind of religiously grounded vocational ethic can be found already among the Chinese Zen masters of the T'ang period. In Tokugawa Japan, such an ethic would have special meaning for the suffering and needy rural population. When times of drought or heavy taxes oppressed the farmers and threatened to precipitate peasant revolts, the Sōtō monks, who were always close to the people and who took part in the social movements of the time, offered the people practical assistance.

The same advice that Shōsan gave to the farmers he also offered to the artisans. But when it came to formulating a Buddhist ethic for the merchants, he ran into special difficulties. Nonetheless, he may be considered the first Buddhist in modern times to have succeeded in this line.[149] Although regarded disdainfully at the start of the Edo period, the merchant's profession grew vigorously and stood in need of its own spiritual direction. It was necessary to show the merchants how they could carry on successfully with their business without falling prey to greed and without having to forfeit the quest for higher, spiritual realities. As capable businessmen they are to work to increase their holdings, but as Buddhists they are not to cling to their profits. Reconciling these two attitudes was no easy matter. To do so, Shōsan made use of the distinction common in the Buddhist philosophy of ancient India between "pure" and "impure" (*sāsrava-anāsrava*; Jpn., *muro-uro*) things (*dharma*) and applied it to the business world as a distinction between "profits with clinging" and "profits without clinging."[150] Nothing runs more counter to the spirit of Buddhism than craving for and then clinging to possessions, be they material or spiritual. Accordingly, those engaged in buying and selling must not allow themselves to be waylaid by self-serving desires. Their success in business must, in the final analysis, serve the common good.

A merchant once asked Shōsan for advice:

> Though I am fortunate to have been given the opportunity to be born into the world of human beings, I find myself, insofar as I go about this pitiful profession, constantly thinking about profits. It truly saddens me that I cannot strive for enlightenment. Teach me the proper skill in means (Skt., *upāya;* Jpn., *hōben*)!

Shōsan replied:

> Those in the business world must first of all cultivate a mind for increasing profits. This attitude means nothing less than turning one's life over to the way of heaven. If, in the course of your trading, you abandon all attachments and put away greed, the heavens will protect you and the gods will favor you with a prosperous life; you will excel in making profits and be so filled with prosperity that you will look down upon the chief men of great [hereditary] wealth. Everything will go well for you. But those who make private desires their exclusive concern and, making distinctions between themselves and others, "get ahead" of these others with [only] a mind to their own profit—on these will fall the curse of heaven. Their calamities will multiply; everyone will detest them . . . and in nothing will their expectations be fulfilled.[151]

In the light of the influence that Suzuki Shōsan had in the Sōtō school at the beginning of the modern age, we can conclude that his teachings on vocational ethics, as they were passed on through Sōtō Zen, had a widespread impact on the general population during the Edo period. As a result, the popular religiosity that grew up around Sōtō did not want for religiously grounded ethical principles. Shōsan's open, wholesome religiosity, his fondness for the *nembutsu* (the invocation of the name of Amida Buddha), and his simple way of life still are very much part of the Sōtō school.

Daigu Ryōkan.   The popular religiosity of Sōtō Zen reached its high point in the person of the poet-monk Daigu Ryōkan (1758–1831).[152] It is rare to find the essence of so unique a figure expressed so aptly in the double name by which he is remembered in Zen history. The two Chinese characters of the name given him by his master signify "good" (*ryō*) and "abundant" (*kan*)—like the abundance of goodness that poured forth from his great heart during his life as a hermit. His other name, *Daigu,* self-bestowed, means "big fool"—the special folly of the child and the saint, of the fool and the wise man. Beneath surface appearances— beneath his highly artistic poetry, his simple, cordial way of dealing with his many friends, his happy games with the village children—there lay a depth that he himself was aware of but was never able to express fully.

As a Buddhist monk, Ryōkan belonged to the school of Sōtō Zen. In 1775, at the age of seventeen, he entered the Sōtō temple of Kōshō-ji in his native town of Izumozaki (in Echigo). He had already completed a course of studies on the Chinese classics at the school (*juku*) of the Confucian scholar Ōmori Shiyō in nearby Jizōdō. At Kōshō-ji he received the tonsure from the abbot, Genjō Haryō. One of the highlights of his monastic formation was the visit of the Sōtō abbot Dainin Kokusen, who was on a lecture trip and who accepted the hospitality of his school's monastery at Izumozaki. Ryōkan was deeply impressed by the personality of Kokusen and accompanied him on the return voyage to Entsū-ji in Tamashima (in the region of Bitchū) in 1779. For some twelve years Ryōkan lived a disciplined monastic life and devoted himself energetically to Zen practice, drinking in the spirit of Zen at the feet of his master, Kokusen, whom he held up as an ideal.

The most important event of his years in the monastic community was the spiritual encounter with the great patriarch of the Sōtō school, Dōgen, in reading the master's works.[153] There he came into touch with the inexhaustible depths of the Buddha reality. Toward the end of his years of study, Master Kokusen confirmed his enlightenment. The certificate reads as follows:

> To Ryōkan, good as foolish, who walks the broadest way
> So free and so untrammeled, none can truly fathom him,
> I grant this certificate with a stick of mountain wood.
> Everywhere he will find quiet rest as inside the walls.[154]

However highly Kokusen held his disciple in esteem, he was not in the end able to get to the bottom of him.

After Kokusen's death in 1791, Ryōkan left Tamashima to begin his travels. We have no precise information as to where he went, but we do know that his journey brought him considerable hardship. His mother had died already in 1783, but when his father committed suicide in 1795, Ryōkan rushed to Kyoto to attend the funeral services. Soon after, he returned home to Echigo. Meantime, his brother was having a hard time as mayor of Izumozaki. At the end of a long search he came upon the really poor hermitage of Gogō-an on the western slopes of the Mount Kugami not far from the Shingon Temple of Kokujō-ji. After staying there for a time, he made it his permanent residence.

Ryōkan's twenty years in Gogō-an, from 1797 to 1817, represent both the middle period of his life and its high point. Far removed from both the monastic community of his school and from worldly concerns, he led a hermit's life in great poverty and solitude. His was also a characteristically religious life lived in obedience to the monastic rule. He begged for his meals with his beggar's bowl[155] and practiced meditation. At the same time, he produced an important body of poetry in which he expressed the feelings that flowed through him during the long nights he passed in those rugged natural surroundings. In all, we have some fourteen hundred of his poems, including about ninety longer poems, four hundred Chinese poems, and a smaller number of Japanese epigrams (*haikai* or *haiku*). Most of his Japanese poems were composed in the classical form of the short verse (*tanka*) or Japanese lyric (*waka*) in five lines of thirty-one syllables (5,7,5,7,7), many of them in the style of the oldest Japanese collection of songs, the *Man'yōshū*. Several of his Japanese compositions also show traces of the influence of the later collections *Kokinshū* and *Shinkokinshū*, as well as of Dōgen's poetry.[156]

Ryōkan's parental home was graced with the air of music. His father I'nan[157] showed considerable poetic talents and his brothers and sisters all had a strong interest in literature. Given his own genuine poetic gifts, it comes as no surprise to find Ryōkan holding a place in the history of Japanese poetry. Japanese literary history lists him among the poets of the *Man'yōshū* renaissance, and while it is true that he himself was particularly taken by the this style of composition, it is hard to categorize him in any particular school.[158] The *Man'yōshū* renaissance during the Tokugawa period begins with Kamo Mabuchi (1697–1769), the master from Agatai whose return to Japanese antiquity opened the way to a renewal of the lyrical arts.[159] As the Japanese literary scholar Hisamatsu Sen'ichi observes, what took place in this movement was "not literally a return to the ancients but a revitalization of the simple, pure spirit of ancient times."[160] Hisamatsu distinguishes four phases of the movement: "first, . . . a desire to return to the ancients; second, academic research into the world of the ancients; third, efforts to express the discovered heritage of the ancients in spirituality and in artistic form; finally, an authentic experience of the spirit of ancient times."[161] He locates Mabuchi in the third phase, and as representative of the last and highest stage he names the poet Ide (or Tachibana) Akemi (1812–1868) and the Sōtō monk Ryōkan. Like Mabuchi, Ryōkan was able to break free of the established patterns of poetic form,[162] but he surpassed the "master of Agatai" in spontaneity and ingenuousness. Ryōkan's strongest and most direct contact with the *Man'yōshū* school was through Mabuchi's disciple Ōmura Mitsue (1753–1816), who visited him and exchanged views in his hermitage in 1801. At his departure, Ryōkan composed a poem for him in which he bade his friend to tarry a while longer since it had begun to drizzle outside.[163]

The Japanese literature of the Tokugawa period was influenced by an influx of Chinese poetry, which Ryōkan took and used to his advantage. In expressing his own inner feelings and experiences, he preferred the Chinese poetic style. In many ways, a dark shadow hovers over his Chinese texts, which speak of "night and solitude," are "imbued with his deepest feelings . . . and in a certain sense serve as his personal diary," whereas, according to Japanese authors, his Japanese poems express more of his surface self.[164] "One should not forget that within this mild, simple Zen monk dwelled an infinitude of darkness and solitude."[165]

Ryōkan's Chinese poems (*kanshi*) contain a good deal of autobiographical material and "reflect the inner concerns of his spirit,"[166] beginning with the solitude that was his constant companion—from the painful, oppressive aloneness of sickness, to quiet resignation, to expansive happiness. His spirited contact with local peasants may have done much to alleviate his loneliness, but they did not take away his solitude.

Ryōkan suffered from a weak constitution and often took sick. He was still relatively young when problems usually associated with old age forced him to change his residence in 1817, relocating his hut to the foot of Mount Kugami near the Shinto shrine of Otogo. During the ten years he spent there he changed little to his previous way of life. His poetic activity showed no signs of regression. As he wrote at the time:

Who can call my poems poems?
My poems are not poems
And only those who know that my poems are not poems
Can speak them with me.[167]

In typical Zen paradox, these words express the unfettered quality of a style that was foreign to the "poetic" conventions of the time. Likewise, he spoke of three things he did not like: poems by poets, calligraphy by calligraphers, and cooking by cooks. While the saying brought Ryōkan a certain notoriety, it did not exactly help his reputation as an artist (he was a excellent calligrapher himself). In his correspondence with friends, the Zen spirit of his artistry finds clear expression.

For the most part, Ryōkan was most fully himself when he was able to forget himself, and this he was able to achieve at play with children. He felt best when surrounded by a circle of little ones. This aspect of his life, more than anything other, won him a place of affection in the hearts of his fellow Japanese that continues to this present day. The enlightened Zen monk who plays hide-and-seek with children and hides behind the light, who unabashedly enjoys it as they keep him waiting, who plays ball with them enthusiastically—this is the monk who has become a permanent and indescribably popular part of the folk tradition of Japan.[168] The secret of Ryōkan's ability to delight in children's games was to be found in the experience of Zen that enabled him to forget himself totally. Playing ball with children "was for him the highest form of Zen."[169]

As his declining health made it increasingly difficult for him to remain in his hut, in 1826 he accepted the invitation of his friend Kimura Motoemon, who placed at his disposal an annex of his house in Shimazaki (in the region of Niigata). In 1828 the northern coast of Japan was devastated by storms— first floods and then in November a powerful earthquake that claimed more than a thousand lives. On that occasion, Ryōkan composed the following verses, still widely cited today, which teach a letting go of one's life come what may:

When you meet with misfortune,
    it is good to meet with misfortune.
When you die,
    it is good to die.
This is the wonderful way
    of escaping misfortune.[170]

His last years were brightened by his meeting with Teishin (b. 1798), the daughter of a lower class samurai. She had been given in marriage at the age of seventeen, but after the premature death of her husband she became a nun and lived in the village temple. When Ryōkan first met her she was twenty-nine and he sixty-nine. A warm master-disciple relationship grew up between them, which they expressed by writing poems for each other.[171] Out of her respect and love for Ryōkan, Teishan cared for him in his final illness and later collected his poems in an anthology entitled *Dew-drops on a Lotus Leaf*.

In our own day Ryōkan has once again began to attract attention on many sides. A more careful study of his work shows the close connection between his thought and feelings and the worldview of Dōgen. While he does not exhibit the religious depth, much less the intellectual acumen, of the patriarch of Sōtō, he certainly belongs among Dōgen's spiritual heirs. We have yet to hear the final word on the significance of Ryōkan's accomplishments.

The foregoing overview of the Zen schools of the Tokugawa period has embraced an unexpectedly large number of interesting events and important personalities, a fact that may seem somewhat surprising in view of the intellectual stagnation that accompanied the tight system of controls throughout this rather ill-reputed period. Thanks above all to the research of Japanese scholars over the last decades, the importance of this era is now beyond doubt. Concentration on internal matters called forth previously inactive strengths among the people and wrought change and renewal in a number of areas. The astonishingly rapid and widely effective reopening of the country at the beginning of the Meiji period may be attributed in large measure to the long period of incubation during which Japan was cut off from the outside world. In any case, this is the historical and intellectual context in which all the events of the Zen schools need to be placed. Strongly grounded in a centuries-old tradition reaching back to China, Zen not only succeeded in sinking roots deep into the soil through a process of radical Japanization, but was also able to interact with the major events of the time and thereby make a significant contribution to a turning point in Japan's intellectual history. The dynamic nature of the events described in this chapter may seem to pale in comparison with the overall sweep of this period, but they clearly belong to the flow of events that ushered in the modern period. Zen history at this time was dominated by the figure of Hakuin, who brought about an organic restructuring of Zen that in turn led to a fundamental internal renewal. This shall be the matter of the next chapter.

AN EXCURSUS ON BASHŌ AND ZEN'S LOVE OF NATURE

Japan's greatest poet is filled with the spirit of Zen. Although Matsuo Bashō (1644–1694)[172] was not a Zen monk, he was strongly influenced by Zen.[173] In his biography, Bashō's encounter with Zen comes relatively late—significantly, at the turning point when his poetry took on a new and unique style that was expressed in the *haikai* or *haiku* and that brought the last period of his life to its richest maturity.

In Bashō's *haiku*, Zen found its most perfect poetic expression. This does not mean that the *haiku* is an exclusively Zen poetic form.[174] Like the Noh theater, the *haiku* does not belong totally and exclusively to Zen. The evolution of the *haiku* began with the "linked verses" (*renga*) that the popular poet Sōgi (1421–1502) had helped popularize during the middle ages and took clearer shape during the Edo period in the three-lined *haiku* (5–7–5) as the first verse (*hokku*) assumed an independent form. Matsunaga Teitoku (1571–1653),[175] the first *haiku* poet who was not at all influenced by Zen, had a relatively easy time forging the *haiku* into a respectable poetic form. In his early years, Bashō stuck rather closely to the pattern set by Teitoku.

Bashō came from the Matsuo clan, a lower-class samurai family. As a child he was called Kinsaku, and as a young man, Munefusa. In his early years he entered the service of Tōdō Yoshitada, the lord of the castle in his birthplace of Ueno in Iga (Mie prefecture). The young lord, only twelve years older than Bashō, had studied *haiku* with Kitamura Kigin (artistic name, Sengin), a teacher from the school of Teitoku. This was Bashō's first contact with this form of poetry. After Yositada's early death, Bashō wandered around aimlessly in Kyoto and the surrounding areas until at last he decided to devote himself to the art of poetry. It is probable that he also studied for a short time with Kitamura Kigin, but once he had made the acquaintance of Nishiyama Sōin, the founder of the Danrin school of the *haiku*, he joined the new teacher and received a literary education at his hands. Having quickly mastered the technique of the Danrin school, he made a number of contributions to the school's collection, which it must be said, however, are of inferior quality. At the time he bore the artistic name of Tōsei.

Bashō's real poetic productivity began when he moved to Edo (1672), where, since he could find no other fitting occupation, he settled down as a *haiku* teacher, opened a school, and gathered a circle of students. These early years were filled with searching and hardships. Finally, he made his breakthrough to a new creative poetic form. He was thirty-five when he wrote his first *haiku* of real merit. He won broad recognition through this nature poem, which foreshadows the style of his mature lyricism:

kare-eda ni	On a withered branch
karasu mo tomarikeri	A crow is perched—
aki no kure.	Autumn evening.[176]

With growing self-confidence, he was able to fill the sparse, rigid seventeen-syllable form with the soul of authentic, inner experience. In 1680 he moved his residence to the Fukagawa section of the city, where his well-to-do disciple Sampū had built him a poet's hermitage. Since it was right next to a banana tree, he called his new home Bashō-an ("Banana-tree Hermitage") and gave himself the poet's name of Bashō. At this time, he began to feel the need to learn more about Zen and soon took up a study of Zen teachings and the practice of Zen meditation with the Rinzai master Butchō in Kompon-ji in Kashima.[177] We do not know just how much progress he made on the path toward enlightenment during the brief period of about one year that he spent with the master. There can be little doubt, however, that he had a natural openness toward Zen and that his mind was able to deeply grasp essential elements of the Zen way.

The great accomplishments that were to bring Bashō the poet's laurel took place during the last decades of his life. Bashō spent much of this period traveling around the country. The image that has been passed down is that of a small man, prematurely aging, with traveler's staff in hand. In autumn of 1684 he set out for his first trip, first to his birthplace of Ueno, then by way of Nagoya to Nara, Ōgaki, and Kyoto. He returned to Edo in the summer of 1685. His diary, *Nozarashi kikō* (also called *Kasshi ginkō*, after the Kasshi period), takes its title from the first lines of its first *haiku* "Nozarashi wo" (literally, "In a field of bones exposed to the weather") and testifies to the poet's free, creative spirit. His journey endowed him with a healthy inner freedom and a confirmation of his poetic calling.

Two peaceful, productive years in Edo followed (1685–1687), and then in quick succession, two journeys—one in autumn of 1687 to the Kashima shrine, and the other, in the same year, by way of Suma, Akashi to Sarashina in the Japanese alps, where he was to have his vision of the autumn moon, now famous in poetic tradition.[178] Both journeys bore fruit—the first in the *Kashima kikō*, the second in two diary reports: the *Oi no kobumi* (also called *Yoshino kikō* or *Udatsu kikō*) and the *Sarashina kikō*. His most profitable travel was to the underdeveloped north in late spring of 1689. He began with a trip to Nikko and from there went on to Sendai and Matsushima, then back to Hiraizumi, the northernmost point that Buddhism had reached during the Heian period, and finally came to the east coast. His return took him along the Japan Sea and then, on a broadly curving path, back to Kyoto. He was gone for 156 days and had covered some 2,000 kilometers. The title of his travelog, *Oku no hosomichi* ("The Narrow Way of Oku"), refers to the northeastern provinces of Japan, while the expression *oku* ("backlands") symbolizes the depths of his experience during the journey. The epitome of his poetic achievements, this work is distinguished by the masterful mixture of tight, picturesque prose in the *haiku* style (*haibun*) with interspersed, structured three-liners.

Bashō then spent two years in Kyoto (1689–1691). The travels that he undertook during this time to Genjūan on Lake Biwa and to Rakushisha (Saga) took on literary form in the *Genjūanki* (1690) and the *Saga nikki* (1691). After his return to Edo in 1691, he found himself in the grip of depression. Despite his weakened state of health, he once again took up his traveler's staff and set out for the southern island of Kyūshū (1694). He fell seriously ill in Osaka and was not able to carry out his plans. His last *haiku*, in which he bade farewell (*jisei*) to this beautiful, ephemeral world, reads as follows:

> *Tabi ni yande*   Sick from the journey
> *yume wa kareno wo*   Chasing on the dry field
> *kake-meguru*   Dreams go round

Zen's love of nature comes to unique expression in Bashō's poetry. The poet is in love with nature and with humanity, but a humanity seen in relation to the cosmos, in an essential bond with nature. Most of his poems make some reference to nature, and that not simply because the rules of *haiku* poetry require that in every *haiku* the seasons must be mentioned or at least implied. In no way would Bashō allow himself to be confined by such rules. But he lived in unity with nature. His artistic works are part of a traditional Japanese style of poetry known as *fūga*. What he has to say about the creative and life-enhancing artistic power of the *fūga* also constitutes his own confession as a poet and as a human being. He speaks of himself as a monk in a robe fluttering in the breeze (*fūrabo*):

> For a long time he loved poetry until at long last it became his fate. At times he wearily thought of giving it up; at other times he felt again that he must excel in it. While this struggle went on, his mind was restless. If he tried for a time to make progress in the world, his poetry stood in the way. If for a time he applied himself to study in order to illumine his own ignorance, he was likewise inhibited. Finally he was powerless and void of all achievement. So he attached himself to this one line [of *fūga*]. What Saigyō seeks to express in the Japanese song (*waka*), Sōgi in the linked verses (*renga*), Sesshū in painting, and Rikyū in the tea ceremony—all these ways are permeated by one single thing.
>
> Those who comprehend *fūga* follow nature and befriend the four seasons. In whatever they see, they behold the flower. In whatever they think, they think the moon. Those to whom a form is not a flower are barbarians. Those whose thoughts are not the moon are like animals. Depart from barbarism and leave the beast behind. Follow nature and return to nature![179]

Of the names mentioned by Bashō as his forerunners, only the last two are Zen disciples in the full sense. Saigyō (1118–1190) had lived as an itinerant monk and poet in closest contact with nature before the arrival of Zen to Japan. Several centuries later the poet-monk Sōgi (1421–1502) of the Tendai school followed in his footsteps. More than any other artist, Sesshū is spiritually akin to Bashō. Both comprehend nature from within; both instinctively respond to the rhythm of life in the changes of the moon and repeatedly find the appropriate term for this pulsation in their art. Bashō is sensitive to and fond of the distinctiveness of the seasons. He sings of the splendor of the morning and of flowers in the spring. But in the Land of the Rising Sun, where the cherry blossoms fade after only a few days, no season speaks so forcefully to the heart as autumn, whose dying beauty is transfigured by the glow of eternity. But not even autumn can break the spirit of the follower of Zen. Death and birth alike belong to the life that comes from nature and is reabsorbed by nature. In many songs Bashō develops variations on the motif of the autumn wind. When he mourns the death of his young poet friend Isshō, the autumn wind breathes the pure sorrow of death:

> *Tsuka mo ugoke* Shake, oh grave!
> *waga nakigoe wa* My wailing voice—
> *aki no kaze*   The autumn wind.[180]

In the mute image of the dry leafless boughs, in the melodious whining of the wind, in the first wave of cold that makes the body shiver, autumn breathes loneliness into the soul, which the poet experiences as he describes it:

Mono ieba	If I but speak
kuchibiru samushi	My cold lips tremble—
aki no kaze	The autumn wind. [181]

White is the color of emptiness and solitude. The poet sees the white of the cliffs, and in an unusual transmutation attributes the whiteness to the autumn wind:

Ishiyama no	White shines the stone
ishi yori shiroshi	Of the mountain rock; whiter yet
aki no kaze.	The autumn wind. [182]

Loneliness is the sentiment in which the soul touches the Absolute. Zen practices the loneliness and silence of emptiness in long, somber hours of meditation. Bashō, who had passed through the hard school of practice, carried this silence within him and attuned his ear to the deepest ground of nature, where all sounds sink into stillness and heighten the awesomeness of the silence. In his travel book *Oku no hosomichi* he tells how one day on his wanderings he encountered a perfect silence in nature. It was then that he composed his most beautiful song on silence, which he introduced with the following lines:

In the district of Yamagata is located a mountain temple named Ryūshaku-ji, which was founded by Jikaku Daishi, and is an unusually pure and quiet place. . . . We ascended to the temple hall on the mountain. Rock towers upon rock, pines and oaks are primeval, earth and stones are ancient and covered with slippery moss. The sliding doors of the rock-based temple buildings were closed. Not a sound could be heard. We wandered through the rocky expanse, crept over the boulders, and worshiped before the sacred Buddha images. The glorious landscape and the far-reaching silence pierced straight to our hearts:

Shizukasa ya	Only silence alone—
iwa ni shimiiru	Into the rocky cliff penetrates
semi no koe	The sound of the cicada.

The noise of the cicadas does not disturb the tranquillity of nature. The motion of life is no hindrance to one who knows, but only heightens the inner silence. "Stillness in motion, motion in stillness," is an ancient Oriental dictum that Zen has made its own. Bashō enters into the silence of nature even as he enters into its motion. In his heart he bears the "longing for wind and clouds." On his journeys he experiences the uncertainty of life, survives its dangers and exertions, yet without the wild spirit of adventure or the gestures of heroism. In all that transpires, his mind preserves the quiet clarity of one who knows. Human life is for him a single peregrination, without beginning or end, from somewhere to somewhere, in keeping with the Buddhist doctrine of the Middle

THE ZEN SCHOOLS DURING THE TOKUGAWA PERIOD

Way that moves back and forth between being and nonbeing, between the eternal
and the transient. All nature is on the move, sun and moon, winds and clouds.
Should not humans join it in this wandering? Thus he begins his famous book
Oku no hosomichi:

> Sun and moon are eternal wanderers. So also do the years journey, coming
> and going. He who passes his life in the floating ship and, as he approaches
> old age, grasps the reins of the horse, journeys daily. The journey is his
> abode. In ancient times many people died while on the road.

Bashō goes on to describe how last autumn he returned to his dilapidated
house on the river but by spring was driven by a relentless daimon to set out
on another journey; the gods of the road were inviting him once again to follow
them . . .

Bashō's poetry casts its nets far and wide. In his selection of themes he
follows a poetic bent informed by Zen. His tastes inclined toward small animals
and flowers, toward the wind, the clouds, and the moon (whose mirror-image
in the water is reminiscent of the human mind). In every particle of dust he
finds the universe. In the frog, the cuckoo, and the sparrow, in the chirping
cicada and in the nightingale that soils the rice cakes on the veranda—in all
he feels the life of the Buddha. Suzuki interprets Bashō's most famous *haiku* as
a kōan.[183] The frog, who with a plunge into the pond vivifies the universe,
discloses the final meaning of reality. "What is life other than a noise that breaks
the silence, a noise of foolish origin and soon to pass?" That is Gundert's interpretation of these famous seventeen syllables:

Furuike ya	The old pond, ah!
kawazu tobikomu	A frog jumps in:
mizu no oto	The water's sound.[184]

Bashō is one of the greatest lyric poets of all times. Because of the intimate
bonds of lyric poetry with language, Bashō's verses can hardly be appreciated
without an adequate knowledge of Japanese. The charm of his humanity comes
through in many simple poems that brighten the happenings of everyday life.
His is the innocent eye of the child. He loves children as he loves flowers:

Ko ni aku to	For one who says
mōsu hito ni wa	"I am tired of children,"
hana mo nashi	There are no flowers.[185]

Though of a thoroughly religious nature, Bashō shows little interest in different varieties of Buddhist doctrine:

Tsukikage ya	The light of the moon!
shimon shishū mo	Four the gates and four the sects,
tada hitotsu	And yet only one.[186]

His religiosity is bound to nature. No exuberant passion explodes in his
lines. Humanity's involvement with history remains outside the scope of his

vision. The human person Bashō is completely immersed in the contemplation of nature and is one with cosmic life. The constrictions imposed on his poetic utterances are conditioned by his worldview. Human life is not a one-time, irrepeatable event; rather it is a moment in the course of nature.[187]

Given the keen appreciation of nature of the Japanese, Zen was able here to take on a new and highly artistic poetic expression, nowhere more perfectly articulated than by Bashō. Whether he is to be called a "nature poet" depends on what one understands by those words.[188] It makes no real difference whether, with Suzuki, one considers Bashō a "most passionate lover of nature" or, with Hoover, a poet "full of all the detached reverence and affection of Zen."[189] From the perspective of intellectual history, it is important that Bashō gave clear expression to Taoist elements, which, as in Chinese Ch'an, play no small role in Japanese Zen.[190] From common Taoist roots there arose in Japan a variety of expressions that, though different in form, were essentially related. Yoshida Shōin (1830–1859), the noble educator who was schooled in Confucianism and prepared the way for the Meiji Restoration, drew strength in his last hours from a turning back to nature; from his prison cell he wrote: "However people may judge, I give myself up to nature. I do not desire death. I do not refuse death."[191] The pioneer of the Kokugaku school, Kamo Mabuchi (1697–1769), who devoted himself energetically to the renewal of Shinto, sees in the "harmony with heaven and earth" the highest ideal of life, which is to be accomplished in conformity to the spontaneous working of nature "of itself."[192] The widely read modern novelist Natsume Sōseki can also be considered a representative of aesthetic naturalism.[193] Zen is not the only element, nor perhaps the primary one, responsible for the naturalistic trend that runs through all of Japanese intellectual life, but it bears strong affinities to the innate Japanese feeling for nature. This is why it was possible for Zen to strike deep roots in Japan and to produce, in its alliance with the Japanese spirit, a rich artistic tradition.

NOTES

1.   See the entries in EJ, vol. 6, pp. 47a,b and Zengaku daijiten, I, p. 123. See also Tsuji Zennosuke, Nihon bukkyōshi, vol. 9, pp. 285–416; Hakugen Yūsen, chap. 2 of vol. 3 of Nihon bukkyōshi, ed. by Ienaga Saburō, Akamatsu Toshihide, and Keishitsu Taisei, pp. 92–94; Imaeda Aishin, Zn no rekishi, pp. 214–21.

2.   See the brief biography in Zengaku daijiten II, p. 860. See also Tsuji, Nihon bukkyōshi, vol. 9, pp. 296ff.

3.   On Fei-yin T'ung-ying and the Wu-teng yen-t'ung chronicle, see Zen Dust, pp. 430–31 and table IX, p. 505.

4.   Tsuji lists a number of names, Nihon bukkyōshi, vol. 9, p. 299ff.

5.   Nihon bukkyōshi, vol. 9, pp. 298ff. On the treatment that Tao-che received at the hands of Yin-yüan, see Minamoto Ryōen's introduction to vol. 17 of Nihon no zengoroku on Tetsugen, pp. 103ff (hereafter abbreviated as Tetsugen goroku).

6. See the brief biographies in EJ, vol. 3, p. 30b, and *Zengaku daijiten* II, 1271. Japanese Buddhist histories generally give him detailed treatment, especially the works of Tsuji Zennosuke and Ui Hakuju.

7. See Tsuji, *Nihon bukkyōshi*, vol. 9, p. 321.

8. See the entry "Itsunen" in EJ, vol. 3, p. 357a,b; Tsuji, *Nihon bukkyōshi*, vol. 9, p. 286. I-jan was the third abbot of Kōfuku-ji.

9. Tsuji, *Nihon bukkyōshi*, vol. 9, pp. 319–20.

10. More than two hundred monks would have attended the talk. The enthusiasm gripped Sōtō and Rinzai monks alike. See *Tetsugen goroku*, pp. 62ff.,

11. The text has been reproduced in full by Tsuji, *Nihon bukkyōshi*, vol. 9, pp. 322–25. A commentary appears in the introduction to the *Tetsugen goroku*, pp. 63ff. On Ryūkei, who became a disciple of Yin-yüan together with some other Japanese monks, see pp. 77, 84, 88.

12. See *Tetsugen goroku*, p. 65.

13. See Tsuji, *Nihon bukkyōshi*, vol. 9, p. 322.

14. He managed the office of *shoshidai*. See *Tetsugen goroku*, p. 67.

15. For the wording of the letter, see Tsuji, *Nihon bukkyōshi*, vol. 9, p. 351.

16. The reference is to Mount Huang-po (Jpn., Ōbaku) is the province of Fukien, on which already in the eighth century a Zen monk had built a cloister, Po-jo-t'ang (Jpn., Hannya-dō), which later was expanded into a temple. In another temple on the same mountain the famous Huang-po Hsi-yün (Jpn., Ōbaku Kiun, d. 850), the master of Lin-chi, had practiced in his youth. Later he constructed another temple on a mountain in the northwest region of the province of Kiangsi that he named Huang-po (Ōbaku) in commemoration of his practice as a young man on the mountain in Fukien. During the Sung period the temple in Fukien was abandoned and fell into ruin. In the year 1614, on the site of the ruins, a new and more impressive temple named Wan-fu-ssu (Jpn., Mampuku-ji) was built. It was here that Yin-yüan Lung-ch'i (Ingen Ryūki) lived before his departure for Japan. The name of the school and temple in Japan are named after the temple and the mountain in China. See *Zen Dust*, pp. 209–10. The official name is Ōbakusan Mampuku-ji; see *Tetsugen goroku*, p. 74.

17. Tsuji, *Nihon bukkyōshi*, vol. 3, p. 93.

18. Because of his zeal in practicing the *nembutsu*, the fourth abbot of Mampuku-ji, Tu-chan Hsing-ying (Jpn., Dokutan Shōkei, 1628–1706) was called "Nembutsu Dokutan." See *Tetsugen goroku*, p. 84.

19. These prescriptions, called *Yoshokugo*, edited by Yin-yüan toward the end of his life, were taken over into the *Ōbaku shingi* (T. no. 2007). See *Tetsugen goroku*, pp. 80ff. The second abbot, Mu-an (Jpn., Mokuan, on whom see below), gave a perspective to the rule and effected certain minor changes. The fifth abbot, the important Kao-ch'üan Hsin-tun (Jpn., Kōsen Shōton, 1633–1695) promulgated a final definitive version of the rule. In the *Taishō* collection of the Sino-Japanese canon, two further works of Yin-yüan have been included: his collected sayings or *Fushō Kokushi goroku* (T. 2605) and his Dharma sayings, *Fushō Kokushi hōgo* (T. 2606). Fushō Kokushi is the title bestowed on Yin-yüan.

20. See the section "Ōbaku sandan kaie" in *Tetsugen goroku*, pp. 75ff.

21. That is, until the year 1740. The fourteenth abbot, Ryūtō Gentō (1663–1746), was the first Japanese to assume the leadership of Mampuku-ji. Since 1786 all the abbots have been Japanese.

22.   The abbot of Myōshin-ji, Gudō Tōshoku (1579–1661), complained about Yin-yüan's breach of courtesy for having failed to pay his respects. The editor of the introduction to the *Tetsugen goroku*, who reports on the incident, comments that Yin-yüan may have completely forgotten to think about this, or that the reason lay in "an unconscious contempt of a monk of a great land toward a monk from a smaller land" (p.85).

23.   See *Tetsugen goroku*, pp. 88ff, 95ff.

24.   The three Chinese Ōbaku masters, Yin-yüan, Mu-an, and Yin-fei are renowned as "the three brushes."

25.   See the entry in EJ, vol. 8, p. 16a, and *Zengaku daijiten* II, p. 918. See also the piece of Akamatsu Shimmyō in *Kōza zen* vol. 4, *Zen no rekishi: Nihon*, pp. 327–36; Akamatsu has also compiled a biography entitled *Tetsugen Zenji*. A collection of his writings, translated into modern Japanese, annotated, and accompanied by an introduction, appears in vol. 17 of *Nihon no zen-goroku* (Tokyo, 1979), edited by Minamoto Ryōen.

26.   On the following see above all the introduction to the *Tetsugen goroku*, which draws its biographical data on Tetsugen from the *Zuiryū kaisan Tetsugen Oshō gyōjitsu* by the disciple Dōsō Keishu (1714). The introduction goes into some detail on Saigin and Gekkan, as well as on the struggles within Pure Land Buddhism; see. pp. 24–33.

27.   *Tetsugen goroku*, pp. 19, 42.

28.   *Tetsugen goroku*, pp. 130–31.

29.   *Tetsugen goroku*, p. 112.

30.   Kengan's teacher Sessō had also been the teacher of Saigin. Sessō, and extraordinary personality, converted from Amida Buddhism to Zen, achieved the great enlightenment, and was invested as chief abbot of Tafuku-ji; see *Tetsugen goroku*, pp. 112–13.

31.   *Tetsugen goroku*, pp. 119ff, 123ff; on the characteristics of the edition of Tetsugen as compared with that of Tenkai, see pp. 167–71.

32.   The Korean edition, *Koryŏ dè čan gÿon* (Jpn. *Kōrai daizōkyō*) is named after the Korean Koryŏ dynasty (918–1392).

33.   In the judgment of one Japanese scholar "modern Japanese Buddhist scholarship begins here." The British scholar Samuel Beal used this Ōbaku edition for his early studies of Sino-Japanese Buddhism. See *Tetsugen goroku*, p. 170–71.

34.   Hubert Durt and Anna Seidel report on this edition in the "Avertissement" to the *Répertoire du Canon Bouddhique Sino-Japonais Édition de Taishō*, pp. 1–7.

35.   The complete title is *Zuiryū-ji Tetsugen Zenji kanaji hōgo*, which is abbreviated as *Tetsugen kana hōgo (Dharma Words in Kana)*; see *Zenmon hōgoshū*, vol. 1, pp. 281–318; for an annotated edition in modern Japanese, see *Tetsugen goroku*, pp. 177–272.

36.   Minamoto Ryōen treats the question in detail in *Tetsugen goroku*, pp. 136ff. 144–48.

37.   See *Tetsugen goroku*, pp. 147, 165ff.

38.   See the essay by D. T. Suzuki, "Dōgen, Hakuin Bankei: Three Types of Thought in Japanese Zen," trans. by N. Waddell, EB 9.1 (1976): 1–17 and 9.2: 1–20. The original appears in *Suzuki Daisetzu zenshū*, vol. 1, pp. 57–83.

39.   See the brief biography in *Zengaku daijiten* II, p. 930; see also Furuta Shōkin, *Kōza zen*, vol. 4, *Zen no rekishi: Nihon*, pp. 79, 81–82. There is also a biography of the disciple of Gudō, Shidō Munan, in EB 3.1 (1970): 122ff.

40.   *Zen no rekishi: Nihon*, p. 82.

41.   See *Nihon no Zen-goroku: Bankei*, pp. 3–4.

42.   See his *Living by Zen*, pp. 111–16, 122–24, 176–77.

43.   Normann Waddell, *The Unborn: The Life and Teaching of Zen Mastesr Bankei*, pp. x–xi. Waddell bases his translation of selections from Bankei's sermons and dialogue on D. T. Suzuki's *Bankei Zenji goroku*, a reproduction of the *Bankei butchi kōzai zenji hōgo*, which first appeared in 1757. The first printing long remained the main source of his work in Japan. The earliest manuscript of the sermons of Bankei is the so-called *Ryūmonji-hon*, extant in a four-volume and a one-volume edition. Fujimoto Tsuchishige has edited the latter, which stems from an unknown disciple of Bankei and was transcribed prior to 1740, as the first basic section of his edition *Bankei Zenji hōgoshū* (Tokyo, 1971). The second part of this edition forms the *Futetsuan-hon* (author and date unknown). Both contain what are referred to in the text as the sermons of Bankei, but are distinguished from one another by marked discrepancies in the wording. They are divided into two sections and shall henceforth be cited as Ia and Ib, IIa and IIb. In addition, particular sections are numbered. The edition also contains two other sections, III and IV, of the same content but shorter. Tamaki Kojirō uses the edition of Fujimoto Tsuchishige in earlier cited work (see note 41). This, currently the best available edition, is henceforth abbreviated as *Bankei hōgoshū*. Fujimoto presents a detailed account of the sources in his standard work on Bankei, *Bankei Kokushi no kenkyū*, pp. 697–705. Much material on Bankei is presented by Akao Ryūji in his comprehensive work *Bankei Zenji zenshū* (hereafter referred to as *Bankei zenshū*. The same author has gathered together anecdotes on Bankei into two volumes in *Bankei Zenji itsuwashū*. He notes in the introduction to the first volume that Bankei's Zen, for all its special character, is also "Japanese Zen," "people's Zen," and "Zen in everyday language." Suzuki's studies on Bankei comprise the first volume of his collected works (see note 38).

44.   Waddell, *The Unborn*, p. ix.

45.   See *Nihon no zen-goroku: Bankei*, pp. 17–18. Umpo Zenjō also practiced with the famous Kaisen Jōki (d. 1582), who served as abbot of various monasteries. Later, because of Umpo's favorable attitude to Takeda Shingen, he incurred the wrath of the powerful Nobunaga, who had his monastery of Erin-ji burned to the ground.

46.   *Bankei hōgoshū* Ia:27–28, pp. 15–16. The portions set in square brackets come from a report in the same collection (III:34, p. 179) and are included to clarify the picture of his affliction. Much of the wording is taking from Waddell, *The Unborn*, pp. 9–10.

47.   *Bankei zenshū*, p. 172. The *Bankei Oshō gyōgōki*, which appears there, was compiled by the disciple Myōzan Soin one year after Bankei's death and was published in 1740. Concerning this, the only biography of Bankei to appear during the Edo period, see pp. 806–807.

48.   The names of some of these masters are given in *Nihon no zen-goroku: Bankei*, p. 23.

49.   Both the *Bankei Oshō gyōgōki* and *Bankei Oshō kinen ryakuroku* (this latter composed by an unknown disciple) contain accounts of an enlightenment experience that Bankei had with Tao-che (see *Bankei zenshū*, pp. 174, 331). As Furuta Shōkin notes, it is more correct to say that Bankei had sought from Tao-che confirmation that his was an experience of enlightenment. The remarks appear in an essay of Furuta's lauding the influence of Tao-che in Japan, "Dōsha Chōgen no raichō to sono eikyō," *Furuta chosakushū*, vol. 2, p. 352.

50.   This episode, appearing in the same source, is also uncertain.

51. Cf. *Bankei hōgoshū* III:24–25, pp. 171–72.

52. See the section on "The Reconciliation with Master Bokuō" in Fujimoto Tsuchi-shige, *Bankei Zenji no kenkyū*, pp. 279–82, edited by Tamaki Kōshirō in *Nihon no zen-goroku: Bankei*, P. 40. See also Furuta Shōkin on the relation between Tao-che and Yin-Yüan, *Furuta chosakushū*, vol. 2, pp. 362ff.

53. The winter practice in 1679 was held at Ryūmon-ji with 60 participants; in 1682 at Jizō-ji with 150 participants; in 1684 at Kōrin-ji with 300 participants; in 1685 at Shūtoku-ji (in the area of Harima) with 90 participants and later in Ryūmon-ji with 130 participants; in the summer of 1686 at Ryūmon-ji with 150 participants; in 1687 at Kōrinji with 150 participants; in 1688 in Fumon-ji (Hirado) with 60 participants; and in 1689 at Sanyū-ji in Okayama with 130 participants. See *Nihon no zen-goroku: Bankei,* pp. 43–48.

54. *Udāna* VIII:3 Translation from *The Minor Anthologies of the Pāli Canon,* part II, trans. by F. L. Woodward (London, 1948), p. 98.

55. *Bankei hōgoshū* Ia:6, p. 6. Translation from Waddell, *The Unborn,* p. 36.

56. *Bankei hōgoshū* Ia:7, p. 6; cf. the entire section.

57. *Bankei hōgoshū* Ia:2, p. 4. Elsewhere he refers to his school as the "Clear-Eyed" sect (*myōgenshū*), Ia:37, *p.* 19. Cf. Waddell, *The Unborn,* pp. 47–48.

58. *Bankei Zenji goroku* 13, p. 24.

59. See *Bankei hōgoshū* III:69, p. 235. On this point see also Tamaki, *Nihon no zen-goroku: Bankei,* p. 131.

60. *Bankei hōgoshū* III:49, pp. 5–6; cf. III:5, p. 169. The Unborn is "the thing just as it is" (*sono mama*), namely, in its "suchness." "What Bankei meant by 'suchness' is not something relative but primordially absolute" (*Suzuki zenshū,* vol. 1, p. 59). See the details Suzuki presents on the absolute quality of the Unborn (pp. 58–59). See also the text to note 94 below.

61. *Bankei hōgoshū* III:49, p. 190. Cf. Ia:42, p. 21. These remarks were made shortly after the persecution of the Christians. Tamaki attributes the uniqueness of his preaching on the "Unborn" to his maturation without being guided along the way (*Nihon no zen-goroku: Bankei,* p. 116).

62. *Bankei hōgoshū* Ib:17, p. 57; the sermon was preached on the morning of 25 September 1690.

63. *Bankei hōgoshū,* Ia:51, p. 34.

64. *Bankei Zenji goroku* Ia:14, p. 26.

65. *Bankei hōgoshū,* Ib:5, p. 49.

66. Cited by Furuta Shōkin in his essay on the development of Japanese Zen, "Nihon zen no hattatsu," which appeared in vol. 2 of *Gendai zen kōza: rekishi to ningen,* pp. 75–76. Compare the detailed advice given an angry monk in *Bankei hōgoshū* Ia:46, pp. 24–29. In several sermons Bankei takes up the question of anger and the conquest of the passions. The story of discord between married people takes up a great deal of space; see Ib:37–42, pp. 75–80.

67. *Bankei hōgoshū* Ia:21, p. 12. These words stand in sharp contrast to his own ascetic efforts.

68. *Bankei hōgoshū,* Ia:46, p. 29.

69. *Bankei hōgoshū* Ia:48, p. 31.

70. *Bankei hōgoshū* Ia:49–50, pp. 31–32.

71. *Bankei hōgoshū* Ia:57, pp. 39–40. English translation, N. Waddell, *The Unborn*, pp. 71–72.

72. *Bankei hōgoshū* Ia:47, pp. 29ff.

73. *Bankei hōgoshū* III:47, p. 189; see also Ia:40, p. 20. English translation, Waddell, *The Unborn*, p. 48.

74. *Bankei Zenji goroku* Ib:31, p. 88.

75. *Bankei hōgoshū* IIb:9, p. 135.

76. *Bankei Zenji goroku* Ia:14, p. 26. English translation, N. Waddell, *The Unborn*, p. 57.

77. *Bankei hōgoshū* IIb:9, p. 135; cf. IIb:47, p. 189.

78. *Bankei hōgoshū* II:16, p. 108. The entire section is relevant. English translation, Waddell, *The Unborn*, p. 54.

79. *Bankei Zenji goroku* Ia:20, p. 37. See Waddell, *The Unborn*, p. 37.

80. *Bankei hōgoshū* IIa:36, p. 127. Suzuki gives a free translation of the passage from the *Hekiganroku* and Bankei's comments on it. He does not hesitate to characterize the kōan as "idle hairsplitting." See his "Dōgen, Hakuin, Bankei," pp. 18–19.

81. *Bankei hōgoshū* IIa:37, p. 127; Ia:54, p. 38.

82. *Bankei hōgoshū* Ia:56, p. 39.

83. Vol. 1, pp. 252–253.

84. "Dōgen, Hakuin, Bankei," pp. 16–17. Suzuki also brings out the Japanese character of Bankei's Zen style.

85. *Ibid.*, p. 19.

86. *Bankei Zenji goroku* Ia:14, pp. 26–27. English translation, Waddell, *The Unborn*, p. 57.

87. For example, see *Bankei hōgoshū* Ia:54, p. 38. Waddell's translation has Bankei refer to them as "worthless old documents," *The Unborn*, pp. 69–70.

88. In a postscript to this edition of Bankei's sermons, Furuta Shōkin lists a number of sharp expressions with which Hakuin rebukes Bankei's Zen (*Bankei Zenji goroku*, p. 291). He himself acknowledges the broad-minded, nonsectarian, liberating style of Bankei (p. 292).

89. *Bankei hōgoshū* Ia:55, pp. 38–39. English translation, Waddell, *The Unborn*, p. 70.

90. *Bankei hōgoshū* IIb:18, p. 140.

91. *Nihon no zen-goroku: Bankei*, pp. 141–42. Tamaki remarks on the report in detail (pp. 45–46). For the version on which the quotation in the text is based, see *Bankei hōgoshū* IV:61, pp. 231–32.

92. *Nihon no zen-goroku: Bankei*, p. 26. See also the version in *Bankei hōgoshū* IV:61, p. 230.

93. *Bankei hōgoshū* IV:61, p. 231. See *Nihon no zen-goroku: Bankei*, pp. 159ff.

94. *Bankei hōgoshū* Ib:9, p. 52; cf. Ib:27–28, pp. 67–68.

95. *Suzuki zenshū*, vol. 1, p. 57.

96. See the brief biography in *Zengaku daijiten* II, p. 742.

97. See the brief biography in *Zengaku daijiten* I, p. 213. He also composed a commentary on the *Heart Sūtra*.

98.   See the brief biography in *Zengaku daijiten* II, p. 395.

99.   Mujaku Dōchū functioned three times as abbot of Myōshin-ji; see Imaeda, *Zenshū no rekishi*, p. 241. Imaeda reads his name *Muchaku;* the *Zengaku daijiten* reads it *Mujaku.*

100.   See the brief biography in *Zengaku daijiten* II, p. 1102. His personal name is listed there as Bunshu; Imaeda and others read it Monju (see *Zenshū no rekishi*, p. 257).

101.   See the brief biography in EJ, vol. 7, p. 89; *Zengaku daijiten* II, pp. 1095–96. The biography of Munan by Tōrei Enji (1721–1792), *Kaisan shidō Munan Zenji anroku*, has been translated into English by Kobori Sōhaku and Norman Waddell; see EB 3.1 (1970): 122–38. On the biography, see also the introduction by Ichihara Toyota to vol. 15 of *Nihon no zen-goroku: Munan Shōju*, pp. 9–23, and Furuta Shōkin, "Shidō Munan," *Furuta chosakushū*, vol. 5, pp. 279–321. For Munan's writings, see the edition prepared by Koda Rentarō, *Shidō Munan Zenji shū (Tokyo, 1940)*. In addition to the main works of Munan, Sokushinki and Jishōki, and the text of the biography of Tōrei, the volume contains sayings, verses, letters, and other material that has been passed down. A modern Japanese rendering of the two main works, along with other material, are contained in *Munan Shōju* mentioned above, pp. 44–233. An English translations of the *Sokushinki* by Kobori and Waddell appeared in EB 3.2 (1970): 89–118; 4.1 (1971): 116–23; 4.2 (1971): 119–27. For an English translation of the *Jishōki*, see Kusumita Priscilla Pederson, EB 8.1 (1975): 96–132. The reason that Munan's name is often pronounced *Bunan* will be explained later. The transcription *Munan* is more common.

102.   See Furuta Shōkin, "Kanagaki dōji Shidō Munan," *Furuta chosakushū*, vol. 3, pp. 245–51. Munan wrote his works in Japanese *kana* style.

103.   In a postscript to his *Jishōki*, Munan writes of his childhood as follows: "I was born in a poor neighborhood and when I was a child was awkward in appearance and weak in constitution. We lived in the village of Fujikawa in Sekigahara in Mino, and my usual occupation was tending the cattle. When I reached the age of fifteen, I traveled with my father to Kyoto and passed the time there until I was twenty. I saw the vicissitudes of this transient world and pondered the teaching of the 'special transmission.' To attain it I shaved off my hair and beard and dyed my robe, and visited teachers asking about the Way. I wandered east and west, sleeping in the dew and lodging in the grasses, and was growing older . . ." (Pederson, *Jishōki*, pp. 131–32).

104.   *Sokushinki*, EB 3.2 (1970): 90–91.

105.   The most important source is the biography composed by the disciple of Hakuin, Tōrei Enji (see note 101), about a hundred years after Munan's time. It is often not difficult to detect legendary elements in the episodes narrated about his life.

106.   See vol. 1 of this work, p.133. This saying is also the beginning of the second case in the kōan collection *Hekiganroku*,

107.   The manuscript contains the hundred cases of the *Hekiganroku* that the Zen master Tōyō Eichō (1429–1504) studied under his teacher Sekkō Shōshin (1408–1486) and copied out in his own hand. That manuscript had been entrusted to the care of Gudō from the Tōyō Eichō line. See *Munan goroku*, p. 16; *Furuta chōsakushū*, p. 287. See also the English translation in EB 3.1 (1970): 129.

108.   EB 3.2 (1970): 89.

109.   EB 3.2 (1970): 116. Munan also cited cases 18 and 37 of the *Mumonkan* (pp. 116–17).

110.   EB 3.2 (1970): 117.

111.   EB 4.2 (1971): 125. The Confucian tinge is clear at the conclusion of the passage cited.

112. EB 3.2 (1970): 108–109.

113. EB 3.2 (1970): 92.

114. EB 3.2 (1970): 94.

115. See the brief biographies in Zen Dust, pp. 213–15; Zengaku daijiten I, p. 100. See also Ichihara Toyota's introduction to vol. 15 of Nihon no zen-goroku, pp. 25–41; his writings, with a translation into modern Japanese, appear on pp. 237–357; Furuta Shōkin, "Shōju Etan," Furuta chōsakushū, vol. 5, pp. 322–52. His works have also been edited by the Shinano Kyōikukai under the title Shōju Rōjin-shū (Tokyo, 1937; reprint, 1975). The volume contains a great many poems as well as a biography by Tōrei Enji (1721–1792).

116. Also known as the Ryōgon-kyō; T. no. 945.

117. The date of the erection of Shōju-an is uncertain according to the chronology (nempu) in the Shōju Rōjin-shū, p. 49.

118. On Ch'en Tsun-su, see vol. 1, p. 230. Cf. Zen Dust, p. 213. On the mother-son relationship, see Furuta chōsakushū, vol. 5, p. 328.

119. Shōju Rōjin-shū, p. 35; see the English translation in Zen Dust, p. 215.

120. See the brief biography in Zengaku daijiten II, p. 932. See Imaeda, Zenshū no rekishi, p. 222.

121. See Kagamishima Genryū in Kōza zen, vol. 4, pp. 115–16. On the Sōtō temples in eastern Japan, see the entry "Kansansetsu" in Zengaku daijiten I, p. 180.

122. See the section on the organization of the Sōtō school during the Edo period in Takeuchi Michio, Sōtōshū kyōdanshi, pp. 90–110, especially pp. 101ff. The title bestowed by the emperor did not eliminate equality among the temples.

123. Detailed statistics on the Sōtō school and the unfortunate friction between Eihei-ji and Sōjō-ji are given by Takeuchi, ibid., pp. 94ff, 101–102.

124. See the brief biography in Zengaku daijiten I, p. 83; Imaeda, Zenshū no rekishi, p. 223. His name is occasionally read Ban'an.

125. See the brief biography in Zengaku daijiten II, p. 725. See also Kagamishima, Kōza zen 4, pp. 117–18; Imaeda, Zenshū no rekishi, p. 225–26.

126. See the brief biography in Zengaku daijiten I, p. 294.

127. See the brief biography in Zengaku daijiten II, pp. 938–39. See also vol. 18 of the collection Nihon no zen-goroku: Manzan, Menzan (Tokyo, 1978). Texts of both masters rendered in modern Japanese are included and annotated by Kagamishima Genryū. All relevant works on the history of Japanese Zen treat Manzan.

128. Cited in Manzan–Menzan zen-goroku, p. 20. The passage appears in DZZ I, p. 341.

129. DZZ I, pp. 446–53.

130. On Manzan's efforts for the renewal of the ancient tradition of transmission, see Kagamishima, Kōza zen, vol. 4, pp 118ff; Tsuji, Nihon bukkyōshi, vol. 9, pp. 441–42. Regarding transmission in the Rinzai school, see note 5 of chapter 17 above.

131. See the brief biography in Zengaku daijiten I, p. 281; see also Kagamishima, Kōza zen, vol. 4, p. 120.

132. See the brief biography in Zengaku daijiten I, pp. 423–24.

133. For details on this series of events, see especiall Tsuji, Nihon bukkyōshi, vol. 9, pp. 454ff.

134. See note 32 above.

135. See the brief biography in *Zengaku daijiten* II, p. 895; Imaeda, *Zenshū no rekishi*, pp. 229–30; Kagamishima, *Kōza zen*, vol. 4, p. 120.

136. Kagamishima clarifies the point of Tenkei's critique of Manzan in his introduction to *Nihon no zen-goroku: Manzan, Menzan*, pp. 62–63; see also Takeuchi, *Sōtōshū kyōdanshi*, pp. 136ff.

137. See Kagamishima, *Nihon no zen-goroku: Manzan, Menzan*, p. 63.

138. Takeuchi presents two lists of names, *Sōtōshū kyōdanshi*, p. 138. See also the section on the commentaries to the *Shōbōgenzō* in MN 15 (1959–60): 219ff, especially p. 221.

139. See the brief biography in *Zengaku daijiten* I, p. 634. Part 2 of vol. 18 of *Nihon no zen-goroku* treats Menzan, with an introduction by Kagamishima. On his commentary to the *Shōbōgenzō*, see the article in *Monumenta Nipponica* referred to in the previous note.

140. See the brief biography in *Zengaku daijiten* II, p. 714.

141. See the brief biography in *Zengaku daijiten* I, p. 89; *Zen Dust*, pp. 417–18; T. 1986(a), 1987(b). See also *Zen Dust*, pp. 416–17.

142. See the brief biography in EJ, vol. 7, p. 283; *Zengaku daijiten* I, p. 547. See also Winston L. King, *Death Was His Kōan: The Samurai-Zen of Susuki Shōsan* (Berkeley, 1986), and Nakamura Hajime, "Suzuki Shōzan and the Spirit of Capitalism in Japanese Buddhism," MN 22 (1967): 1–14. Shōsan's collected works, *Suzuki Shōsan zenshū*, were edited by Suzuki Tesshin (Tokyo, 1957). See also vol. 14 of *Nihon no zen-goroku*, ed. by Fujiyoshi Jikai, which includes the text of Shōsan's first work, *Mōanjō* (a Buddhist confrontation with Confucian thought), and the important three-part collection known as the *Roankyō*, edited by the disciple Echū. Other of Shōsan's works worthy of mention are his *Banmin tokuyō* (an ethic for the various classes of society), *Fumoto no kusawake* (a manual for monks), *Ha-kirishitan* (an anti-Christian tract, thirty-one extant copies of which are preserved in Sōtō temples in Kyūshū). For a list and description of the complete works of Shōsan, see W. King, *Death Was His Kōan*, pp. 373–74, and Nakamura Hajime, *Kinsei nihon no hihanteki seishin*, pp. 13–21. Nakamura also treats the same question in his book *Nihon shūkyō no kindaisei*. Recently, a short memorial essay has been issued by a group interested in Shōsan under the title *Suzuki Shōsan: sono ashiato* (Nagoya, 1983).

143. *Suzuki Shōsan zenshū*, p. 162.

144. Cited in Nakamura, *Kinsei nihon no hihanteki seishin*, p. 72.

145. Nakamura refers to the work as Shōsan's "first major work," and the disciple Echū as "the first Dharma writing of the master" (*ibid.*, p. 71). The text is contained in *Suzuki Shōsan zenshū*, pp. 61–72.

146. *Suzuki Shōsan zenshū*, p. 64.

147. *Suzuki Shōsan zenshū*, pp. 68–69. English translation, King, *Death Was His Kōan*, pp. 240–42.

148. In the works cited earlier in note 141, Nakamura draws attention to the value of work in Shōsan's thought. In a Buddhist cemetery I once saw the unmarked grave of a bodhisattva inscribed with the words "A sweating bodhisattva" ("Ase wo kakeru bosatsu").

149. In addition to his work ethic, Nakamura draws attention to Shōsan's critical attitude as a sign of a new age.

150. See Nakamura, *Kinsei nihon no hihanteki seishin*, pp. 98–99; "Suzuki Shōsan and the Spirit of Capitalism," pp. 10–11.

151. *Suzuki Shōsan zenshū*, p. 71; English translation, W. King, *Death Was His Kōan*, p. 249.

152. See the brief biography in EJ, vol. 6, p. 342; *Zengaku daijiten* II, pp. 1281–82. An introductory study in English has been published by Burton Watson, *Ryōkan: Zen Monk-Poet of Japan*. For an English rendition of his Chinese and Japanese poems, complete with introduction and biographical sketch, see Noboyuki Yuasa, *The Zen Poems of Ryōkan*. The complete works were edited in two volumes by Tōgō Toyoharu in *Zenshaku Ryōkan shishū*, the first volume of which contains the Chinese poems with commentary, the second the Japanese poems. See also the annotated edition of the poems by Iida Rigyō. Vol. 20 of *Nihon no zen-goroku* contains a rendition of the Chinese poems into modern Japanese, with commentary and introduction by Iriya Yoshitaka. An earlier, suggestive work by Jakob Fischer, *Dew-drops on a Lotus Leaf* includes a selection of poems and numerous legendary anecdotes about Ryōkan. The first-rate study by Takemura Makio, *Ryōkan no shi to Dōgen-zen* (with a foreword by Tamaki Kōshirō) strives for a more profound appreciation of this Zen poet.

153. See the first chapter of Takemura, *Ryōkan no shi to Dōgen-zen*, pp. 7–39.

154. The Chinese verses appear in *Ryōkan zengoroku*, p. 39; the English translation comes from Yuasa, *The Zen Poems of Ryōkan*, pp. 29–30.

155. He used a misshapen begging bowl whose lack of proper form symbolized his own sinfulness. Once he lost his bowl and exerted himself might and main until he found it (see Yuasa, *The Zen Poems of Ryōkan*, p. 36). The begging rounds were something holy for him, consistent with his general religious appreciation of poverty. Oral tradition has it that he cut an opening in the floor of his hut to allow a sprouting tree to grow freely.

156. *The Zen Poems of Ryōkan*, p. 10. Yuasa lists the influences of the poets of the *Man'yōshū* and later collections, pp. 8ff.

157. I'nan is his pen name; his full name is Yamamoto Jirōzaemon Yasuo.

158. He was familiar with the commentary on the *Man'yōshū* composed by Katō (or Tachibana) Chikage (1735–1808), a student of Kamo Mabuchi. *Ibid.*, p. 6.

159. See my monograph, *Kamo Mabuchi: Ein Beitrag zur japanischen Religions- und Geistesgeschichte*, as well as the following essays and translations: "Die Erneuerung des Liederweges durch Kamo Mabuchi," MN 6 (1943): 110–45; "Kamo Mabuchi und das *Man'yōshū*," MN 9 (1953): 34–61; "*Uta no kokoro no uchi* (auch *Kaikō*) und *Niimanabi*," MN 4 (1941): 192–206, 566–84.

160. Cited in his three-volume work on the history of Japanese literature, *Nihon bungaku hyōronshi*, vol. 2, p. 735.

161. *Nihon bungaku hyōronshi*, vol. 2, p. 735.

162. See the letter of Mabuchi (cited in his *Zenshū*, vol. 10, p. 442; see also MN 6 (1943): 128. Mabuchi's definition of the poem as "words of the heart" that "express in outward form what the heart senses and feel within" (*Zenshū*, vol. 10, p. 293) applies to Ryōkan's poetry.

163. The English translation is in Yuasa, *The Zen Poems of Ryōkan*, p. 62.

164. See Takemura, *Ryōkan no shi to Dōgen-zen*, p. 62.

165. *Ryōkan no shi to Dōgen-zen*, p. 62.

166. In the words of a *Kambun* poem cited by Takemura (Ryōkan no shi to Dōgenzen, p. 88), *shinchū no mono wa shasuru*. Takemura notes fittingly: "The world mirrored in Ryōkan's poetry is infinitely deep. . . . He did not immerse himself in the inner core

of poetry as deeply as Bashō. Compared with Bashō, he is too religious a thinker; compared with Dōgen, he is too much the poet" (p. 190).

167.   Cited in *Ryōkan zen-goroku*, p. 21. Takemura also writes on this "paradox of the non-poem" (*Ryōkan no shi to Dōgen-zen*, pp. 87–88). Regarding the shrine of Otogo, see Yuasa, *The Zen Poems of Ryōkan*, p. 36.

168.   D. T. Suzuki relates the anecdote, in full and final form, in which Ryōkan waited for an entire night in his hiding place in the field for the children to come, noting that the veracity of the "somewhat extreme" story is suspect (*Zen and Japanese Culture*, p. 373).

169.   Yuasa, *The Zen Poems of Ryōkan*, p. 36

170.   *Ryōkan zen-goroku*, p. 53. The same source also makes reference to the natural disasters referred to in the text.

171.   Many of their verses read like love poems. Yuasa dismisses as "insignificant" the perennial question as to whether their mutual attraction was really one of love (*The Zen Poems of Ryōkan*, p. 41).

172.   See the entries by Ueda Makoto in EJ, vol. 1, pp. 144–45; and in the *Biographical Dictionary of Japanese Literature*, ed. by Sen'ichi Hisamutsu; Robert Aitken, *A Zen Wave: Bashō's Haiku and Zen*, pp. 209ff; Thomas Hoover, *Zen Culture*, pp. 204–208; D. T. Suzuki, *Zen and Japanese Culture*, pp. 215–67. There is a rich mine of material on Bashō in Japanese. The Kadokawa Shoten of Tokyo published a ten-volume edition of his collected works (*Kōhon Bashō zenshū*) between 1962 and 1969. See also the nine-volume collection *Bashō kōza* (Tokyo, 1944–1951); Yamamoto Kenkichi, *Bashō: sono kanshō to hihyō*, 3 volumes. Satō En gives a detailed presentation of Bashō's relations with Buddhism in his *Bashō to bukkyō*.

173.   "The connection between the art of Bashō's *haiku* and Zen Buddhism is particularly noteworthy," reports the editor of the section on Bashō in *Sources of Japanese Tradition*, ed. by Wm. Theodore de Bary, p. 457. See also p. 456 for a passage from Basho's *Kashima kikō*, in which he speaks of being "neither priest nor layman, bird nor rat, but something in between."

174.   On the history of the *haiku*, see R. H. Blythe, *A History of Haiku*, 2 vols.; Harold G. Henderson, *An Introduction to Haiku*; Kenneth Yasuda, *The Japanese Haiku*. See also entries in the bibliography on Japanese literature (in both Japanese and Western languages).

175.   See the essay by Donald Keene, "Matsunaga Teitoku and the Beginning of Haikai Poetry," in his *Landscapes and Portraits: Appreciations of Japanese Culture*, pp. 71–93.

176.   English translation from Aitken, who also reports on the merits and weaknesses of the piece (*A Zen Wave*, pp. 28–29.) Some have seen in this *haiku*, characteristic of his turn to his own unique style, an expression of his Zen enlightenment, but this is pure speculation. See E. Sato, *Bashō to bukkyō*, pp. 52–53.

177.   See E. Sato, *Bashō to bukkyō*, pp. 47–60. The section of the chapter on Zen Master Butchō and Bashō, dealing specifically with Bashō's practice of Zen, appears on pp. 52–58.

178.   Hammitzsch has done German translations of the *Kashima kikō* in MN 2.2 (1936): 86–93; *Nozarashi kikō (Kasshi ginkō)* in NOAG 75 (1953): 3–24; *Sarashina kikō*, NOAG 79 (1956): 103–109; *Oi no kobumi (Udatsu kikō)* in *Sino-Japonica: Festschrift André Wedemeyer* (Leipzig, 1956), pp. 74–106. He has also done translations of four *haibun* in SL

4.2 (1954) and three texts of Bashō's addressed to his students in NOAG 14.3 (1963–64). For an English translation of the travel books *Nozarashi kikō* and *Sarashina kikō*, see D. Keene, *Landscapes and Portraits*, pp. 94–108, 109–130. An early German translation of the *Oku no hosomichi* was done by H. Ueverschaar in MOAG 29. (1935); and an English translation by Nobuyuki Yuasa, *Bashō: The Narrow Road to the Deep North and Other Travel Sketches* (Baltimore, 1966).

179.   From the *Udatsu kikō*.

180.   Translation from Aitken, who draws attention to the influence of the Chinese poet Tu Fu that he discerns in this poem (*A Zen Wave*, pp. 149–50). Compare the study by Fumiko Fujikawa, "The Influence of Tu Fu on Bashō," MN 20.3–4 (1965): 381.

181.   According to the view of Iwata Kurō, there is a didactic element at work in this poem that is not uncommon in Bashō, since cold lips can mean, in the popular mind, punishment for mistakes in speech (*Bashō no haiku, haibun*, p. 94).

182.   From the *Oku no hosomichi*.

183.   Suzuki, *Zen and Japanese Culture*, pp. 238–39.

184.   Wilhelm Gundert, *Die japanische Literatur*, p. 123.

185.   This *haiku* is attributed to Bashō but there is no certainty as to its authenticity; it belongs to the *haiku* of didactic content and seems to have been inspired by a poem from the *Man'yōshū*. See Aitken, *A Zen Wave*, p. 79.

186.   This *haiku*, taken from the *Sarashina kikō*, was composed by Bashō as he stood before Zenkō-ji, a temple in Nagano belonging to the Tendai school. The second line is interpreted variously, but clearly has to do with the various doctrines and rites practiced in the temple. See Donald Keene, *Landscapes and Portraits*, p. 120.

187.   The Protestant theologican Kitamori Kazō, in a critical study based on Kierkegaard's categories, refers to the aesthetic-religious feeling of Bashō, whose "pseudo-religion" was an "enemy" of true religion. See his *Ajia ni okeru kirisutokyō* (Tokyo, 1959), p. 119.

188.   Suzuki calls Bashō a "nature poet" (*Zen and Japanese Culture*, p. 230); Hoover finds in his work "nature poetry at its finest" (*Zen Culture*, p. 208); Ueda Shizuteru speaks of a "mystical unity with nature" (EJ, vol. 1, p. 245). Such quotations could be multiplied effortlessly. Against this view, however, Aitken rejects the categorization of Bashō as a nature poet (*A Zen Wave*, p. 18), referring to Donald Keene's attack on this "popular misconception." Keene is correct in pointing out that Bashō never describes scenes in his *haiku* and that even his prose (*haibun*) is sparing in its allusions to the beauties of nature (*Portraits and Landscapes*, pp. 123–24). A corresponding remark by Wolfman Naumann on Bashō leans in the same direction: "The editor of first-rate travelogs expresses himself most scornfully on the value of descriptions of natural scenery (some great examples he deems unattainable), but justifies his reports from the province with the lingering power of the experience of nature and contact with history . . ." (JH, col. 1008). Bashō, "the man now considered Japan's finest poet, who finally brought Zen to Japanese poetry" (Hoover, *Zen Culture*, p. 204), is the best poetic interpreter of Zen's feeling towards nature.

189.   Suzuki, *Zen and Japanese Culture*, p. 254; Hoover, *Zen Culture*, p. 208.

190.   Compare the remark of Miyakawa Hisayuki: "The influence of Chuang-tzu on poetry was as great in Japan as it was in China. The master of the seventeen-syllable *haiku*, Matsuo Bashō, was so influenced by the interpretation of Chuang-tzu through the Sung scholar Lin Hsi-i (Jpn., Rin Kitsu) that he took the standpoint of Sung Confucianism

as his starting point and equated *t'ai-chi* (Jpn., *taikyoku,* the Absolute) with *tsao-hua* (Jpn., *zōka,* nature), thus achieving a unity with the All." From the entry on Taoism in JH, col. 1659.

191.   See my article "Yoshida Shōin: Ein Beitrag zum, Verständnis der geistigen Quellen der Meijierneuerung," MN 1 (1938): 375.

192.   Particularly in his chief work, *Kokuikō;* see my work, *Kamo Mabuchi: Ein Beitrag zur japanischen Religions-und Geistesgeschichte,* pp. 268–303.

193.   See Kitamori, *Ajia ni okeru kiritusokyō,* pp. 123ff.

9

Hakuin

Hakuin (1685–1768)[1] is one of the greatest figures of Japanese Buddhism. His significance is most evident in the impact he had on subsequent history. After him, nearly all Japanese Rinzai masters belonged to his line and practiced what may be called "Hakuin-Zen." His achievements represent a turning point in the history of Japanese Zen inasmuch as he put an end to the decline that had set in the Zen movement since the end of the medieval period. He also laid new foundations for the Rinzai school. He was the first to develop a system for applying the practice of kōan to enlightenment, a system that his disciples would bring to perfection. At the same time, he invigorated and consummated the work that Bankei and Munan had begun in expanding Rinzai Zen among the common people.

His sharply defined and intense personality embraces a wide range of talents and qualities. The many strong tensions within his character often seem to overpower the central unity of his personality. Marked from childhood by a sensitivity that bordered on the pathological, he concentrated incredible willpower into his struggle to experience the depths of his self. His spiritual gifts were mixed with intellectual clarity and sharpness, with musical inclinations, and with no small artistic talent. He took the intellectual life seriously and made every effort to secure broad knowledge and education for himself and his disciples. His stern manner with his disciples, which did not shrink from harsh measures, was surpassed only by his warm concern for the poorly educated rural population caught so often in situations of extreme suffering.

LIFE AND ENLIGHTENMENT EXPERIENCES

The historical sources for Hakuin's biography are not entirely reliable. Essentially all the information we have on the life of this great Zen master has been furnished by himself. The first description of his life and work, which forms the basis for all the others, stems from his disciple Tōrei Enji (1721–1792),[2] who composed his work from oral communications with his master as well as from autobiographical comments in the master's writings. Principal among the latter is Hakuin's late autobiographical work, the *Itsumadegusa*, written between 1765 and 1766.[3] It is only natural that the eighty-one-year old master was not completely consistent in all his details. Indeed, there are often stark contradictions and exaggerations. As experience shows, many events take on a different shape when they are later recorded in fixed form. Nonetheless, the sources for Hakuin's life, personally colored though they be, provide us with a picture that is not only lively and clear but also historically sound. In the earlier accounts we encounter an outstanding Zen master with a penchant for ecstatic experiences who pressed on with boldness and determination to unsuspected heights and abysmal depths. His accounts are distinguished by spiritual strength, interior perspicacity, and high literary merit.

Hakuin began and ended his life in the nondescript village of Hara in Suruga in the district of Shizuoka. His mother's family belonged to the Nichiren sect. His father came from the samurai class and was adopted into his mother's family by marriage. The child, named Iwajirō, was the youngest in a family of five children, physically frail but intellectually gifted. From earliest childhood he displayed unusual religious sensibilities. The mere view of clouds rapidly changing over the sea could make him sorrowful, and as early as the age of four he had inklings of the transiency of all earthy things. "Is there anything in the world that does not change?" he is said to have asked his mother. "For thousands of years in this world," she replied, "the teaching of the Buddha has not changed."[4] He loved to listen to the stories of the Buddha that his mother told him. His parental home was frequented by an aged ascetic named Kyūshimbō, who took a liking to the young Hakuin and, recognizing his greatness, exhorted him to become a "land of bliss" for all.

Hakuin's strongest spiritual impressions came from his pious mother. She once took him along to a temple where a famous Nichiren monk was giving a lecture. The sermon on the "eight hot hells" completely shook the young boy, a mischievous child who took special delight in catching insects and small birds and killing them. He was so smitten by fear of the terrible retributions meted out for such deeds that he was seized with a fit of trembling. For a long time afterward the fear of hell did not leave him. Once when he was taking a bath with his mother, who loved hot water, his attention was caught by the fire loudly crackling beneath the tub.[5] He was reminded of hell and began to cry, pleading with his mother to tell him how he might escape the fires of hell. She consoled him with the words: "Kannon (Avalokiteśvara) is full of mercy and will certainly save you." Convinced that he could escape hell only as a monk, he resolved, already at his young age, to abandon the world. His parents, however, did not immediately consent to his plans.

With increased fervor Hakuin devoted himself to Buddhist piety. He was particularly impressed by the wondrous promise of the Lotus Sūtra that neither fire nor water can harm the ascetic who is protected by magic formulas. For several days he zealously recited the dhāraṇī of the sūtra. Then, putting his luck to the test, he took a glowing iron rod from the hearth and touched it to his thigh. The blistering pain let him know that no great changes had taken place within him.[6]

When his parents finally gave their consent for him to enter monastic life, Hakuin, who was fifteen years old at the time, betook himself to the Zen temple of his native village, Shōin-ji.[7] The abbot, Tanrei Sōden, received him warmly and granted him the tonsure, bestowing on him the monastic name of Ekaku. When Tanrei fell ill shortly thereafter, Ekaku traveled to Daishō-ji in the nearby town of Numazu, there to continue his training under the master Sokudō. He did not, however, reach his desired goal. Life in the temple proved to be a disappointment, and the parables of the *Lotus Sūtra*, praised so highly as the king of the sūtras, could not satisfy his longings. He began to doubt whether the law of the Buddha could bring him liberation. His inner distress increased.

In his nineteenth year, having read the story of the tragic death of the Zen master Yen-t'ou Chüan-huo (Jpn., Gantō Zenkatsu, 828–887) at the hands of brigands, he fell into pure despair.[8] It was a state of despair that threw his entire spiritual life into serious jeopardy. Driven by inner unrest and a thirst for knowledge, he left the monastery where he was living[9] and turned his attentions to art—especially to poetry and painting—where he thought he might find not only distraction and consolation, but some satisfaction for his spiritual longings. His travels brought him to the Zuiun-ji in Mino (in the province of Gifu), where the abbot, the poet-monk Baō, effectively stimulated his literary talent. A religious experience he had at Zuiun-ji reawakened him to his search.[10] One summer's day, the abbot had carried the many Buddhist, Confucian, and Taoist volumes of his library outdoors to let them air out in the sun. At the sight of these treasures of diverse wisdom, Hakuin suddenly felt himself at a complete loss. Whom should he choose as his guide: Master K'ung, the Buddha, or the sages of Taoism? Praying fervently to all the guardian gods of the Dharma, he reached for a volume. It turned out to be a collection of Zen stories from the Ming period, a treasurehouse of ancient wisdom. There he read of the famous Rinzai master Shih-shuang Ch'u-yüan (986–1039), who meditated day and night without interruption and who, when threatened by drowsiness, bored his flesh with a sharp awl in order to arouse his mind through the pain. For the first time, Hakuin's zeal for Zen practice was awakened. Repentant for having strayed from the straight path, he resolved to dedicate himself totally and exclusively to the practice of Zen until he attained full enlightenment. At that time news of his mother's death reached him. His first impulse was to go home to her grave, but on second thought he felt that it would be more in keeping with her spirit if he would dedicate himself completely to the realization of his religious ideal.

Once again, in 1706, he set out to visit temples, with no other thought in mind than to practice Zen. In the Jōkō-ji monastery of Wakasa (in the region of Fukui) he became acquainted with the collection of sayings of the Chinese Rinzai master Hsü-t'ang Chih-yü (Jpn., Kidō Chigu, 1185–1269), and at Shōshū-ji in Iyo (Shikoku) he learned of the *Busso sankyō*[11], a three-part work that was a favorite among Zen Buddhists. In these two temples he had his first enlightenment experiences.[12] During this period he devoted himself day and night to the practice of the kōan *mu* from the well-known opening case of the *Mumonkan*. All his efforts failed to produce a breakthrough.

This first, itinerant period of Hakuin's life came to an end in 1708, when he paid a visit to his home in Hara.[13] He did not stay long and was soon again on the road, this time to the Eigan-ji in Echigo (in the region of Niigata), where he attended Shōtetsu's lectures on the *Ninden ganmoku*,[14] a text in which the Five Ranks figure prominently. This was the occasion for a powerful experience.

But when, much to his regret, the master did not recognize his enlightenment, he left the monastery disheartened. For the rest of his life, Hakuin gave great importance to this experience, as is clear in his description we find of it in the *Orategama*:

> The spring of my twenty-fourth year found me in the monk's quarters of the Eigan-ji in Echigo, pursuing my strenuous studies. Night and day I did not sleep; I forgot both to eat and rest. Suddenly a great doubt manifested itself before me. It was as though I were frozen solid in the midst of an ice sheet extending tens of thousands of miles. A purity filled my breast and I could neither go forward nor retreat. To all intents and purposes I was out of my mind and the *mu* alone remained. Although I sat in the lecture hall and listened to the master's lecture, it was as though I were hearing a discussion from a distance outside the hall. At times it felt as though I were floating through the air.
>
> This state lasted for several days. Then I chanced to hear the sound of the temple bell and I was suddenly transformed. It was as if a sheet of ice had been smashed or a jade tower had fallen with a crash. Suddenly I returned to my senses. I felt then that I had achieved the status of Yen-t'ou, who through the three periods of time encountered not the slightest loss [although he had been murdered by bandits]. All my former doubts vanished as though ice had melted away. In a loud voice I called: "Wonderful, wonderful. There is no cycle of birth and death through which one must pass. There is no enlightenment one must seek. The seventeen hundred kōan handed down from the past have not the slightest value whatsoever." My pride soared up like a majestic mountain, my arrogance surged forward like the tide. Smugly I thought to myself: "In the past two or three hundred years no one could have accomplished such a marvelous breakthrough as this."[15]

Hakuin wrote these lines forty years after the event. His first strong experience struck deep roots in his memory. Two phases of the psychological process can be clearly discerned in his description. First, a state of tension is established in the practice of the kōan; this Hakuin decribes as the "Great Doubt." The mind is under pressure to the point of explosion. A resolution is achieved in the form of an ecstatic experience that Hakuin explains by analogies. It is experienced as a liberation, a clarity, and a delight. Although the experience shows some essential characteristics of *satori*, it is not yet perfect. In the ecstasy that follows, traces of the "I" are still evident. For this reason the humiliation he received from master Shōtetsu was entirely appropriate. Indeed, it was a favor.

Driven to the point of depression, Hakuin at first sought in vain to have his experience confirmed by a number of other masters.[16] As fate would have it, he came into contact with Dōju Sōkaku (1679–1730), the only disciple of the old master of Shōju-an, Dōkyō Etan; like Hakuin, Sōkaku was attending the lectures in Eigan-ji. Both of them would meet and talk after the lectures and soon became aware of their common interests and inclinations. Sōkaku urged that they visit his master Shōju Rōjin, whom he held in the highest regard and could not praise enough. He also recommended that Hakuin read the Chinese Zen sources.

Humbled but still driven by inner conviction, Hakuin set out with Sōkaku in April of 1708 for the hermitage of Shōju-an in Shinano (in the province of Nagano). They came upon the old master chopping wood near his hut. At first, he did not even do them the favor of a glance. After Sōkaku introduced his companion, the three of them entered the hermitage. Hakuin immediately presented the master with his enlightenment verses and then waited for his evaluation. What followed is one of those unique scenes, full of originality, wit, and crudeness, that have been part of the Zen tradition since the days of the great masters of the T'ang era. Hakuin's report reads as follows:

> The master, holding my verse in his left hand, said to me: "This verse is what you have learned from study. Now show me what your intuition has to say," and he held out his right hand.
>
> I replied: "If there were something intuitive that I could show you, I'd vomit it out," and I made a gagging sound.
>
> The master said: "How do you understand Chao-chou's *mu?*"
>
> I replied: "What sort of place does *mu* have that one can attach arms and legs to it?"
>
> The master twisted my nose with his fingers and said: "Here's someplace to attach arms and legs." I was nonplused and the master gave a hearty laugh. "You poor hole-dwelling devil!" he cried. I paid him no attention and he continued: "Do you think somehow that you have sufficient understanding?"
>
> I answered: "What do you think is missing?"
>
> Then the master began to discuss the kōan that tells of Nan-ch'üan's death. I clapped my hands over my ears and started out of the room. The master called after me: "Hey, monk!" and when I turned to him he added: "You poor hole-dwelling devil!" From then on, almost every time he saw me, the master called me a "poor hole-dwelling devil."[17]

Thus did their first meeting end. Hakuin practiced further. Was it not the notoriety and unyielding severity of the enlightened old master that had drawn him to this hermitage in the first place? How could he give up halfway? The merciless training was reaching its climax. Hakuin recalls:

> One evening the master sat cooling himself on the veranda. Again I brought him a verse I had written. "Delusions and fancies," the master said. I shouted his words back at him in a loud voice, whereupon the master seized me and rained twenty or thirty blows with his fists on me, and then pushed me off the veranda.
>
> This was on the fourth day of the fifth month after a long spell of rain. I lay stretched out in the mud as though dead, scarcely breathing and almost

unconscious. I could not move; meanwhile the master sat on the veranda roaring with laughter. After a short while I regained consciousness, got up, and bowed to the master. My body was bathed in perspiration. The master called out to me in a loud voice: "You poor hole-dwelling devil!"

After this I devoted myself to an intensive study of the kōan of the death of Nan-ch'üan, not pausing to sleep or eat. One day I had a kind of awakening and went to the master's room to test my understanding, but he would not approve it. All he did was call me a "poor hole-dwelling devil."[18]

Hakuin now entered the final phase of practice. His understanding of enlightenment did not satisfy the master. Again and again he had to hear himself called a "poor hole-dwelling devil," which hinted indirectly at the imperfection of his enlightenment. Like the devil in a dark cave, his mind was unwittingly imprisoned in his own ego. He trained desperately. When his efforts still proved in vain, he began to think secretly of leaving the hermitage to try his luck elsewhere. But one day, while seeking alms in a neighboring village, the change suddenly took place. In his autobiography, *Itsumadegusa*, Hakuin gives a detailed description of the event:

Still deeply dejected, I took up my begging bowl early the next morning and went into the village below Iiyama castle. My mind was hard at work on my kōan. It never left them. I stood before the gate of a house, my bowl in my hand, lost in a kind of trance.

A voice from within yelled, "Go on! Go somewhere else!" But I was so preoccupied I didn't even notice it. This must have angered the resident of the house, because she suddenly appeared, flourishing a broom upside down in her hand. She flew at me, flailing out wildly, whacking away at my head as if she were bent on dashing my brains out. My sedge hat lay in tatters, I was knocked down and ended heels up on the ground. I lost consciousness and lay there like a dead man.

All the neighbors, alarmed by the noise, appeared with apprehensive looks on their faces. "Oh, now look what that crazy old crone has done!" they cried, and vanished behind locked doors. There was total silence, not a stir or sign of life anywhere. Some people who happened to be passing by approached me in wonderment. They grabbed hold of me and propped me rightside up.

"What's wrong! What happened?" they exclaimed.

As I regained consciousness, my eyes opened, and as they did, I found that the unsolvable and impenetrable kōan I had been working on—all those poisoned cat's paws—were completed cut through. Right to the root. They had suddenly ceased to exist. I clapped my hands and laughed great shouts of laughter, frightening the people who had gathered around me.

"He's lost his mind." "A crazy monk," they shouted, and shrank back from me. They turned heel and ran off without looking back.

I picked myself up from the ground, straightened my robes, and fixed the remnants of my hat back on my head. With a blissful smile on my face, slowly and exultantly I began to walk back toward Narasawa. As I did, I saw an old man beckoning to me.

"Honorable priest," he said. "You were really knocked out back there."

I gave him a faint smile, but spoke not a word in return. He offered me something to eat and drink, and sent me on my way.

I smiled elatedly all the way back through the gates of Shōju's hermitage. The master was standing on the veranda. He took one look at me and said, "I see that something good has happened to you. Try to tell me about it."

I advanced to where he was standing, and related at length what I had come to realize. He took his fan and stroked my back with it . . .[19]

In the *Orategama*, Hakuin describes the same episode more briefly and emphasizes that the kōan on the death of Nan-ch'üan, among others, suddenly became clear to him. The old master laughed as he heard the experience reported, and from that point on, Hakuin stresses, he no longer called him "a poor hole-dwelling devil."[20]

After a stay of eight months, Hakuin left Shōju-an. At his departure, the old abbot urged him to gather some capable disciples, but not too many; two or three would be sufficient to carry on the old Zen style. Hakuin went to his ailing former master Sokudō of Daishō-ji in Numazu. He then set out on another pilgrimage. As his practice intensified, his ecstatic experiences increased also, but his physical constitution was too weak to bear the incredible strain this caused him. He suffered a serious nervous breakdown that brought him to the verge of despair. He went to see the hermit Hakuyū (1646–1709), who taught him a psychological treatment for the so-called "Zen sickness" that restored him to health. We will have more to say of this in connection with his work, the *Yasen kanna*.

Immediately after his cure, he had further powerful experiences. Toward the end of the *Yasen kanna*, he writes:

And not only were my illnesses healed, also all those things which are difficult to believe, difficult to penetrate, difficult to understand, difficult to enter into, and which until then I had been unable to grasp with my hands or feet or to reach with my teeth—those things I now understood intuitively at once, penetrating them to their roots, piercing them to their depths. Thus I experienced the great joy six or seven times. And beside this, I forgot how many times I have experienced the little enlightenments, the joys which make one dance. For the first time I realized the meaning of those words [of Miao-hsi[21]] saying that in Paradise one will experience great enlightenment eighteen times, but the little enlightenments are too numerous to mention. In real truth I have not been deceived.[22]

Hakuin gives an account of still other experiences from this period. Once he was overcome by the Great Joy while he was reading some verses from the Chinese Zen master Hsü-t'ang Chih-yü. It was as if a ray of light had lighted a dark path, and he cried out in a loud voice, "Today for the first time I have entered into the word *samādhi*."[23] In another instance he was traveling in the vicinity of Ise. The rain was falling heavily and the water had reached his knees. At that point he suddenly understood the deep meaning of some verses of Ta-hui that he had read earlier. So enraptured did he become that he could not hold himself erect and fell into the water. A passerby, watching all of this in amazement, gave him a hand. Hakuin laughed out loud for joy so that the bystanders took him for a madman. Or again, sitting in nightly meditation one winter in the Zen hall at a rural temple, he heard the snow falling outside and experienced enlightenment. On other occasions, while doing walking meditation (kinhin) in a monks' hall in Mino, he underwent ecstatic experiences that surpassed all previous experiences.[24]

In this context, Hakuin gives us accounts of two experiences that belong to a later period. After his return to Shōin-ji he had an extraordinary experience that led him to higher levels of understanding. His description is unusual and informative:

> I came to this dilapidated temple when I was thirty-two. One night in a dream my mother came and presented me with a purple robe made of silk. When I lifted it, both sleeves seemed very heavy, and on examining them I found an old mirror, five or six inches in diameter, in each sleeve. The reflection from the mirror in the right sleeve penetrated to my heart and vital organs. My own mind, mountains and rivers, the great earth seemed serene and bottomless. The mirror in the left sleeve, however, gave off no reflection whatsoever. It surface was like that of a new pan that had yet to be touched by flames. But suddenly I became aware that the luster of the mirror from the left sleeve was innumerable times brighter than the other. After this, when I looked at all things, it was as though I were seeing my own face. For the first time I understood the meaning of the saying, "The Tathāgata sees the Buddha nature within his eye."[25]

The mystical experience here described begins as a dream, which then passes over into an awakened state of extraordinary clarity. The mother, the purple monastic robe, the two mirrors, and the light—all these elements of the mystic dream are of great significance for Hakuin's inner life. In an overwhelming flood of light he beholds the nature of all things, a vision that he understands as beholding his own countenance, which is identical with the Buddha nature.

When he was over forty-one, Hakuin had another experience, also described in the Orategama, which numbers among the greatest enlightenments of his life. One autumn evening, as he was reading from the Lotus Sūtra, his concentration was interrupted by the buzzing of an insect. He writes:

> Suddenly I penetrated to the perfect, true, ultimate meaning of the Lotus. The doubts I had held initially were destroyed and I became aware that the understanding I had obtained up to then was greatly in error. Unconsciously I uttered a great cry and burst into tears.[26]

In Hakuin's own descriptions of his experiences, we are faced with the fact that there are degrees and stages in Zen enlightenment as well as different psychic tones. It would appear that in the imperfect stages of enlightenment, the emotional element, accentuated in concentration and ecstasy, dominates, while on the higher levels of experience, intuitive insights open up. Once he had risen to higher levels, he comprehended the inadequacies and errors of his initial experiences.

In his hasty sketches of his experiences, Hakuin looks like an ecstatic in an almost constant state of agitation. Enlightenment comes to him when he is walking, standing, or seated in meditation and he is seized in rapture. The word *oboezu* ("unexpectedly" or "unconsciously") occurs frequently in his writings. Experiences surprise him and take hold of him at unexpected moments. In the enlightened state he is beside himself. Immeasurable jubilation wells up in his heart and breaks out in involuntary shouting and spontaneous dancing. Each time Hakuin is astonished, as if for the first time, at the great force with which the experience grips him.

Our extended consideration of Hakuin's own reports of his experiences provides many valuable insights into the psychology of Zen. Because of his extremely emotional temperament, his keen sensitivity to psychic impressions, and his ecstatic disposition, his autobiographical testimonies occupy an extremely important place in the history of Zen. Why, one might ask, did the master so often and so extensively talk about himself—especially in the final accounts contained in his three-part work, the *Itsumadegusa?* There is no clear answer to the question, but neither are we without grounds for speculation. His readiness to take up the pen grew out of the literary skills he had gathered during his years of systematic study, as well as from his ability to explore the world of inner reflection. His wide knowledge of Zen literature, which is full of so many original Zen masters, must also have encouraged him to record his own experiences. He must have drawn considerable assurance from the hope shining before his inner eye that his writings would prompt future generations to courageous commitments on the way of Zen. In reading Hakuin one cannot escape the impression that his accounts are meant to present the figure of the mature master as an embodiment of the ideal Buddhist person—that is, the bodhisattva ideal.

The final years of his life can be summarized briefly. After long years of moving about, news of his father's fatal sickness brought him back home for good. In 1716 he settled permanently at Shōin-ji. The temple, located not far from his birthplace, was, as the name indicates, by a pine grove. It was there that Hakuin's religious career had begun. He found the temple in a state of disrepair, but guided it to become the center of the strongest Buddhist movement of the Tokugawa period. Once Myōshin-ji had accorded him rank, the right to succession, and the name Hakuin, his fame spread throughout all Japan. For half a century he was active in this small rural temple in Hara. From far and wide disciples came to him to be guided on the way to enlightenment. Much of his time he devoted to the local farmers, whom he counseled in their many different needs. He undertook frequent journeys in order to spread the authentic teachings of Zen across the country. His activity never let up until he passed away peacefully at the ripe old age of eighty-three.

THE ZEN SICKNESS

An important aspect of Hakuin's life not referred to in the foregoing account is his repeated bouts with illness caused by tuberculosis of the lungs combined with a nervous ailment. This illness overcame him soon after his first great experience of enlightenment, as he continued his practice with unstinting zeal. He paid little attention to these psychosomatic disturbances until they had quite overwhelmed and incapacitated him. He turned to doctors and teachers for help but no one seemed able to help. Finally, he came to Hakuyū, an aged hermit, in the lonely mountains near Shirakawa in Yamashiro (now part of Kyoto) who helped restore him to health.

In the *Yasen kanna* Hakuin describes the visit graphically and tells how the old man's remedies wrought their cure.[27] He presents Hakuyū as an almost mythic figure, veiled in miraculous powers. As the local people said, his years contained three or four lifetimes. In his mountain retreat, far from all human dwellings, he was cut off from all human contact. People were not sure whether he was really a sage or a fool. Those in the surrounding villages considered him to be a legendary immortal of Chinese antiquity. It was only with the greatest difficulty that Hakuin was able to find him. Friendly villagers showed him a mountain river, which he followed, then crossed, and finally made his way up a rocky incline to a cave whose entrance was marked by a curtain waving in the breeze. As he stood there, a shiver passed through his body and he had to pause to compose himself before looking, with fear and hesitation, behind the curtain. There, in the hush of evening light, he saw the upright body of the hermit, clad in a loose-fitting linen robe, his eyes staring straight ahead. Lying on the table were copies of the *Chung-yung, Lao-tzu,* and the *Diamond Sūtra.*[28] Hakuin's description has prompted doubts, which have only been resolved in recent times, regarding the actual existence of this strange old hermit.[29] Hakuyū is indeed a historical personality who came to Hakuin's aid in his extreme need.

Immediately after arriving and making a formal greeting, Hakuin described to the hermit the symptoms of his sickness and how he experienced their effects in his daily routine:

> But later, when reflecting on my daily life, activity and non-activity had become entirely out of harmony. I could not decide whether to do a thing or to omit it. So I said to myself: I will try once more, courageously and with thoroughness, even if it cost my life.
>
> In this state, I set my teeth, fixed my eyes clearly, and determined even to forego sleep and food. And then, before I had spent many months in that strenuous way, my heart began to make me dizzy, my lungs became dry, both my legs felt as cold as if they were immersed in ice and snow. My ears were filled with a ringing as of the rushing waters of a swift river in a deep canyon. My liver felt weak, and in my behavior I experienced many fears. My spirit was distressed and weary, and whether sleeping or waking I always became lost in wild fancies. Both armpits were perpetually bathed in sweat, and my eyes were continually filled with tears.[30]

The thousand phenomena that Hakuin beheld night and day suggest visions and hallucinations, and hence a state of psychic overstimulation that is well known in Zen and of which the Zen masters warn, calling it the "domain of the devil" *(makyō)*. In describing the symptoms of his illness, Hakuin uses ancient Chinese physiological concepts according to which the head is cool and the lower body warm in the healthy person. In his case, the bodily fire mounts upwards to heat the head while the lower body, the legs, and the feet become cool. Recovery therefore depends entirely on thoroughly heating the lower part of the body through strong, deep breathing, in order to overcome the natural tendency of fire to rise and of water to sink.

Hakuyū leads his visitor into a precise knowledge of the essence of Taoist medical wisdom:

> The perfect man always supplied energy to the lower [bodily organs]. When these lower organs are thus provided with energy, the seven misfortunes do not operate in the body, nor can the four evils invade it from the outside. The bodily defenses are sufficiently strong so that the heart and mind are healthy. The mouth does not know the taste of drugs, nor does any part of the body have to experience the pains of acupuncture or moxacautery.[31]

He formulates a basic principle:

> Generally speaking, the way of nourishing one's life requires that the upper part be always kept cool and the lower part warm.[32]

And again:

> One must know that the main thing in nourishing one's life is to fill the lower part with the original energy.[33]

From his examination of the physical condition of his visitor and patient, Hakuyū was clearly able to tell that Hakuin's problems were rooted in the extremes of his meditational and ascetic pratices. In such a case, he emphasized, the usual means of acupuncture, moxa, and medicine would be of no help. The sole remedy is the healing practice of introspection *(naikan)*.

Through the autosuggestive practice of introspection, one channels the original life energy of one's entire body into the navel *(sairin)*, the center of breathing *(kikai)*, the parts below the navel *(tanden)*, and the loins and legs down to the soles of the feet.[34] With full inner participation and effort, one seeks to come to as perfect a realization as possible of the following image:

> This space below my navel,
>> my loins and legs down to the soles of my feet,
>> are in truth my original face.
>> There is no need of any nostrils.
> This space below my navel
>> is in truth my original home.
>> There is no need of any visits from my home.

This space below my navel
  is in truth the Pure Land of my heart.
There is no need of any other splendor.
This space below my navel
  is in truth the Amida who am I.
There is no need of preaching the Law to me.[35]

The ocean of breath or the center of breathing is located beneath the navel. There lies the center of gravity where one's vital powers are collected by meditation; the healing of the sick organism must proceed from this point. The original countenance, the true home, the Pure Land, and Amida are all identical with the Buddha nature. They are not to be sought somewhere without, but are to be made actual in one's own self.

The most remarkable method of autosuggestion is the so-called "butter method," which Hakuyū explained and urgently recommended. For the proper use of this method, he gave Hakuin the following instructions:

If the ascetic while meditating has the four elements out of harmony and feels his body and spirit to be wearied, he must rouse himself and let the following ideas come into his mind, If, for instance, he were to place some deliciously scented pure, clean, soft butter as large as a duck's egg on his head he will feel a delicate sensation. His head will become all moist. The moist feeling will seem to sink deeper and go lower and lower to both shoulders and both arms, to both breasts, to the diaphragm, the lungs, the liver, and the stomach, till at last will reach the bottom of the spine and the buttocks. Then everything accumulated within the breast, the pains in the loins, the pains in the bowels will, as one desires it, flow downwards like water till there will be felt a clear sensation of energy circulating all round the whole body, warming both the legs, and reaching right down to the very soles of the feet . . .[36]

Practitioners are supposed to bring forth this image over and over to conquer tiredness and regain the fullness of their life-energy.

For such advice, Hakuyū was able to appeal to his own experience. As he states, in his early years, he was the victim of many sicknesses for which the usual medical treatments were of no avail. Only when he tried "this wonderful butter method" did he regain his health and attain a harmonious physical condition that could be harmed by neither hunger nor cold nor any kind of insult and that he enjoyed for many years.

In his treatise Yasen kanna, Hakuin makes mention of still other autosuggestive techniques of Chinese Taoists and hermits in which proper breathing and the warming of the lower parts of the body play a key role. Such methods were popular already from the early years of Chinese Buddhism. In his grand treatise on meditation, the Maka shikan (Chin., Mo-ho chih-kuan, T. 1911), the patriarch of the Tendai school Chih-i (538–597) teaches various breathing procedures to promote healing; he also recommends using the autosuggestive image of a bean in the center of one's navel. From his Chinese master Ju-ching, Dōgen learned how to place one's heart in the left hand during practice.

Hakuin's visit to the hermit Hakuyū bore abundant fruit. By conscientiously following the recommended instructions he was completely restored to health within about three years; these same methods' were to prove extremely helpful in directing the many disciples who also contracted serious health problems as a result of excessive zeal in their practice. In such cases, the best remedies were introspection and the butter method.

Whereas the *Yasen kanna* reports exclusively on Zen sickness and its remedies, pertinent autobiographical passages from the *Orategama* are integrated in a broader context. Hakuin knew well how to integrate the Taoist elements he had learned from Hakuyū into his understanding of the way of Zen, and makes frequent mention of the advantage of using curative autosuggestive methods to make progress along the path to enlightenment. By seriously applying the method of introspection, Hakuin found that

> the serious disease from which I suffered, that up until then I had found so difficult to cure, gradually cleared up like frost and snow melting beneath the rays of the morning sun. The problems with those vile kōan—kōan difficult to unravel, difficult to enter—kōan that up to then had been impossible for me to sink my teeth into, now faded away with the passing of my disease.[37]

Although the regaining of health is itself of preeminent value, Hakuin also experienced that "during your practice of introspection, without your seeking it and quite unconsciously, you will attain, how many times I cannot tell, the benefits of enlightenment experiences."[38]

Physical health may not be one's actual objective, but it is at least a necessary condition for the fruitful practice of Zen. As Hakuin writes, "Even if by the powers of introspection you could live eight hundred years, as did P'eng Tsu, if you do not have the eye to see into your own nature, you are no more than an aged demon fit only to guard corpses."[39] There is also a spiritual Zen sickness that befalls Zen disciples who go astray in their search. This "great Zen sickness"[40] arises from ignorance and illusion, and finally from false distinctions. The only remedy for this sickness is the authentic, radical practice that the ancient masters taught and exemplified. While he warns against erroneous ways, Hakuin clarifies his own understanding of Zen practice. It is noteworthy that it is in this context that he speaks of "Zen sickness." For him, the physical and the spiritual are inextricably bound together.

KŌAN PRACTICE BEFORE AND AFTER ENLIGHTENMENT

Hakuin's Zen is known as the kōan-Zen par excellence in the history of Japanese Zen. More than any other Zen master he stylized kōan practice and stressed its primary importance for following the Zen way. But this does not mean that kōan practice constituted the center and whole meaning of his spirituality. For Hakuin as well, when all is said and done, kōan are only a means, even if a unique and superlative means. Convinced that the experience of enlightenment is the goal of one's efforts, he stands in the best of Zen tradition as it originated from its founder Bodhidharma and from the Sixth Patriarch, Hui-neng. With Hui-neng, he holds up "seeing into one's own nature" (Jpn., kenshō) as the essence of Zen enlightment. As he writes in a letter, "Nothing surpasses the unique and clear insight into one's own nature and original being."[41] He describes the spiritual state that is attained in enlightenment eloquently:

> If in this way you do not let the matter rest until you have once awakened clearly to it and if throughout the twelve divisions of the day you exert yourself fiercely in the twelve forms of deportment associated with them and proceed striving unremittingly, then before you know it you will transcend the realm of deluded thoughts and the state where before and after are cut off will manifest itself to you. Then the state of mind in which you are not a man, not a woman; not wise, not stupid; you do not see birth, you do not see death; and in which there is only vast emptiness, where distinction between night and day is not seen and the body and mind are lost, will many times be present.[42]

Enlightenment is described here as an insight into the identity of one's own nature with all reality in an eternal now, as a vision that removes all distinctions. This enlightenment is the center and goal of the Zen way. Hakuin prefers the term "seeing into one's nature," which for him means ultimate reality. The Buddha nature and the cosmic Buddha body, wisdom (prajñā), and emptiness (śūnyatā), the original countenance one had before one was born, and other expressions from the rich palette of Mahāyāna terms were all familiar to him from his continued study of the sūtras and Zen literature. Deeply rooted in Mahāyāna thought and far removed from any form of sectarianism, he saw a fundamental unity among all the different schools of Japanese Buddhism. His deep knowledge of the teachings of the Wisdom sūtras was clearly reflected in his widely read commentary of the Heart Sūtra, one of the shortest and most popular texts of its kind.[43] He interprets his own experiences of enlightenment in the light of this sūtra, which is an authentic hymn of praise of transcendent wisdom.

This broadminded approach to Mahāyāna admits of many paths to the same goal. Besides meditation and concentration, Buddhism also recognizes the recitation of sūtras, invocation of the Buddha's name, and magic formulas. Hakuin himself permits variety in practice, as long as it is undertaken with total commitment and strict concentration of the mind. One who goes about kōan practice—even as important and effective a kōan as that of Chao-chou's mu—in a haphazard way will not reach the goal even after ten or twenty years. By contrast, one who undertakes seriously the exclusive practice of the nembutsu (invocation of the name of the Buddha) is able to reach a deep level of concentration.[44] Serious practice means letting go of all passions and concepts; it means refusing to cling to any desire, including the desire for enlightenment or for the Pure

Land. Practice in this sense is basically identical with seeing into one's own nature. Deception and trickery are exposed. Those who go about their practice with the thought that through the pious invocation of the Buddha's name they can attain, if not enlightenment, then at least the joy of the paradise beyond, are deceiving themselves. The *nembutsu* practice of the devotees of Amida, as well as the invocation of sūtra titles by the followers of Nichiren are, like the practice of kōan, only means and aids on the way to the enlightened vision of unity.

Hakuin stresses emphatically the incomparable power of Zen meditation and kōan practice. As his own experience made clear for him, among all forms of practice the kōan take precedence. This is due to the state of psychological tension brought about through struggle with a kōan, a tension that can usher in a high degree of enlightenment. The element of doubt has a decisive role to play in this process. The power of doubt produced by the kōan is directly proportional to the force of the subsequent experience of enlightenment. "At the bottom of great doubt lies great awakening. If you doubt fully you will awaken fully."[45] The enlightenment experience is thus conditioned by doubt. Hakuin is convinced that "if those who study Zen are able to make the Great Doubt appear before them, a hundred out of a hundred, a thousand out of a thousand, will without fail attain awakening."[46] He describes the state of doubt with reference to his own experience:

> When a person faces the great doubt, before him there is in all directions only a vast and empty land without birth and without death, like a huge plain of ice extending ten thousand miles. As though seated within a vase of lapis lazuli surrounded by absolute purity, without his senses he sits and forgets to stand, stands and forgets to sit. Within his heart there is not the slightest thought or emotion, only the single word *mu*. It is just as though he were standing in complete emptiness. At this time no fears arise, no thoughts creep in, and when he advances single-mindedly without retrogression, suddenly it will be as thought a sheet of ice were broken or a jade tower had fallen. He will experience a great joy, one that never in forty years has he seen or heard.[47]

Hakuin urged the hesitant among his disciples to exert themselves boldly. The state of concentration of the Great Doubt is within the reach of everyone. No special outward circumstances are necessary. One must only undertake the exercises with real energy.

> You may ask how one can make this great doubt appear. Do not favor a quiet place, do not shun a busy place, but always set in the area below the navel Chao-chou's *mu*. Then, asking what principle this *mu* contains, if you discard all emotions, concepts, and thoughts, and investigate single-mindedly, there is no one before whom the great doubt will not appear.[48]

On one's practice, one must of course be prepared to put out great effort and put up with pain. Yet there is nothing that brings greater joy than breaking through to the realms of rebirth from within the cycle of this transitory world (saṃsāra). The transition from the Great Doubt to the Great Enlightenment is indescribable. It takes place through the "Great Dying." Hakuin elucidates the process by way of an analogy:

> If you wish accordance with the true, pure non-ego, you must be prepared to let go your hold when hanging from a sheer precipice, to die and return again to life. Only then can you attain to the true ego of the four nirvāṇa virtues.
>
> What is "to let go your hold when hanging from a sheer precipice"? Supposing a man should find himself in some desolate area where no man has ever walked before. Below him are the perpendicular walls of a bottomless chasm. His feet rest precariously on a patch of slippery moss, and there is no spot of earth on which he can steady himself. He can neither advance nor retreat; he faces only death. The only things he has on which to depend are a vine that he grasps by the left hand and a creeper that he holds with his right. His life hangs as if from a dangling threat. If he were suddenly to let go his dried bones would not even be left.
>
> So it is with the study of the Way. If you take up one kōan and investigate it unceasingly your mind will die and your will will be destroyed. It is as though a vast, empty abyss lay before you, with no place to set your hands and feet. You face death and your bosom feels as though it were afire. Then suddenly you are one with the kōan, and both body and mind are cast off. This is known as the time when the hands are released over the abyss. Then when suddenly you return to life, there is the great joy of one who drinks the water and knows from himself whether it is hot or cold. This is known as rebirth in the Pure Land. This is known as seeing into one's own nature. You must push forward relentlessly and with the help of this complete concentration you will penetrate without fail to the basic source of your own nature. Never doubt that without seeing into your own nature you cannot become a Buddha; without seeing into your own nature there is no Pure Land.[49]

This description of kōan practice is reminiscent of the fifth case of the *Mumonkan* collection, which presents a man holding on to the branch of a tree with his teeth while someone standing below asks him about the meaning of Bodhidharma's coming from the West—in other words, about the nature of reality. This no-exit situation, essential for the kōan, presses the Great Doubt to its limits until the student, after painfully wrestling, breaks through to the Great Enlightenment, which gives rise in turn to the Great Joy. The Great Doubt, the Great Enlightenment, and the Great Joy—these three characterize the psychological process of the way of Zen.

In the passage cited above Hakuin clearly compares the vision of enlightenment with the direct attainment of a state of consciousness that is free of all illusion. In the actual moment of experience the subject is as certain of the experience as one drinking water knows whether it is hot or cold.[50] Later reflection does not possess this same nondeceptive certainty inasmuch as it lacks the quality of directness.

Even before his own enlightenment, Hakuin was acquainted with a number of kōan cases.[51] He devoted himself intensely to Chao-chou's kōan on *mu* mentioned above. During the first period of his teaching in Shōin-ji, he customarily assigned this kōan to his disciples as their first practice. Later he preferred the kōan on "the sound of one hand clapping," which he discovered on his own and commented on extensively in a work called *Yabukōji* (written in 1753, printed in 1792).[52] In one part of the work, ostensibly a letter to an unknown lady of high social standing, Hakuin describes his kōan as follows:

> What is the Sound of the Single Hand? When you clap together both hands a sharp sound is heard; when you raise the one hand there is neither sound nor smell. Is this the High Heaven of which Confucius speaks?[53] Or is it the essentials of what Yamamba describes in these words: "The echo of the completely empty valley bears tidings heard from the soundless sound?"[54] This is something that can by no means be heard with the ear. If conceptions and discriminations are not mixed within it and it is quite apart from seeing, hearing, perceiving, and knowing, and if, while walking, standing, sitting, and reclining, you proceed straightforwardly without interruption in the study of this kōan, then in the place where reason is exhausted and words are ended, you will suddenly pluck out the karmic root of birth and death and break down the cave of ignorance. Thus you will attain to a peace in which the phoenix has left the golden net and the crane has been set free of the basket.[55]

Hakuin praises the high quality of the state of enlightenment attained through practicing the kōan of the sound of one hand clapping; this kōan gives access to the spiritual heights of the Buddhas and the patriarchs.

After the attainment of enlightenment, kōan practice occupies the most important place in Zen practice. As Hakuin states in his autobiography, when he was setting out on his path the old man of Shōju-an urged him not to relent in his practice but to commit all his energies to advancing along the way of Zen.[56] He was also warned about people who sit in silent enlightenment like tree stumps and was told to keep up his "hidden practice and secret efforts" (*sengyō mitsugyō*) as opposed to just sitting in the "Zen of silent enlightenment" (Jpn., *mokushō zen*; Chin., *mo-chao ch'an*), a practice popular in China during the Sung period. Taking the admonitions of his master to heart, Hakuin carried on a continuous practice of kōan while visiting temples and masters throughout the land.

After enlightenment, his practice of Zen was directed in a special way against the "Zen of silent enlightenment," which had been practiced extensively in both Rinzai and Sōtō monasteries since the middle ages. The disagreement between the two outlooks goes back to the conflict that once raged in China between Ta-hui Tsung-kao (1089–1163), the protagonist of the "Zen of beholding the kōan" (Jpn., *kanna-zen*; Chin., *k'ang-hua ch'an*), and Hung-chih Ch'eng-chüeh (1091–1157), the representative of *mokushō-zen*.[57] Hakuin was well aware of the historical background. Ta-hui had his full sympathy; his vigorous hefty attacks on the "Zen of silent enlightenment" were directed mainly against the contemporary Japanese disciples who practiced this particular form of Zen. Hakuin could not sit back and attribute the downfall of Zen in Japan to chance or to the will of heaven. The downfall of Zen, he believes, is promoted by those people whose mind and wisdom are as dark as ash, the erroneous partisans of the *nembutsu* within the Zen school, and the false Zen of silent enlightenment.[58]

In view of his otherwise tolerant character, Hakuin's rejection of the "Zen of silent enlightenment" might seem surprising. His vehement polemics were aimed exclusively at Zen monks who sat in their monasteries and enjoyed a deceptive tranquillity. In such people Hakuin could see little sign of the dynamic quest that is born of the Great Doubt; because of their lack of vitality, he compares them to cold ashes. As he says, they

> foolishly take the dead teachings of no-thought and no-mind, where the mind is like dead ashes with wisdom obliterated, and make these into the essential doctrines of Zen. They practice silent, dead sitting as though they were incense burners in some old mausoleum and take this to be the treasure place of the true practice of the patriarchs.[59]

He finds little to distinguish such worthless colleagues from those fresh upstarts who, like well-groomed howling dogs, reject and degrade the kōan of the ancients; they are opinionated hardheads of low-grade intelligence who never really accomplish anything.[60]

In such passages, which are not infrequent in his writings, Hakuin paints in extremely lurid colors the deplorable situation of Zen in his days. He was vexed by what he considered an abandonment of the authentic way of Zen. When he includes "no-thinking" and "no-mind" among the weaknesses of the "Zen of silent enlightenment," he is by no means intending to disqualify the similar negative expressions of the Chinese Zen masters of the T'ang period, who embodied the purest expression of Zen tradition. In the same treatise, the *Yabukōji*, he expresses the highest esteem for the patriarchs and masters mentioned in the chronicle *Keitoku dentōroku* and lists a number of them by name.

In his opinion, kōan represent the highest form of Zen practice. Not only should these examples of the ancients be used to get a first grasp of enlightenment, they are necessary for all subsequent stages of Zen practice. The many disciples who gathered around Hakuin in the small monastery of Shōin-ji led a rigid monastic life. No matter how often and how intensely they had experienced enlightenment, no matter how far they had advanced in their spiritual life, all, without exception, had to devote themselves industriously to the practice of kōan. Here we have the beginnings of the systematization of kōan practice that has been associated with Hakuin's name. We may assume that a large number of the examples of the ancients that had been transmitted in the pertinent kōan collections made up the daily fare of Hakuin's disciples. Hakuin held the Five

Ranks in special esteem and composed a penetrating commentary on this formula, which for him closes and crowns the system of kōan.[61]

Although Hakuin is regarded as the originator of the systematic practice of kōan that is followed today in Rinzai monasteries, the details of his actual contribution to the systematization are not clear. Most likely he selected from among the large number of kōan those that he found to be especially helpful and then determined a sequence for adopting them in practice. We do not know whether Hakuin categorized the kōan according to content and form. The most important thing for him was to break through the Great Doubt. Resolving a kōan depended not so much on particular answers but on whether the student attained a state of consciousness that overcame discursive thought. The individual steps in the development of the kōan system are not known; only in the third generation of Hakuin's disciples did this development come to term. Naturally, the systematic use of kōan requires the help of an experienced master who can recognize the spiritual maturity of his successful disciples and grant them, often only after long years of hard practice, the rank of master. Hakuin owes his prominent place in Japanese Zen to the kōan system that was named after him and that continues to this day to occupy a central place in the Rinzai school.

WORKING AMONG THE PEOPLE

The stages of Zen's implantation in Japan reach over several centuries and extend in all directions. The aristocratic qualities that characterized the Rinzai Zen of the Kamakura and Muromachi periods found expression in doctrine, monastic life, daily practice, as well as in the cultural realm, especially in the arts. While Rinzai Zen was especially popular among the urban population, Sōtō was better received in rural areas, at the price, however, of becoming adulterated with different syncretistic practices that tarnished the purity of Dōgen's Zen. It was during the Edo period that Rinzai first began to make inroads into the religious life of Japan's general populace. Munan and Bankei can be considered Rinzai's first popular masters, but it was Hakuin that achieved the decisive breakthrough in making Rinzai available to the general population. His village temple of Shōin-ji in Hara became the most influential Rinzai center during the second half of the Edo period.

The activities that Hakuin carried out from his rural temple of Shōin-ji had two sides. First and foremost, the master guided his disciples along the path to enlightenment in his own unique way, making particular use of the kōan. We touched on this in the previous section and in what follows we will have more to say about his disciples. Yet Hakuin was not only abbot for his disciples; he also served as spiritual father for wide circles of the rural population. With his own roots in the common people, he is of the most popular personalities of Japanese Buddhism.[62] Early on in his formation, during his many travels through the land, he became acquainted with numerous local customs, learned how to speak the language of the people, and made contact with different levels of society. His choice of residence in Hara was an option to live among the people. He renounced the abbot's chair of the great Myōshin-ji, a post readily available to a man of his stature. He turned down not only the honors and amenities of such a position, but also the intellectual stimulation that life in the capital offered a leading thinker. His sole motivation was the Zen ideal that he found in the ancient chronicles of the classical Chinese masters of early times.

Numerous stories are told of how the abbot of Shōin-ji shared his life with the common people[63] and proved to be an eminently successful popular educator. With his gift for translating the Buddhist precepts into moral values for everyday life, he constantly urged the faithful to live a morally virtuous life both at home and in the marketplace. His numerous popular writings, composed in simple *kana* style, are seasoned with songs and poems that make for easy memorization, thus enabling illiterate people to learn their lessons simply by hearing them. In his "Song of the Weeds" he urges farmers to cut off their passions at the roots, as if they were weeds.[64] This poem, like many others, belonged to the genre of rural songs popular at the time. Hakuin knew how to blend inspirational language with a good sense of humor. His poetry overcame the limitations of the farmers' education. Particularly renowned are his deeply touching "Songs for Grinding Corn."[65] In his "Song of an Old Woman Grinding Corn," he compares her with the Buddha nature that is identical to the self, and has her begin her song: "How grateful we are for the grace of heaven and earth, for heat and cold, and for night and day, which are all so necessary!" At the end, the old woman bids farewell with the words: "If the old woman deeply explores her heart, the way of the patriarchs will not fail. Do not grow weak! Stay healthy! The old woman now takes her leave of thee."[66]

In his song "In Praise of Filial Love,"[67] Hakuin extols reverence for one's parents as a fundamental social virtue, explaining that children should be grateful to those from whom they have received their bodies. Because Confucian ethics had become so integral a part of Japanese popular wisdom, however, there is no cause for seeing any distinctively Confucian quality in Hakuin's poems and songs. Even the originally Confucian saying about "encouraging good and punishing evil" (Jpn., *kanzen chōaku*) had become part and parcel of the Japanese ways of thinking. Hakuin brought moral maxims to life through numerous Buddhist stories about good and bad karma.[68] Through his integrity and goodness, his simplicity and persuasiveness, Hakuin won the hearts of the simple people and helped them in their religious strivings.

His efforts at providing spiritual direction for the rural population were aimed especially at raising ethical standards, and to do this he drew on ancient Japanese traditions, Confucian ethics, and also traditional Buddhist ethical models. When it came to religious practices, he was even more adaptive. Given his total commitment to Zen, he was naturally interested in promoting the Rinzai school. He was not at all happy about the introduction of the *nembutsu* practice in many Japanese Zen monasteries. Though fundamentally not opposed to the Pure Land school, in his own temple he taught and practiced only the Zen way to enlightenment. He therefore demanded of his disciples a resolute adherence to the proven Zen practices of *zazen* and the kōan, clearly rejecting the *nembutsu* as a "side practice" (*sōshu*) in Zen monasteries. "As I said before," he writes, "if you cannot attain to Zen, then when you face death, try to be reborn in the Pure Land. Those who try to practice both at the same time will be able to obtain neither the fish nor the bear's paw, but instead will cultivate the karma of birth and death, fail to cut off the root of life and will never be able to attain the joy of enlightenment."[69] For Hakuin, there was no question about combining both practices; his monks were devoted solely to the way of Zen.

Nonetheless, Hakuin was prepared to make concessions for his lay disciples. He saw little sense or good in trying to disabuse the rural population of its dependence on invoking the name of Amida. In his view, the invocation of Amida, essentially a Mahāyāna practice, was an aid for attaining insight into one's true nature (*kenshō*). All the mythical embellishments he considered to be artificial means (Skt., *upāya*; Jpn., *hōben*). He consistently urged his hearers to seek the 'Pure Land' in their own nature.

Hakuin has been accused of self-contradiction in his attitudes toward faith in Amida and the *nembutsu* practice. Such accusations are groundless. He was convinced that there are different paths to the goal of Mahāyāna, namely the attainment of Buddhahood. Zen's approach through *zazen* and the kōan is extremely effective, but it is not the only way:

> Studying Zen, calling the name, even reading and reciting sūtras, all are aids in the path toward seeing the Way. They are like the staves that travelers use to aid them in their journeys.[70]

Such an approach shows a fundamental tolerance toward the different forms of Mahāyāna Buddhism. In the case of the *nembutsu*, Hakuin found himself faced with a situation that called for careful distinctions. Within his own temples he insisted on strict observance of Zen practice, but at the same time he could not ignore the dominant practice of invoking the name of Amida throughout Edo-period Japan. In choosing the right means for attaining enlightenment, one had to take into consideration the different inclinations and capacities of people. Along this line he writes:

> Techniques such as these are called the "talons and teeth of the Cave of Dharma" and the "supernatural talisman that wrests life from death." They are of great benefit to people of superior talents. Those of medium or inferior talents leave such things alone and quite disregard them. The people of the Pure Land school, in fact, are opposed to them. But the Pure Land is still a teaching to which veneration is due. Amida Buddha, with the skillful concentrated practice of great compassion, on the basis of his forty-eight vows, was endowed with the three minds and four practices. These techniques were established solely for those of medium and inferior talents . . .[71]

It is not easy to make coherent sense out of Hakuin's nuanced statements about Zen and the *nembutsu*. At play here is his understanding of the essence of Mahāyāna and its various forms and schools, including the Zen school. His distinction between the way in which monks and the laity are to be led along the way of Zen is clear, but his more popular approach to the simple people can be misunderstood in that a number of ideas come together in the way he dealt with them.[72]

Hakuin's intimate familiarity with the *Lotus Sūtra* stems from his childhood years. His pious mother was a devotee of the Nichiren school and accordingly was whole heartedly devoted to this sūtra. The chapter on Kannon—who was really the bodhisattva Avalokiteśvara transformed by popular piety into the Mother of Mercy—made a particularly deep impression on the young boy's docile spirit; in him these seeds of popular piety would eventually grow to full maturity.

Hakuin was already an adult when a deep experience having to do with the *Lotus Sūtra* made clear to him why this sūtra was so beloved by the Japanese people. In the first part of a long letter to an aged Nichiren nun he wrote about this sūtra.[73] Taking the five characters that make up its title—*Myō-hō ren-ge kyō*—he summarized them in the two characters *myō-hō* ("wonderful Dharma") and then condensed them in turn into the single character *shin* ("heart") to expresses the whole breadth of the universe compressed into the self.

Hakuin repeatedly stressed that the *Lotus Sūtra* should hold a special place in the sacred scriptures of Buddhism. "Outside the mind there is no *Lotus Sūtra* and outside the *Lotus Sūtra* there is no mind."[74] The title *Myōhō-renge-kyō* is a hymn of praise for the wondrous powers of the One Mind. It is

> called the *Lotus Sūtra*, or the Buddha of Infinite Life; in Zen it is called the Original Face, in Shingon the Sun Disc of the Inherent Nature of the Letter A, in Ritsu the Basic, Intangible Form of the Precepts. Everyone must realize that there are all different names for the One Mind.[75]

It is no easy thing to adhere with all one's strength to the *Lotus Sūtra*, whose faithful advocates in Japan extolled it as the quintessence of all Buddhist teachings, indeed of all religions.[76] Although Hakuin is not to be numbered among such advocates, he did consider this sūtra to be a means of attaining unity with the Buddha and of acquiring Buddhahood.

The popular roots that nourished his zeal and devotion for the *Lotus Sūtra* deepened through his well-known devotion to Kannon, whose picture, according to tradition, the boy Hakuin greatly honored. Kannon, the bodhisattva of mercy, was particularly highly regarded as the source of life; a long life was the coveted gift of this bodhisattva. Among the numerous versions of the *Kannon Sūtra* is an abridged text—*Emmei jikku Kannon-gyō reigenki (Report in Ten Statements on the Wonderous Powers of the Kannon Sūtra for a Long Life)*, whose recitation Hakuin highly recommended.[77] Easily memorized because of its brevity, the text could be repeated continuously by the farmers as they went about their work. Miraculous accounts were added as examples and inspired even more zealous practice.

Besides preaching and writing, Hakuin also made use of art to spread the message of Rinzai Zen.[78] Even in his early years he showed signs of his talents for ink painting and calligraphy. His artistic gifts matured along with his religious experience, but it was only when he was fifty years of age that his unique, unconventional, raw style came unto its own, and only ten years later did it reach its full flower. All his works were stamped with his own immediate experience. Through his paintings he was able to reach the illiterate farmers whom he could not affect with his writings, even though these writings were composed in a simple form in the Japanese *kana* style.

Among the many themes of his paintings, religious subjects predominate. His self-portrait, with his oversized eyes peering out into the distance, is particularly well known. Almost all of his paintings of Zen masters, especially that of the patriarch Bodhidharma, are characterized by the expressive look in the eyes. But it is perhaps in his Kannon paintings that Hakuin touched the soul of the people most directly. His paintings of the "Kannon in a Lotus Pond" ("Renchi no Kannon"), of which we have many variations from his later years, was most likely his own invention. The last picture of this series—a white figure on a black background—bears the following inscription written in the master's hand:

> The Eye of Compassion watches over sentient beings,
> The Sea of Blessings is beyond measure
> The eighty-three-year-old Buddhist monk drew this.[79]

In the history of Japanese art, Hakuin falls in the period following the great flowering of Zen art. He may not have reached the heights of the Zen painters of the Muromachi period, but some of his ink paintings and calligraphy clearly deserve to be counted as masterpieces.[80] He used art mainly to further the Zen movement. A few decades later, the same was done by Sengai Gibon (1750–1837) from the district of Mino, a disciple of the Rinzai master Gessen Zenne. Sengai spent a large part of his life in Shōfuku-ji in Hakata. The many works of this productive artist contributed in no small measure to the spread of Zen.[81]

HAKUIN'S DISCIPLES AND HAKUIN'S ZEN

Soon the small rural temple of Shōin-ji was no longer able to handle the ever-growing number of disciples gathering around the eminent master. In the surrounding area monks' halls and smaller establishments arose to broaden Hakuin's circle of influence. Although the names of many disciples have been passed down in tradition, it is not easy to distinguish between monks, disciples (*monka*), and Dharma heirs.[82] Community life was structured according to strict rules; besides the central practices of *zazen* and the kōan, all the monks had to devote themselves daily to the recitation of sūtras and the study of Buddhist scriptures, especially those from the Zen tradition. There was also daily manual labor and begging. Overall guidance and responsibility was in the hands of the master, whose zeal for the spread of Buddhism was transmitted to his disciples. They supported his extensive activity as a lecturer and helped with the composition of his works, as many titles produced by Hakuin in the temple attest.

Prominent among Hakuin's disciples was Tōrei Enji (1721–1792),[83] who was born in Kanzaki in the region of Shiga and, according to the customs of the time, as a young boy was turned over to the local temple to be educated. When he was seventeen he traveled to Daikō-ji, where he was ordained a monk by the active, widely known Rinzai master Kogetsu Zenzai (1667–1751) without, however, becoming one of the master's disciples.[84] Kogetsu Zenzai became the head of a Rinzai line that for a while assumed a certain prominence, stood in some rivalry with Hakuin's line, and then disappeared. Kogetsu's name appears frequently in connection with Hakuin's disciples.

Tōrei Enji's youth was for the most part filled with travels around the country, in which he visited different temples and had numerous experiences of enlightenment. In 1743 he arrived at Shōin-ji in Hara and began a friendship with Hakuin that was to prove decisive for his whole life. Tradition does not actually speak of a master-disciple relationship between them. Over the years the friendship between the two grew deeper and deeper. Tōrei's first visit to Shōin-ji did not last long before the illness of his mother called him home for two years. He was in the fullness of manhood when he traveled to Kyoto to submit himself to a program of rigorous asceticism. He attained enlightenment but damaged his health in the process. After reporting to Hakuin what had happened, he remained in the capital for some time devoting himself zealously to the study of Buddhist scriptures. It was at this time that he completed his first important work, the *Shūmonmujintō-ron* (1748, T. 2575), which evoked great praise from his master Hakuin. Meanwhile, his health improved enough for him to undertake the journey to Hara. Hakuin received him warmly and soon made him one of his Dharma heirs and in 1759 appointed him superior over the rather neglected temple of Ryūtaku-ji near Mishima in the region of Shizuoka. This temple came to earn a place of special affection in the eyes of the master, and indeed, during the last years of his life Hakuin made it the center of his lecturing.

Tōrei was active in Ryūtaku-ji for some twenty years. He restored the temple buildings, composed foundational works on the history of Hakuin-Zen, and set up as founding abbot his master Hakuin, who had passed away in the meantime. Built on a hill at the foot of Mount Fuji, Ryūtaku-ji is one of the most beautiful temple complexes in eastern Japan.

Besides Tōrei Enji, one of the most prominent of Hakuin's first disciples was the painter monk Suiō Genro (1716–1789).[85] Although older than Tōrei, he followed his example in making the acquaintance of Hakuin. Hakuin recognized Suiō's superior artistic techniques and happily consented to become his student. Tōrei was also given to ink painting but, like Suiō, was unable to attain Hakuin's spontaneous creativity. Although Suiō never did show the qualities of a Zen master (in his old age he turned to drink), at Tōrei's recommendation he was appointed abbot of Shōin-ji for a term. Suiō sent all the novices to Tōrei, who was in charge of Hakuin-Zen during this first period.[86]

Gasan Jitō[87] (1727–1797) played an important part in the subsequent development of Hakuin's Zen movement. Although he did not belong to the close circle of disciples and was probably not even one of Hakuin's Dharma heirs,[88] this extraordinary man enabled Hakuin-Zen to assume and retain the leading position in the Rinzai school during the modern period.

Born in Ōshū in northeastern Japan, Gasan was a young man when he joined Gessen Zenne (1702–1781), a disciple and successor of Kogetsu Zenzai whom we alluded to earlier, in the Zen temple of Kōken-in in Miharu (present-day Fukushima prefecture), which belonged to the Kogetsu line. He did not remain long, however, but was soon off on a pilgrimage that brought him into contact with many different monasteries and masters. He was thirty years old when he returned to Gessen, who at that time was living in Hōrin-ji in Nagata in the province of Musashi (now part of Kanagawa prefecture), not far from Edo. It was there that he met Hakuin, who had traveled from his village temple in Hara to eastern Japan and was spending a few days in Edo.

At first Gasan was not at all well-disposed toward Hakuin and his movement. In time, however, he gave some thought to traveling to Hara at last to get to know, or at least encounter, the famous master and his methods of teaching. But his teacher Gessen strongly urged him not to do this. So the years passed rather uneventfully until Hakuin once again came to Edo to lecture. Though the historical sources are not entirely clear about the circumstances, we do know that Gasan was moved, and then strongly attracted and encouraged, by Hakuin's lectures. Hakuin hesitated to accept him as a disciple and is reported to have thrown Gasan out of his quarters three times. At that time, Hakuin was eighty-one, which means that after Gasan was accepted as a disciple, there remained only three years for the master, now failing from old age and sickness, to instruct his new disciple. We may assume, therefore, that Gasan's training fell mainly to Tōrei. Tradition has it that after Hakuin's death, Gasan remained for some time with Tōrei and received from him the certificate of enlightenment (inka). Even though Gasan's name does appear in later lists of Hakuin's Dharma heirs, it is very doubtful that he was formally received by the master among his successors.[89]

Not much is known of Gasan's whereabouts and activity during the first years after Hakuin's death. He did maintain contacts with his early master Gessen Zenne until the latter's death in 1781. Later he showed up in the Zen temple of Rinshō-in in Edo, where his work was extraordinarily effective. Hundreds flocked to hear his lectures. He was a powerful preacher who saw as his main task the promotion of Hakuin's Zen. He received frequent calls to assume the abbot's office in different Rinzai temples and for a while presided over Shōin-ji in Hara. He died in 1797 while taking a cure at the famous hot springs of Atami on Japan's east coast.

Although Gason Jitō's name is not often mentioned in histories of Japanese Zen, this eloquent and energetic man is doubtless one of the key figures in the development of Hakuin's Zen. Unlike other Rinzai lines, Hakuin's line was named the Kokurin-ha after the literary name of the master.[90] This line owes its stability mainly to Gasan. The unusually large number of students who flocked to his lectures are an indication of what must have been his strong, attractive personality. The two lines of Hakuin's Zen that are still active today stem from Gasan's disciples Inzan Ien (1751–1814) and Takujū Kosen (1760–1833), who under their master's guidance were able to imbibe and pass on the spirit and method of Hakuin's Zen.

Inzan Ien[91] was born in Echizen in the region of Fukui. Having been entrusted as a child to Kōtoku-ji in Mino, he became a monk under the abbot Rōzan (d. 1781). He was sixteen when he began his Zen studies under Bankoku, a disciple of Bankei Yōtaku, but after three years he moved to Hōrin-ji in Nagata near Edo, where he followed a rigid Zen practice for seven years under Gessen Zenne. He then set out for Baisen-ji in Mino, where his first teacher, Rōzan, had meanwhile taken up residence. After his teacher's death, Inzan spent a time in Baisen-ji until he heard about the successes of Gasan Jitō, who was working out of Gessen Zenne's temple. Gasan Jitō came to recognize Inzan as one of his Dharma heirs. Inzan's fame spread far and wide, and he served for a short time as abbot of Myōshin-ji. One of his best known disciples was Taigen Shigen (1768–1837), whose own famous disciple, Gisan Zenrai (1802–1878) accompanies his masters Inzan and Taigen on the list of abbots of Myōshin-ji. Inzan left behind a collection of sayings that was published only in 1942.

Born in Tsushima near Nagoya, Takujū Kosen[92] made various attempts to become a monk before he was received among the disciples of Gasan Jitō in the Hōrin-ji at the young age of twenty. With all his energy, he devoted himself to the practice of the kōan; on one occasion he went for some nineteen days without food or sleep to mull over the kōan mu, the opening case of the Mumonkan. His zeal in the monks' hall bore abundant fruit. After fourteen years of practice Gasan recognized him as his Dharma heir. Takujū then returned to Sōken-ji in Nagoya, where he had begun his monastic life. For twenty years he devoted himself to meditation and study in his solitary retreat. When he was appointed abbot of Myōshin-ji in Kyoto in 1813 and invested with the purple robes, he was at the height of his career, one of the most influential religious leaders of his time. He led many monks and prominent lay people pursuing Hakuin's path of enlightenment. Through his disciple Sozan Genkyō (d. 1868), who was also abbot of Myōshin-ji and master of one of Takujū's monks' halls in Nagoya, the line continued to the first year of the Meiji period (1868). In his old age, Takujū felt drawn to return to the starting point of his religious path. Within the confines of Sōken-ji, he had a quiet hermitage built that served him as the final station of his rich life.

The two Hakuin lines are identical in teachings and method; the differences between them are unimportant. Contrasts such as there are stem mainly from the opposing temperaments of their founding figures. Inzan Ien, a man of powerful naturalness, confronted and pursued his disciples, while the quiet, balanced Takujū preferred a more steady and methodical sort of progress. Toward the end of the Edo period, all the larger Rinzai monasteries were directed by masters from these two lines and continued to preserve their doctrinally insignificant peculiarities. As a result, there was no want of tensions and mutual accusations.

In Japan, Rinzai Zen became Hakuin-Zen, an indication of Hakuin's incomparable role in the history of Japanese Zen. The characteristics that Hakuin impressed into the Rinzai schools are clearly present in his own personality and work. It is worth our while to summarize the different qualities of Hakuin that we have discussed in the preceding pages.

First of all, Hakuin was rooted in the tradition of Japanese Rinzai that came from the great Japanese masters Nampo Shōmyō (Daiō Kokushi), Shūhō Myōchō (Daitō Kokushi), and Kanzan Egen. Insofar as the word is allowable in Zen, we may say that Hakuin, in his words and writings, developed the "orthodox" line. This is evident in both of his chief literary works written in Chinese kanbun style, Kaian kokugo and Keisō dokuzui.[93] Compiled, edited, and published by his disciples, both these collections make hard demands of their readers in the breadth of their content and in the difficulty of their language. They constitute the backbone of Hakuin's work. Hakuin's commentary on Shūhō Myōchō's collection of sayings, the Daitōroku, constitutes the core of the Kaian kokugo (T. 2574). The Keisō dokuzui contains Hakuin's collections of sayings, with the enriching addition of other materials.[94]

The second characteristic of Hakuin's Zen is the kōan system, which the master promoted so intensely. Though Hakuin considered the kōan to be only a means, their practical and indissoluble bonds with the experience of enlightenment in fact make them the keystone of his approach. He presented his disciples with the incomparable advantages of kōan practice both before and after enlightenment, and insisted on the faithful use of kōan. The Zen that is practiced in the monks halls under his care is authentic kōan-Zen. Though completed by his disciples, the systematization of kōan practice is really his work. A careful and reliable description of the practice of Hakuin's kōan system has yet to be provided, even though it remains important, even indispensable, for a proper historical evaluation of Hakuin-Zen.

Finally, mention must also be made of the popularity of Hakuin's Zen. In the complex phenomenon that is Hakuin's form of Zen, an endearing geniality, an adaptability to customs and attitudes of ordinary people, a strong ethical concern, an openness to different religious practices, and a self-expression in popular, down-to-earth language are all blended together. It is doubtful whether without Hakuin's efforts on behalf of the common people the formalistic and stiff Rinzai school could have freed itself from its rigidity and become a broadly effective popular religion by the end of the Edo period.[95]

Still much loved in Japan's contemporary Rinzai monasteries is Hakuin's "Hymn to Zazen" ("Zazen wasan"), which is one of the strongest expressions in Japanese Buddhism of the Mahāyāna spirit. A reflection of the master's own experience, the hymn begins with this verse:

> Sentient beings are intrinsically Buddha.
> It is just as it is with ice and water—
> Apart from water there is no ice,
> Apart from sentient beings there is no Buddha . . .

This uniform, free-flowing outpouring, burning with inner passion, ends with these verses:

> The gate of the oneness of cause and effect opens,
> The non-dual, non-triple road lies straight ahead.
> The formless form now being your form,
> Going or returning you go not elsewhere;
> The thoughtless thought now being your thought,
> Singing and dancing are the voice of the Dharma.
> How vast and unobstructed the empty sky of samādhi!
> How perfect and bright the moon of the Four Wisdoms!
> At this moment, what is there more for you to seek,
> With nirvāṇa itself manifest before you?
> This very place, this is the Lotus Land;
> This very body, this is Buddha.[96]

NOTES

1.   See the entries in EJ, vol. 3, p. 88 and Zengaku daijiten I, p. 191. Zen Dust treats the figure of Hakuin in detail. Philip Yampolsky's The Zen Master Hakuin: Selected Writings (New York, 1971) includes an appendix with a list of the works of Hakuin. For Hakuin's original works, see the eight-volume edition Hakuin Oshō zenshū (Tokyo, 1934, reprinted 1967). There is a wealth of material on Hakuin in Japanese. For his biography see Rikugawa Taiun, Hakuin Oshō shōden. See also the collection Nihon no zen-goroku, vol. 19 on Hakuin, edited by Kamata Shigeo (hereafter Hakuin zen-goroku). See also the essay by Tsūyama Sōkaku in vol. 4 of Zen, Zen no rekishi: Nihon, pp. 289–308. Several essays on Hakuin also appear in the collected works of Furuta Shōkin.

The dates of Hakuin are given as 1685–1768 according to the old calendar, and 1686–1769 according to the new. (In the new calendar, New Year's day falls in February of the old calendar.) According to the old calendar, Hakuin was born and died in December. It is not uncommmon for differences in the calendar to cause such discrepancies in the dating of authors. In general, though not always, I have tried to follow the old calendar, as is the custom in the Japanese literature.

2.   Ryūtaku kaiso Jinki Dokumyō Zenji nenpu, a chronological biography of Hakuin edited by Tōrei Enji. See Hakuin zenshū, vol. 1, pp. 1–78. Compare Rikugawa Taiun, Hakuin Oshō shōden, pp. 443–546. Jinki Dokumyō is the posthumous title granted Hakuin shortly after his death by the emperor.

3.   Hakuin zenshū, vol. 1, pp. 149–230. Hakuin's writings include several autobiographical passages, particularly in Orategama (Hakuin zenshū, vol. 5, pp. 107–246), Yabukōji (vol. 5, pp. 319–340), and Yasen kanna jōkan (vol. 5, pp. 341–366).

4.   Thus recounts Tsūyama, Zen no rekishi: Nihon, p. 289.

5.   See Orategama, afterword to the kanbun in letter 3, Hakuin zenshū, vol. 5, p. 203. For an English translation of Orategama see Yampolsky, Zen Master Hakuin, pp. 29–157.

6.   Orategama, in Hakuin zenshū, vol. 5, p. 203. Concerning belief in miracles among adherents to the Lotus Sūtra, see Itsumadegusa (Hakuin zenshū, vol. 1, p. 159) as well as the chronological biography prepared by Tōrei (vol. 1, pp. 5–6).

7.   Shōin-ji was founded as a branch temple of Engaku-ji in Kamakura.

8.   *Oategama*, see *Hakuin zenshū*, vol. 5, p. 204; cf. Yampolsky, *Zen Master Hakuin*, p. 117.

9.   The allusion is to Zensō-ji; see *Hakuin zen-goroku*, p. 23.

10.   See *Zen Dust*, pp. 23–24; Tsūyama, *Zen no rekishi: Nihon*, pp. 290–91, where the passage from Tōrei's chronological biography is cited.

11.   See *Hakuin zenshū*, vol. 5, p. 204; on the text see *Hakuin zen-goroku*, p. 251, and Yampolsky *Zen Master Hakuin*, p. 117, n. 30.

12.   See *Hakuin zen-goroku*, p. 251; Yampolsky, *Zen Master Hakuin*, p. 117.

13.   See *Hakuin zen-goroku*, p. 24.

14.   See vol. 1, p. 214.

15.   *Hakuin zenshū*, vol. 5, pp. 204–205; Yampolsky, *Zen Master Hakuin*, p. 118.

16.   What transpired during the period between his stays in Eigan-ji and Shōju-an cannot be clearly established. See *Zen Dust*, p. 24, and Tsūyama, *Zen no rekishi: Nihon*, pp. 294–95. In the *Oategama*, the description of the experience is followed by a trip to Shōju-an. The mediation of Sōkaku is not mentioned but appears in other sources.

17.   *Oategama*, in *Hakuin zenshū*, vol. 5, pp. 204ff; Yampolsky, *Zen Master Hakuin*, pp. 118–19. Compare the report in the chronological biography of Tōrei, vol. 1, pp. 18–19.

18.   See *Hakuin zenshū*, vol. 5, pp. 205–206; Yampolsky, *Zen Master Hakuin*, pp. 119–20.

19.   *Hakuin zenshū*, vol. 1, pp. 169–70. Compare the report in the chronological biography of Tōrei (p. 20). Norman Waddell has published an English translation of the *Itsumadegusa* in EB 15.2 (1982): 71–109, 16.1 (1983): 107–39. The quotation appears in 15.2 (1982): 99–100.

20.   The sources fail to present a clear expression of Dōkyō Etan's recognition of the enlightenment experience. This fact has led to a controversy among Japanese historians of Zen. Rikugawa takes the question up in his detailed biography of Hakuin and offers seven reasons that for him shed doubt on or preclude acknowledgement (*Hakuin Oshō shōden*, pp. 43ff). *Hakuin zengoroku* reports the controversy (vol. 19, pp. 30–31). Most authors admit that Hakuin's experience was confirmed by his master. Yampolsky points out the uncertainty of the approval (*Zen Master Hakuin*, p. 12).

21.   Ta-hui Tsung-kao (Jpn., Daie Sōkō), named after the monastery of Miao-hsi-an (Jpn., Myōki-an).

22.   *Yasen kanna jōkan*, in *Hakuin zenshū*, vol. 5, p. 364. The English translation is by R. D. M. Shaw and Wilhelm Schiffer, MN 13 (1957–58): 101–27. Quotation on p. 126.

23.   See the explanation in *Hakuin zen-goroku*, p. 255 (note). The note refers to the *Mumonkan*, case 24. The expression is there interpreted differently.

24.   *Oategama*, in *Hakuin zenshū*, vol. 5, pp. 206–207.

25.   *Hakuin zenshū*, vol. 5, p. 207; Yampolsky, *Zen Master Hakuin*, p. 121.

26.   *Hakuin zenshū*, vol. 5, p. 207; Yampolsky, *Zen Master Hakuin*, pp. 121–22.

27.   *Yasen kanna jōkan*, in *Hakuin zenshū*, vol. 5, pp. 349–66. See also the introduction to the text.

28.   The *Chung-yung* is one of the Four Books of Confucianism The three volumes represent the three religions of China: Confucianism, Taoism, and Buddhism.

29.   See the study by Itō Kazuo in *Zen bunka* 6 (November, 1956): 40–48.

30.   *Hakuin zenshū*, vol. 5, p. 349; English translation, MN 13 (1957): 112–13.

31.   *Hakuin zenshū*, vol. 5, p. 354. English translation, MN 13 (1957): 117. Hakuin likens the defense of the body to the defense of territory.

32.   *Hakuin zenshū*, vol. 5, p. 354; English translation, MN 13 (1957): 118.

33.   *Hakuin zenshū*, vol. 5, p. 335; English translation, MN 13 (1957): 119.

34.   The center of breathing lies some three cm. beneath the navel; beneath it is the lower body. See the description in *Orategama*, letter 1; English translation by Yampolsky, *Zen Master Hakuin*, p. 43.

35.   Foreword to the *Yasen kanna*, in *Hakuin zenshū*, vol. 5, pp. 343–44; English translation, MN 13 (1957): 109. The important foreword (pp. 341–47) contains almost all the important themes of the work.

36.   *Yasen kanna*, in *Hakuin zenshū*, vol. 5, p. 361; English translation, MN 13 (1957): 124.

37.   *Orategama*, in *Hakuin zenshū*, vol. 5, pp. 109–10; Yampolsky, *Zen Master Hakuin*, p. 32.

38.   *Hakuin zenshū*, vol. 5, p. 110; Yampolsky, *Zen Master Hakuin*, pp. 32–33.

39.   *Hakuin zenshū*, vol. 5, p. 128; Yampolsky, *Zen Master Hakuin*, p. 51.

40.   *Hakuin zenshū*, vol. 5, p. 140.

41.   *Yabukōji*, in *Hakuin zenshū*, vol. 5, p. 320.

42.   *Hakuin zenshū*, vol. 5, p. 321; Yampolsky, *Zen Master Hakuin*, pp. 160–61. The reference to times and postures expresses the necessity of unbroken practice.

43.   *Hannya shingyō dokugochū* (also known as the *Dokugo shingyō*), edited in 1741 and printed in 1760. See Yampolsky, *Zen Master Hakuin*, p. 225; Rikugawa, *Hakuin Oshō shōden*, pp. 197–98. A new, annotated edition was published by Shibayama Zenkei in 1964.

44.   *Orategama zokushū*, in *Hakuin zenshū*, vol. 5, p. 213.

45.   *Hakuin zenshū*, vol. 5, p. 231; Yampolsky, *Zen Master Hakuin*, p. 144.

46.   *Hakuin zenshū*, vol. 5, pp. 231–32; Yampolsky, *Zen Master Hakuin*, p. 144.

47.   *Hakuin zenshū*, vol. 5, p. 232; Yampolsky, *Zen Master Hakuin*, pp. 144–45.

48.   *Hakuin zenshū*, vol. 5, pp. 232–33; Yampolsky, *Zen Master Hakuin*, p. 145.

49.   *Hakuin zenshū*, vol. 5, pp. 222–23; Yampolsky, *Zen Master Hakuin*, pp. 135–36.

50.   The comparison of the immediacy of the enlightenment experience with sense perception appears also in case 23 of the *Mumonkan*.

51.   See for example the reference in Hakuin's autobiographical work *Itsumadegusa*, in *Hakuin zenshū*, vol. 1, p. 169.

52.   The work is also known by the title *Sekishu no onjō* (*The Sound of One Hand*); see *Hakuin zenshū*, vol. 5, pp. 319–40; see also vol. 4, pp. 385–404.

53.   For the play on a quotation from the Chinese classic, *The Book of Poetry*; see *Hakuin zen-goroku*, p. 324.

54.   The quotation is not exact. See Yampolsky, *Zen Master Hakuin*, p. 164; for an explanation of the "soundless sound," see *Hakuin zen-goroku*, p. 325.

55.   *Hakuin zenshū*, vol. 5, pp. 324–25; Yampolsky, *Zen Master Hakuin*, p. 164.

56.   On the following, see the *Itsumadegusa* in *Hakuin zenshū*, vol. 1, p. 171.

57.   Concerning this confrontation, see vol. 1, pp. 256–261.

58.   *Yabukōji*, in *Hakuin zenshū*, vol. 5, p. 337.

59.   *Yabukōji*, in *Hakuin zenshū*, vol. 5, p. 331; Yampolsky, *Zen Master Hakuin*, p. 170.

60.   *Yabukōji*, in *Hakuin zenshū*, vol. 5, p. 331.

61.   Hakuin probably heard about the Five Ranks through Shōju Rōjin. Convinced of the importance of the formula, he devoted himself to the text, and produced a detailed commentary in his work *Keisō dokuzui* (*Hakuin zenshū*, vol. 2, pp. 1–302). See the translation of part of his commentary (pp. 81–88) in *Zen Dust*, pp. 63–72 and the comments on p. 299. Hakuin also makes reference to the Five Ranks in his *Hōkan ishō* (*Hakuin zenshū*, vol. 1, pp. 231–66). On the following, see *Zen Dust*, pp. 35–72, which also presents the different types of kōan.

62.   On the following, see Furuta Shōkin's essay "Hakuin no minshūzen," in his *Zenshū*, vol. 5, pp. 78–106.

63.   See for example Naoki Kimihiko, *Hakuin Zenji: Kenkōhō to itsuwa.*

64.   *Kusatori-uta*, in *Hakuin zenshū*, vol. 6, pp. 263–68. On this and the following text see Rikugawa, *Hakuin Oshō shōden*, pp. 212–16.

65.   *Shushin obaba konabiki-uta*, in *Hakuin zenshū*, vol. 6, pp. 231–38.

66.   *Shushin obaba konabiki-uta*, in *Hakuin zenshū*, vol. 6, pp. 231–38.

67.   *Kōdō wasan*, in *Hakuin zenshū*, vol. 6, pp. 285–90.

68.   See the section on "Instruction in Karmic Histories" in Furuta Shōkin, "Hakuin no minshūzen," pp. 86–92.

69.   *Orategama zokushū*, in *Hakuin zenshū*, vol. 5, p. 231; Yampolsky, *Zen Master Hakuin*, pp. 143–44.

70.   *Orategama zokushū*, in *Hakuin zenshū*, vol. 5, p. 218; Yampolsky, *Zen Master Hakuin*, p. 132.

71.   *Orategama zokushū*, in *Hakuin zenshū*, vol. 5, pp. 229; Yampolsky, *Zen Master Hakuin*, p. 142. The three spiritual postures are deep sincerity, deep determination for rebirth in the Pure Land, and the resolution to transfer one's own merits to the service of others. The four performances are cultivating deep esteem for the Buddha and all sentient beings, calling on the name of Amida, practicing the *nembutsu* unceasingly, and practicing throughout one's whole life. See Yampolsky, *Zen Master Hakuin*, p. 142. On the "talons and teeth of the Cave of Dharma" referred to in the first sentence of the quotation, see *Zen Dust*, pp. 278–79.

72.   The Japanese Buddhologist Furuta Shōkin has researched Hakuin's joint practice of the *nembutsu* and Zen, and come to a not entirely satisfactory conclusion:

Hakuin clearly loathed the joint practice (*sōshu*) of Zen and *nembutsu*. In fact, he strongly criticized the protagonists of the joint practice. Nevertheless, permission to carry on practices of the Pure Land that omit contemplation of one's nature are an undeniable characteristic of Hakuin's Zen. The intellectual element in Zen tends to leave the masses behind. In this regard Hakuin was able to encourage a reversal of the trend. Karmic histories and spiritual experiences were certainly foreign to Zen. Through them Hakuin brought Zen close to the people. At the same time he bound Zen more tightly to the people through elements of the doctrine of the Pure Land. Inasmuch as he permitted the "reprehensible" doctrine of the Pure Land, he worked for the expansion and strengthening of Zen. One should not be too quick to judge from the two apparently contradictory positions toward the doctrine of the Pure Land found in various parts of his writings that Hakuin involved himself in a contradiction. He did not. He repudiated strongly what had to be repudiated; what was acceptable he accepted without hesitation (*Furuta Shōkin chosakushū* vol. 5, p. 105).

73.   *Orategama* III, in *Hakuin zenshū*, vol. 5, pp. 171–209.

74.   *Orategama* III, in *Hakuin zenshū*, vol. 5, p. 171; Yampolsky, *Zen Master Hakuin*, p. 87.

75.   *Orategama* III, in *Hakuin zenshū*, vol. 5, pp. 172–73; Yampolsky, *Zen Master Hakuin*, p. 88.

76.   *Orategama* III, in *Hakuin zenshū*, vol. 5, p. 136.

77.   Hakuin encouraged the recitation of this text in his work *Hebiichigo* (*Hakuin zenshū*, vol. 5, pp. 401–50). One has to recite the text two or three hundred times in order to experience its marvelous powers (p. 405). See the explanatory footnote in Yampolsky, *Zen Master Hakuin*, p. 185.

78.   See the books referred to in the foregoing chapter on Japanese art. Y. Awakawa, *Zen Painting*, and K. Brasch, *Zenga*, draw particular attention to the impact that Hakuin's painting had on the common people.

79.   See plate 33 in Brasch, *Zenga*; the plate and inscription also appear in *Zen Dust*.

80.   Hisamatsu Shin'ichi is particularly fond of Hakuin's picture of the ape; see its accompanying commentary in *Zen and the Fine Arts*, pp. 64–65. He also touched on Hakuin's calligraphy (plates 6 and 7), commentary, pp. 67ff.

81.   See pictures 114–18 in Y. Awakawa and the brief biography on p. 178; see also K. Brasch, plates 91–103 and the brief biography on pp. 120ff. See also D. T. Suzuki's brief monograph, *Sengai: The Zen Master*, edited by Eva van Hoboken.

82.   On this difference, see Rikugawa, *Hakuin Oshō shōden*, pp. 128ff and also his detailed list of Hakuin's disciples.

83.   See the biographical data in *Zen Dust*, pp. 218ff.

84.   On Kogetsu Zenzai and his line, see Imaeda Aishin, *Zenshū no rekishi*, pp. 242–43; see further the essay by Furuta Shōkin in his *Chosakushū*, vol. 5, pp. 148–55.

85.   See Rikugawa, *Hakuin Oshō shōden*; cf. Brasch, *Zenga*, p. 131.

86.   See Imaeda, *Zenshū no rekishi*, p. 247.

87.   A brief biography appears in *Zen Dust*, pp. 220–21.

88.   On the following see also the chapter on Gasan in Rikugawa, *Hakuin Oshō shōden*, pp. 173ff. Entry into the room of the master signifies in the Rinzan school a request for acceptance into discipleship, which Hakuin is said to have refused to Gasan on several occasions.

89.   Rikugawa (*Hakuin Oshō shōden*, p. 175) concludes the comment with the remark that Gasan could not have been designated the Dharma heir of Hakuin in the strict sense.

90.   *Zen Dust*, p. 23; see also Imaeda, *Zenshū no rekishi*, p. 243.

91.   See the brief biography in *Zen Dust*, pp. 221–22; cf. Imaeda, *Zenshū no rekishi*, pp. 247–48.

92.   See the brief biography in *Zen Dust*, pp. 222–23; cf. Imaeda, *Zenshū no rekishi*, pp. 248–49.

93.   See *Hakuin zenshū*, vol. 3, pp. 15–378, and vol. 5, pp. 1–302. See also Yampolsky, *Zen Master Hakuin*, pp. 226–27; Rikugawa, *Hakuin Oshō shōden*, p. 199. For a detailed treatment of the two texts, see *Zen Dust*, pp. 366–68.

94.   See the relevant material in *Keisō dokuzui shūi* (*Hakuin zenshū*, vol. 2, pp. 305–64).

95.   In the view of Furuta Shōkin, Hakuin-Zen owes its origins and blossoming above all to the popular characteristics. Furuta thinks that Zen in the elevated, classical style of Daitō Kokushi and Kanzan would, without Hakuin's orientation, probably not have been acceptable to the common folk. "Hakuin," he writes "esteemed Daitō, which is why his style of Zen is extraordinarily strict. But he did not simply transmit Zen after the manner of Daitō. It is indeed said that Zen is aristocratic while the doctrine of the Pure Land popular, but this appellation does not fit in the case of Hakuin's Zen." The popular Zen of Hakuin is, as Furuta stressed, particularly important in modern Japan, where religious ignorance and indifference are the general role. Sympathetically he asks, "Are not all the above mentioned points [regarding popular characteristics] given too little attention?" See the final section of his detailed essay in his *Chosakushū*, vol. 5, pp. 105–106.

96.   A complete German translation appears in Ōhasama-Faust, *Zen: Der lebendige Buddhismus in Japan*, pp. 62–3; the English translation here is taken from *Zen Dust*, pp. 251ff.

10

Modern Movements

The Meiji Restoration, the most significant event in modern Japanese history, was both an end and a beginning. In terms of foreign policy it marked the end of the long period of isolation and the opening of Japan to the outside world. In terms of internal politics, it brought about the removal of the Tokugawa shogunate and restored the emperor system. Intellectually and culturally, it witnessed the beginning of Japan's modern period as the nation took its place in the international community of nations. This complete restructuring was forced on Japan by elements inside the country and out. The long prevalent view that Japan was in a state of total economic and psychic depletion as a result of more than two hundred years of isolation simply does not do justice to the facts. The view collapses under the weight of careful research into the Tokugawa period compiled over the past decades by competent scholars. The truth is that the ill effects of a bureaucratic and ossified system of government had oppressed the people, while the mounting threat from outside forces was a cause of great concern for those with the nation's welfare at heart. The presence of vigorous and vital forces is evident from the numerous capable persons who guided the fortunes of the nation from the beginning of the reconstruction with energetic commitment and bold wisdom. To be sure, there was a contradiction latent in the two broad principles that guided the ruling figures of the time—that is, restoration of the old order (fukko) and renewal through modernization (ishin)—but such attitudes helped prevent or slow down extremist developments. There were no bloody revolutions. Uprisings and countermovements were successfully suppressed. The decisive early years from the beginning of the Meiji government in 1868 (under a fifteen-year-old emperor!) to the proclamation of the constitution in 1889 and the convocation of parliament in the following year make fascinating drama. Grounded in its two principles, Japan set itself up as a constitutional monarchy and as such took its rightful place in the modern world.

THE ZEN SCHOOLS IN THE NEW ORDER OF THE MEIJI PERIOD

Naturally, there were religious dimensions to the sweeping new beginnings of the Meiji period (1868–1912) that were to influence and change the direction of the whole of Japan's religious life.[1] The Zen schools must be considered here in the broader context of Japanese Buddhism. The first decisive decrees of the new government during the opening year of the Meiji era established a new governmental department for Shinto and brought about the separation of Shinto and Buddhism (*shinbutsu bunri*).[2] Both decrees unsettled the Buddhists, who felt that their religion was being neglected in favor of Shinto. Anti-Buddhist tendencies became all the clearer as a vigorous popular movement armed with the slogan "Down with Buddhism!" (*haibutsu kishaku*) began to take shape in the political background.

These anti-Buddhist currents had originated during the Tokugawa period with the Confucians, who enjoyed a dominant influence on the ruling powers of the time and who in their writings carried on a resolute polemic against Buddhism throughout the period. Joining ranks with the Confucians was a Shinto reform movement known as the Kokugaku ("national learning").[3] But intellectual differences are not sufficient to explain the widespread discontent with Buddhist temples and monks.[4] It was in response to the moral laxity, corruption, and arrogance of not a few Buddhist monks that a certain bitterness and anger toward Buddhism had grown up among the people, and toward the end of the Tokugawa period these sentiments had reached the boiling point. Riots broke out at various places.[5] Fukuda Gyōkai (1805–1888), a member of Hōnen's school of Pure Land Buddhism (Jōdoshū) and a person of impeccable reputation who was "honored as the greatest Buddhist of the Meiji period,"[6] describes the situation in this way:

> At the present, provincial temples are being destroyed; people are withdrawing their memberships and this causes temple revenues to decline; priests are gladly returning to secular life. Although there is no demand to destroy Buddhism, there probably has been nothing to compare with this situation in the fourteen or fifteen centuries during which Buddhism has been in Japan. In my opinion, there will be an imperial rescript eradicating Buddhism within five to seven years.[7]

People across the nation feared that Buddhism in Japan was about to be destroyed. The government was not planning to go that far, however.[8] The nation's rulers were merely seeking to put Shinto in a prominent place and to make it the national religion. Although pursued vigorously for a time, this goal was never fully realized and eventually abandoned altogether.

As mentioned, a department of Shinto was added to the seven other principal ministries of the government in 1871. Not only were Buddhist ceremonies forbidden at the imperial court, but it was also decreed that all future memorial services for imperial ancestors as well as burial ceremonies for members of the imperial house were to be carried out according to Shinto rituals. Buddhist statues and paintings were removed from the imperial palace. Despite these measures, within a year, the Ministry of Shinto (Jingishō) was changed into the "Ministry for Religion and Education" (Kyōbushō) and Buddhism was included therein. Buddhist priests also figured among the "national priests" who were commissioned to teach the "three principles" or "doctrines" of the "Great Teaching" (*daikyō*). Formulated by the government as an expression of the Japanese religious worldview, these principles required (1) respect for the gods (*kami*) and a patriotic devotion to the nation, (2) recognition of "the reason of heaven" and "the way of humanity," and (3) reverence toward the emperor and submission to authority.[9]

A national institute known as the Daikyō-in was founded in 1872 to explain and propagate this "Great Teaching." It was staffed by Shinto and Confucian scholars as well as by Buddhists and other national educators. Besides embodying the fundamental Shinto vision and the core of Confucian ethics, the principles of the teaching were broadened to include lists of eleven and seventeen rules. These regulations were of contemporary political and social importance and were intended to promote the "prompt modernization" of the nation.[10] In any case, one is hard put to find anything Buddhist there. It is no surprise, therefore, that the Buddhists were not very happy with this new decree, even though it did give them a participatory voice in policy matters and introduced a new organizational order. Each of the Buddhist schools was represented in the Daikyō-in by its head,[11] with the Zen schools of Rinzai, Sōtō, and Ōbaku at first represented jointly by one of their most prominent figures, Yuri Tekisui (1822–1899), the abbot of Tenryū-ji in Kyoto. Soon the Sōtō school was represented on its own, the abbots of the major temples of Eihei-ji and Sōji-ji alternating annually in the post. At first subsumed in the Rinzai school, the Ōbaku school was finally granted independent organizational identity in 1876. The Rinzai school received recognition for nine of its lines of tradition, all stemming from major temples in Kyoto and Kamakura. Through later divisions, the number of these lines increased, so that by the end of the Meiji period, some fourteen Rinzai schools were recognized officially.[12] Other Buddhist schools also eventually found satisfactory arrangements for institutional recognition by the new government.

The Daikyō-in may be considered a first, unsatisfactory step by the Meiji government in the direction of a more moderate political position toward religion. The idea was sharply criticized by Shimaji Mokurai (1838–1911), a member of the True Pure Land Buddhist sect (Jōdo Shinshū) and one of the leading political critics in the Buddhist world at the time. In a letter he sent to the government while accompanying the Iwakura mission in Europe, he urged the dismantling of the Daikyō-in and the separation of religion and state,[13] a position he pressed resolutely upon returning to Japan. After further discussions back and forth, the Daikyō-in was dissolved in 1875, and two years later the Ministry for Religion and Education followed suit. The path was cleared for a new constitution that would imitate other modern governments in guaranteeing religious freedom.

Buddhism had passed the critical first years of the Meiji period relatively well. Most painful for many Buddhists was their separation from Shinto, since they had become accustomed to good relations with this indigenous religion of the kami and accepted it as part of their own religiosity. Buddhist monks who served Shinto shrines were now forced by governmental decrees either to change their robes and become Shinto priests or—a decision many found preferable—to return to the lay state. A further decree did away with the requirement of monastic celibacy and permitted the eating of meat and fish. The option for marriage, which Shinran had introduced into the True Pure Land school against great opposition, now became common practice in all Japanese Buddhist schools, including Zen. The number of unmarried Rinzai monks today is small. In Zen monasteries charged with the formation of future priests, a vegetarian diet is still observed. Having had to experience secular influences since its beginnings, Japanese Buddhism was able to draw on the open-minded spirit of Mahāyāna Buddhism and adjust quite easily to the urgings of the Meiji government that it adapt to the ways of the world.

Serious-minded Buddhists took the claims of their opponents, especially the spontaneous dissatisfaction expressed by the people, as an opportunity for personal reflection and inner renewal. Fukuda Gyōkai, whom we mentioned earlier, called for a radical reform:

> Buddhists regret *haibutsu kishaku,* but not because temples have been destroyed. It is not because we now have less food and clothing. It is not because we have lost our government stipend. We grieve before heaven and man that we have lost the greatest Good. In order to regain this Good, and for this reason only, priests should pray for the elevation of truth and the prevention of *haibutsu kishaku.* [14]

In addition to popular discontent, the disposition of the government provided Japanese Buddhists with further incentive for self-examination, and in many instances, for genuine conversion. The new official structures, first enforced by the worldly authorities and then restated by the Buddhists themselves, opened up new possibilities for joint action and international contacts. The new structures provided a focal point for the kind of mutual interactions that have become indispensable in the modern world.

MASTERS OF THE RINZAI SCHOOL

The tremors of reform that Hakuin had sent through the Rinzai school at the height of the Tokugawa period persisted for several generations through the two lines of Inzan and Takujū. The masters of these lines embodied a Zen tradition that had survived intact and was strong enough to resist the storms of the present. The Rinzai masters of the early Meiji period found themselves very much caught up in the deep-reaching political changes of the new government as well as in the confusion of the popular anti-Buddhist movements. In what follows we will have a look at how some of these representative Rinzai monks defended their school against the menaces facing Buddhism. Not only did they effectively wield the traditional spirit of Zen in defense of Buddhism, they also succeeded in making contributions of their own to the political reawakening going on in the nation. [15]

In the early years of the Meiji era, very few Buddhists were able to comprehend just how new and different the events that were taking place around them were. From the beginning there was concern about the Christian threat that came with the opening of the nation to the West. The end of the Christian persecution, which the government had decreed in 1873 in response to the demands of the Western powers, stirred up deep-seated antipathy against the foreign religion. At the same time, the Christian challenge was something of a boon insofar as it aroused in many Buddhists a new religious zeal and an appreciation for traditional values. Moreover, Buddhism was assimilating new cultural concerns resulting from the changing times. These new influences were summarized in the motto *bunmei kaika* ("civilization and enlightenment"). A number of Rinzai masters showed early signs of accepting the new intellectual spirit. Shimaji Mokurai, the first Japanese Buddhist to clearly and openly grasp what was going to be necessary, was from the True Pure Land sect. The Rinzai masters, however, needed more time to open themselves to the new age, but by the end of the Meiji period, the new spirit had permeated nearly all of Japanese Buddhism, and the Rinzai school played a key role in making this posible.

In the Inzan line of Hakuin-Zen, treated in the previous chapter, a split occurred between Inzan Ien's two chief disciples, Taigen Shigen (1768–1837) and Tōrin Sōju (d. 1837). Each of the resulting branches produced a large number of important masters. It is said of Taigen that he meditated with great zeal day and night after he had overcome the devil of sleep by pricking his skin with needles. He achieved a high degree of enlightenment. The headquarters for his work was Sōgen-ji in Okayama, where he trained numerous disciples in a program of rigid discipline. Among his disciples were the two prominent masters Gisan Zenrai (d. 1877) and Daisetu Shōen (d. 1855). Gisan, who became his successor at Sōgen-ji, was renowned as a master of great virtue (*daitoku*) and attracted a large number of disciples. He was abbot of Myōshin-ji three times and of Daitoku-ji twice. Because of him, Sōgen-ji earned a place in the history of the Rinzai school. Its fame was due mainly to his three disciples Ekkei Shuken (1809–1883), Tekisui Giboku (1822–1899), and Kōsen Sōon (1816–1892), who did very important work during the first half of the Meiji period in Myōshin-ji, Tenryū-ji, and Engaku-ji.

Ekkei Shuken[16] came from Takahama in Wakasa (in the region of Fukui), and was only nine years old when he received his first introduction to Zen in a local temple. At seventeen he began a pilgrimage, in the course of which he met Okayama Gisan, who became his lifetime master and under whom he attained enlightenment. Ekkei carried on his postenlightenment practice in Shō-koku-ji under the aged Master Daisetsu, who like Gisan was a disciple of Taigen, who in turn had also practiced under Takujū, the founder of the second major line of Hakuin-Zen. Ekkei later traveled to Myōshin-ji and became a member of this community that produced so many great names in Zen history. He set up a Zen hall for the monks' meditation. A man of upright and unassuming character, he enjoyed the respect of his disciples and the high esteem of the ordinary people. To a great extent it was his efforts that enabled Myōshin-ji to remain, despite the difficult times, a broadly influential center of Rinzai Zen.

Tekisui Giboku[17] stands out as the first Rinzai monk to appear in the history of the Meiji period. After the initial religious decrees in the fifth year of the Meiji government were modified to halt what was virtually a persecution of Buddhism, and after the Shinto Ministry was changed into the Ministry for Religion and Education, which now included Buddhists, Tekisui was called on to be the representative of the three Zen schools of Rinzai, Sōtō, and Ōbaku. Little is known of his term of office, but his appointment is a clear sign of the leading position he held in Zen Buddhism at the time.

Tekisui is a popular figure in contemporary Rinzai Zen. Many stories about him and his disciple Gasan Shōtei (1852–1900) have been passed on. Born in Kyoto, he took his first steps in Zen Buddhism in a number of different temples in his home area. At eighteen, having heard of Gisan's work in Sōgen-ji, he left for Okayama, where, after ten years of intense training, the master recognized his experience of enlightenment. Tekisui returned to Kyoto in 1849 and stayed for about ten years in a little-known temple of which in time he became abbot.

In 1863 he had occasion to visit Tenryū-ji on the occasion of a celebration. Tekisui remained at Tenryū-ji even after belligerent unrest broke out in the following year and the temple buildings had been burned to the ground in one of the clashes. He and his disciple Gasan escaped with their lives. When the conflict was over, the monks set about rebuilding the temple under Tekisui's direction. It was not the best of times and the work moved ahead slowly. Tekisui continued to hold his lectures in the devastated temple complex. In 1871 he was appointed abbot of Tenryū-ji and in the following year became head of the Tenryū-ji line. A leader in the struggle against the *haibutsu kishaku* movement and a zealous defender of Buddhism, he traveled up and down the country while the new buildings were being erected in Kyoto, urging all to adhere faithfully to the Buddha's message. One of his main concerns was to gather new members for the line and he was particularly pleased when the Dharma hall, connected to the monks' hall, was finally finished.

Ryōen Genseki (1842–1918) was one of Tekisui's most outstanding disciples. He first met his master in 1868 as a young monk in search of the Way, and attained enlightenment shortly after he was accepted into the circle of Tekisui's disciples. After only four years of practice the master charged him with the direction of a rural temple; Tekisui also took Ryōen on a trip to Tokyo in 1879 and entrusted him with securing the necessary funds for the reconstruction of Tenryū-ji. Tekisui opened a new monks hall in Kyoto in 1883, and Ryōen took over the direction of a meditation hall in 1889. There he lectured on the collected sayings of the Sung period Zen master Hsü-t'ang Chih-yü. Known for their high literary quality, the lectures were collected and published in 1913 under the title *Kidōroku.*[18]

In 1892 Tekisui resigned as abbot in order to make way for his disciple Ryōen. A few years later, however, in order to further the rebuilding of the temple, Ryōen requested the master to reassume the abbot's office. In 1899, the year in which the reconstruction of the temple was finally completed, Master Tekisui died. The relatively young Gasan succeeded him but died himself the following year, which meant that the care of the temple once again fell into the hands of Ryōen, who presided over the monastery for a second term from 1901 to 1913. Toward the end of his life Ryōen undertook a long journey to Korea and China. A quiet and retiring man by nature, he impressed everyone with his strong, inwardly rich personality. His memory is still very much alive today.[19]

The most important of Gisan's disciples is Kōsen Sōon (known by his family name of Imakita Kōsen),[20] a powerful figure in the Rinzai school during the Meiji era. Highly gifted and broadly educated, experienced in Zen meditation and well versed in the ways of the world, he had an enduring influence, took a bold part in the historical events of the time, and made sound provisions for the future. The effects of his efforts extend to our present day through his disciple Kōgaku Sōen (usually called Shaku Sōen, 1859–1919) and Sōen's disciple, Suzuki Daisetsu (D. T. Suzuki, 1870–1966) who authored a large, detailed monograph on Kōsen.[21]

Fifty years after his meeting with Imakita Kōsen, Suzuki Daisetsu's memories of the great Zen master were still fresh. It was only a year before Kōsen's death that the twenty-year-old student Suzuki was summoned by one of the monks, Hirota Tenshin (d. 1924, destined to become famous later), from his lay dormitory in Engaku-ji to meet the abbot. Suzuki describes the occasion as follows:

> . . . Master Kōsen approached from inside the monastery. As is evident from the oil painting that today hangs there, the master was of an imposing physical build. What I said and what the master said I have since completely forgotten. Only one thing remains in my memory. When I responded "Kanazawa in Kaga" to his question about where I had been born, the master said, "People from the North are persevering." Whether he encouraged me with something like "Carry on," I don't remember. Nor do I remember the impression I had of the master's personality. Yet I do remember that one morning after *zazen* the master was taking his morning meal on the veranda facing the "Pond of the Wondrous Fragrance," seated on a chair facing a crude desk. It was all so simple. He helped himself to some thin rice gruel, which he poured from an earthen kettle into a bowl. Whether a fragrance arose, I don't know any more. In any case, an earthen kettle was there. And without much ado, he pointed to a chair on the other side of the desk and said, "Sit down there." Today I can't remember at all what we talked about. But deeply impressed in my heart is the picture of the master sitting there so unpretentiously and forthrightly.[22]

Imakita Kōsen was born in Settsu of a prominent family. His father was a Confucian who initiated his son into the study of Confucianism and the reading of the Chinese classics as a little boy. At the height of his studies, between the ages of thirteen and eighteen, he joined the school of the learned Confucian Fujisawa Tōgai (1794–1869) who, as it turned out, took a greater interest in the teachings of Lao-tzu than in those of K'ung-tzu (Confucius) and Meng-tzu (Mencius). Under Fujisawa the young man learned to value intuition and inner experience, and perhaps acquired an interest for Zen. At age twenty-four, already quite well educated and experienced, he decided to enter a Zen monastery. He was soon knocking at the gate of Shōkoku-ji in Kyoto, hoping to practice under Daisetsu Shōen (1797–1855), well known for his extreme rigor, which, it was said, forced many of his novices to leave the monastery. Kōsen endured the strenuous practice for seven years, after which Daisetsu sent him to Sōgen-ji in Okayama, where he earned the seal of enlightenment (*inka*) under Gisan. After his enlightenment, Kōsen continued his practice, studied under various masters, and presided over a number of smaller Zen temples. One report describes his enlightenment in the style of Hakuin. He writes:

One night during *zazen* practice the boundary between before and after suddenly disappeared. I entered into the blessed realm of the totally wondrous. It was as if I had arrived at the ground of the Great Death, with no memory of the existence of anything, not even of myself. All I remember is an energy in my body that spread out over ten times ten-thousand worlds and a light that radiated endlessly. At one point, as I took a breath, seeing and hearing, speaking and moving suddenly became different from what they had normally been. As I sought for the highest principle and the wondrous meaning of the universe, my own self became clear and all things appeared bright. In this abundance of delight, I forgot that my hands were moving in the air and my feet were dancing.[23]

As this passage shows, Kōsen was well acquainted with the ecstasy of enlightenment. He had the experience that was necessary for a Zen master to be able to guide his disciples.

Imakita Kōsen's mature work may be divided into two equal periods covering respectively his years as abbot of Eikō-ji in Iwakuni (1858–1875) and then of Engaku-ji in Kamakura (1875–1892). In both Rinzai temples he served as superior, maintained order and discipline, devoted himself with special care to the direction of his disciples, and added new buildings to the temple complexes. While at Eikō-ji he enjoyed a period of rather quiet work and was able to find a good deal of spare time for writing. His long hymn on the Chinese graph for "nothingness"—"Muji no uta"—is still chanted in monks halls to encourage intense practice.

Kōsen devoted much time to the composition of his famous work, the *Zenkai ichiran* (*A Wave on the Zen Sea*), completed in 1862. The work earned him the secure place in Zen literature that he enjoys to this day. Dedicated to the feudal lord of Iwakuni and written mainly for Confucian scholars and samurai, the *Zenkai ichiran* is comprised of an argument between Confucianism and Buddhism, naturally from a Buddhist perspective. According to Kōsen, the ways of Ju (Confucianism) and Butsu (Buddhism) are fundamentally the same; indeed, even Shinto and Taoism can be included in the "great Way" of Eastern religions. Kōsen's own experience and practice of Zen assured him that it was possible to combine Confucianism and Buddhism, since it had confirmed his conviction of the unity of ultimate reality. While still holding firm to the Zen insistence on the transmission of mind without words and scriptures, the well-read Zen abbot also stressed the value of academic studies. The thirty sections that make up the *Zenkai ichiran* include Chinese sayings, which Kōsen interprets in a Buddhist sense without denying their original meaning. He was convinced that he had uncovered the deepest meaning of Confucianism and Buddhism. In three appendices he explains that the knowledge of nature contains all knowledge, that the Confucians of the Sung period were mistaken when they defamed Buddhism, and that when the ancient sages followed the Buddha-Dharma, they were following the Way (*tao*).

While he was on leave from Eikō-ji, Kōsen spent some time in Zuiō-ji in

Hagi, close to the influential daimyō of the Mori clan. At this time (1868–1871) the anti-Buddhist movement was at its height. Kōsen did not bend under these attacks but mustered all his strength to prepare a defense. With his optimistic rhetoric, he convinced lay Buddhists that Buddhism would protect itself against the onslaughts of the age and in the end would prove its saving power. After returning to Eikō-ji, Kōsen heard of the new regulation that required capable men to serve as officials of the newly formed ministry of education (Kyōdōshoku) and to communicate the government's views to the people in contemporary fashion. This required Kōsen to hold lectures on the three principles referred to above. He did so, but interpreted them in a way suited to Buddhists. He also was charged with overseeing popular education in the district of Yamaguchi.

In 1875 the Daikyō-in in Tokyo was dissolved and the Buddhist schools acquired a limited degree of independence. Kōsen was called to Tokyo to oversee the organization of the Rinzai school, which included ten temples, eight in Kyoto and two in Kamakura. This organization developed into a Zen school that, however, did not meet with any further success. In 1877 Kōsen was appointed abbot of Engaku-ji and therefore resigned as director of the Zen school in order to devote himself fully to his responsibilities as abbot. He developed an active program for the Buddhist laity of the area, while the number of monastic disciples continued to grow. In 1881 he constructed a new monks' hall. As the center of Rinzai Zen in the Kantō area, his monastery was held in high regard.

During the last decades of his life, Kōsen held a number of different offices and honors. His intellectual gifts propelled him into a position of leadership that extended beyond the Rinzai school and into all of Japanese Buddhism. He understood the historical situation to be one of "change" and "new beginnings" (tempuku kaishi), but in the midst of all the change he adhered resolutely to the content of Buddhist tradition, particularly in its Zen form. Affected as he was by the spirit of modern civilization and the Enlightenment, he sought to enrich his solid Eastern formation through contact with Western perspectives. He sprinkled his conversations with English terms and was interested in European philosophers such as Plato and Kant. Even so, and in spite of his tolerance for Shinto, Confucianism, and Taoism, he was convinced that the sole religious way suited to the welfare of the Japanese people was Buddhism. He did not take a friendly posture toward Christianity, which he considered a foreign religion. His interest in politics extended beyond the effects of politics on religion; he belonged to a group of Buddhist monks formed to prepare for the new parliament. Although he was not entirely free of the effects of the centuries-long isolation, he could be called "the most progressive Zen figure during the first phase of the Meiji era."[24]

During the early Meiji period, special attention is due Ogino Dokuon (1819–1895),[25] mainly because of his courageous opposition to the government regulations against Buddhism. Dokuon was born in Bizen (Okayama prefecture), and after the usual education in Buddhist temples chose as his master Daisetsu Shōen, abbot at Shōkoku-ji. Known as "the devil" or "the demon," Daisetsu made use of shouting and beatings to urge his disciples on to more intense practice. The moving account of the enlightenment that Dokuon experienced under Shōen is in the best Chinese tradition. He had to spend an entire year struggling with the kōan on the Buddha nature of a dog. One day, when he went in to report his progress, he found the master was petting a cat seated on his knee. The master made no comment on Dokuon's report. Even when Dokuon repeated his findings, the master remained silent. The disciple bowed and left the room. Outside, he bowed once again. At that point he heard the thunderous cry "*Katsu!* This numbskull comes for Zen guidance and then leaves before the master can say 'yes' or 'no'."[26] Such is the treatment Dokuon endured for fourteen years. He preserved, spending cold winter nights sitting in meditation on a stone, until one day Daisetsu happily confirmed his enlightenment. Later, in 1879, he became the master's successor in Shōkoku-ji.

In 1872, at a time when the government attitude to Buddhism was beginning to thaw, Dokuon was officially appointed as director of the joint Zen schools in the Daikyō-in. He was expected to assist in reeducating the people concerning the newly formulated three principles. Not at all happy with this commission, he continued to preach the Buddhist doctrine of rebirth. Chided by a Shinto official, he answered:

> In the house of Buddha, one does not hide hells or heavens but shows them for all to see. Those who open their eyes will see immediately. But when there is no one who has seen the high plains of heaven (*takama-ga-hara*) nor the underworld, then one cannot see hells and heavens. Have you ever undertaken a journey to the high plains of heaven?"[27]

In vain did Dokuon registered his complaints with the Ministry of Religion and Education, pointing out how necessary it was to train virtuous, capable, and well-educated monks to be superiors of the different temples. But even if his efforts met with little success at the time, they were not completely useless. Dokuon can clearly be counted among the boldest of Buddhist monks taking part in the religious struggles of those years.

The bond between asceticism and study that characterized so many Rinzai masters took on special significance in the case of Tankai Genshō (1811–1898).[28] Tankai came from Mino (in the province of Gifu) and joined the line of Hakuin-Zen that had originated with Takujū Kosen (1760–1833). In his early years he undertook a program of rigorous asceticism in the Rinzai monasteries of his home area under Shunnō Zen'etsu in Eiho-ji (or Kokeizan) and under Settan Shōboku (1801–1873) in Zuiryū-ji. The hard practice took its toll on his health. After a period in a local hermitage in the region of Yamanashi (1848–1854), his search at last came to term under Master Karyō Zuika (1793–1859) in Hōrin-ji (in the district of Kanagawa). From early on, Tankai had been attracted by the spiritual tradition of the Rinzai line, which was eminently embodied in Takujū's scholarly and learned disciple Myōki Sōseki (1774–1848). As abbot of Hōrin-ji, Myōki's disciple Karyō carried on in the spirit of his master. Tankai became a worthy member of this tradition, and Karyō soon made him his Dharma heir. After

Karyō's early death, Tankai became abbot at Hōrin-ji, an office he held for many years (1859–1872).

Amidst the difficulties of the age, Tankai proved his mettle. The trials that he faced convinced him all the more that if the monks and laity of the Rinzai school were to persevere, they needed sound intellectual training and an unwielding strength of character. On his many travels throughout the country he observed the signs of the new age. Well aware that an upheaval was imminent, he continually urged his listeners to be prepared both to defend the old and to take on the new. After the first storms that had threatened to expel all Buddhists from public positions had subsided, the government issued further stabilizing decrees the following year, reinforcing the authority of the competent Tankai. Having been appointed to a position of leadership in the Daikyō-in in 1872, he also spent a year as abbot in the influential Rinzai temple of Myōshin-ji (1873–1874). His chief concern in the years that followed was with education. He established study centers and gave lectures that earned him widespread popularity. He did not limit himself to expositions on Zen literature, but spoke also about the sūtras, especially the *Diamond Sūtra* and the popular *Lotus Sūtra*, thus fostering the people's great devotion to Kannon.

In the spring of 1891 the aging monk began work on a monks' hall on Kokeizan. After its completion, he turned it over to his foremost disciple Dokutan Sōsan (1840–1917). Tankai had taken great care in preparing more than ten disciples to carry on his work. The exceptional understanding that these men showed for the times in which they were living not only gave stability to the Rinzai school but also redounded to the overall welfare of Japanese Buddhism during the agitation of the Meiji era.

ADJUSTMENTS WITHIN THE SŌTŌ SCHOOL

The anti-Buddhist movement (*haibutsu kishaku*) that prevailed at the beginning of the Meiji period, driven as it was more by emotion than by reason, wrought widespread devastation amid the Sōtō temples widely scattered through the rural areas.[29] The reasons for this bitterness toward a religion that had greatly benefited the rural population often lay in personal animosities that were frequently the result of abuses in the temples. In some areas, the violence assumed menacing proportions. Temples went up in flames and monks and nuns were forced to return to the lay state. As already stated, such actions were often provoked by governmental decrees. Still, the cumulative individual losses did not amount to a serious threat to the numerical and widespread strength of the Sōtō school in Japan.

The organizational measures that the Meiji government had taken against Buddhism stopped short in mid-course. The total exclusion of Buddhism from the public life of the nation lasted but a short while. Moreover, the intentionally repressive decision to consolidate the three Zen Buddhist schools was soon abandoned, and in 1869 the Sōtō school regained its independence. At the beginning of the Meiji period internal animosities reaching back into the distant past also reappeared in the Sōtō school. As already explained in a previous chapter, during the Edo period conflicts between the two main temples of Eihei-ji and Sōji-ji led to a legalized equality between the two centers.[30] With its rich tradition, Eihei-ji's prominence was not merely titular. This delicate balance was disturbed at the beginning of the Meiji era when the abbot of Eihei-ji, Gaun Dōryū (d. 1871), proposed to the new government that his monastery once again be charged with the overall direction of the Sōtō school. For a government intent on centralized control, the proposal was not unattractive. The government's hasty approval triggered immediate and vigorous opposition from the numerically stronger members of the Sōji-ji temple; they simply could not accept that their temple, together with the many smaller temples that it had founded and now directed, were all to become branch temples (matsuji) of Eihei-ji. The government's overhasty approval of Eihei-ji's proposal was forthwith withdrawn. Tedious negotiations dragged on within the Sōtō school. The government proposed a decree adjusted to the new situation, but it did not meet with the immediate approval of all parties. Finally, at the wish of the government, a treaty (kyōwa meiyaku) was proposed and then promulgated in 1879.[31] The main point in the agreement was that the two main temples of Eihei-ji and Sōji-ji were to have equal say in the governance of the Sōtō school. For the rest, life in the monasteries remained the same.

The establishment of a central bureau for the entire school (Sōtōshūmukyoku) was extremely important for the unity and preservation of order within the school. All temples were under the direction of this bureau, which was also authorized to resolve differences between the two main temples. Reexamined in 1902–1904 and then finally promulgated in 1906, this organizational structure for the Sōtō school has remained in effect to the present day, to the basic satisfaction of all members of the school.

Before the Meiji period, there had been no recognized general system of education in Japan. The high level of general education that had nevertheless been maintained since the middle ages was due to the efforts of Buddhists and Confucians, and in no small measure to the educational programs of Zen temples. The development of an educational system was one of the top priorities for the Meiji government, particularly since in Japan "to a degree hardly found anywhere else, education was considered a means to social advancement."[32] From the first days of the Meiji era, the Sōtō school felt itself obliged to contribute to the government's educational program. If in the past smaller school programs attached to individual temples had been considered adequate, now a general educational system became the goal, even if this meant that the system would stay dependent on the temples in the beginning. Experienced monks from both main temples formed a commission whose first decision was the establishment of new schools that soon were opening their doors to both Sōtō and non-Sōtō students.

In the 1870s the Sōtō institutions included all the existing forms of schools, from the elementary to the professional level. During this decade the state educational system took shape and became compulsory for everyone.[33] This forced certain adaptations on the Sōtō schools, and numerous changes had to be introduced. It is interesting that the subjects taught in Sōtō schools included not only Zen Buddhist doctrine and Chinese studies, but also English and mathematics. The model of dedication and virtue held up for the students in these schools was the venerable figure of Dōgen, the founder of Sōtō.

The reality did not, however, conform to the ideal. The institutions that had developed out of the monastery schools were unable to meet the students' expectations. Once again, a mood of unrest was growing. At first, the main problem was the students' dissatisfaction with the teaching staff, whom they found incapable of keeping pace with the demands of the times. Eventually more serious difficulties were expressed concerning the overall aims of education and the lifestyle it was promoting. Such discontent reached a climax in 1899 and 1900, when Sōtō's best known educational institution, the Sōtōshū Daigakurin, was forced temporarily to close its doors. Students were dismissed and teachers were relieved of their posts. In the conflict between a monastic style of education and modern educational demands, the latter won out. Conservative, feudalistic values were replaced by newer, Western methods. New subjects were added to the curriculum—comparative religions, philosophy, literature, and foreign languages. A new and freer lifestyle allowed eating meat, drinking beer, and wearing modern dress. Occasional confrontations did not hold back the systematic expansion of Sōtōshū Daigakurin, which was later renamed Sōtōshū Daigaku. After purchasing more land needed for its development, the school eventually became Komazawa University of Tokyo. In much the same way, the Rinzai school began with small undertakings and eventually developed into Hanazono University of Kyoto. Both universities have made great contributions to maintaining the academic stature of Zen in the modern age.

The religious vigor of Sōtō was by no means equal to the widespread activity of the some fifteen thousand temples throughout the nation. At the beginning of the new era an inner renewal was also called for. Those in responsibility adhered faithfully to the tradition of their founder, Dōgen. The renewal of Zen meditation was promoted mainly by the two monks' halls (sōdō), accommodating about fifty novices each, that were established at the temples of Eihei-ji and Sōji-ji. Later the number was raised to eighty-five novices. The original monastic ideal of Dōgen, considered the fountainhead of Sōtō Buddhism's vitality, was to be preserved at all costs. It was clear that the number of monks trained in the main temples did not suffice to maintain the numerous rural temples, whose continuance was determined by heredity within local families.

Prominent lay Buddhists devoted themselves to the general revival of the Sōtō school. Foremost among them was Ōuchi Seiran (1845–1919), a well-educated and energetic Buddhist journalist, who in addition to four newspapers also published a number of his own works. This virtuous friend and supporter of the Sōtō school helped found a benefactors' association known as the Sōtō-fushūkai, which made use of conferences, educational courses, and publications to engage the active participation of monks and laity as much as possible. The association met with internal opposition, probably because it raised expectations that were too demanding for most of the faithful. Certain problems may also have come from people associated with Eihei-ji, since the majority of the as-sociation's members were attached to Sōji-ji.[34] The rivalry between the two main temples continued for some time to be a source of unrest within the Sōtō school.

One of the achievements of the Sōtō school during the Meiji period that had broad, positive effects was the publication of the *Shushōgi*,[35] a text that presented the main teachings of Sōtō Zen in easily understandable language. Nearly all the selections contained in the work's five chapters were taken from Dōgen's *Shōbōgenzō*. Although the manuscript was the result of collaborative efforts between Eihei-ji and Sōji-ji, the bulk of the work was done by lay people, especially Ōuchi Seiran. All those involved took great pains to maintain fidelity to the original teachings of Dōgen. Meditation and enlightenment were not extolled and details of monastic living were omitted in order to focus more clearly on the main elements of Zen Buddhist teaching. Thus the *Shushōgi* pro-vided the Sōtō school with an authoritative text of great religious and practical value. Relying as it did on Dōgen's writings, it offered an effective introduction to the thought of this great master, who has been presented to the West as a central figure in Zen.

OPENING TO THE WEST

The relatively short Meiji era, which began with the liberation of Japan from its insular isolation and after two victorious wars (against China and Russia) led to the inclusion of Japan among the world powers, can be considered one of the most important periods of world history. Following on the heels of the political and economic reopening came a marked intellectual and cultural growth. During this era Zen Buddhism took an important turn, a consideration of which will end our presentation. In what follows, special note will be made of the abundant openings to modernity that characterized the Meiji period.

Despite the difficulties of the first years of the new era, the religious leaders of Japan soon realized that they had to make the most of the changing situation. This momentous national event of reopening was also of importance for Japan's religions, which had always felt obliged to further the welfare of the state. As already mentioned, Shimaji Mokurai accompanied the first group of Japanese politicians on a trip through the United States and Europe to acquire the knowl-edge from the West that so many Buddhists desired. He also hoped to return home with firsthand knowledge of India. Many Japanese Buddhists followed his example.

Interestingly, the opening-up of Japanese Buddhism during the Meiji period coincided with the general revival of Buddhism in Asia stimulated by the West through the efforts of its scholars.[36] The West seemed to have an insatiable thirst for knowledge of the East, while Asia wanted to profit from Western science. This phenomenon also affected the area of religion. Theravāda Buddhism was the first to step into the arena of Western academia. Thanks to the opening to the West during the Meiji period, Japanese scholars were able to make an early contribution to Buddhist research.

In this context, three Japanese Buddhists, none of whom belonged to the Zen school, attained international renown. Nanjō Bun'yū (1849–1927) from Higashi Hongan-ji in Kyoto and Takakusu Junjirō (1866–1945) from Nishi Hongan-ji in Kyoto both studied at Oxford under Max Müller (1823–1900), the pioneering Indologist of the time. Both of them earned the good pleasure and trust of their teacher Nanjō Bun'yū's catalog of Chinese translations of the Buddhist *tripiṭaka*, which he dedicated to his teacher, was published in Oxford in 1883. Properly codified and provided with Chinese characters, it became a standard resource for Buddhist research.[37] England honored its author with membership in the Royal Asiatic Society of London, while in Japan he was known as the nation's first qualified specialist in Sanskrit. Under the direction of Takakusu Junjirō the monumental one-hundred-volume edition of the Sino-Japanese canon of Buddhist scriptures appeared in Japan.[38]

There were different grounds for the fame of Anesaki Masaharu (1873–1949), the polished Buddhist scholar known for his extraordinary linguistic and artistic gifts. Through his lecture tours in America and England he contributed greatly to the good name of Japanese scholarship. In Japan he is known for establishing the library of the Imperial University (now Tokyo University) and for founding the university's Department of Comparative Religions and the Society for the History of Religions. His *History of Japanese Religion*, written in English, is still regarded as a masterpiece.[39]

During the Meiji period, a variety of reasons prompted monasteries of different Buddhist schools to send their young monks to the West. There was a general conviction that the expansion of intellectual horizons would be of no small value for the future of Buddhism. Although the monks were sent primarily to learn, at the same time they also brought to the West Buddhist teachings, rituals, and customs previously unknown there. We read about little-known Sōtō monks[40] whose influence in the West was small and yet who made possible a genuine, if inadequate, contact with Zen Buddhism. For the most part, academic concerns were dominant. At this time, too, three significant Sōtō scholars, all working together, traveled abroad to pursue a rigorous and extremely fruitful program of study. The oldest of them, Nukariya Kaiten (1867–1934), made use of his methodological studies in America and Europe to become the first to communicate Zen in modern form.[41] His influence on the younger Kimura Taiken (1881–1930), who at that time was studying Indian Buddhism in London under the direction of C. A. F. Rhys-Davids, led to an expansion of Buddhist studies within the Sōtō school. At the height of his productivity as professor at the Imperial University in Tokyo, Kimura was considered one of the best of Japan's Buddhologists.[42] His successor at the university, Ui Hakuju (1882–1963), studied in Germany and England and went on to become an authority on the various aspects of Buddhism's historical roots in India. A scholar of balanced historical judgment, he was acclaimed for his research into the now internationally recognized field of Zen history.

Another intellectual movement during the first half of the twentieth century that has only indirect links with Buddhism but is colored by the spirit of Zen also finds its historical roots in the Meiji period. The renowned "Kyoto school" of philosophy traces its origins to Nishida Kitarō (1870–1945), whose philosophical explorations combine elements of Eastern and Western intellectual traditions. Nishida's spiritual roots, as those of many of his best known disciples and successors, were in Zen. These latter include Hisamatsu Shin'ichi (1889–1980), Tanabe Hajime (1885–1962), and the current leading figure of the school, Nishitani Keiji (1900–). The opening that took place during the Meiji period made it possible for the Kyoto philosophers to appropriate the intellectual content of Western tradition and with it to take creative steps towards an East-West philosophy. To explore this philosophy further would take us beyond the limits of this book.[43]

The World Parliament of Religions held in Chicago in 1893, which brought together representatives of many religions from across the globe, also provided Zen with an opportunity to take its first steps in the West. Renowned spiritual leaders from Asia provided the congress with an aura that was as exotic as its was spiritual. Foremost among these leaders was the Indian Swami Vivekānanda (1862–1902), whose moving lecture became the clarion call of the meeting. Standing in the shadow of Vivekānanda, mainly because of his difficulties with English, was Kōgaku Sōen (also known as Shaku Sōen, 1859–1919), the abbot of the Zen monastery of Engaku-ji in Kamakura, who provided the West with its first knowledge of Zen Buddhism. When his disciple Suzuki Daisetsu translated the manuscript of his talk into English, the value of what he had to say was widely recognized. During those memorable days, the West began to hear and speak about Zen for the first time.

Shaku Sōen, a disciple and Dharma heir of Imakita Kōsen, numbers among the Rinzai masters of the Hakuin line. His master esteemed him highly and instructed him not only in the tradition of Rinzai Zen but also in the spirit of the modern age. With his master's permission, he interrupted his monastic life and spent three years of study at Keiō University, which had been founded by the eminent scholar Fukuzawa Yukichi (1835–1901). After his master Kōsen died and he took over as abbot, Sōen gathered around him important disciples and promoted, with lasting effects, Zen's lay movement. As a well known figure in Japan, he was invited to attend the World Parliament. What might have been lacking in the glamor of his external appearance was more than compensated for by the religious power of his personality. He was surpassed only by his ingenious disciple Suzuki Daisetsu, who gave him a place in the religious history of the world.

Sōen's activity in Kamakura, like that of his many disciples, was carried out within the framework of Zen leadership of the time. His greatest achievements were in his efforts to make Zen known throughout the world. In this context, four of his disciples deserve special mention. Tetsuō Sōkatsu (1870–1954), who had already practiced under Imakita Kōsen, attained enlightenment under Shaku Sōen. He made trips to Siam and Burma. In Japan he devoted himself especially to the religious education of the laity. In 1906 he traveled to California, where he remained for only four years. His disciple Sasaki Shigetsu (known as Sōkei-an Rōshi, 1882–1945) transferred his sphere of activity to New York, where he founded the First Zen Institute of America in 1931, an organization that Ruth Fuller Sasaki was later to direct for many years. Senzaki Nyogen (1876–1958), a direct disciple of Shaku Sōen, worked for many years in San Francisco and Los Angeles and promoted Zen through his writings.

Zen's real breakthrough to the West was pioneered by Suzuki Daisetsu, who was prepared for this role by the years he spent in America during the Meiji period. At the time of the World Parliament of Religions in Chicago, Shaku Sōen had met the publisher and philosopher of religion Paul Carus (1852–1919), who, having completed a book on the Buddha, wanted to focus his work as a publisher on research in Far Eastern religions. In a letter to Shaku Sōen he explained his plans and asked him to recommend a suitable young Japanese who could work with him. Suzuki Daisetsu was chosen and immediately set off for the United States; from 1897 to 1908 he lived in the Carus's home in La Salle, Illinois. This ten-year stay with the Carus Publishing House provided the young Suzuki with a methodic, scientific formation that enabled him to speak effectively to the West.

Suzuki's main task was to help Paul Carus in his project of translating the *Tao-te ching* of Lao-tzu. Though he also had other small projects, such as articles and translations, he still found considerable free time for personal study. Totally committed to the service of Zen, he served as translator for his master, Shaku Sōen, during his lecture tour of America in 1905. These lectures appeared in Suzuki's English translation *Sermons of a Buddhist Abbot*.[44] Suzuki also promoted the cause of Zen in his article, "The Zen Sect of Buddhism."[45] His most important academic work during this period was his book *Outlines of Mahāyāna Buddhism*,[46] which was an indirect introduction to his literary works on Zen Buddhism.

Suzuki's first stay in America came to an end in 1908. After a brief stay in New York, he returned to Japan by way of Europe and in 1910 became a professor at the Gakushū-in University. The following year he married the American Beatrice Erskine Lane, who shared his academic interests and assisted him until her death in 1939. In 1912, still during the Meiji period, he undertook a trip to England at the invitation of the Swedenborg Society. The first phase of Suzuki's life ended with the Meiji era. He occupies an important place among the Japanese who fostered their nation's opening to the West. The period that follows takes us out of history and into the present.

NOTES

1. On the following, see especially Joseph M. Kitagawa, *Religion in Japanese History*, pp. 177–261; see also the collection *Japanese Religion in the Meiji Era*, edited by Hideo Kishimoto, translated and annotated by John F. Howes, in particular the opening chapter by Kishimoto and Wakimoto Tsuneya, "Introduction: Religion during Tokugawa," pp. 1–33, and chap. 3, "Buddhism" by Masutani Fumio and Undō Yoshimichi, pp. 101–169.

2. The edict (*Shinbutsu hanzen no rei*) is dated 20 April 1868.

3. Among those belonging to the school are Kada Azumamaro (1669–1736), Kamo Mabuchi (1697–1769), Motoori Norinaga (1730–1801), and Hirata Atsutane (1776–1843). On Mabuchi's low estimation of Buddhism see Dumoulin, *Kamo Mabuchi: Ein Beitrag zur japanischen Religions- und Geistesgeschichte*, pp. 160–63. Since Motoori Norinaga, who stressed the veneration of the native gods (*kami*), the study of Japanese classics (*kokugaku*) has come to represent the unity of cult and state (*saisei itchi*). Hirata Atsutane fought most vigorously against Buddhism.

4. For examples of gross abuses in Buddhism already during the Tokugawa period, see Kishimoto, *Japanese Religion in the Meiji Era*, pp. 108–109.

5. See Kitagawa, *Religion in Japanese History*, p. 226. Cf. also the detailed account in Kishimoto, *Japanese Religion in the Meiji Era*, pp. 114–24. In the region of Satsuma, for instance, 1,066 Buddhist temples were destroyed and 2,964 priests were laicized through the anti-Buddhist people's movement and in consequence of the harsh measures of the regime.

6. See Kishimoto, *Japanese Religion in the Meiji Era*, p. 126. Similarly, the Ritsu master Shaku Unshō (1827–1909) was highly esteemed.

7. Cited in Kishimoto, *Japanese Religion in the Meiji Era*, p. 111.

8. On 2 November, 1868, the regime expressly denied harboring plans to dissolve Buddhism. See Kishimoto, *Japanese Religion in the Meiji Era*, p. 50.

9. For the Japanese wording, see Takeuchi Michio, *Nihon no zen*, p. 344.

10. See Kishimoto, *Japanese Religion in the Meiji Era*, pp. 70–71, as well as the lists given there. The "rash modernization" is stated in no. 12 of the seventeen-item list.

11. On the following see Takeuchi, *Nihon no zen*, pp. 344ff.

12. Takeuchi cites the nine lines and then names the attached lines (*Nihon no zen*, p. 345).

13. The unity of cult and state (*saisei itchi*) was a sore point. It is worth noting that during the Meiji period the difference between state Shinto and the Shinto religion arose. The regime "defined Shinto as a national cult of ancestor veneration and 'not as a religion' " (Kishimoto, *Japanese Religion in the Meiji Era*, p. 131).

14. Cited in Kishimoto, *Japanese Religion in the Meiji Era*, p. 126.

15. On the following see essays collected in *Meiji no zenjō*, issued by the editorial staff of the Japanese journal *Zen bunka*, where the majority of the articles had originally appeared.

16. See the essay by Kimura Shinzuō in *Meiji no zenjō*, pp. 25–45.

17. See Ogisu Jundō in the introduction to *Meiji no zenjō*, p. 15. Cf. also the essay on Tekisui Giboku and his disciple Ryōen Genseki, by Hirata Seikō, 121–35.

18. See *Meiji no zenjō*, p. 133; for the description of this work in ten volumes see *Zen Dust*, pp. 361–62.

19. See *Meiji no zenjō*, pp. 134–35.

20. It is customary nowadays for Zen masters to use their family names. In the biographies of bygone days this was indeed known but not widely practiced. With Imakita (or Imagita) Kōsen the turn to the modern age is announced. See on this the essay by Furuka Shōkin in *Meiji no zenjō*, pp. 67–99; see also *Zen Dust*, pp. 224–25.

21. Japanese edition of the collected works of Suzuki Daisetsu, vol. 26, pp. 1–217.

22. *Ibid.*, pp. 14–15.

23. Cited in Kishimoto Hideo, *Shinkō to shugyō no shinri* (Tokyo, 1975), p. 48.

24. Furuka Shōkin, in *Meiji no zenjō*, p. 98.

25. On this point, see the essay by Ogisu Jundō in *Meiji no zenjō*, pp. 101–17.

26. Ogisu, *Meiji no zenjō*, p. 104.

27. Ogisu, *Meiji no zenjō*, p. 110.

28. See the essay by Furuta Shōkin, *Meiji no zenjō*, pp. 47–66.

29. See Takeuchi, *Nihon no zen*, pp. 149ff; cf. Imaeda, *Nihon bukkyōshi* III, pp. 278ff.

30. See note 122 of chap. 21 above.

31. See the wording of the Japanese text in Takeuchi, *Nihon no zen*, pp. 164–67.

32. Klaus Luhmer, *Schule und Bildungsreform in Japan*, vol. 1, p. 31.

33. For an overview of the legal regulations, see Luhmer, *Schule und Bildungsreform in Japan*, vol. 1, p 275; cf. pp. 80ff.

34. See Takeuchi, *Nihon no zen*, pp. 194–95.

35. A German translation with an extended bibliography was published by K. Ishimoto and E. Naberfeld in *Monumenta Nipponica* 6 (1943), pp. 355–66. An English translation by Nukariya Kaiten appeared in 1896 under the title *Principles of Practice and Enlightenment of the Sōtō Sect* (later in an edition by the publishing house of Sōtō school itself). The introduction in the *Monumenta Nipponica* translation recounts the origin of the text. The meaning of the text in the light of Christian spirituality is the subject of chapter of my *Östliche Meditation und christliche Mystik*, pp. 257–77.

36. See *Buddhism in the Modern World*, ed. by H. Dumoulin. Several of the contributions point out the significance of Western science for the renewal of Buddhism in Asia during the twentieth century.

37. *A Catalogue of the Chinese Translation of the Buddhist Tripitaka: The Sacred Canon of the Buddhists in China and Japan*, compiled by order of the Secretary of State for India by Bunyiu Nanjio (Oxford, 1883).

38. *Taishō shinshū daizōkyō* (Tokyo, 1924–35). On this edition see the report in *Répertoire du Canon Bouddhique Sino-Japonais*, ed. by Paul Demiéville, Hubert Durt, and Anna Seidel.

39. *History of Japanese Religion* (London, 1930).

40. See Takeuchi, *Nihon no zen*, pp. 203–204. Takeuchi singles out the Sōtō monk Yamazaki Kaiei, who studied in the United States in 1901.

41. Among his numerous writings on Zen, the most important is the two-volume work *Zengaku shisōshi*.

42. *Kimura Taiken zenshū*, 6 volumes.

43. Recent years have seen a number of works by and about the Kyoto school in English. See especially the brief account and bibliographical references in Hans Waldenfels, *Absolute Nothingness*, (New York, 1979), pp. 35–46, 190ff.

44. *Sermons of a Buddhist Abbot: Addresses on Religious Subjects* (Chicago, 1906).

45. "The Zen Sect of Buddhism," Journal of the Pali Text Society, 1906–1907, pp. 8–43; see also *Studies in Zen*, pp. 11–47.

46. *Outlines of Mahāyāna Buddhism* (London, 1907).

Epilogue

This second volume makes up a seamless garment with the first. Japanese Zen Buddhism appears as the legitimate continuation of the Chinese Ch'an movement, which for its part took shape from Indian and Chinese sources. A historical overview of Zen as a characteristic Asian movement spanning many centuries illustrates the spirit of the Eastern hemisphere. From the viewpoint of the history of religions, Zen takes its place within the history of Buddhism, despite a variety of other influences and dependencies. Having found a ready reception in Japan, Zen experienced fresh impulses that enriched it and enabled it to expand into new areas. The pluralism of the Zen way that fascinates us today was already evident during the medieval period of Japan. We have pointed out how Zen found a new fulfillment in Japan. For all the trust contained in that claim, when we consider the vigorous growth of Zen in the West at present, it is hard to see how Japan's contributions can represent the final word in the history of Zen.

The aim of this volume was to trace the history of Zen in Japan. Relations with other Buddhist schools were examined only insofar as they had a direct bearing on that story. Given its own numerous strengths, Zen itself occupies a pivotal place within the history of Japanese Buddhism in general. According to official statistics of 1980 (which admittedly are not entirely reliable), the Sōtō school is ranked after the True Pure Land School (Jōdo Shinshū) as the second largest Buddhist group in Japan, numbering 14,699 temples and 6,748,616 adherents. The elitist Rinzai school counts some 6,000 temples and a few million members. But far more important than such numbers is the unquestionable inner strength of the Japanese Zen movement.

Over the course of the centuries, creative energies emerged from within Japanese Zen Buddhism that have continued to enrich the intellectual and cultural life of the nation. We have mentioned a large number of important masters, but certainly not all of them. The most prominent place has been given to Dōgen, Bankei, and Hakuin, three religious figures of extraordinary stature who succeeded in articulating the fruits of their experiences and reflection. This ability to express themselves in an intellectually powerful and moving manner is one of the chief qualities of Zen persons who may in the broad sense of the term be spoken of as originators. An entire chapter was devoted to Japanese art—both in the form of great art and the daily art of the "ways"—which continue to speak to people and touch their lives, and which the Japanese count among their inalienable national treasures.

Zen is deeply embedded in Japanese history. It has followed Japan to the heights of its glory and to the depths of its decline. It has formed the great personalities of Japanese history and admonished them. It has provided consolation to its people in their nearly unbroken suffering and oppression. Without Zen, Japanese history clearly would not be what it is. For all that, we must be careful of exaggeration. A well-educated Japanese friend once asked me, "How could so many unhappy things have taken place in our country since the Kamakura period if Zen were really possessed of the wondrous powers that Westerners attribute to it?" Such words introduce a relativizing note to the meaning of Zen for Japanese history and point to the limits of any spiritual movement in regard to mounting historical developments. At the same time, my friend's observations should not, however, diminish the extensive dimensions of Zen's contribution to the intellectual history of Japan.

In the twentieth century, the history of Zen has entered a new epoch marked by communication with the West. Already different phases to this new period are discernible. Out of the living tradition of Japan, Zen is introducing two opposing forces into the process of history: on the one hand, there is a conservative adherence to what is considered essential; and on the other, an amazing openness to new impulses, external stimuli, changes of direction, and turns. In view of our contemporary global upheaval, Zen has an important role to play in the East-West encounter. While the external course of events may seem to be running a different course and at a different pace, the encounter of the East with the dominant intellectual currents of the West is giving birth to new directions that promise to issue forth a new synthesis for the future. The primary points of contact between the two cultures would seem to include modern psychology with its many different schools; philosophy with its no less rich abundance of perspectives, from existentialism by way of phenomenology and ontology up to linguistic analysis and hermeneutics; the natural sciences and anthropology, especially in their evolutionary orientations, which lead to an interest in the study of the future. In all these areas of encounter, Zen can contribute its own perspectives and unique experiences. And of course, Zen is also a fitting partner in the increasingly important dialogue among world religions.

I have made every effort to keep this overview of Zen within a historical framework, in particular, within the bonds of religious and intellectual history. The size of volume two demanded that I draw to a close at the gates of the twentieth century. But there was also a second, more important reason for doing so. It became increasingly clear to me that the new epoch brought about by Zen's entry into the Western world would require a fundamental shift in the manner of treating Zen history. In the previous section I touched on this question, which during the last few decades has been taking shape in a flood of literature. It is a question that makes the topic of Zen in the twentieth century a fascinating study. But to present a historical summary of such a study seems to me, at least for now, impossible. The present development of Zen is marked by a constantly expanding pluralism. How far can such pluralism go without destroying the essence of Zen? Within what limits can this pluralism still be called "Buddhist"? Or is it even desirable that Zen remain within the context of Buddhism? Is it reaching for a new universality? Such questions would have to be taken up in a proper treatment of Zen in the twentieth century. They do not yet belong to a history of Zen Buddhism.

Nevertheless, insofar as this study claims to be a history, it has something to say not just to the specialist but to contemporary men and women as well. During the long centuries of its history, Zen has produced and nourished sources of life-giving energy—sources that continue to provide opportunities for a deeper spiritual life. This study of the past can be a valuable help for us as we step into the future.

Appendixes

Abbreviations

AM	*Asia Major*
AMG	*Annales du museé Guimet*, Paris
AS	*Asiatische Studien*, Bern
BEFEO	*Bulletin de l'Ecole Français de l'Extrème Orient*
Bi-yän-lu I-III	W. Gundert, *Bi-yän-lu: Meister Yüan-Wu's Niederschrift der Smaragdende Felswand*, 3 vols. (Munich: Hanser, 1964–1973)
Ch'en, *Buddhism in China*	Kenneth S. Ch'en, *Buddhism in China: A Historical Survey*. (Princeton, 1964)
Chin.	Chinese
Chinese Philosophy II	Fung Yu-lan, *A History of Chinese Philosophy*, vol. 2 (Princeton, 1953)
Chūgoku zenshūshi	Yanagida Seizan, *Chūgoku zenshūshi* [*History of the Zen School in China*], vol. 3 of *Zen no rekishi* [*History of Zen*], ed. by D. T. Suzuki and K. Nishitani (Tokyo, 1974), pp. 1–108.
DZZI–II	*Dōgen Zenji zenshū*, ed. by Ōkubo Dōshu, 2 vols. (Tokyo; 1969–1976)
EB	*The Eastern Buddhist*, Kyoto
EJ	*Kōdansha Encyclopedia of Japan*. 9 vols. (Tokyo, 1983)
Enō kenkyū	*Enō kenkyū* [*Studies on Hui-neng: Foundational Studies on the Life and Sources of Hui-neng*], ed. by the Association for Zen Research in Komazawa University (Tokyo, 1978)
Entretiens de Lin-tsi	*Entretiens de Lin-tsi*, translated with a commentary by Paul Demiéville (Paris, 1972)

Essays I-III	D. T. Suzuki, *Essays in Zen Buddhism*, ed. by Christmas Humphreys, 3 vols. London, 1970)
Imaeda II	*Nihon bukkyōshi*, vol. 2, *Chūsei*, chap. 3, edited by Imaeda Aishin
JA	*Journal Asiatique*, Paris
JAOS	*Journal of the American Oriental Society*
JH	*Japan Handbuch*, ed. by Horst Hammitzsch (Wiesbaden, 1981).
Jpn.	Japanese
Kōsōden	*Biographies of Eminent Monks (Kaoseng chuan)*, compiled by Hui-chiao. T. 2059, vol. 50, Nj. 1490
KJW	*Kleines Wörterbuch der Japanologie*, ed. by Bruno Lewin (Wiesbaden, 1968)
MN	*Monumenta Nipponica*, Tokyo
MOAG	*Mitteilungen der Deutschen Gesellschaft für Natur- und Völkerkunde Ostasiens*. Tokyo
Mochizuki, *Bukkyō daijiten*	Mochizuki Shinkō, *Bukkyō daijiten* [Cyclopedia of Buddhism] (Tokyo 1932–1936), 10 vols.
MS	*Monumenta Serica*, St. Augustin.
N	*Nippon: Zeitschrift für Japanologie*. Berlin and Tokyo
Nj	*A Catalogue of the Chinese Translation of the Buddhist Canon of the Buddhists in China and Japan*, compiled by Nanjō Bun'yū (Oxford, 1883; Tokyo, 1929)
NOAG	*Nachrichten der Deutschen Gesellschaft für Natur- und Völkerkunde Ostasiens*
OE	*Oriens Extremus*, Wiesbaden
Record of Lin-chi	*The Recorded Sayings of Ch'an Master Lin-chi Hui-chao of Chen Prefecture*, translated by Ruth Fuller Sasaki (Kyoto, 1975)
Rinzairoku	*Rinzairoku* [Discourses of Lin-chi], with an introduction and commentary by Yanagida Seizan, *Butten kōza* [Lectures on Buddhism], vol. 30 (Tokyo, 1972)

S	*Saeculum: Jahrbuch für Universalgeschichte*, Freiburg im Breisgau and Munich
Shoki	Yanagida Seizan, *Shoki zenshū shisho no kenkyū* [*Researches in the Early History of the Zen School*] (Kyoto, 1967)
SK	*Shūkyō kenkyū* [*Religious Studies*], Tokyo
Skt.	Sanskrit
SL	*Sinologica*, Basel
Sōdai jugaku	Kusumoto Bun'yū, *Sōdai jugaku no zenshisō kenkyū* [*Studies on Zen Ideas in Confucianism during the Sung Period*] (Nagoya, 1980)
Sō kōsōden	*Biographies of Eminent Monks Compiled during the Sung Period (Sung kao-seng chuan)* T. 2060, vol. 50
SPSR	*The Social and Political Science Review (Peking)*
T.	*Taishō shinshū daizōkyō* [Taishō Tripiṭaka in Chinese], ed. by J. Takakusu, K. Watanabe, G. Ono, et al. (Tokyo, 1922–1933), 85 vols.
The Development of Chinese Zen	H. Dumoulin, *The Development of Chinese Zen after the Sixth Patriarch in the Light of the Mumonkan*, translated and annotated by Ruth Fuller Sasaki (New York, 1953)
TP	*T'oung Pao*, Leiden
TRE	*Theologische Realenzyklopädie*, Berlin
Yampolsky	Philip Yampolsky, *The Platform Sūtra of the Sixth Patriarch: The Text of the Tun-huang Manuscript with Translation, Introduction, and Notes* (New York, 1967)
Z.	*Dainihon zokuzōkyō* (Kyoto, 1905–1912), 75 vols.
ZB	*Zen bunka*, Kyoto
Zen Dust	Isshū Miura and Ruth Fuller Sasaki, *Zen Dust: The History of the Kōan and Kōan Study in Rinzai Zen* (New York, 1966)

Zengaku daijiten I–III

Zengaku daijiten [Cyclopedia of Zen], edited by Komazawa University (Tokyo, 1978), 3 vols.

Zengaku jiten

Zengaku jiten [Dictionary of Zen], edited by Jimbo Nyoten and Inoue Jisaku (Kyoto, 1944).

Zenshūshi I-III

Ui Hakuju, *Zenshūshi kenkyū* [Studies in the History of Zen] (Tokyo, Iwanami, 1939–1943), 3 vols.

ZMR

Zeitschrift für Missionswissenschaft und Religionswissenschaft, Munster

Zoku kōsōden

Further Biographies of Eminent Monks, compiled by Tao-hsüan. T. 2060, vol. 50; Nj. 1493, 3 vols.

ZB

Zen bunka [Zen Culture], Kyoto

Appendix 2

Chronological Table

Nara	710–794
Heian	794–1192
Kamakura	1185–1333
Nambokuchō	1333–1392
Muromachi (Ashikaga)	1338–1573
Azuchi-Momoyama	1573–1600
Edo (Tokugawa)	1600–1868
Meiji	1868–1912
Taishō	1912–1926
Shōwa	1926–1989

CHINESE CHARACTERS

Aikuōzan (A-yü-wang-shan) 阿育王山
ajikan fushō 阿字觀不生
Andō Bun'ei 安藤文英
Anesaki Masaharu 姉崎正治
ango 安居
A'nin 阿忍
Ankoku-ji 安國寺
Anyō-in 安養院
Araki Murashige (Settsu) 荒木村重 (攝津)
Ashikaga-Gakkō 足利學校
Awa Kenzō 阿波研造
awase (mono-) 合せ
A-yü-wang-shan see Aikuōzan

Baisen-ji 梅泉寺
Baiyū Jikushin 梅峰竺信
Baizan Mompon 梅山聞本
Banjin Dōtan 萬仞道坦
Bankei Oshō gyōgōki 盤珪和尚行業記
Bankei Oshō kinen ryakuroku 盤珪和尚記念略錄
Bankei Yōtaku 盤珪永琢
Bankoku 萬國
Banmin tokuyō 萬民德用
Banzui 萬瑞
Bashō, see Matsuo Bashō
Bassui Tokushō 拔隊得勝
Bemmeiron 辨明論
bendō (pan-tai) 辨道
Bendōhō 辨道法
Bendōwa 辨道話

Biyō Shingi (Pei-yung ch'ing-kuei) 備用清規
bōkatsu 棒喝
Bokkei Saiyo 墨谿采譽
Bokuō Sogyū 牧翁祖牛
Bokusai 墨齋
bokuseki 墨跡
bonnō 煩惱
bōzu 坊主
Budda-ji 佛陀寺
Bukan, see Feng-kan
Buke shohatto 武家諸法度
Bukkō-ha 佛光派
Bukkō Zenji 佛光禪師
bunan 無難
buppō 佛法
Buppō daimeiroku 佛法大明錄
bushidō 武士道
busshinhō 佛心法
busshō-kū 佛性空
busshō-mu 佛性無
busshō-u 佛性有
Bussō 佛僧
Busso sankyō 佛祖三經
Butchi Kōsai Zenji 佛智弘濟禪師
Butchō 佛頂
butsuden 佛殿
butsudō 佛道
Butsugen-ha 佛眼派
Butsugen Zenji 佛眼禪師
Butsu no on-inochi 佛の御いのち
Buttsū-ji 佛通寺

cha-bana 茶花

cha-ire 茶入

chajin 茶人

chakin 茶巾

Chang-lu Tsung-i 長蘆宗賾

chanoyu 茶ノ湯

Ch'an-yüan ch'ing-kuei, see Zen'on
    shingi

chashaku 茶杓

chashitsu 茶室

chatei 茶亭

chawan 茶碗

Chi-fei Ju-i (Sokuhi Nyoichi)

chia-ch'a see shozan

Chiao-ting ch'ing-kuei, see Kōtei shingi

Chidon Kūshō 凝鈍空性

Ch'ien-yen Yüan-chang 千巖元長

Chigotsu Daie 癡兀大慧

Chiji shingi 知事清規

Ch'ing-cho Cheng-ch'eng (Seisetsu
    Shōchō) 清拙正澄

Ching-t'ang Chueh-yüan (Kyōdō
    Kakuen) 鏡堂覺圓

Ching-te-ling-yin-ssu, see Keitoku Reiin-ji

Ching-tz'u-pao-en-kuang-hsiao-ssu, see
    Jōjihōonkōkō-ji

chinsō 頂相

Chi-t'an Tsung-le 季潭宗泐

Chi-yüan, see Jakuen

Chō Densu 兆殿(典)司

Chōen-ji 長圓寺

Chōgen 重源

Chōjirō 長次郎

Chōkai 澄海

chokushimon 勅使門

Chokushū hyakujō shingi (Chih-hsiu
    pai-chang ch'ing-kuei) 勅修百丈
    清規

Chōraku-ji 長樂寺

chōrō 長老

Chōshō-ji 長勝寺

Chūgan Engetsu 中巖圓月

Chūhō-ha 中峰派

Chu-hsien Fan-hsien (Jikusen Bonsen)
    竺仙梵僊

Daian-ji 大安寺

Daibutsu-ji 大佛寺

Daichidoron 大智度論

Daichi Sokei 大智祖繼

Daichū Sōshin 大蟲宗岑

Daien Hōkan Kokushi 大圓寶鑑國師

Daigaku (Ta-hsüeh) 大學

daigidan 大疑團

Daigu Ryōkan 大愚良寛

Daigu Sōchiku 大愚宗築

daihonzan 大本山

Daihonzan-Eiheiji-han 大本山永平寺版

Daiji-ji 大慈寺

Daijō-ji 大乘寺

Daikaku-ha 大覺派

Daikaku Zenji 大覺禪師

Daikaku Zenji goroku 大覺禪師語錄

Daikan-ha 大鑑派

Daikan Zenji 大鑑禪師

Daikō-ji 大光寺

Daikyō-in 大教院

Daikyū Oshō goroku 大休和尚語錄

Daikyū Shōnen, see Ta-hsiu Cheng-nien

Daimin Kokushi 大明國師

Daimyō-ji 大明寺

Dainichi-kyō 大日經

Dainichi Nōnin 大日能忍

Dainin Kokusen 大忍國仙

Daiō Kokushi 大應國師

Dairyō Gumon 大了愚門

Daisen-in 大僊院

Daisetsu Shōen 大拙承演

Daisetsu Sonō 大拙祖能

daishi 大師

Daishō-ji 大聖寺

daisu 臺子

Daitetsu Sōrei 大徹宗令

Daitō Kokushi 大燈國師

Daitoku-ji 大德寺

Daitokuji-ha 大德寺派

Daitōroku 大燈

danka 檀家

dannotsu 檀越

Danrin 談林

Danrin-ji 檀林寺

dempō no deshi 傳法の弟子

Dengyō Daishi 傳教大師

denkai no deshi 傳戒の弟子

Denkōroku 傳光録

Dōgen Oshō Kōroku 道元和尚廣錄

Dōgen Shamon 道元沙門

dōjuku 同宿

Dōju Sōkaku 道樹宗覺

Dokuan Genkō 獨庵玄光

Dokugo shingyō 毒語心經

doku-sesshin 獨接心

Dokutan Shōkei, see Tu-chan Hsing-jung

Dokutan Sōsan 毒湛匝三

Dōkyō Etan 道鏡慧端

Donchū Dōhō 曇仲道芳

Don'ei Eō 曇英慧應

Donki 曇希

Dōsen Risshi, see Tao-hsüan Lü-shih

Dōsha Chōgen, see Tao-che Ch'ao-yüan

dōshin 道心

Dōshō 道昭

Dōsō Dōai 道叟道愛

Dōson 道荐

Dōsui, see Tao-sui

ehō 衣法

Eichō, see Shakuen Eichō

Eifuku-an 永福庵

Eifuku-ji 永福寺

Eigan-ji 英巖寺

Eigen-ji 永源寺

Eihei-ji 永平寺

Eiheiji-han 永平寺版

Eihei-ji sanso gyōgōki 永平寺三祖行業記

Eihei kōroku 永平廣録 see Dōgen Oshō kōroku

Eihei shingi 永平清規

Eihei shitsuchū monjo 永平室中聞書

Eihei shoso gakudōyōjinshū 永平初祖學道用心集

Eiho-ji 永保寺

Eikō-ji 永興寺

Eishō-ji (Bitchū) 永祥寺

Eishō-ji (Kokura) 永照寺

Ejō, see Koun Ejō

Ekan, see Kakuzen Ekan

Ekkei Shuken 越溪守謙

Emmei jikku kannon-gyō reigenki 延命十句觀音經靈驗記

Emmyō, see Hottō Emmyō Kokushi

Engaku-ji 圓覺寺

engyō 圓教

Enkiri-dera 縁切寺

en-mitsu-zen-kai 圓密禪戒

Ennō 圓能

Enryaku-ji 延暦寺

Entsū-ji 圓通寺

Enyū-ji 圓融寺

Enzū Daiō Kokushi goroku 圓通大應國師語錄

Erin-ji 慧林寺

Etsu 悦

Eun 慧雲

Fei-yin T'ung-jung (Hiin Tsūyō) 費隠通容

Feng Hu-tzu 風湖子

Feng-kan (Bukan) 豊干

Gisan Zenrai 儀山善來

Gishin 義信

Gitai 義諦

Giten Genshō 義天玄詔

Giun 義雲

Giun goroku 義雲語録

Giyō Hōshū 岐陽方秀

godaizan 五台山

Gogō-an 五合庵

Gohō Kaion 五峰海音

goka (kōka) 後架

Gokei Sōton 悟溪宗頓

Gongai Sōchū 言外宗忠

Gokuraku-ji 極樂寺

gotsu-gotchi 兀兀地

Gottan Funei, *see* Wu-an P'u-ning

gozan (wu-shan) 五山

gozan-sōrin 五山叢林

Guchū Shūkyū 愚中周及

Gudō Tōshoku 愚堂東寔

Gyōben 堯辨

Gyōgi 行基

Gyōhyō 行表

Gyōji 行持

gyōjūzaga 行住坐臥

Gyokuryū-ji 玉龍寺

Gyokushitsu Sōhaku 玉室宗珀

Gyōyū, *see* Taikō Gyōyū

haboku 破墨

Hachidainingaku 八大人覺

haibun 俳文

haibutsu kishaku 潑佛毀釋

Hagakure 葉隱

haikai 俳偕

haiku 俳句

Hajaku-ji 波著寺

hakku 八句

Hakuhō Genteki 白峰玄滴

Hakusen-an 泊船庵

Hakuun Egyō 白雲慧曉

Hakuyū 白幽

Hannyadō (Po-jo-t'ang) 般若堂

Hannya shingyō dokugochū 般若心經
  毒語註

hanshinbutsu 汎神佛

Hariya Sekiun 針谷夕雲

Hatano Tokimitsu 波多野時光

Hatano Yoshishige 波多野義重

hatsuboku 潑墨

hattō 法堂

Hayashi Razan 林羅山

Hebiichigo 邊鄙以知吾

Heki Danjō Masatsugu 日置彈正正次

Hekigan kyūjūge 碧巖九十偈

Henshō goi zusetsu 偏正五位圖説

Henshō goi zusetsu kitsunan 偏正五位圖
  説詰難

Hi'in Tsūyō, *see* Fei-yin T'ung-jung

Hirota Tenshin 廣田天心

Hisamatsu Shin'ichi 久松眞一

hishaku 柄杓

hi-shiryō 非思量

hōgo 法語

hōjō 方丈

Hōkan ishō 寶鑑貽照

hokku 發句

Hōkō-ha 法皇派

Hōkō-ji 方廣寺

Hokuzan (Pei-shan) 北山

Hōkyō-ji 寶慶寺

Hōkyōki 寶慶記

hombunnin 本分人

Honda Toshizane 本多利實

Hōnen 法然

Hongan-ji 本願寺

honji 本寺

Honkō Kokushi 本光國師

honshin 本心

honzon 本尊

Hōon-ji 報恩寺

Hōrin-ji 寶林寺

Hōryū-ji 法隆寺

hōsen 法戰

Hosokawa Fujitaka (Yūsai) 細川藤孝
  (幽齋)

Hosokawa Tadaoki (Sansai) 細川忠興
  (三齋)

Hosshō-ji 法勝寺

hossu 拂子

Hotoke 佛

hotsu bodaishin 發菩提心

hotsu mujōshin 發無上心

Hottō Emmyō Kokushi 法燈圓明國師

Hottō-ha 法燈派

Hottō Kokushi zazengi 法燈國師坐禪
  儀

hou 鉢盂

Hōzan Tōzen 鳳山等膳

Hōzō-in 寶藏院

Hsia Kuei 夏珪

Hsi-an 齊安

Hsiao-jan (Yūzen) 翛然

Hsiao-yin Ta-hsin 笑隱大訢

hsin, see shin

hsin-chen t'o-lo, see shinjin datsuraku

Hsing-sheng-wan-shou-ssu, see
  Kōshōmanju-ji

Hsü-an Huai-ch'ang (Koan Eshō) 虛庵
  懷敞

Huan-chu ch'ing-kuei, see Genjū shingi

Huang T'ing-chien (Kō Teiken) 黃庭堅

Hui-yüan (Eon) 慧遠

ichidaiji 一大事

Ichige Sekiyu 一華碩由

Ichiō Inkō 一翁院豪

ichiryū sōjō 一流相承

Ide (Tachibana) Akemi 井手(橘)曙覽

I-jan (Itsunen) 逸然

ike-bana 生け花

Ikenobō Sen'ō 池坊專應

Ikka myōju 一顆明珠

ikkōto 一向徒

Ikkyū Sōjun 一休宗純

I-k'ung (Gikū) 義空

Imakita Kōsen, see Kōsen Sōon

I'nan 以南

inga 因果

Ingen Ryūki, see Yin-yüan Lung-ch'i

ino 維那

intoku no soshi 陰德の祖師

Inzan Ien 隱山惟琰

Ishi 伊子

ishi-dōrō 石燈籠

Ishin Sūden 以心崇傳

Ishō Tokugan 惟肖得巖

Issan Kokushi goroku 一山國師語錄

isshi inshō 一師印證

isshiki rikka 一色立花

Isshi Monju 一絲文守

isshō sangaku no daiji 一生參學の大
  事

isu-zō 椅子像

Itsumadegusa 壁生草

Itsuzan Sojin 逸山祖仁

Itsunen, see I-jan

Ittō Shōteki 一凍紹滴

Iwajirō 岩次郎

Jakuen (Chi-yüan) 寂圓

Jakushitsu Genkō 寂室元光

Jien 慈圓

jihi 慈悲

jijuyū 自受用

Jikaku Daishi 慈覺大師

Jikiō Chikan 直翁智侃

Jikuin 竺印

Jikusen Bonsen, *see* Chu-hsien Fan-hsien

Jimbō Nyoten 神保如天

jingikan 神祇官

jingishō 神祇省

Jinshi Eison 神子榮尊

Jinshin inga 深信因果

jippō jūji sei 十方住持制

Jippō Ryōshū 實峰良秀

jiriki 自力

jisei 辭世

jisha 侍者

Jishō-ji 慈照寺

Jishōki 自性記

jissetsu (shih-ch'a) 十刹

Jitsuen 實圓

Jiun Myōi 慈雲妙意

jō 丈

Jōchi-ji 淨智寺

Jōdo Shinshū 淨土眞宗

Jōei-ji 常榮寺

Jōjihōonkōkō-ji (Ching-tz'u-pao-en-kuang-hsiao-ssu) 淨慈報恩光孝寺

Jōjū-ji 淨住寺

Jōko-ji 淨居寺

Jōkō-ji 常高寺

Jōman-ji 城滿寺

Jōmyō-ji 淨妙寺

Jōraku-ji 常樂寺

Joro 如露

Josetsu 如拙

jubutsu itchi 儒佛一致

Jufuku-ji 壽福寺

jūhōi 住法位

jūji seido 住持制度

Jukai 受戒

Juō Sōhitsu 授翁宗弼

Jūshiya Sōchin 十四屋宗陳

Jūshiya Sōgo 十四屋宗悟

Jushūyōdōki 十宗要道紀

jūundō 重雲堂

Kagen-ji 嘉元寺

Kage-ryū 陰流

Kaian kokugo 槐安國語

kairitsu 戒律

Kaisan Shidō Mu'nan Anju Zenji anroku 開山至道無難菴主禪師行錄

Kaisen Jōki 快川紹喜

Kaiun 海雲

kaiyūshiki teien 回遊式庭園

Kaizen-ji 開善寺

kaji-kitō 加持祈禱

Kajō 家常

Kakekomi-dera 驅込寺

Kakua 覺阿

Kakuan 覺晏

Kakubutsu 覺佛

Kakukai 覺海

Kakuzen Ekan 覺禪懷鑑

kama 釜

Kambun-shōbōgenzō 漢文正法眼藏

Kameyama Rikyū 龜山離宮

kami 神

Kamiizumi Musashi no Kami Nobutsuna 上泉武藏守信綱

Kamo Mabuchi 加茂眞淵

kana-gaki dōji 假名書童子

Kana-hōgo 假名法語

Kan'ami 觀阿彌

Kana-shōbōgenzō 假名正法眼藏

Kangan Giin 寒巖義尹

kanji 官寺

Kannondōri-in 觀音導利院

Kanō Masanobu 狩野正信

Kanō Motonobu 狩野元信

kansansatsu 關三利

kanshi 漢詩

kansu 監寺

Kanzan Egen 關山慧玄

Kao-ch'üan Hsing-tun (Kōsen Shōton)
　高泉性激

Kaō Sōnen 可翁宗然

karayō 唐様

kare-sansui 枯山水

Karyō Zuika 迦陵瑞迦

Kashima kikō 鹿島紀行

Kasō Sōdon 華叟宗曇

Kasshi Ginkō 甲子吟行

Katsudō Fukan 瞎堂普觀

Katsudō Honkō 瞎道本光

Katsura Rikyu 桂離宮

Katsuro 瞎驢

Keian Genju 桂庵玄樹

Keichū 契沖

Keisei sanshoku 溪聲山色

Keisen Sōryū 景川宗隆

Kei Shoki 啓書記

Keisō dokuzui 荊叢毒蘂

Keisō dokuzui shūi 荊叢毒蘂拾遺

Keitoku reiin-ji (Ching-te-ling-yin-ssu)
　景德靈隱寺

Keizan Jōkin 瑩山紹瑾

Keizan shingi 瑩山清規

Kenchō-ji 建長寺

kendō 劍道

Kengan 賢巖

Kennin-ji 建仁寺

Ken'ō 謙翁

kenshō jōbutsu 見性成佛

kenshō reichi 見性靈知

Kenzei (Tendai monk) 見西

Kenzei (Sōtō monk) 建撕

Kenzeiki 建撕記

kesa kudoku 袈裟功德

Kesō Sōdon 華叟宗曇

Ketsudō Nōshō 傑堂能勝

Kian Soen 規菴祖圓

Kichijō-ji 吉祥寺

Kichizan Minchō 吉山明兆

Kidōroku, see Kidō Oshō goroku (vol. 1)

ki-e 歸依

Kie buppōsō-hō 歸依佛法僧寶

kikai 氣海

kikan 機關

kikan-kōan 機關公案

Kimura Motoemon 木村元衞門

Kimura Taiken 木村泰賢

Kinchū narabini kuge shohatto 禁中竝公
　家諸法度

kinhin 經行

kinin-guchi 貴人口

Kinkaku-ji 金閣寺

Kinoshita Katsutoshi (Chōshōshi) 木下
　勝俊(長嘯子)

Kippō-ji 吉峰寺

Kisei Reigen 希世靈彦

Kisen Seidō 希先西堂

Kissa yōjōki 喫茶養生記

kitai-zen 期待禪

Kitamuki Dōchin 北向道陳

Kitamura Kigin 北村季吟

Koan Eshō, see Hsü-an Huai-ch'ang

Kōbō Daishi 弘法大師

Kobori Enshū 小堀遠州

Kōdō wasan 孝道和讚

Kōen 公圓

Kōfuku-ji (Nara, Harima) 興福寺

Kōfuku-ji (Higo) 廣福寺

Kōgai 劫外

kogaku 古學

Kōgaku-an 向嶽庵

Kōgaku-ji 向嶽寺

Kōgaku Sōen 洪嶽宗演 (Shaku Sōen 釋宗演)

Kogaku Sōkō 古岳宗亘

Koga Michichika 久我通親

Kōgen-ji 高源寺

kōgetsudai 向月臺

Kōgetsu Sōgan 江月宗玩

Kogetsu Zenzai 古月禪材

Kohō-an 孤篷庵

Kohō Kakumyō 孤峰覺明

Kōhō Kennichi 高峰顯日

Kōin 公胤

Kojiki 古事記

kōka, see goka

Kokan Shiren 虎關師鍊

Koke-dera 苔寺

Kokei-an 虎溪庵

Kokeizan 虎溪山

Kōken-in 高乾院

Kokinshū 古今集

Kōkoku-ji 興國寺

kokū 虛空

Kokubun-ji 國分寺

kokugaku 國學

Kokujō-ji 國上寺

Kokutai-ji 國泰寺

Kokyō Myōsen 古鏡明千

koma 小間

komusō 虛無僧

Kōmyōzozammai 光明藏三昧

Konchi-in 金地院

Kongō dōka 金剛幢下

Kongōzammai-in 金剛三昧院

Konishi Yukinaga 小西行長

Konpon-ji 根本寺

Kōri-ji (Kuan-li-ssu) 廣利寺

Kōrin-ji 光林寺

Kosen Ingen 古先印元

Kōsen Shōton, see Kao-ch'üan Hsing-tun

Kōsen Sōon 洪川宗溫 (Imakita Kōsen 今北洪川)

Kōshōhōrin-ji 興聖法林寺 (Kōshō-ji 興聖寺)

Kōshō-ji (Echigo) 光照寺

Kōshō-ji (Uji) 興聖寺

Kōshōmanju-ji (Hsing-sheng-wan-shou-ssu) 興聖萬壽寺

Kōshō Shōtō Kokushi 高照正燈國師

kōso 高祖

Kō Teiken, see Huang T'ing-chien

Kōtei shingi (Chiao-ting ch'ing-kuei) 校定清規

Kōtoku-ji (Hyūga) 皇德寺

Kōtoku-ji (Fukuoka, Mino) 興德寺

Kōtoku-ji goroku 興德寺語錄

Koun Ejō 孤雲懷弉

Kōzen 晃全

Kōzen Daitō Kokushi 興禪大燈國師

Kōzen gokokuron 興禪護國論

Kōzen-ji 光禪寺

Kōzenki 興禪記

Kūa 空阿

Kuan-li-ssu, see Kōri-ji

Kuei-shan Ling-yu 偽山靈祐

kufū (ku-fung) 工夫

ku-fung, see kufū

Kūin-ji 空印寺

Kūkai 空海

Kūkoku Myōō 空谷明應

Ku-lin Ch'ing-mao (Kurin Seimu) 古林清茂

Kundaikan souchōki 君臺觀左右帳記

kuri 庫裡

Kurin Seimu, see Ku-lin Ch'ing-mao

Kuroda Yoshitaka (Josui) 黒田孝高 (如水)

kusatori-uta 草取り歌

Kusharon 俱舍論

Muin Emban 無隱圓範

Mujaku Dōchū 無著道忠

muji no uta 無字の歌

Mujin Shōtō 無塵省燈

mujō-busshō 無常佛性

mujokushin 無濁心

Mujū Dōgyō 無住道曉

Mukan Fumon 無關普門

Mukan Gengo 無關玄悟

Mukei 夢閨

mukyoku 無極

Mukyoku Shingen 無極志玄

Mukyū Tokusen 無及德詮

Mumon Gensen 無文元選

mu-mu 無無

mumyō 無明

Munefusa 宗房

Murata Jukō 村田珠光

muro 無漏

musa 無作

mushi dokugo 無師獨悟

mushin munen 無心無念

Musō Kokushi, see Musō Soseki

Musō Kokushi nempu 夢窓國師年譜

musō muchaku 無相無著

Musō Shōgaku nempu 夢窓正覺年譜

Musō Soseki 夢窓疎石

Mutan Sokan 無端祖環

Mutei Ryōshō 無底良韶

mutekatsu 無手勝

Mutō Shūi 無等周位

Muzō Jōshō 無象靜照

Myōgen-shū 明眼宗

Myō-hō-renge-kyō 妙法蓮華經

myōkaku 妙覺

Myōki-an (Miao-hsi-an) 妙喜庵

Myōkō Sōei 明江宗叡

Myōōkyō-ji 妙應教寺

Myōshin-ji 妙心寺

Myōshin-ji-ha 妙心寺派

Myōshō-ji 妙勝寺

myōshu honshō 妙修本證

myōtei mondō 妙貞問答

Myōyū 明融

Myōzen 明全

nage-ire 投入れ

naikan 内觀

Nambōroku 南坊錄

Nambō Sōkei 南坊宗啓

Nan'ei Kenshū 南英謙宗

Nanjō Bun'yū 南条文雄

Nankei Sōgaku 南景宗嶽

Nanrin-ji 南林寺

Nan-shan, see Nanzan

Nansō-ji 南宗寺

Nanzan (Nan-shan) 南山

Nanzan Shiun 南山士雲

Nanzen-ji 南禪寺

Negorō-ji 根來寺

Nihon Darumashū 日本達磨宗

nijiri-guchi 躙口

nikkamon 日華門

ningyō jōruri 人形淨瑠璃

ninshitsu 忍室

Nippō Sōshun 日峰宗舜

Nishiari Bokuzan 西有穆山

Nishida Kitarō 西田幾多郎

Nishitani Keiji 西谷啓治

Nishiyama Sōin 西山宗因

Niten-ichi-ryū 二天一流

Nitō-ryū 二刀流

Nō (Noh) 能

Nōami 能阿彌

norito 祝詞

Nozarashi kikō 野ざらし紀行

Nukariya Kaiten 忽滑谷快天
Nyohō-ji 如法寺
Nyojō Oshō goroku 如淨和尚語錄
Nyorai zenshin 如來全身
nyūdō 入道

Ōbaku-ban 黃檗版
Ōbaku sandan kaie 黃檗三壇戒會
Ōbaku shingi 黃檗清規
ōbō 王法
Odagiri Ichiun 小田切一雲
Oda Urakusai 織田有樂齋
Ogasawara Nagahide 小笠原長秀
Ogasawa-ryū 小笠原流
Ogasawara Sadamune 小笠原貞宗
Ō Gishi, see Wang Hsi-chih
Oi no kobumi 笈の小文
Okada Gihō 岡田宜法
Ō Kenshi, see Wang Hsien-chih
Oku no hosomichi 奧の細道
Ōmori Shiyō 大森子陽
Ōmura Mitsue 大村光枝
on inochi 御いのち
Onjō-ji 園城寺
Orategama 遠羅天釜
Oribe-ryū 織部流
Ōsen Keizan 橫川景三
Ōshiken 奧旨軒
Otogo (Shrine) 乙子
Ōtomo Chikaie 大友親家
Ōtomo Kōhaiki 大友興廢記
Ōtomo Yoshishige (Sōrin) 大友義鎮
　(宗麟)
Ōuchi Seiran 大內青巒

pan-tai, see bendō
Pei-shan, see Hokuzan
Pei-yung ch'ing-kuei, see Biyō Shingi
Po-jo-t'ang, see Hannyadō

Raihai tokuzui 禮拜得髓
Raku (ceramics) 樂
Rankei Dōryū, see Lan-hsi Tao-lung
Rashō-mon 羅生門
reichi 靈知
reikon 靈魂
Reirōshū 玲瓏集
Reiun-in 靈雲院
Renchi no Kannon 蓮池の觀音
renga 連歌
Rennyo 蓮如
richi 理致
Ri-ki sabetsuron 理氣差別論
rikka (tatebana) 立華
rikkoyō 六古窯
rinka (ringe) 林下
Rinsen-ji 臨川寺
Rinsen Kakun 臨川家訓
Rinshō-in 麟祥院
rishōtō 利生塔
Rissen-ji 立川寺
Roankyō 驢鞍橋
Rōbai-an 老梅庵
rōbashin 老婆心
Rōben 良辨
rōhachi-sesshin 臘八攝心
roji 露地
Rokuon-in 鹿苑院
Rokuon-ji 鹿苑寺
Rōzan 老山
rufubon 流布本
Ryakuō Shishō Zenji 曆應資聖禪寺
Ryōan Emyō 了菴慧明
Ryōan-ji 龍安寺
Ryōen Genseki 龍淵元碩
Ryōgongyō 楞嚴經
Ryōkan, see Daigu Ryōkan
Ryōkan Hōgen 良觀法眼
Ryōnen Myōzen 了然明全

Ryōshō-ji 龍翔寺
Ryūmon-ji 龍門寺
Ryūshaku-ji 立石寺
Ryūshū Shūtaku 龍湫周澤
Ryūtaku-ji 龍澤寺
Ryūzan-an 龍山庵
Ryūtō Gentō 龍統元棟
Ryūzan Tokken 龍山德見

Saga nikki 嵯峨日記
Saigin 西吟
Saigyō 西行
Saihō-ji (Wakayama) 西方寺
Saihō-ji (Kyōto) 西芳寺
Saihō yuikai 西芳遺誡
Saijō-ji 最乘寺
Saikin-ji 西金寺
sairin 臍輪
saisei itchi 祭政一致
Saishō Shōtai 西笑承兌
Sakuteiki 作庭記
Sambyaku kosoku 三百古則
Sammai-ō-zammai 三昧王三昧
sammon 山門
Sanbon 參本
Sanchū 參註
sandai sōron 三代相論
sangaku 散樂
Sanjōnishi Sanetaka 三條西實隆
sanjūshichihon bodaibumpō 三十七品
　　菩提分法
Sankon zazensetsu 三根坐禪説
San'e-in 三會院
San'e-in yuikai (ikai) 三會院遺
　　誡
Sanrin 山林
Sansō Eun 山叟慧雲
sansui 山水
Sanyū-ji 三友寺

Sarashina Kikō 更級紀行
sarugaku 猿樂
Sasaki Shigetsu 佐々木指月 (Sōkeian
　　Rōshi 曹溪庵老師
Sasaki Sadatsuna 佐々木定綱
Satsuma gakuha 薩摩學派
seigo 省悟
Seisetsu Shōchō, see Ch'ing-cho Cheng-
　　ch'eng
Seishō-ji 青松寺
Seizan Jiei 青山慈永
Seizan yawa 西山夜話
Sekishitsu Zenkyū 石室善玖
Sekishu no onjō 隻手の音聲
Sekisō Keisho, see Shih-shuang Ch'ing-
　　chu
Sekkō Sōshin 雪江宗深
Sembutsu-ji 選佛寺
Sen'e 詮慧
Sengai Gibon 仙厓義梵
Sengaku-ji 泉岳寺
seng-lu, see sōroku
senjō 洗淨
Senkōbō 千光房
Senkō Kokushi 千光國師
senmen 洗面
Senmen betsubon 洗面別本
Sen no Rikyū 千利休
sesshin 接心
Sesshin sesshō 説心説性
Sesshū Tōyō 雪舟等楊
Sessō 雪窓
Sesson Shūkei 雪村周繼
Sesson Yūbai 雪村友梅
Seta Kamon 瀬田掃部
Setsudō Sōboku 拙堂宗朴
Settan Shōboku 雪潭紹璞
shaku 尺
Shakuen Eichō 釋圓榮朝

shakuhachi 尺八

Shaku Sōen, *see* Kōgaku Sōen

Shaku Unshō 釋雲照

shami 沙彌

shariden 舍利殿

Sharisōdenki 舍利相傳記

Shasekishū 沙石集

shen-hsin t'o-lo, *see* shinjin datsuraku

Shibayama Kenmotsu 芝山監物

Shidōan 至道庵

Shidō Munan 至道無難

shie jiken 紫衣事件

shigajiku 詩畫軸

Shigetsu E'in 指月慧印

shih-ch'a, *see* jissetsu

Shih-shuang Ch'ing-chu (Sekisō Keisho) 石霜慶諸

Shi-hsi Hsin-yüeh 石溪心月

shiitake 椎茸

shiji zazen 四時坐禪

shikan taza 只管打坐

Shimaji Mokurai 島地默雷

Shimazu Nisshinsai 島津日新斎

shin (hsin) 信

shinbutsu bunri 神佛分離

Shinchi Kakushin 心地覺心

Shingaku 心學

Shingei 眞藝

Shingon-in 眞言院

shinji-ike 心字池

shinjin datsuraku (shen-hsin t'o-lo) 身心脱落

shinjin datsuraku (hsin-chen t'o-lo) 心塵脱落

Shinjin meinentei 信心銘拈提

Shinji-shōbōgenzō 眞字正法眼藏

Shinju-an 眞珠庵

Shin-kage-ryū 神陰流

Shinkokinshū 新古今集

Shinnō 眞能

Shinran 親鸞

shinshō 心性

shinsō 新草

Shintō 神道

Shin-yagyū-ryū 新柳生流

shiroku-benrei-bun 四六駢儷文

shiryō 思量

shishi menju 師資面授

shissui 直歲

shitsuu-busshō 悉有佛性

shōbō 正法

Shōbōgenzō 正法眼藏

Shōbōgenzō benbenchū 正法眼藏辨辨註

Shōbōgenzō benchū narabini chōgen 正法眼藏辨註竝調絃

Shōbōgenzō chūkai 正法眼藏註解

Shōbōgenzō goshō 正法眼藏御抄

Shōbōgenzō keiteki 正法眼藏啓迪

Shōbōgenzō kyakutai ichijisan 正法眼藏却退一字參

Shōbōgenzō monge 正法眼藏聞解

Shōbōgenzō naippō 正法眼藏那一寶

Shōbōgenzō sambyakusoku 正法眼藏三百則

Shōbōgenzō shisōtaikei 正法眼藏思想大系

Shōbōgenzōshō 正法眼藏抄

Shōbōgenzō shōtenroku 正法眼藏涉典錄

Shōbōgenzō wagoshō 正法眼藏和語鈔

Shōbōgenzō wagotei 正法眼藏和語梯

Shōbōgenzō zuimonki 正法眼藏隨聞記

Shōbō-ji 正法寺

Shōbōzan Myōshin-ji 正法山妙心寺

shodō 書道

Shōfuku-ji 聖福寺

Shōgen Sūgaku, *see* Sing-yüan Ch'ung-
  yüeh

shōgyoku 小玉

shohō 書法

Shōichi goroku 聖一語錄

Shōichi-ha 聖一派

Shōichi kana hōgo 聖一假名法語

Shōichi Kokushi 聖一國師

Shōin-ji 松蔭寺

shoin-zukuri 書院造り

Shōji 生死

Shōju-an 正受庵

Shōju Etan 正受慧端

shojitsu 書術

Shōkan-ji 正觀寺

Shōkei 祥啓

Shōkin-tei 松琴亭

Shōkoku-ji 相國寺

Shōmyō-ji 稱名寺

Shōnankattōroku 湘南葛藤錄

Shōnen-ji 唱念寺

Shosha Negi Kannushi hatto 諸社禰宜
  神主法度

shōshi 正師

Shōshū-ji 正宗寺

Shoshū jiin hatto 諸宗寺院法度

Shōtetsu 性徹

Shuryōgon sammaikyō 首楞嚴三昧經

shozan (chia-ch'a) 諸山

Shūgaku-in 修學院

Shugendō 修驗道

Shūgetsu 秋月

shugyō 修行

Shūhō Myōchō 宗峰妙超

Shukke kudoku 出家功德

Shukō-an 珠光庵

Shūmon mujintōron 宗門無盡燈論

shūmon no aratame 宗門の改め

Shunjō 俊芿

Shunjū 春秋

Shunnō Zen'etsu 春應禪悅

Shun'oku Myōha 春屋妙葩

Shun'oku Sōen 春屋宗園

Shun'u-an 春雨庵

Shūon-an 酬恩庵

shuryō 衆寮

Shuryō shingi 衆寮箴規

Shushin obaba konabiki-uta 王心お婆々
  粉引歌

shushō 修證

Shushōgi 修證義

shuso 首座

shūtō fukko 宗統復古

Shūtoku-ji 周德寺

sō 草

Sōami 相阿彌

sōan 草庵

Sōeki Rikyū 宗易利休

Sōfuku-ji (Sūfuku-ji) 崇福寺

Sōfuku-ji goroku 崇福寺語錄

Sōgen-ji 曹源寺

Sōgi 宗祇

Sōgo 宗吾

Sōhō Sōgen 雙峯宗源

Sōji-ji 總持寺

Sōkaku Zenji 宗覺禪師

Sōkeian Rōshi, *see* Sasaki Shigetsu

Sōken-ji 總見寺

Sokudō 息道

Sokuhi Nyoichi, *see* Chi-fei Ju-i

Sokushinki 卽心記

Sokushin zebutsu 卽心是佛

Sōkyō-ji, *see* Sugyō-ji

Sonnō Sōeki 損翁宗益

sōrin 叢林

sōroku (seng-lu) 僧錄

Sōsen-ji 總泉寺

sōsho 草書

sōshu 雙修

Sōtan 宗湛

Sōtōfushūkai 曹洞扶宗會

Sōtōshū Daigakurin 曹洞宗大學林

Sōtōshūmukyoku 曹洞宗務局

Sōtōshū nikka seiten 曹洞宗日課聖典

Sozan Genkyō 蘇山玄喬

Sozan Kōnin, see Su-shan Kuang-jen

Sūden, see Ishin Sūden

Sugitani Muneshige 杉谷宗重

Sugyō-ji 宗鏡寺

Sugyōroku 宗鏡

suibokuga 水墨畫

Suiō Genro 醉翁元盧

sukiya 數寄屋

Sung-yüan Ch'ung-yüeh (Shōgen Sūga-ku) 松源崇岳

Su-shan Kuang-jen (Sozan Kōnin) 疎山光仁

Suzuki Shōsan 鈴木正三

Tafuku-ji 多福寺

Ta-hsiu Cheng-nien (Daikyū Shōnen) 大休正念

Ta-hsüeh, see Daigaku

Taiaki 太阿記

Taigen Shigen 太元孜元

Taigen Sōshin 太源宗眞

taigo-zen 待悟禪

Taihakuzan (T'ai-po-shan) 太白山

Taikan (Daikan) shingi 大鑑清規

Taikō-an 退耕庵

Taikō Gyōyū 退耕行勇

taimitsu 台密

T'ai-po-shan, see Taihakuzan

taiso 太祖

Taitaiko-goge-jarihō 對大己五夏闍梨法

Taiyō Bonsei 太容梵清

Taizō-in 退藏院

Takakusu Junjirō 高楠順次郎

Takayama Ukon 高山右近

Takeno Jōō 武野紹鷗

Takuan Sōhō 澤庵宗彭

Takujū Kosen 卓洲胡僊

Tanabe Hajime 田邊元

tanden 丹田

Tan-hsia T'ien-jan (Tanka Tennen) 丹霞天然

Tan'ishō 歎異鈔

tanka 短歌

Tankai Genshō 潭海玄昌

Tanka Tennen, see Tan-hsia Tien-jan

Tanrei Sōden 單嶺宗傳

Tao-che Ch'ao-yüan (Dōsha Chōgen) 道者超元

Tao-hsüan Lü-shih (Dōsen Risshi) 道璿律師

Tao-sui (Dōsui) 道邃

tariki 他力

tatebana 立華

Teishin 貞心

Tekisui Giboku 滴水宜牧

Temmoku 天目

Temmokuzan, see T'ien-mu-shan

tempuku kaishi 顚覆開始

Tendai-in 天台院

Tendō-keitoku-ji (T'ien-t'ung-ching-te-ssu) 天童景德寺

Tendō Nyojō Zenji goroku 天童如淨禪師語錄

Tendōsan (T'ien-t'ung-shan) 天童山

Tengugeijutsuron 天狗藝術論

tenka daiichi 天下第一

Tenkai 天海

Tenkei Denson 天桂傳尊

Tenryū-ji 天龍寺

Tenryū-ji bune 天龍寺船

Tenryū Shishō Zenji 天龍資聖禪寺

Tentaku-ji 天澤寺

tenzo 典座

Tenzo kyōkun 典座教訓

tera-koya 寺小屋

tera-uke 寺請

Tetsugen-ban 鐵眼版

Tetsugen Dōkō 鐵眼道光

Tetsuō Sōkatsu 輟翁宗活

Tettō Gikō 徹翁義亨

Tettsū Gikai 徹通義介

T'ien-mu-shan (Temmokuzan) 天目山

T'ien-t'ung-ching-te-ssu see Tendō-
keitoku-ji

T'ien-t'ung-shan, see Tendōsan

tobi-ishi 飛び石

tōcha 鬪茶

Tōdai-ji 東大寺

tōdō 東堂

tōdōi 東堂位

Tōenken 投淵軒

Tōfuku-ji 東福寺

Tōgan Ean 東嚴慧安

Tōgudō 東求堂

Tōhoku-an 東北菴

Tōhoku-ji 東北寺

Tōho Sōchū 董甫宗仲

Tōji-ji 等持寺

Tōjō goisetsu 洞上五位説

Tōjō ungetsu-roku 洞上雲月録

Tōkai-ji 東海寺

Tōkai yawa 東海夜話

Tōkei-ji 東慶寺

Tōkei Tokugo 桃溪德悟

tokonoma 床間

Tokuhō Zenketsu 特芳禪傑

Tokuō Myōshū 禿翁妙周

Tokuō Shunka 得翁俊可

Tōmyō Enichi, see Tung-ming Hui-jih

Tōrei Enji 東嶺圓慈

Tōrin Sōju 棠林宗壽

Tōryō Eiyo, see Tung-ling Yun-wu

tōsu 東司

Tōyō Eichō 東陽英朝

Tōzan Tanshō 東山湛照

Tōzen-ji 東禪寺

Tsu-an Chih-chien 足庵智鑑

Tsuda Sōkyū 津田宗及

Tsūgen Jakurei 通幻寂靈

Tsukahara Bokuden 塚原卜傳

tsukubai 蹲

tsūsu 都寺

Tu-chan Hsing-ying (Dokutan Shōkei)
獨湛性瑩

Tung-li Hung-hui 東里弘會

Tung-ling Yun-wu (Tōryō Eiyo) 東陵
永璵

Tung-ming Hui-jih (Tōmyō Enichi) 東明
惠日

Tung-yuan Te-hui 東陽德輝

u-busshō 有佛性

Udatsu kikō 卯辰紀行

Uji 有時

ukiyoe 浮世繪

ukiyo-zōshi 浮世草子

Umpo Zenjō 雲甫全祥

Ungan-ji 雲巖寺

Ungo-an 雲居庵

Ungo-ji 雲居寺

Ungo kiyō 雲居希膺

Unju-ji 雲樹寺

Unkoku-an 雲谷庵

unshin-jishin 渾身似信
unsui 雲水
Unshū 雲舟
uro 有漏
ushin 有心

wabi 佗び
waka 和歌
wa-kei-sei-jaku 和敬清寂
Wang Hsi-chih (Ō Gishi) 王義之
Wang Hsien-chih (Ō Kenshi) 王獻之
Wan-nien-ssu, see Mannenji
Wanshi-ha 宏智派
Wan-shou ch'an-ssu, see Manjuzen-ji
wayō 和様
wen-tzu, see monji
Wu-an P'u-ning (Gottan Funei) 兀菴普寧
Wu-chi Liao-p'ai 無際之派
Wu-hsüeh Tsu-yüan (Mugaku Sogen) 無學祖元
Wu-ming Hui-hsing 無明慧性
wu-shan, see gozan

Yabukōji 藪柑子
yabusame 流鏑馬
Yagyū Tajima no Kami Munenori 柳生但馬守宗矩
Yagyū Tajima no Kami Muneyoshi 柳生但馬守宗嚴
Yakuō Tokken 約翁德儉
yakuseki 藥石
Yamaga Sokō 山鹿素行
Yamamba 山姥
Yamamoto Tsunetomo 山本常朝
Yamanoue no Sōji-ki 山上宗二記
Yamanoue Sōji 山上宗二
yamato-e 大和畫

Yamazaki Kaiei 山崎快英
Yaran s. Yeh-lan
Yasen Kanna 夜船閑話
Yeh-lan (Yaran) 也嬾
Yen-kuan Ch'i-an 鹽官齊安
Yin-yüan Lung-ch'i (Ingen Ryūki) 隱元隆琦
yōji 楊枝
Yōjōbō 葉上房
Yōjō (ryū) 葉上（流）
Yōjō taimitsu 葉上台密
Yōkō-ji (Kyoto) 永興寺
Yōkō-ji (Noto) 永光寺
yokushitsu 浴室
Yoshino kikō 芳野紀行
Yōshō-an 陽松庵
Yoshokugo 預囑語
Yōshun-an 陽春庵
Yōsō Sōi 養叟宗頤
Yōtaku-ji 永澤寺
Yüeh-shan Hung-tao 藥山弘道
yūgen 幽玄
yuibutsu yobutsu 唯佛與佛
Yuien 唯圓
yuikai 遺誡
Yuri Tekisui 由利滴水
Yūzen, see Hsiao-jan

Zazengi 坐禪儀
Zazenron 坐禪論
zazen-seki 坐禪石
Zazenshin 坐禪箴
Zazen wasan 坐禪和讚
Zazen yōjinki 坐禪用心記
Zeami Motokiyo 世阿彌元清
ze-busshō 是佛性
Zekkai Chūshin 絶海中津
zen-cha ichi-mi 禪茶一味
Zen-in 禪院

Zen'ebō Shōkū 善慧房證空

Zenjō-ji 禪定寺

Zenkai ichiran 禪海一瀾

Zenki 全機

zenkizu 禪機圖

Zenkō-ji 禪興寺

zenkyō itchi 禪教一致

Zennō-ji 善應寺

Zen'on shingi (Ch'an-yüan ch'ing-kuei)
    禪苑清規

zenrin 禪林

Zenrin-ji 禪林寺

Zenrin kushū 禪林句集

zenritsugata 禪律方

zenritsugata tōnin 禪律方頭人

Zensō-ji 禪叢寺

Zōsan Junkū 藏山順空

Zōsō Rōyo 藏叟朗譽

zōsu 藏主

Zuikei Shūhō 瑞谿周鳳

Zuimonki, see Shōbōgenzō zuimonki

Zuiō-ji 隨鷗寺

Zuiryū-ji 瑞龍寺

Zuiryū-ji Tetsugen Zenji kanaji hōgo
    瑞龍寺鐵眼禪師假名字法語

Zuiryū Kaisan Tetsugen Oshō gyōjitsu
    瑞龍開山鐵眼和尚行實

Zuisen-ji 瑞泉寺

Appendix 4
Genealogical Tables

Table I.   Planting of the Rinzai school in Japan

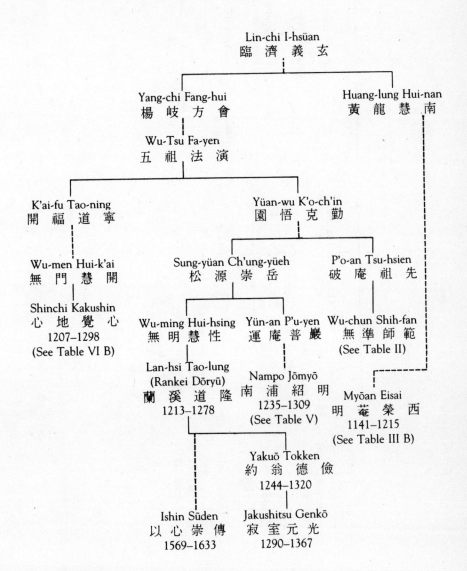

Table II.   The Beginnings of the Gozan movement

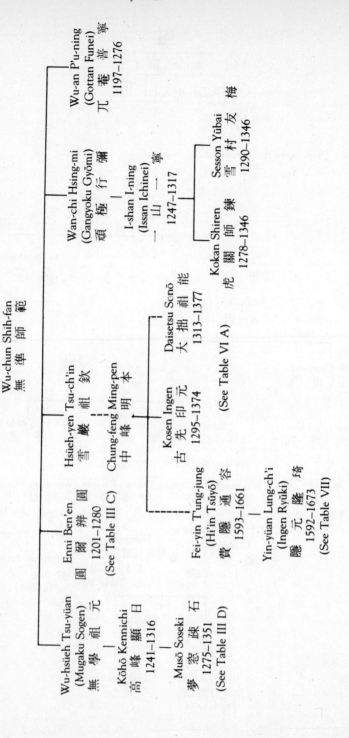

Table III.   Zen Lines of the Early Period

A.   Japanese Bodhidharma School

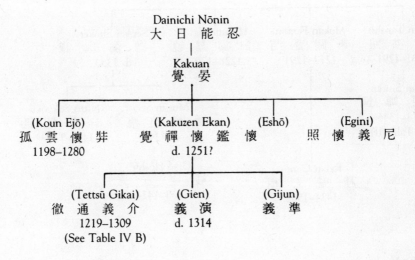

Dainichi Nōnin
大 日 能 忍

Kakuan
覺 晏

(Koun Ejō) 孤 雲 懷 弉 1198–1280

(Kakuzen Ekan) 覺 禪 懷 鑑 懷 d. 1251?

(Eshō) 照 懷

(Egini) 義 尼

(Tettsū Gikai) 徹 通 義 介 1219–1309 (See Table IV B)

(Gien) 義 演 d. 1314

(Gijun) 義 準

B. The Disciples of Myōan Eisai

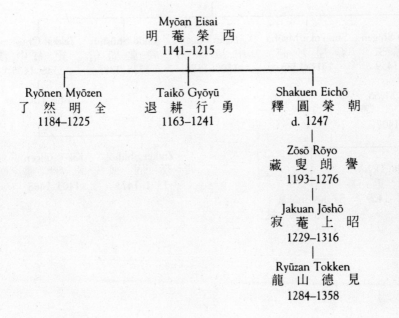

Myōan Eisai
明 菴 榮 西
1141–1215

Ryōnen Myōzen 了 然 明 全 1184–1225

Taikō Gyōyū 退 耕 行 勇 1163–1241

Shakuen Eichō 釋 圓 榮 朝 d. 1247

Zōsō Rōyo 藏 叟 朗 譽 1193–1276

Jakuan Jōshō 寂 菴 上 昭 1229–1316

Ryūzan Tokken 龍 山 德 見 1284–1358

C. The Shōichi Line

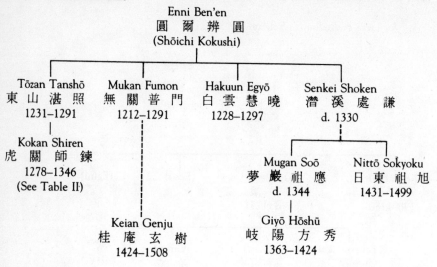

Enni Ben'en
圓 爾 辨 圓
(Shōichi Kokushi)

Tōzan Tanshō
東 山 湛 照
1231–1291

Kokan Shiren
虎 關 師 鍊
1278–1346
(See Table II)

Mukan Fumon
無 關 普 門
1212–1291

Keian Genju
桂 庵 玄 樹
1424–1508

Hakuun Egyō
白 雲 慧 曉
1228–1297

Senkei Shoken
潛 溪 處 謙
d. 1330

Mugan Soō
夢 巖 祖 應
d. 1344

Giyō Hōshū
岐 陽 方 秀
1363–1424

Nittō Sokyoku
日 東 祖 旭
1431–1499

D. The Musō-Line

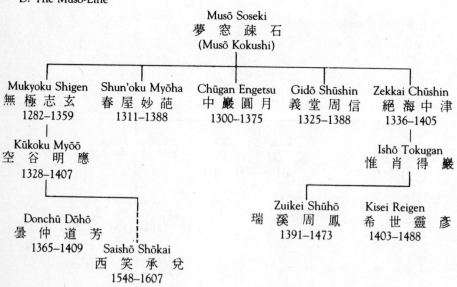

Musō Soseki
夢 窓 疎 石
(Musō Kokushi)

Mukyoku Shigen
無 極 志 玄
1282–1359

Kūkoku Myōō
空 谷 明 應
1328–1407

Donchū Dōhō
曇 仲 道 芳
1365–1409

Shun'oku Myōha
春 屋 妙 葩
1311–1388

Saishō Shōkai
西 笑 承 兌
1548–1607

Chūgan Engetsu
中 巖 圓 月
1300–1375

Gidō Shūshin
義 堂 周 信
1325–1388

Zekkai Chūshin
絕 海 中 津
1336–1405

Ishō Tokugan
惟 肖 得 巖

Zuikei Shūhō
瑞 溪 周 鳳
1391–1473

Kisei Reigen
希 世 靈 彥
1403–1488

Table IV.   Dōgen and his School

A.   Beginnings

B.   Dōgen and his Disciples

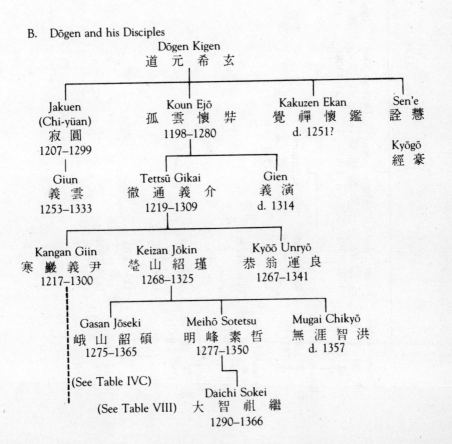

C. The Gasan Line

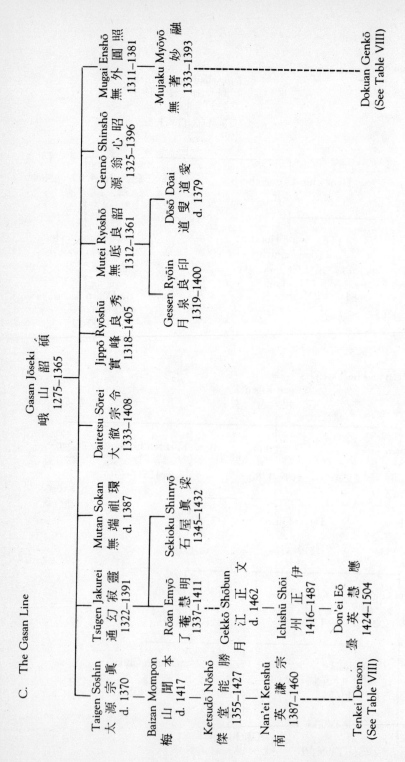

Gasan Jōseki
峨 山 韶 碩
1275–1365

Taigen Sōshin
大 源 宗 眞
d. 1370

Tsūgen Jakurei
通 幻 寂 靈
1322–1391

Baizan Mompon
梅 山 聞 本
d. 1417

Rōan Emyō
了 菴 慧 明
1337–1411

Ketsudō Nōshō
傑 堂 能 勝
1355–1427

Gekkō Shōbun
月 江 正 文
d. 1462

Nan'ei Kenshū
南 英 謙 宗
1387–1460

Ichishū Shōi
州 正 伊
1416–1487

Don'ei Eō
曇 英 慧 應
1424–1504

Tenkei Denson
(See Table VIII)

Mutan Sokan
無 端 祖 環
d. 1387

Sekioku Shinryō
石 屋 眞 梁
1345–1432

Daitetsu Sōrei
大 徹 宗 令
1333–1408

Jippō Ryōshū
實 峰 良 秀
1318–1405

Gessen Ryōin
月 泉 良 印
1319–1400

Mutei Ryōshō
無 底 良 韶
1312–1361

Dōsō Dōai
道 叟 道 愛
d. 1379

Gennō Shinshō
源 翁 心 昭
1325–1396

Mugai Enshō
無 外 圓 照
1311–1381

Mujaku Myōyō
無 著 妙 融
1333–1393

Dokuan Genkō
(See Table VIII)

Table V.   The Main Lines of the Rinzai School

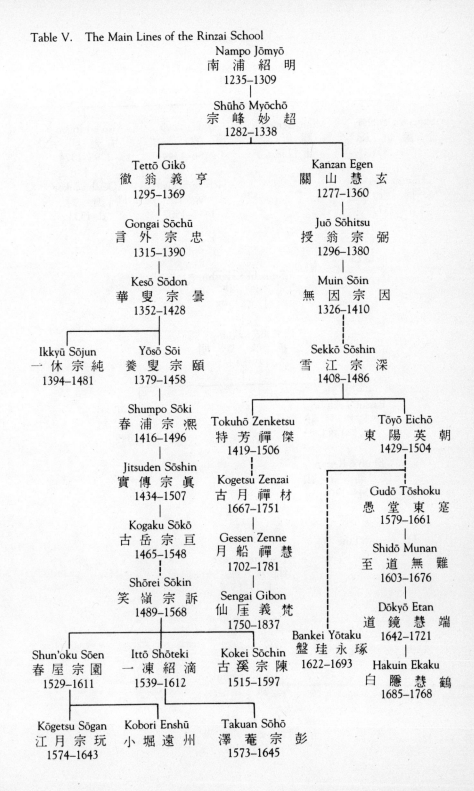

Nampo Jōmyō
南 浦 紹 明
1235–1309

Shūhō Myōchō
宗 峰 妙 超
1282–1338

Tettō Gikō
徹 翁 義 亨
1295–1369

Kanzan Egen
關 山 慧 玄
1277–1360

Gongai Sōchū
言 外 宗 忠
1315–1390

Juō Sōhitsu
授 翁 宗 弼
1296–1380

Kesō Sōdon
華 叟 宗 曇
1352–1428

Muin Sōin
無 因 宗 因
1326–1410

Ikkyū Sōjun
一 休 宗 純
1394–1481

Yōsō Sōi
養 叟 宗 頤
1379–1458

Sekkō Sōshin
雪 江 宗 深
1408–1486

Shumpo Sōki
春 浦 宗 熙
1416–1496

Tokuhō Zenketsu
特 芳 禪 傑
1419–1506

Tōyō Eichō
東 陽 英 朝
1429–1504

Jitsuden Sōshin
實 傳 宗 眞
1434–1507

Kogetsu Zenzai
古 月 禪 材
1667–1751

Gudō Tōshoku
愚 堂 東 寔
1579–1661

Kogaku Sōkō
古 岳 宗 亘
1465–1548

Gessen Zenne
月 船 禪 慧
1702–1781

Shidō Munan
至 道 無 難
1603–1676

Shōrei Sōkin
笑 嶺 宗 訴
1489–1568

Sengai Gibon
仙 厓 義 梵
1750–1837

Dōkyō Etan
道 鏡 慧 端
1642–1721

Bankei Yōtaku
盤 珪 永 琢
1622–1693

Shun'oku Sōen
春 屋 宗 園
1529–1611

Ittō Shōteki
一 凍 紹 滴
1539–1612

Kokei Sōchin
古 溪 宗 陳
1515–1597

Hakuin Ekaku
白 隱 慧 鶴
1685–1768

Kōgetsu Sōgan
江 月 宗 玩
1574–1643

Kobori Enshū
小 堀 遠 州

Takuan Sōhō
澤 菴 宗 彭
1573–1645

Table VI.   The Collateral Lines of Rinzai Zen
A.   The Genjū Line

(Chung-feng Ming-pen)
中 峰 明 本

Sengan Genchō 千 巖 元 長 1284–1357	Muin Genkai 無 隱 元 晦 d. 1358	Onkei Soyū 遠 溪 祖 雄 1286–1344	Kosen Ingen 古 先 印 元 1295–1374
Daisetsu Sonō 大 拙 祖 能 1313–1377		Ichige Sekiyu 一 華 碩 由 1441–1507	Gesshū Jukei 月 舟 壽 桂 d. 1333

B.   The Hottō Line

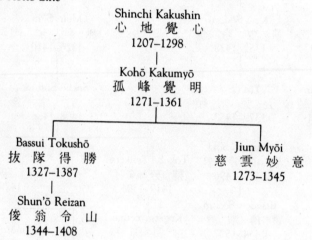

Shinchi Kakushin
心 地 覺 心
1207–1298

Kohō Kakumyō
孤 峰 覺 明
1271–1361

Bassui Tokushō 拔 隊 得 勝 1327–1387	Jiun Myōi 慈 雲 妙 意 1273–1345
Shun'ō Reizan 俊 翁 令 山 1344–1408	

C.   The Gettan Line

Nampo Jōmyō
南 浦 紹 明
1235–1309

Hōō Soichi
峰 翁 祖 一
1274–1357

Daichū Sōshin
大 蟲 宗 岑

Gettan Sōkō
月 菴 宗 光
1326–1389

D.   The Sekkō Line

Sekkō Sōshin
雪 江 宗 深
1408–1486

Keisen Sōryū
景 川 宗 隆
1426–1500

Gokei Sōton
悟 溪 宗 頓
1416–1500

Tokuhō Zenketsu
特 芳 禪 傑
1419–1506

Tōyō Eichō
東 陽 英 朝
1429–1504
(See Table V)

Tenshō Sōju
天 縱 宗 受
d. 1512

Daikyū Sōkyū
大 休 宗 休
1468–1549

Daichū Sōshin·
大 蟲 宗 岑
1512–1599

Mujaku Dōchū
無 著 道 忠
1653–1744

·A master of the same name appears in Table VI C.

Table VII.   The Ōbaku School

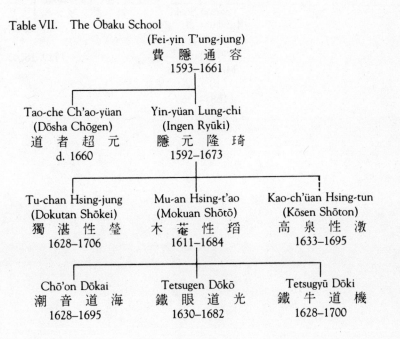

(Fei-yin T'ung-jung)
費 隱 通 容
1593–1661

Tao-che Ch'ao-yüan
(Dōsha Chōgen)
道 者 超 元
d. 1660

Yin-yüan Lung-chi
(Ingen Ryūki)
隱 元 隆 琦
1592–1673

Tu-chan Hsing-jung
(Dokutan Shōkei)
獨 湛 性 瑩
1628–1706

Mu-an Hsing-t'ao
(Mokuan Shōtō)
木 菴 性 瑫
1611–1684

Kao-ch'üan Hsing-tun
(Kōsen Shōton)
高 泉 性 激
1633–1695

Chō'on Dōkai
潮 音 道 海
1628–1695

Tetsugen Dōkō
鐵 眼 道 光
1630–1682

Tetsugyū Dōki
鐵 牛 道 機
1628–1700

Table VIII.   The Sōtō School in Modern Times

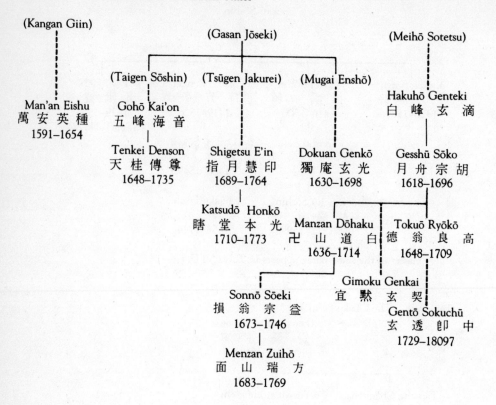

Table IX.   The Line of Hakuin

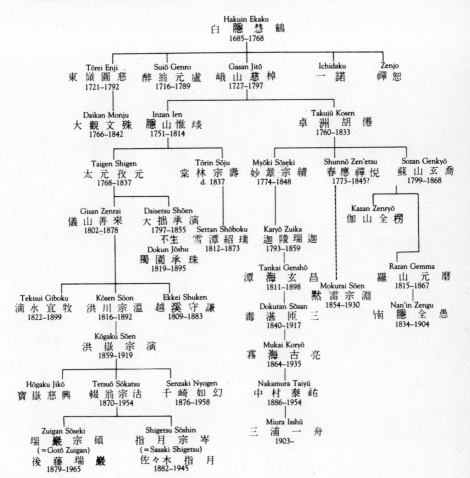

Bibliography

CHINESE AND JAPANESE SOURCES

TEXTUAL COLLECTIONS

Dainihon kōtei zōkyō 大日本校訂藏經 *(Manji daizōkyō)* 卍字大藏經 36 cases. Kyoto, 1902–1905.

Dainihon zokuzōkyō 大日本續藏經. 750 vols. in 150 cases. Kyoto, 1905–1912. [Abbreviated in text and below as Z.]

Nihon no zen-goroku 日本の禪語錄. 20 vols. Tokyo, 1977–78.

Taishō shinshū daizōkyō 大正新修大藏經. 85 vols. Tokyo, 1924–1932. [Abbreviated in text and below as T.]

Zenmon hōgoshū 禪門法語集. 3 vols. Tokyo, 1977.

Zenmon sōtōshū hōgozenshū 禪門曹洞宗法語全集. 2 vols. Tokyo, 1978.

Zen no goroku 禪の語錄. 19 vols. to date. Tokyo, 1969–.

WORKS IN THE BUDDHIST CANON

[For the reader's convenience, the Japanese reading of the title of each Chinese text cited in this section appears in parentheses immediately following the Chinese title.]

Ch'an-men shih-tzu ch'eng-hsi-t'u (Zenmon shishi shōshūzu) 禪門師資承襲圖. Z.2:15,5.

Ch'an-yüan chu-ch'üan-chi tu-hsü (Zengen shosenshū tojo) 禪源諸詮集都序. T.2015, vol. 48.

Ch'uan-fa cheng-tsung chi (Dembō shōshūki) 傳法正宗記. T.2078, vol. 51.

Ch'uan fa-pao chi (Den hōbōki) 傳法寶紀. T.2838, vol. 85.

Chao-che liu-men (Shōshitsu rokumon) 小室六門. T.2009, vol. 48.

Chao-lun (Jōron) 肇論. T.1858, vol. 45.

Cheng-tao-ko (Shōdōka) 證道歌 T.2014, vol. 48

Chia-t'ai pu-teng lu (Katai futōroku) 嘉泰普燈錄 Z.2B:10, 1–2.

Chien-chung ching-kuo hsü-teng lu (Kenchū seikoku zokutōroku) 建中靖國續燈錄. Z.2B:9, 1–2.

Chin-kang ching (Kongōkyō) 金剛經. T.235, vol. 8.

Ching-te ch'uan-teng lu (Keitoku dentōroku) 景德傳燈錄. T.2976, vol. 51.

Chung-feng Ho-shang kuang-lu (Chūhō Oshō kōroku) 中峰和尚廣錄. *Dainihon kōtei zōkyō*, vol. 31.

Daikaku Zenji goroku 大覺禪師語錄. T.2547, vol. 80.

Daikan shingi 大鑑清規. T.2577, vol. 81.

Daitō Kokushi goroku 大燈國師語錄. T.2566, vol. 81.

Denkōroku 傳光錄. T.2585, vol. 82.

Eihei shingi 永平清規. T.2584, vol. 82.

Fen-yang Wu-te Ch'an-shih yü-lu (Fun'yō Mutoku Zenji goroku) 汾陽無德禪師語錄 T.1992, vol. 47.

Fu-chou Ts'ao-shan Pen-chi Ch'an-shih yü-lu (Bushū Sōzan Honjaku Zenji goroku) 撫州曹山本寂禪師語錄 . T.1987B, vol. 47.

Fukanzazengi 普勸坐禪儀 . T.2580, vol. 82.

Fushō Kokushi goroku 普照國師語錄 . T.2605, vol. 82.

Fushō Kokushi hōgo 普照國師法語 . T2606, vol. 82.

Gakudōyōjinshū 學道用心集 . T2581, vol. 82.

Giun Oshō goroku 義雲和尚語錄. T.2591, vol.82.

Goke sanshōyōromon 五家參詳要路門 . T.2576, vol. 81.

Hsin-hsin-ming (Shinjinmei) 信心銘 . T.2010, vol. 48.

Hsü kao-seng chuan (Zoku kōsōden) 續高僧傳 . T.2060, vol. 50.

Hsü-t'ang Ho-shang yü-lu (Kidō Oshō goroku) 虛堂和尚語錄 . T.2000, vol. 47.

Hung-chih Ch'an-shih kuang-lu (Wanshi Zenji kōroku) 宏智禪師廣錄 . T.2001, vol. 48.

Jen-t'ien yen-mu (Ninden gammoku) 人天眼目 . T.2006, vol. 48.

Ju-ching Ho-shang yü-lu (Nyojō Oshō goroku) 如淨和尚語錄 . T.2002A, vol. 48.

Kaian kokugo 槐安國語 . T.2574, vol. 81.

Kao-seng chuan (Kōsōden) 高僧傳. T.2059, vol. 50.

Keizan shingi 瑩山清規 . T2589, vol. 82.

Ku-tsun-su yü-lu (Kosonshuku goroku) 古尊宿語錄 . Z.2:24,1.

Kuei-shan Ling-yu Ch'an-shih yü-lu (Isan Reiyū Zenji goroku) 潙山靈祐禪師語錄 . T.1989, vol. 47.

Kōmyōzō sammai 光明藏三昧 . T.2590, vol. 82.

Kōzen gokokuron 興禪護國論 . T.2543, vol. 80.

Le-tao ko (Rakudōka) 樂道歌 . In *Ching-te ch'uan-teng lu*, T.51.461c–462a.

Leng-ch'ieh ching (Ryōgakyō) 楞伽經 . T.670, vol. 16.

Leng-ch'ieh shih-tzu chi (Ryōga shijiki) 楞伽師資記 . T.2837, vol. 85.

Li-tai fa-pao chi (Rekidai hōbōki) 歷代法寶記 . T.2075, vol. 51.

Lin-chi lu (Rinzairoku) 臨濟錄 . T.1958, vol. 47.

Liu-tsu t'an ching (Rokuso dankyō) 六祖壇經 . T.2007, vol. 48.

Lo-yang ch'ieh-lan chi (Rakuyō garanki) 洛陽伽藍記 . T.2092, vol. 51.

Musō Kokushi goroku 夢窓國師語錄 . T.2555, vol. 80.

Ōbaku shingi 黃檗清規 . T.2607, vol. 82.

Pai-chang ch'ing-kuei (Hyakujō shingi) 百丈清規 . T.2025, vol. 48.

Pai-chang kuang-lu (Hyakujo kōroku) 百丈廣錄 . In *Ssu-chia yü-lu*.

P'ang Chü-shih yü-lu (Hō Koji goroku) 龐居士語錄 . Z.2B:25,1.

Pao-ching san-mei ko (Hōkyō zammai-ka) 寶鏡三昧歌. In *Tung-shan Wu-pen Ch'an-shih yü-lu*, T.47.515.

Pi-yen lu (Hekiganroku) 碧巖錄 . T.2003, vol. 48.

Shinjinmei nentei 信心銘拈提 . T.2587, vol. 82.

Shōbōgenzō 正法眼藏 . T.2582, vol. 82.

Shōichi Kokushi goroku 聖一國師語錄 . T.2544, vol. 80.

Shou-leng-yen ching (Shuryōgongyō) 首楞嚴經 . T.945, vol. 19.

Ssu-chia yü-lu (Shike goroku) 四家語錄 . Z.2:24,5.

Sung kao-seng chuan (Sō kōsōden) 宋高僧傳. T.2061, vol. 50.

Ta-an-pan shou-i ching (Daiampanshuikyō) 大安般守意經 . T.602, vol. 15.

Ta-fang-kuang-fo hua-yen ching (Daihō kōbutsu kegongyō) 大方廣佛華嚴經. T.278, vol. 9 (Buddhabhadra, trans.); T.279, vol. 10 (Śikṣānanda, trans.); T.293, vol. 10 (Prajñā, trans.)

Ta-hui Ch'an-shih yü-lu (Daie Zenji goroku) 大慧禪師語錄. T.1998A, vol. 47.

Ta-pan nieh-p'an ching (Daihatsu nehangyō) 大般涅槃經. T.374–378, vol. 12.

Ta-sheng ch'i-hsin lun (Daijō kishinron) 大乘起信論. T.1666, vol. 32.

Ta-sheng ta-i-chang (Daijō daigishō) 大乘大義章. T.1856, vol. 45.

T'ien-sheng kuang-teng lu (Tenshō kōtōroku) 天聖廣燈錄. Z.2B:,8, 4–5.

Ts'an-t'ung-ch'i (Sandōkai) 參同契. In *Ching-te ch'uan-teng lu*, T.51.459b.

Ts'ao-shan Yüan-cheng Ch'an-shih yü-lu (Sōzan Ganshō Zenji goroku) 曹山元證禪師語錄. T.1987A, vol. 42.

Tsu-t'ing shih-yüan (Sotei jion) 祖庭事苑. Z.2:18,1.

Tsui-shang-sheng lun (Saijōjōron) 最上乘論. T.2011, vol. 48.

Tsung-ching lu (Shūkyōroku) 宗鏡錄. T.2016, vol. 48.

Ts'ung-jung lu (Shōyōroku) 從容錄. T.2004, vol. 48.

Tsung-men lien-teng hui-yao (Shūmon rentō eyō) 宗門聯燈會要. Z.2B:9,3–5.

Tsung-men shih-kuei lun (Shūmon jikkiron) 宗門十規論. Z.2:15.

Tung-shan Wu-pen Ch'an-shih yü-lu (Tōzan Gohon Zenji goroku) 洞山悟本禪師語錄. T.1986A, vol. 47.

Wei-mo ching (Yuimakyō) 維摩經. T.475, vol. 14.

Wu-chia cheng-tsung tsan (Goke shōjūsan) 五家正宗贊. Z.2B:8,5.

Wu-men kuan (Mumonkan) 無門關. T.2005, vol. 48.

Wu-teng hui-yüan (Gotō egen) 五燈會元. Z.2B:10,5

Wu-teng yen-t'ung (Gotō gentō) 五燈嚴統. Z.2B:12,1–5.

Wu-tsu Fa-yen Ch'an-shih yü-lu (Goso Hōen Zenji goroku) 五祖法演禪師語錄. T.1995, vol. 47.

Yüan-chüeh ching (Engakukyō) 圓覺經. T.842, vol. 17.

Yüan-chüeh ching ta-shu ch'ao (Engakukyō daishoshō) 圓覺經大疏鈔. Z.1:14,3–5;15,1.

Yüan-jen lun (Genninron) 原人論. T.1886, vol. 45.

Yün-men K'uang-chen Ch'an-shih kuang-lu (Ummon Kyōshin Zenji kōroku) 雲門匡眞禪師廣錄. T.1988, vol. 47.

Zazenyōjinki 坐禪用心記. T.2586, vol. 82.

OTHER SELECTED PRIMARY SOURCES

Bankei Zenji goroku 盤珪禪師語錄. Suzuki Daisetsu 鈴木大拙 ed. Tokyo, 1941.

Bankei Zenji hōgoshū 盤珪禪師法語集. Fujimoto Tsuchishige 藤本槌重, ed. Tokyo, 1971.

Bankei Zenji itsuwashū 盤珪禪師逸話集. Akao Ryōji 赤尾龍治, ed. 2 vols. Tokyo, 1975.

Chao-lun 肇論. *Jōron kenkyū* 肇論研究. Tsukamoto Zenryū 塚本善隆, ed. Kyoto, 1955.

Denkōroku (Kanchū denkōroku) 冠註傳光錄. Komine Chisan 孤峰智粲, ed. Tokyo, 1934; reprint, 1937.

Kenseiki 建撕記. *Sōtōshū zensho* 曹洞宗全帅, vol. 17. Tokyo, 1929.

Kōzen gokokuron 興禪護國論. In *Chūsei zenka no shisō* 中世禪家の思想, vol 16 of *shisō taikei* 日本思想大系 Yanagida Seizan 柳田聖山, ed. Tokyo, 1972.

Lin-chi lu. Rinzairoku 臨濟錄. Yanagida Seizan, ed. *Butten kōza* 佛典講座, vol. 30. Tokyo, 1972.

Muchū mondo 夢中問答. *Zengaku taikei* 禅学大系: *sorokubu* 祖録部, vol. 4. Tokyo, 1910; reprint, 1977.

Musō Kokushi nempu 夢窓國師年譜 (*Musō Shōgaku nempu* 夢窓正覺年譜). *Zoku gunshoruiju* 續群書類聚, vol. 9b. Tokyo, 1905; reprint, 1957.

Pao-lin chuan. Hōrinden 寶林傳. Yanagida Seizan, ed. (combined edition with the *Ch'uan-teng yü-ying chi* [*Dentōgyokueishū* 傳燈玉英集]). Kyoto, 1975.

Pi-yen lu 碧巖錄. *Hekiganroku daikōza* 碧巖錄大講座, vols 1–12. Katō Totsudō ed. Tokyo, 1939–1940.

Sōkei Daishi betsuden 曹溪大師別傳. In *Enō kenkyū* (see below).

Tsu-t'ang chi. Sodōshū 祖堂集. Yanagida Seizan, ed. Kyoto, 1974.

Wu-chia yü-lu. Goke goroku 五家語錄. Yanagida Seizan, ed. Kyoto, 1974. Edited from the MS in Komazawa University.

Wu-men kuan. Mumonkan 無門關. Edited with commentary by Hirata Kōji 平田高士. *Zen no goroku*, vol. 18. Tokyo, 1969.

———. *Hekiganroku daizōka*, vols. 13–15. Katō Totsudō, ed. Tokyo, 1940.

COMPLETE WORKS OF SELECTED ZEN MASTERS

Bankei Zenji zenshū 盤珪禪師全集. Akao Ryōji, ed. Tokyo, 1976.

Dōgen Zenji zenshū 道元禪師全集. Ōkubo Dōshū 大久保道舟, ed. 2 vols. Tokyo, 1969–1976. Includes the following works:

    Eihei kōroku 永平廣錄 (also, *Dōgen Oshō kōroku* 道元和尚廣錄)

    Eihei shitsuchū monjo 永平室中聞書

    Eihei shoso gakudōyōjinshū 永平初祖學道用心集

    Shōbōgenzō **正法眼藏**

    Shōbōgenzō sambyakusoku 正法眼藏三百則

    Shōbōgenzō zuimonki 正法眼藏隨聞記

    Tenzo kyōkun 典座敎訓

Hakuin Oshō zenshū 白隱和尚全集. Gotō Kōson 後藤光村, ed. 8 vols. Tokyo, 1934–1935.

Hakuin Zenji-shū 白隱禪師集. Tokiwa Daijō 常盤大定, ed. Tokyo, 1938.

Ryōkan zenshū 良寛全集. Ōtsuka Kasoku 大塚花束, ed. Tokyo, 1924.

Shidō Munan Zenji-shū 至道無難禪師集. Kōda Rentarō 公田連太郎. Tokyo, 1968.

Shōju Rōjin-shū 正受老人集. Shinano Kyōikukai. 1937; reprint, Tokyo, 1975.

Suzuki Shōsan Dōnin zenshū 鈴木正三道人全集. Suzuki Tesshin 鈴木鉄心, ed. Tokyo, 1962.

Takuan Oshō zenshū 澤菴和尚全集. Takuan Oshō Zenshū Kankōkai, ed. 6 vols. Tokyo, 1928–1930.

ENCYCLOPEDIAS AND LEXICONS

Bukkyōgo daijiten 佛教語大辭典. Nakamura Hajime 中村 元 , ed. 3 vols. Tokyo, 1966–1968.

Bussho kaisetsu daijiten 佛書解説大辭典. Ono Gemmyō, 小野玄妙, ed. 12 vols. Tokyo, 1932–1936

Chūgoku gakugei daijiten 中国学芸大事典. Kondō Haruo 近藤春雄, ed. Tokyo, 1978.

Konsaisu bukkyō jiten コンサイス佛教辭典. Ui Hakuju 宇井伯壽, ed. Tokyo, 1938.

Kan-wa shin daijiten 漢和新大辭典. Haga Gōtarō 芳架剛太郎 , ed. Tokyo, 1934.

Bukkyō daijiten 佛教大辭典. Mochizuki Shinkō 望月信亨 , ed. Rev. ed. 10 vols. Tokyo, 1958–1963.

Nihon kokugo daijiten 日本国語大辞典. 20 vols. Tokyo, 1973–1976.

Répetoire du Canon Bouddhique Sino-Japonais: Fascicule Annexe due Hōbōgirin 大正大藏經總索引一法寶義林. Paul Démieville, editor in chief. Tokyo, 1931; rev. ed., 1978.

Shin bukkyō jiten 新佛教辭典. Nakamura Hajime, ed. Tokyo, 1962.

Zengaku daijiten 禪學大辭典. Komazawa University, eds. 3 vols. Tokyo, 1978.

Zengaku jiten 禪學辭典. Jimbō Nyoten, ed. Kyoto, 1944.

Zenrin meiku jiten 禪林名句辭典. Iida Rigyō, ed. Tokyo, 1975.

SECONDARY SOURCES: GENERAL STUDIES

Araki Kengo 荒木見悟. *Bukkyō to jukyō* 佛教と儒教. Kyoto, 1976.

Ebizawa Arimichi 海老沢有道. *Kindai nippon bunka no tanjō* 近代日本文化の誕生. Tokyo, 1956.

Hisamatsu Sen'ichi 久松潜一. *Nihon bungaku hyōronshi* 日本文学評論史. 3 vols. Tokyo, 1936–1938.

Hisamatsu Shin'ichi, ed. *Gendai zen kōza* 現代禅講座. 6 vols. Tokyo, 1956.

Ienaga Saburō 家永三郎, Akamatsu Toshihide 赤松俊秀, Keishitsu Taisei 圭室諦成, eds. *Nihon bukkyōshi* 日本佛教史. 3 vols. Kyoto, 1967.

Kagamishima Genryū 鏡島元隆 and Tamaki Kōshirō 玉城康四郎, eds. *Kōza Dōgen* 講座道元. 7 vols. Tokyo, 1979–1981.

Komazawa University, eds. *Enō kenkyū* 慧能研究. Tokyo, 1978.

Nakamura Hajime. *Nihon shūkyō no kindaisei* 日本宗教の近代性. Tokyo, 1964.

———. *Kinsei nihon no hihanteki seishin* 近世日本の批判的精神. Tokyo, 1965.

Nishimura Eshin 西村恵信 and Nara Yasuaki, 奈良康明 eds. *Nihon bukkyō kisokōza* 日本仏教基礎講座. 7 vols. Tokyo, 1978–1980.

Sakaino Kōyō 境野黄洋. *Shina bukkyō seishi* 支那佛教精史. Tokyo, 1935.

Suzuki Daisetsu 鈴木大拙 and Nishitani Keiji 西谷啓治. *Kōza zen* 講座禅. 8 vols. Tokyo, 1967–1968.

Tokiwa Daijō 常盤大定. *Shina bukkyō no kenkyū* 支那佛教の研究. 3 vols. Tokyo, 1938–1943.

Tsuji Zennosuke 辻善之助. *Nihon bukkyōshi* 日本佛教史. 11 vols. Tokyo, 1944–1953.

Uehara Senroku 上原専禄, et al., eds. *Gendai bukkyō kōza* 現代佛教講座. 5 vols. Tokyo, 1955.

Ui Hakuju 宇井伯壽 *Indo tetsugakushi* 印度哲學史. Tokyo, 1935.

———. *Shina bukkyōshi* 支那佛教史. Tokyo, 1936.

SECONDARY SOURCES: MONOGRAPHIC STUDIES ON ZEN AND JAPANESE BUDDHISM

Akiyama Hanji 秋山範二. *Dōgen no kenkyū* 道元の研究. Tokyo, 1935.

Akizuki Ryōmin 秋月龍珉. *Dōgen nyūmon* 道元入門. Tokyo, 1970.

Daihonzan Eihei-ji 大本山永平寺 eds. *Ejō Zenji kenkyū* 懷奘禅師研究. Eihei, 1981.

Etō Sokuō 衛藤卽應. *Shūso to shite no Dōgen Zenji* 宗祖としての道元禪師. Tokyo, 1944.

Etō Tarō 江藤太郎. "Dōgen no tetsugaku to Haideggā [Heidegger] 道元の哲学とハイデッガー." *Risō* 理想 349 (June, 1962):1–11.

Furuta Shōkin 古田紹欽. *Nihon bukkyō shisōshi no shomondai* 日本仏教思想史の諸問題. Tokyo,1964.

———. *Zen shisōshiron—Nihon zen* 禅思想史論—日本禅. Tokyo, 1966.

———. *Zensō no shōji* 禅僧の生死. Tokyo, 1971.

———. *Furuta Shōkin chosakushū* 古田紹欽著作集. 14 vols. Tokyo, 1981.

———. *Nihon zenshūshi no nagare* 日本禅宗史の流れ. Kyoto, 1983.

———. *Kyūdō to fūga* 求道と風雅. Tokyo, 1984.

Fujimoto Tsuchishige 藤本槌重. *Bankei Kokushi no kenkyū* 盤珪国師の研究. Tokyo, 1971.

Habito, Ruben. "Busshinron no tenkai 仏身論の展開." SK 52 (1978):1–21.

Hayashi Taiun 林 岱雲. "Bodaidaruma-den no kenkyū 菩提達磨傳の研究." SK 9 (1932):444–458.

———. *Nihon zenshūshi* 日本禅宗史. Tokyo, 1977.

Hu Shih (Ko Teki) 胡 適. *Shina zengaku no hensen* 支那禪學の變遷 Tokyo, 1936.

Iida Rigyō 飯田利行, ed. *Ryōkan shishūyaku* 良寛詩集譯. Tokyo, 1969.

Imaeda Aishin 今枝愛真. *Zenshū no rekishi* 禅宗の歴史 Tokyo, 1966.

———. "Kamakura-zen no seiritsu 鎌倉禅の成立." In *Ajia bukkyōshi, Nihon-hen* アジア仏教史, vol. 4. Nakamura Hajime, Kasahara Kazuo 笠原一男, and Kanaoka Shūyū 金岡秀友 eds. Tokyo, 1969.

———. *Chūsei zenshūshi no kenkyū* 中世禅宗史の研究. Tokyo, 1970.

Kawamura Kōdō 河村孝道. "Shōbōgenzō kenkyū josetsu 正法眼蔵研究序説." *Komazawa Daigaku Bukkyōgakubu Kenkyū Kiyō* 23 (1965): 108–125;24 (1966): 52–72.

Kimura Taiken 木村泰賢. *Kimura Taiken zenshū* 木村泰賢全集. *Kimura Taiken Zenshū Kankō Iinkai*, ed. 6 vols. Tokyo, 1937–1939.

Kinomiya Yasuhiko 木宮泰彦. *Eisai Zenji* 栄西禅師. Tokyo, 1977.

Kusumoto Bun-yū 久須本文雄. *Sōdai jugaku no zen-shisō kenkyū* 宋代儒学の禅思想研究. Nagoya, 1980.

Masunaga Reiho 増永靈鳳. *Zenjō shisōshi* 禪定思想史. Tokyo, 1944.

———. *Eihei Shōbōgenzō—Dōgen no shūkyō* 永平正法眼藏—道元の宗敎. Tokyo, 1956.

Masutani Fumio 増谷文雄. *Rinzai to Dōgen* 臨済と道元. Tokyo, 1971.

Matsuda Bugyō 松田奉行. *Takuan* 沢庵. Tokyo, 1978.

Matsumoto Bunsaburō 松本文三郎. *Daruma no kenkyū* 達磨の研究. Tokyo, 1942.

Minakami Tsutomu 水上 勉. *Ryōkan* 良寛. Tokyo, 1984.

Nakamura Hajime中村 元. "Zen ni okeru seisan to kinrō no mondai 禅における生産と勤労の問題." ZB 1 (1955): 27–35;3 (1956):7–15.

Nakaseko Shōdō中世古祥道. *Dōgen Zenji-den kenkyū* 道元禅師伝研究. Tokyo, 1979.

Namimoto Sawaichi 浪本澤一. "Rinka no zensha jakushitsu genkō 林下の禅者寂室元光." *Daihōrin* 大法林 4(1982):60–65.

Naoki Kimihiko直木公彦. *Hakuin Zenji—kenkōhō to itsuwa*白隠禅師―健康法と逸話. Tokyo, 1975.

Nishi Yoshio 西 義雄 ed. *Daijō bosatsudō no kenkyū* 大乗菩薩道の研究. Kyoto, 1968.

Nukariya Kaiten忽滑谷快天. *Zengaku shisōshi* 禪學思想史. Tokyo, 1923.

Ōkubo Dōshū大久保道舟. *Dōgen Zenji-den no kenkyū* 道元禪師傳の研究. Tokyo, 1966.

Ōmori Sōgen大森曹玄. *Ken to zen* 剣と禅. Tokyo, 1977.

Rikugawa Taiun 陸川堆雲. *Kōshō Hakuin Oshō shōden* 考証白隠和尚詳伝. Tokyo, 1963.

Rinoie Masafumi李家正文. *Ōbaku sanketsu egoku Dōmyō Zenji-den* 黄檗三傑慧極道明禅師伝. Tokyo, 1981.

Sakurai Yoshirō桜井好朗and Fukuma Kōchō 福間光超, eds. *Ikkyū, Rennyo* 一休・蓮如. *Nihon meisō ronshū*日本名僧論集, vol. 10. Tokyo, 1983.

Sugawara Tōzen菅原洞禅. *Nihon zenmon iketsu-den*日本禅門偉傑伝. Tokyo, 1977.

Suzuki Daisetsu. *Suzuki Daisetsu zenshū* 鈴木大拙全集. Hisamatsu Shin'ichi, et al., eds. 32 vols. Tokyo, 1968–1970.

Takemura Makio竹村牧男. *Ryōkan no shi to Dōgen-zen*良寛の詩と道元禅. Tokyo, 1978.

Takeuchi Michio竹内道雄. *Sōtōshū kyōdanshi* 曹洞宗教団史. Tokyo, 1971.

———. *Nihon no zen*日本の禅. Tokyo, 1976.

———. *Koun Ejō Zenji-den* 孤雲懷奘禅師伝. Tokyo, 1982.

Tanabe Hajime 田邊 元. *Shōbōgenzō no tetsugaku shikan* 正法眼藏の哲學私觀. *Tanabe Hajime zenshū* vol. 5. Nishitani Keiji, et al., eds. Tokyo, 1963, pp. 443–94.

Tamamura Takeji玉村竹二. *Musō Kokushi* 夢窓國師. Tokyo, 1958.

———. "Shoki Myōshinji-shi no ni-san giten 初期妙心寺史の二三疑点" *Nihon zenshūshi ronshū*日本禅宗史論集, vol. 2.2 Kyoto, 1981, pp. 267–306.

Ui Hakuju宇井伯壽. *Zenshūshi kenkyū* 禪宗史研究. 3 vols. Tokyo, 1939–1943.

Watsuji Tetsurō 和辻哲郎. "Shamon Dōgen 沙門道元." *Watsuji Tetsurō-shū* 和辻哲郎集. Tokyo, 1974, pp. 3–69.

Yamanouchi Chōzō山内長三. *Hakuin san no eseppō*白隠さんの絵説法. Tokyo, 1984.

Yanagida Seizan柳田聖山. *Shoki zenshūshisho no kenkyū* 初期禅宗史書の研究. Kyoto, 1967.

———. *Rinzai no kafū* 臨済の家風. Tokyo, 1967.

———. "Dōgen to Rinzai 道元と臨済." *Risō* 513(Feb., 1976): 74–89.

———. "Shinzoku chōshi no keifu 新続灯史の系譜." *Zengaku kenkyū* 禅学研究59 (Nov., 1978): 1–39.

———. *Ikkyū—Kyōunshū no sekai* 一休―「狂雲集」の世界. Kyoto, 1980.

Yokoyama Hideya横山秀哉. "Zenshū no shichi dō garan 禪宗の七堂伽藍." ZB 2.4(1956): 40–45.

Zenbunka 禅文化. *Meiji no zenjō* 明治の禅匠. Kyoto, 1981.

MISCELLANEOUS WORKS

Bashō kōza 芭蕉講座. 9 vols. Tokyo, 1944–1951.

Horiguchi Sutemi 堀口捨巳. *Rikyū no cha* 利休の茶. Tokyo, 1978.

Iwata Kurō 岩田九郎. *Bashō no haiku, haibun* 芭蕉の俳句・俳文. Tokyo, 1966.

Komiya Toyotaka 小宮豊隆, ed. *Kōhon Bashō zenshū* 校本芭蕉全集. 10 vols. Tokyo, 1962–1969.

Nishimura Tei 西村貞. *Kirishitan to chadō* キリシタンと茶道. Kyoto, 1948.

Ōmori Sōgen 大森曹玄 and Terayama Katsujō 寺山葛常. *Tesshū to shodō* 鐵舟と書道. Tokyo, 1979.

Satō En 佐藤圓. *Bashō to bukkyō* 芭蕉と仏教. Tokyo, 1969.

Terayama Katsujō. *Sanshū oyobi nanshū no sho* 三舟及び南洲の書. Tokyo, 1982.

Terayama Tanchū 寺山旦中. *Hitsu-zendō* 筆禅道. Tokyo, 1983.

Yamamoto Kenkichi 山本健吉. *Bashō—sono kanshō to hihyō* 芭蕉―その鑑賞と批評 3 vols. Tokyo, 1955.

WORKS IN WESTERN LANGUAGES

TRANSLATIONS OF TEXTS

Zen Anthologies

Ch'an and Zen-Teaching. Ed. and trans. by Lu K'uan Yü C[harles Luk.] 3 vols. London 1960–62. Contains English translations of the *Heart Sūtra* and the *Diamond Sūtra,* lengthy sections from the Zen chronicles *Keitoku dentōroku* and *Gotō egen* as well as from the *Gotō zammai* of Tungshan Liang-chieh, and the Yüan text of the *Platform Sūtra.*

Manual of Zen Buddhism. Ed. by Daisetz Teitaro Suzuki. Kyoto, 1935. This handbook of Zen texts contains not only prayers, vows, and magical formulas but complete translations of the *Heart Sūtra* and the *Kannon Sūtra;* portions of the *Diamond Sūtra,* the *Laṅkāvatāra Sūtra,* and the *Śūraṅgama Sūtra;* and various texts of Chinese and Japanese Zen.

Timeless Spring: A Soto Zen Anthology. Ed. and trans. by Thomas Cleary. New York, 1980. A selection of texts from Zen chronicles and collections of sayings having to do with the Sōtō school of Zen.

Zen—Der lebendige Buddhismus in Japan. Ed. by Otto Faust and trans. into German by Shūej Ōhasama. Foreword by Rudolf Otto. Stuttgart, 1925. Contains selected kōan from the *Hekiganroku* and *Mumonkan,* as well as the texts of the *Shinjinmei, Shōdōka,* and *Zazen wassan.*

Zen Flesh, Zen Bones. Ed. by Nyogen Senzaku and Paul Repps. Tokyo, 1957. Contains 101 Zen stories, the collection of Zen kōan, the *Mumonkan,* K'uo-an Shih-yüan's text of the Ten Oxherding Pictures, and some pre-Zen materials.

Indian Buddhism

Aṣṭasāhasrikā prajñāpāramitā sūtra (in 8000 Lines). Trans. by E. Conze. Bolinas, Cal., 1973.

Avataṃsaka (Kegon) Sūtra. Trans. into German from Chinese, with introduction, by Torakazu Doi. 4 vols. Tokyo 1978–83. Contains a complete German translation of the Chinese text of the 60 volumes and 934 books of the *Buddhabhadra* (T. 278, vol. 9).

Dhammapada. Trans. into German by Karl Eugen Neumann. Jena, 1923. Trans. into English by Narada Thera. London, 1954.

Diamond Sūtra (Vajracchedikā Prajñāpāramitā sūtra). Trans. into German by Max Walleser, under the title *Prajñāpāramitā: Die Vollkommenheit der Erkenntnis.* Göttingen-Leipzig, 1914. Trans. into English (together with the *Heart Sūtra*) by E. Conze, under the title *Buddhist Wisdom Books.* London, 1958. Walleser's translation also includes a portion of the "Great Prajñāpāramitā sūtra in 100,000 lines" (*Śatasāhasrikā prajñāpāramitā sūtra).*

Heart Sūtra (Hrdaya prajñāpāramitā sūtra). Trans. into German by Max Walleser, under the title *Prajñāpāramitā.* Trans. into English by E. Conze, under the title *Buddhist Wisdom Books.* London, 1958.

Lankāvatāra sūtra. Sanskrit text trans. by D. T. Suzuki. London, 1932, 1968.

Mahāparinibbāna sutta. Trans. into German by Karl Eugen Neumann, under the title *Die letzen Tage Gotama Buddhas.* Munich, 1911; Zürich, 1956. Also by H. Beckh, under the title *Der Hingang des Vollendeten (Parinibbāna sutta).* Stuttgart, 1960.

Mahāprajñāpāramitā śāstra: Le Traité de la Grande Vertu de Sagesse de Nāgārjuna. French trans. with commentary. Bibliothèque du Muséon No. 8. 5 vols. Louvain, 1949–80.

Mūlamadhyamaka kārikā. Trans. by K. K. Inada. Tokyo, 1970.

Satipatthāna sutta. Der Heilsweg buddhistischer Geistesschulung: Die Lehre von der Vergegenwärtigung der Achtsamkeit. Pāli text trans. into German by Nyanaponika. Konstanz, 1950.

Selected Sayings from the Perfection of Wisdom. London, 1955. An anthology of prajñāpāramitā texts.

Three Short Prajināpāramitā Texts. Trans. by E. Conze. London, 1973. Contains 19 texts.

Śūrangama sūtra. Trans. by Lu K'uan yü (Charles Luk). Abridged commentary by Ch'an Master Hanshan. London, 1966.

Vasumitra. On the 18 sects of early Indian Buddhism. Trans. by J. Masuda, in *Origins and Doctrines of Early Buddhist Schools.* AM 2 (1925).

Vimalakīrti sūtra. Trans. into German by Jakob Fischer and Takezō Yokota. Tokyo, 1944. Trans. into English by: H. Idumi, EB 2–4 (1922–28); Lu K'ian Yü, Berkeley, 1972; and R. A. F. Thurman, from Tibetan, London, 1976. Trans. into French by E. Lamotte, under the title *L'Enseignement de Vimalakīrti,* Bibliothèque du Muséon, No. 51. Louvain, 1962.

Visuddhi magga: Oder der Weg zur Reinheit von Buddhaghosa. Trans. from Pāli into German by Nyanatiloka. Munich, 1931; Konstanz, 1975.

Chinese Zen Texts

Chao-lun. Trans., with commentary, by Walter Liebenthal, under the title *The Book of Chao.* Peking, 1948.

Hekiganroku (Pi-yen lu). Trans. into German by Wilhelm Gundert, under the title *Bi-yän-lu: Meister Yüan-wu's Niederschrift von der Smaragdenen Felswand.* 3 vols. Munich, 1960–73. Trans. into English by T. and J. C. Cleary, 3 vols., London, 1977; also by Katsuki Sekida, under the title *Two Zen Classics: Mumonkan and Hekiganroku,* Tokyo, 1977.

Huang-po: Enryōroku (Wan-ling lu). Trans. into English by John Blofeld, under the title *The Zen Teaching of Huang-po.* London, 1958. Trans. into German by Robert Zean, under the title *Die Zen-Lehre des chinesischen Meisters Huang-po.* Weilheim, 1960.

Keitoku dentōroku (Ching-te ch'uan-teng lu). T. 2076, vol. 51. Partially trans., with introductory annotations, by Chan Chung-Yuan, under the title *Original Teachings of Ch'an Buddhism.* New York, 1969.

Kōsōden. T. 2059, vol. 50. First three books trans. into French by R. Shih. Bibliothèque du Muséon, No. 54. Louvain, 1968.

Lhasa, Acts of the Council of. Trans. from Chinese into French, with commentary, by Paul Démieville, under the title *Le Concile de Lhasa: Une Controverse sur le quiétisme entre bouddhistes de l'Inde et de la China au VIIIème siècle de l'ère chrétienne.* Paris, 1952.

Mumonkan (Wu-men-kuan). Trans. into German, with commentary, by H. Dumoulin, under the title *Mumonkan—Die Schranke ohne Tor: Meister Wu-men's Sammlung der 48 Kōan,* Mainz, 1975; also by Walter Liebenthal, under the title *Ch'an-tsung Wu-men kuan: Zutritt nur durch die Wand,* Heidelberg, 1977. Trans. into English by: R. H. Blyth, Tokyo, 1966; Zenkei Shibayama, under the title *Zen Comments on the Mumonkan,* New York, 1974; Koun Yamada, under the title *Gateless Gate,* Los Angeles, 1979; and Katsuki Sekida, under the title *Two Zen Classics: Mumonkan and Hekiganroku,* Tokyo, 1977.

P'ai chang Huai-hai: Records of the Life of Ch'an Master Pai-chang Huai-hai. Trans. by Yi T'ao-t'ien. EB 9-1 (1975):42–73.

P'ang: A Man of Zen—The Recorded Sayings of Layman P'ang. Trans. from Chinese by Ruth Fuller Sasaki, Yoshitaka Iriya, and Dana R. Fraser. New York, 1971, 1976.

Rinzairoku (Lin-chi lu). Trans. into English by Ruth Fuller Sasaki, under the title *The Recorded Sayings of Ch'an Master Lin-chi Hui-chao of Chen Prefecture,* Kyoto, 1975; also by Irmgard Schloegel, under the title *The Zen Teaching of Rinzai,* Berkeley, 1976. Trans. into French, with commentary, by Paul Demiéville, under the title *Entretiens de Lin-tsi.* Paris, 1972.

Rokuso dankyō (Liu-tsu t'an ching). Tunhuang text trans. by Wing-tsit Chan, New York, 1963; also by P. B. Yampolsky, New York, 1967.

Shen-hui. Trans. into English by Walter Liebenthal, under the title "The Sermon of Shen-hui." AM 3 (1952):132–35. Trans. into French by Jacques Gernet, Hanoi, 1949.

Shōdōka (Cheng-tao-ko). T. 2014. Vol. 48. Trans., with commentary, by Walter Liebenthal. In *Monumenta Serica* 6 (1941):1–39. See also the Zen anthologies *Ch'an and Zen Teaching,* pp. 103–45, and *Manual of Zen Buddhism,* pp. 106–21 (see above).

Tongo yōmon (Tun-wu yao-men), by Ta-chu Hui-hai. Trans. by John Blofeld, under the title *The Path to Sudden Attainment: A Treatise of the Ch'an School of Chinese Buddhism by Hui Hai of the T'ang Dynasty.* London, 1948; reprinted in 1962 under the title *The Zen Teaching of Hui Hai on Sudden Illumination.*

Japanese Zen Texts
(alphabetical by author)

Bankei Yōtaku. Trans., with commentary, by Norman Waddell, under the title *The Unborn: The Life and Teaching of Zen Master Bankei, 1622–1693.* San Francisco, 1984.

Bashō. See Matsuo Bashō.

Bassui Tokushō. Collected sayings and letters, trans. by Philip Kapleau, under the title *The Three Pillars of Zen*. Tokyo, 1965.

Dōgen Kigen. *Gakudōyōjinshū*. Trans. into French by Hoang-Thi-Bich. Geneva, 1973.

———. *Fukanzazengi*. Trans. into German by H. Dumoulin. MN 14 (1958):429–36. Trans. into English by Norman Waddell and Abe Masao, EB 6-2 (1973):115–28; Yūhō Yokoi and Daizen Victoria, in *Master Dōgen: An Introduction with Selected Writings*, Tokyo, 1976; and Francis Dojun Cook, in *How to Raise an Ox: Zen Practice as Taught in Zen Master Dōgen's Shōbōgenzō*, Los Angeles, 1978, pp. 95–99.

———. *Hōkyōki*. Trans. by Norman Waddell, EB 10-2 (1977):102–39; 11 (1978):66–84; also by T. J. Kodera, in *Dōgen's Formative Years in China*, London, 1980.

———. *Shōbōgenzō*. Trans. by Kōsen Nishiyama and John Stevens. 4 vols. Sendai, 1975–83. Particular books (or chapters) of the *Shōbōgenzō*:

Genjōkōan. Trans. into German by H. Dumoulin, MN 15 (1960):425–40; also by Ryō-suke Ōhashi and Hans Brockard, *Philosophisches Jahhrbuch* 83 (1976):402–15. Trans. into English by Waddell and Abe. EB 5-2 (1972):129–40.

Uji. Trans. into German by Kōichi Tsujimura. In G. Condrau, ed., *Festschrift Medard Boss*. Bern, 1973. Trans. into English by Philip Kapleau, in *The Three Pillars of Zen*; also by Norman Waddell, EB 12-1 (1979):114–29.

Other books, trans. by Norman Waddell and Abe Masao, may be found in *The Eastern Buddhist*: Bendōwa 4 (1971):124–57; Ikka myōju 4 (1971):108–18; Zenki and Shōji 5 (1972):70–80; Sammai-ō-zammai 7 (1974):118–23; Busshō 8 (1975):87–105; 9 (1976):71–87.

See also books trans. by Francis Dojun Cook, in *How to Raise an Ox*, Los Angeles, 1978: Keisei sanshoku, Hotsu mujōshin, Shukke, Raihai tokuzuui, Shunjū, Shinjin inga, Nyorai zenshin, Gyōji, and Kajō.

The 12 books of the "New Manuscript" (see notes 99 and 111 of chapter 2) may be found in Yokoi and Victoria, in *Master Dōgen*. The book Dōtoku (also from the *Shōbōgenzō*) has been translated, with commentary, by Sakamoto Hiroshi, EB 16-1 (1983):90–105.

———. *Shōbōgenzō zuimonki*. Partially trans. into German by N. Iwamoto. Tokyo, 1943. Trans. into English by Reihō Masunaga, in *A Primer of Soto Zen*, Honolulu, 1972; also by Thomas Cleary, in *Record of Things Heard*, Boulder, Col., 1960.

———. *Tenzō kyōkun*. Trans. by Thomas Wright, in *Zen Master Dōgen and Kōshō Uchiyama*. New York, 1983.

———. *Eiheigenzen-ji shingi*. Trans. by Yūhō Yokoi, under the title *Regulations for Monastic Life*. Tokyo, 1973.

Hakuin Ekaku. *Orategama, Orategama zokushū, Yabukōji, Hebiichigo*. Trans. by Philip Yampolsky. In *Zen Master Hakuin: Selected Writings*. New York, 1971.

———. *Yasen kanna*. Trans. by R. D. M. Shaw and Wilhelm Schiffer, under the title "A Chat on a Boat in the Evening." MN 13 (1956):101–27.

———. *Itsumadegusa*. Trans. by Norman Waddell, under the title "Wild Ivy: The Spiritual Autobiography." EB 15-2 (1982):71–109; 16-2 (1983):107–39.

Han-shan shih. Trans. from Chinese into German by Stephan Schuhmacher, under the title *Han Shan: 150 Gedichte vom Kalten Berg*. Düsseldorf, 1977.

Ikkyū Sōjun. Trans. (from the text Gaikotsu) by R. H. Blyth, under the title "Ikkyū's

Skeletons." EB 6-1 (1973):111–25. Reprinted in F. Franck, ed. *The Buddha Eye*, pp. 75–85. New York, 1982.

Im Garten der schönen Shin (collection of poems). Trans., with commentary, by Shuichi Kato und Eva Thom. Düsseldorf, 1979.

Keizan Jōkin. *Zazenyōjinki*. Trans. into German by H. Dumoulin. MN 13 (1957):147–64. Trans. into English by Thomas Cleary, under the title *Timeless Spring*, pp. 112–25. Tokyo, 1980.

Matsuo Bashō. The following texts have been translated into German by Horst Hammitzsch: *Kashima kikō*, N 2 (1936);86–93; *Nozarashi kikō (Kasshi ginkō)*, NOAG 75 (1953):3–24; *Sarashina kikō*, NOAG 79 (1956):103–9; *Oi no kobumi (Udatsu kikō)*, in *Sino-Japonica: Festschrift André Wedemeyer*, Leipzig, 1956, pp. 74–106; four *haibun* in Sl 4 (1954); and three texts to disciples, in MOAG 14 (1963–64).

―――. *Oku no hosomicho*. Trans. into German by H. Ueberschaar. MOAG 19 A. Tokyo, 1935.

―――. *Nozarashi kikō* and *Sarashina kikō*. Trans. by Donald Keene. In *Landscapes and Portraits*, pp. 94–108, 109–30. Tokyo, 1971.

―――. *Oku no hosomichi*. Trans. by Nobuyuki Yuasa. In *Bashō: The Narrow Road to the Deep North and Other Travel Sketches*. Baltimore, 1966.

Musō Soseki. *Rinsen kakun*. Trans. by M. Collcutt. In *Five Mountains*, pp. 149–65. London, 1981.

Ryōkan. *The Zen Poems of Ryōkan*. Trans., with introduction, notes, and biographical sketch, by Nobuyuki Yuasa. Princeton, 1981. See also Burton Watson, *The Zen Monk-Poet of Japan*, New York, 1977.

Shidō Munan. *Sokushinki*. Part 1 trans. by Kobori Sōhaku and Norman Waddell. EB 3-2 (1970):89–118. Parts 2 und 3 trans. by Kobori Sōhaku. EB 4-1 (1971):116–23; 4-2:119–27.

―――. *Jishōki*. Trans. by Kusumita Priscilla Pedersen. EB 8-1 (1975):96–132.

―――. *Shushōgi* (Principles of Practice and Enlightenment). Trans. into German by K. Ishimoto and E. Naberfeld. MN 6 (1943):355–69.

―――. Tōrei Enji. *Kaisan Shidō Munan Anju Zenji anroku* (Biography of Shidō Munan). Trans., with introduction, by Kobori Shōhaku and Norman Waddell. EB 3 (1970):122–38.

―――. Tōyō Eichō. *Zenrin kushū*. In *Zen Dust*, pp. 79–122. New York, 1966.

Zeami. *Die geheime Überlieferung des Nō: Aufgezeichnet von Meister Seami*. Trans. into German, with commentary, by Oskar Benl. Frankfurt, 1961.

Miscellaneous Translations

Fabian. *Myōtei mondō*. Trans. into French by Pierre Humberclaude. MN 1 (1938):515–48; 2 (1939):237–67.

Frois, Luis. *Die Geschichte Japans 1549–1578*. Trans. from Portuguese into German, with commentary, by G. Schurhammer and E. A. Voretzsch. Leipzig, 1926.

Kamo Mabuchi. *Uta no kokoro no uchi*. Trans. into German by H. Dumoulin. MN 4 (1941):192–206.

―――. *Niimanabi*. Trans. into German by H. Dumoulin, MN 4 (1941):566–84.

Rodrigues, João. *Account of Sixteenth Century Japan.* Trans. from Portuguese by Michael Cooper. In *This Island of Japan.* Tokyo, 1973.

Shissai Chozan. *geijitsuron.* Trans. into German by Reinhard Kammer. In *Die Kunst der Bergdämonen: Zen-Lehre und Konfuzianismus in der japanischen Schwertkunst.* Weilheim, 1969.

Reference Works and Lexicons

Bary, Wm. Theodore de, ed. *Sources of Chinese Tradition.* New York, 1960.

——. *Sources of Japanese Tradition.* New York, 1958.

Daitō Shuppansha, *Japanese-English Buddhist Dictionary.* Tokyo, 1965.

Hammitzsch, Horst, ed. *Japan-Handbuch.* Wiesbaden, 1981.

Hisamitsu Sen'ichi, ed. *Biographical Dictionary of Japanese Literature.* Tokyo, 1976.

Lewin, Bruno, ed. *Kleines Wörterbuch der Japanologie.* Wiesbaden, 1968.

Miura, Isshū, and Sasaki, Ruth Fuller. *Zen Dust: The History of the Kōan and Kōan Study in Rinzai (Lin-chi) Zen.* New York, 1966.

Munsterberg, Hugo. *Dictionary of Chinese and Japanese Art.* New York, 1981.

Nanjio, Bunyiu. *A Catalogue of the Chinese Translation of the Buddhist Tripitaka: The Sacred Canon of the Buddhists in China and Japan.* Oxford, 1883.

Papinot, E., *Historical and Geographical Dictionary of Japan.* Tokyo, 1942.

Reischauer, Edwin O., ed. *Kodansha Encyclopedia of Japan.* 9 vols. Tokyo, 1983.

GENERAL WORKS

Anesaki, M. *History of Japanese Religion.* London, 1930.

Bareau, A. "Der indische Buddhismus." In *Die Religionen der Menschheit,* vol. 13, pp. 1–215. Stuttgart, 1964.

Bechert, H. "Buddhismus." In TRE, vol. 7, pp. 317–35.

Beckh, H. *Buddha und seine Lehre.* Reprint. Stuttgart, 1958.

Bellah, R. N. *Tokugawa Religion.* Boston, 1957.

Bersiihand, R. *Geschichte Japans.* Stuttgart, 1963.

Boxer, C. R. *The Christian Century in Japan, 1549–1650.* Berkeley, 1967.

Burton, C. *The Philosophers of China.* New York, 1962.

Chan, Wing-tsit. *A Source Book of Chinese Philosophy.* Princeton, 1963.

Chang, Carsun. *The Development of Neo-Confucian Thought.* 2 vols. New Haven, 1963.

Ch'en, K. *Buddhism in China: A Historical Survey.* Princeton, 1964.

Conze, E. *Buddhism: Its Essence and Development.* New York, 1951.

Cooper, M. *Rodrigues the Interpreter: An Early Jesuit in Japan and China.* Tokyo, 1974.

Dumoulin, H., ed. *Buddhismus der Gegenwart.* Freiburg, 1970.

Eder, M. *Geschichte der japanischen Religion.* 2 vols. Nagoya, 1978.

Eichhorn, W. *Die Religionen Chinas.* Stuttgart, 1973.

Eliade, M. *Yoga: Immortality and Freedom.* Princeton, 1973.

Filliozat, J. "Le Bouddhisme." *Manuel des Études Indiennes.* Vol. 2. Hanoi, 1953.

Frauwallner, E. *Die Philosophie des Buddhismus.* Vol. 2. Berlin, 1969.

Fung, Yu-lan. *A History of Chinese Philosophy.* Vol. 2. Princeton, 1953.

Graf, O. *Tao und Jen: Sein und Sollen im Sungchinesischen Monismus.* Wiesbaden, 1970.

Gundert, W. *Die japanische Literatur.* Potsdam, 1929.

———. *Japanische Religionsgeschichte.* Tokyo, 1935.

Hackmann, H. *Chinesische Philosophie.* Munich, 1927.

Hall, J. W. *Das japanische Kaiserreich.* Frankfurt, 1968.

Hauer, J. W. *Der Yoga: Ein indischer Weg zum Selbst.* Stuttgart, 1958.

Kitagawa, J. *Religion in Japanese History.* New York, 1966.

Lamotte, E. *Histoire du bouddhisme indien.* Bibliothèque du Muséon, No. 43. Louvain, 1967.

Laures, J. *Takayama Ukon und die Anfänge der Kirche in Japan.* Münster, 1954.

Luhmer, K. *Schule und Bildungsreform in Japan.* 3 vols. Tokyo, 1972.

Nakamura, H. "Die Grundlehren des Buddhismus: Ihre Wurzeln in Geschichte und Tradition." In *Buddhismus der Gegenwart,* ed. by H. Dumoulin, pp. 9–34. Freiburg, 1970.

———. *Ways of Thinking of Eastern Peoples: India-China-Tibet-Japan.* Ed. by P. Wiener. Rev. English trans. Honolulu, 1964.

Oldenberg, H. *Buddha: His Life, His Doctrine, His Order.* New Delhi, 1971.

Regamey, C. "Der Buddhismus Indiens." In *Christus und die Religionen der Erde,* vol. 3. Freiburg, 1951.

Samson, G. B. *A History of Japan 1334–1615.* London, 1961.

———. *A History of Japan 1615–1867.* London, 1963.

———. *Japan: A Short Cultural History.* New York, 1943.

Schlingloff, D. *Die Religion des Buddhismus.* 2 vols. Berlin, 1962, 1963.

Schurhammer, G. *Francis Xavier: His Life, His Times.* Vol. 4. Rome, 1982.

Schütte J. F. *Valignano's Mission Principles for Japan.* Vol. 1, part 1 (1573–1580). Saint Louis, 1980.

Takaskusu, J. *The Essentials of Buddhist Philosophy.* Honolulu, 1947.

Thomas, E. J. *The Life of Buddha as Legend and History.* London, 1927.

———. *The History of Buddhist Thought.* London, 1933.

Winternitz, M. *Geschichte der indischen Literatur.* Vol. 2. Leipzig, 1913; Stuttgart, 1968.

Zürcher, E. *The Buddhist Conquest of China.* 2 vols. Leiden, 1972.

MONOGRAPHS AND INDIVIDUAL STUDIES

Buddhism

Bareau, A. "Les Premiers Conciles bouddhiques." AMG 60 (1955).

———. *Les Sectes bouddhiques du Petit Véhicule.* Saigon, 1955.

Bielefeldt, Carl. "Recarving the Dragon: History and Dogma in the Study of Dōgen." In *Dōgen Studies,* ed. by W. R. LaFleur. Honolulu, 1985.

Chang, G. C. C. *The Buddhist Teaching of Totality: The Philosophy of Hwa Yen.* London, 1971.

Conze, E. *Buddhist Thought in India.* London, 1962.

———. *The Prajñāpāramitā Literature.* The Hague, 1960.

———. *Thirty Years of Buddhist Studies.* London, 1967.

Demiéville, P. Choix d'études bouddhiques. Leiden, 1973.

Dumoulin, H. Begegnung mit dem Buddhismus: Eine Einführung. Freiburg, 1978.

———."The Consciousness of Guilt and the Practice of Confession." In Festschrift Gershom Scholem. Jerusalem, 1967.

Dutt, S. Early Buddhist Monachism. Bombay, 1960.

Faure, Bernard. "The Daruma-shū, Dōgen, and Sōtō." MN 42-1 (1987):25–55.

Glasenapp, H. von. Buddhistische Mysterien: Eine religionsgeschichtliche Untersuchung. Stuttgart, 1940.

Heiler, F. Die buddhistische Versenkung. Munich, 1918.

Jong, J. W. de. Buddhist Studies. Ed. by G. Schopen. Berkeley, 1979.

Kasulis, Thomas. "The Incomparable Philosopher: Dōgen and How to Read the Shō-bōgenzō." In Dōgen Studies, ed. by W. R. LaFleur, pp. 83–98. Honolulu, 1985.

Keith, J. B. Buddhist Philosophy in India and Ceylon. Oxford, 1923.

King, W. L. Buddhism and Christianity: Some Bridges of Understanding. London, 1963.

———. Death Was His Kōan: The Samurai Zen of Suzuki Shōosan. Berkeley, 1986.

Lubac, H. de Aspects du bouddhisme. Paris, 1951.

Matsumoto, T. Die Prajñāpāramitā-Literatur. Stuttgart, 1932.

Matsunaga, D. & A. Foundation of Japanese Buddhism. Tokyo, 1976.

Murti, T. R. V. The Central Philosophy of Buddhism: A Study of the Mādhayamika System. London, 1970.

Nara, M. Tempel und Schreine. Kyoto, 1978.

Nishitani Keji. Religion and Nothingness. Trans. by Jan Van Bragt. Berkeley, 1982.

Reischauer, E. O. Die Reisen des Mönches Ennin: Neun Jahre im China des neunten Jahrhunderts. Stuttgart, 1963.

Rhys Davids, C. A. F. A Buddhist Manual of Psychological Ethics. London, 1900; reprinted 1975.

Robinson, R. H. Early Mādhamika in India and China. London, 1967.

Rosenberg, O. Die Probleme der buddhistischen Philosophie. Heidelberg, 1924.

Saigusa, M. Studien zum Mahāprajñāpāramitā (upadeśa) śāstra. Tokyo, 1969.

Schmidt-Glintzer, H. Die Identität der buddhistischen Schulen und die Kompilation buddhistischer Universalgeschichten in China. Wiesbaden, 1982.

Schurhammer, G. Die Disputation des P. Cosme de Torres, S. J., mit den Buddhisten in Yamaguchi im Jahre 1951. Tokyo, 1929.

Shimizu, M. Das "Selbst" im Mahāyāna-Buddhismus in japanischer Sicht und die "Person" im Christentum im Licht des Neuen Testaments. Leiden, 1981.

Stcherbatsky, Th. The Conception of Buddhist Nirvāna. Leningrad, 1927.

Streng, F. J. Emptiness: A Study in Religious Meaning. Nashville, 1967.

Suzuki, B. L. Mahayana Buddhism. London, 1948.

Suzuki, D. T. Outlines of Mahāyāna Buddhism. Chicago, 1908.

———. Studies in the Lankavatara Sūtra. London, 1930.

———. "The Essence of Buddhism," The Essentials of Zen Buddhism. Ed. by Bernhard Philips. New York, 1962.

Takeuchi, Y. The Heart of Buddhism: In Search of the Timeless Spirit of Primitive Buddhism. Trans. by J. Heisig. New York, 1983.

Vallée-Poussin, L. de la. *Nirvāna.* Paris, 1925.

Visser, M. W. de. *Ancient Buddhism in Japan.* Vol. 1. Leiden, 1935.

Walleser, M. *Die Sekten des alten Buddhismus.* Heidelberg, 1927.

Watanabe, S. *Japanese Buddhism: A Critical Appraisal.* Tokyo, 1970.

Welborn, G. R. *The Buddhist Nirvana and Its Western Interpreters.* Chicago, 1968.

Wright, A. F. *Buddhism in Chinese History.* London, 1971.

Zen Buddhism

Abe Masao. *Zen and Western Thought.* Ed. by William R. LaFleur. Honolulu, 1985.

Chang Chung-yuan. *Tao, Zen und schöpferische Kraft.* Düsseldorf, 1975.

Collcutt, M. *Five Mountains: The Rinzai Zen Monastic Institution in Medieval Japan.* London, 1981.

Covell, J. C., with Sobin Yamada. *Unraveling Zen's Red Thread: Ikkyu's Controversial Way.* New Jersey, 1980.

Dumoulin, H. *Zen Enlightenment: Origins and Meaning.* Trans. by John Maraldo. Tokyo, 1979.

Dumoulin, H., with R. F. Sasaki. *The Development of Chinese Zen after the Sixth Patriarch.* New York, 1953.

Enomiya-Lassalle, H. M. *Zen-Buddhismus.* Cologne, 1966.

Fischer, J. *Dew-Drops on a Lotus Leaf.* Tokyo, 1954.

Gernet, J. "Biographie du Maître de Dhyāna Chen-houei du Hotsö." JA 249 (1951):29–60.

———. *Entretiens du Maître de Dhyāna Chen-houei du Ho-tsö.* Hanoi, 1949.

———. "Complément aux Entretiens du Maître de Dhyāna Chen-houei." BEFEO 14 (1954):453–66.

Heinemann, R. K. *Der Weg des Übens im ostasiatischen Mahāyāna: Grundformen seiner Zeitrelation zum Übungsziel in der Entwicklung bis Dōgen.* Wiesbaden, 1979.

Hisamatsu, S. *Die fünf Stände von Zen-Meister Tōsan Ryōkai.* Trans. into German and ed. by Ryōsuke Ohashi and Hans Brockard. Pfullingen, 1980.

Hoffman, Yoel, trans. *The Sound of One Hand: 281 Zen Koans with Answers.* New York, 1975.

Humphreys, C. *Zen Buddhism.* London, 1949.

Izutsu, Toshihiko. *Toward a Philosophy of Zen Buddhism.* Boulder, Colo., 1982.

Kadowaki, J. K. *Zen and the Bible: A Priest's Experience.* Trans. by Joan Rieck. London, 1980.

Kammer, R. *Die Kunst der Bergdämonen: Zen-Lehre und Konfuzianismus in der japanischen Schwertkunst.* Weilheim, 1969.

Kapleau, P. *The Three Pillars of Zen: Teaching, Practice, Enlightenment.* Tokyo, 1965.

Kasulis, T. P. *Zen Action—Zen Person.* Honolulu, 1981.

Kim, Hee-Jin. *Dōgen Kigen—Mystical Realist.* Tucson, 1975.

Kodera, T. J. *Dōgen's Formative Years in China.* London, 1980.

Ku, Y. H. *History of Zen.* Pennsylvania, 1979.

Lai, Whalen, and Lancaster, Lewis R., eds. *Early Ch'an in China and Tibet.* Berkeley, 1983.

Leggett, T. *Zen and the Ways*. London, 1978.

Masunaga, R. *The Soto Approach to Zen*. Tokyo, 1958.

Miura Isshū and Sasaki, R. F. *The Zen Kōan*. Kyoto, 1965.

Nishimura Eshin. *Unsui:A Diary of Zen Monastic Life*. Honolulu, 1973.

Shaku Sōen. *Sermons of a Buddhist Abbot: Addresses in Religious Subjects*. Chicago, 1906.

Sung-peng Hsu. *A Buddhist Leader in Ming China: The Life and Thought of Han-shan Te-ch'ing*. University Park, Pa., 1979.

Suzuki, D. T. *An Introduction to Zen Buddhism*. New York, 1964.

———. *Essays in Zen Buddhism*. 3 vols. London, 1927, 1933, 1934.

———. *The Training of the Zen Buddhist Monk*. Kyoto, 1934.

———. *Living by Zen*. London, 1972.

———. *Studies in Zen*. London, 1955.

———. *Zen and Japanese Culture*. Princeton, 1959.

———. *The Zen Doctrine of No Mind*. London, 1969.

Suzuki, D. T., with Erich Fromm and Richard de Martino. *Zen Buddhism and Psychoanalysis*. New York, 1960.

Verdu, A. *Abstraktion und Intuitions als Wege zur Wahrheit in Yoga und Zen*. Munich, 1965.

———. *Dialectical Aspects in Buddhist Thought: Studies in Sino-Japanese Mahāyāna Idealism*. Kansas, 1974.

Waldenfels, H. *Absolute Nothingness: Foundations for a Buddhist-Christian Dialogue*. Trans. by J. W. Heisig. New York, 1980.

Watts, A. *The Way of Zen*. New York, 1957.

Wu, C. H. *The Golden Age of Zen*. Taipei, 1967.

Wunderle, F. *Schritte nach Innen*. Freiburg, 1975.

Yampolsky, Ph. *The Zen Master Hakuin: Selected Writings*. New York–London, 1971.

Art

Aitken, R. *A Zen Wave: Bashō's Haiku and Zen*. Tokyo, 1978.

Akiyama, T. *Japanische Malerei*. Geneva, 1977.

Armbruster, G., and Brinker, H., eds. *Mit Pinsel und Tusche: Meisterwerke japanischer Schreibkunst*. Munich, 1975.

Awakawa, Y. *Die Malerei des Zen-Buddhismus*. Vienna, 1970.

Blyth, R. H. *A History of Haiku*. 2 vols. Tokyo, 1964.

Brasch, K. *Zenga*. Tokyo, 1961.

Brinker, H. *Die zen-buddhistische Bildnismalerei in China und Japan von den Anfängen bis zum Ende des 16. Jahrhunderts: Eine Untersuchung zur Ikonographie, Typen- und Entwicklungsgeschichte*. Wiesbaden, 1973.

———. *Zen in der Kunst des Malens*. Bern, 1985.

Castile, Rand. *The Way of Tea*. Tokyo, 1971.

Covell, J., and Yamada Sōbin, eds. *Zen at Daitokuji*. Tokyo, 1974.

Engel, D. H. *Japanese Gardens for Today*. Tokyo, 1959.

Glaser, C. *Die Kunst Ostasiens*. Leipzig, 1922.

Goepper, R. "Kalligraphie." In JH, pp. 788–94.

Hammitzsch, H. *Chadō—Der Teeweg: Eine Einführung in den Geist der japanischen Lehre vom Tee*. Munich, 1958; reprintd 1977, under the title *Zen in der Kunst der Teezeremonie*.

Hayakawa, M. *The Garden Art of Japan*. Tokyo, 1973.

Hayashiya, T., Nakamura, M., and Hayashiya, S. *Japanese Arts and the Tea Ceremony*. Tokyo, 1974.

Henderson, H. G. *An Introduction to Haiku*. New York, 1958.

Herrigel, E. *Zen in the Art of Archery*. New York, 1957.

Herrigel, G. L. *Der Blumenweg*. Weilheim, 1970.

Hisamatsu, S. *Zen and the Fine Arts*. Tokyo, 1971.

Hoover, T. *Zen Culture*. London, 1978.

Immoos, T., and Halpern, E. *Japan: Tempel, Gärten und Paläste*. Cologne, 1974.

Immoos, T., and Mayer, Fred. *Japanisches Theater*. Zürich, 1975.

Itoh, T. (text), und Iwamiya, T. (photographs). *Imperial Gardens of Japan*. Tokyo, 1970.

Kanazawa, H. *Japanese Ink Painting: Early Zen Masterpieces*. Tokyo, 1979.

Keene, D. *Appreciations of Japanese Culture*. Tokyo, 1981.

———. *Some Japanese Portraits*. Tokyo, 1978.

Kuck, L. E. *One Hundred Kyoto Gardens*. London, 1936.

Kümmel, O. *Die Kunst Ostasiens*. Berlin, 1922.

Ledderose, L. *Mi Fu and the Classical Tradition of Chinese Calligraphy*. Princeton, 1979.

Munsterberg, H. *Zen-Kunst*. Cologne, 1978.

———. *Zen and Oriental Art*. Tokyo, 1965.

Naitō, A. (text) and Nishikawa, T. (photographs). *Katsura: Ein Ort der Besinnung*. Stuttgart, 1978.

Nakata, Y. *The Art of Japanese Calligraphy*. Tokyo, 1973.

Newsom, S. *A Thousand Years of Japanese Gardens*. Tokyo, 1953.

Okakura, K. *The Book of Tea*. New York, 1900; reprinted 1968.

Pageant of Japanese Art. Vol. 2 (painting). Tokyo, 1953. Vol. 6 (architecture and gardens. Tokyo, 1953.

Ponsonby-Fane, R. A. B. *Kyoto: The Old Capital of Japan*. Kyoto, 1956.

Richie, D., and Weatherby, M., eds. *The Master's Book of Ikebana*. Tokyo, 1966.

Rodrigues, J. *Arte del Cha*. Trans. from Portuguese into Spanish by J. L. Alvarez-Taladriz. Tokyo, 1954.

Schaarschmidt-Richter, I. *Der japanische Garten*. Würzburg, 1979.

———. "Schriftkunst." In *KWJ*, pp. 395–400.

Schwalbe, H. *Acht Gesichter Japans im Spiegel der Gegenwart*. Tokyo, 1970.

Seckel, D. *Einführung in die Kunst Ostasiens*. Munich, 1960.

———. *Buddhistische Kunst Ostasiens*. Stuttgart, 1957.

———. *Kunst des Buddhismus*. Baden-Baden, 1963.

———. "Jenseits des Bildes: Anikonische Symbolik in der buddhistischen Kunst." In *Abhandlungen der Heidelberger Akademie der Wissenschaften*. Heidelberg, 1976.

———. *Buddhistische Tempelnamen in Japan*. Stuttgart, 1985.

Shibayama Zenkei. *Zen im Gleichnis und Bild*. Munich, 1974.

Suzuki, D. T. *Sengai: The Zen Master.* Ed. by Eva van Hoboken. London, 1971.

Tamura, T. *Art of Landscape Garden in Japan.* Tokyo, 1935.

Tsujimura, K., and Buchner, H. *Der Ochs und sein Hirt: Eine Altchinesische Geschichte.* Pfullingen, 1958., English ed. of this work trans. by M. H. Trevor, under the title *The Ox and His Herdsman.* Tokyo, 1969.

Warner, L. *The Enduring Art of Japan.* Cambridge, 1952.

Yasuda, K. *Japanese Haiku.* Tokyo, 1957.

Miscellanea

Beky, G. *Die Welt des Tao.* Munich, 1972.

Bruce, J. P. *Chu Hsi and His Masters.* London, 1923.

Buber, M. *Schriften zum Chassidismus.* Vol. 3 of his *Werke.* Munich, 1963.

Ching, J. *To Acquire Wisdom: The Way of Wang Yang-ming.* New York, 1976.

Dumoulin, H. *Kamo Mabuchi: Ein Beitrag zur japanischen Religions- und Geistesgeschichte.* Tokyo, 1943.

———. *Östliche Meditation und christliche Mystik.* Munich, 1966.

Nakamura, H. "Ansätze modernen Denkens in den Religionen Japans." *Zeitschrift für Religions- und Geistegeschichte* 23 (1982).

Pacheco, D. "Fate of a Christian Daimyo." In *Great Historical Figures of Japan,* ed. by Murakami Hyōe and T. J. Harper. Tokyo, 1978.

Scholem, G. *Judaica.* Frankfurt, 1963.

Schurhammer, G. *Gesammelte Schriften.* Vols. 3 and 4. Lisbon, 1964, 1965.

PERIODICAL LITERATURE

Abe Masao. "Dōgen on Buddha Nature." EB 4-1 (1971):28–71.

Anesaki Masaharu. "The Writings of Fabian the Apostate Irman." In *Proceedings of the Imperial Academy* 8 (London, 1929):307–10.

Benl, O. "Der Zen-Meister Dōgen in China." NOAG 79/80 (1956):67–77.

———. "Musō Kokushi (1275–1351): Ein japanischer Zen-Meister." OE 2 (1955):86–108.

———."Die Anfänge der Sōto-Mönchsgemeinschafte." OE 7 (1960):31–50.

Bodart, B. M. "Tea and Counsel: The Political Role of Sen Rikyū." MN 32 (1977):49–74.

Ching, J. "The Goose Lake Monastery Debate (1175)." *Journal of Chinese Philosophy* 1 (1974):161–78.

Dumoulin, H. "Bodhidharma und die Anfänge des Ch'an-Buddhismus." MN 7 (1951):67–83.

———."Die religiöse Metaphysik des japanischen Zen-Meisters Dōgen." S 12 (1961):205–36.

———."Das Problem der Person im Buddhismus: Religiöse und künstlerische Aspekte." S 31-1 (1980):78–91.

———. "Die Geschichte der japanischen Manyōshūforschung von der Heianzeit bis zu den Anfängen der Kokugaku." MN 8 (1952):67–98.

———. "Kamo Mabuchi und das Manyōshu." MN 9 (1953):34–61.

———. "Die Erneuerung des Lidederweges durch Kamo Mabuchi." MN 6 (1943):110–45.

———. "Yoshida Shōin: ein Beitrag zum Verständnis der geistigen Quellen der Meijierneuerung." MN 1 (1938):350–77.

Gernet, J. "Techniques de recueillement, religion et philosophie, à propos du Jingzuo Neo-Confucéen," BEFEO 69 (981):289–305.

Hammitzsch, H. "Zum Begriff 'Weg' im Rahmen der japanischen Künste." NOAG 82 (1957):5–14.

Heinemann, R. K. "Zokugo in Dōgens Shōbōgenzō I: Das Hilfswort-jaku." OE 15 (1968):101–19.

———. "Zokugo in Dōgens Shōbōgenzō II: Die Uji-hakkiu." OE 15 (1968):179–90.

———. "Zokugo in Dōgens Shōbōgenzō III: Dōji-hosshin." OE 16 (1969):169–79.

———. "Zokugo in Dōgens Shōbōgenzō IV: Meitōrai-Meitōda." OE 18 (1971):67–83.

Hu Shih, "Development of Zen-Buddhism in China." SPSR 15 (1932):475–505.

Hu Shih and Suzuki, D. T. "Ch'an (Zen) Buddhism in China: Its History and Method." Philosophy East and West 3 (1953):3–46.

Kataoka, Y. "Takayama Ukon." MN 1 (1938):451–64.

King, W. L. "Suzuki Shōsan, Wayfarer." EB 1 (1938):451–64.

Laures, J. "Notes on the Death of Ninshitsu." MN 8 (1952):407–11.

Liebenthal, W. "Was ist chinesischer Buddhismus?" AS 6 (1952):116–29.

———. "Shih Yüan's Buddhism as Set Forth in His Writings." JAOS 70 (1950):243–59.

———. "Chinese Buddhism during the 4th and 5th Century." MN 11 (1955):44–83.

———. "A Biography of Chu Tao-sheng." MN 11 (1955):284–316.

———. "The World Conception of Chu-Tao-sheng." MN 12 (1956):65–103.

———. "The World Conception of Chu-Tao-sheng Texts." MN 12 (1956):241–68.

Maraldo, J. C. "The Hermeneutics of Practice in Dōgen and Francis of Assisi." EB 14-2 (1981):22–44.

Nakamura, H. "Suzuki Shōsan and the Spirit of Capitalism in Japanese Buddhism." MN 22 (1967):1–14.

Pelliot, P. "Notes sur quelques artistes de Six Dynasties et des T'ang." TP 22 (1923):215–91.

Schmithausen, L. "Spirituelle praxis und philosophische Theorie im Buddhismus." ZMR 57 (1973):161–86.

———. "Die ier Konzentrationen der Aufmerksamkeit: Zur geschichtlichen Entwicklung einer spirituellen Praxis des Buddhismus." ZMR 60 (1976):241–66.

Seckel, D. "Interpretation eines Zen-Bildes." NOAG 77 (1952):44–45.

———. "Shākyamunis Rückkehr aus den Bergen: Zur Deutung des Gemäldes von Liang K'ai." AS 8/9 (1965):35–72.

———. "Soziale und religiöse Aspekte der japanischen Teekeramik." NOAG 126 (1979):19–36.

Suzuki, D. T. "The Zen Sect of Buddhism." Journal of the Pāli Text Society (London, 1906–7):8–43.

————. "Dōgen, Hakuin, Bankei: Three Types of Thought in Japanese Zen." EB 9.1 (1976):1–17; 9.2:1–20.

Tsukamoto, Z. "The Dates of Kumārajīva and Seng-chao Reexamined." In *Silver Jubilee Volume of the Jinbun Kagaku Kenkyusho*, pp. 568–584. Kyoto, 1954.

Verdu, A. "The 'Five Ranks' Dialectic of the Sōtō-Zen School in the Light of Kuei-feng Tsung-mi's 'ariya-shiki' Scheme." MN 21 (1966):125–70.

Yanagida, S. "The Life of Lin-chi I-hsüan." EB 5-2 (1972):70–94.

Yün-hua, J. "Tsung-mi: His Analysis of Ch'an Buddhism." TP 58 (1972):1–54.

Indexes

Index of Names and Titles

Index of Terms and Subjects